Macmillan/McGraw-Hill READING

Mc Graw Hill Macmillan McGraw-Hill
New York Farmington

Contributors
The Princeton Review, Time Magazine, Accelerated Reader

The Princeton Review is not affiliated with Princeton University or ETS.

RFB&D
learning through listening

Students with print disabilities may be eligible to obtain an accessible, audio version of the pupil edition of this textbook. Please call Recording for the Blind & Dyslexic at 1-800-221-4792 for complete information.

Macmillan/McGraw-Hill
A Division of The ***McGraw·Hill*** *Companies*

Published by Macmillan/McGraw-Hill, a division of The McGraw-Hill Companies, Inc., Two Penn Plaza, NY, NY 10121

Printed in the United States of America

2, Bk.2, U.2
2 3 4 5 6 7 8 9 073/043 05 04 03 02

Macmillan/McGraw-Hill READING

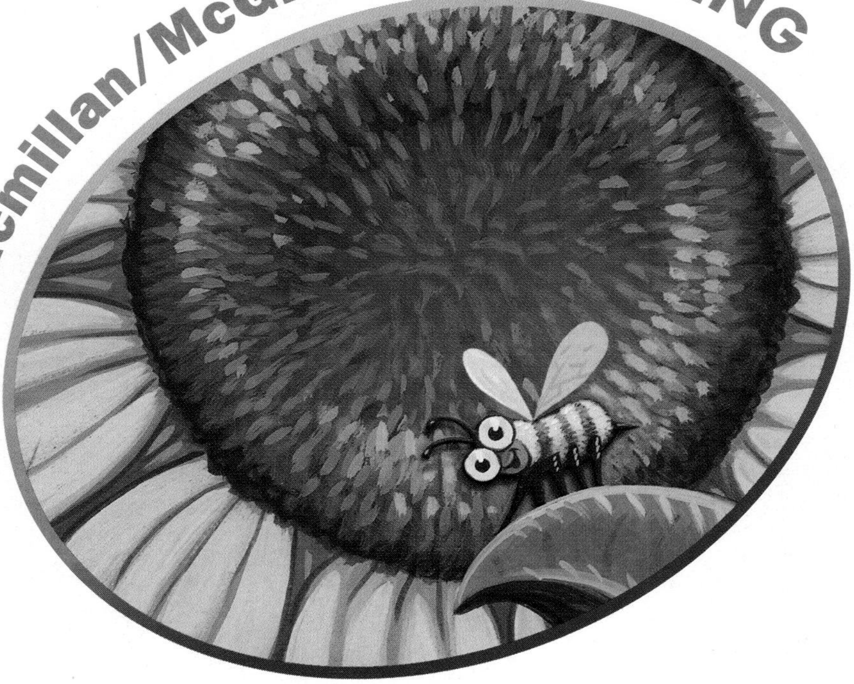

Authors

James Flood

Jan E. Hasbrouck

James V. Hoffman

Diane Lapp

Donna Lubcker

Angela Shelf Medearis

Scott Paris

Steven Stahl

Josefina Villamil Tinajero

Karen D. Wood

Macmillan McGraw-Hill

New York Farmington

Selected Quizzes Prepared by Accelerated Reader

Managing the

Classroom

TEACHING TIP

MANAGEMENT

Provide children in each group with their own list of centers they will go to. Children can check off each center after finishing their work. Early finishers can read a book from the Reading Center.

Sample Management Plan

Group 1	Group 2	Group 3	Group 4
With Teacher	Reading or Writing Workstation	Working with Words Station	Cross-Curricular or Computer Station
Reading or Writing Workstation	**With Teacher**	Cross-Curricular or Computer Station	Working with Words Station
Working with Words Station	Cross-Curricular or Computer Station	**With Teacher**	Reading or Writing Workstation
Cross-Curricular or Computer Station	Working with Words Station	Reading or Writing Workstation	**With Teacher**

Creating WORKSTATIONS

Establishing independent workstations and other independent activities is a key to helping you manage the classroom as you meet with small groups.

Reading

Set up a classroom library including the Leveled Books and other independent reading titles that have been previously read during small-group instruction. See the Theme Bibliography on pages T88–T89 for suggestions. Include titles based on discussions of students' fiction and nonfiction preferences.

- Self-Selected Reading
- Paired Reading
- Student Anthology selection from the Listening Library

Writing

Focus the unit's writing projects on expository writing. Weekly writing assignments are found at the end of each selection. The unit writing process project, Expository Writing, can also be the focus of the Writing Station. Equip the Writing Station with the following materials:

- Samples of published expository writing
- Expository Writing samples, available in the **Teacher's Writing Resource Handbook**, pages 24–25

Computer

Students can access the Internet to complete the Research and Inquiry activities suggested throughout the unit. Look for Internet connections in the following Research and Inquiry projects:

- Find Out More project at the end of each selection
- Cooperative Theme Project: Solving Riddles
- Cross-Curricular Activities
- Bringing Groups Together project

promise success explore

Working with Words

Selection Vocabulary

Create a simple "racetrack" that includes a starting space and finish line, with blank spaces in between. Also supply two toy cars and a pile of selection vocabulary word cards. Have partners pick cards from the pile. For each accurately defined word, they may advance their cars one space until they reach the finish line.

High-Frequency Words

Create word cards for these high-frequency words: *men, think, better, present, read, stand*. Have students copy the words, then list as many rhyming words as they can think of under each word.

TEACHING TIP

MANAGEMENT

If the classroom space is limited, incorporate workstation suggestions into a class assignment chart.

Shelve materials for each project in the classroom and distribute them as you assign an activity.

Have students work in groups, in pairs, or independently at their desks.

Cross-Curricular STATIONS

Set up a Cross-Curricular Station to help extend selection concepts and ideas. Cross-Curricular activities can be found throughout the unit.

Science

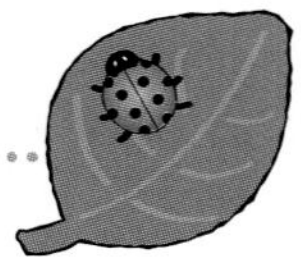

- Voices, 136
- Heart Rates, 156
- What's in a Breath?, 184
- An Imprint Investigation, 220

Social Studies

- Animal Farmers, 134
- Map Skills, 160
- Learning about Deserts, 194
- Prehistoric Life, 218

Math

3 + 2

- Time, 166
- Graph Transportation, 200
- Which Is More? Which Is Less?, 222

Art

- Make Scenery, 140
- Ball Flip Book, 162
- What Can You Share?, 190
- Make Imprints, 228

Additional Independent Activities

The following independent activities offer students practice exercises to help reinforce the concepts and skills taught within the unit.

PUPIL EDITION: READER RESPONSE

Story Questions to monitor student comprehension of the selection. The questions are leveled, progressing from literal to critical thinking.

Story Activities related to the selection. Four activities are always provided: one writing activity, two cross-curricular activities, and a research and inquiry activity in the Find Out More project that encourages students to use the Internet for research.

LEVELED PRACTICE

Each week, Reteach, Practice, and Extend pages are offered to address the individual needs of students as they learn and review skills.

McGraw-Hill Reading

Theme Chart

GRADE LEVEL	Experience	Connections
	Experiences can tell us about ourselves and our world.	Making connections develops new understandings.
Kindergarten	**My World** We learn a lot from all the things we see and do at home and in school.	**All Kinds of Friends** When we work and play together, we learn more about ourselves.
Subtheme 1	**At Home**	**Working Together**
Subtheme 2	**School Days**	**Playing Together**
1	**Day by Day** Each day brings new experiences.	**Together Is Better** We like to share ideas and experiences with others.
2	**What's New?** With each day, we learn something new.	**Just Between Us** Family and friends help us see the world in new ways.
3	**Great Adventures** Life is made up of big and small experiences.	**Nature Links** Nature can give us new ideas.
4	**Reflections** Stories let us share the experiences of others.	**Something in Common** Sharing ideas can lead to meaningful cooperation.
5	**Time of My Life** We sometimes find memorable experiences in unexpected places.	**Building Bridges** Knowing what we have in common helps us appreciate our differences.
6	**Pathways** Reflecting on life's experiences can lead to new understandings.	**A Common Thread** A look beneath the surface may uncover hidden connections.

MULTI-AGE Classroom

Using the same global themes at each grade level facilitates the use of materials in multi-age classrooms.

Themes: Kindergarten – Grade 6

Six Units IN EVERY GRADE

Expression	Inquiry	Problem Solving	Making Decisions
There are many styles and forms for expressing ourselves.	By exploring and asking questions, we make discoveries.	Analyzing information can help us solve problems.	Using what we know helps us evaluate situations.
Time to Shine We can use our ideas and our imagination to do many wonderful things.	**I Wonder** We can make discoveries about the wonders of nature in our own backyard.	**Let's Work It Out** Working as part of a team can help me find a way to solve problems.	**Choices** We can make many good choices and decisions every day.
Great Ideas	**In My Backyard**	**Try and Try Again**	**Good Choices**
Let's Pretend	**Wonders of Nature**	**Teamwork**	**Let's Decide**
Stories to Tell Each one of us has a different story to tell.	**Let's Find Out!** Looking for answers is an adventure.	**Think About It!** It takes time to solve problems.	**Many Paths** Each decision opens the door to a new path.
Express Yourself We share our ideas in many ways.	**Look Around** There are surprises all around us.	**Figure It Out** We can solve problems by working together.	**Starting Now** Unexpected events can lead to new decisions.
Be Creative! We can all express ourselves in creative, wonderful ways.	**Tell Me More** Looking and listening closely will help us find out the facts.	**Think It Through** Solutions come in many shapes and sizes.	**Turning Points** We make new judgments based on our experiences.
Our Voices We can each use our talents to communicate ideas.	**Just Curious** We can find answers in surprising places.	**Make a Plan** Often we have to think carefully about a problem in order to solve it.	**Sorting It Out** We make decisions that can lead to new ideas and discoveries.
Imagine That The way we express our thoughts and feelings can take different forms.	**Investigate!** We never know where the search for answers might lead us.	**Bright Ideas** Some problems require unusual approaches.	**Crossroads** Decisions cause changes that can enrich our lives.
With Flying Colors Creative people help us see the world from different perspectives.	**Seek and Discover** To make new discoveries, we must observe and explore.	**Brainstorms** We can meet any challenge with determination and ingenuity.	**All Things Considered** Encountering new places and people can help us make decisions.

UNIT 2

Contents

Figure It Out

We can solve problems by working together.

The Bremen Town Musicians 130A

by ***The Brothers Grimm,*** *retold* ***by Margaret H. Lippert***
illustrated by ***Mary Grand Pré***

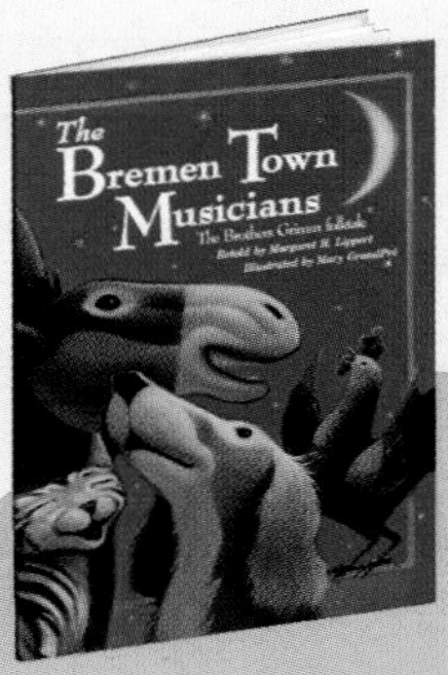

PLAY

SKILLS

Phonics	Comprehension	Vocabulary	Study Skill
• **Review** /âr/*are;* /ôr/*or, ore;* /îr/*ear*	• **Introduce** Summarize	• **Introduce** Suffixes	• Various Texts: Follow Directions

Our Soccer League 150A

a photo essay by ***Chuck Solomon***

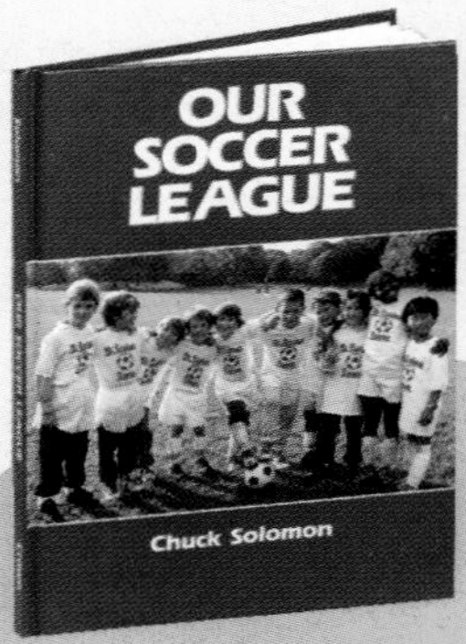

NONFICTION

SKILLS

Phonics	Comprehension	Vocabulary	Study Skill
• **Review** /ü/*oo, ue, ew;* /ôr/*or, ore*	• **Introduce** Sequence of Events	• **Review** Context Clues	• Various Texts: Read a Newsletter

SKILLS

Phonics	Comprehension	Vocabulary	Study Skill
• **Review** /ər/, /ən/, /əl/; /ü/; /ôr/; /îr/	• **Review** Summarize	• **Review** Suffixes	• Various Texts: Use a Calendar

REALISTIC FICTION

SKILLS

Phonics	Comprehension	Vocabulary	Study Skill
• **Review** /ou/; /oi/; /ər/, /ən/, /əl/; /âr/	• **Review** Sequence of Events	• **Review** Context Clues	• Various Texts: Interpret Signs

NONFICTION

TIME FOR KIDS

SKILLS

Phonics	Comprehension	Vocabulary	Study Skill
• **Review** /ou/; /oi/; /ər/, /ən/, /əl/; /ü/	• **Review** Sequence of Events • **Review** Summarize	• **Review** Context Clues • **Review** Suffixes	• Various Texts: Read an Advertisement

NONFICTION

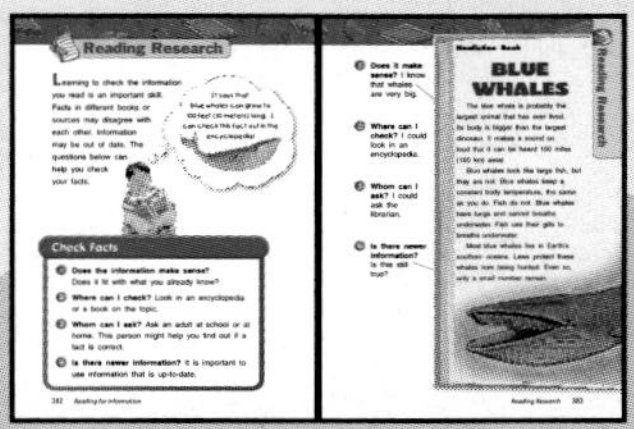

INFORMATIONAL TEXT

UNIT 2

Unit Planner

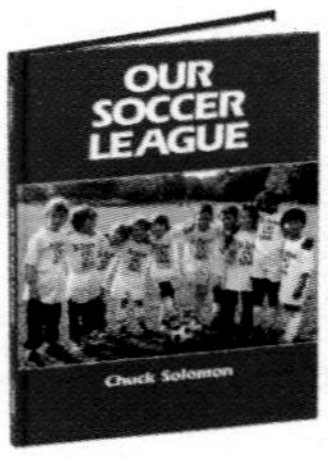

	WEEK 1 Bremen Town Musicians	WEEK 2 Our Soccer League
Leveled Books	Easy: *The Chief's Daughter and the Hunting Dog* Independent: *Why Lizard Stretches His Neck* Challenge: *The Voice of the Sea*	Easy: *Coyotes Rule!* Independent: *Playing Your Best* Challenge: *Teammates for Life*
Tested Skills	**Phonics** Review /âr/*are*; /ôr/*or, ore*; /îr/*ear*, 130G–130H Review /âr/*are*; /ôr/*or, ore*; /îr/*ear*, 149E–149F, 149G–149H **Comprehension** Introduce Summarize, 149I–149J **Vocabulary** Introduce Suffixes, 149K–149L **Study Skills** Various Texts, 148	**Phonics** Review /ü/*oo, ue, ew*, 150G–150H Review /ü/*oo, ue, ew*, 179E–179F Review /ü/*oo, ue*; /ôr/*or, ore*, 179G–179H **Comprehension** Introduce Sequence of Events, 179I–179J **Vocabulary** Review Context Clues, 179K–179L **Study Skills** Various Texts, 178
Minilessons	**Vowel Sounds:** /ô/*a*, 135 **Make Inferences,** 137 **Context Clues,** 139 **Summarize,** 141	**Phonics and Decoding:** Long *o*, 157 **Make Inferences,** 159 **Context Clues,** 161 **Main Idea,** 165
Language Arts	**Writing:** Expository Writing, 149M **Grammar:** Pronouns, 149O **Spelling:** Words with *c, k,* and *ck,* 149Q	**Writing:** Expository Writing, 179M **Grammar:** *I* and *Me, We* and *Us,* 179O **Spelling:** Words with Blends, 179Q
Activities		
Curriculum Connections	Read Aloud: "The Bundle of Sticks," 130E Phonics Rhyme: "Try a Little Music," 130/131 Social Studies: Animal Farmers, 134 Science: Voices, 136 Art: Make Scenery, 140	Read Aloud: "The Great Ball Game," 150E Phonics Rhyme: "Game Time," 150/151 Health: Heart Rates, 156 Social Studies: Map Skills, 160 Science & Art: Ball Flip Book, 162 Math: Time, 166
CULTURAL PERSPECTIVES	Variant Tales, 142	Soccer Facts, 158

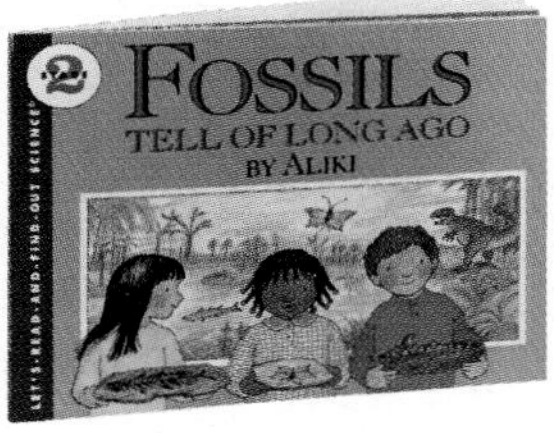

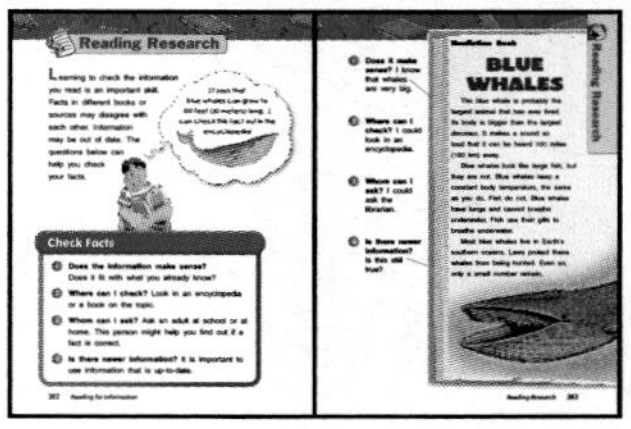

WEEK 3 The Wednesday Surprise	WEEK 4 Fossils Tell of Long Ago	WEEK 5 Are You a Fossil Fan?	WEEK 6 Review, Writing, Reading Information, Assessment
Easy: *Farmer Brown's Birthday Surprise* Independent: *Sequoyah* Challenge: *The Light of One Candle*	Easy: *I Live at the Museum* Independent: *Learn About Your World* Challenge: *At the Museum*	*Self-Selected Reading of Leveled Books*	*Self-Selected Reading*
Phonics Review /ər/*er*; /ən/*en*; /əl/*le*, 180G–180H, 211E–211F Review /ər/, /ən/, /əl/; /ü/; /ôr/; /îr/, 211G–211H **Comprehension** Review Summarize, 211I–211J **Vocabulary** Review Suffixes, 211K–211L **Study Skills** Various Texts, 210	**Phonics** Review /ou/*ow, ou* and /oi/*oi, oy*, 212G–212H, 235E–235F Review /ou/, /oi/; /ər/, /ən/, /əl/; /âr/, 235G–235H **Comprehension** Review Sequence of Events, 235I–235J **Vocabulary** Review Context Clues, 235K–235L **Study Skills** Various Texts, 234	**Phonics** Review /ou/; /oi/; /ər/, /ən/, /əl/; /ü/, 236G–236H **Comprehension** Review Sequence of Events, 245E–245F Review Summarize, 245G–245H **Vocabulary** Review Context Clues, 245I–245J Review Suffixes, 245K–245L **Study Skills** Various Texts, 244	**Assess Skills** /âr/*ar*; /ôr/*or, ore*; /îr/*ear* /ü/*oo, ue, ew* /ər/*er*; /ən/*en*; /əl/*le* /ou/*ow, ou* and /oi/*oi, oy* Summarize Sequence of Events Suffixes Context Clues **Assess Grammar and Spelling** Review Pronouns, 247I Review Spelling Patterns, 247J **Unit Progress Assessment** **Standardized Test Preparation** **Reading Research** 247A
Suffixes, 187 **Context Clues,** 193 **Phonics and Decoding:** Consonant Blends/pr/*pr*, 197 **Summarize,** 199 **Making Inferences,** 201	**Decoding Multisyllabic Words,** 219 **Phonics and Decoding,** /j/*ge* and /s/*ce*, 221 **Form Generalizations,** 225 **Main Idea,** 229		
Writing: Expository Writing, 211M **Grammar:** Possessive Pronouns, 211O **Spelling:** Words with Blends, 211Q	**Writing:** Expository Writing, 235M **Grammar:** Pronoun-Verb Agreement, 235O **Spelling:** Words with Blends, 235Q	**Writing:** Expository Writing, 245M **Grammar:** Contractions, 245O **Spelling:** Words from Social Studies, 245Q	**Unit Writing Process:** Expository Writing, 247C
Read Aloud: "Reading to Me," 180E Phonics Rhyme: "To Market! To Market!" 180/181 Science: What's in a Breath? 184 Art: What Can You Share? 190 Social Studies: Learning About Deserts, 194 Math: Graph Transportation, 200 Birthday Celebrations Around the World, 202	Read Aloud: "The Dinosaur Who Lived in My Backyard," 212E Phonics Rhyme: "Digging," 212/213 Social Studies: Prehistoric Life, 218 Science: An Imprint Investigation, 220 Math: Which Is More? Which Is Less? 222 Art: Make Imprints, 228 Dinosaurs, 226	Read Aloud: "Gotta Find a Footprint," 236E Phonics Rhyme: "When You're an Archeologist," 236/237	GROUP **Cooperative Theme Project** **Research and Inquiry:** Solving Riddles, 129

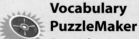

LITERATURE

LEVELED BOOKS

Easy:

- ***The Chief's Daughter and the Hunting Dog***
- ***Coyotes Rule!***
- ***Farmer Brown's Birthday Surprise***
- ***I Live at the Museum***

Independent:

- ***Why Lizard Stretches His Neck***
- ***Playing Your Best***
- ***Sequoyah***
- ***Learn About the World***

Challenge:

- ***The Voice of the Sea***
- ***Teammates for Life***
- ***The Light of One Candle***
- ***At the Museum***

THEME BIG BOOK

Share *Six Crows* to set the unit theme and make content-area connections.

LISTENING LIBRARY

Children can listen to an audio recording of the student selections and poetry.

Macmillan/McGraw-Hill

Intervention

Easy Leveled Books
Skills Intervention Guide
Phonics Intervention Guide

SKILLS

LEVELED PRACTICE

Practice: Practice for phonics, comprehension, vocabulary and study skills; plus practice for instructional vocabulary and story comprehension. Take-Home Story included for each lesson.

Reteach: Reteaching opportunities for students who need more help with each assessed skill.

Extend: Extension activities for vocabulary, comprehension, story and study skills.

TEACHING CHARTS

Instructional charts for modeling vocabulary and tested skills. Also available as **transparencies.**

WORD BUILDING MANIPULATIVE CARDS

a b c Letter and word cards to utilize phonics and build instructional vocabulary.

LANGUAGE SUPPORT BOOK

ESL Parallel lessons and practice for students needing language support.

PHONICS/PHONEMIC AWARENESS PRACTICE BOOK

Additional practice focusing on key phonetic elements.

FLUENCY ASSESSMENT

Evaluation and practice for building reading fluency.

LANGUAGE ARTS

GRAMMAR PRACTICE BOOK

Provides practice for grammar and mechanics lessons.

SPELLING PRACTICE BOOK

Provides practice with the word list and spelling patterns. Includes home involvement activities.

DAILY LANGUAGE ACTIVITIES

Provide brief practice and reinforcement of grammar, mechanics, and usage skills. Available as **blackline masters** and **transparencies.**

WRITING PROCESS TRANSPARENCIES

Model stages of the writing process.

HANDWRITING HANDBOOKS

For instruction and practice.

McGraw-Hill School **TECHNOLOGY**

Phonics CD-ROM Provides phonics support.

interNET* CONNECTION** Extend lesson activities through research and inquiry ideas. Visit ***www.mhschool.com/reading.

Vocabulary PuzzleMaker Provides practice with instructional vocabulary.

Handwriting CD-ROM Provides practice activities.

Mind Jogger Videos Review grammar and writing skills.

Resources for
Meeting Individual Needs

UNIT 2	EASY	ON-LEVEL	CHALLENGE	LANGUAGE SUPPORT
 *The Bremen Town Musicians*	**Leveled Book:** *The Chief's Daughter and the Hunting Dog* Reteach, 169–176 **Alternate Teaching Strategies,** T64–T76 **Writing:** Draw an Event, 149M–149N Phonics CD-ROM Intervention	**Leveled Book:** *Why Lizard Stretches His Neck* Practice, 169–176 **Alternate Teaching Strategies,** T64–T76 **Writing:** Posters, 149M–149N Phonics CD-ROM	**Leveled Book:** *The Voice of the Sea* Extend, 169–176 **Writing:** Write a Review, 149M–149N Phonics CD-ROM	**Teaching Strategies,** 132A, 132C, 137, 138, 149N Language Support, 181–189 **Alternate Teaching Strategies,** T64–T76 **Writing:** Write a Report, 149M–149N Phonics CD-ROM
 *Our Soccer League*	**Leveled Book:** *Coyotes Rule!* Reteach, 177–184 **Alternate Teaching Strategies,** T64–T76 **Writing:** Sports Illustrated, 179M–179N Phonics CD-ROM Intervention	**Leveled Book:** *Playing Your Best* Practice, 177–184 **Alternate Teaching Strategies,** T64–T76 **Writing:** Soccer Scenes, 179M–179N Phonics CD-ROM	**Leveled Book:** *Teammates for Life* Extend, 177–184 **Writing:** New Setting, 179M–179N Phonics CD-ROM	**Teaching Strategies,** 152A, 152C, 153, 155, 157, 163, 173, 179N Language Support, 190–198 **Alternate Teaching Strategies,** T64–T76 **Writing:** Write a Team-Player Guide, 179M–179N Phonics CD-ROM
 *The Wednesday Surprise*	**Leveled Book:** *Farmer Brown's Birthday Surprise* Reteach, 185–192 **Alternate Teaching Strategies,** T64–T76 **Writing:** Characterization, 211M–211N Phonics CD-ROM Intervention	**Leveled Book:** *Sequoyah* Practice, 185–192 **Alternate Teaching Strategies,** T64–T76 **Writing:** Book Recommendation, 211M–211N Phonics CD-ROM	**Leveled Book:** *The Light of One Candle* Extend, 185–192 **Writing:** Diary Entry, 211M–211N Phonics CD-ROM	**Teaching Strategies,** 182A, 182C, 183, 185, 191, 195, 211N Language Support, 199–207 **Alternate Teaching Strategies,** T64–T76 **Writing:** Write About a Book, 211M–211N Phonics CD-ROM
 *Fossils Tell of Long Ago*	**Leveled Book:** *I Live at the Museum* Reteach, 193–200 **Alternate Teaching Strategies,** T64–T76 **Writing:** Invitation, 235M–235N Phonics CD-ROM Intervention	**Leveled Book:** *Learn About the World* Practice, 193–200 **Alternate Teaching Strategies,** T64–T76 **Writing:** Caption, 235M–235N Phonics CD-ROM	**Leveled Book:** *At the Museum* Extend, 193–200 **Writing:** News Bulletin, 235M–235N Phonics CD-ROM	**Teaching Strategies,** 214A, 214C, 215, 217, 224, 235N Language Support, 208–216 **Alternate Teaching Strategies,** T64–T76 **Writing:** Write a Speech, 235M–235N Phonics CD-ROM
 *Are You a Fossil Fan?*	**Review** Reteach, 201–208 **Alternate Teaching Strategies,** T64–T76 **Writing:** Make a Poster, 245M–245N Phonics CD-ROM Intervention	**Review** Practice, 201–208 **Alternate Teaching Strategies,** T64–T76 **Writing:** Write an Interview, 245M–245N Phonics CD-ROM	**Review** Extend, 201–208 **Writing:** Apply for a Job, 245M–245N Phonics CD-ROM	**Teaching Strategies,** 238A, 238C, 239, 245N Language Support, 217–225 **Alternate Teaching Strategies,** T64–T76 **Writing:** Write a Report, 245M–245N Phonics CD-ROM

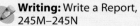

UNIT 2

Unit Assessment

INFORMAL

Informal Assessment

- Phonics, 130H, 145, 149F, 149H; 150H, 175, 179F, 179H; 180H, 207, 211F, 211H; 212H, 231, 235F, 235H; 236H, 241, 245F, 245H
- Comprehension, 144, 145, 149J; 174, 175, 179J; 206, 207, 211J; 230, 231, 235J; 240, 241
- Vocabulary, 149L, 179L, 211L, 235L, 245J, 245L

Performance Assessment

- Scoring Rubrics, 149N, 179N, 211N, 235N, 245N
- Research and Inquiry, 128J, 247
- Listening, Speaking, Viewing Activities, 130E, 130, 132C, 132–145, 149D, 149M–N; 150E, 150, 152C, 152–175, 179D, 179M–N; 180E, 180, 182C, 182–207, 211D, 211M-N; 212E, 212, 214C, 214–231, 235D, 235M–N; 236E, 236, 238C, 238–241, 245D, 245M–N
- Portfolio, 149N, 179N, 211, 235, 245N
- Writing, 149M–N, 179M–N, 211M–N, 235M–N, 245M–N, 247C–H
- Fluency, 146, 176, 208, 232, 242

Leveled Practice

Practice, Reteach, Extend

- **Phonics and Decoding**
  /âr/are; /ôr/or, ore; /îr/ear, 169, 173, 174, 182, 190, 198
  /ü/oo, ue, ew, 177, 181, 182, 190, 201
  /ər/er; /ən/en; /əl/le, 185, 189, 190, 198, 201
  /ou/ow, ou; /oi/oi, oy, 193, 197, 198, 201
- **Comprehension**
  Summarize, 175, 191, 206
  Sequence of Events, 183, 199, 205
- **Vocabulary Strategies**
  Suffixes, 176, 192, 208
  Context Clues, 184, 200, 207
- **Study Skills**
  Various Texts, 172, 180, 188, 196, 204

FORMAL

Selection Assessments

- **Skills and Vocabulary Words**
  The Bremen Town Musicians, 41–42
  Our Soccer League, 43–44
  The Wednesday Surprise, 45–46
  Fossils Tell of Long Ago, 47–48
  Are You a Fossil Fan? 49–50

Unit 2 Test

- **Phonics and Decoding**
  /âr/are; /ôr/or, ore; /îr/ear
  /ü/oo, ue, ew
  /ər/er; /ən/en; /əl/le
  /ou/ow, ou and */oi/oi, oy*
- **Comprehension**
  Summarize
  Sequence of Events
- **Vocabulary Strategies**
  Suffixes
  Context Clues

Grammar and Spelling Assessment

- **Grammar**
  Pronouns, 159–160
- **Spelling**
  Unit 2 Assessment, 159–160

Fluency Assessment

- Fluency Passages, 46–49

Diagnostic/Placement Evaluation

- Informal Reading Inventories
- Running Record
- Phonemic Awareness Assessment
- Placement Tests

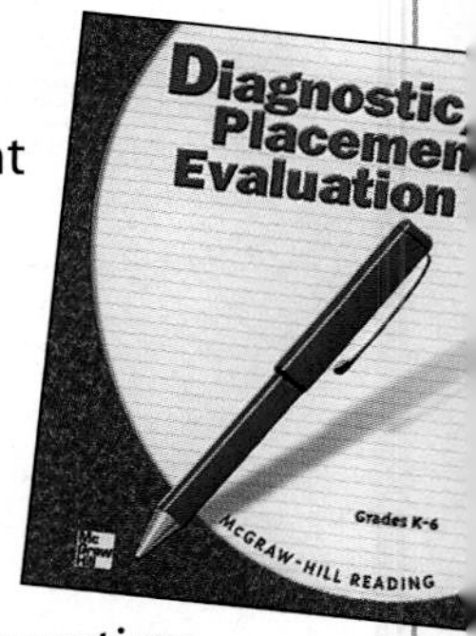

Test Preparation

- Test Power, 149, 179, 211, 235, 245
- Additional standardized test preparation materials available

Reading Test Generator

- Assessment Software

Assessment Checklist

Student .... **Grade** ....

Teacher ....

	The Bremen Town Musicians	Our Soccer League	The Wednesday Surprise	Fossils Tell of Long Ago	Are You a Fossil Fan?	Assessment Summary
LISTENING/SPEAKING						
Participates in oral language experiences						
Listens and speaks to gain knowledge of culture						
Speaks appropriately to audiences for different purposes						
Communicates clearly						
READING						
Uses phonological awareness strategies, including • blending, segmenting, deleting, substituting sounds						
Uses a variety of word identification strategies: • Phonics and decoding: /âr/*are;* /ôr/*or, ore;* /îr/*ear*						
• Phonics and decoding: /ü/*oo, ue, ew*						
• Phonics and decoding: /ər/*er;* /ən/*en;* /əl/*le*						
• Phonics and decoding: /ou/*ow, ou,* and /oi/*oi, oy*						
• Suffixes						
• Context Clues						
Reads with fluency and understanding						
Reads widely for different purposes in varied sources						
Develops an extensive vocabulary						
Uses a variety of strategies to comprehend selections: • Summarize						
• Sequence of Events						
Responds to various texts						
Analyzes the characteristics of various types of texts						
Conducts research using various sources: • Various Texts						
Reads to increase knowledge						
WRITING						
Writes for a variety of audiences and purposes						
Composes original texts using the conventions of written language such as capitalization and penmanship						
Spells proficiently						
Composes texts applying knowledge of grammar and usage						
Uses writing processes						
Evaluates own writing and writing of others						

+ Observed   – Not Observed

Introduce the Theme

Figure It Out

We can solve problems by working together.

DISCUSS THE THEME Write the theme statement on the board. Read it aloud with children. Share with them an example of how you have worked with someone to solve a problem. Ask:

- How can people work together to solve problems?
- Can you think of stories or movies that illustrate groups of people working together to solve problems?
- Have you ever worked with others to solve a personal problem? What was the problem? How did you solve it?
- Have you ever needed to do research to solve a problem? What types of problem solving might involve research?

SHARE A STORY Use the Big Book *Six Crows* to help establish the unit theme.

Have children discuss how this fable of the crows and the farmer relates to the theme Figure It Out.

PREVIEW UNIT SELECTIONS Have children preview the unit by reading the selection titles, paging through the stories, and looking at the illustrations. Ask:

- How might these selections relate to the theme Figure It Out?
- Do you think that learning how to solve problems can be taught in literature about imaginary people and imaginary events? Why or why not?
- Which selection looks most interesting to you? Why?

Have children work in small groups to brainstorm a list of ways that the stories, poems, and the *Time for Kids* magazine article relate to the theme Figure It Out.

THEME CONNECTIONS

Each of the five selections relates to the unit theme Figure It Out, as well as to the global theme of Problem Solving.

The Bremen Town Musicians A group of singing animals outwits a gang of robbers.

Our Soccer League Each team works together to outplay the other during a soccer game.

The Wednesday Surprise A girl helps her grandmother learn how to read.

Fossils Tell of Long Ago Fossils give clues about animals and plants from long ago.

Are You a Fossil Fan? A boy has learned about the past by digging up fossils.

Activity

Research and Inquiry

Theme Project: Solving Riddles Have teams of children work together to create riddles. They can make up their own riddles or find them in books. Encourage children to choose a theme for their riddles, such as nature, family life, or school experience. Then teams will challenge each other to solve their set of riddles.

Make a Resource Chart Ask children to brainstorm some questions they would need to answer in order to prepare their riddles. Then have them create a three-column chart. In the first column have them list questions they need to answer to prepare their riddles. Have them list possible resources in the second column. In the third column they will record their research findings.

Present Your Puzzles When each team has written at least three riddles, they will think about how to present them to the rest of the class. The teams may present their riddles orally, write them on cards, or print and illustrate them on posters that can then be displayed around the classroom.

QUESTIONS	POSSIBLE RESOURCES	ANSWERS
• What is a riddle? • Where can riddles be found? • What is a surprising fact about my riddle topic?	• dictionary • joke books, riddle books • text book, reference book	

See **Wrap Up the Theme,** page 246.

Research Strategies

Children may wish to look for examples of riddles in the library. Share these research tips:

- Use the subject card catalog to find books about your topic.
- Write down the title of the book, listed below the topic.
- Jot down the author of the book, listed below the title of the book.
- Write down the call numbers; they will help you locate the book in the library.
- Remember that there can be more than one book about a topic.

*inter***NET** CONNECTION Children can learn more riddles by visiting ***www.mhschool.com/reading.***

Poetry

Read the Poem

READ ALOUD Read "What Is It?" by Eve Merriam aloud to children. Afterward, ask:

- How does this poem relate to the unit theme, Figure It Out?
- Do you think that this poem is a riddle? Why or why not?
- Which words in the poem will help you "figure it out" and why?

Listening Library Children can listen to an audio recording of the poem.

PARTNER READING Assign partners. PARTNERS Have children alternate reading stanzas of "What Is It?" to each other. Encourage partners to work together to decode difficult or unfamiliar words.

Learn About Poetry

ONOMATOPOEIA Explain that onomatopoeia means a word whose sound suggests the sound it refers to, such as *buzz* and *hiss*.

- Have children find and discuss examples of onomatopoeia in the poem "What Is It?"
- Ask children: Does onomatopoeia make this poem seem more alive? How?

Point out that the poet uses both real and made-up words in the poem.

ASSONANCE Explain that assonance is the repetition of a vowel sound without the repetition of consonants, as in *stony* and *snowy*.

- Have children find examples of assonance in the poem "What Is It?"
- Point out the words *teeth, eat,* and *speak* in the first stanza. Ask, *Do these words sound the same? How?*

Discuss other ways in which the use of assonance contributes to the feeling, flow, and structure of the poem.

MEET THE POET

ABOUT EVE MERRIAM
Children may be interested to learn that Eve Merriam began to write her own poems when she was about seven or eight. Today Eve Merriam is the author of more than fifty books for adults and children. Her writing includes poetry, plays, fiction, and nonfiction. She has been honored with numerous awards including the National Council of Teachers of English Award in 1981 for excellence in poetry for children.

READ TOGETHER

UNIT 2

Figure it Out

What Is It?

It has no teeth,
so it can't eat a carrot.
It can't speak a word,
so it isn't a parrot.

It woggles and goggles
and scrunches its eyes.
It squawks and it yawps,
it burps and it cries.

It waggles its fingers,
it snuffles its nose.
Let's wait for a while
And watch how it grows.

by Eve Merriam

129

WRITE A POEM

Poetry Activity Have children write a poem about a baby. They can use the same format as "What Is It?" or you may choose to model another poem for them to follow. You may wish to begin the process by inviting children to interview their parents and other caretakers about what they were like as babies. Have them write down key descriptive words for their poems. Invite them to bring in photos of themselves as babies.

WRITING

Who Is it? Bulletin Board Have children submit their poems and baby photos for a bulletin board. Make sure names are not included. Entitle the bulletin board, Who Is it? Challenge children to identify their classmates as babies.

Poetry

STANZA Explain that a *stanza* is a group of lines in a poem. Point out that each stanza is set apart by a line of space.

Copy the poem, "What Is it?," onto the chalkboard or chart paper. Invite a volunteer to read the first stanza aloud, and then circle it with chalk or a marker. Repeat this process for identifying the remaining stanzas. Use a different colored chalk or marker for each stanza.

Assign children to groups. Have each group write an additional stanza for this poem. Discuss with groups how they can write a stanza for placement at the beginning, middle, or end of the poem. Have groups share stanzas with the class. Ask, *How do stanzas make poems easier to read?*

Oral Response

SMALL-GROUP DISCUSSIONS Have children share personal responses to the poem and discuss these questions:

GROUP

- Why is the poem called "What Is It?"
- Can you guess what "it" is?
- What do *woggle* and *goggle* mean? Are they real words?
- What do *squawk* and *yawp* mean? What might you squawk and yawp about?
- Do the sounds some of the words make help the poem flow smoothly? How?
- Is the poem fun to read? Why or why not?

Lesson Overview

Reaching All Learners

Concept
- Plays

Phonics
- Variant Vowels: /âr/, /ôr/, /îr/

Vocabulary
- daughter
- music
- scare
- third
- voice
- whistle

Anthology

The Bremen Town Musicians

Selection Summary **In this play, four animals who have been forced from their homes figure out how they can start a new life together.**

Rhyme applies to phonics

Listening Library

INSTRUCTIONAL pages 132–149

About the Authors Jacob and Wilhelm Grimm, who were born in Germany more than 200 years ago, were the first authors to write down the folktale *The Bremen Town Musicians.* The Brothers Grimm collected many folk and fairy tales to ensure that these wonderful stories would never be forgotten.

About the Illustrator Mary GrandPré has illustrated several books for children, including *Pockets,* the award-winning *Chin Yu Min and the Ginger Cat, Batwings and the Curtain of Night,* and *The Thread of Life: Twelve Old Italian Tales.*

Same Concept, Skills and Vocabulary!

Leveled Books

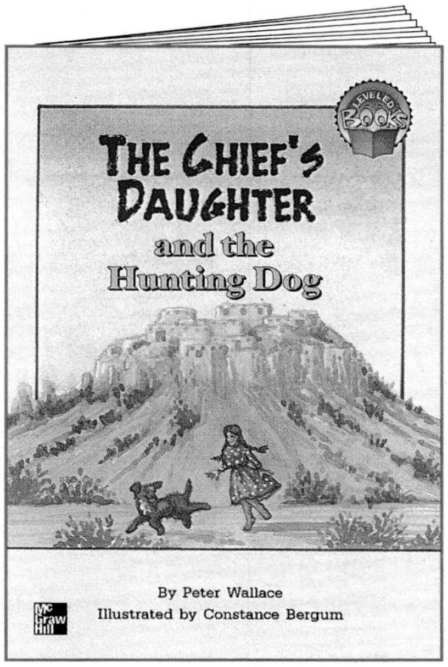

EASY
Lesson on pages 149A and 149D
DECODABLE

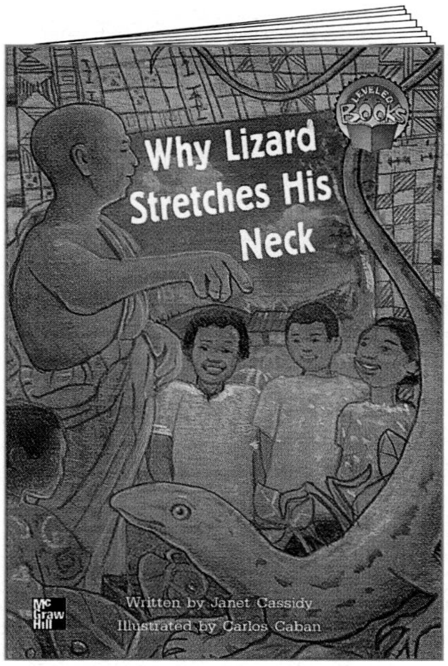

INDEPENDENT
Lesson on pages 149B and 149D
Take-Home version available

CHALLENGE
Lesson on pages 149C and 149D

Leveled Practice

EASY
Reteach, 169–176 Blackline masters with reteaching opportunities for each assessed skill

INDEPENDENT/ON-LEVEL
Practice, 169–176 Workbook with Take-Home stories and practice opportunities for each assessed skill and story comprehension

CHALLENGE
Extend, 169–176 Blackline masters that offer challenge activities for each assessed skill

Quizzes Prepared by Accelerated Reader

Social Studies	Animal Farmers, *134*
Science	Voices, *136*
Art	Make Scenery, *140*
Language Arts	Read Aloud, *130E*
Cultural Perspectives	Folktales, *142*
Writing	Write a Report, *146*
Research and Inquiry	Find Out More, *147*
Internet Activities	www.mhschool.com/reading

Suggested Lesson Planner

READING AND LANGUAGE ARTS	**DAY 1** *Focus on Reading and Skills*	**DAY 2** *Read the Literature*
● **Phonics Daily Routines**	Daily **Phonics** Routine: **Fluency,** 130H **Phonics** CD-ROM	Daily **Phonics** Routine: **Discriminating,** 132A **Phonics** CD-ROM
● **Phonological Awareness** ● **Phonics** /âr/, /ôr/, /îr/ ● **Comprehension** ● **Vocabulary** ● **Study Skills** ● **Listening, Speaking, Viewing, Representing**	**Read Aloud: Fable,** 130E "The Bundle of Sticks" ☑ **Develop Phonological Awareness,** 130F /âr/*are*; /ôr/*or, ore*; /îr/*ear* ☑ **Review** /âr/*are*; /ôr/*or, ore*; /îr/*ear*, 130G–130H **Teaching Chart 141** **Reteach, Practice, Extend,** 169 **Phonics/Phonemic Awareness Practice Book,** 113–116 **Read** **Apply** /âr/*are*; /ôr/*or, ore*; /îr/*ear*, 130/131 "Try a Little Music" ⓘ Intervention Program	**Build Background,** 132A Develop Oral Language **Vocabulary,** 132B–132C *daughter scare voice* *music third whistle* **Word Building Manipulative Cards** **Teaching Chart 142** **Reteach, Practice, Extend,** 170 **Read** **Read the Selection,** 132–145 Comprehension ☑ /âr/*are*; /ôr/*or, ore*; /îr/*ear* **Genre:** Play, 133 **Cultural Perspectives,** 142 ⓘ Intervention Program
● **Curriculum Connections**	**Link** Language Arts, 130E	**Link** Language Arts, 132A
● **Writing**	✏ **Writing Prompt:** Do you have a favorite singer or musician? Describe what it is you like about this person.	✏ **Writing Prompt:** What other stories have you read about a talking animal? Tell what the animal did or what happened to it. 📓 **Journal Writing** Quick-Write, 145
● **Grammar**	**Introduce the Concept: Pronouns,** 149O Daily Language Activity: Write the correct pronoun. **Grammar Practice Book,** 129	**Teach the Concept: Pronouns,** 149O Daily Language Activity: Write the correct pronoun. **Grammar Practice Book,** 130
● **Spelling** *c, k, ck*	**Pretest: Words with** *c, k,* **and** *ck,* 149Q **Spelling Practice Book,** 129, 130	**Explore the Pattern: Words with** *c, k,* **and** *ck,* 149Q **Spelling Practice Book,** 131

Meeting Individual Needs

☑ = Skill Assessed in Unit Test

ⓘ Intervention Program Available

Read EVERY DAY

DAY 3 Read the Literature	DAY 4 Build Skills	DAY 5 Build Skills
Daily Phonics Routine: **Segmenting,** 147 Phonics CD-ROM	Daily Phonics Routine: **Identifying,** 149F Phonics CD-ROM	Daily Phonics Routine: **Writing,** 149H Phonics CD-ROM
Rereading for Fluency, 144 **Story Questions and Activities,** 146–147 **Reteach, Practice, Extend,** 171 **Study Skills,** 148 ☑ **Various Texts** **Teaching Chart 143** **Reteach, Practice, Extend,** 172 **Test Power,** 149 Read **Read the Leveled Books,** 149A–149D Guided Reading ☑ */âr/are; /ôr/or, ore; /îr/ear* ☑ **Instructional Vocabulary** ⓘ Intervention Program	Read **Read the Leveled Books and Self-Selected Books** ☑ **Review** */âr/are; /ôr/or, ore; /îr/ear,* 149E–149F **Teaching Chart 144** **Reteach, Practice, Extend,** 173 **Language Support,** 186 **Phonics/Phonemic Awareness Practice Book,** 113–116 ☑ **Review** */âr/are; /ôr/or, ore; /îr/ear,* 149G–149H **Teaching Chart 145** **Reteach, Practice, Extend,** 174 **Language Support,** 187 **Phonics/Phonemic Awareness Practice Book,** 113–116 **Minilessons,** 135, 137, 139, 141 ⓘ Intervention Program	Read **Read Self-Selected Books** ☑ **Introduce Summarize,** 149I–149J **Teaching Chart 146** **Reteach, Practice, Extend,** 175 **Language Support,** 188 ☑ **Introduce Suffixes,** 149K–149L **Teaching Chart 147** **Reteach, Practice, Extend,** 176 **Language Support,** 189 **Listening, Speaking, Viewing, Representing,** 149N Illustrate the Reports Radio Report **Minilessons,** 135, 137, 139, 141 ⓘ Intervention Program
Activity **Social Studies,** 134	Activity **Science,** 136	Activity **Art,** 140
Writing Prompt: Write a short story about a group of animals who play on a sports team together. **Expository Writing,** 149M Prewrite, Draft	**Writing Prompt:** Write a conversation between the animals in the story after they get rid of the robbers. **Expository Writing,** 149M Revise **Meeting Individual Needs for Writing,** 149N	**Writing Prompt:** Write a story about an animal and a person who work together or help each other. **Expository Writing,** 149M Edit/Proofread, Publish
Practice and Write: Pronouns, 149P Daily Language Activity: Write the correct pronoun. **Grammar Practice Book,** 131	**Review and Practice: Pronouns,** 149P Daily Language Activity: Write the correct pronoun. **Grammar Practice Book,** 132	**Assess and Reteach: Pronouns,** 149P Daily Language Activity: Write the correct pronoun. **Grammar Practice Book,** 133, 134
Practice and Extend: Words with *c, k,* and *ck,* 149R **Spelling Practice Book,** 132	**Proofread and Write: Words with *c, k,* and *ck,*** 149R **Spelling Practice Book,** 133	**Assess and Reteach: Words with *c, k,* and *ck,*** 149R **Spelling Practice Book,** 134

Link
Language Arts

Read Aloud

The Bundle of Sticks

a fable by Aesop retold by Stephanie Calmenson

One evening, a Father who was about to set off on a long journey gathered his children together and said, "There is something important I want you to know. But rather than tell you in words, I will show you what I mean."

The Father handed a bundle of sticks to his Eldest Son.

"I want you to break this bundle of sticks in two," he said.

"Yes, Father," said the Eldest Son. He took the bundle in his hands and, with a mighty effort, tried to break the sticks. Again and again he tried. But he could not do it.

"It is no use, Father," he said. "I cannot break the bundle in two."

"Pass the bundle to your Sister and let her try," the Father said.

The Sister took her turn trying to break the bundle of sticks, but could not do it either.

"Now let your Youngest Brother try," said their Father.

Continued on page T2

Oral Comprehension

LISTENING AND SPEAKING Ask children to think of families as you read this fable aloud. When you have finished, ask, *What did the Father mean by the bundle of sticks?* Then ask, *Could this apply to other people besides brothers and sisters? Why or why not?*

GENRE STUDY: FABLE Discuss the literary devices and techniques used in *The Bundle of Sticks.*

- Discuss the characters in the fable. Ask: *Do you know much about them?* As a class, list what is known about each character.
- Ask children to describe the setting of the story. Ask: *Is the setting important to the fable? Why might it be a good thing that the setting is not clear?*
- Discuss the moral of the story. Determine how the moral is supported throughout the fable.

Activity Illustrate that there is "strength in numbers" by having each child roll a strip of paper into a tight log, securing it with glue or paste. Then have the class or small groups get together and see what they can build with their logs. (a cabin, a raft, other structures)

▶ **Visual/Spatial**

Develop Phonological Awareness

Blend Sounds

Phonemic Awareness

MATERIALS
- paper square
- common classroom materials

Teach Tell children that they are going to play a guessing game. Then say: *I'm thinking of a shape. It has four equal sides. It is a* /s/-/kw/-/âr/. *What shape am I thinking of?* (square) Hold up a square and repeat the word.

Practice Continue the guessing game with other items found in the classroom, or items that you bring in, such as: *corn, book, page, head, horn, coat, desk,* and *fork.*

Segment Sounds

Phonemic Awareness

MATERIALS
- Word Building Boxes
- self-stick notes
- pictures of fruits and vegetables

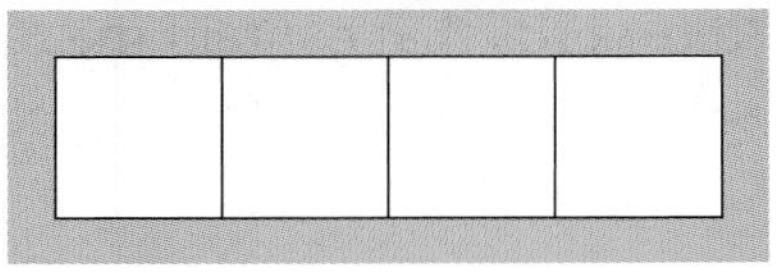

Teach Tape pictures on the board that show a category, for example, foods. Draw a four-box grid underneath each picture. If *corn* is one of the words count the number of sounds you hear in *corn.* Place a self-stick note in a box for each sound as you say, /k/-/ôr/-/n/. Repeat with *bread.*

Practice Have volunteers say words that fit in the category. Distribute Word Building Boxes with four sections and counters to each child. Have them place counters in each box for the sounds they hear in: *bean, water, turkey, lime, rice, apple, pea, kiwi,* and *beet.*

Delete Sounds

Phonemic Awareness

MATERIALS
- colored blocks

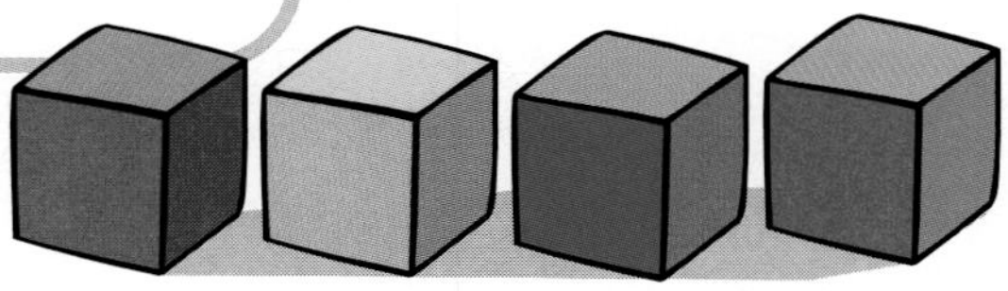

Teach Give each child a set of four colored blocks. Say the word *sport* /s/-/p/-/ôr/-/t/ and place four blocks in front of you. Then say: /s/-/ôr/-/t/. Remove the second block and ask, *If I leave off the* /p/ *sound in* sport, *what new word do we make?* (sort)

Practice Continue the exercise with these words: *score*/without the *c, stay*/without the *t, smear*/without the *m, store*/without the *t, flare*/without the *l, play*/without the *l.*

INFORMAL ASSESSMENT

Observe children as they blend, segment, and delete sounds. If children have difficulty, see Alternate Teaching Strategies on p. T64.

Review /âr/ are; /ôr/ or, ore; /îr/ ear

TESTED OBJECTIVES

Children will:

- identify /âr/ *are*; /ôr/ *or ore*; /îr/ *ear*.
- blend and read words with /âr/ *are*, /ôr/ *or*, *ore*, and /îr/*ear*.
- review initial and final consonants.

MATERIALS

- letter, variant vowel, and digraph cards from the **Word Building Manipulative Cards**
- **Teaching Chart 141**

Skills Finder

/âr/ *are*; /ôr/ *or*, ore; /îr/ *ear*

Introduce	B1: 192G-H
Review	B1: 215E-F; B2: 130G-H, 149E-F, 149G-H
Test	B1: Unit 2

SPELLING/PHONICS CONNECTIONS

See the 5-Day Spelling Plan, pages 149Q–149R.

TEACHING TIP

SPELLING PATTERNS

To remind children that the letter *r* works with a vowel or vowels to spell a unique sound, have them circle the vowel-and-r spelling pattern in each word on the **Teaching Chart** and underline the letter *r* in each.

TEACH

Identify and Read Words with /âr/ *are*, /ôr/ *or*, *ore*, and /îr/ *ear*

Tell children they will review words in which letter combinations made up of vowels and the letter *r* spell the sounds /âr/, /ôr/, and /îr/. Write the following sentence on the chalkboard and ask children to underline the words with the /âr/, /ôr/, and /îr/ sounds: *Do you care that the new store is not near us?*

BLENDING Model and Guide Practice with /âr/*are*, /ôr/*or*, *ore*, and /îr/*ear* Words

- Display **Teaching Chart 141.** Read aloud the word *spare*. Underline the letters *are* in *spare*. Tell children this letter combination spells the /âr/ sound.
- Run your finger under *spare*, blending the letters to read the word again. Have children repeat.
- Repeat this procedure, introducing the letter combinations *or/ore* and *ear* in the second and third columns.
- Write the words *short, near, care, scare, store, dear, fear, morning* and *stare* on the chalkboard.
- With children, read aloud each word.
- Ask children to identify the words that contain the /âr/ sound. Have volunteers write them under *spare* in the first column on the chart.

are	or/ore	ear
spare	more	hear
care	store	near
stare	short	fear
scare	morning	dear

Teaching Chart 141

Use the Words in Context

Use the words in sentences to reinforce their meanings. Example: *I care about animals.*

Repeat the Procedure

Follow the same procedure to assign /ôr/ and /îr/ words from the board to the second and third columns of the chart respectively.

PRACTICE

LETTER SUBSTITUTION
Build /âr/ *are*, /ôr/ *or*, *ore*, and /îr/ *ear* Words

PARTNERS

Have partners use letter cards to build the words *care*, *shore*, and *near*. Then, have them replace the *sh* in *shore* with a *b* to form *bore*. Ask children to work with the following letter cards: *m*, *f*, *c*, *l*, *s*, *t*, to build as many /âr/, /ôr/, and /îr/ words as possible. Have children determine if pairs of words rhyme. ▶ **Visual/Linguistic**

s h b o r e

ASSESS/CLOSE

Decode and Read /âr/ *are*, /ôr/ *or*, *ore*, and /îr/ *ear* Words

To assess children's ability to decode and read /âr/, /ôr/, and /îr/ words, observe their work on the Practice activity. Then have children read the phonics rhyme on page 131 in their anthologies and identify words with the sounds /âr/, /ôr/, and /îr/.

ADDITIONAL PHONICS RESOURCES

Phonics/Phonemic Awareness Practice Book, pages 113–116

McGraw-Hill School TECHNOLOGY

Phonics CD-ROM activities for practice with Blending and Word Building

Meeting Individual Needs for Phonics

EASY

Name ________ Date ______ **Reteach 169**

/âr/ are; /ôr/ or, ore; /îr/ ear

Look at the spellings for these sounds.
/âr/ as in **stare** **/îr/** as in **near** **/ôr/** as in **born** or **store**

Choose letters from the list below and write them on the line to complete a word. Answers may vary.

are ear or ore

1. c are ful
2. st or m
3. sc are d or scored
4. n ear or nor
5. f or or fear, fore, or fare
6. h ear or hare
7. sh or t
8. t ore or tear
9. st or yteller
10. m or ning
11. m ore or mare
12. sh are or shore or shear

12 Book 2.2/Unit 2 **The Bremen Town Musicians** **At Home:** Have children write a short poem using the words on this page. 169

Reteach, 169

ON-LEVEL

Name ________ Date ______ **Practice 169**

/âr/ are; /ôr/ or, ore; /îr/ ear

Write a word from the box to complete each sentence.

careful scared story for stored morning more hear

1. Kitty waited for Sally.
2. The loud noise scared us.
3. Mom reads me a story every night.
4. I am careful when I ride my bike.
5. We eat breakfast every morning.
6. I'm cold, so put on more heat.
7. Luis wanted to hear the song.
8. The clothes are stored in the closet.

8 Book 2.2/ Unit 2 **The Bremen Town Musicians** **At Home:** Invite children to write a story using words from the box. 169

Practice, 169

CHALLENGE

Name ________ Date ______ **Extend 169**

/âr/ are; /ôr/ or, ore; /îr/ ear

Help Sam find the gold. Circle all the words with the *ear* sound. Then draw a path.

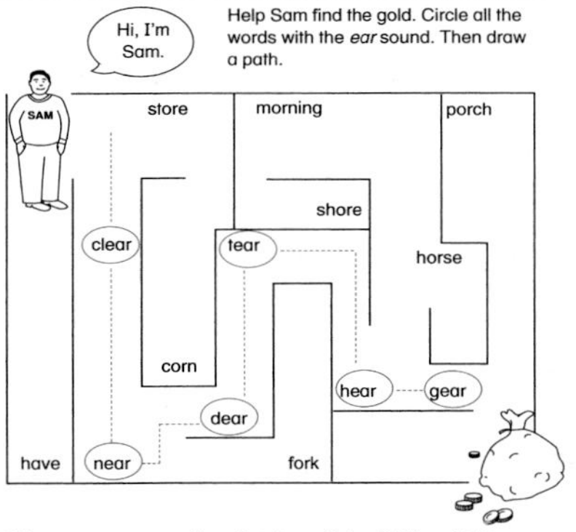

Write two sentences telling what Sam will do with his gold. Use words from the maze.

Sam will buy corn.

Sam will buy a hare.

Book 2.2/Unit 2 **The Bremen Town Musicians** **At Home:** Invite children to make a maze using the words *careful, scared, scary, dare, hare, mare*, and *dared* along the path. Have them put other words in the maze to make the maze tricky. They can give their maze to a friend to solve. 169

Extend, 169

Daily Routines

DAY 1 **Fluency** Write the following words on the chalkboard: *hear*, *score*, *morning*, *fare*. Point to each word, asking children to blend the sounds silently. Ask a volunteer to read aloud each word.

DAY 2 **Discriminating** Say aloud the following pairs of words: *car/care*; *horn/phone*; *sport/cot*; *hear/hide*. Ask children to raise their hands when they hear /âr/, /ôr/, or /îr/ words.

DAY 3 **Segmenting** Write these words: *care*, *story*, *spear*. Ask children to underline the letters in each word that spell /âr/, /ôr/, or /îr/ sounds. Ask children to suggest other words with the same vowel sounds and spellings.

DAY 4 **Identifying** Play "Simon Says" with r-controlled-variant-vowel words. When children hear a word with an /âr/, /ôr/, or /îr/ sound, they should take one step forward.

DAY 5 **Writing** Have partners write riddles whose answers contain /âr/, /ôr/, and /îr/ words. Have one partner say the riddle and the other partner answer it. Tell children to switch roles.

TESTED OBJECTIVES

Children will blend and read words with /âr/*are;* /ôr/*or, ore;* /îr/*ear.*

Apply /âr/ are; /ôr/ or, ore; /îr/ ear

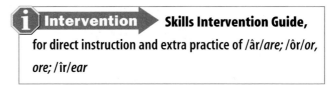

Try a Little Music
If you feel sad or scared today,
Try a little music.
If things don't seem to go your way,
Try a little music.
You'll feel better when you hear
That music pouring in your ear.
So tum your drum
And toot your flute,
And try a little music.
130
131

Anthology pages 130–131

Read and Build Fluency

READ THE POEM Play the audio recording of "Try a Little Music." Encourage children to focus on the words *pouring, scared, ear* and *hear* as they read along silently. Point out how the recorded voice pauses or stops appropriately. For auditory modeling, engage children in a shared reading as you track the print.

PARTNERS **REREAD FOR FLUENCY** Encourage partners to take turns reading the poem aloud to each other. Promote fluent reading by reminding children to read the lines as if they were telling a story to a friend. Mention how important it is for them to vary their intonation and read with expression.

Dictate and Spell

JOURNAL **DICTATE WORDS** Say *scared* aloud. Then segment it sound by sound. Repeat the word and use it in a sentence, such as, *Are you scared of the dark?* Have children say the word aloud and write the letters to make the whole word. Repeat with *pouring* and the /îr/ word *hear.* Ask children to name other words with a vowel and the letter *r* to segment, from the poem or elsewhere.

Intervention **Skills Intervention Guide,** for direct instruction and extra practice of /âr/*are;* /ôr/*or, ore;* /îr/*ear*

Build Background

Link
Language Arts

Concept: Plays

Evaluate Prior Knowledge

CONCEPT: PLAYS Ask children to share what they know about plays. Ask children to describe plays they have attended, or in which they have performed. Use the following activities to build additional background about plays.

CREATE A CHART FOR PLAYS Discuss what plays have in common with stories. Then have children list things that are special about plays. Create a two-column chart.
▶ **Linguistic**

SAME AS STORIES	DIFFERENT FROM STORIES
characters plot	act it out costumes scenery music audience actors

Graphic Organizer 31

CREATE A SCENE Have children GROUP WRITING work in small groups to act out a scene from a favorite story, fairy tale, or television show, or encourage children to create a short scene of their own. Have them write a list of the characters in the scene and a script that includes one or two lines of dialogue for each character. Children can perform their short scenes for the class.

Develop Oral Language

THE ELEMENTS OF A PLAY Help ESL children understand words in the chart by displaying, labeling, and discussing illustrations depicting the elements of a play. You may wish to use programs, posters, or ads for actual plays. Have children pantomime what an audience does at the end of a play. ▶ **Kinesthetic**

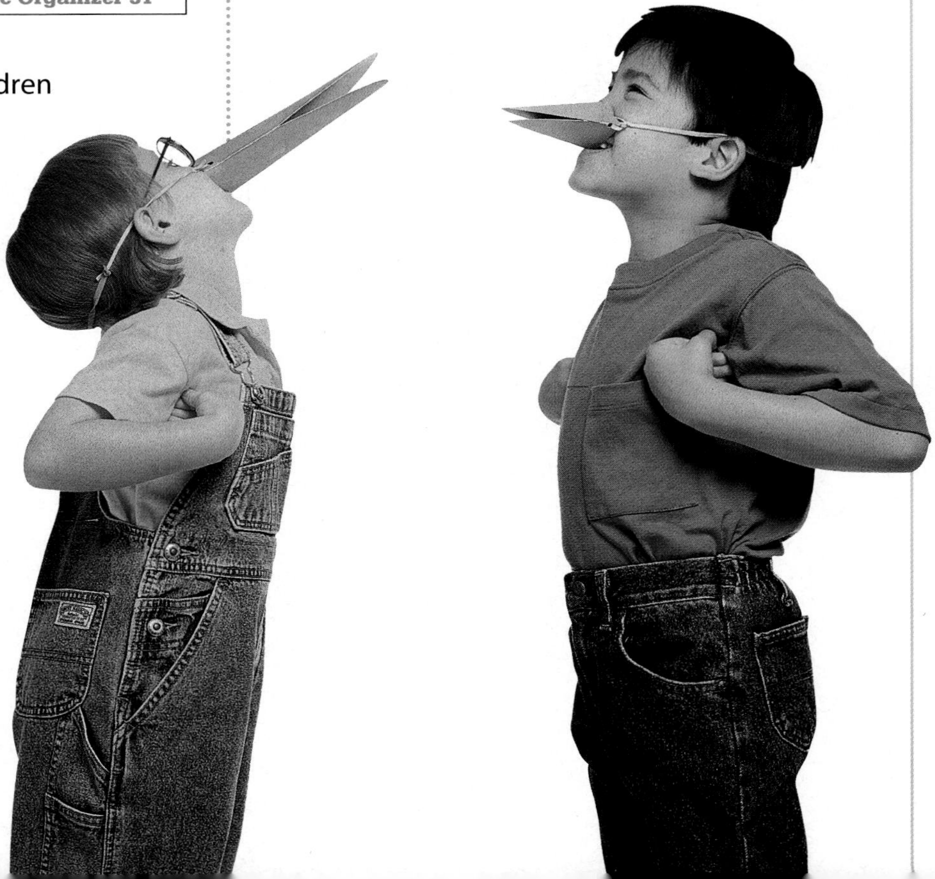

Anthology and Leveled Books

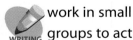

DAILY Phonics ROUTINES

DAY 2 **Discriminating** Say aloud the following pairs of words: *car/care; horn/phone; sport/cot; hear/hide*. Ask children to raise their hands when they hear /âr/, /ôr/, or /îr/ words.

Phonics CD-ROM

LANGUAGE SUPPORT

Use the **Language Support Book**, pages 181–184, to help build background.

TESTED OBJECTIVES

Children will use context and structural clues to determine the meanings of vocabulary words.

Definitions

music (p. 144) sounds that have melody, harmony, or rhythm, made by instruments or a voice

voice (p. 135) sound made by the vocal cords

whistle (p. 141) to make a high-pitched sound by blowing air through pressed lips.

scare (p. 139) to frighten

third (p. 144) something in position number three when things are placed in order

daughter (p. 135) a parent's female child

Story Words

These words from the selection may be unfamiliar. Before children read, have them check the meanings and pronunciations of the words in the Glossary, beginning on page 390, or in a dictionary.

- storyteller, p. 134
- musicians, p. 135
- miller, p. 136
- envy, p. 137

music
voice
whistle
scare
third
daughter

Vocabulary

Teach Vocabulary in Context

Identify Vocabulary Words Display **Teaching Chart 142** and read the passage with children. Have volunteers circle each vocabulary word and underline other words that are clues to its meaning.

The Three Singers

1. Three animals wanted to make beautiful music by singing. **2.** Each sang the words with a lovely voice. **3.** But instead of singing, one animal put his lips together and began to whistle, making a sharp, squeaky sound. **4.** The other animals asked him to stop—they were afraid the loud noise would scare people away. **5.** They asked him three times to stop. After the third time, he finally did. **6.** One day, the animals sang for the king's youngest daughter. She enjoyed their singing so much that she asked her father the king to give them a reward!

Teaching Chart 142

Discuss Meanings Ask questions like these to help clarify word meanings:

- When you listen to the radio, what kind of music do you like best?
- Do you talk with a loud voice or a quiet one?
- Can you whistle and sing at the same time? Can you whistle and walk at the same time?
- What kinds of stories or movies might scare people?
- What is the third letter of the alphabet?
- If there are two girls and one boy in a family, how many daughters are there?

Activities

Practice

Word Scramble

WRITING · PARTNERS

Have children choose vocabulary cards from a pile and rewrite their words, scrambling the letters. Have partners exchange papers and unscramble the letters to write the vocabulary words correctly. Then have children orally define the words.

▶ **Logical/Linguistic**

music   third   voice

Word Building Manipulative Cards

Write Context Sentences

WRITING · PARTNERS

Have partners write context sentences, leaving a blank for each vocabulary word. Ask children to exchange papers and fill in the blanks or use vocabulary cards to show answers. Have children refer to their Glossary as needed.

Assess Vocabulary

Identify Word Meaning in Context

WRITING · GROUP

Help children form small groups, and give each group a list of vocabulary words. Ask the groups to write riddles for their words. For clues, children can use antonyms or synonyms of the words or tell where and when they might use or hear the words. Have groups exchange and solve riddles.

SPELLING/VOCABULARY CONNECTIONS

See Spelling Challenge Words, pages 149Q–149R.

LANGUAGE SUPPORT

See the **Language Support Book**, pages 181–184, for teaching suggestions for **Vocabulary**.

Vocabulary PuzzleMaker

Provides vocabulary activities.

Meeting Individual Needs for Vocabulary

EASY

Name__________ Date______ **Reteach 170**

Vocabulary

Find the word in the box below that completes each sentence. Write the letter of the answer on the line in front of the sentence.

daughter   music   scare   third   voice   whistle

e **1.** Your ___ sounds very nice when you sing. **a.** whistle

c **2.** I like to ___ my friends in the dark. **b.** daughter

f **3.** This is the ___ time Rick saw the movie. **c.** scare

a **4.** I heard the wind ___ around the corner. **d.** music

d **5.** Lou plays beautiful ___ on his piano. **e.** voice

b **6.** That girl is the ___ of my teacher. **f.** third

170 **At Home:** Encourage children to write a story using the vocabulary words in the box. Book 2.2/Unit 2 The Bremen Town Musicians 6

Reteach, 170

ON-LEVEL

Name__________ Date______ **Practice 170**

Vocabulary

scare   third   daughter   music   voice   whistle

Read each sentence. Choose a word from the box that means almost the same thing as the words in dark type. Write it on the line.

1. They took their (**girl child**) to the movies. daughter
2. Alex can (**make a sound with his lips**). whistle
3. John lost his key for the (**three in a row**) time. third
4. The children (**make people afraid**) with their masks. scare
5. I love to play (**nice sounds**) on the guitar. music
6. Luke has a strong speaking (**sound from his mouth**). voice

170 **At Home:** Have children make up questions using three of the vocabulary words. Book 2.2/Unit 2 The Bremen Town Musicians 6

Practice, 170

ON-LEVEL

Lina Saves the Play

At the play, Lina was scared. Still, she said her lines. But Sandy did not turn on the music, and José did not wake Maria. Luckily, Lina whistled the song and woke the daughter.

Everyone yelled, "More! More!"

"You saved the day, Lina," said Mrs. Rose.

At Home: Have children write about a time they were scared, and what they did to get through their fear.

4 170a

Practice, 170a Take-Home Story

CHALLENGE

Name__________ Date______ **Extend 170**

Vocabulary

daughter   music   scare   third   voice   whistle

Write a word from the box that answers each riddle.

1. She is not a son. daughter
2. You blow through me to make a high sound. whistle
3. I am between the second and the fourth. third
4. You need me to sing, talk, or whisper. voice
5. Musicians read me to play their instruments. music
6. This is what you get when someone sneaks up on you. scare

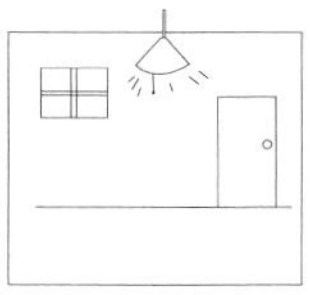

Write a title for this scene.

Title: The Music Room

170 **At Home:** Invite children to write the vocabulary words on individual cards. Put them in a stack facing down. Have children choose a card and use the word in a sentence. Book 2.2/Unit 2 The Bremen Town Musicians

Extend, 170

Comprehension

Prereading Strategies

PREVIEW AND PREDICT Read aloud the name of the play. Explain to children that plays are meant to be acted out, but they can also be read like a story. Then take a **picture walk** through the illustrations. Discuss with children how the pictures give clues about what will happen in the play.

- How do you think a play might be different from a story? *Genre*
- What clues do the title and pictures give about this play's characters and setting?
- What do you think the play will be about?

Have children record in a chart their predictions about what will happen in the story.

PREDICTIONS	WHAT HAPPENED
The play is about a group of animals who take a trip together.	

SET PURPOSES Ask children what they would like to learn from reading the story. For example:

- Why do the animals leave?
- Why do they chase the men?

READ TOGETHER

The Brothers Grimm

Jacob and Wilhelm Grimm were born in Germany more than 200 years ago. They heard old fairy tales from friends and shopkeepers. They wrote down all the stories so they would not be forgotten. Some of the fairy tales the Brothers Grimm collected are *Rapunzel*, *Hansel and Gretel*, and *Little Red Riding Hood*. Jacob and Wilhelm worked closely together. Jacob said, "Up to the very end, we worked in two rooms next to each other, always under one roof."

Meet Margaret H. Lippert

Margaret Lippert is a professional storyteller. She has retold many classic tales and has also written new stories.

Meet Mary GrandPré

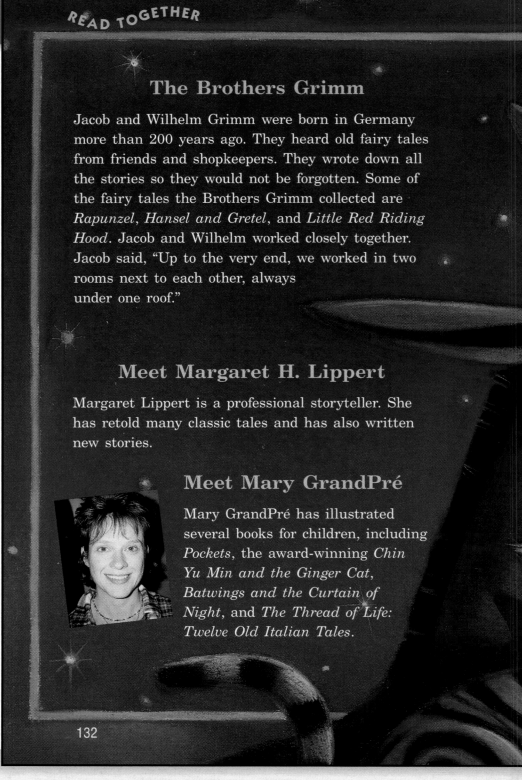

Mary GrandPré has illustrated several books for children, including *Pockets*, the award-winning *Chin Yu Min and the Ginger Cat*, *Batwings and the Curtain of Night*, and *The Thread of Life: Twelve Old Italian Tales*.

132

Meeting Individual Needs • Grouping Suggestions for Strategic Reading

EASY

Read Together Read the play aloud with children. Model the strategy of changing voices for each speaker's dialogue to help children keep track of characters and events. Comprehension and Intervention prompts offer additional help with decoding, vocabulary, and comprehension.

ON-LEVEL

Guided Instruction Before reading the story with the class, you may want to have children read the story first on their own. Use the Comprehension prompts as you read the story with children. Afterwards, have children reread the story using their stick puppets to help them keep track of the characters and sequence of events.

CHALLENGE

Read Independently After reading, have children retell the story and tell whether they thought each animal had good reasons for leaving home.

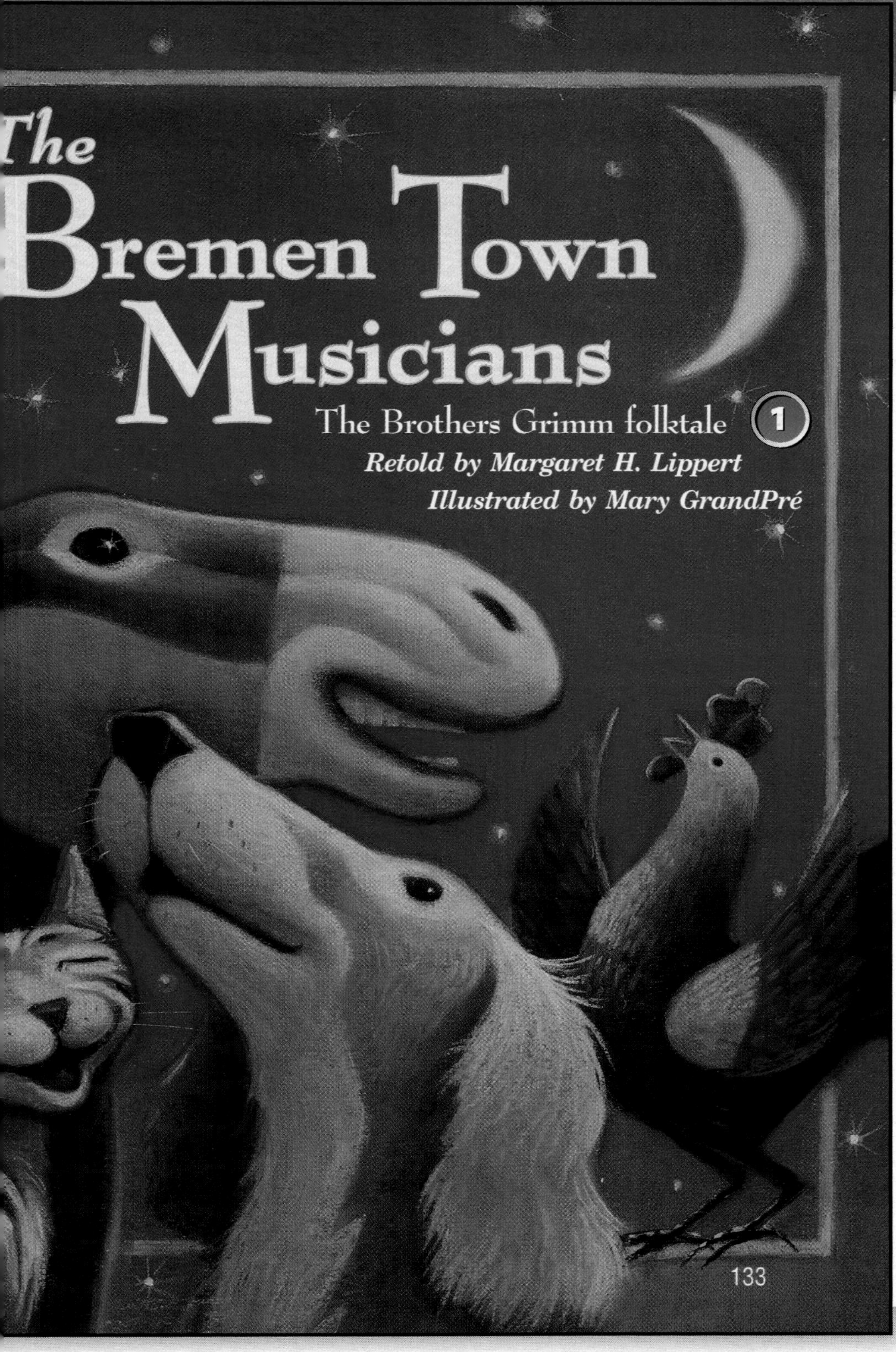

Comprehension

Phonics Apply /âr/, /ôr/ and /îr/ Sounds

STRATEGIC READING One part in the play we are going to read is the storyteller. Let's create stick puppets to help us remember and understand the play's characters and plot. We'll add pictures of characters, things, and places that seem important.

1 This page lists information about the author and illustrator. It also gives information about the Brothers Grimm. What does it mean that Margaret H. Lippert "retold" this story? (She turned an old folk tale into a play.) *Author*

Genre

Play

Explain that a play:

- often has a plot that revolves around a central conflict and its resolution.
- is largely composed of dialogue between characters.
- may have more than one setting.
- may be divided into acts and scenes.

Activity After children read *The Bremen Town Musicians,* select volunteers to identify the conflict(s) and resolution(s) in the plot. Ask them to provide examples of features that make this selection a play, such as the presence of dialogue, changing settings, and different acts. Assign roles to volunteers and have them read aloud their parts.

LANGUAGE SUPPORT

Blackline masters of the stick puppets can be found in the **Language Support Book**.

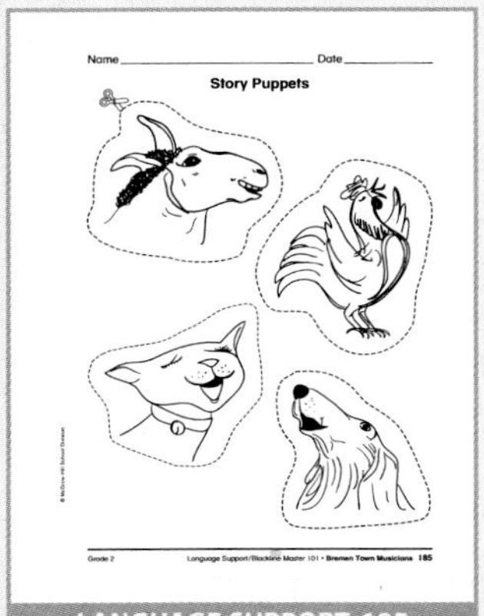

LANGUAGE SUPPORT, 185

Comprehension

2 Phonics /ôr/ *or* Which character speaks first on this page? Say that character's name aloud. (Storyteller) Which letters make the /ôr/ sound? (*or*) Let's run a finger under this word as we blend the sounds and read it. ***Blending/Graphophonic Cues***

3 What problem does the donkey have? (The farmer is planning to sell him because he is too old to work.) Why would no one want to buy an old donkey? (The donkey might be too old to work hard.) ***Make Inferences***

TEACHING TIP

MANAGEMENT Have children begin with their story puppets face down in front of them. When each new character is introduced, ask them to pick up the puppet. After a character has been introduced, but the puppet is not in use, ask children to rest that puppet face up.

The Players

Donkey	Boss
Dog	Muscles
Cat	Curly
Rooster	Storyteller

ACT ONE

2 **Storyteller:** There was once a farmer who had a donkey. The donkey had worked hard for many years, but now he was getting too old to work. One day the farmer was talking to a friend about selling his donkey, and the donkey heard him.

3 **Donkey:** I can't believe that after all my hard work, the farmer has decided to sell me. No one will want to buy an old donkey like me. I think I will run away to Bremen Town and be a musician there.

134

Activity

Cross Curricular: Social Studies

ANIMAL FARMERS Tell children that animals on farms often have jobs to do, even dogs and cats.

RESEARCH AND INQUIRY Invite children to look through books about farm life to learn more about what jobs an animal might do in a day at the farm. Children can work in groups to create schedules showing what a farm animal's day is like.

▶ **Linguistic/Logical**

interNET CONNECTION Children can learn more about the lives of farm animals by visiting ***www.mhschool.com/reading.***

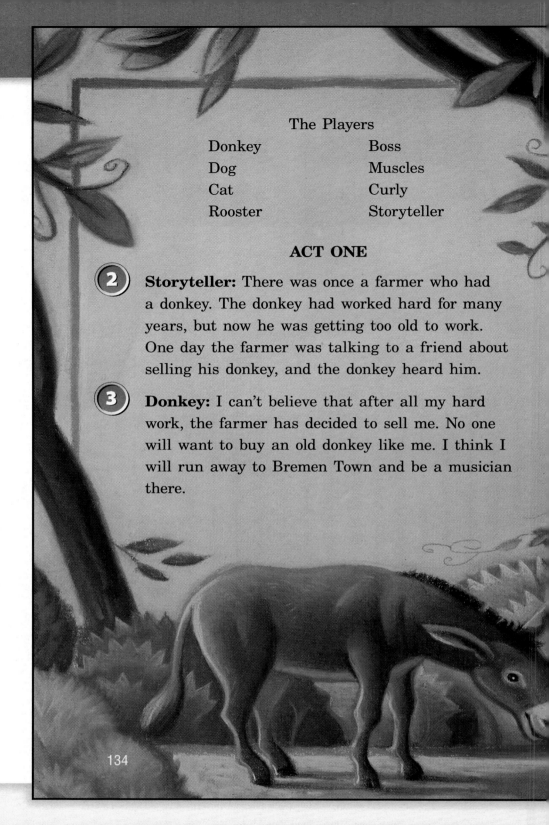

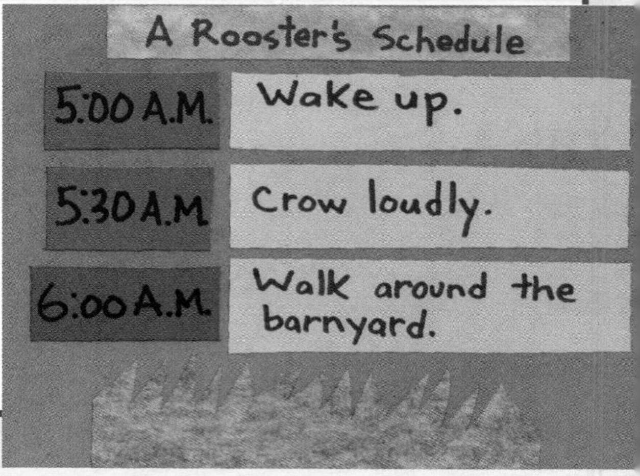

A Rooster's Schedule
5:00 A.M.
Wake up.
5:30 A.M.
Crow loudly.
6:00 A.M.
Walk around the barnyard.

Storyteller: So in the morning the donkey set off down the road to Bremen. Soon he came to a dog lying in the road.

Donkey: Why are you lying in the road? (4)

Dog: I need to rest. I have just run a long, long way and I am very tired.

Donkey: Where are you going?

Dog: I don't know. I am running away because my master is angry with me. I am getting old and can't run as fast as I once could. Last night when I let a fox run off with a nice, plump chicken, my master told his daughter to kiss me good-bye. He said that I am no longer worth the food I eat, so I decided to run away. (5)

Donkey: Why don't you come with me? I am going to Bremen to be a musician in the town band. You, too, have a beautiful voice. We can be in the town band together. I'll bray and you'll bark, and they will invite us to join.

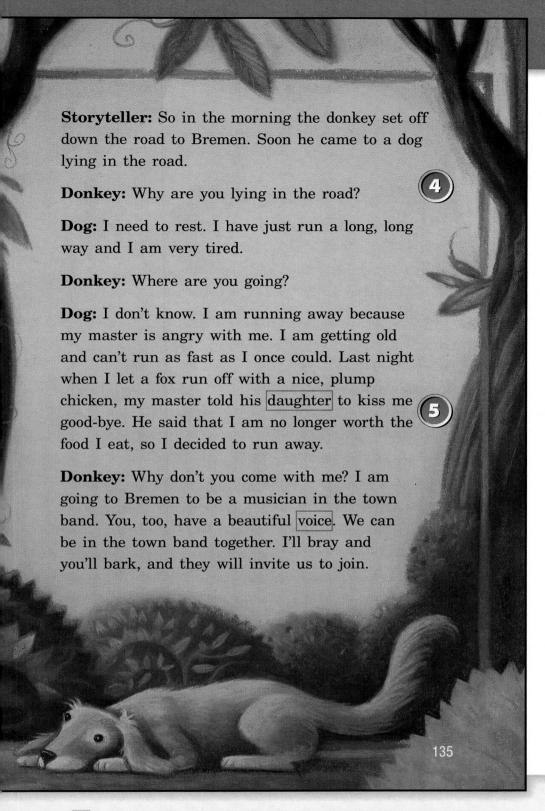

135

Comprehension

4 What problem does the dog have? Compare the dog's problem to the donkey's problem. (Both animals' owners think they are too old to be of any use.) ***Plot/Compare and Contrast***

5 The dog says he "let a fox run off with a nice, plump chicken," and that because of this, his master decided that he was no longer worth having around. What work did the dog do for the farmer? (kept the farm safe from wild animals) ***Draw Conclusions***

P/I READ WORDS WITH /oi/ *oi* Read aloud the last word of the third sentence in the last paragraph. (*voice*) What is the vowel sound in this word? (/oi/)

P/I PREVENTION/INTERVENTION

READ WORDS WITH *oi* Write on the chalkboard: *Did he toil all day in the soil?* Read aloud the sentence. Ask children if any words in it have the same vowel sound that is in the word *voice*.

- Underline *toil* and *soil*. Circle the letters *oi* in each word, and explain to children that these letters work together to spell the sound /oi/. Run your hand under each word as you blend the sounds together. Have children repeat after you.
- Write these sentences on the chalkboard: *He wrapped it in foil so it would not spoil. She made a choice to make some noise.* Invite volunteers to read each sentence aloud, underline the words that contain the /oi/ sound, and circle the letters that spell the sound. ***Graphophonic Cues***

Minilesson

REVIEW/MAINTAIN

Vowel Sounds: /ô/ spelled *a*

Make the /ô/ sound, and ask children to find two words with this sound on page 134. Write *talking, all* on the chalkboard, and run a finger under the letters as you blend the word. Next to *talking* and *all*, write *walk* and *wall*. Blend and read aloud each word, inviting children to repeat after you. Ask:

- What vowel sound can be heard in each of these words? (/ô/)
- Which letters spell the /ô/ sound?

Activity Ask children to brainstorm a list of other words containing /ô/ spelled *a*.

Phonics CD-ROM Have children use the interactive phonics activities for reinforcement.

Comprehension

6 Why was the cat sad? (The master was going to toss the cat in the lake.) Act out the scene from page 136 where the donkey meets the cat. Use expressions and movements to show how the animals feel. *Pantomime*

7 What animals are now on their way to Bremen Town to become musicians? Let's hold up puppets for the characters we have met so far. (donkey, dog, and cat)

Fluency

READ WITH EXPRESSION

Have partners take turns reading page 143 aloud to each other with expression appropriate to each character. Invite children to first consider how each character is feeling in this part of the story. Tell children to make sure that their reading reflects these feelings. Remind them that the storyteller is not a character in the action, so he or she should speak with the voice of an onlooker.

Storyteller: So the dog and the donkey went along together. Soon they came to a cat who was looking very sad.

Donkey: Why are you so sad?

6 **Cat:** I am about to die. Last night I heard the miller talking to his family. He said he doesn't want me anymore because I am getting too old to catch mice. My teeth are not as sharp as they once were, so the mice get away. The miller said he is going to toss me into the lake tomorrow, and I can't swim.

Donkey: Don't be sad any longer. Come along with us. We are off to Bremen Town to be musicians in the town band. With your beautiful meow, you can be in the band, too.

7 **Storyteller:** So the cat followed the donkey and the dog down the road. Before long they saw a rooster crowing.

136

Activity

Cross Curricular: Science

VOICES The donkey praises the animals' voices. Have children think about their voices. Explain that when we speak or sing, our lungs, lips, tongue, voice box (or larynx), and brain all work together to produce sound. Have partners try the following experiments and record their results:

- Try to talk without moving your lips.
- Try to talk without moving your tongue.
- Put your finger on your throat so you can feel your larynx vibrate as you talk, as you sing a low note, and as you sing a high note.

▶ **Linguistic/Kinesthetic/Musical**

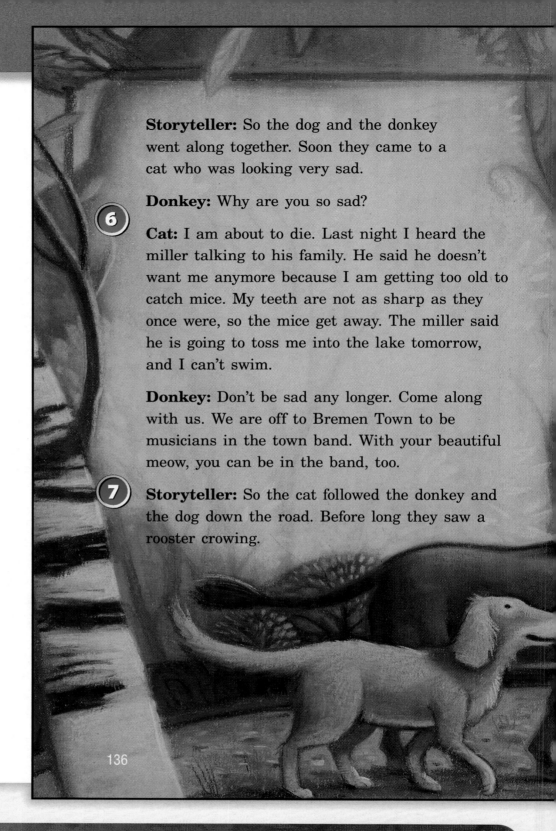

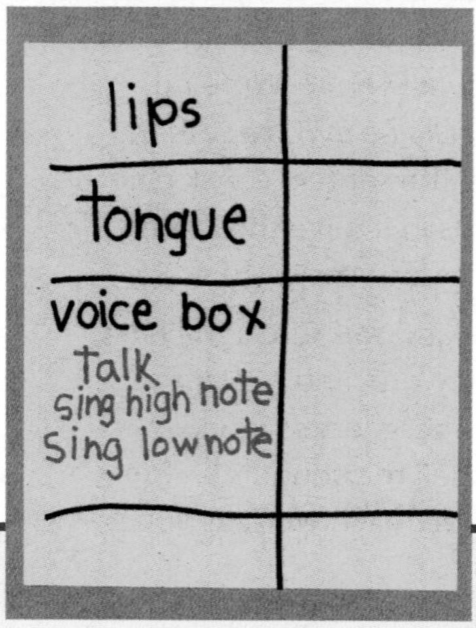

Donkey: I never heard a rooster crowing so late in the morning. What is the matter?

Rooster: Soon I will leave the earth, and this is my last song. I just heard the farmer tell his wife that I am getting old and sleep too late to wake them up in the morning. He told her to make me into soup for the family dinner.

8

9

Donkey: Why, then, you must come with us! We are going to Bremen to be musicians in the town band. With your crowing to add to my braying, the dog's barking, and the cat's meowing, we will be the envy of all the other musicians there.

Storyteller: So the rooster decided to join the donkey, the dog, and the cat, and they all went down the road together.

137

Comprehension

8 Which character in the play did we meet first? Second? Third? Fourth? (donkey, dog, cat, rooster) Let's place our puppets in front of us in the order we met them. ***Sequence of Events/Story Props***

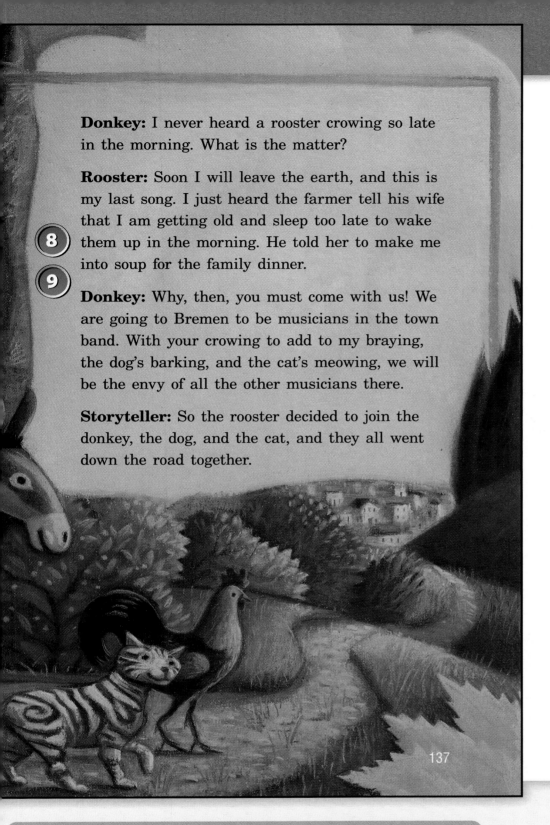

9 What is the main problem all of the animals are facing? How are the animals solving their problem? (Their masters think they are too old and want to get rid of them. They are running away to become musicians.) ***Plot/Problem and Solution***

LANGUAGE SUPPORT

ESL On separate cards, write the name of each animal pictured on pages 132–133. Invite ESL children to share with the class the names for these animals in their native languages. Write these names in a different color on the cards below the English words. Shuffle the cards and have children choose a card, say the English name for that animal, and point to that animal in the picture.

Minilesson

REVIEW/MAINTAIN

Make Inferences

Remind children that readers can make inferences about characters or events based on information in the story.

- Have children reread page 136. Invite them to make an inference about the cat. Ask: How do you think the cat feels after talking to the donkey? (happy)
- Ask them to explain how they made this inference. (The cat feels better because she found a friend with the same problem; the donkey says kind things to her.)

Activity Invite children to infer why the donkey and the dog become friends so quickly. Ask them to explain how they made this inference. (Both animals have run away, and maybe they can help each other.)

Comprehension

10 How do you think the animals are feeling after traveling all day? (hungry and tired) What do you predict will happen next? *Make Inferences*

11 Why does the donkey tell the other animals to hide in the bushes?

MODEL Let's see if the donkey is going to look in the window of a strange house. The animals don't know who will be inside. I think the donkey wants the other animals to be safe while he checks the house. *Critical Thinking*

SELF-MONITORING STRATEGY

REREADING Rereading a part of the story that you didn't understand the first time can help make events in the plot clearer.

MODEL I don't understand how the musicians found that house in the woods. I'll reread that section. Now I see—they saw a light far away and walked towards it until they came to the house.

ACT TWO

Storyteller: The friends traveled on and on, but they did not reach Bremen that day. When it began to get dark, they decided to look for a place to spend the night. Way back in the woods they saw a little light. They went toward it, into the
10 dark woods, hoping to find shelter. After a long time they saw a house through the trees.

Donkey: There must be someone at home. You hide behind this clump of bushes, while I go and
11 look through the window.

Storyteller: The donkey went to the house and peeked in the window. There he saw a band of robbers eating dinner. On the table were stacks of gold coins and plates piled high with food. The donkey got an idea.

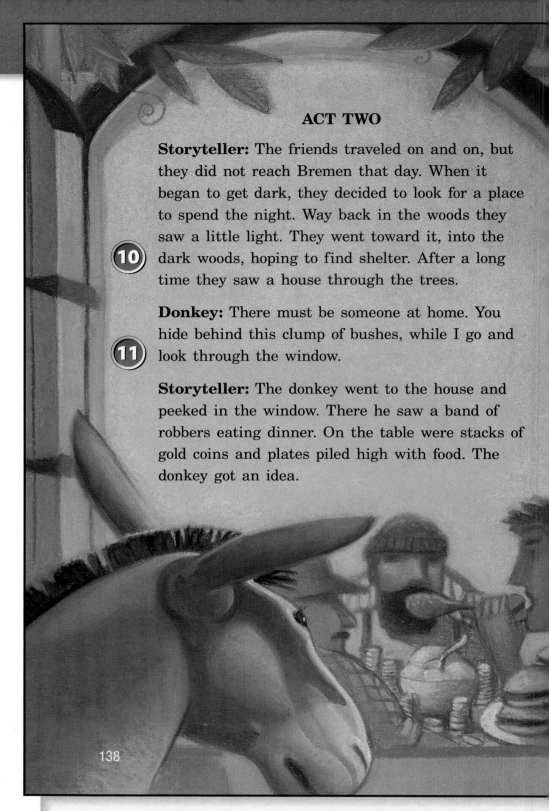

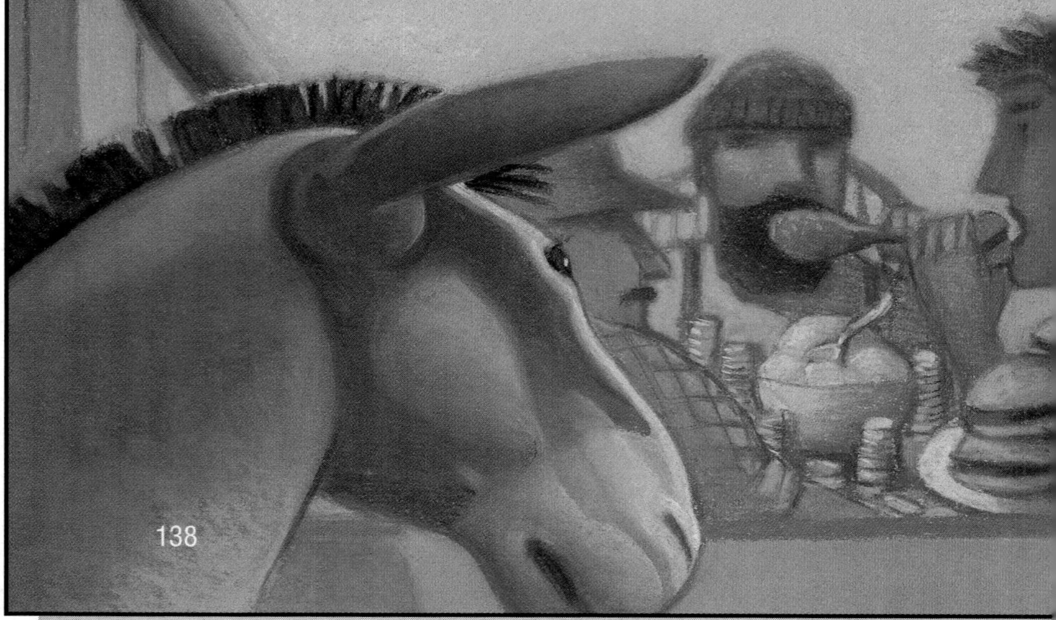

138

LANGUAGE SUPPORT

ESL Children may have difficulty understanding the word *toward* on page 138. To help them, write *toward* on the chalkboard and underline the letters *to*. Invite children to stand. Beckon with your hand as you invite them to walk *toward you*. Now write *backward* on the board, underlining the small word *back*. Pantomime how to walk backward and ask children to walk backward. Guide them to understand that the little words *to* and *back* help explain the meaning of *toward* and *backward*.

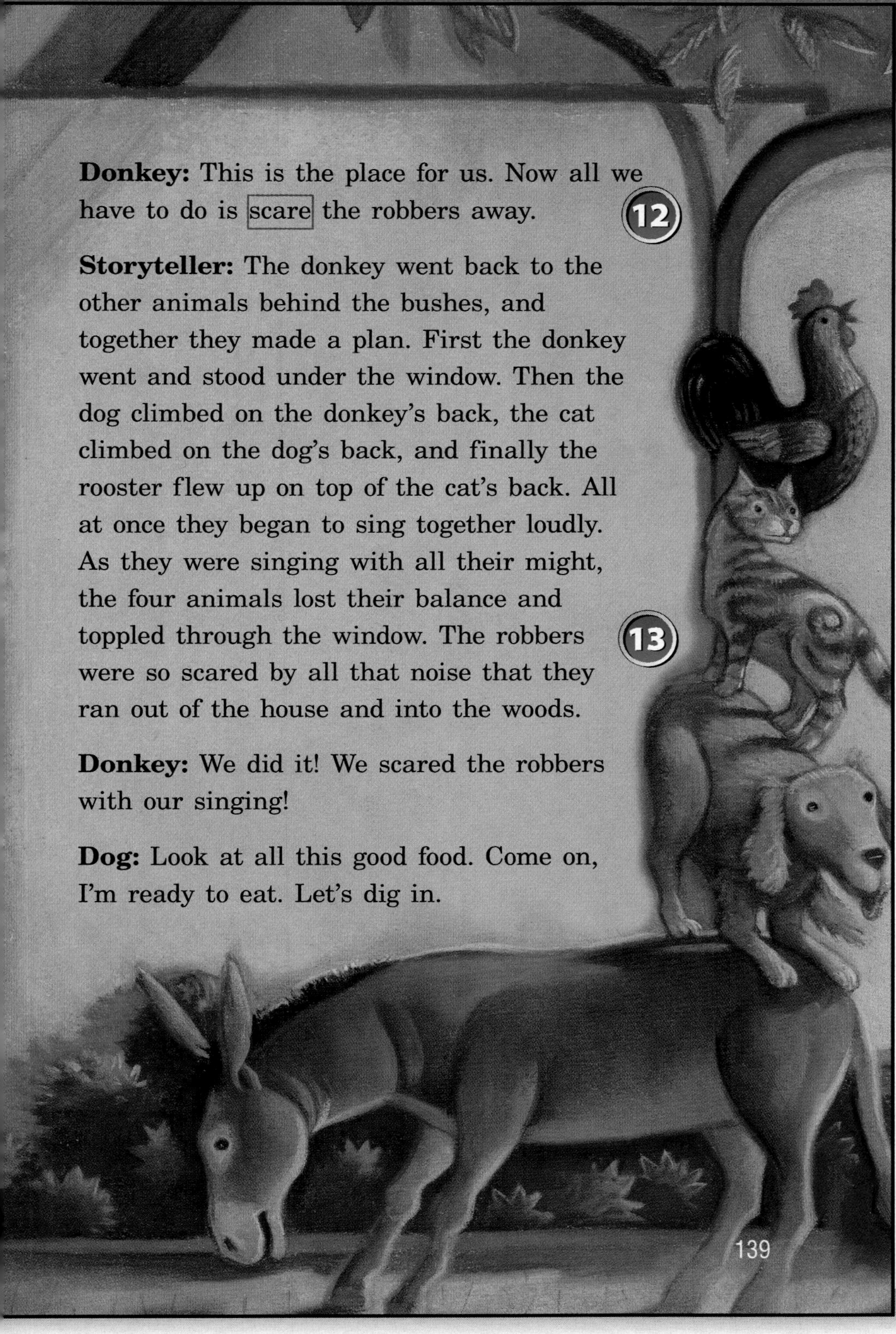

Donkey: This is the place for us. Now all we have to do is scare the robbers away. **12**

Storyteller: The donkey went back to the other animals behind the bushes, and together they made a plan. First the donkey went and stood under the window. Then the dog climbed on the donkey's back, the cat climbed on the dog's back, and finally the rooster flew up on top of the cat's back. All at once they began to sing together loudly. As they were singing with all their might, the four animals lost their balance and toppled through the window. The robbers **13** were so scared by all that noise that they ran out of the house and into the woods.

Donkey: We did it! We scared the robbers with our singing!

Dog: Look at all this good food. Come on, I'm ready to eat. Let's dig in.

139

Comprehension

12 **Phonics** ***/âr/are*** Let's read aloud the donkey's second line on this page. Is there a word in this sentence that contains the /âr/ sound? (*scare*) Let's run a finger under this word as we blend the sounds and read it. ***Blending/Graphophonic Cues***

13 Why do you think the animals fell through the window? Use your puppets to show what happened. ***Story Props***

P/I **APOSTROPHES** Find the words *Let's* and *I'm* on page 139. What do they mean? (Let us, I am)

P/I PREVENTION/INTERVENTION

APOSTROPHES Write on the chalkboard *I'm* and *let's*. Circle the apostrophes in each word. Elicit that apostrophes are used in these words because they are contractions, words created by uniting two words into one (*I* and *am*, *let* and *us*) and leaving out certain letters. Explain that in contractions, the apostrophe stands for letters that were dropped when the contractions were formed. Prompt children to tell you what letters were dropped from *I'm* and *let's*. (*a* and *u*)

Write on the chalkboard the word pairs *she is*; *we are*; *that is*. Ask children to create contractions from each pair. (*she's, we're, that's*) ***Syntactic Cues***

Minilesson

REVIEW/MAINTAIN

Context Clues

Remind children that the familiar words around unfamiliar words can give clues to the unfamiliar words' meaning. Write the following sentence on the chalkboard and have children read it silently. *When the big, yellow zargle drove into the parking lot, all the children got on it and rode back to school.*

- Point out that the underlined word is a nonsense word. Ask children to use context clues to figure out the meaning of *zargle*. (school bus) Help them to recognize as clues the words *big*, *yellow*, *drove* and the phrase *got on it and rode back to school*.

Activity Have partners use context clues to help them figure out the meaning of *shelter* on page 138.

Comprehension

14 Why does the cat decide to sleep in front of the fireplace? (It is warm.) Do you think most cats like to sleep where it is warm? (yes) ***Form Generalizations***

15 Remind children that in some make-believe stories, animals do things that only people can do in real life. This is called *personification*. Ask children to name examples of personification found in this play. (The animals talk, sing, sit at the table to eat, and so on.) ***Author's Craft***

TEACHING TIP

BACKGROUND INFORMATION On a map of Germany, point out the town of Bremen, which has a monument in honor of the Bremen Town musicians. Show pictures of the German countryside to children. Encourage children to compare and contrast the pictures to the setting of the play.

Storyteller: Then the cat, the dog, the donkey, and the rooster all sat down at the table and ate until they were full.

14 **Cat:** My, but I'm tired. The fireplace is still warm. I think I'll curl up and go to sleep there.

Dog: I think I'll sleep here in this cozy spot behind the door.

15 **Donkey:** I'll go outside and sleep in front of the house.

Rooster: I think I'll take my nap up on the roof. Good night, all!

140

Activity

Cross Curricular: Art

MAKE SCENERY One of the things that makes a play seem real is a backdrop—artwork on the stage that depicts the setting in which a scene is taking place. For example, one backdrop for *The Bremen Town Musicians* might show the forest.

Activity Have children choose a scene from the play to draw or paint a backdrop for, using a roll of butcher paper. Encourage children to look at story illustrations, reread the story, and use their imaginations.

▶ **Spatial/Kinesthetic**

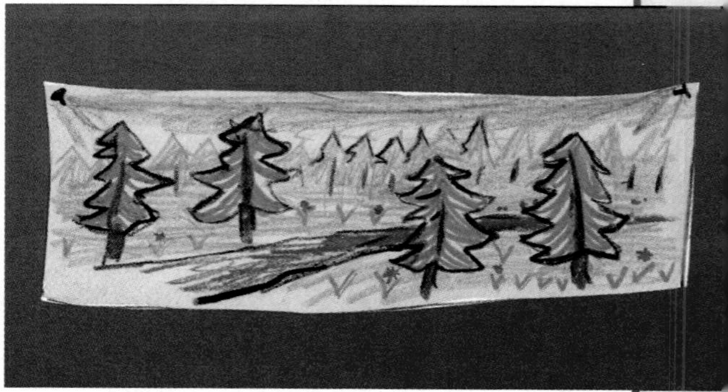

Storyteller: It was not long before all the animals were asleep. (16) As the robbers began to think about the tasty dinner and the shiny gold they left behind, they decided they had made a mistake and had been scared away too quickly. They went back to the house and discovered that it was dark and quiet. (17)

Boss: It looks as though our house is empty now. Let's go back in.

Muscles: No so fast, Boss. One of us should go in first to be sure all of them are gone. How about it, Curly?

Curly: Don't look at me, Muscles. I always have to do all the hard work.

Boss: He's right. You go ahead, Muscles. Look all around. If everything seems fine, whistle. When we hear you whistle, we'll come in. Good luck, and be careful.

Curly: Don't forget to open the front door slowly so it doesn't squeak. (18)

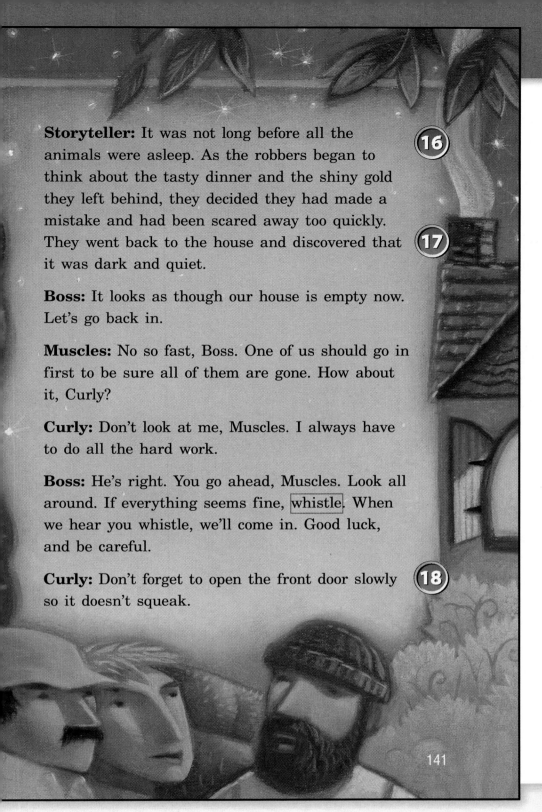

141

Comprehension

(16) Were the animals awake or asleep when the robbers decided to go back to the house? (asleep) ***Sequence of Events***

(17) Why did the robbers decide to go back to the house ? (They thought about the dinner and the gold they had left behind.) ***Cause and Effect***

(18) **Phonics** **/âr/*are* and /îr/*ear*** Can you find the words *hard* and *hear* on this page? Which of these words contains the /îr/ sound? (*hear*) Now find the words *scared* and *squeak*. Which of these words contain the /âr/ sound? (*scared*) ***Graphophonic Cues***

P/I **READ WORDS WITH /ē/** Why did Curly say to open the door slowly? (so it wouldn't squeak)

P/I PREVENTION/INTERVENTION

READ WORDS WITH /ē/ Write *squeak* on the chalkboard. Run your hand underneath the word as you blend the sounds together aloud. Have children repeat after you. Ask:

- Which letters in this word spell the /ē/ sound? (*ea*)
- Can you think of any other words in which the *ea* letter combinations stand for the /ē/ sound? (*read, flea, speak*) ***Graphophonic Cues***

Minilesson

REVIEW/MAINTAIN

Summarize

Review that summarizing a story or play means telling about the main characters and the most important events. Ask pairs of children to summarize the events of the play up to the end of page 141. Have each pair use their story puppets to help them act out events that have taken place.

Activity Have children create comic strips, with each box containing a main event or idea from the story.

Comprehension

19 **Phonics** ***/ôr/ore*** Can you find a word on this page that contains the /ôr/ sound? *(more)* Which letters in this word spell the /ôr/ sound? *(ore)* ***Segmenting/ Graphophonic Cues***

Storyteller: Boss and Curly waited behind a clump of trees while Muscles went into the house. They were listening for a whistle, but Muscles never whistled. He was careful, but when he opened the front door it did squeak a little.

The cat opened her eyes. Muscles saw the cat's eyes gleaming like fire. He came closer to the fireplace to get more light, but instead he got the fright of his life. The cat jumped up and scratched him with her claws. As Muscles backed out of the door, the dog grabbed him by the leg. Then the donkey chased him out into the yard. **19**

142

CULTURAL PERSPECTIVES

Variant tales explain that it is not unusual for similar folktales to be found in different cultures. The story of Cinderella can be found in Algonquin and Ojibway Indian, Korean, Chinese, French, German, Italian, Filipino, Zimbabwean, and Egyptian cultures.

RESEARCH AND INQUIRY Help children use the library or Internet to find versions of the Cinderella story from different cultures.

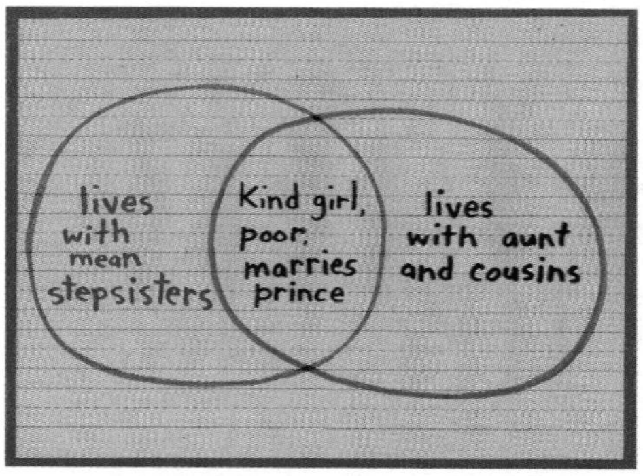

Muscles: Help! Help! I'm going to die.

Rooster (from the roof): COCK-A-DOODLE-DOO!

Storyteller: Muscles ran away and banged right into the other robbers, who were still standing behind the trees.

Boss: What happened? You look awful.

Muscles: I FEEL awful. My leg is bleeding and I'm hurting all over. I envy you, Curly. You have all the luck.

Curly: Well, don't be shy. Tell us what happened.

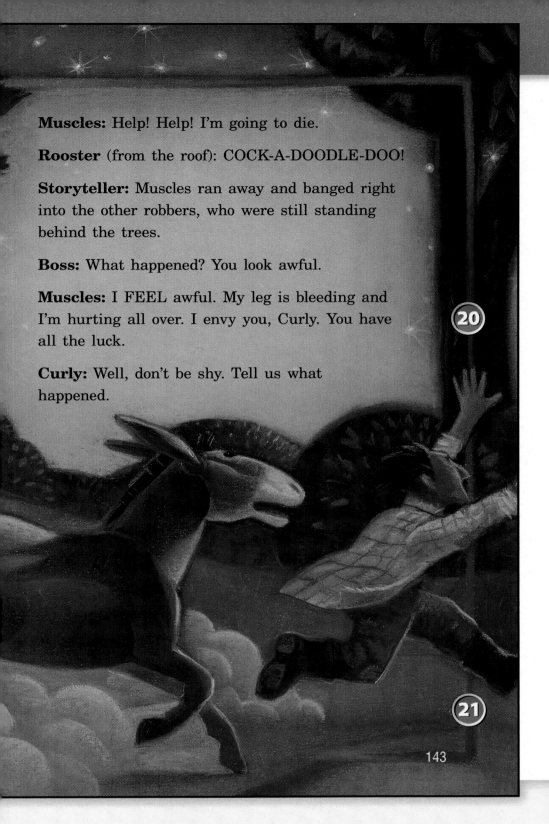

143

Comprehension

20 Think about the robber characters in the story. Find an example of where they have real qualities. Are the robbers described in a way that they can be both good and bad, or are they only described as bad? ***Character Analysis***

21 Some words sound like what they mean, such as *purr* or *boom*. These kinds of words are called *onomatopoeia*. Find some examples in the play. (*meow, cock-a-doodle-doo, squeak*) ***Author's Craft***

Comprehension

22 What words did Muscles think he heard from the roof? ("Catch that man, now, do!") What did he really hear? (The rooster saying cock-a-doodle-doo!) ***Make Inferences***

23 Why do you think the robbers never came back? (They were scared.) ***Critical Thinking***

RETELL THE STORY Ask children to work as a group to retell the story, either using their puppets or taking parts and acting out the play. If they choose to act out the play, children who are not speaking can represent parts of the scenery, such as clumps of bushes, trees, the fireplace, and so on. Children may also wish to act out the scenery in front of the backdrop they created during the Art activity.

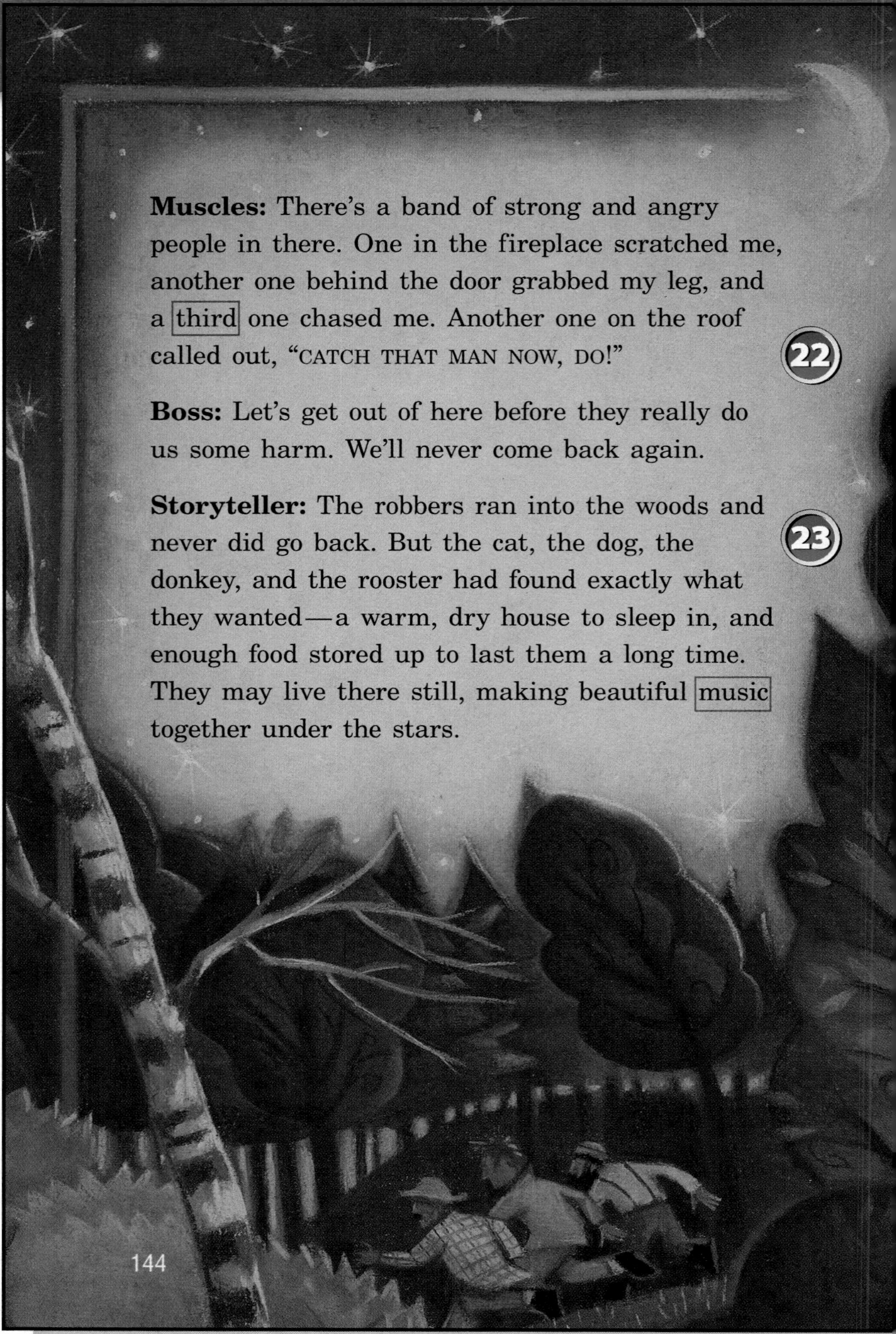

Muscles: There's a band of strong and angry people in there. One in the fireplace scratched me, another one behind the door grabbed my leg, and a third one chased me. Another one on the roof called out, "CATCH THAT MAN NOW, DO!" **22**

Boss: Let's get out of here before they really do us some harm. We'll never come back again.

Storyteller: The robbers ran into the woods and never did go back. But the cat, the dog, the donkey, and the rooster had found exactly what they wanted—a warm, dry house to sleep in, and enough food stored up to last them a long time. They may live there still, making beautiful music together under the stars. **23**

144

STUDENT SELF-ASSESSMENT

Have children ask themselves the following questions to assess how they are reading:

- Did I use what I know about the characters to help me read their parts with expression?
- Did the puppets help me to keep track of the main characters?
- How did I use what I know about letter sounds and word meanings to help me read and understand unfamiliar words?

TRANSFERRING THE STRATEGIES

- How can these strategies help me to understand other stories and plays?

REREADING FOR *Fluency*

GROUP

Children who need fluency practice can take turns reading aloud while the rest of the group follows along silently.

READING RATE When you evaluate reading rate, have children read aloud from the story for one minute. Place a stick-on note after the last word read. Count words read. To evaluate children's performance, see Running Record in the **Fluency Assessment** book.

i Intervention For leveled fluency passages, lessons, and norms charts, see **Skills Intervention Guide**, Part 5, Fluency.

Comprehension

Return to Predictions and Purposes

Reread children's predictions about the story. Discuss the predictions, noting which need to be revised. Then ask children if the story answered the questions they had before they began reading it.

PREDICTIONS	WHAT HAPPENED
The play is about a group of animals who take a trip together.	Four animals run away to be musicians, because their masters think they are too old to be useful anymore.

INFORMAL ASSESSMENT

HOW TO ASSESS

/âr/, /ôr/, AND /îr/ Have children turn to page 141 and read the last word in the fifth paragraph. Then have them point to and read the second word in the third line of the paragraph.

PLOT Ask children to explain the main problem between the animals and their owners. Then have them explain the main problem between the animals and the robbers.

FOLLOW UP

/âr/, /ôr/ AND /îr/ Continue to point out and model blending of /âr/, /ôr/, and /îr/ words.

PLOT If children are having trouble explaining the animals' problems, ask: Why did each animal leave its home? What did the animals have that the robbers wanted?

LITERARY RESPONSE

QUICK-WRITE Invite children to use their journals to record their thoughts on the play. These questions can help them get started:

JOURNAL

- Which part of the story did you like best? Why?
- Do you think the animals were right to scare away the robbers and keep the house and the food? Why or why not?
- What would you like or dislike about living in a house with four friends?

ORAL RESPONSE Have children discuss what they think might happen to the animals in the future.

Story Questions

Have children discuss or write answers to the questions on page 146.

Answers:

1. The donkey sees a band of robbers, food, and gold. *Literal/Plot*
2. Their owners think they are useless because they are old. *Inferential/Plot*
3. The animals work together to trick the robbers. *Inferential/Main Idea*
4. Possible answers: This story is about animals running away and joining together to start a new life. *Critical/Summarize*
5. The characters in both stories work together to accomplish their goals—finding a new home and raising money. *Compare and Contrast/Reading Across Texts*

Write a Report For a full writing process lesson related to this writing suggestion, see the lesson on expository writing on page 149M.

Story Questions & Activities

READ TOGETHER

1. What does the donkey see through the window?
2. Why have the animals run away from home?
3. How are four old farm animals able to stand up to a band of robbers?
4. What is this story mostly about?
5. The characters in "The Bremen Town Musicians" and "Lemonade for Sale" both have something they want to do. What do they want to do? How do they do it?

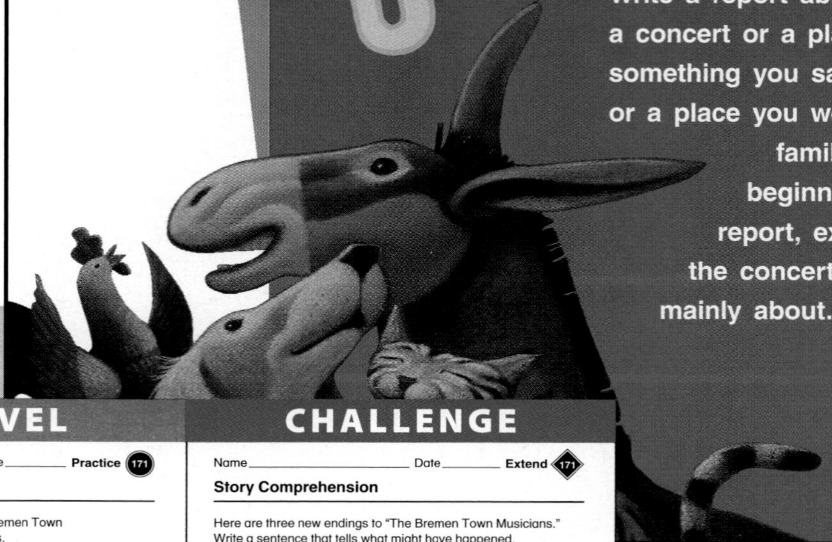

Write a Report

Write a report about going to a concert or a play. It could be something you saw at school or a place you went with your family. At the beginning of your report, explain what the concert or play was mainly about.

Meeting Individual Needs

EASY

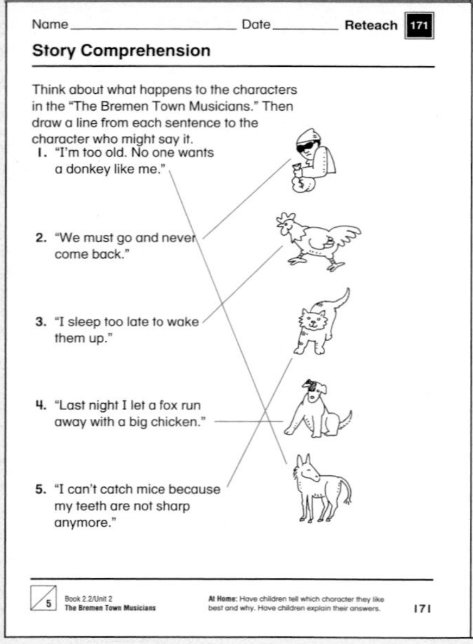

Name________ Date______ Reteach 171

Story Comprehension

Think about what happens to the characters in the "The Bremen Town Musicians." Then draw a line from each sentence to the character who might say it.

1. "I'm too old. No one wants a donkey like me."
2. "We must go and never come back."
3. "I sleep too late to wake them up."
4. "Last night I let a fox run away with a big chicken."
5. "I can't catch mice because my teeth are not sharp anymore."

5 Book 2.2/Unit 2 The Bremen Town Musicians

At Home: Have children tell which character they like best and why. Have children explain their answers. 171

Reteach, 171

ON-LEVEL

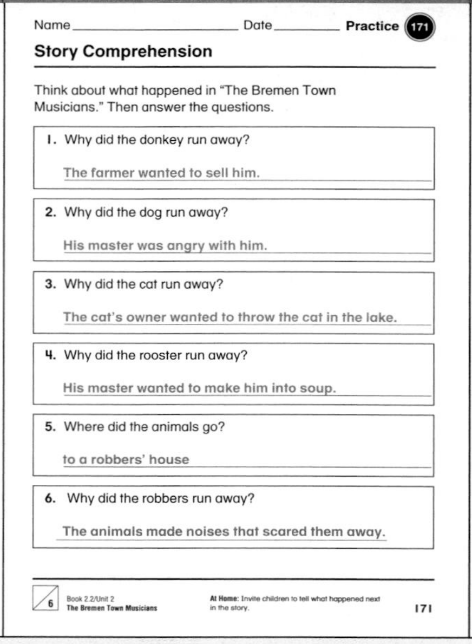

Name________ Date______ Practice 171

Story Comprehension

Think about what happened in "The Bremen Town Musicians." Then answer the questions.

1. Why did the donkey run away?
   The farmer wanted to sell him.
2. Why did the dog run away?
   His master was angry with him.
3. Why did the cat run away?
   The cat's owner wanted to throw the cat in the lake.
4. Why did the rooster run away?
   His master wanted to make him into soup.
5. Where did the animals go?
   to a robbers' house
6. Why did the robbers run away?
   The animals made noises that scared them away.

6 Book 2.2/Unit 2 The Bremen Town Musicians

At Home: Invite children to tell what happened next in the story. 171

Practice, 171

CHALLENGE

Name________ Date______ Extend 171

Story Comprehension

Here are three new endings to "The Bremen Town Musicians." Write a sentence that tells what might have happened.

Answers will vary. Sentences should relate to the picture.

Book 2.2/Unit 2 The Bremen Town Musicians

At Home: Have children draw a picture and write a sentence showing what might have happened to each animal if they had never met each other. 171

Extend, 171

Picture a Band

In "The Bremen Town Musicians," the four animals use their voices as musical instruments. Suppose you were going to start a band. Draw a picture of the instruments in your band. Label each instrument.

Make a Mask

Choose one character from "The Bremen Town Musicians." Make a mask for that character. You can use the directions on page 148 to help you.

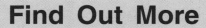

Find Out More

The animals in the play use their voices as instruments. There is a kind of music where people use just their voices to make songs. This is called *a cappella* singing. It means singing without instruments. What kind of music do you like best? Find out how and where it started. Did it come from another country? Is it a new type of music? Has it been around for a hundred years?

147

DAILY Phonics ROUTINES

DAY 3 **Segmenting** Write these words: *care, story, spear*. Ask children to underline the letters in each word that spell /âr/, /ôr/, or /îr/ sounds. Ask children to suggest other words with the same vowel sounds and spellings.

Phonics CD-ROM

Story Activities

Picture a Band

Materials: markers or crayons, poster paper

ONE Have children brainstorm a list of instruments and discuss the physical features of each before they draw. You may wish to have them create posters for different kinds of instruments.

Make a Mask

Materials: paper bags, scissors, paper plates, yarn or string, glue, paints, markers

ONE Encourage children to use a variety of materials to create masks depicting different characters from the play. Masks may be made from paper bags that go over the head, or from paper plates, which can be tied over the face; both may have decorations painted or glued on.

Find Out More

RESEARCH AND INQUIRY Bring to class recordings of various types of music and ask children to bring in recordings of their favorite music. Play parts of various selections, and help children to describe and discuss the music they hear (instrumental, lots of bass, lots of horns, focused on vocalist, and so on).

interNET CONNECTION Children may find out where different kinds of music originated by visiting ***www.mhschool.com/reading***.

FORMAL ASSESSMENT

After page 147, see Selection Assessment.

Study Skills

VARIOUS TEXTS

TESTED OBJECTIVES Children will follow step-by-step directions to make something.

PREPARE Display **Teaching Chart 143**

TEACH Explain that reading a set of directions completely before beginning a project helps make sure that you understand all the steps and have all the materials needed.

PRACTICE Have children answer questions 1–5. Then review answers as a group:

1. grocery bag, paper, scissors, glue, pencils or paint **2.** Draw or paint whiskers, a mouth, and a tongue on the bag. **3.** No, you have to cut the shapes out before gluing them in place. **4.** Answers will vary, but may include bigger ears, different nose. **5.** Answers will vary, but may include a paper cone or triangle.

ASSESS/CLOSE Have each child write step-by-step directions for a familiar task.

STUDY SKILLS

READ TOGETHER

Follow Directions

The directions tell how to make a cat mask.

1. Find a large grocery bag. Cut eye holes about 3 inches from the top.
2. Cut a nose shape out of paper. Cut two ear shapes out of paper.
3. Glue the nose and ears into place.
4. Draw or paint whiskers, a mouth, and a tongue on the bag.

1. What materials do you need to make the cat mask?
2. What is the last step in the directions?
3. Could you do step 3 before you do step 2? Explain.
4. Suppose you wanted to make a dog mask. How might it be different from the cat mask?
5. Suppose you wanted to make a rooster mask. How could you make the rooster's beak?

Meeting Individual Needs

EASY

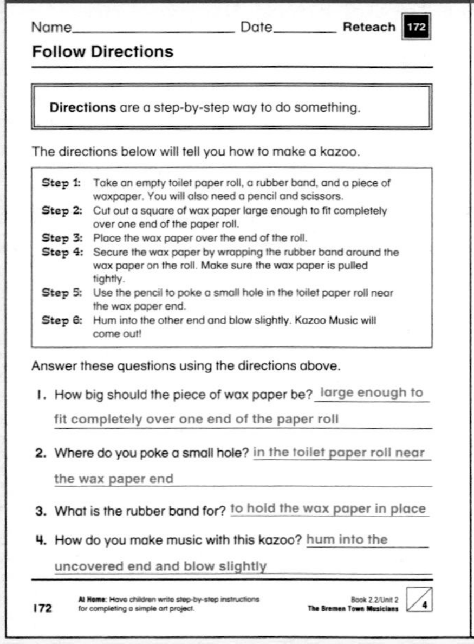

Name________ Date______ Reteach 172

Follow Directions

Directions are a step-by-step way to do something.

The directions below will tell you how to make a kazoo.

Step 1: Take an empty toilet paper roll, a rubber band, and a piece of waxpaper. You will also need a pencil and scissors.
Step 2: Cut out a square of wax paper large enough to fit completely over one end of the paper roll.
Step 3: Place the wax paper over the end of the roll.
Step 4: Secure the wax paper by wrapping the rubber band around the wax paper on the roll. Make sure the wax paper is pulled tightly.
Step 5: Use the pencil to poke a small hole in the toilet paper roll near the wax paper end.
Step 6: Hum into the other end and blow slightly. Kazoo Music will come out!

Answer these questions using the directions above.

1. How big should the piece of wax paper be? large enough to fit completely over one end of the paper roll
2. Where do you poke a small hole? in the toilet paper roll near the wax paper end
3. What is the rubber band for? to hold the wax paper in place
4. How do you make music with this kazoo? hum into the uncovered end and blow slightly

172 **At Home:** Have children write step-by-step instructions for completing a simple art project. Book 2.2/Unit 2 **The Bremen Town Musicians** 4

Reteach, 172

ON-LEVEL

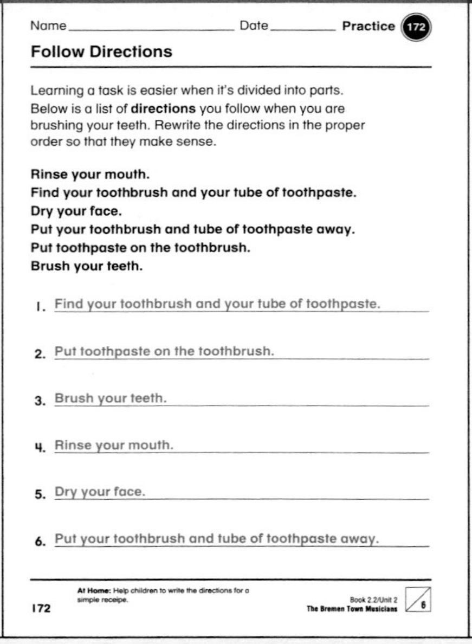

Name________ Date______ Practice 172

Follow Directions

Learning a task is easier when it's divided into parts. Below is a list of **directions** you follow when you are brushing your teeth. Rewrite the directions in the proper order so that they make sense.

Rinse your mouth.
Find your toothbrush and your tube of toothpaste.
Dry your face.
Put your toothbrush and tube of toothpaste away.
Put toothpaste on the toothbrush.
Brush your teeth.

1. Find your toothbrush and your tube of toothpaste.
2. Put toothpaste on the toothbrush.
3. Brush your teeth.
4. Rinse your mouth.
5. Dry your face.
6. Put your toothbrush and tube of toothpaste away.

172 **At Home:** Help children to write the directions for a simple receipe. Book 2.2/Unit 2 **The Bremen Town Musicians** 6

Practice, 172

CHALLENGE

Name________ Date______ Extend 172

Follow Directions

Think about something you know how to do. Write the steps that tell how to do it.
You can write directions for:
- Making a puppet
- Solving a math problem
- Writing a story
- Drawing an animal
- Or anything you choose!

Follow These Steps

Look for directions that are complete and in proper sequence.

Give your directions to a partner to follow. See if your partner can follow the steps. Change your directions if you have to.

172 **At Home:** Have children draw pictures with missing parts. Ask them to write directions for drawing in the parts in the picture. Book 2.2/Unit 2 **The Bremen Town Musicians**

Extend, 172

TEST POWER

Pay attention to the details in the story.

DIRECTIONS:

Read the story. Then read each question about the story.

SAMPLE

Building a Tree House

Mark was happy. It was Saturday. On Saturdays, Kim came over to work on the tree house.

Mark's father picked out a big tree in the backyard. Then, they bought wood and nails. Mark's father showed them how to use a hammer.

Every week Mark and Kim worked on the tree house. First, they built the floor. Then, they built the walls and roof. Now, the tree house was almost finished.

Kim brought a rug. They put it on the tree house floor.

Kim and Mark sat down on the rug. They looked around at their new tree house. They felt very proud. They had built it all by themselves!

1 Where did Kim and Mark build their tree house?

- ○ In Mark's bedroom
- ○ In Kim's backyard
- ● In Mark's backyard
- ○ In the woods

2 What is the best summary for this story?

- ○ Mark and Kim put a rug in their tree house.
- ○ Mark and Kim are brother and sister.
- ● Mark and Kim built a tree house in Mark's backyard.
- ○ Mark and Kim worked very hard on Saturdays.

149

Test Power

THE PRINCETON REVIEW

Read the Page

Explain to children that you will be reading this story as a group. You will read the story, and they will follow along in their books.

Request that children put pens, pencils, and markers away, since they will not be writing in their books.

Discuss the Questions

QUESTION 1: Instruct children to look back to the passage and find some mention of the place where Mark and Kim are building the house. The answer is at the end of the third sentence.

QUESTION 2: Remind children that the title often has clues to the story's main idea. The story is about Mark and Kim building a tree-house. Direct children to the story's last line.

Leveled Books

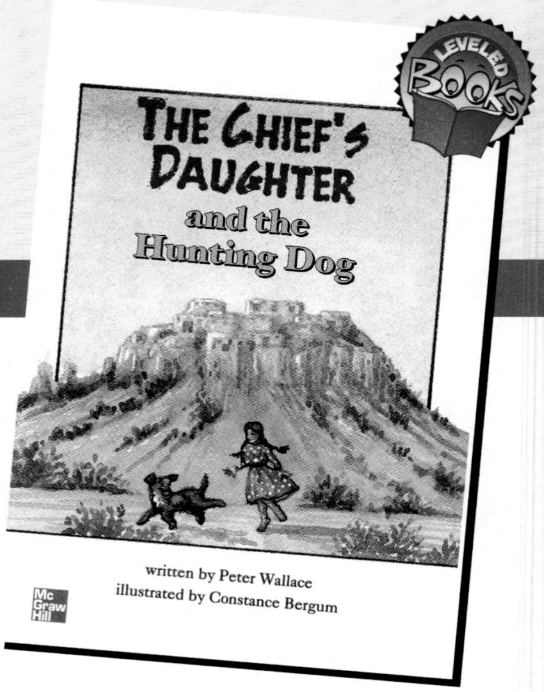

EASY

The Chief's Daughter and the Hunting Dog

☑ **Phonics** Variant Vowels: /âr/, /ôr/, /îr/

☑ **Instructional Vocabulary:** ***daughter, music, scare, third, voice, whistle***

Intervention Skills

Intervention Guide, for direct instruction and extra practice of phonics and vocabulary

Answers to Story Questions

1. She wants a dog so the people of her village can hunt better.
2. She compliments her and gives her gifts.
3. Yes. She seems like a responsible person who cares about people and animals.
4. How the Chief's daughter got a hunting dog for her village.
5. The Bremen Town Musicians dislike humans, as they have been cast out by their owners. The Great Dogs are willing to help humans.

The Story Questions and Activity below appear in the Easy Book.

Story Questions and Writing Activity

1. Why does the Chief's Daughter want a dog?
2. Why does Auntie Dog become nice to Chief's Daughter?
3. Do you think Chief's Daughter will keep her promise to be kind to the dog? Why do you think so?
4. What is this play mostly about?
5. How is the relationship between the Bremen Town Musicians and humans different from that of the Great Dogs and humans in this play?

Mesa Model

Look at the illustration of the mesa village on page 2. Make a model of a mesa out of clay.

from *The Chief's Daughter*

Guided Reading

PREVIEW AND PREDICT Discuss the illustrations through page 7. As you take the **picture walk**, have children predict what the play will be about.

SET PURPOSES Have children make posters that show why they want to read *The Chief's Daughter and the Hunting Dog*. They may want to learn more about the dog that the girl discovers.

READ THE BOOK Use the following prompts as children read, or after they have read the play independently.

Page 2: Read the third sentence. What word has the /îr/ sound? *(near)* Which letters make the /îr/ sound? *(ear)* ***Phonics and Decoding***

Pages 5–7: Do you think this play is about real life or about make-believe things? How can you tell? (Make-believe; Old Spider Woman sends a dream and changes into a spider.) ***Fantasy and Reality***

Page 7: Find the word *third*. If you are third in line, how many people are in front of you? ***Instructional Vocabulary***

Pages 11–12: What kind of creature is Auntie Dog? (kind, warm) What makes you think so? (She speaks kindly and gives Daughter a dog.) ***Character***

Page 16: Imagine that you are talking to someone who has never read this play. Now that you have finished it, tell that person what the play is about. ***Summarize***

RETURN TO PREDICTIONS AND PURPOSES Have children review their predictions and purposes for reading. Did they find out what they wanted to know?

LITERARY RESPONSE Discuss these questions:

- What did you like best about this play?
- Did you admire Old Spider Woman? Why or why not?

Also see the story questions and activity in *The Chief's Daughter and the Hunting Dog*.

See the **Phonics CD-ROM** for practice using words with /âr/, /ôr/, and /îr/ sounds.

Leveled Books

INDEPENDENT

Why Lizard Stretches His Neck

- ☑ Phonics Variant Vowels: /âr/, /ôr/, /îr/
- ☑ Instructional Vocabulary: ***daughter, music, scare, third, voice, whistle***

Guided Reading

PREVIEW AND PREDICT Take a **picture walk** through page 7. See if children can predict what the play will be about by studying the illustrations. Chart their ideas.

SET PURPOSES Have children write one or two sentences describing why they want to read *Why Lizard Stretches His Neck.*

READ THE BOOK Use the following questions as children read, or after they have read the play independently.

Page 5: Find a word on this page with the /ôr/ sound. *(more)* What letters stand for /ôr/? *(ore)* Can you find another word on this page with /ôr/? *(for)* How is /ôr/ spelled? *(or) Phonics and Decoding*

Page 6: What are the most important things that have happened in the play so far? *Summarize*

Page 7: Find the word *daughter*. If you are someone's daughter, raise your hand. If you are not someone's daughter, what would you be? (someone's son) *Instructional Vocabulary*

Page 11: What kind of character do you think Lizard is? (mean, tricky) Why do you think so? (He doesn't tell Chief that Anansi was the one that found out the name.) *Character*

Page 16: Why does lizard need to keep stretching his neck? (so he can watch out for Anansi) *Make Inferences/Summarize*

RETURN TO PREDICTIONS AND PURPOSES Have children review their predictions and purposes for reading. Did they find out what they wanted to know?

LITERARY RESPONSE Discuss these questions:

- What was your favorite part of the play? Would you recommend it to a friend? Why or why not?
- Would you like to have a friend like Lizard? Why or why not?

Also see story questions and activity in *Why Lizard Stretches His Neck.*

See the Phonics **CD-ROM** for practice using words with /âr/, /ôr/, and /îr/ sounds.

Answers to Story Questions

1. He had to guess her name.
2. He wanted to find out her name and win her for his wife.
3. He knew Lizard had tricked him when he found out that Lizard was marrying the Chief's daughter.
4. The story is mostly about why Lizard stretches his neck—he is watching out for Kwaku Anansi, who he tricked.
5. Answers will vary.

The Story Questions and Activity below appear in the Independent Book.

Story Questions and Writing Activity

1. What did someone have to do to marry the Chief's daughter?
2. Why did Anansi creep into the daughter's hut?
3. When did Anansi know that Lizard had tricked him?
4. What is this story mostly about?
5. Both this play and *The Bremen Town Musicians* used a storyteller to tell some of the story. Why do you think this was done?

Learn About Lizards

Read about lizards in an encyclopedia or a science book. Draw a picture of a lizard and write something you found out about lizards.

from *Why Lizard Stretches His Neck*

Leveled Books

CHALLENGE

The Voice of the Sea

- ☑ Phonics Variant Vowels: /âr/, /ôr/, /îr/
- ☑ Instructional Vocabulary: ***daughter, music, scare, third, voice, whistle***

Guided Reading

PREVIEW AND PREDICT Discuss the illustrations through page 7 of the play. As you take the **picture walk**, have children predict what the play will be about.

SET PURPOSES Have children draw pictures that show the reasons why they want to read *The Voice of the Sea*. For example, children may draw pictures of pirates on a boat in the middle of the sea.

READ THE BOOK Use the following questions as children read or after they have read the story independently.

Page 4: Find and read aloud a word that means *frighten*. *(scare)* What vowel sound do you hear? (/âr/) What letters stand for the sound? *(are)* ***Phonics and Decoding***

Page 6: Do you think Captain Tom meant for the map to be found? Why or why not? (No, because he tells the audience that he hid it.) ***Make Inferences***

Pages 8–9: What generalization can you form about all the pirates except Pirate Jenny? (They are greedy and want the treasure for themselves.) ***Form Generalizations***

Page 12: Find the word *whistle*. Is a whistle something you see or hear? ***Instructional Vocabulary***

Page 16: Try to retell the play of *The Voice of the Sea* in your own words. What are the most important things to tell about what happened in the play? ***Summarize***

RETURN TO PURPOSES AND PREDICTIONS Have children review their predictions and purposes for reading. Did they find out what they wanted to know?

LITERARY RESPONSE Discuss these questions:

- Did you enjoy reading the play? How was it different from reading a story?
- Can you think of other stories or movies about pirates?

Also see the story questions and activity in *The Voice of the Sea*.

See the Phonics **CD-ROM** for practice using words with /âr/, /ôr/, and /îr/ sounds.

Answers to Story Questions

1. She's Captain Tom's daughter.
2. They have been at sea a long time.
3. She knows how to get others to work together.
4. You need to work together with others to get anything done.
5. Students will probably suggest the musicians; they don't fight as much.

The Story Questions and Activity below appear in the Challenge Book.

Story Questions and Writing Activity

1. Who is Pirate Jenny?
2. Why do the pirates want to go home?
3. Why might Jenny be a good pirate captain?
4. What is the main idea of this story?
5. Who would you rather have help you solve a problem, the pirates or the Bremen Town Musicians?

Your Own Ship

What if you were the captain of a ship? Write a few sentences from your ship's log.

from *The Voice of the Sea*

Activities

Bringing Groups Together

Anthology and Leveled Books

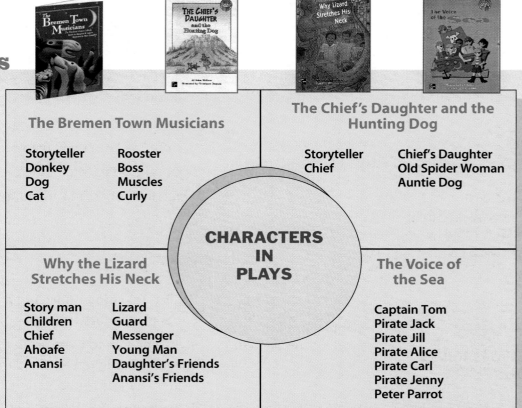

Connecting Texts

CHARACTERS
Write the story titles on the four corners of a chart. In the middle of the chart, write the words *Characters in Plays*. Ask children in each reading level to identify the characters in the play they read. Print the names of the characters under the appropriate story titles. (Be sure to include the narrator figure.)

Use the chart to talk about the different characters and the function of the narrator in the plays.

CHARACTERS IN PLAYS

The Bremen Town Musicians
Storyteller, Donkey, Dog, Cat, Rooster, Boss, Muscles, Curly

The Chief's Daughter and the Hunting Dog
Storyteller, Chief, Chief's Daughter, Old Spider Woman, Auntie Dog

Why the Lizard Stretches His Neck
Story man, Children, Chief, Ahoafe, Anansi, Lizard, Guard, Messenger, Young Man, Daughter's Friends, Anansi's Friends

The Voice of the Sea
Captain Tom, Pirate Jack, Pirate Jill, Pirate Alice, Pirate Carl, Pirate Jenny, Peter Parrot

Viewing/Representing

GROUP PRESENTATIONS Divide the class into four groups, one for each of the four books read in the lesson. Have each group dramatize a scene from the story assigned. Have each group present their scene to the rest of the class.

AUDIENCE RESPONSE Ask children to pay attention to each group's presentation and to ask questions after the dramatization.

Research and Inquiry

MORE ABOUT FOLKTALES: Three of the selections are folktales. Invite children to discover more about folktales by:

- looking at classroom picture books and school library books that focus on folktales.
- listening to folktales on audiocassettes.

*inter***NET** **CONNECTION** Go to ***www.mhschool.com/reading*** for more information about folktales.

Review /âr/ are; /ôr/ or, ore; /îr/ ear

TESTED OBJECTIVES

Children will:

- **review words with /âr/*are*, /ôr/*or*, *ore*, and /îr/*ear*.**
- **build and read words with /âr/*are*, /ôr/*or*, *ore*, and /îr/*ear*.**

MATERIALS

- **Teaching Chart 144**

Skills Finder

/âr/ are; /ôr/ or, ore; /îr/ ear

Introduce	B1: 192G-H
Review	B1: 215E-F; B2: 130G-H, 149E-F, 149G-H
Test	B1: Unit 2

ALTERNATE TEACHING STRATEGY

/âr/, /ôr/, /îr/ WORDS

For a different approach to teaching this skill, see page T65.

PREPARE

Listen for /âr/, /ôr/, /îr/ Tell children they will review letter combinations that spell /âr/, /îr/, and /ôr/ sounds.

Have children clap when they hear a word that rhymes with the words *bare*, *store*, or *clear* as you read each sentence aloud:

- *bare*: Take good care of the mare.
- *store*: Have a nap, but try not to snore.
- *clear*: If you come near, I might hear you better.

TEACH

BLENDING Model and Guide Practice with /âr/, /ôr/, and /îr/ Words

- Display **Teaching Chart 144** and read aloud the word *care* as you underline the letters *are*.
- Invite children to write *are* in the blanks in the next two examples. Encourage children to blend the sounds together in each word and read the words *stare* and *bare*.
- In the bottom box, have children identify which letter or letters could be added to the letters *are* to form more /âr/ words. (*mare, dare*)

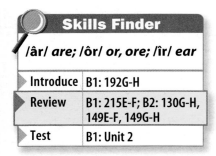

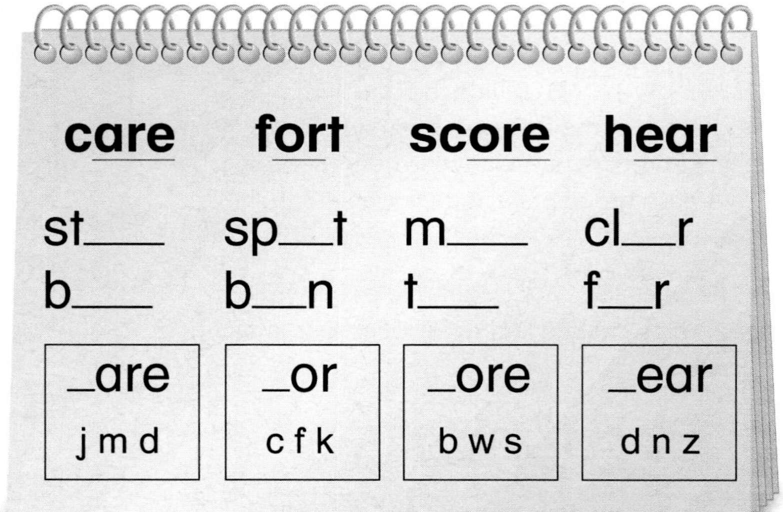

Teaching Chart 144

Use the Words in Context Use the words in sentences to reinforce their meanings. Example: *Don't stare at the sun.*

Repeat the Procedure Repeat the procedure to complete the other columns and boxes on the chart.

PRACTICE

DISCRIMINATING Identify and Write Words with /âr/, /ôr/, /îr/ Sounds

GROUP

Invite children to play "Word Bingo." Ask each child to draw on a piece of paper a 3-by-3 grid of squares. When they hear an /âr/, /ôr/, or /îr/ word, they should write it into a box of their choice. Encourage children to write each word family in its own row. The first child to list three /âr/, /ôr/, or /îr/ words in a row wins. If they've got a row of one word family they get Bingo Plus. Read aloud the following words one at a time: *fear, fake, clear, clean, hear, help, score, stay, fort, fell, more, most, sort, stain, scare, risk, rare, sell, stare.*

▶ **Spatial/Linguistic/Auditory**

ASSESS/CLOSE

Read Words with /âr/, /ôr/, /îr/ Sounds

To assess children's ability to recognize /âr/, /ôr/, and /îr/ words, observe their work on the Practice activity. Ask each child to read aloud three words from his or her completed bingo squares.

ADDITIONAL PHONICS RESOURCES

Phonics/Phonemic Awareness Practice Book, pages 113–116

McGraw-Hill School TECHNOLOGY

Phonics CD-ROM activities for practice with Discriminating and Segmenting

DAILY Phonics ROUTINES

DAY 4 **Identifying** Play "Simon Says" with r-controlled-vowel words. When children hear a word with an /âr/, /ôr/, or /îr/ sound, they should take one step forward.

Phonics CD-ROM

SPELLING/PHONICS CONNECTIONS

See the 5-Day Spelling Plan, pages 149Q–149R.

Intervention **Skills**

Intervention Guide, for direct instruction and extra practice of /âr/ *are;* /ôr/ *or, ore;* /îr/ *ear*

Meeting Individual Needs for Phonics

EASY

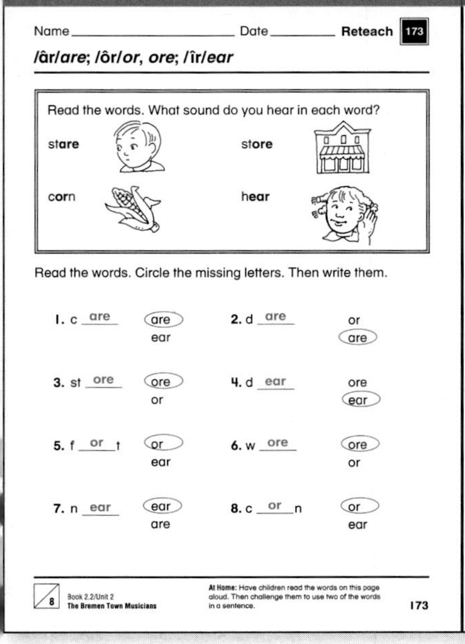

Name______ Date______ **Reteach** 173

/âr/are; /ôr/or, ore; /îr/ear

Read the words. What sound do you hear in each word?

stare store

corn hear

Read the words. Circle the missing letters. Then write them.

1. c are — (are) ear
2. d are — or (are)
3. st ore — (ore) or
4. d ear — ore (ear)
5. f or t — (or) ear
6. w ore — (ore) or
7. n ear — (ear) are
8. c or n — (or) ear

Book 2.2/Unit 2 The Bremen Town Musicians

At Home: Have children read the words on this page aloud. Then challenge them to use two of the words in a sentence.

173

Reteach, 173

ON-LEVEL

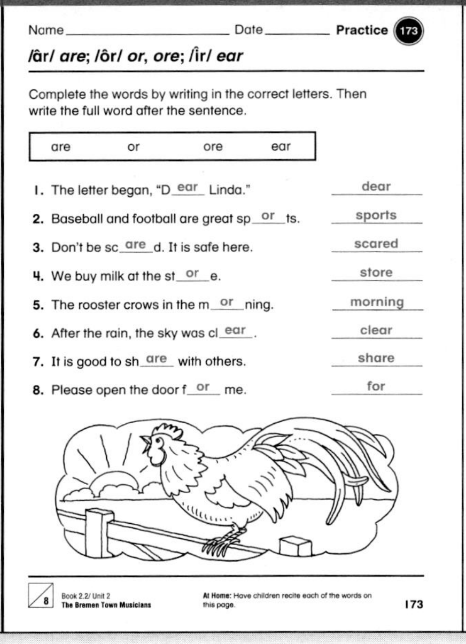

Name______ Date______ **Practice** 173

/âr/ are; /ôr/ or, ore; /îr/ ear

Complete the words by writing in the correct letters. Then write the full word after the sentence.

are or ore ear

1. The letter began, "D ear Linda." dear
2. Baseball and football are great sp or ts. sports
3. Don't be sc are d. It is safe here. scared
4. We buy milk at the st or e. store
5. The rooster crows in the m or ning. morning
6. After the rain, the sky was cl ear . clear
7. It is good to sh are with others. share
8. Please open the door f or me. for

Book 2.2/ Unit 2 The Bremen Town Musicians

At Home: Have children recite each of the words on this page.

173

Practice, 173

CHALLENGE

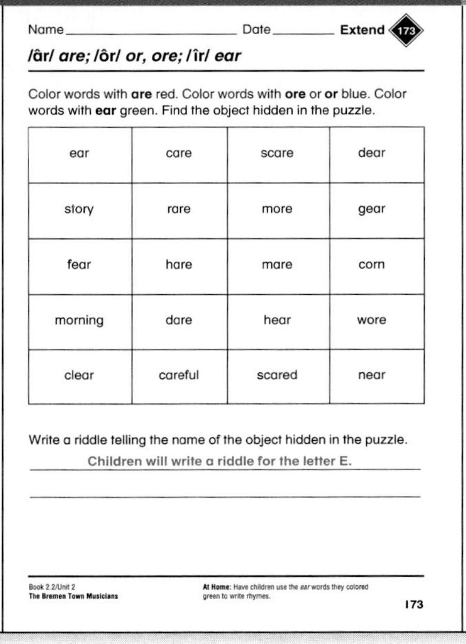

Name______ Date______ **Extend** 173

/âr/ are; /ôr/ or, ore; /îr/ ear

Color words with **are** red. Color words with **ore** or **or** blue. Color words with **ear** green. Find the object hidden in the puzzle.

ear	care	scare	dear
story	rare	more	gear
fear	hare	mare	corn
morning	dare	hear	wore
clear	careful	scared	near

Write a riddle telling the name of the object hidden in the puzzle.

Children will write a riddle for the letter E.

Book 2.2/Unit 2 The Bremen Town Musicians

At Home: Have children use the *ear* words they colored green to write rhymes.

173

Extend, 173

LANGUAGE SUPPORT

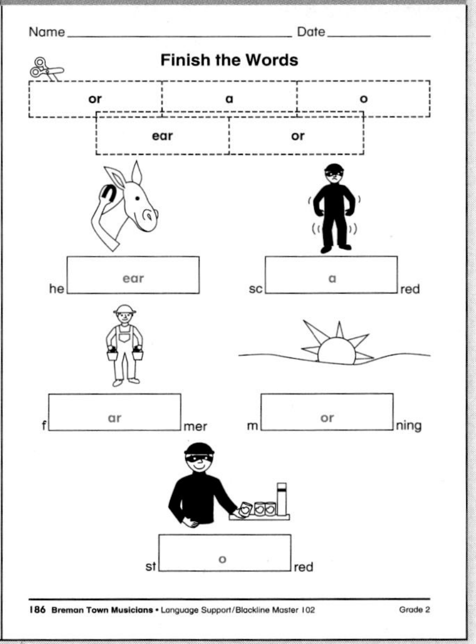

Name______ Date______

Finish the Words

or a o

ear or

he ear

sc a red

f ar mer

m or ning

st o red

186 **Breman Town Musicians** • Language Support/Blackline Master 102 Grade 2

Language Support, 186

Review /âr/ are; /ôr/ or, ore; /îr/ ear

TESTED OBJECTIVES

Children will:

- review /âr/*are*, /ôr/*or*, *ore*, /îr/*ear*.
- discriminate and read words with /âr/*are*, /ôr/*or*, *ore*, and /îr/*ear*.

MATERIALS

- Teaching Chart 145

Skills Finder

/âr/ are; /ôr/ or, ore; /îr/ ear

Introduce	B1: 192G-H
Review	B1: 215E-F; B2: 130G-H, 149E-F, 149G-H
Test	B1: Unit 2

TEACHING TIP

SPELLING PATTERNS

Help children recognize spelling patterns in words with *are, or,* and *ear.* Write a three-column chart on the board. Label the columns *are, or, ear.* Brainstorm a list of words to write under each column. Have children underline common letters in each set of words.

PREPARE

Discriminate /âr/*are*; /ôr/*or*, *ore*; /îr/*ear*

Write on the chalkboard the following groups of words and invite volunteers to circle the word that contains the /âr/, /ôr/, or /îr/ sound:

- head, hear, haul
- scared, skate, school
- stem, steep, story
- mine, more, map

TEACH

BLENDING Model and Guide Practice with /âr/ /ôr/ and /îr/ Words

- Display **Teaching Chart 145.**
- Call on children to fill in the first blank with an /ôr/ word. Underline the letters that spell /ôr/. Use the clues in parentheses to prompt these answers.
- Invite children to read aloud the completed sentences.

1. Dean left for school one ________. (early in the day) (morning)
2. He was not ________ to walk alone. (afraid) (scared)
3. At school they read his favorite ________, *The Bremen Town Musicians*. (folktale, play) (story)
4. He sat in the front so he could ________ the teacher read. (listen to) (hear)
5. The hour went so quickly! It was too ________. (not long) (short)

Teaching Chart 145

Use Words in Context

- Have children write their own sentences to reinforce the meaning of the word *morning*. Example: *The morning is my favorite time of day.*

Repeat the Procedure

- Repeat the procedure to complete the remaining sentences.

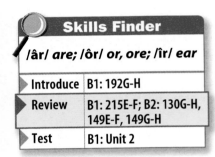

PRACTICE

WORD BUILDING Build /âr/*are*; /ôr/*or, ore*; /îr/*ear* Words with a Word Scramble

GROUP

Have children work in groups to brainstorm two words with /âr/ spelled *are*, two words with /îr/ spelled *ear*, and two words with /ôr/ spelled *or* or *ore*. Have children mix up the letters in each word, creating a list of word scrambles. Then have groups exchange lists and work together to unscramble each other's words. Encourage children to use their knowledge of spelling patterns to unscramble the words.

▶ **Spatial/Linguistic**

ASSESS/CLOSE

Read /âr/, /ôr/*or*, and /îr/ Words and Use in Sentences

Observe children's work on the Practice activity to ensure they are able to build and write /âr/, /îr/, and /ôr/ words. Have each child read aloud one unscrambled /âr/, one unscrambled /îr/, and one unscrambled /ôr/ word to ensure he or she is comfortable blending these sounds. Ask children to use the words in a silly sentence.

ADDITIONAL PHONICS RESOURCES

Phonics/Phonemic Awareness Practice Book, pages 113–116

McGraw-Hill School TECHNOLOGY

Phonics CD-ROM activities for practice with Blending and Decoding

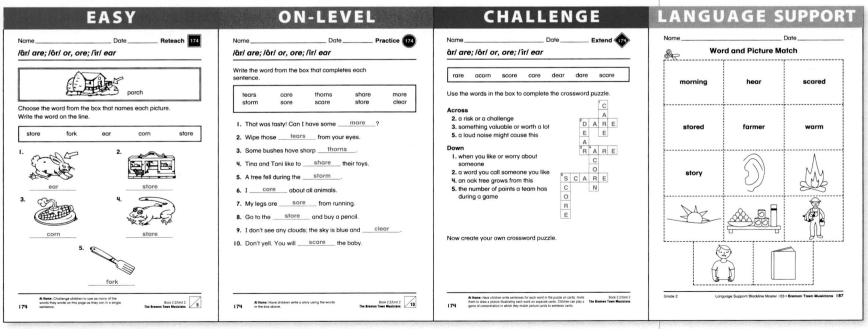

DAILY Phonics ROUTINES

DAY 5 **Writing** Have partners write riddles whose answers contain /âr/, /ôr/, and /îr/ words. Have one partner say the riddle and the other partner answer it. Tell children to switch roles.

Phonics CD-ROM

ALTERNATE TEACHING STRATEGY

/âr/, /ôr/, /îr/ WORDS

For a different approach to teaching this skill, see page T65.

Intervention ▶ Skills

Intervention Guide, for direct instruction and extra practice of /âr/ *are;* /ôr/ *or, ore;* /îr/ *ear*

Meeting Individual Needs for Phonics

EASY

Name ______ Date ______ Reteach 174

/âr/ are; /ôr/ or, ore; /îr/ ear

porch

Choose the word from the box that names each picture. Write the word on the line.

store fork ear corn stare

1. ear
2. store
3. corn
4. stare
5. fork

At Home: Challenge children to use as many of the words they wrote on this page as they can in a single sentence.

174 Book 2.2/Unit 2 The Bremen Town Musicians 5

Reteach, 174

ON-LEVEL

Name ______ Date ______ Practice 174

/âr/ are; /ôr/ or, ore; /îr/ ear

Write the word from the box that completes each sentence.

tears	care	thorns	share	more
storm	sore	scare	store	clear

1. That was tasty! Can I have some more?
2. Wipe those tears from your eyes.
3. Some bushes have sharp thorns.
4. Tina and Toni like to share their toys.
5. A tree fell during the storm.
6. I care about all animals.
7. My legs are sore from running.
8. Go to the store and buy a pencil.
9. I don't see any clouds; the sky is blue and clear.
10. Don't yell. You will scare the baby.

At Home: Have children write a story using the words in the box above.

174 Book 2.2/Unit 2 The Bremen Town Musicians 10

Practice, 174

CHALLENGE

Name ______ Date ______ Extend 174

âr/ are; /ôr/ or, ore; /îr/ ear

rare acorn score care dear dare scare

Use the words in the box to complete the crossword puzzle.

Across
2. a risk or a challenge
3. something valuable or worth a lot
5. a loud noise might cause this

Down
1. when you like or worry about someone
2. a word you call someone you like
4. an oak tree grows from this
5. the number of points a team has during a game

CARE, DARE, DEAR, RARE, ACORN, SCARE, SCORE

Now create your own crossword puzzle.

At Home: Have children write sentences for each word in the puzzle on cards. Invite them to draw a picture illustrating each word on separate cards. Children can play a game of concentration in which they match picture cards to sentence cards.

174 Book 2.2/Unit 2 The Bremen Town Musicians

Extend, 174

LANGUAGE SUPPORT

Name ______ Date ______

Word and Picture Match

morning	hear	scared
stored	farmer	warm
story		

Grade 2 Language Support/Blackline Master 103 • Bremen Town Musicians 187

Language Support, 187

TESTED OBJECTIVES

Children will summarize a story by telling about its most important characters and events.

Skills Finder

Summarize

Introduce	B2: 149I-J
Review	B2: 211I-J, 245G-H
Test	B2: Unit 2
Maintain	B2: 271, 303, 323

TEACHING TIP

MAIN IDEA Remind children that when they summarize a story they should tell about the main idea of the story. Tell students that sometimes the main idea is not directly stated; it is implied. When the main idea is implied, they must decide what the story is about by using clues from the text.

SELF-SELECTED Reading

Children may choose from the following titles.

ANTHOLOGY

- *The Bremen Town Musicians*

LEVELED BOOKS

- *The Chief's Daughter and the Hunting Dog*
- *Why Lizard Stretches His Neck*
- *The Voice of the Sea*

Bibliography, pages T88–T89

Introduce Summarize

PREPARE

Demonstrate Summarizing Tell children that to summarize a story is to retell it in a quick or short way including only important events and characters. Say: A family takes a vacation by car around the United States. Ask: What story that you know did I just retell? *(The Best Vacation Ever)* Tell children that what you just did was summarize the story.

TEACH

Read "The Concert" and Model the Skill Display **Teaching Chart 146** and read it aloud to children. Ask them to think what their answer might be if someone asked them what the story is mainly about.

The Concert

The dog, the cat, the donkey, and the rooster decided it was time to share their beautiful songs with others. Many people helped them. A farmer told them they could perform in his empty barn. The carpenter gave the donkey planks of wood to make benches for people to sit on. A teacher from the school helped the cat print posters announcing the concert. Finally, on the day of the concert, the rooster crowed to let the town know it was time to come to the barn. The musicians sang the best they had ever sung. The townspeople were very happy, and the musicians were very proud.

Teaching Chart 146

Ask a volunteer to find and circle the names of the main characters. Then have children underline up to four sentences that give important information about the story.

MODEL The donkey, dog, cat, and rooster—the musicians—are the main characters in the story. The story is mainly about the musicians having a concert, so I will include that in my summary. I think it is important to talk about how everybody felt about the concert. I'll underline that part, too. I may also want to say that many people helped, but I don't need to give all the information about what each of those characters did.

PRACTICE

Make a Chart Have children refer to **Teaching Chart 146** in order to make a Main Character/Important Events chart. Point out that the main characters take part in the important events.

PARTNERS

▶ **Linguistic**

Main Characters	Important Events
Dog, Donkey, Cat, Rooster	Give a concert

ASSESS/CLOSE

Read and Assess Summaries Ask children to choose a story the class has read this year and work together to summarize what happened in it, using no more than three sentences.

ALTERNATE TEACHING STRATEGY

SUMMARIZE

For a different approach to teaching this skill, see page T67.

Intervention ▶ Skills

Intervention Guide, for direct instruction and extra practice in summarizing

Meeting Individual Needs for Comprehension

EASY

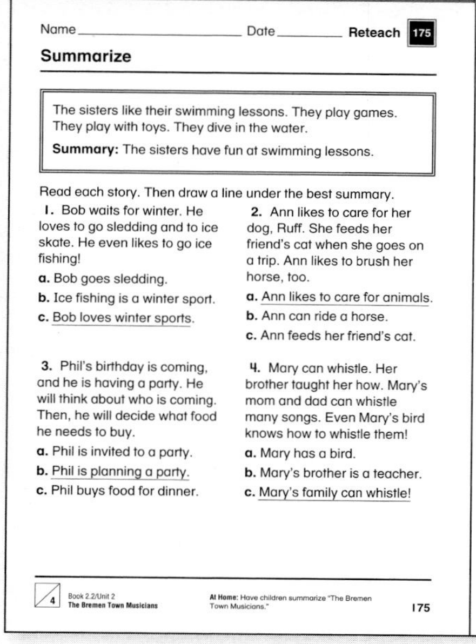
Name________ Date______ Reteach 175

Summarize

The sisters like their swimming lessons. They play games. They play with toys. They dive in the water.

Summary: The sisters have fun at swimming lessons.

Read each story. Then draw a line under the best summary.

1. Bob waits for winter. He loves to go sledding and to ice skate. He even likes to go ice fishing!
   a. Bob goes sledding.
   b. Ice fishing is a winter sport.
   c. Bob loves winter sports.
2. Ann likes to care for her dog, Ruff. She feeds her friend's cat when she goes on a trip. Ann likes to brush her horse, too.
   a. Ann likes to care for animals.
   b. Ann can ride a horse.
   c. Ann feeds her friend's cat.
3. Phil's birthday is coming, and he is having a party. He will think about who is coming. Then, he will decide what food he needs to buy.
   a. Phil is invited to a party.
   b. Phil is planning a party.
   c. Phil buys food for dinner.
4. Mary can whistle. Her brother taught her how. Mary's mom and dad can whistle many songs. Even Mary's bird knows how to whistle them!
   a. Mary has a bird.
   b. Mary's brother is a teacher.
   c. Mary's family can whistle!

4 Book 2.2/Unit 2 The Bremen Town Musicians — At Home: Have children summarize "The Bremen Town Musicians." 175

Reteach, 175

ON-LEVEL

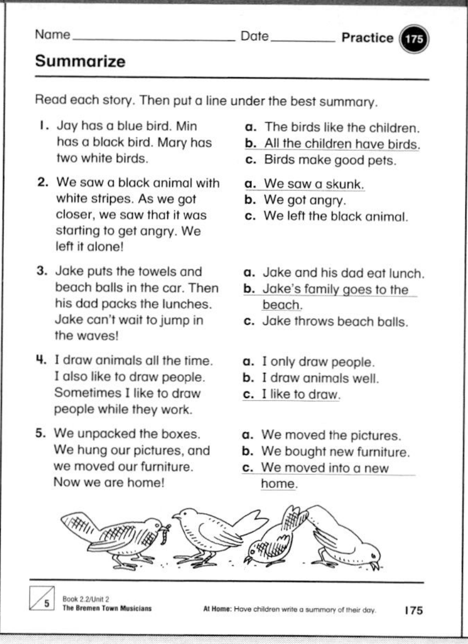
Name________ Date______ Practice 175

Summarize

Read each story. Then put a line under the best summary.

1. Jay has a blue bird. Min has a black bird. Mary has two white birds.
   a. The birds like the children.
   b. All the children have birds.
   c. Birds make good pets.
2. We saw a black animal with white stripes. As we got closer, we saw that it was starting to get angry. We left it alone!
   a. We saw a skunk.
   b. We got angry.
   c. We left the black animal.
3. Jake puts the towels and beach balls in the car. Then his dad packs the lunches. Jake can't wait to jump in the waves!
   a. Jake and his dad eat lunch.
   b. Jake's family goes to the beach.
   c. Jake throws beach balls.
4. I draw animals all the time. I also like to draw people. Sometimes I like to draw people while they work.
   a. I only draw people.
   b. I draw animals well.
   c. I like to draw.
5. We unpacked the boxes. We hung our pictures, and we moved our furniture. Now we are home!
   a. We moved the pictures.
   b. We bought new furniture.
   c. We moved into a new home.

5 Book 2.2/Unit 2 The Bremen Town Musicians — At Home: Have children write a summary of their day. 175

Practice, 175

CHALLENGE

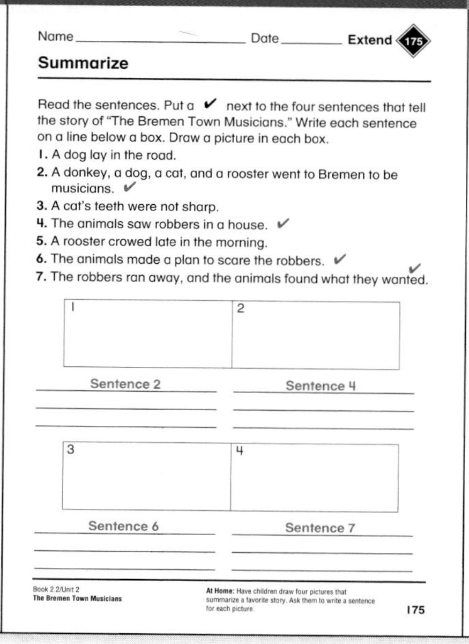
Name________ Date______ Extend 175

Summarize

Read the sentences. Put a ✔ next to the four sentences that tell the story of "The Bremen Town Musicians." Write each sentence on a line below a box. Draw a picture in each box.

1. A dog lay in the road.
2. A donkey, a dog, a cat, and a rooster went to Bremen to be musicians. ✔
3. A cat's teeth were not sharp.
4. The animals saw robbers in a house. ✔
5. A rooster crowed late in the morning.
6. The animals made a plan to scare the robbers. ✔
7. The robbers ran away, and the animals found what they wanted. ✔

1 | 2

Sentence 2 | Sentence 4

3 | 4

Sentence 6 | Sentence 7

Book 2.2/Unit 2 The Bremen Town Musicians — At Home: Have children draw four pictures that summarize a favorite story. Ask them to write a sentence for each picture. 175

Extend, 175

LANGUAGE SUPPORT

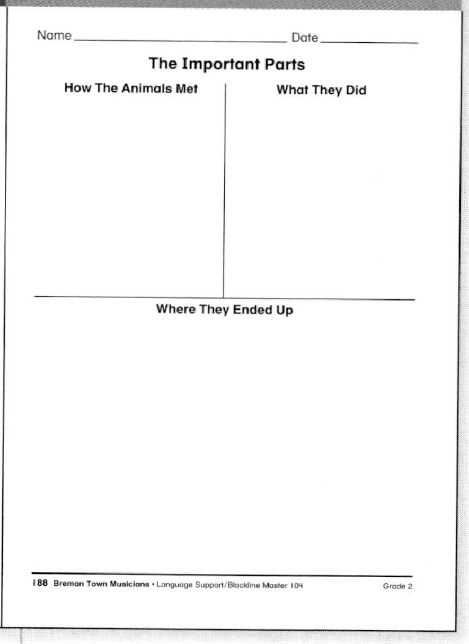
Name________ Date______

The Important Parts

How The Animals Met | **What They Did**

Where They Ended Up

188 Breman Town Musicians • Language Support/Blackline Master 104 — Grade 2

Language Support, 188

Introduce Suffixes

TESTED OBJECTIVES

Children will:

- use derivational endings to help recognize and understand words.
- read and write words with suffixes *-ly* and *-ful*.
- learn how suffixes *-ly* and *-ful* change word meaning.

MATERIALS

- Teaching Chart 147

Skills Finder

Suffixes

Introduce	B2: 149K-L
Review	B2: 211K-L, 245K-L
Test	B2: Unit 2
Maintain	B2: 355

TEACHING TIP

MULTISYLLABIC WORDS Explain that word parts like suffixes usually form separate syllables. Remind children that when they come across an unfamiliar word, the first thing to do is to cover any obvious affixes. Then they should try to pronounce the base word. Next, they should blend all the word parts in sequence. The complete word should be close enough to the real word that they will be able to recognize it.

PREPARE

Discuss Meanings of Suffixes Write the word *slowly* on the chalkboard. Underline its base word (*slow*) and circle the suffix (*-ly*). Tell children the ending *-ly* is called a suffix, and that adding a suffix to the end of a word changes the word's meaning. They can figure out the meaning of a word if they know the meaning of its base word and its suffix. Explain: The suffix *-ly* means "in a certain way." The suffix *-ful* means "having" or "full of." So, *slowly* means "in a slow way." *Careful* means "full of care."

TEACH

Identify Base Words and Suffixes Have children read the passage on **Teaching Chart 147** and then model the skill beginning with the word *kindly*.

The Horse and the Rabbit

The man spoke kindly about the horse. "Isn't she pretty?" he asked. "Yes," I said, "she is beautiful. I see that you are careful with her." Suddenly, a rabbit ran by. The rabbit was fast. It ran by so quickly that no one else saw it!

Teaching Chart 147

MODEL I see the word *kindly*. I know that the suffix *-ly* means "in a certain way." I know the base word *kind* means *nice*. So *kindly* must mean "in a kind way."

Underline the words with suffixes (*kindly, beautiful, careful, suddenly, quickly*). Have children circle suffixes in the underlined words and give meanings for each one.

PRACTICE

Form Words with *-ly* and *-ful*

GROUP

On the chalkboard, list the following base words in one column: *joy*, *fear*, *thought*. Above them, write the suffix *-ful*. In another column, list the words *soft*, *smooth*, *loud*, with the suffix *-ly* above them. Challenge groups to form new words using the base words and suffixes on the chalkboard. Invite groups to share aloud the words they've created. Ask volunteers to tell the meanings of the new words.
▶ **Linguistic**

ASSESS/CLOSE

Write a Suffix Story

Have each group work together to write a brief story using at least six of the words they've created. Invite groups to read their stories aloud.

ALTERNATE TEACHING STRATEGY

SUFFIXES *-ly* AND *-ful*

For a different approach to teaching this skill, see page T68.

Intervention Skills

Intervention Guide, for direct instruction and extra practice of suffixes

Meeting Individual Needs for Vocabulary

EASY

Name ____________ Date ________ **Reteach 176**

Suffixes

The **suffixes -ly** and **-ful** change the meaning of the word to which they are added. The suffix **-ly** means "in a (base word) manner"; **-ful** means "full of (base word)."

Write the word from the box that has the opposite meaning of the underlined word.

quietly	slowly	beautiful	careful	useful

1. I am not careless. I am careful.
2. I am not ugly. I am beautiful.
3. I am not talking loudly. I am talking quietly.
4. I am not going quickly. I am going slowly.
5. We are not useless. We are useful.

176 **At Home:** Ask children to add **-ful** or **-ly** to each of the following words and to use them in sentences: **hope, sad, friend,** and **thought.** Book 2.2/Unit 2 **The Bremen Town Musicians** 5

Reteach, 176

ON-LEVEL

Name ____________ Date ________ **Practice 176**

Suffixes

You can add **-ful** and **-ly** to some words to make new words.

thank + **-ful** = thankful quick + **-ly** = quickly

Thankful means "full of thanks." Quickly means "in a quick way."

Read each sentence. Write a word with **-ful** or **-ly** that means the same as the underlined words in each sentence.

1. My mom drives in a slow way past the school. slowly
2. Please be full of care when you cross the street. careful
3. The circus tent was full of color. colorful
4. The storm came in a sudden way from the west. suddenly
5. We are full of hope that the rain will stop soon. hopeful
6. Lulu tiptoed in a quiet way past the baby. quietly
7. My little brother smiled in a shy way. shyly
8. Everyone at the party was full of joy. joyful

176 **At Home:** Ask children to add **-ly** or **-ful** to these words to make new words: **eager, glad, firm, fear.** Book 2.2/Unit 2 **The Bremen Town Musicians** 8

Practice, 176

CHALLENGE

Name ____________ Date ________ **Extend 176**

Suffixes

suddenly	fearful	careful	luckily	beautiful
slowly	brightly	loudly	quickly	thankful

Add the suffix **-ly** or **-ful** to each word in dark type so the story makes sense. Use words from the box.

It was a **beauti** ful summer day. The sun shone **bright** ly. I was **care** ful to wear my sunglasses when I went outside. It got hot **quick** ly. I took my time and walked **slow** ly toward the beach. **Sudden** ly, lightning flashed across the sky. Thunder rumbled **loud** ly. I was **fear** ful that my day at the beach would be spoiled. **Lucki** ly, the storm only lasted for five minutes. Boy, was I **thank** ful!

Write two more sentences telling what happened next. Use two words from the box. **Sample answers given.**

I spent a beautiful day on the beach.

I had so much fun that the day went quickly.

176 **At Home:** Have children write a short story using three or four words with **-ful** and **-ly** suffixes. Book 2.2/Unit 2 **The Bremen Town Musicians**

Extend, 176

LANGUAGE SUPPORT

Name ____________ Date ________

Completing Sentences

quickly	suddenly
beautiful	careful

1. The animals all had beautiful voices.
2. The animals suddenly fell through the window.
3. The robbers had been scared away too quickly.
4. The head robber told the big robber to be careful.

Grade 2 Language Support/Blackline Master 105 • **Breman Town Musicians** 189

Language Support, 189

GRAMMAR/SPELLING CONNECTIONS

See the 5-Day Grammar and Usage Plan on pronouns, pages 149O–149P.

See the 5-Day Spelling Plan on words with *c*, *k*, and *ck*, pages 149Q–149R.

TEACHING TIP

Technology Use the formatting tool on your computer to add italics to your story. Writers use italics for words they want read with extra energy and feeling.

Handwriting Remind children to print legibly. Ask: *Is your handwriting neat and easy to read? Have you left the correct amount of space between letters and words?* See Handwriting pages T74–T79.

Handwriting CD-ROM

Expository Writing

Prewrite

WRITE A REPORT Present this writing assignment: Write a report about going to a concert or a play. It could be something you saw at school or a place you went with your family. Explain what the concert or play was mainly about at the beginning.

MAKE A LIST OF INFORMATION Have children brainstorm about information they want to include in their reports. Suggest that they answer the questions: *Who? What? When? Where? Why?*

Strategy: Create a Chart Have children record notes in a 5-row chart, as below:

Who?	my family
What?	the marching band
When?	last Saturday
Where?	my sister's high school
Why?	honor the girls' soccer team

Graphic Organizer 31

Draft

USE THE CHART Children should include the information from their charts near the beginning of their report. Then they should tell what the play or concert was about. Ask them to arrange the information in an order that will make sense to a reader. Encourage children to use descriptive language that will make the reader feel as though he or she were at the performance. Remind children that a report tells about facts or things that really happened, so they should not include made-up details. The report should also include a title.

Revise

SELF-QUESTIONING Ask children to assess their drafts.

- Did I begin by telling what the concert or play was mainly about?
- Did I include the details listed on my chart?
- Did I use descriptions to help the reader to "see" and "hear" what the event was like?
- Did I stick to the facts and not make up anything?
- Did I include a title for my report?

PARTNERS Have partners trade reports. They may want to ask their partners the questions listed above.

Edit/Proofread

CHECK FOR ERRORS Children should reread their reports to check spelling, grammar, and punctuation.

Publish

SHARE THE REPORTS You may wish to compile children's reports into a "magazine" about concerts and plays, and make copies children can bring home and save. Have the class vote on a title for the magazine.

The High School Band

by Aviva Fredericks

Last Saturday, I went to a concert at my sister's high school. The marching band played songs to honor the girls' soccer team's winning season. My favorite song was "I Love a Parade." The band sounded great. In one song, the drum sounded like thunder and we had to cover our ears! There were about 20 people in the band. After they played, the crowd stood up and clapped.

Presentation Ideas

ILLUSTRATE THE REPORTS Encourage children to add information to their reports by drawing pictures of the event they saw. Have them add captions that tell what's happening in their drawings.

▶ **Viewing/Representing**

RADIO REPORT Using their reports as guides, have children deliver a "radio report" on the event they saw. Encourage children to review the performance and suggest whether others might like to attend an event like it. Invite audience members to "call in" with questions.

▶ **Speaking/Listening**

Consider children's creative efforts, possibly adding a plus (+) for originality, wit, and imagination.

Scoring Rubric

Excellent	Good	Fair	Unsatisfactory
4: The writer • clearly identifies at the beginning of the report what performance he or she saw and what it was about. • answers the questions *who, what, where, when,* and *why.* • uses descriptive language creatively.	**3:** The writer • clearly identifies at the beginning of the report what performance he or she saw. • answers some of the questions *who, what, where, when,* and *why.* • uses some descriptive language.	**2:** The writer • identifies what performance he or she saw, but not at the beginning of the report. • answers only one or two of the questions *who, what, where, when,* and *why.* • includes elements of fiction in the report.	**1:** The writer • does not clearly identify what performance he or she saw. • does not answer the questions *who, what, where, when,* and *why.* • writes a fiction story instead of a report.

Incomplete 0: The writer leaves the page blank or fails to respond to the writing task. The student does not address the topic or simply paraphrases the prompt. The response is illegible or incoherent.

Meeting Individual Needs for Writing

EASY

Draw an Event Encourage each child to draw a series of pictures depicting an event. One picture might show who was there; another might show what he or she saw; another might show where the event took place, and so forth. Have them add captions explaining their drawings.

ON-LEVEL

Posters Invite children to create posters for a performance they have recently seen. Before they begin, prompt children to identify what information the posters should contain. *(who, what, where, when, why?)*

CHALLENGE

Write a Review Invite children to write a review of a concert, movie, or television show they have seen recently. Have them include facts about the event, their opinion of it, and reasons for their opinion. Invite children to read their reviews to the class.

Listening and Speaking

LISTENING Have children

- listen for details that will help determine their interest in attending a similar performance.
- list questions to "call in" and ask.
- listen carefully to try to picture the performance from start to finish.

SPEAKING Encourage children to

- speak clearly and at a volume that others can hear from across the room.
- make the report sound as if it were a radio report by varying the intonation in the voice.

LANGUAGE SUPPORT

ESL Figurative language may be confusing to some children. Share this example from the report on page 149M: *In one song, the drum sounded like thunder . . .* Explain that the performance didn't have real thunder. The writer used thunder to tell how the drum sounded. Encourage children to use some sentences that tell what things *sounded like* and *looked like.*

PORTFOLIO Invite children to include their reports, or another writing assignment, in their portfolios.

5 Day Grammar and Usage Plan

LANGUAGE SUPPORT

As you explain what a pronoun is, make sure children understand the meaning of *take the place of* and *replace*. Demonstrate by using each child's name as a subject in a sentence. Have the children replace the child's name with the pronoun *he* or *she*.

DAILY LANGUAGE ACTIVITIES

Write the Daily Language Activities on the chalkboard each day, or use **Transparency 21**. For each sentence, have children orally replace the subject noun or noun plus pronoun with a pronoun.

Day 1

1. A woman writes a story about animals. She
2. The man has a donkey. He
3. The town is named Bremen. It

Day 2

1. The dog and I are getting old. We
2. The farmer's wife makes soup. She
3. The mice got away. They

Day 3

1. The story is about animals. It
2. The animals plan to go. They
3. The miller's son has a cat. He

Day 4

1. The donkey and I play music. We
2. "Cat played well," the dog told the cat. You
3. Four animals are singing. They

Day 5

1. The house is old. It
2. The animals and I live there. We
3. The people ran away. They

Daily Language Transparency 21

DAY 1 Introduce the Concept

Oral Warm-Up Read this sentence aloud: *They were known as the Bremen Town Musicians.* Ask children whom *They* refers to in the sentence.

Introduce Pronouns Review: A noun is a word that names a person, place, or thing. Present:

Pronouns

- A pronoun is a word that takes the place of a noun or nouns.
- A pronoun must agree with the noun it replaces.
- The pronouns *I, he, she, it,* and *you* can take the place of a singular noun.

Present the Daily Language Activity. Then have children list examples of nouns and the pronouns that can replace them. Model the activity first.

WRITING Assign the daily Writing Prompt on page 130C.

Name ________________ Date ________ LEARN Grammar 129

Pronouns

- A **pronoun** is a word that takes the place of a noun or nouns.
- A pronoun must agree with the noun it replaces.
- The pronouns *I, he, she, it,* and *you* can take the place of a singular noun.

She put her hat on. She put it on her head.
He took his hat off. I saw him.
Did you see him?

Look at the underlined noun. Choose the pronoun that could be used in its place. Mark the answer.

1. Billy only eats spinach.
   ⓐ He ⓑ She
2. Billy loves spinach.
   ⓐ he ⓑ it
3. Billy's mother gave him rice.
   ⓐ He ⓑ She
4. Billy's dad gave him pie.
   ⓐ He ⓑ She
5. Billy gave the pie to the dog.
   ⓐ he ⓑ it

5 Book 2.2/Unit 2 Bremen Town Musicians

Extension: Have children continue the story about Billy, using the pronouns *I, he, she, it,* and *you*.

129

GRAMMAR PRACTICE BOOK, PAGE 129

DAY 2 Teach the Concept

Review Pronouns Ask children what a pronoun is, and have them name singular pronouns as you list them on the chalkboard.

Introduce Plural Pronouns Review: A plural noun names more than one person, place, or thing. Present:

Pronouns

The pronouns *we, you,* and *they* can take the place of a plural noun or more than one noun or pronoun.

Present the Daily Language Activity. Then write the following sentence on the chalkboard: *The dogs howled at the moon.* Have children write another sentence about the dogs, using a pronoun. (Example: They barked loudly.) Repeat with this sentence: *The dog and I played together.*

WRITING Assign the daily Writing Prompt on page 130C.

Name ________________ Date ________ PRACTICE AND LEARN Grammar 130

Pronouns

- The pronouns *we, you,* and *they* can take the place of a plural noun.

Beans are good for you. Ned and I are friends.
They are good for you. We are friends.

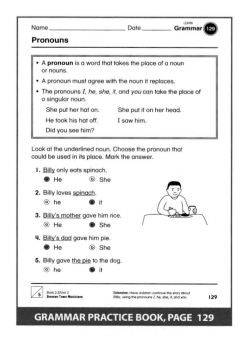

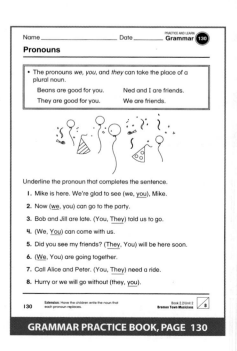

Underline the pronoun that completes the sentence.

1. Mike is here. We're glad to see (we, you), Mike.
2. Now (we, you) can go to the party.
3. Bob and Jill are late. (You, They) told us to go.
4. (We, You) can come with us.
5. Did you see my friends? (They, You) will be here soon.
6. (We, You) are going together.
7. Call Alice and Peter. (You, They) need a ride.
8. Hurry or we will go without (they, you).

130 **Extension:** Have the children write the noun that each pronoun replaces.

Book 2.2/Unit 2 Bremen Town Musicians 8

GRAMMAR PRACTICE BOOK, PAGE 130

DAY 3 Review and Practice

Learn from the Literature Review pronouns. Read the following sentences on page 124 of *The Bremen Town Musicians:*

> **I am going to Bremen to be a musician in the town band. You, too, have a beautiful voice. We can be in the town band together.**

Point out that the donkey is talking to the dog. Ask a child to identify the pronouns. Then, ask a child to identify the nouns they replace. (I—donkey; you—dog; we—donkey, dog)

Identify Pronouns Present the Daily Language Activity. Then ask volunteers to find and read aloud a sentence from *The Bremen Town Musicians* that includes pronouns. Ask others to identify the pronoun or pronouns in the sentence.

WRITING Assign the daily Writing Prompt on page 130D.

Name ____________ Date ________ REVIEW AND PRACTICE Grammar 131

Writing Pronouns

- A **pronoun** is a word that takes the place of a noun or nouns.
- A pronoun must agree with the noun it replaces.
- The pronouns *I, he, she, it,* and *you* can take the place of a singular noun.
- The pronouns *we, you,* and *they* can take the place of a plural noun.

Replace each underlined word or words with a pronoun. Then write the sentence.

1. Joe and Pam wrote a song together.
   They wrote a song together.
2. Pam wrote the music.
   She wrote the music.
3. Joe wrote the words.
   He wrote the words.
4. The song is funny.
   It is funny.
5. You and I can sing it.
   We can sing it.

5 Book 2.2/Unit 2 Bremen Town Musicians

Extension: Have children say sentences with proper nouns. Have other children substitute *he, she,* and *they* for them.

131

GRAMMAR PRACTICE BOOK, PAGE 131

DAY 4 Review and Practice

Review Pronouns List the characters from *The Bremen Town Musicians* on the chalkboard. Ask each child to write a sentence about one of the characters, or a sentence that one of the characters might say, that includes a pronoun. Model an example. Have volunteers read their sentences aloud and ask others to identify the pronoun(s).

Mechanics and Usage Before children begin the daily Writing Prompt on page 130D, review the use of quotation marks. Display and discuss:

> **Quotation Marks**
>
> Use quotation marks at the beginning and end of what a person says.

WRITING Assign the daily Writing Prompt on page 130D.

Name ____________ Date ________ MECHANICS Grammar 132

Using Quotation Marks

- Use quotation marks at the beginning and end of what a person says.
  "Go home," Jon told the dog.

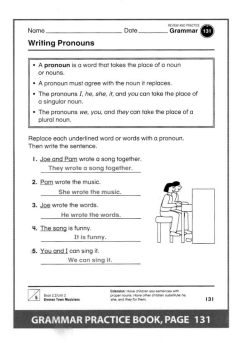

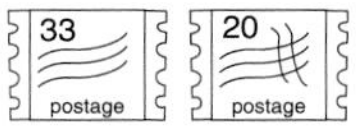

Read each sentence. Correct it.
Write the correct sentence on the line.

1. I need a stamp for this letter, Cindy said.
   "I need a stamp for this letter," Cindy said.
2. Let's go to the post office, Marc said.
   "Let's go to the post office," Marc said.
3. I'll buy stamps there, Cindy said.
   "I'll buy stamps there," Cindy said.
4. So will I, Marc said.
   "So will I," Marc said.
5. I like to collect stamps, said Cindy.
   "I like to collect stamps," said Cindy.

132

Extension: Have children write their own dialogues using quotation marks.

Book 2.2/Unit 2 Bremen Town Musicians 5

GRAMMAR PRACTICE BOOK, PAGE 132

DAY 5 Assess and Reteach

Assess Use the Daily Language Activity and page 133 of the **Grammar Practice Book** for assessment.

Reteach Have children write each rule about pronouns from the lesson grammar concepts on an index card.

Organize the class into groups, and have each group imagine that they are "The Bremen Town Musicians." As each group acts out a scene based on the play, have the class listen for and name pronouns.

List the pronouns and the nouns they refer to on the word wall.

Use page 134 of the **Grammar Practice Book** for additional reteaching.

WRITING Assign the daily Writing Prompt on page 130D.

Name ____________ Date ________ TEST Grammar 133

Test

A. Read each sentence. Write the pronoun that can take the place of the underlined words.

1. Aunt Doris is coming to visit. She
2. Aunt Doris will stay one week. She
3. Uncle Nate is staying home. He
4. Uncle Nate and Aunt Doris live in New York. They
5. "Uncle Nate will come later," said Aunt Doris. He
6. Uncle Nate and Aunt Doris like to travel. They

B. Read each pair of lines. Write the pronoun that can take the place of the underlined words.

7. Aunt Doris brought a big bag.
   The big bag was heavy. It
8. Uncle Nate gave me something special.
   Uncle Nate wants me to give it to you. He
9. Uncle Nate and Aunt Doris went to the museum.
   The museum was very interesting. It
10. Uncle Nate and Aunt Doris went home.
    Uncle Nate and Aunt Doris had a good time. They

10 Book 2.2/Unit 2 Bremen Town Musicians

133

GRAMMAR PRACTICE BOOK, PAGE 133

GRAMMAR PRACTICE BOOK, PAGE 134

5 Day Spelling Plan

LANGUAGE SUPPORT

ESL Spanish speakers may need help associating the /k/ sound with the *k* and *ck* spellings. Write the words *bake, work, kind,* and *sick* on the chalkboard, using a different color chalk for the *k* and *ck*.

DICTATION SENTENCES

Spelling Words

1. I can come too.
2. That is a hard act to follow.
3. The work is hard.
4. Wish for good luck.
5. I like to ride my bike.
6. She is kind to me.
7. You can wake him up this morning.
8. The girl knows how to bake.
9. She was sick all day.
10. That book cover is best.

Challenge Words

11. Her daughter is away.
12. The music is loud.
13. She is in the third grade.
14. Her voice is high.
15. He can whistle a tune.

DAY 1 Pretest

Assess Prior Knowledge Use the Dictation Sentences at left and **Spelling Practice Book** page 129 for the pretest. Allow students to correct their own papers. If students have trouble, have partners give each other a midweek test on Day 3. Students who require a modified list may be tested on the first five words.

Spelling Words		Challenge Words
1. **come**	6. kind	11. **daughter**
2. **act**	7. **wake**	12. **music**
3. **work**	8. bake	13. **third**
4. **luck**	9. sick	14. **voice**
5. **like**	10. cover	15. **whistle**

*Note: Words in **dark type** are from the story.*

Word Study On page 130 of the **Spelling Practice Book** are word study steps and an at-home activity.

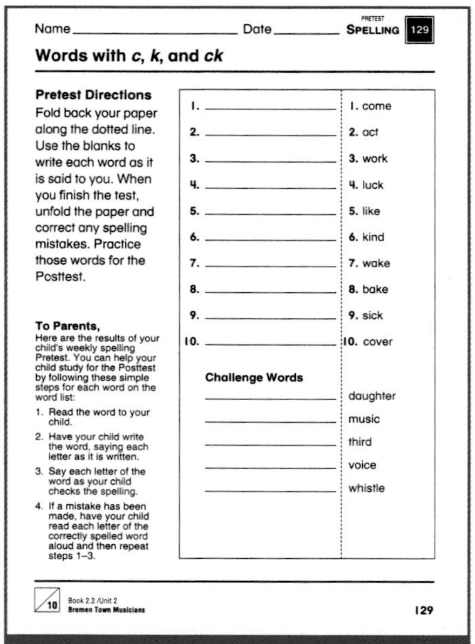

Name ______ Date ______ PRETEST SPELLING 129

Words with *c*, *k*, and *ck*

Pretest Directions
Fold back your paper along the dotted line. Use the blanks to write each word as it is said to you. When you finish the test, unfold the paper and correct any spelling mistakes. Practice those words for the Posttest.

1. ______	1. come
2. ______	2. act
3. ______	3. work
4. ______	4. luck
5. ______	5. like
6. ______	6. kind
7. ______	7. wake
8. ______	8. bake
9. ______	9. sick
10. ______	10. cover
Challenge Words	
______	daughter
______	music
______	third
______	voice
______	whistle

To Parents,
Here are the results of your child's weekly spelling Pretest. You can help your child study for the Posttest by following these simple steps for each word on the word list:
1. Read the word to your child.
2. Have your child write the word, saying each letter as it is written.
3. Say each letter of the word as your child checks the spelling.
4. If a mistake has been made, have your child read each letter of the correctly spelled word aloud and then repeat steps 1–3.

10 Book 2.2 /Unit 2 Bremen Town Musicians 129

SPELLING PRACTICE BOOK, PAGE 129

WORD STUDY STEPS AND ACTIVITY, PAGE 130

DAY 2 Explore the Pattern

Sort and Spell Words Say the words *come, kind, wake,* and *luck*. Ask students what sound they hear at the beginning of the first two words and the end of the second two. /k/ Write the words and circle the spellings of /k/.

Ask students to read aloud the ten spelling words before sorting them according to the spelling pattern.

Words with		
c	***k***	***ck***
come	work	luck
act	like	sick
cover	kind	
	wake	
	bake	

Spelling Patterns Ask students which spelling of /k/ appears only at the end of a word or syllable and never at the beginning of a word *(ck)*. Have them find other words ending with *ck* and add them to the word wall.

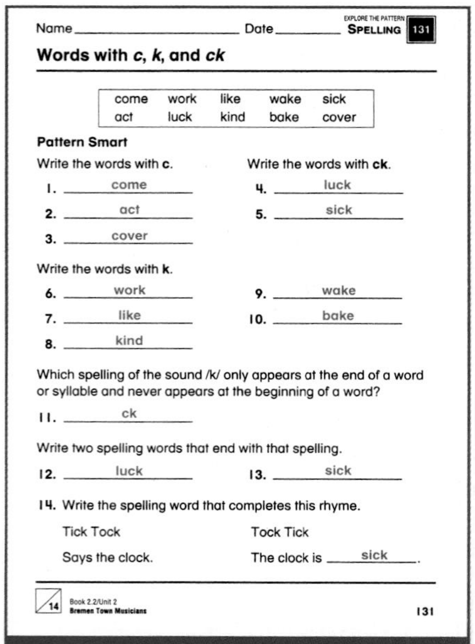

Name ______ Date ______ EXPLORE THE PATTERN SPELLING 131

Words with *c*, *k*, and *ck*

come	work	like	wake	sick
act	luck	kind	bake	cover

Pattern Smart

Write the words with **c**.
1. come
2. act
3. cover

Write the words with **ck**.
4. luck
5. sick

Write the words with **k**.
6. work
7. like
8. kind
9. wake
10. bake

Which spelling of the sound /k/ only appears at the end of a word or syllable and never appears at the beginning of a word?
11. ck

Write two spelling words that end with that spelling.
12. luck 13. sick

14. Write the spelling word that completes this rhyme.
Tick Tock Tock Tick
Says the clock. The clock is sick.

14 Book 2.2/Unit 2 Bremen Town Musicians 131

SPELLING PRACTICE BOOK, PAGE 131

Words with *c*, *k*, and *ck*

DAY 3 — Practice and Extend

Word Meaning: Synonyms Remind students that a synonym is a word that means the same thing as another word. Ask students to think of synonyms for as many of the spelling words as they can (examples: bake– cook, roast; sick–ill; cover–lid; kind–nice).

Glossary Have partners:

- write each Challenge Word.
- look up each Challenge Word and read each example sentence.
- write a new sentence for each Challenge Word.

DAY 4 — Proofread and Write

Proofread Sentences Write these sentences on the chalkboard, including the misspelled words. Ask students to proofread, circling incorrect spellings and writing the correct spellings. There are two spelling errors in each sentence.

> I (licke) to (bayk). (like, bake)
>
> I can (kome) to (wurk). (come, work)

Have students create additional sentences with errors for partners to correct.

WRITING Have students use as many Spelling Words as possible in the daily Writing Prompt on page 130D. Remind students to proofread their writing for errors in spelling, grammar, and punctuation.

DAY 5 — Assess and Reteach

Assess Students' Knowledge Use page 134 of the **Spelling Practice Book** or the Dictation Sentences on page 149Q for the posttest.

Personal Word List If students have trouble with any words in the lesson, have them add to their personal list of troublesome words in their journals. Have students write a context sentence for each word.

Students should refer to their word lists during later writing activities.

SPELLING PRACTICE BOOK, PAGE 132

Name _____ Date _____ PRACTICE AND EXTEND SPELLING 132

Words with *c*, *k*, and *ck*

| come | work | like | wake | sick |
| act | luck | kind | bake | cover |

Write the words that complete each sentence.

1. My father rides the bus to ____ **work** ____
2. What ____ **kind** ____ of sandwich do you want?
3. You should ____ **cover** ____ your mouth when you sneeze.
4. Tony likes to ____ **bake** ____ cookies.
5. It's time to ____ **wake** ____ up from your nap.
6. Is Maria ____ **sick** ____ with a cold?

Word Meaning
Say it another way. Draw a line from each spelling word to the word that means almost the same.

7. kind — cook
8. cover — ill
9. bake — lid
10. sick — nice

Challenge Extension: Have students write fill-in sentences using the words. They may exchange with a partner to complete the sentences.

132 Book 2.2/Unit 2 Bremen Town Musicians

SPELLING PRACTICE BOOK, PAGE 133

Name _____ Date _____ PROOFREAD AND WRITE SPELLING 133

Words with *c*, *k*, and *ck*

Proofreading Activity
There are six spelling mistakes in the paragraph below. Circle each misspelled word. Write the words correctly on the lines below.

It takes a lot of (werk) to make cookies. Pat asked her friend May to (cume) help. "What (keind) shall we make?" May asked. "I like chocolate chip!" Pat said. Pat's father put the cookies in the oven to (backe). "(Waok) me when they are done," he said. Pat told May to (cuver) some cookies and take them home to her mother.

1. **work** 2. **come** 3. **kind**
4. **bake** 5. **Wake** 6. **cover**

Writing Activity
Write a recipe using four spelling words. Circle the spelling words in your recipe.

Book 2.2/Unit 2 Bremen Town Musicians 133

SPELLING PRACTICE BOOK, PAGE 134

Name _____ Date _____ POSTTEST SPELLING 134

Words with *c*, *k*, and *ck*

Look at the words in each set. One word in each set is spelled correctly. Use a pencil to color in the circle in front of that word. Before you begin, look at the sample sets of words. Sample A has been done for you. Do Sample B by yourself. When you are sure you know what to do, you may go on with the rest of the page.

Sample A
- (A) taak
- (B) tayk
- ● take
- (D) teake

Sample B
- ● cage
- (F) caage
- (G) caje
- (H) cayge

1. (A) akt / (B) ackt / ● act / (D) acck
2. (E) waik / (F) wacke / (G) wayke / ● wake
3. ● kind / (B) kined / (C) kaned / (D) keind
4. ● come / (F) kome / (G) cume / (H) kum
5. (A) lauk / (B) luk / ● luck / (D) louck

6. (E) cowver / ● cover / (G) cuver / (H) coover
7. (A) woirk / ● work / (C) worck / (D) worek
8. ● bake / (F) beik / (G) bayk / (H) baik
9. (A) seak / (B) sikc / (C) seeck / ● sick
10. (E) leik / ● like / (G) licke / (H) lyke

134 Book 2.2/Unit 2 Bremen Town Musicians

Reaching All Learners

Concept
- Team Sports

Comprehension
- Summarize

Phonics
- Variant Vowels /ü/ *oo, ue, ew*

Vocabulary
- coaches
- field
- score
- stretches
- throws
- touch

Game Time
Toot! Toot! The whistle blows.
It's time to start the game.
Red team runs on the field.
Blue team does the same.
Zoom! Zoom! The ball goes fast.
Blue team makes a score.
Boom! Boom! the band plays loudly.
And all the people roar.

Rhyme applies to phonics

Anthology

Our Soccer League

Selection Summary **Children will find out about soccer while playing along with the Falcons and the Sluggers.**

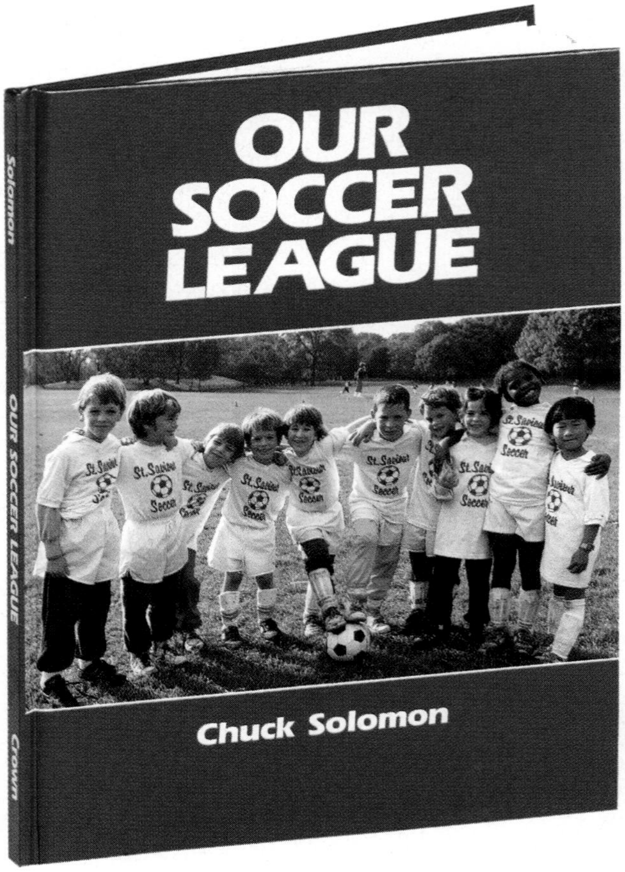
OUR SOCCER LEAGUE
Chuck Solomon
Solomon
OUR SOCCER LEAGUE
Crown

Listening Library

INSTRUCTIONAL pages 152–179

About the Author/Illustrator Professional sports photographer Chuck Solomon says he wanted to write *Our Soccer League* because soccer is such a good sport for children. "It's not too rough, and running is good exercise," he says. "Besides, both boys and girls can play it."

Same Concept, Skills and Vocabulary!

Leveled Books

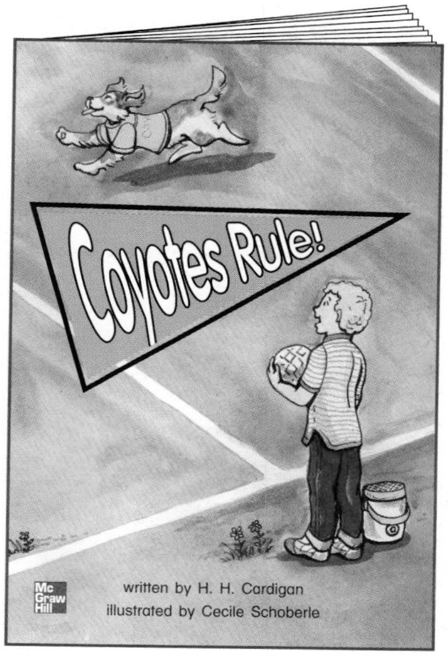

EASY
Lesson on pages 179A and 179D
DECODABLE

INDEPENDENT
Lesson on pages 179B and 179D
Take-Home version available

CHALLENGE
Lesson on pages 179C and 179D

Leveled Practice

EASY
Reteach, 177–184 Blackline masters with reteaching opportunities for each assessed skill

INDEPENDENT/ON-LEVEL
Practice, 177–184 Workbook with Take-Home stories and practice opportunities for each assessed skill and story comprehension

CHALLENGE
Extend, 177–184 Blackline masters that offer challenge activities for each assessed skill

Quizzes Prepared by Accelerated Reader

WORKSTATION Activities

Social Studies . . . Map Skills, *160*
Science/Art. . . . . . . Ball Flip Book, *162*
Math. . . . . Time, *166*
Health . . . . Heart Rates, *156*
Language Arts . . Read Aloud, *150E*
Writing. . . . . Write a Game Guide, *176*
Cultural Perspectives . . . . . Soccer, *158*
Research and Inquiry . . . . . . Find Out More, *177*
Internet Activities. . . . . www.mhschool.com/reading

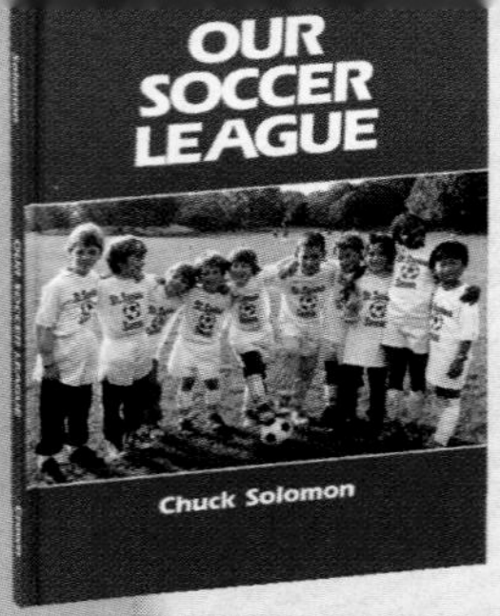

Suggested Lesson Planner

READING AND LANGUAGE ARTS	DAY 1 Focus on Reading and Skills	DAY 2 Read the Literature
Phonics Daily Routines	Daily Phonics Routine: Segmenting, 150H Phonics CD-ROM	Daily Phonics Routine: Fluency, 152A Phonics CD-ROM
Phonological Awareness Phonics /ü/ Comprehension Vocabulary Study Skills Listening, Speaking, Viewing, Representing	**Read Aloud: Myth,** 150E "The Great Ball Game" ☑ **Develop Phonological Awareness,** 150F /ü/*oo, ue, ew* ☑ **Review /ü/*oo, ue, ew*,** 150G–150H **Teaching Chart 148** **Reteach, Practice, Extend,** 177 **Phonics/Phonemic Awareness Practice Book,** 117–120 Read **Apply /ü/*oo, ue, ew*,** 150/151 "Game Time" Intervention Program	**Build Background,** 152A Develop Oral Language **Vocabulary,** 152B–152C *coaches* *score* *throws* *field* *stretches* *touch* **Word Building Manipulative Cards** **Teaching Chart 149** **Reteach, Practice, Extend,** 178 Read **Read the Selection,** 152–175 Comprehension ☑ /ü/*oo, ue, ew* ☑ Summarize **Genre: Narrative Nonfiction,** 153 **Writer's Craft: Suspense,** 172 **Cultural Perspectives,** 158 Intervention Program
Curriculum Connections	Link **Language Arts,** 150E	Link **Social Studies,** 152A
Writing	**Writing Prompt:** Every team wants to win all the time. No team does. Describe how it feels to be on the winning team. Describe how it feels to be on the losing team.	**Writing Prompt:** Have you ever been on the same team with a close friend or relative? Tell about the experience. **Journal Writing** Quick-Write, 175
Grammar	**Introduce the Concept: *I* and *Me*, *We* and *Us*,** 179O Daily Language Activity: Use *I* and *me* correctly. **Grammar Practice Book,** 135	**Teach the Concept: *I* and *Me*, *We* and *Us*,** 179O Daily Language Activity: Use *we* and *us* correctly. **Grammar Practice Book,** 136
Spelling *Blends*	**Pretest: Words with Blends,** 179Q **Spelling Practice Book,** 135,136	**Explore the Pattern: Words with Blends,** 179Q **Spelling Practice Book,** 137

Meeting Individual Needs

☑ = Skill Assessed in Unit Test

ⓘ Intervention Program Available

Read EVERY DAY

DAY 3 Read the Literature

Daily Phonics Routine:
Blending, 177

Phonics CD-ROM

Rereading for Fluency, 174

Story Questions and Activities, 176–177
Reteach, Practice, Extend, 179

Study Skills, 178
☑ **Various Texts**
Teaching Chart 150
Reteach, Practice, Extend, 180

Test Power, 179

Read **Read the Leveled Books,** 179A–179D
Guided Reading
☑ ***/ü/oo, ue, ew***
☑ **Summarize**
☑ **Instructional Vocabulary**

ⓘ Intervention Program

Activity **Health,** 156; **Social Studies,** 160

Writing Prompt: Write a letter to a friend telling about a sporting event you went to or would like to see. Who did you go with? How did you get there?

Expository Writing, 179M
Prewrite, Draft

Practice and Write: *I* and *Me*, *We* and *Us*, 179P
Daily Language Activity: Use *me* and *us* correctly.

Grammar Practice Book, 137

Practice and Extend: Words with Blends, 179R

Spelling Practice Book, 138

DAY 4 Build Skills

Daily Phonics Routine:
Discriminating, 179F

Phonics CD-ROM

Read **Read the Leveled Books and Self-Selected Books**

☑ **Review /ü/*oo, ue, ew*,** 179E–179F
Teaching Chart 151
Reteach, Practice, Extend, 181
Language Support, 195
Phonics/Phonemic Awareness Practice Book, 117–120

☑ **Review /ü/*oo, ue*; /ôr/*or, ore*,** 179G–179H
Teaching Chart 152
Reteach, Practice, Extend, 182
Language Support, 196
Phonics/Phonemic Awareness Practice Book, 117–120

Minilessons, 157, 159, 161, 165, 171

ⓘ Intervention Program

Activity **Science/Art,** 162

Writing Prompt: Imagine you are a famous athlete. Explain how you and your coach or team prepare for a big game.

Expository Writing, 179M
Revise

Meeting Individual Needs for Writing, 179N

Review and Practice: *I* and *Me*, *We* and *Us*, 179P
Daily Language Activity: Use *I* and *me*, *we* and *us* correctly.

Grammar Practice Book, 138

Proofread and Write: Words with Blends, 179R

Spelling Practice Book, 139

DAY 5 Build Skills

Daily Phonics Routine:
Writing, 179H

Phonics CD-ROM

Read **Read Self-Selected Books**

☑ **Introduce Sequence of Events,** 179I–179J
Teaching Chart 153
Reteach, Practice, Extend, 183
Language Support, 197

☑ **Review Context Clues,** 179K–179L
Teaching Chart 154
Reteach, Practice, Extend, 184
Language Support, 198

Listening, Speaking, Viewing, Representing, 179N
Recruit Players
Make a Poster

Minilessons, 157, 159, 161, 165, 171

ⓘ Intervention Program

Activity **Math,** 166

Writing Prompt: It's hard for members of a team to get along all the time. Write some advice for teammates about getting along with each other.

Expository Writing, 179M
Edit/Proofread, Publish

Assess and Reteach: *I* and *Me*, *We* and *Us*, 179P
Daily Language Activity: Use *I* and *me*, *we* and *us* correctly.

Grammar Practice Book, 139–140

Assess and Reteach: Words with Blends, 179R

Spelling Practice Book, 140

Link
Language Arts

Read Aloud

The Great Ball Game

a Muskogee myth retold by Joseph Bruchac

Long ago the Birds and Animals had a great argument.

"We who have wings are better than you," said the Birds.

"That is not so," the Animals replied. "We who have teeth are better."

The two sides argued back and forth. Their quarrel went on and on, until it seemed they would go to war because of it.

Then Crane, the leader of the Birds, and Bear, the leader of the Animals, had an idea.

"Let us have a ball game," Crane said. "The first side to score a goal will win the argument."

"This idea is good," said Bear. "The side that loses will have to accept the penalty given by the other side."

So they walked and flew to a field, and there they divided up into two teams.

On one side went all those who had wings. They were the Birds.

On the other side went those with teeth. They were the Animals.

Continued on pages T2–T3

Oral Comprehension

LISTENING AND SPEAKING Read this myth aloud. Ask children, as you read, to use clues in the text to draw conclusions about the animals. When you have finished, ask, "How would you describe the bat?" Then ask, "Which words in the story helped you draw that conclusion?"

GENRE STUDY: MYTH Discuss the literary devices and techniques used in *The Great Ball Game.*

- Tell children that myths often explain the origin of something in nature. Ask: *What does this myth explain?*
- Determine the setting of the myth. In what time period does the myth take place?
- Discuss the characters in *The Great Ball Game.* Are the characters realistic? Ask: *Could the story have really taken place? Why or why not?*

Activity Have students re-enact *The Great Ball Game.* On a soccer field, divide the class into two teams. Tell one team that they are the Birds, the other that they are the Animals. Explain that they will play a soccer game in which the Birds can only use their hands, and the Animals can only use their feet. When the Birds have the ball, they cannot move–they can simply throw the ball to another player. Choose an Animal player by chance to be the Bat. The Bat starts playing in the second half, and can use both hands and feet.

▶ **Visual/Spatial**

Develop Phonological Awareness

Blend Sounds

Phonemic Awareness

MATERIALS
- Phonics Picture Posters

Teach Display three pictures, for example, *bread, baby, book.* Say the sounds of one of the picture names. Tell children to point to the picture and blend the sounds to say the picture name. Continue by having children blend the sounds for the other two pictures.

Practice Follow the same procedure using: *whale, cane, train; sink, nine, nest; bee, seal, leaf.*

Segment Sounds

Phonemic Awareness

MATERIALS
- Word Building Boxes from *Word Building Cards*
- paper circles for each child

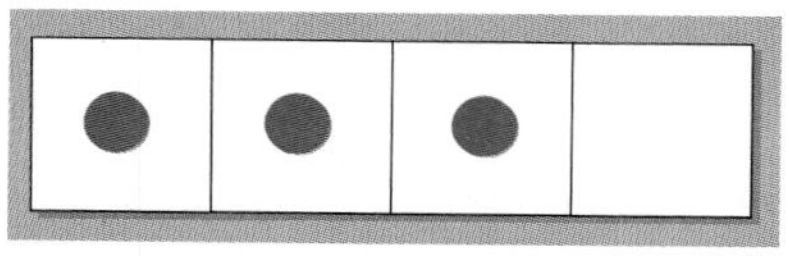

Teach Say the word *food.* Then say the sounds /f/-/ü/-/d/, sliding a paper circle into a word box for each sound. Count the word boxes and tell children the word *food* has three sounds.

Practice Distribute a set of Word Building Boxes and colored paper circles to each child. Have them continue to segment and count the sounds in the following words: *true, room, stop, cool, dew, race, noon,* and *new.*

Delete Sounds

Phonemic Awareness

MATERIALS
- colored blocks

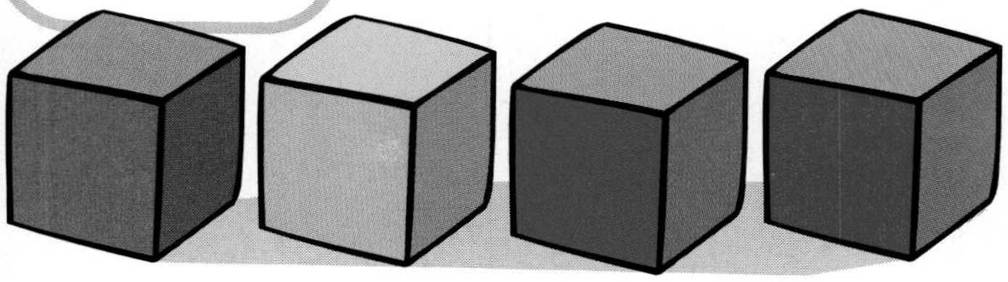

Teach Give each child a set of four colored blocks. Say the word *blue.* Segment the word, placing a block for each sound. Then say /b/-/ü/ and remove the second block. Ask: *If I take out the /l/ sound, what word do we get?* (boo)

Practice Repeat the exercise, as children use their blocks with these words:

drew/without the *r*	*bloom*/without the *l*
skip/without the *k*	*spoon*/without the *p*
trip/without the *r*	*brag*/without the *r*

INFORMAL ASSESSMENT

Observe children as they blend, segment, and delete sounds. If children have difficulty, see Alternate Teaching Strategies on p. T69.

Review /ü/ oo, ue, ew

TESTED OBJECTIVES

Children will:

- identify /ü/*oo, ue, ew*.
- segment and read words with /ü/*oo, ue, ew*.

MATERIALS

- **Teaching Chart 148**

Skills Finder

/ü/ oo, ue, ew

Introduce	B1: 128G-H
Review	B1: 155E-F; B2: 150G-H, 179E-F, 179G-H
Test	B1: Unit 2

SPELLING/PHONICS CONNECTIONS

See the 5-Day Spelling Plan, pages 179Q–179R.

TEACHING TIP

SPELLING PATTERNS

Help children recognize that the spelling patterns *oo, ue,* and *ew* all make the same sound /ü/. After completing the teaching chart, read each word aloud. Have children repeat the vowel sound as you point to the letters that make the vowel sound in each word.

PREPARE

Listen for Words with /ü/

- Read the following sentence aloud. Ask children to clap when they hear the /ü/ sound. *My bluebird flew right out of the room.*

TEACH

BLENDING Model and Guide Practice with *oo* Words

- Display **Teaching Chart 148**. Tell children they will build words in which the letters *oo, ue,* and *ew* stand for the vowel /ü/. Write the letters *oo* in the first example to form the word *food*. Blend the sounds together to read the word *food*. Repeat, asking children to listen to the vowel sound, and to identify it as /ü/.
- Review that the /ü/ sound is represented by the letters *oo*.
- Model the first example in columns 2 and 3, blending the sounds in each word with children.

oo	ue	ew
f oo d	bl ue	f ew
br oo m	tr ue	kn ew
st oo l	cl ue	gr ew
tr oo p	d ue	dr ew

Teaching Chart 148

Use the Word in Context

- Have volunteers use the word in a sentence to reinforce its meaning. Example: *I love to eat French food.*

Repeat the Procedure

- Follow the same procedure to complete the rest of the words in column 1 and to form words for the *ue* and *ew* sounds in columns 2 and 3.

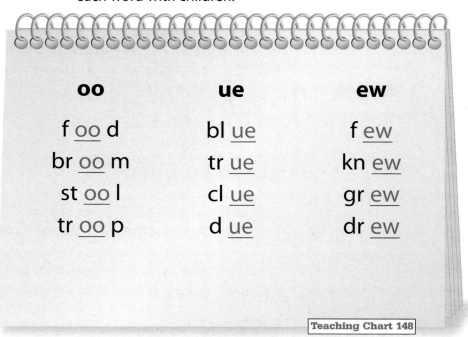

PRACTICE

WORD BUILDING
Building Words with the /ü/ Sound

PARTNERS

Use letter and variant vowel cards to build the word *glue*. Blend the sounds together and read the word aloud. Ask children to blend the sounds and read after you. Then have children work with partners to build and read the words *groom, noon, spoon, blue, blew, flew*.
▶ **Interpersonal/Linguistic**

ASSESS/CLOSE

Read and Sort /ü/ Words

To assess children's ability to build and read /ü/ words, have each child write his or her /ü/ words from the Practice activity on index cards, and make a class word wall sorted by the different spelling patterns for /ü/. Then have children read the phonics rhyme on page 150/151 in their anthologies. Finally, have them use the cards to brainstorm more words with /ü/.
▶ **Interpersonal/Linguistic**

ADDITIONAL PHONICS RESOURCES

Phonics/Phonemic Awareness Practice Book, pages 117–120

McGraw-Hill School TECHNOLOGY

Phonics CD-ROM activities for practice with Decoding and Building

Meeting Individual Needs for Phonics

EASY

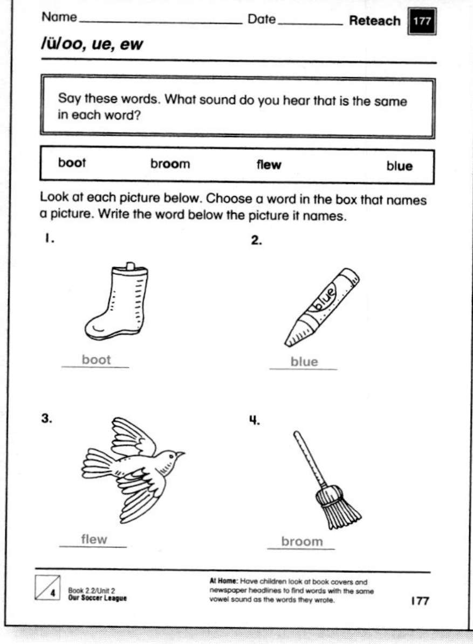

Name ______ Date ______ Reteach 177

/ü/oo, ue, ew

Say these words. What sound do you hear that is the same in each word?

boot broom flew blue

Look at each picture below. Choose a word in the box that names a picture. Write the word below the picture it names.

1. boot
2. blue
3. flew
4. broom

4 Book 2.2/Unit 2 **Our Soccer League**

At Home: Have children look at book covers and newspaper headlines to find words with the same vowel sound as the words they wrote.

177

Reteach, 177

INDEPENDENT

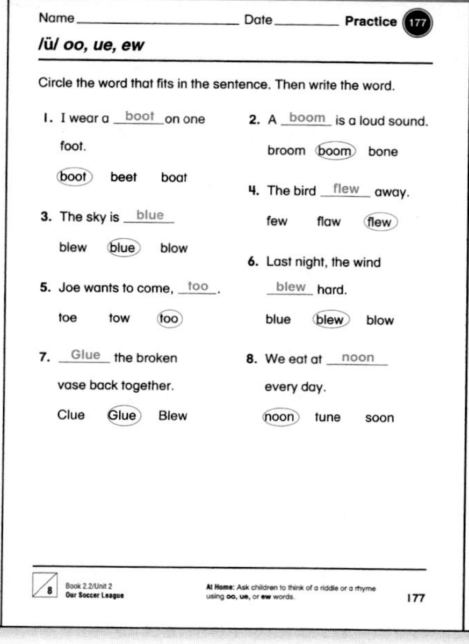

Name ______ Date ______ Practice 177

/ü/ oo, ue, ew

Circle the word that fits in the sentence. Then write the word.

1. I wear a __boot__ on one foot.
boot beet boat
2. A __boom__ is a loud sound.
broom boom bone
3. The sky is __blue__.
blew blue blow
4. The bird __flew__ away.
few flaw flew
5. Joe wants to come, __too__.
toe tow too
6. Last night, the wind __blew__ hard.
blue blew blow
7. __Glue__ the broken vase back together.
Clue Glue Blew
8. We eat at __noon__ every day.
noon tune soon

8 Book 2.2/Unit 2 **Our Soccer League**

At Home: Ask children to think of a riddle or a rhyme using **oo, ue,** or **ew** words.

177

Practice, 177

CHALLENGE

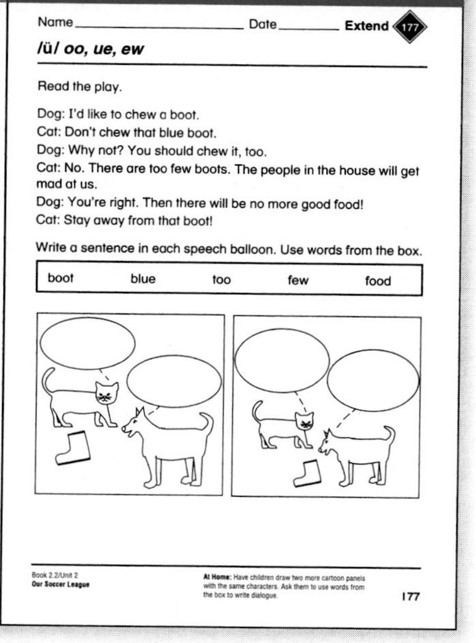

Name ______ Date ______ Extend 177

/ü/ oo, ue, ew

Read the play.

Dog: I'd like to chew a boot.
Cat: Don't chew that blue boot.
Dog: Why not? You should chew it, too.
Cat: No. There are too few boots. The people in the house will get mad at us.
Dog: You're right. Then there will be no more good food!
Cat: Stay away from that boot!

Write a sentence in each speech balloon. Use words from the box.

boot blue too few food

Book 2.2/Unit 2 **Our Soccer League**

At Home: Have children draw two more cartoon panels with the same characters. Ask them to use words from the box to write dialogue.

177

Extend, 177

Daily Routines

DAY 1 **Segmenting** Write two words with different spelling patterns for /ü/ on the board (for example: *grew, glue*). Have a volunteer identify and underline the letters in each word that stand for the /ü/ sound.

DAY 2 **Fluency** Write a list of /ü/ words such as *stool, dew, knew*, and *true*. Point to each word, asking children to blend the sounds silently. Ask a volunteer to read aloud each word.

DAY 3 **Blending** Write the spelling of each sound in *tooth* as you say it. Have children repeat after you. Ask children to blend the sounds to read the word. Repeat with *true, tool*, and *drew*.

DAY 4 **Discriminating** Say a list of words, some containing /ü/ (for example: *foot, pool, sit, mother, jewel*). Have children listen for the /ü/ sound and clap their hands each time they hear it.

DAY 5 **Writing** Have children write a nonsense sentence or rhyming triplet using each of the spellings of the /ü/ sound. For example: *I once knew a blue groom.*

TESTED **OBJECTIVES**

Children will segment and read words with /ü/*oo, ue, ew.*

Apply /ü/oo, ue, ew

Game Time
Toot! Toot! The whistle blows,
It's time to start the game.
Red team runs on the field,
Blue team does the same.
Zoom! Zoom! The ball goes fast,
Blue team makes a score.
Boom! Boom! the band plays loudly,
And all the people roar.
150
151

Anthology pages 150–151

Read and Build Fluency

READ THE POEM Before you and the children read "Game Time," review the /ü/ sound in *zoom* and *blue.* Model fluent reading by expressively reading the poem aloud as children track the text. Then, for auditory modeling, ask children to echo your reading style, reminding them to put real feeling in their voices as they read the words *toot, zoom,* and *boom.*

GROUP **REREAD FOR FLUENCY** Encourage fluency by choral reading the selection with children. Have them read aloud with you. Gradually fade your voice out as children become more fluent. Ask them to repeat certain words or phrases, echoing your tone and expression.

Dictate and Spell

JOURNAL **DICTATE WORDS** Say the word *toot* and segment it into its three individual sounds. Repeat the word and use it in a sentence, for example, "The horn will toot at dinner time." Have children say the word. Then direct them to write down the letter or letter patterns for each sound until they make the entire word. Continue the exercise with other words from the poem, such as *blue* and *boom.* Then use words outside the poem, such as *food, clue,* and *grew.*

Intervention **Skills Intervention Guide,** for direct instruction and extra practice of /ü/*oo, ue, ew*

Build Background

Link
Social Studies

Concept: Team Sports

Evaluate Prior Knowledge

CONCEPT: TEAM SPORTS Ask children which sports they play by themselves and which they play as a team. Discuss with them that being part of a team means that everyone works together.

DIAGRAM DIFFERENCES Brainstorm with children how team sports and individual sports are different and alike. Have children create a Venn diagram of the differences and similarities. ▶ **Spatial/Interpersonal**

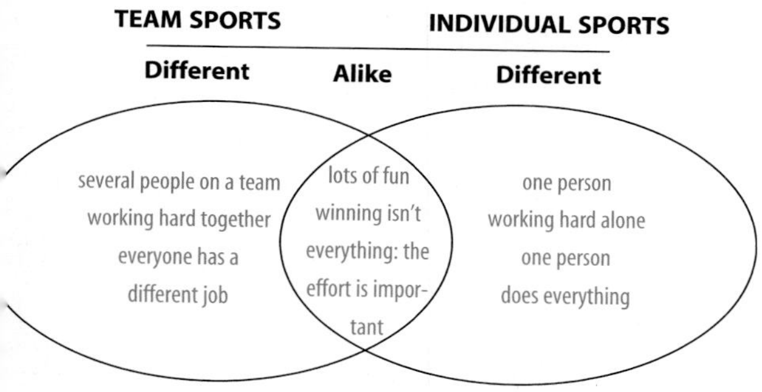

Graphic Organizer 14

EXPLAIN A SAYING Write on the chalkboard: *It's not whether you win or lose, it's how you play the game.* Have children write a brief paragraph explaining what this means to them.

WRITING ONE

Develop Oral Language

CONNECT WORDS AND ACTIONS Have

ESL

children pantomime their favorite sports for the rest of the group. Ask the other children in the group to identify the sport and, if possible, the position, such as pitcher on a baseball team. After the sport and/or position has been identified, have the child write the name of the sport on the chalkboard in his or her native language. Then have a volunteer write the sport name in English and read it aloud. Have the group repeat the word. ▶ **Kinesthetic/Linguistic**

Anthology and Leveled Books

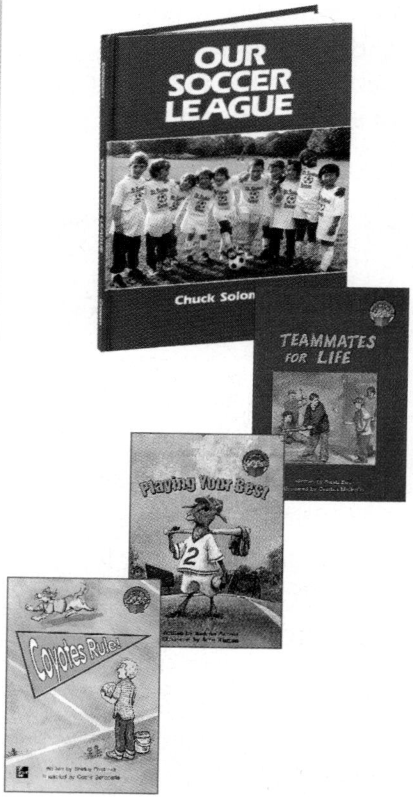

DAILY Phonics ROUTINES

DAY 2 **Fluency** Write a list of /ü/ words such as *stool, dew, knew,* and *true.* Point to each word, asking children to blend the sounds silently. Ask a volunteer to read aloud each word.

Phonics CD-ROM

LANGUAGE SUPPORT

Use the **Language Support Book, pages 190–193,** to help build background.

TESTED OBJECTIVES

Children will use context and structural clues to determine the meanings of vocabulary words.

Definitions

coaches (p. 156) teachers or trainers of athletes or performers

field (p. 154) an area of land on which a game is played

score (p. 158) to make a point or points in a game or test

stretches (p. 154) to spread out one's arms, legs, or body to full length

throws (p. 157) to send up into or through the air

touch (p. 154) to put a hand or other part of the body on or against something

Story Words

These words from the selection may be unfamiliar. Before children read, have them check the meanings and pronunciations of the words in the Glossary, beginning on page 390, or in a dictionary.

- dribble, p. 154
- goalie, p. 154
- intercept, p. 157
- out-of-bounds, p. 158
- halftime, p. 160
- collide, p. 162

coaches
field
score
stretches
throws
touch

Vocabulary

Teach Vocabulary in Context

Identify Vocabulary Words Display **Teaching Chart 149** and read the passage with children. Have volunteers circle each vocabulary word and underline other words that are clues to its meaning.

Playing Soccer

1. From the sidelines, the coaches shout out advice about the best way to play the game. **2.** You can hear them saying, "Don't touch the ball with your hands!" a lot. **3.** Of course, we like it best when we score and get a point. **4.** When that happens, we run across the grass on the field to high-five each other. **5.** Moira throws the ball in when it goes out of bounds. It flies out of her hands and through the air. **6.** Scott stretches his leg as far as he can and kicks the ball to me.

Teaching Chart 149

Discuss Meanings Ask questions like these to help clarify word meanings:

- How are coaches like teachers?
- Would you rather touch something smooth or something rough?
- How do you score a point in baseball? in football?
- What does a soccer field look like? a baseball field?
- Who can show how an athlete stretches before a game?
- What parts of the body does a pitcher use to throw the ball?

Activities

Practice

Illustrate Meanings PARTNERS Have partners choose vocabulary cards from a pile. Then have them draw a picture for each word and display the drawings to their partners to be identified. ▶ **Spatial/Linguistic**

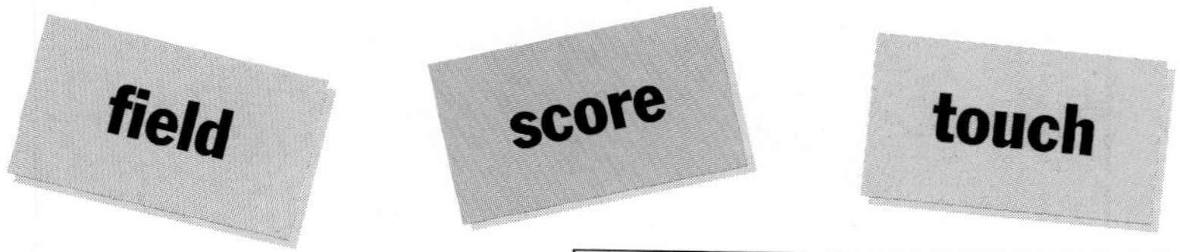

Word Building Manipulative Cards

Write Illustrated Sentences ONE WRITING Have children write context sentences on the chalkboard, taping their illustrations up in place of the vocabulary word. Ask volunteers to identify each word and underline the context clues. ▶ **Linguistic/Interpersonal**

Assess Vocabulary

Identify Word Meaning in Context PARTNERS WRITING Invite children to write three or more questions that use vocabulary words. Ask them to include context clues in each question they write. Then have children exchange questions and write answers to their partners' questions. The partners' answers should include the vocabulary words whenever possible.

SPELLING/VOCABULARY CONNECTIONS

See Spelling Challenge Words, pages 179Q–179R.

LANGUAGE SUPPORT

See the **Language Support Book**, pages 190–193, for teaching suggestions for Vocabulary.

Vocabulary PuzzleMaker

Provides vocabulary activities.

Meeting Individual Needs for Vocabulary

EASY

Name________ Date________ Reteach 178

Vocabulary

Choose a word from the box to complete each sentence. Write the word on the line.

coaches field score stretches throws touch

1. Sue __throws__ a softball very far.
2. Please don't __touch__ the wet paint.
3. We did sit-ups and __stretches__ on the floor.
4. Ben added up the __score__ to see who won.
5. Our parents are the __coaches__ of our team.
6. Tall grass grew in the __field__.

178 At Home: Ask children to draw a picture for one of the vocabulary words. Book 2.2/Unit 2 Our Soccer League 6

Reteach, 178

ON-LEVEL

Name________ Date________ Practice 178

Vocabulary

Circle the word that answers the riddle. Then write the word on the line.

coaches field score stretches throws touch

1. These are good to do before you play sports. __stretches__
   field (stretches) objects
2. This is what David does with a ball. __throws__
   (throws) whistles scares
3. You can do this to a table, a book, or a chair. __touch__
   sleep score (touch)
4. We are the people who run the team. __coaches__
   (coaches) police nurses
5. This is what happens when a ball goes in the goal. __score__
   safe (score) wild
6. I am the place where ball games are played. __field__
   house barn (field)

178 At Home: Have children make up riddles using some of the words that they didn't circle. Book 2.2/Unit 2 Our Soccer League 6

Practice, 178

ON-LEVEL

The Blue Birds

"Now we are going to lose big time!" I say.
"That's not true! Wait and see," says Martha.
Boom! Ted hits the ball! Then Joe hits the ball! Then I hit a home run, too! We win!
"You see," says Martha. "I knew you were a good team all along. You just had to believe in yourselves!"

At Home: Have children draw a picture and write a few sentences about their favorite sport. Who is their favorite player? Why?

178a

Practice, 178a Take-Home Story

CHALLENGE

Name________ Date________ Extend 178

Vocabulary

touch stretches score coaches throws field

Use the clues in the soccer balls to name a word from the box.

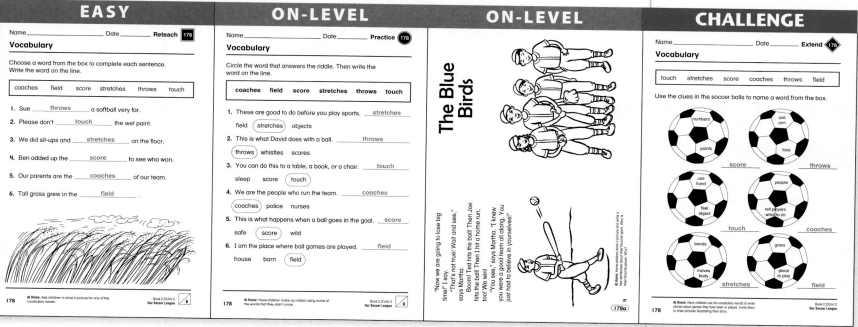

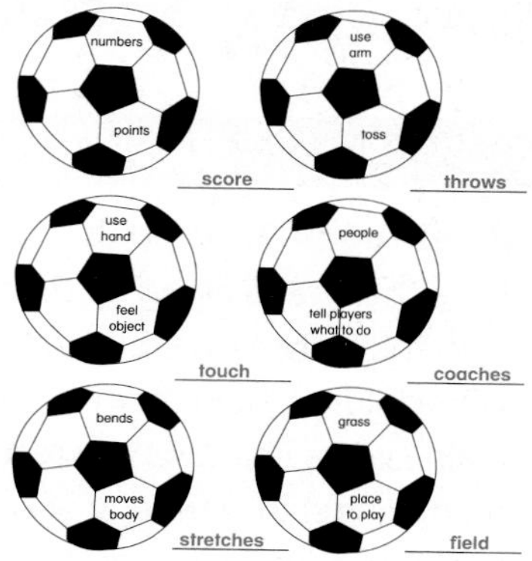

__score__ __throws__
__touch__ __coaches__
__stretches__ __field__

178 At Home: Have children use the vocabulary words to write stories about games they have seen or played. Invite them to draw pictures illustrating their story. Book 2.2/Unit 2 Our Soccer League

Extend, 178

Comprehension

Prereading Strategies

PREVIEW AND PREDICT Have children read the title and take a **picture walk** through the photographs, looking for details that might help them summarize the story at various points.

- What are the characters doing in the story?
- Will this be a folktale or a nonfiction story? How can you tell? (The photographs are of real children.) ***Genre***
- What is this story most likely about?

Have children make and chart predictions about the story.

PREDICTIONS	WHAT HAPPENED
The story will be about a soccer game.	
The story will tell how to play soccer.	

SET PURPOSES Ask children what they want to find out as they read the story. For example:

- How is soccer played?
- What does it take to be part of a team?
- Who will win the game?

Meeting Individual Needs • Grouping Suggestions for Strategic Reading

EASY

Read Together Read the story aloud or have them read along by themselves with the **Listening Library.** As you read with children, help them to fill in the Main Events chart. As you read with children, model the strategy of summarizing the story at various points to reinforce children's understanding of the plot.

ON-LEVEL

Guided Instruction Read the story with children, choosing from the Comprehension questions. Have them use the Main Events chart to record meaningful information during reading.

CHALLENGE

Read Independently Have children set purposes before they read. Remind children that as they read they should stop periodically to summarize the story. Explain that summarizing will reinforce their understanding of the story and help point out any areas that might be misunderstood. After reading, have children use their Main Events charts to summarize the story.

WE'RE THE FALCONS.
WE PLAY SOCCER!
1
St. Saviour Soccer
153

Comprehension

Phonics Apply /ü/ oo, ue, ew

Apply Summarize

STRATEGIC READING Before we begin reading, let's set up a Main Events chart so we can record important information from the story.

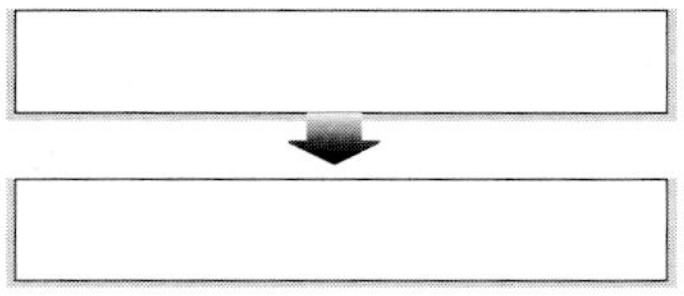

1 Do you think the children on pages 152 and 153 will make a good team? Why? (They look like they know each other, and like each other, so they probably play well together.) ***Make Inferences***

Genre

Narrative Nonfiction

Explain that narrative nonfiction:

- gives facts about a topic in time order.
- includes photographs and graphics, such as charts.
- is presented in the form of a story.

Activity When children have read *Our Soccer League,* challenge them to cite examples of time order words from the selection. Have them explain how the use of the scoreboard and the time clock helps to show the order in which events happen in the story. Then point out the game-play chart on page 156. Encourage volunteers to discuss how this chart might help readers better understand the story.

LANGUAGE SUPPORT

The blackline master on the right can be found in the **Language Support Book.**

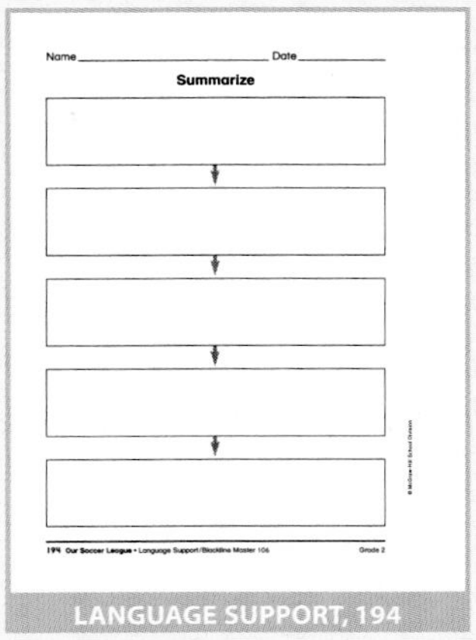
Name ____ Date ____
Summarize

LANGUAGE SUPPORT, 194

Comprehension

2 Phonics /ü/ Let's read the second sentence together. What word has /ü/ sound? *(blue)* Which two letters make that sound? (*ue*) Now let's read the first sentence in the last paragraph. Can anyone find the word with the /ü/ sound? (*too*) Which letters make the /ü/ sound in this word? (*oo*) ***Graphophonic Cues***

3 Where does this story take place? (outdoors, on a soccer field) Why do you think this is the setting for the story? (Because a soccer game takes a lot of room to play, so it makes sense for the game to take place outdoors.) ***Setting***

P/I **PHONICS/DECODING** Read the last paragraph on this page. What word contains the /sk/ sound? (*scoring*)

Today the game is with our friends, the Sluggers. They wear blue shirts. (2)

First everyone stretches.

(3) (4)

Then we practice.

In soccer, you dribble the ball with your feet.

You pass to your teammates.

And you try to kick the ball through the goal, if you can.

Goalies need practice, too. They stop the other team from scoring, and they're the only players on the field who can touch the ball with their hands.

154

P/I PREVENTION/INTERVENTION

PHONICS/DECODING Read aloud the last paragraph on this page again. Have children raise their hand when they hear a word that starts with the sound /sk/ (*scoring*).

Write *scoring* on the chalkboard, and underline the blend *sc*. Explain that the *s* and *c*, together, make the /sk/ sound. Let children say the word *scoring* several times emphasizing the /sk/ sound. Then brainstorm other words that begin with the *sc* blend. (Examples: scab, scare, scalp, scale, scar, scarf) ***Graphophonic Cues***

Comprehension

4 What do the children need to do before they start playing? (stretch) Why do the children need to stretch? (to warm up their muscles) How do you know they stretch before playing? (The words and illustrations in the story show the children stretching before the game.) ***Make Inferences***

5 Who is the person in the photograph at the bottom of this page? (the goalie) What clues in the story tell you? What picture clues tell you? (The story says that goalies are the only players that can touch the ball with their hands. The person in the photograph is touching the ball with his hands, so he must be the goalie.) ***Draw Conclusions***

LANGUAGE SUPPORT

ESL The meaning of the word *dribble* may be difficult for some children to understand. First write the definition on the chalkboard: *to move a ball along by bouncing or kicking it.*

Then, clear a space in the classroom. Have children form a circle around the cleared space. Give a wadded-up piece of paper to a child. Call on a volunteer, who will say to the child with the ball of paper, "Dribble the ball to me." Then have the child with the paper place the ball on the floor and gently tap it across the clearing with his or her feet.

Comprehension

6 Who wants to be a sports announcer and tell us what happens on this page in the order in which it happens? ***Role-Play***

7 What does it mean for the coaches to give the players their positions for the kickoff? What on this page helps you to know? (The chart shows where the players stand during the kickoff.) Why would playing in a certain position be important in soccer? (to cover the field) ***Critical Thinking***

TEACHING TIP

MANAGEMENT When children are asked to sit on the floor in a large group, they tend to "bunch up," distracting others by touching and poking. To help eliminate this, it is a good idea to put lines of tape on the floor to accommodate all of the children and ask them to sit inside the tape lines.

6 It's game time!

7 The coaches give us our positions for the opening kickoff.

The Sluggers kick off and burst downfield. They charge to the goal. There's a goal kick.

156

Activity

Cross Curricular: Health

HEART RATES Point out that soccer is a running game, and that running is an aerobic exercise which makes the heart beat faster.

Activity Have children take their own pulse by placing their two middle fingers on the inside of their wrist and counting the total number of beats in the time it takes to count off fifteen seconds. Then have all children without health problems do two minutes of calisthenics. Have them take their pulse again and discuss any changes.

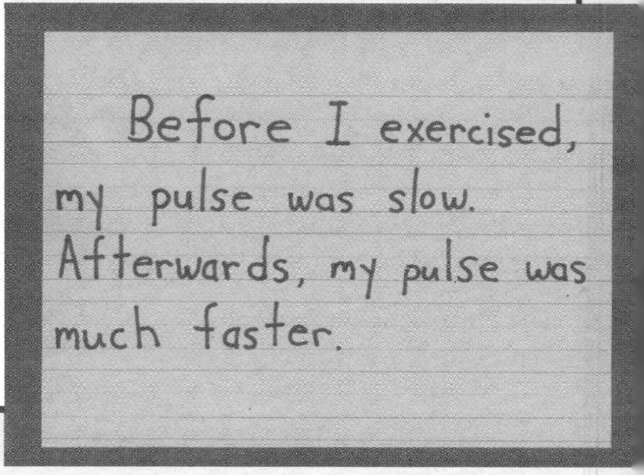
Before I exercised,
my pulse was slow.
Afterwards, my pulse was
much faster.

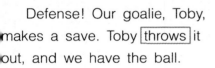

Defense! Our goalie, Toby, makes a save. Toby throws it out, and we have the ball.

Eric dribbles to midfield . . . with the Sluggers in pursuit. Eric passes . . .

but a Slugger intercepts! He gets his foot behind the ball . . . and boots it! **8**

The Sluggers have the ball.

157

Comprehension

8 **Phonics** **/ü/** Read the third paragraph on this page. Which two words are spelled with *oo*? (*foot* and *boots*) Run your finger under each word and blend the sounds together, as you read them aloud. Do they sound the same? Which word has the /ü/ sound? (*boots*) ***Blending/Graphophonic Cues***

LANGUAGE SUPPORT

ESL Monitor comprehension of sports terms throughout the reading. After completing each page, help children explain and demonstrate what each new word means. For example, a *goalie* can defend an imaginary goal, a student can mime *dribbling* a ball, and another student can mime *intercepting* the ball. Write these new words on the board and ask children to say the word in their first language, if possible.

Minilesson

REVIEW/MAINTAIN

Long *o*

Have children pronounce the words *coaches*, *opening*, and *goal* on page 156.

- Ask children what vowel sound these words have in common. (/ō/) Write the words on the board.
- Have a volunteer come to the board and underline the letters that spell the long *o* sound in each word. (*oa, o*)

Activity Brainstorm with children other words with long *o*, using these two spellings.

Phonics CD-ROM Have children use the interactive phonics activities on the CD-ROM for more reinforcement.

Comprehension

9 **SUMMARIZE** Can you tell me, in your own words, what has happened so far in the story? Remember to keep your summary short, and try to talk about just the main events. After we discuss this, we can start our charts. ***Main Events***

MODEL Maybe if I look back at the pages I've already read it will be easier to keep track of the things that have happened. I see that after stretching and practice, the game starts. The ball goes back and forth between the teams, is kicked out of bounds, and the Falcons make the first goal.

SUMMARIZE

The story tells how to play soccer while a real game is being played. In the game, the ball is kicked out of bounds and the Falcons score.

But then it is kicked out-of-bounds. Whenever a team puts the ball out, the other team throws it back in.

Moira throws it in for us.

"Don't use your hands, Johnny!"

9 Eric booms it.

10 Score! It's one to nothing,

11 Falcons.

Teams	1st half	2nd half	Final
Falcons	1		
Sluggers			

158

CULTURAL PERSPECTIVES

Share these facts about soccer:

- Millions of people in more than 140 countries play soccer.
- In most countries the game of soccer is called *football*.

RESEARCH AND INQUIRY Have children find out other soccer facts to share with the class.

▶ **Linguistic/Interpersonal**

interNET CONNECTION Children can learn more about soccer by visiting ***www.mhschool.com/reading.***

In 1998 France won the World Cup.

But not for long.

The Sluggers bounce right
ack and tie the game.

It's now one to one.

Teams	1st half	2nd half	Final
Falcons	1		
Sluggers	1		

159

Comprehension

10 Do you have enough information to make a prediction about who will win this game? Explain your answer. (I could guess who will win, but there is not enough information to predict. Anything could happen.) ***Make Predictions***

11 **Phonics** Find the word *booms* on page 158. How is the /ü/ sound spelled in this word? (*oo*) ***Graphophonic Cues***

P/I **PHONOLOGICAL AWARENESS** Raise your hand every time you hear the *ou* sound in this sentence: *But then it is kicked out of bounds.*

P/I PREVENTION/INTERVENTION

PHONOLOGICAL AWARENESS
Repeat the term *out-of-bounds*, this time emphasizing the /ou/ sound. Model blending the sounds together to read the words. Then encourage children to blend the sounds with you as they emphasize the /ou/ sound, too, in the words *out* and *bounds.*

Then repeat the process with each of the following sentences. Ask children to raise their hands when they hear the /ou/ sound.

- We shout cheers when the team wins. (shout)
- The Sluggers bounce right back and tie the game. (bounce)
- The baby weighed 7 pounds 11 ounces. (ounces) ***Graphophonic Cues***

Minilesson

REVIEW/MAINTAIN

Make Inferences

Remind children that the author doesn't always tell in words what the characters are feeling.

- Ask children if they think the Sluggers are excited about making the tying goal. What makes them think so? (The boy in the photograph on page 159 is holding up his hand, proudly pointing out the Sluggers's score.)
- Have them brainstorm a list of words to describe how the Sluggers feel.

Activity Have children write in the first person what the boy might be thinking in this illustration.

Comprehension

(12) What happens after the Sluggers tie the game? (The teams take a ten-minute break.) What happens during the break? (The players drink fluids.) Point to the photograph that shows this. Why might it be a good idea for the teams to rest and drink fluids? ***Draw Conclusions***

TEACHING TIP

BACKGROUND INFORMATION Tell children that when we play or exercise, our bodies use up energy. We get energy from the foods we eat and drink. Sugary foods give us energy for only a short period of time. Vitamins, proteins, and complex carbohydrates give us more lasting energy.

The score is still tied at one to one when the coaches call halftime.

Whew! It feels good to take a break.

After a ten-minute rest . . .

(12) we're back to the game!

160

Activity

Cross Curricular: Social Studies

MAP SKILLS Tell children that one of the most famous soccer players in the world is the Brazilian, Pelé. Display a map of South America.

RESEARCH AND INQUIRY Have partners:

- locate Brazil.
- name the countries and the ocean that border Brazil.

▶ **Interpersonal/Spatial**

We charge down to the
lugger's goal.

Olivier's kick is wide . . . (13)

and the Sluggers take
he ball.

161

Comprehension

13 What is the reason the Sluggers are able to take the ball? (Because Olivier's kick is wide.) ***Cause and Effect***

P/I **WORD MEANING** Read the first sentence on this page. Do you know what the word *charge* means in this sentence? What other word could you use instead? (*run*)

P/I PREVENTION/INTERVENTION

ORD MEANING Ask children what
word with the same or almost the
ame meaning as another word is
alled. (synonym) Point out that in the
irst sentence on page 161, *charge* can
e considered a synonym for *run*.

Have children come up with synonyms for the following words:

- gift (present)
- large (big)
- hurry (rush)

Semantic Cues

Minilesson

REVIEW/MAINTAIN

Context Clues

Review that context clues can help provide the meaning of an unfamiliar word or term. Have children reread page 160. Remind them that context clues are not always in the same sentence as the unfamiliar word. Ask them what context clues help them find the meaning of the word *halftime*. (take a break, ten-minute rest, back to the game)

Activity Have children write a context sentence using the word *halftime*.

Comprehension

14 What happened when the two players collided? (The ball became anybody's ball.) What do you predict will happen next? *Cause and Effect*

SELF-MONITORING STRATEGY

ASK FOR HELP Sometimes it is a good idea to ask another classmate or a teacher for help if you are confused about what you are reading. If you clarify your questions early on, you understand what you are reading better and enjoy it more.

MODEL I'm not sure how to summarize a story with so many things happening in it. Can someone help me find the main ideas of the story?

Here comes our defense at midfield.

The two players collide.

14 It's anybody's ball.

The Sluggers and Falcons **15** battle for the ball.

The ball goes up . . .

162

Activity

Cross Curricular: Science/Art

BALL FLIP BOOK Children can make flip books that animate a soccer ball. Tell children that they will be making an optical illusion, in this case flip books that animate a soccer ball.

- Distribute ten 2″ x 3″ pieces of paper to each child. Have children draw a soccer ball in the center of the first page.
- For each consecutive page, children should draw a soccer ball slightly to the right of the one on the previous page.
- Help children staple one side of the pages together and show how to flip the pages to make the soccer ball move.

▶ **Kinesthetic/Spatial**

163

Comprehension

15 What problem are the Falcons faced with on page 161? (The Sluggers have the ball.) How do they try to solve that problem on page 162? (They send in their defense to try and get the ball.) Are they successful? (We don't know yet.) ***Problem and Solution***

LANGUAGE SUPPORT

ESL Help those children needing additional ıstruction to understand the word ıidfield. Write *mid* and *field* on the halkboard. Ask children what word ıid reminds them of. Point out that it ; a shortened version of the word *middle*. Have children point to the middles of various items in the classroom, such as a notebook, a desk, the chalkboard. Then ask what they think *midfield* means. Explain that *midfield* means *the middle of the field*.

Comprehension

16 What causes the Falcons to get a free kick? (One of the Sluggers touched the ball with his hand.) What word on this page is a clue that this is the cause? (*since*) ***Cause and Effect***

17 Point to the photograph that shows you what a hand ball is. What clues does the text give you that a hand ball is against the rules? (The other team gets a free kick.) ***Draw Conclusions***

Fluency

READ WITH A PARTNER

PARTNERS Have partners take turns reading pages 162 and 164 to each other. Before partners begin reading to each other, demonstrate reading the sentences with ellipses for the entire class. Encourage children to end the sentences with ellipses on an up note, instead of the down note with which they would normally end a sentence, in order to get across the feeling of suspense.

Joely kicks it . . .

16 Oh, no! "Hand ball!" Since a Slugger touched the ball, we get a free kick.

17

164

Jonathan booms it and we ave control again.

No one scored, and the ock is running out. Only five inutes are left in the game. (18)

Comprehension

(18) **SUMMARIZE** Can you summarize in your own words what has happened in the story since we made our last summary? Remember not to get too stuck on details, and to keep events in order.

MODEL I know that right now the score is tied and there are only five minutes left in the game. During the second half of the game there was a battle over who would get the ball, and then one of the Sluggers touched the ball with his hand which got a free kick for the Falcons.

(P/I) **WORD STRUCTURE** Look at pages 164 and 165. Let's find the verbs on these pages. (*kicks, touched, booms, scored, running*) How do the different endings change the tense of each verb?

Minilesson

REVIEW/MAINTAIN

Main Idea

Call on volunteers to tell the main idea of the story—what it is mainly about. Remind children that they should focus on the main events of the story, not every detail.

Activity Have children write one sentence which explains the main idea of the story. For example: Soccer is tiring, but it is lots of fun and very rewarding to play.

P/I PREVENTION/INTERVENTION

/ORD STRUCTURE Review with hildren the following inflectional ndings: Add *-s* to a verb when talking bout someone doing something in ne present; *-ed* creates the past tense f a verb; *-ing* is the present tense of a erb. Write *kicks, touched, booms, cored,* and *running* on the chalkboard. lave volunteers underline the infleconal ending in each word and circle ne base word.

Have children look through the selection to locate other words with inflectional endings. Ask them to think about how the ending changes the time the action is taking place. ***Semantic Cues***

Comprehension

(19) How many minutes are left in the game on page 166? (five) How can you tell? (The clock shows the time left.)
Critical Thinking

TEACHING TIP

VERIFYING FACTUAL INFORMATION
Have children research soccer terms and rules in books, encyclopedias, and other resources. Ask children to determine if the information in the text is true based on their research. Encourage children to use soccer terms as they write their own story to go with the illustrations on pages 166–167.

Activity

Cross Curricular: Math

TIME Have children point out how long five minutes is on a wall clock or watch. Have them experiment to see how long five minutes really is.

Invite children to write without stopping the phrase "Time marches on" while a timekeeper watches the clock, calling "one minute. . . two minutes", up to five minutes. Then have children count how many words they wrote during the five minutes, and write the number on a strip of paper. Make a number wall of children's word counts.

▶ **Logical/Linguistic**

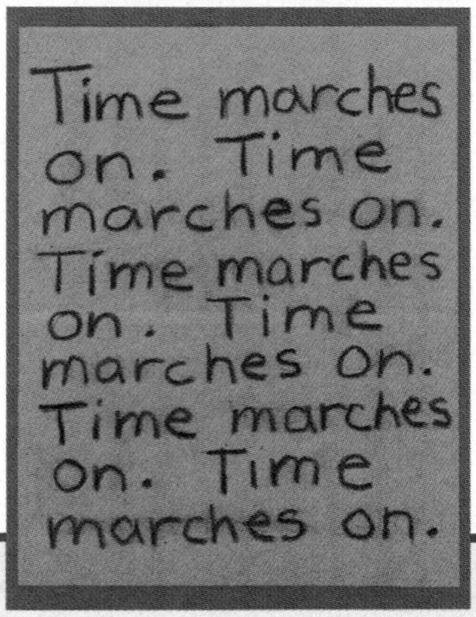

Time marches on. Time marches on. Time marches on. Time marches on. Time marches on.

Comprehension

20 Time is starting to run out. Based on what you've read about how hard each team is trying to win, and how easily the ball can get out of a player's control, what might the players be thinking? What might they be feeling? (They are probably thinking they should try even harder, but they could be worried about making mistakes that would cause the other team to score. They must be very excited.) ***Make Inferences***

21 Which team do all the children on this page belong to? (the Sluggers) How do you know? (The Sluggers wear blue shirts.) ***Details***

Comprehension

22 How many minutes are left in the game on pages 168 and 169? (three on 168; two on 169) Do you think the game is moving quickly? What makes you think so? ***Use Photographs***

23 Look at pages 166–169— the pages with the time clock in the corner. How are these pages different from most of the other pages you have looked at and read so far? (There is just one photograph on each page, not a collage, and there is little, or no, writing on these pages.) ***Compare and Contrast***

24 What do the photographs on these pages make you think about soccer? Does it look exciting? Boring? Active? Restful? What makes you think this? ***Form Generalizations***

Visual Literacy

VIEWING AND REPRESENTING

Discuss the photo on page 163. Ask children what they look at first in the photo. Suggest that they might be drawn to look at the ball before they look at anything else. Tell them that the ball is the focal point of the photograph.

Have children look back at the photos on the pages they have already read. Is the ball often a focal point in the photos? (yes) Ask them why they think the photographer used the ball as a focal point in so many of the photos. (That's what the players are focused on; that's where the action of the story is.)

2:00
Out-of-bounds on a header.
St. Savi
Socc
25
169

Comprehension

WORD MEANING Look at the word *header* on this page. What is the base word? (*head*) How does this help you know what a *header* is?

25 What has the boy in this photograph just done? (hit the soccer ball with his head) What happened to the ball? (It went out of bounds.) ***Cause and Effect***

PREVENTION/INTERVENTION

VORD MEANING Point out the vord *header* on this page. Ask a volun-eer to underline the base word. (*head*) Remind children that the inflectional nding *-er* means *a person or thing that oes something*. Based on this, ask chil-ren to define *header*. (the use of one's ead to hit the ball)

Encourage children to also use context clues in the picture to identify the word. Tell children to notice that the ball has bounced off of the boy's head. Remind children that soccer players can touch the ball with every part of their body except their hands. ***Semantic Cues***

Comprehension

(26) Who would like to be the sportscaster, and tell us about the events that happened on pages 168, 169, and 170? Remember to name the team of the players pictured, and to keep things in time order. *Role-Play*

TEACHING TIP

MANAGEMENT As students read aloud, make observations about fluency and decoding skills to determine where help may be needed. Classify problems by type, such as

- reading rate.
- fluency, accuracy, and expression.
- decoding, using letter-sound correspondences.
- recognizing common vowel spelling patterns.

Ted throws it in.

The Sluggers boot the ball
(26) into the open field.

170

1:00
John's set . . . boom! 27
Score! It's two to one, Sluggers! 28
29
171

Comprehension

27 Who scored a goal on this page? (John) How do you think he feels? Let's all make a face to show how we think John feels after scoring a goal. ***Pantomime***

28 Can you make a prediction about which team is most likely to win this game? What information are you basing your prediction on? ***Make Predictions***

29 **Phonics** ***/ü/ oo*** Can you find the words with the /ü/ sound on pages 170–71? (*boot and booms*) How is /ü/ spelled in these words? (*oo*) ***Graphophonic Cues/ Blending***

Minilesson

REVIEW/MAINTAIN

Homophones

Review the meaning of homophones, words that look and sound alike but have different meanings.

- Read aloud, *The Sluggers boot the ball into the open field.* Have children think about how the word *boot* is used in the sentence. Ask, *Is it a noun or a verb?*
- Have children replace the word *boot* with another word that means the same thing.

Activity Have children work with a partner to create sentences that contain the word *boot*. Encourage children to use *boot* as a noun and *boot* as a verb.

Comprehension

30 Can you summarize the story from the last summary to when the clock runs out? After we discuss your summaries, we will add to our charts.

MODEL The last summary ended with the Falcons getting a free kick after a hand ball by the Sluggers. With five minutes left in the game, the ball goes from team to team. With two minutes left, the Falcons put the ball out of bounds, which gives the Sluggers control of the ball. They score, and the Falcons lose.

SUMMARIZE

The story tells how to play soccer while a real game is being played. In the game, the ball is kicked out of bounds and the Falcons score.

The Sluggers tie the score. In the second half of the game there is an exciting battle for the ball.

In the last five minutes of the game, the ball is fought for, hit out of bounds, and taken control of by the Sluggers.

Writer's Craft

SUSPENSE

Explain: Suspense is a build-up of excitement about a story's outcome that is felt by the reader. An author can create suspense by maintaining a high degree of tension throughout the story and by keeping the end a surprise.

Direct children's attention to anthology pages 172–173. Ask, *At what point in the story do we find out who wins the game? Does the story end like you thought it would? How would the story change if we knew who won?*

WRITING Draw the main events in *Our Soccer League*. Show a clock with each picture that tells how much time is left before the game ends.

We try our best to tie the score . . .

30 but the clock runs out.

172

Teams	1st half	2nd half	Final
Falcons	1	0	1
Sluggers	1	1	2

Comprehension

31 What is the final score of the game? (Sluggers, two; Falcons, one.) If you had forgotten that you knew the score from reading the story, how else could you find out? (from the scoreboard printed on page 173) *Critical Thinking*

32 How is the game in the story like a real soccer game? Give examples from the story to support your answer. *Compare and Contrast*

LANGUAGE SUPPORT

ESL Read the second part of the sentence on page 72. Ask volunteers what the phrase *lock runs out* means. Point out that he clock doesn't literally rush off the ield! Tell children this is an expression, r a phrase whose meaning cannot be nderstood from the ordinary meanngs of the words in it. *The clock runs out* means that there is no more time. Other expressions are: *You're pulling my leg*, meaning *You're trying to trick me*, and *That was a close call,* meaning *Something bad almost happened.*

Comprehension

33 **SUMMARIZE** Let's make our final summary of the story, based on the summaries we have made for the beginning, the middle, and the end. Is there anything we should add to our charts?

The story tells how to play soccer while a real game is being played. In the game, the ball is kicked out of bounds and the Falcons score.
The Sluggers tie the score. In the second half of the game there is an exciting battle for the ball, and the Falcons get a free kick after the Sluggers make a hand ball.
In the last five minutes of the game, the ball is fought for, hit out of bounds, and taken control of by the Sluggers who score the winning goal.

RETELL THE STORY Ask children to work in groups of three to retell the story. Have them divide the story into the three parts of their Summary charts. After children decide what they will say, have each child in the group tell one part. *Summarize*

STUDENT SELF-ASSESSMENT

Have children ask themselves the following questions to assess how they are reading:

- How did summarizing the story at certain points help me to understand the story as a whole?
- How did using what I know about letter sounds and word meanings help me read and understand unfamiliar words?

TRANSFERRING THE STRATEGIES

- How can I use these strategies to help me read other stories?

The Sluggers celebrate . . .

and we give ourselves a cheer.

When you play a great game . . .

everybody wins!

33

174

REREADING FOR *Fluency*

PARTNERS Have partners read their favorite sections of the story to each other.

READING RATE When you evaluate reading rate, have children read aloud from the story for one minute. Place a stick-on note after the last word read. Count words read. To evaluate children's performance, see Running Record in the **Fluency Assessment** book.

Intervention For leveled fluency passages, lessons, and norms charts, see **Skills Intervention Guide**, Part 5, Fluency.

READ TOGETHER

MEET CHUCK SOLOMON

"I wanted to write *Our Soccer League* because soccer is such a good sport for children," says Chuck Solomon. "Soccer doesn't require much equipment, it's not too rough, and running is good exercise. Besides, both girls and boys can play it together."

Mr. Solomon wrote this book to show children how to play soccer. He said, "I also wanted to show the excitement and feelings you get when you play the game.

"I photographed this book during an actual game, just as it happens in the book. As I was taking pictures, an editor was writing what was happening. After I developed the photographs, I wrote the story. It was important for me to tell the story just the way it happened."

175

LITERARY RESPONSE

QUICK-WRITE Have children write what they like, about soccer based on what they learned in the story.

JOURNAL

ORAL RESPONSE Have children think about the words on page 174, as they answer the following questions:

- How would you feel if your team lost? Won?
- If you were the coach of a soccer team, what would you say to your team before the game?
- If you were the coach, what would you say if your team won? What would you say if your team lost?

Comprehension

Return to Predictions and Purposes

Reread children's predictions about the story. Discuss the predictions, noting which needed to be revised.

PREDICTIONS	WHAT HAPPENED
The story will be about a soccer game.	The Falcons and the Sluggers play an exciting soccer game.
The story will tell how to play soccer.	Many of the rules of soccer are explained in the story.

INFORMAL ASSESSMENT

HOW TO ASSESS

Phonics **/ü/** Have children look back at the entire story, finding words with the /ü/ sounds spelled *oo* and *ue*. Have them write each word and underline the letters that spell the /ü/ sound.

SUMMARIZE Have children summarize another story which they have read recently.

FOLLOW UP

Phonics **/ü/** For children having difficulty locating /ü/ words in the story, have them work with a partner to find and read aloud the words.

SUMMARIZE For children who are having difficulty ask: *What are the main events in the story?*

Story Questions

Have children discuss or write answers to the questions on page 176.

1. The Sluggers. *Literal/Details*
2. They played a good game. *Inferential/Make Inferences*
3. They show the players in action and make it easier to follow the game. *Inferential/Use Photographs*
4. Soccer is a game that everyone enjoys playing, whether they win or lose. *Critical/Summarize*
5. Possible answer: Jamaica would tell Luka not to touch the ball with her hands unless she/he is playing goalie. *Critical/Reading Across Texts*

Write a Game Guide For a full writing process lesson see **Expository Writing** page 179M.

Story Questions & Activities

READ TOGETHER

1. Which team wins the soccer game?
2. Why do you think the Falcons give themselves a cheer at the end of the game?
3. How are the photographs important to the story?
4. What is the main idea of this selection?
5. Imagine that Jamaica is teaching Luka to play soccer. What are some of the things she would tell her about how to play the game?

Write a Game Guide

Choose a favorite sport, game, or activity. Write a guide that explains how to play, do, or make what you chose. What are the rules of the game or the steps for the activity? What does each player do?

Meeting Individual Needs

EASY

Name____________ Date______ **Reteach 179**

Story Comprehension

In "Our Soccer League," you learned many things about the game of soccer. Read each statement. Then circle **T** if the sentence is true, or **F** if it is false.

1.	"Our Soccer League" tells about a game.	(T)	F
2.	In soccer, you dribble with your feet.	(T)	F
3.	Goalies can touch the ball.	(T)	F
4.	Everyone can touch the ball.	T	(F)
5.	Soccer is a team sport.	(T)	F
6.	Only boys play soccer.	T	(F)
7.	When you run out of bounds, it is called a "header."	T	(F)
8.	The game is over when time runs out.	(T)	F
9.	The Sluggers are a baseball team.	T	(F)
10.	The Falcons lose the game.	(T)	F

10 Book 2.2/Unit 2 **Our Soccer League**

At Home: Have students suggest a new title for the story and draw a picture of one of the scenes. 179

Reteach, 179

ON-LEVEL

Name____________ Date______ **Practice 179**

Story Comprehension

Think about the story "Our Soccer League." Draw pictures to show six things you learned about soccer. Write a label for each picture. **Answers will vary.**

1. Possibly: the goalie
2. Possibly: foot dribble
3. Possibly: the goal
4. Possibly: header
5. Possibly: pass
6. Possibly: hand ball

6 Book 2.2/Unit 2 **Our Soccer League**

At Home: Have children pretend to be sports announcers, announcing the players and moves in a soccer game. 179

Practice, 179

CHALLENGE

Name____________ Date______ **Extend 179**

Story Comprehension

Sample answers are shown.

Write a sentence to answer the questions.

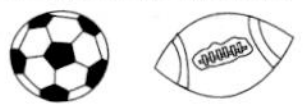

1. What if a soccer ball were the size of a marble? Would it be easy or hard to play soccer with such a small ball?
   It would be hard to play soccer with such a small ball.
2. What if a soccer ball were shaped like a football? Would it be easy or hard to play soccer with a differently shaped ball?
   It would be hard to play soccer with a football.
3. What if there were only two people on each team? Could soccer still be played? How?
   You could play soccer with two people if the two people took turns trying to make a goal and being the goalie.
4. What would happen if it started to rain or snow during the game? Write what you think would happen.
   If it rained or snowed during the game, the field would be slippery.
5. Would you like to be a goalie? Why or why not?
   I would like to be goalie because I like to stop the ball from going in the net.
6. What if there were no coaches? Write what you think would happen during a game.
   If there were no coaches, the players might lose the game.

Book 2.2/Unit 2 **Our Soccer League**

At Home: Have children make a poster advertising a soccer game. Ask them to make up names for teams, and to include the place, time, date, and fun facts about the players. 179

Extend, 179

Make a Tally Chart About Favorite Sports

Which sport is the favorite of your class? Write down a guess. Then have a class vote to check your guess. Make a tally chart that shows how many votes each sport gets.

Describe a Sport

Find photographs of people playing a sport you like. What do the pictures tell you? Describe the action in the photographs. How is the sport you chose different from soccer? How is it like soccer?

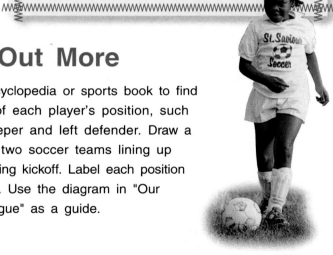

Find Out More

Use an encyclopedia or sports book to find the name of each player's position, such as goal keeper and left defender. Draw a diagram of two soccer teams lining up for an opening kickoff. Label each position on the field. Use the diagram in "Our Soccer League" as a guide.

177

Story Activities

Make a Tally Chart about Favorite Sports

Materials: paper, colored markers

GROUP Have the class brainstorm a list of sports. Ask them to write down which sport they think is the favorite in their class. Then take a class vote to find out which sport is the favorite. Have the class make a tally chart showing the results of the vote.

Describe a Sport

Materials: magazines, scissors, poster board, glue

ONE Have children look through magazines for photographs of sports. They should cut out photographs and paste them to a piece of poster board. Have them write about their sport, answering the questions on this page.

Find Out More

RESEARCH AND INQUIRY Provide encyclopedias and sports books for partner research. Invite children to draw a diagram similar to the one in *Our Soccer League*.

PARTNERS

interNET CONNECTION Have children go to ***www.mhschool.com/reading*** for more information on sports.

DAILY Phonics ROUTINES

DAY 3 **Blending** Write the spelling of each sound in *tooth* as you say it. Have children repeat after you. Ask children to blend the sounds to read the word. Repeat with *true, tool,* and *drew.*

Phonics CD-ROM

FORMAL ASSESSMENT

After page 177, see Selection Assessment.

Study Skills

VARIOUS TEXTS

TESTED OBJECTIVES Children will learn about the different parts of a newsletter.

PREPARE Read the newsletter with children. Display **Teaching Chart 150.**

TEACH Tell children that a newsletter is a newspaper that deals with one subject, published for people involved in that subject. Ask a volunteer to identify the subject of this newsletter.

PRACTICE Have children answer questions 1–5. Review the answers with them. **1.** Soccer Today! **2.** Michael Tyler **3.** Fairview County Soccer Club Goes to Moscow! **4.** It was colder. **5.** parades, banners, and proud parents

ASSESS/CLOSE Have children think of a subject for a newsletter. Ask them to name their newsletters, and write a headline.

STUDY SKILLS

READ TOGETHER

Read a Newsletter

SOCCER TODAY!
The Soccer Newsletter of Fairview County — **October 15**

Fairview County Soccer Club Goes to Moscow!
by Michael Tyler

In August, kids from the Fairview County Soccer Club went to Russia! The Fairview players were part of a special event. They played in the first game of a new soccer league for kids.

In some ways, the game they played was like opening games at home. There were parades, banners, and proud parents. But there was one big difference. It is a lot colder in Moscow than it is in Fairview County. That's because Moscow is farther north than Fairview County.

The weather was the only thing that was cold. The people in Moscow were warm and friendly. They look forward to meeting other kids from the U.S.

Use the newsletter to answer the questions.

1. What is the name of this newsletter?
2. Who wrote the article about the soccer club's trip?
3. What is the headline of this article?
4. How was Moscow different from Fairview County?
5. In what ways did Moscow seem like home?

Meeting Individual Needs

EASY

Name________ Date______ Reteach 180

Read a Newsletter

A **newsletter** is like a small newspaper. It is usually written about one topic, such as a club, a sport, or a neighborhood.

GIRLS BASKETBALL DIGEST
The B-Ball Newsletter of Kennedy Grade School — January 2000

Division Winners Rule
by Kenesha Winterly
The Kennedy hoopsters marched right through the Winter Tournament. Six straight victories! That makes us the winners of our division!
Joleen Larsen led the way with sixteen points in the last three games. Yours truly scored the most points ever. Two! Luckily, the rest of the team scored a lot more points.

Dates To Keep In Mind:
Feb. 4: Practice for Playoffs 4 P.M.
Feb. 6: First playoff game 1 P.M.
March 16: Awards party 7 P.M.

Don't Forget
Coach Remington says all uniforms must be returned to her office after the last game. They must be cleaned and folded. Go Kennedy Girls!

Use the information in the newsletter to answer these questions.

1. When is the first play-off game? Feb. 6, 1 p.m.
2. How many points did Joleen Larsen score in the last three games? 16
3. What is the date of this newsletter? January 2000
4. What did Coach Remington say? all uniforms must be returned to her office after the last game

180 **At Home:** Invite children to produce a newsletter about the neighborhood. Book 2.2/Unit 2 **Our Soccer League** 4

Reteach, 180

ON-LEVEL

Name________ Date______ Practice 180

Read a Newsletter

Different **newsletters** are aimed at different readers.

Newsletter #1

CHESS CLUB NEWS
by Peter Kingsley
The final match of the chess tournament was played Tuesday after school. Tanya Quigly went head to head with Victor Sing. The winner was the first to gain three points. A win was worth one point. A draw was worth a half point. Victor won the first match. Tanya pulled out a tie in the second. And then Tanya got a checkmate in sixteen moves in the third. But Victor won two straight games. They were both close but Victor is our new champion!

Newsletter #2

GABRIEL STREET BLOCK ASSOCIATION NEWSLETTER
Block clean-up Saturday! All day!
Be there or be square! Bring a friend!
Take pride in our block. The city is sending a special garbage truck just for us. The vacant lot will be cleared. Trees will be planted. Bus benches will be painted. Gabby's Deli is bringing sandwiches. If you have anything to bring to the block yard sale, call Tom 555-2345. A clean block is a happy block!!

Use the information in the two newsletters above to answer the questions that follow.

1. Which newsletter was written for the people who lived in a certain area? #2
2. Which newsletter told who wrote it? #1
3. Who won the final match of the chess club? Victor Sing
4. When is the big block clean up? Saturday all day
5. What is the main idea of each newsletter?
   Newsletter #1: to tell who won the big chess match
   Newsletter #2: to tell about the block clean-up

180 **At Home:** Have children write newsletters about their lives to send to family and friends. Book 2.2/Unit 2 **Our Soccer League** 5

Practice, 180

CHALLENGE

Name________ Date______ Extend 180

Read a Newsletter

Read the newsletter. Write a word or words to complete the article. Illustrate the newsletter. Sample answers given.

Banner: Barnhart Elementary School Newsletter

Date: November, 2000

Headine: Barnhart Tigers Win Again!

By-line: by June Moon

Article: Last Saturday, the Barnhart Tigers soccer team beat the Hollyville Heroes. The score was 3 to 2. It was a very exciting game! In the beginning, the goalie of the Tigers blocked two kicks. People were cheering for the Tigers. Then the Heroes scored two goals in a row. It looked bad for the Tigers, until they scored three goals and won the game.

180 **At Home:** Invite children to create a newsletter about themselves. Ask them to illustrate their pages, and to interview friends and family members for quotes about themselves to include in the newsletter. Book 2.2/Unit 2 **Our Soccer League**

Extend, 180

TEST POWER

Ask yourself the questions again, but use your own words.

DIRECTIONS:

Read the story. Then read each question about the story.

SAMPLE

A Surprise Visitor

Elsa finished her homework. Her father was washing the dishes. Her mother had gone to dinner with a friend. She had left more than an hour ago and would be home soon.

"Can I help with the dishes?" Elsa asked her father. Just then, the front doorbell rang. Elsa's father walked to the front door. "Who is it?" he asked politely.

"It's a surprise," said a voice from outside. Elsa's father looked through the peephole. There was Elsa's mother and Elsa's grandma.

"Surprise!" yelled her grandma as Elsa ran to give her a hug.

1 Which is the best summary for this story?

- ○ Elsa has a surprise birthday party.
- ○ Elsa and her dad have dinner together.
- ● Elsa has a surprise visitor.
- ○ Elsa's grandma moves away.

2 What happens after Elsa's father opens the door?

- ○ Elsa sees her neighbor.
- ● Elsa sees her grandma.
- ○ Elsa runs to hide.
- ○ Elsa's father sees his brother.

Test Power

THE PRINCETON REVIEW

Read the Page

Explain to children that you will be reading this story as a group. You will read the story, and they will follow along in their books.

Request that children put pens, pencils, and markers away, since they will not be writing in their books.

Discuss the Questions

QUESTION 1: Remind children that the title often has clues to the main idea of the story. Also point out to them that the story ends with a surprise.

QUESTION 2: Children should reread the story beginning with the opening of the door. Ask: *What happens next in the story?*

Leveled Books

EASY

Coyotes Rule!

- ☑ Variant Vowels /ü/
- ☑ Summarize
- ☑ Instructional Vocabulary: ***coaches, field, score, stretches, throws, touch***

Intervention **Skills**

Intervention Guide, for direct instruction and extra practice of vocabulary and comprehension

Guided Reading

PREVIEW AND PREDICT As children look at the title and the illustrations, ask them to predict what the story will be about.

SET PURPOSES Have children write sentences describing why they want to read *Coyotes Rule!*

READ THE BOOK Use questions like the following as children read or after they have read the story independently.

Page 2: Find a word with the /ü/ sound. *(school)* How is the /ü/ sound spelled in this word? *(oo)* ***Phonics and Decoding***

Page 6: What did Justin tell his sister when she asked him about soccer? (He said he didn't want to play.) What happened just before Justin met his sister on the way home from school? (He wasn't picked for the team.) ***Sequence of Events***

Page 7: Find the word *coach.* What does a coach do? Try to use the word *coaches* in a sentence. ***Instructional Vocabulary***

Page 16: What would you say the story *Coyotes Rule!* was about? ***Summarize***

Page 16: How were the Coyotes doing during the second half of the game? (They were winning.) What was happening in the game at the end of the first half? (Neither team scored, but the Coyotes were less tired than the Bears.) ***Sequence of Events***

RETURN TO PREDICTIONS AND PURPOSES Discuss children's predictions and purposes for reading. Did they find out what they wanted to know?

LITERARY RESPONSE Discuss these questions:

- Is it more important to win the game or to have fun playing it?
- How do you think it feels not to be picked for a team?
- Also see the story questions and activity in *Coyotes Rule!*

See the **Phonics CD-ROM** for practice with the /ü/ sound.

Answers to Story Questions

1. He loves soccer, but he is not a good player.
2. Yes, she listens to Justin, then suggests what he would be good at.
3. Carlos knows Justin has made mistakes in the past; the other kids think Justin is a poor player.
4. A boy who gets cut from the team finds a way to help his team win.
5. Answers will vary.

The Story Questions and Activity below appear in the Easy Book.

Story Questions and Writing Activity

1. What is Justin's problem at the beginning of the story?
2. Do you think Rachel gives Justin good advice?
3. Justin is Carlos's friend. Why does Carlos cut Justin from the team?
4. What is this story mostly about?
5. If Justin were on one of the teams in *Our Soccer League*, how would the game have been different? Explain.

Your Own Team

Think of a sport or a game you like and come up with a plan for winning it. Add a diagram or drawing of the team winning.

from *Coyotes Rule!*

Leveled Books

INDEPENDENT

Playing Your Best

- Variant Vowels /ü/
- Summarize
- Instructional Vocabulary: *coaches, field, score, stretches, throws, touch*

Guided Reading

PREVIEW AND PREDICT Take a **picture walk** through page 5 of the story. Have children predict what the story will be about from the illustrations.

SET PURPOSES Have children write why they want to read *Playing Your Best*. For example: I want to learn how to play a good game of baseball.

READ THE BOOK Have children read the story independently. When they finish, return to the text to apply strategies.

Page 4: Find a word with the /ü/ sound. *(knew)*. What letters make the /ü/ sound in this word? *(ew)* ***Phonics and Decoding***

Page 4: What happened when the boy in the story was seven years old? (joined the Blue Jays) What was happening before the boy joined this team? (couldn't play baseball well no matter how hard he tried) ***Sequence of Events***

Page 8: Find the word *stretches*. What does a stretch look like? How do you think stretching helps in the game of baseball? ***Instructional Vocabulary***

Page 16: If someone asked you what the story *Playing Your Best* was about, what would you tell them? (It's about a boy who is not a good ball player, but he keeps practicing and doesn't give up.) ***Summarizing***

Page 16: What happened during the last game the boy played in the story? (He was out, tagged at second base) ***Plot***

RETURN TO PREDICTIONS AND PURPOSES Discuss children's predictions and purposes for reading. Did they find out what they wanted to know?

LITERARY RESPONSE Discuss these questions:

- Where do you think the word *teamwork* comes from?
- What do you think the boy learned during the last game?

Also see the story questions and activity in *Playing Your Best*.

See the Phonics **CD-ROM** for practice with the /ü/ sound.

Answers to Story Questions

1. He couldn't play baseball very well.
2. He is sure that he will mess up, his team will lose, and it will be his fault.
3. The next batter might have hit a home run, driving Billy home, and giving the team the two runs they needed to win the game.
4. A kid handles not being a very good ball player.
5. Answers will vary.

The Story Questions and Activity below appear in the Independent Book.

Story Questions and Writing Activity

1. Why was Billy always the last one to be picked for a ball game?
2. The score was 5 to 4. The Hawks were winning. It was Billy's turn at bat. Why does he think this is "terrible luck"?
3. What might have happened if Billy had stayed on first base instead of trying to go to second base?
4. What is this story mostly about?
5. How is being on a baseball team similar to and different from being on a soccer team like the one in *Our Soccer League*?

Playing Your Best

Working with two or three classmates, choose a scene or scenes from this story to dramatize. Make sure you have enough time to rehearse your scene.

from *Playing Your Best*

Leveled Books

CHALLENGE

Teammates for Life

- ☑ **Variant Vowels /ü/**
- ☑ **Summarize**
- ☑ **Instructional Vocabulary:** ***coaches, field, score, stretches, throws, touch***

Guided Reading

PREVIEW AND PREDICT Discuss the illustrations and title of the story. Have children predict what the story will be about.

SET PURPOSES Have children write two or three questions they hope to answer by reading *Teammates for Life*. For example, children may want to learn about the rules of stickball.

READ THE BOOK Use questions like the following after children have read the story independently.

Page 3: Find a word that has the /ü/ sound. *(broomstick)* What letters stand for /ü/? *(oo)* ***Phonics and Decoding***

Page 7: Find the word *touched*. Touch your nose. Now touch your toes. ***Instructional Vocabulary***

Page 10: What do the Semanons do together these days? (play golf, watch sports events, go to concerts and movies) What did they do together when they were boys? (played stickball) ***Compare and Contrast***

Page 16: If one of the Semanons calls another member of the group to say that he has hurt himself and is in the hospital, what do you think the other Semanons will do? (Visit him in the hospital because they help each other.) Why do you think so? ***Make Predictions***

Page 16: How would you describe what this story is about to someone who might be interested in reading it? ***Summarize***

RETURN TO PREDICTIONS AND PURPOSES Discuss children's predictions and their purposes for reading. Did they find out what they wanted to know?

LITERARY RESPONSE Discuss these questions:

- What was your favorite part of the story?
- Can you describe the feelings of teammates toward each other?

Also see the story questions and activity in *Teammates for Life*.

See the Phonics **CD-ROM** for practice with the /ü/ sound.

Answers to Story Questions

1. The Bronx
2. Yes; they go to sporting events together and they still play stickball.
3. More pleasant, less expensive, his friends really care.
4. A group of men are still close friends and still work like a team after more than 40 years because of what they learned as children.
5. Answers will vary.

The Story Questions and Activity below appear in the Challenge Book.

Story Questions and Writing Activity

1. Where did Yiggy and the other members of the "Semanons" grow up?
2. Now that the "Semanons" are grown-ups, do they still like sports? How do you know?
3. How does it help a "Semanon" to have his friends help him move to a new home instead of using a moving company?
4. What is the main idea of this book?
5. How are the players in *Our Soccer League* like the members of "Semanon?"

Home Sweet Home

The kind of co-op apartment building Yiggy lived in when he was a boy asked for teamwork from everybody. Do you think you would like to live in that kind of place? Why or why not?

from *Teammates for Life*

Activities

Bringing Groups Together

Anthology and Leveled Books

Connecting Texts

SPORTS CHART
Write the story titles at the four corners of the chart. Write sports terms in the middle of the chart. Have children name the sport, equipment, uniform, game rules, and so on, that pertain to the particular sport central to each story. List these words under the appropriate story titles. Draw a line from the words *sports terms* to the words children list below the titles.

Use the chart to talk about different kinds of sports and things associated with those sports.

SPORTS TERMS

Our Soccer League	*Coyotes Rule!*
soccer	soccer
soccer ball	coach
kick	score
ball	goal
Playing Your Best	***Teammates for Life***
baseball	stickball
bat	broomstick
strike	street
bases	schoolyard

Viewing/Representing

GROUP PRESENTATIONS Divide the class into four groups, one for each of the four books read in the lesson. Have each group play a mock game of the game described in their story.

AUDIENCE RESPONSE Ask children to watch the demonstrations and ask questions about the different games.

Research and Inquiry

MORE ABOUT SPORTS Have children ask themselves, What else would I like to know about soccer, stickball, baseball, and other sports? Then invite them to do the following:

- Look at classroom picture books and school library books to learn more about sports.
- Invite an athlete or coach to talk to the class about his/her particular sport.
- Arrange a field trip to a local sporting event.

*inter*NET CONNECTION Have children log on to ***www.mhschool.com/reading*** for links to web pages.

TESTED **OBJECTIVES**

Children will:

- identify /ü/*oo, ue, ew*.
- blend and read words with /ü/*oo, ue, ew*.

MATERIALS

- **Teaching Chart 151**

Skills Finder

/ü/ *oo, ue, ew*	
Introduce	B1: 128G-H
Review	B1: 155E-F; B2: 150G-H, 179E-F, 179G-H
Test	B1: Unit 2

ALTERNATE TEACHING STRATEGY

/ü/*oo, ue, ew*

For a different approach to teaching this skill, see page T70.

Review /ü/oo, ue, ew

PREPARE

Review Symbols for the /ü/ Sound Say the sentence, "I threw my good, blue boots into the pool." Ask children how many /ü/ sounds they hear. (four) Write the sentence on the chalkboard and have volunteers circle the symbols for /ü/.

TEACH

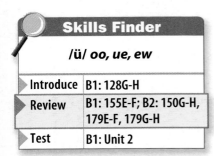

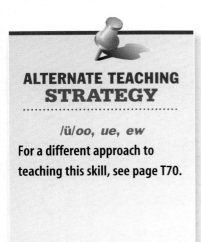

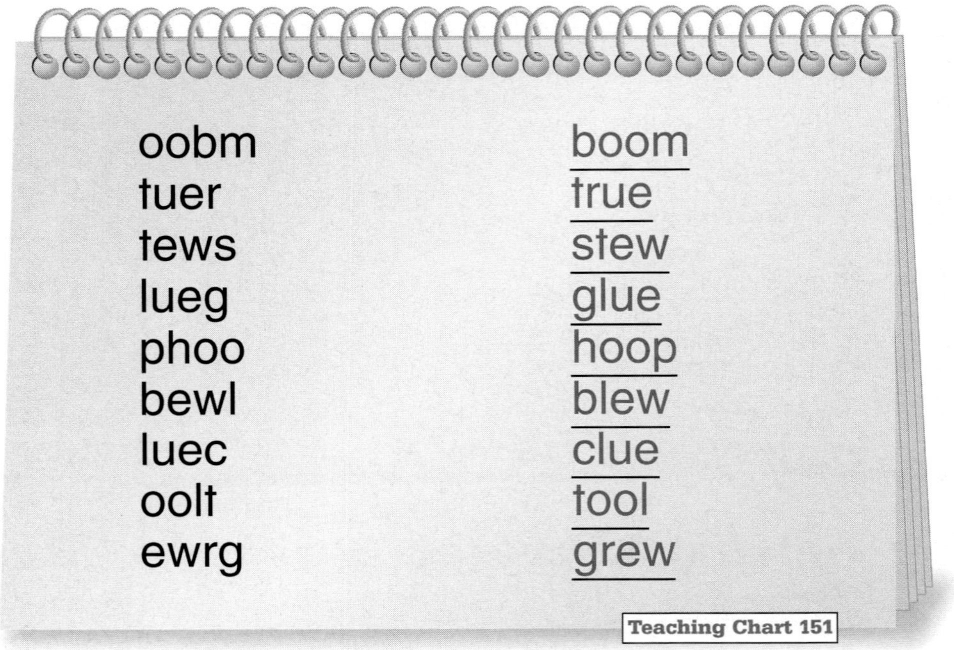
oobm
tuer
tews
lueg
phoo
bewl
luec
oolt
ewrg
boom
true
stew
glue
hoop
blew
clue
tool
grew
Teaching Chart 151

BLENDING Model and Guide Practice with /ü/ Words

- Display **Teaching Chart 151**. Tell children they will use their knowledge of the /ü/ sound and its symbols to identify words with *oo, ue,* and *ew*.
- Explain to children that the words on the left are all words with the /ü/ sound, only the letters have been scrambled. Their knowledge of the symbols for /ü/ will help them unscramble the words correctly.
- Work with children to unscramble the first word on the **Teaching Chart** to form the word *boom.*

Use the Word in Context Have volunteers use the unscrambled word in a sentence to reinforce its meaning. Example: *I heard a boom of thunder last night.*

Repeat the Procedure Follow the same procedure to unscramble the remaining words on the chart.

PRACTICE

DISCRIMINATING
Identify Words with the /ü/ Sound
ONE

Have children draw a three-by-three grid on a sheet of paper, with enough space inside each box for them to write a word. Read aloud the nine unscrambled words from **Teaching Chart 151** and the following words: *story, cart, tall,* and *snore.* Mix up the order of the words as you read them aloud. Children should write each word with /ü/ that they hear into their grid. ▶ **Auditory/Linguistic**

ASSESS/CLOSE

Group Words with *oo, ue,* and *ew*

To assess children's ability to identify and discriminate words with *oo, ue,* and *ew,* observe their work on the Practice activity. Then ask children to label three columns on paper with *oo; ue; ew*. Then have them sort the words in their grid into the appropriate columns according to the symbols for /ü/.

ADDITIONAL PHONICS RESOURCES

Phonics/Phonemic Awareness Practice Book, pages 117–120

McGraw-Hill School TECHNOLOGY

Phonics CD-ROM

activities for practice with Blending and Discriminating

DAILY Phonics ROUTINES

DAY 4 **Discriminating** Say a list of words, some containing /ü/ (for example: *foot, pool, sit, mother, jewel*). Have children listen for the /ü/ sound and clap their hands each time they hear it.

Phonics CD-ROM

SPELLING/PHONICS CONNECTIONS

See the 5-Day Spelling Plan, pages 179Q–179R.

Intervention Skills

Intervention Guide, for direct instruction and extra practice of /ü/ *oo, ue, ew*

Meeting Individual Needs for Phonics

EASY	ON-LEVEL	CHALLENGE	LANGUAGE SUPPORT

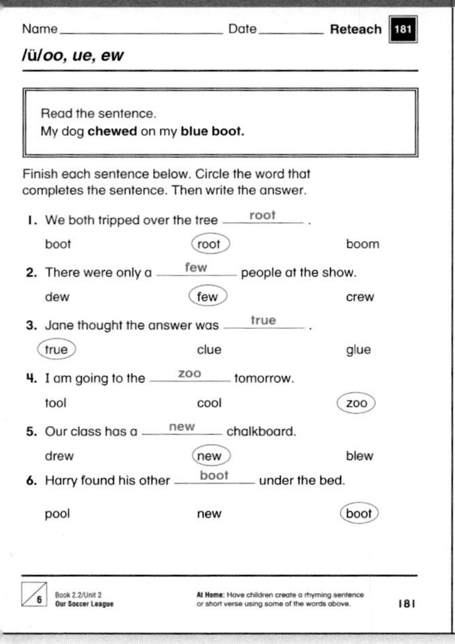
Name ______ Date ______ Reteach 181
/ü/oo, ue, ew

Read the sentence.
My dog **chewed** on my **blue boot.**

Finish each sentence below. Circle the word that completes the sentence. Then write the answer.

1. We both tripped over the tree root. — boot, (root), boom
2. There were only a few people at the show. — dew, (few), crew
3. Jane thought the answer was true. — (true), clue, glue
4. I am going to the zoo tomorrow. — tool, cool, (zoo)
5. Our class has a new chalkboard. — drew, (new), blew
6. Harry found his other boot under the bed. — pool, new, (boot)

6 Book 2.2/Unit 2 Our Soccer League — At Home: Have children create a rhyming sentence or short verse using some of the words above. 181

Reteach, 181

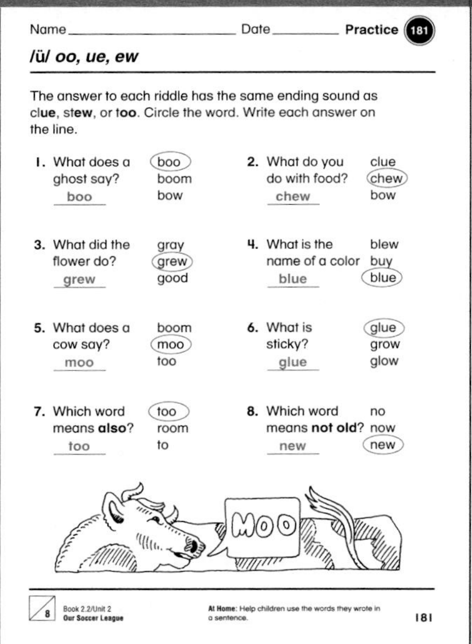
Name ______ Date ______ Practice 181
/ü/ oo, ue, ew

The answer to each riddle has the same ending sound as **clue, stew,** or **too**. Circle the word. Write each answer on the line.

1. What does a ghost say? (boo) boom bow — boo
2. What do you do with food? clue (chew) bow — chew
3. What did the flower do? gray (grew) good — grew
4. What is the name of a color? blew buy (blue) — blue
5. What does a cow say? boom (moo) too — moo
6. What is sticky? (glue) grow glow — glue
7. Which word means **also**? (too) room to — too
8. Which word means **not old**? no now (new) — new

8 Book 2.2/Unit 2 Our Soccer League — At Home: Help children use the words they wrote in a sentence. 181

Practice, 181

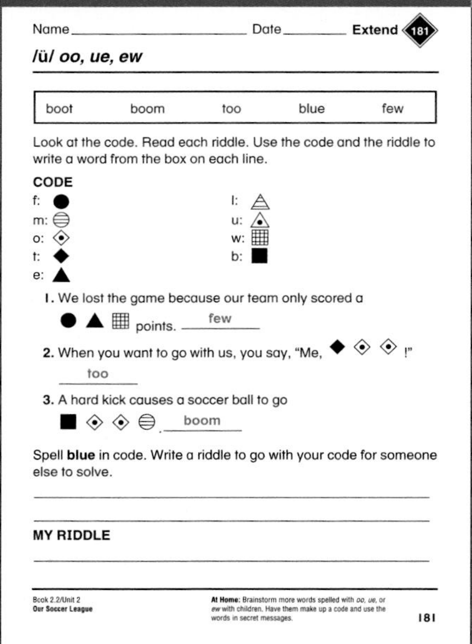
Name ______ Date ______ Extend 181
/ü/ oo, ue, ew

boot boom too blue few

Look at the code. Read each riddle. Use the code and the riddle to write a word from the box on each line.

CODE
f: ● m: ⊖ o: ◈ t: ◆ e: ▲ l: △ u: ▵ w: ▦ b: ■

1. We lost the game because our team only scored a ● ▲ ▦ points. few
2. When you want to go with us, you say, "Me, ◆ ◈ ◈ !" too
3. A hard kick causes a soccer ball to go ■ ◈ ◈ ⊖ . boom

Spell **blue** in code. Write a riddle to go with your code for someone else to solve.

MY RIDDLE

Book 2.2/Unit 2 Our Soccer League — At Home: Brainstorm more words spelled with oo, ue, or ew with children. Have them make up a code and use the words in secret messages. 181

Extend, 181

Name ______ Date ______
Circle the Picture

1. The player boots the ball.
2. You can play, too!
3. Boom! The player scored!
4. The blue team has the ball.

Grade 2 — Language Support/Blackline Master 107 • Our Soccer League 195

Language Support, 195

TESTED **OBJECTIVES**

Children will:

- review /ü/*oo, ue;* /ôr/*or, ore.*
- blend and read words with /ü/ and /ôr/.

MATERIALS

- Teaching Chart 152
- **Word Building Manipulative Cards**
- index cards

Skills Finder

/ü/ oo, ue, ew

Introduce	B1: 128G-H
Review	B1: 155E-F, 155G-H; B2: 150G-H, 179E-F
Test	B1: Unit 2

Review /ü/ oo, ue; /ôr/ or, ore

PREPARE

Identify Symbols for the /ü/ and /ôr/ Sounds Remind children that the /ü/ sound can be spelled with *oo* or *ue*, and that the /ôr/ sound can be spelled with *or* or *ore*. Have them brainstorm words with these sounds and symbols, write their responses on the chalkboard, and blend and read each word aloud with the class.

TEACH

BLENDING Model and Guide Practice with /ü/*oo, ue* and /ôr/*or, ore* Words

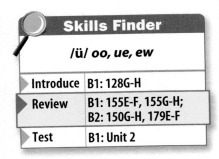

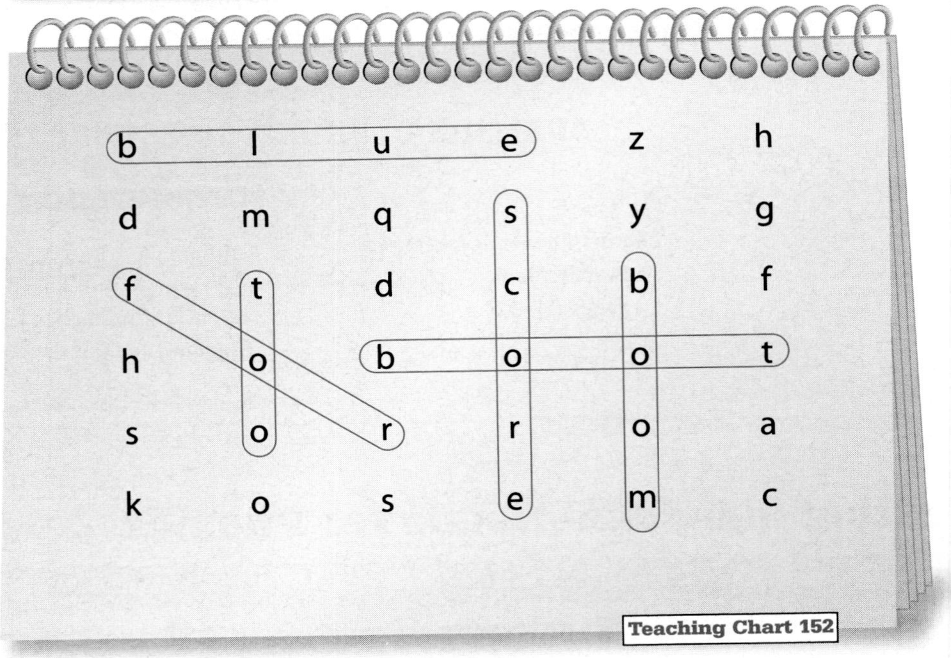

- Display **Teaching Chart 152**. Explain to children that they must find all the real words with the /ü/ and /ôr/ sounds on the chart. Words can be formed in any direction.
- Write the letters *ue* on the chalkboard.
- Circle the word *blue*. Then ask a volunteer to write on the chalkboard the word you have circled, blending it and reading it aloud.

b l ue → blue

Use the Word in Context Have volunteers use the circled word in a sentence to reinforce its meaning. Example: *Blue is the color of the sea and the sky.*

Repeat the Procedure Follow the same procedure, having children find, circle, blend, and read the remaining words on the chart.

PRACTICE

WORD BUILDING
Build and Write /ü/*oo, ue* and /ôr/ *or, ore* Words
GROUP

Have children work in small groups. Have each group use letter, variant vowel, and digraph cards to build as many words with /ü/*oo, ue* as they can. Have children fold a paper in half vertically and label the columns *oo* and *ue.* Ask each child to list the words the group builds under the appropriate word family. Repeat with /ôr/*or, ore*. Have each child in a group choose a word for each of the two sounds and underline the /ü/ and /ôr/ sound. ▶ **Linguistic/Interpersonal**

ASSESS/CLOSE

Read and Sort /ü/*oo, ue* and /ôr/ *or, ore* Words

Observe children's work on the Practice activity to assess their ability to build and write words with /ü/*oo, ue* and /ôr/*or, ore*. Ask each child to blend and read aloud the two words they wrote on index cards in the Practice activity. Have children make a word wall of their index cards sorted by sounds. Then have children read the Phonics Rhyme on pages 150/151 in their anthologies.

ADDITIONAL PHONICS RESOURCES

Phonics/Phonemic Awareness Practice Book, pages 117–120

McGraw-Hill School TECHNOLOGY

Phonics CD-ROM
activities for practice with Blending and Discriminating

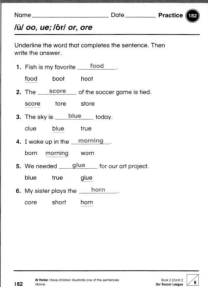

DAILY Phonics ROUTINES

DAY 5 **Writing** Have children write a nonsense sentence or rhyming triplet using each of the spellings of the /ü/ sound. For example: *I once knew a blue groom.*

Phonics CD-ROM

ALTERNATE TEACHING STRATEGY

/ü/ AND /ôr/

For a different approach to teaching this skill, see pages T65 and T70.

Intervention ▶ Skills

Intervention Guide, for direct instruction and extra practice of /ü/ *oo, ue, ew;* /ôr/ *or, ore*

Meeting Individual Needs for Phonics

EASY

Name ________ Date ______ **Reteach 182**

/ü/ oo, ue; /ôr/ or, ore

(thorn) corn

Circle the word that names each picture. Then write the word.

1. fork (boot) — boot
2. (glue) story — glue
3. zoo (corn) — corn
4. (core) moon — core

182 **At Home:** Have children write a sentence using one of the words they circled. Book 2.2/Unit 2 **Our Soccer League** 4

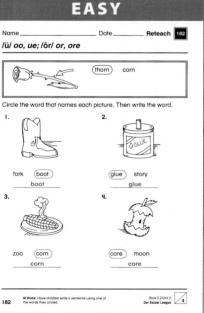

Reteach, 182

ON-LEVEL

Name ________ Date ______ **Practice 182**

/ü/ oo, ue; /ôr/ or, ore

Underline the word that completes the sentence. Then write the answer.

1. Fish is my favorite __food__.
   food boot hoot
2. The __score__ of the soccer game is tied.
   score tore store
3. The sky is __blue__ today.
   clue blue true
4. I wake up in the __morning__.
   born morning worn
5. We needed __glue__ for our art project.
   blue true glue
6. My sister plays the __horn__.
   core short horn

182 **At Home:** Have children illustrate one of the sentences above. Book 2.2/Unit 2 **Our Soccer League** 6

Practice, 182

CHALLENGE

Name ________ Date ______ **Extend 182**

/ü/ oo, ue; /ôr/ or, ore

boot	for	score	blue	boom	too

Write a sentence about each picture. Use one word from the box in each sentence. **Answers: Sample sentences are given.**

1. This present is for you.
2. The score is 44 to 23.
3. The blocks went boom.
4. The boot fell out of the box.
5. May I have some cheese too?
6. The sky is blue today.

182 **At Home:** Have children make a crossword puzzle for the words in the box. Ask them to write clues for each word. Suggest that they use the sentences they wrote to help them. Book 2.2/Unit 2 **Our Soccer League**

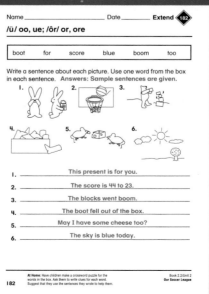

Extend, 182

LANGUAGE SUPPORT

Name ________ Date ______

What Did You Say?

Score	boot	for	blue

I [boot] the ball.

I am the coach [for] the Eagles.

[Score] team!

I play on the [blue] team.

196 **Our Soccer League** • Language Support/Blackline Master 108 Grade 2

Language Support, 196

TESTED OBJECTIVES

Children will recognize sequence of events.

MATERIALS
- **Teaching Chart 153**

Skills Finder

Sequence of Events

Introduce	B2: 179I-J
Review	B2: 235I-J, 245E-F
Test	B2: Unit 2
Maintain	B1: 207, 229

TEACHING TIP

SEQUENCE OF EVENTS
After an initial discussion of Teaching Chart 153, have children actively participate while the chart is read aloud. Have small groups of children act out the sequence of events as you read the paragraph. Discuss how word clues signaled the change from one event to another.

SELF-SELECTED Reading

Students may choose from following titles.

ANTHOLOGY
- *Our Soccer League*

LEVELED BOOKS
- *Coyotes Rule!*
- *Playing Your Best*
- *Teammates for Life*

Bibliography, pages T88–T89

Introduce Sequence of Events

PREPARE

Discuss Steps in Bedtime Routine Have children think about the steps they go through when they get ready for bed at night. Ask: What do you do first? What do you do next? What is the last thing you do before you fall asleep?

TEACH

Define and Model Sequence of Events Tell children that writers often use key words such as *first, then, during, after,* and *soon* to let readers know when events take place. Display **Teaching Chart 153**. Have children pay attention to the word clues as you read the paragraph aloud.

Soccer Saturday

Every Saturday our team plays soccer against another team. **(1)** First, we stretch before playing. **(3)** Soon, we work on hard moves. **(2)** Before that, we pass the ball back and forth so we get used to playing as a team. **(4)** Then, both teams take their starting positions and the game begins. **(5)** Next, everyone is running around and kicking the ball, trying to make a goal. **(6)** One team wins in the end, but no matter who wins, everyone has fun.

Teaching Chart 153

Ask children which words helped them to understand the sequence of events.

MODEL Words like *first* and *before* help me to see that the events in the story happen in a certain order. I will look for other words that are time order clues.

Identify an Implied Sequence of Events Cover the words that signal sequence of events on the **Teaching Chart**. Reread the passage on the chart without these words. As a class, determine which sentences can be rearranged, and which cannot. Determine if there is an implied sequence of events that must take place in order for the passage to make sense. For example, certain activities take place before the game, during the game, or after the game.

PRACTICE

Number Sentences GROUP Have children circle the words in the chart that helped them know the order of events. Then point out that one sentence on the chart is not in the right order. Ask children to identify the out-of-order sentence. Call on volunteers to write a number next to each sentence to show the correct sequence. ▶ **Logical/Linguistic**

ASSESS/CLOSE

Write Bedtime Routines in Time Order Have children describe their bedtime routines in three or four sentences. Encourage them to use word clues such as *first, next, then, after,* and *finally.*

ALTERNATE TEACHING STRATEGY

SEQUENCE OF EVENTS

For a different approach to teaching this skill, see page T71.

Intervention **Skills**

Intervention Guide, for direct instruction and extra practice of sequence of events

Meeting Individual Needs for Comprehension

EASY

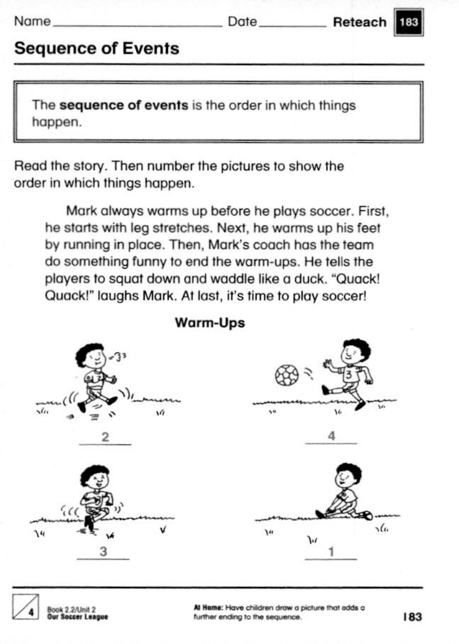
Name ________ Date ________ **Reteach 183**

Sequence of Events

The **sequence of events** is the order in which things happen.

Read the story. Then number the pictures to show the order in which things happen.

Mark always warms up before he plays soccer. First, he starts with leg stretches. Next, he warms up his feet by running in place. Then, Mark's coach has the team do something funny to end the warm-ups. He tells the players to squat down and waddle like a duck. "Quack! Quack!" laughs Mark. At last, it's time to play soccer!

Warm-Ups

2 4 3 1

4 Book 2.2/Unit 2 **Our Soccer League** **At Home:** Have children draw a picture that adds a further ending to the sequence. 183

Reteach, 183

ON-LEVEL

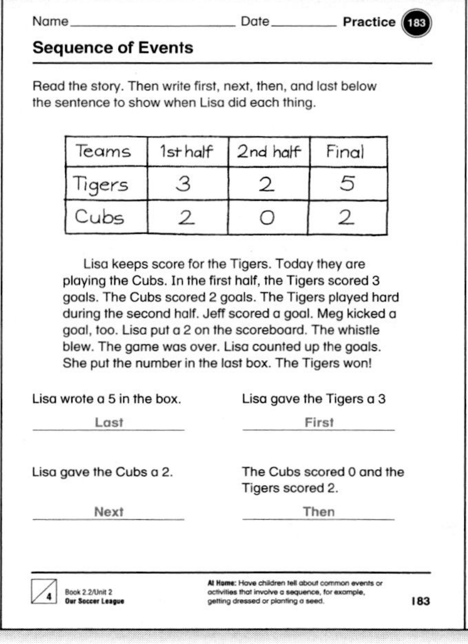
Name ________ Date ________ **Practice 183**

Sequence of Events

Read the story. Then write first, next, then, and last below the sentence to show when Lisa did each thing.

Teams	1st half	2nd half	Final
Tigers	3	2	5
Cubs	2	0	2

Lisa keeps score for the Tigers. Today they are playing the Cubs. In the first half, the Tigers scored 3 goals. The Cubs scored 2 goals. The Tigers played hard during the second half. Jeff scored a goal. Meg kicked a goal, too. Lisa put a 2 on the scoreboard. The whistle blew. The game was over. Lisa counted up the goals. She put the number in the last box. The Tigers won!

Lisa wrote a 5 in the box. Last

Lisa gave the Tigers a 3 First

Lisa gave the Cubs a 2. Next

The Cubs scored 0 and the Tigers scored 2. Then

4 Book 2.2/Unit 2 **Our Soccer League** **At Home:** Have children tell about common events or activities that involve a sequence, for example, getting dressed or planting a seed. 183

Practice, 183

CHALLENGE

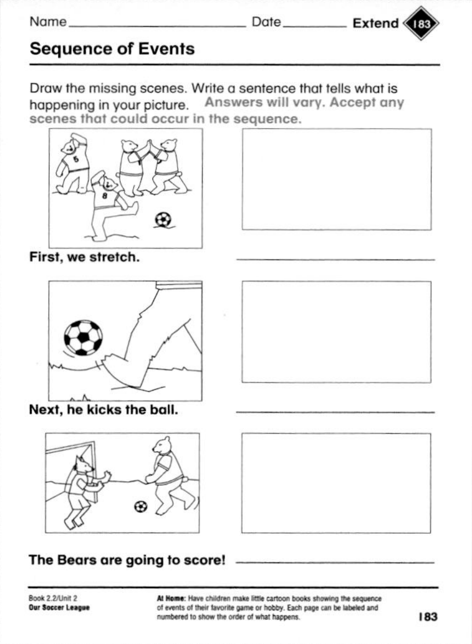
Name ________ Date ________ **Extend 183**

Sequence of Events

Draw the missing scenes. Write a sentence that tells what is happening in your picture. Answers will vary. Accept any scenes that could occur in the sequence.

First, we stretch.

Next, he kicks the ball.

The Bears are going to score!

Book 2.2/Unit 2 **Our Soccer League** **At Home:** Have children make little cartoon books showing the sequence of events of their favorite game or hobby. Each page can be labeled and numbered to show the order of what happens. 183

Extend, 183

LANGUAGE SUPPORT

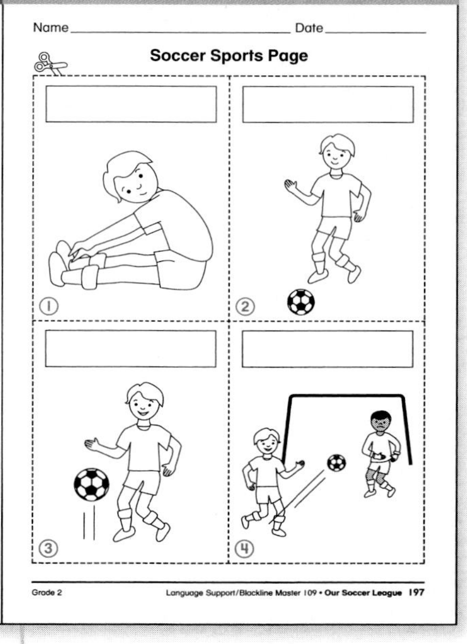
Name ________ Date ________

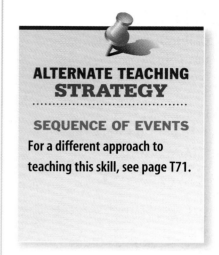

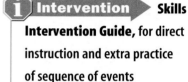

Soccer Sports Page

① ② ③ ④

Grade 2 Language Support/Blackline Master 109 • **Our Soccer League** 197

Language Support, 197

Review Context Clues

TESTED OBJECTIVES

Children will recognize and use context clues to find word meaning.

MATERIALS

- **Teaching Chart 154**
- **index cards**

Skills Finder

Context Clues	
Introduce	B1: 91K-L
Review	B1: 113K-L, 123I-J; B2: 179K-L, 245I-J
Test	B1: Unit 1
Maintain	B2: 139, 193, 269, 295

TEACHING TIP

MANAGEMENT To provide practice with previous vocabulary words, place those words on a word wall or bulletin board. Write each word on a card of colored construction paper. Place words alphabetically. Do at least one daily activity in which children use a word in a sentence. Ask other children to determine the meaning of the word based on context clues from the spoken sentence.

PREPARE

Discuss Using Context Clues to Understand Specialized Vocabulary

Remind children that when they come across an unfamiliar word during their reading, they can use context clues to find that word's meaning. Context clues are very useful for understanding vocabulary that deals with a specific topic, such as sports.

TEACH

Read the Passage and Model the Skill

Have children read the passage on **Teaching Chart 154** with you.

Let's Go, Falcons!

The Falcons' goalie is ready for action. She waits for a chance to stop the ball so the other team won't score. "The second part of the game is always so exciting," she thinks, glad that halftime is over. Her friend dribbles the ball across the field, using only her feet. She tries to pass the ball to a teammate, but, all of a sudden, a Slugger intercepts it! He steals the ball and kicks it toward the goal, but it flies off the field and out-of-bounds. The Falcons' goalie sighs, still ready for action.

Teaching Chart 154

Have children use context clues to determine word meaning.

MODEL I'm not sure what *intercepts* means. I'll look at the words nearby to see if I can figure out what it means. A Slugger steals the ball on its way to a Falcon, so I think *intercepts* means something like *taking something on its way to somewhere else*.

PRACTICE

Use Context Clues to Find Word Meanings

ONE

Have volunteers circle unfamiliar words and underline context clues to identify their meanings. Then have children write each word on index cards, along with a definition for the word based on the context clue. Have them look up the words in the Glossary, beginning on page 374, to verify word meanings. ▶ **Linguistic/Logical**

ASSESS/CLOSE

Write Context Clues

Write the following words on the chalkboard: *pass, bounce, tie, charge*. Have partners take two of the words and write a sentence with a context clue for each word. They may first look up the word in their Glossaries, if necessary. Have them trade papers, and have each partner circle the word, underline the context clue, and write a definition for the word based on the context clue.

ALTERNATE TEACHING STRATEGY

CONTEXT CLUES

For a different approach to teaching this skill, see page T74.

Intervention **Skills**

Intervention Guide, for direct instruction and extra practice of context clues

Meeting Individual Needs for Vocabulary

EASY

Name_______________ Date_________ **Reteach** 184

Context Clues

Sometimes you can find the meaning of a word you do not know by reading other words nearby.

I went to the **market** to get bananas and soap.

The words "to get bananas and soap" tell you that a **market** is a place that sells things.

Read each sentence. Figure out the meaning of the underlined word. Draw a line from the sentence to the word that tells the meaning of the underlined word.

1. There are many people, cars, and buildings in Oakland.	a fun food
2. Many people watched a ball game at the stadium.	big field
3. A player carried the ball down the field to make a touchdown.	a person who checks rules
4. Some people we knew were sitting in the bleachers.	a set of seats
5. The referee blew a whistle when a player broke the rules.	a big city
6. At the show my sister and I enjoyed a big bag of popcorn.	a way to score

184 **At Home:** Show children a newspaper article and ask them to guess the meaning of unfamiliar words by using clues from the surrounding words. Book 2.2/Unit 2 **Our Soccer League** 6

Reteach, 184

ON-LEVEL

Name_______________ Date_________ **Practice** 184

Context Clues

Read each sentence. You can find clues about the meaning of the underlined word by reading the rest of the sentence. Color in the circle next to the word's definition.

1. In this game you throw a ball through a basket.
   - ● an open net on a metal ring
   - ⓑ a swimming pool
2. At halftime, we take a break.
   - ⓐ a young player
   - ● when the game is half over
3. The score is ten to twelve.
   - ● the number of points made in a game
   - ⓑ a very big number
4. The coach helps us learn to throw.
   - ⓐ a special throw
   - ● a teacher in sports
5. The players charge down the court.
   - ⓐ pay for with a credit card
   - ● run fast

184 **At Home:** Read a picture caption from the sports section of your newspaper and help your child learn new words by using clues given in words and pictures. Book 2.2/Unit 2 **Our Soccer League** 5

Practice, 184

CHALLENGE

Name_______________ Date_________ **Extend** 184

Context Clues

Write new sentences using each of the underlined words or phrases in the story.

Teams	1st half	2nd half	Final
Bears	1	0	1
Tigers	0	1	1

What an exciting game! In the first half, the Bears charge to the goal. They run so fast! Then there is a kick to the goal. Barney Bear boots the ball through the goal. The goalie, Tina Tiger, makes a save. There is no point scored this time. Then the Tigers kick the ball out-of-bounds. The Bears get to throw it back in to the field. Then Barney scores. In the end, the Tigers tie the game.

Answers will vary. Look for sentences that use the underlined words or phrases correctly.

184 **At Home:** Brainstorm a list of words used in a sport, such as *base hit, shortstop,* and *foul* used in baseball. Have children use the words to write a short story about the game. Book 2.2/Unit 2 **Our Soccer League**

Extend, 184

LANGUAGE SUPPORT

Name_______________ Date_______________

Word and Picture Match

stretches	throw	tie	score
pass	dribble	field	kick

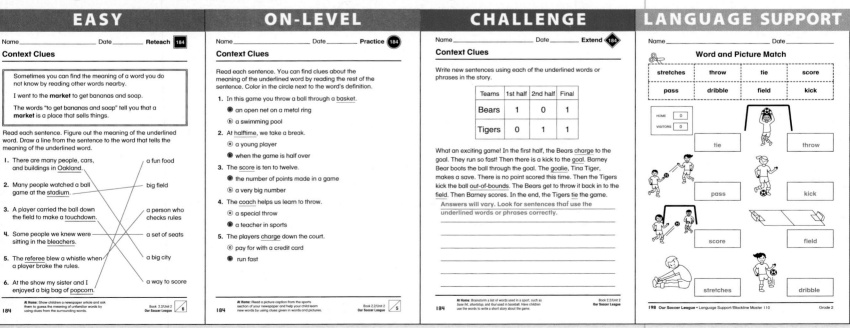

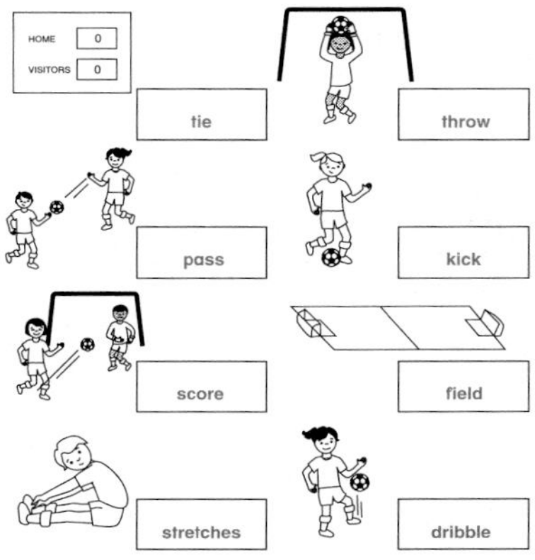

198 Our Soccer League • Language Support/Blackline Master 110 Grade 2

Language Support, 198

GRAMMAR/SPELLING CONNECTIONS

See the 5-Day Grammar and Usage Plan on *I, me, we, us,* pages 179O–179P.

See the 5-Day Spelling Plan on words with blends, pages 179Q–179R.

TEACHING TIP

Technology Review your drafts carefully to see that the ideas flow smoothly and one thing leads to another. If not, try moving paragraphs or sentences around by cutting and pasting text.

Paragraphs Remind children that each idea should have its own paragraph. As thoughts move from one to the next, remember to start a new paragraph by indenting handwritten paragraphs or starting a new line on computer-generated paragraphs.

Handwriting CD-ROM

Expository Writing

Prewrite

WRITE A TEAM-PLAYER GUIDE Present this writing assignment: Choose a favorite sport, game, or activity. Write a guide that explains how to play, do, or make what you chose. What are the rules of the game or the steps for the activity? What does each player do?

DRAMATIZE Once children have made their selections, have them pretend to play or do their activity. Point out that dramatizing their activity will help them put their ideas in order.

Strategy: Make a Chart Have children make a chart to organize the details of their activity. To help them get started, suggest the following categories for the left-hand column of their charts, but point out that not all the categories will be necessary for each choice:

- Number of players
- Names of special positions
- Rules
- Steps

Draft

FREE WRITE Guide children to draft their ideas without self-editing. They can consult their charts to keep the steps in order. Encourage them to use active, vivid language that will help the reader understand what it is like to play the game.

Revise

TAKE TIME OUT Encourage children to put their drafts aside while they take a break. Afterward, they should read their work to make sure they have included all the steps. Tell them that a fresh eye can often help them see how to improve their writing.

PARTNERS Have children trade guides with a partner to get feedback.

Edit/Proofread

CHECK FOR ERRORS Children should reread their guides for spelling, grammar, and punctuation.

Publish

SHARE THE GUIDES Have children form groups based on whether they wrote about a sport, a game, or another type of activity. Have them bind their guides into a "magazine" for each category. Groups can illustrate and title their magazines.

Red Light, Green Light is my favorite game. Here's how you play it.

First, get five or six friends to play with you. You can play with fewer people, but it's not as much fun.

Choose a leader. The leader stands away from everyone else. When the leader turns her or his back to the other players and yells out "Red light, green light! One, two, three!" everyone runs toward the leader. When the leader finishes yelling, and quickly turns around again, everyone has to stop moving. If the leader sees you move, you're out. Keep doing this until someone tags the leader, and that person becomes the new leader.

You should try it. It's lots of fun.

Presentation Ideas

RECRUIT PLAYERS Have children take turns trying to convince the class to participate in their sport, game, or activity. Have the class choose the most convincing speaker.
▶ **Speaking/Listening**

MAKE A POSTER Have children make a poster that shows the steps for doing their chosen activity, game or sport. Or they may draw pictures of the equipment needed, with short explanations alongside them.
▶ **Viewing/Representing**

Consider children's creative efforts, possibly adding a plus for originality, wit, and imagination.

Scoring Rubric

Excellent	Good	Fair	Unsatisfactory
4: The writer • clearly explains a specific task, in a logical, detailed sequence. • uses vivid language that engages the reader. • sums up the guide with a strong conclusion.	**3:** The writer • clearly explains a specific task. • presents the steps in a logical sequence, with some detail. • sums up the guide with a reasonable conclusion.	**2:** The writer • introduces the basic idea of the task, but is somewhat vague. • presents some steps in a process, but they may be unclear, or incomplete. • sums up the guide with a weak or vague conclusion.	**1:** The writer • fails to introduce the task. • presents no steps to explain the task. • does not conclude the guide.

Incomplete 0: The writer leaves the page blank or fails to respond to the writing task. The student does not address the topic or simply paraphrases the prompt. The response is illegible or incoherent.

Meeting Individual Needs for Writing

EASY

Sports Illustrated Have children draw a picture of their favorite sport, game, or activity. At the bottom of the drawing, have them write a sentence explaining why they like it.

ON-LEVEL

Soccer Scenes Invite children to draw a scene from the soccer game in *Our Soccer League,* showing the players in action. Have them place speech balloons above each player's head, so they can write what the players are thinking while they play.

CHALLENGE

New Setting Have children write about what the soccer game in *Our Soccer League* would be like if it were played on a sandy beach, instead of a field of grass. They should describe, in detail, how the game would be different. Challenge children to think about the many ways sand could affect the players.

Viewing and Speaking

VIEWING Have children
- look for details in the poster that show the steps for playing or making the activity.
- find details that describe the materials needed.
- close their eyes and visualize the activity taking place.

SPEAKING Encourage children to
- use gestures to demonstrate the activity.
- use transition words to describe the process in a clear manner.
- communicate the information with enthusiasm to encourage others to participate.

LANGUAGE SUPPORT

ESL Assist children needing additional instruction with sequencing the steps in their task. Have them write the steps on the chalkboard, in whatever order they think of them. Then, using self-stick notes with numbers written on them, have them number the steps in the order they must be followed.

PORTFOLIO Invite children to include their guides in their portfolios.

5 Day Grammar and Usage Plan

LANGUAGE SUPPORT

ESL Give a pencil to a child and say: *Give the pencil to me.* Write the sentence on the chalkboard and identify the pronoun. Repeat a similar activity with other children in the class using the pronouns *we* and *us*. Say: *Give the books to them. Bring the books to us.*

DAILY LANGUAGE ACTIVITIES

Write the Daily Language Activities on the chalkboard each day or use **Transparency 22**. Have children orally correct the use of *I, me, we,* and *us* in the sentences.

Day 1
1. She gave it to I. me
2. Me have the ball. I
3. You can kick the ball to I. me

Day 2
1. Us went down the field. We
2. She can throw it for we. us
3. Us can run into open field. We

Day 3
1. The ball bounced to Sam and I. me
2. The ball now goes to we. us
3. He is too fast for I. me

Day 4
1. Us win the game. We
2. Me and Lou battle for the ball. Lou and I
3. The ball comes toward Ben and I. me

Day 5
1. I and Mary will take you there. Mary and I
2. That was a goal for we. us
3. Me and Tim had fun! Tim and I

Daily Language Transparency 22

DAY 1 Introduce the Concept

Oral Warm-Up Write the following on the chalkboard: *I know that girl. That girl knows me.* Have children identify the pronouns you used to talk about yourself.

Introduce *I* and *Me* Ask children to identify the subject and the predicate in each sentence above. Then present:

I* and *Me

- Use *I* in the subject part of a sentence.
- Use *me* in the predicate part.
- Name yourself last when talking about yourself and another person.

To illustrate the last point, ask children what is wrong with this sentence: *I and Kim went to school. Kim and I.*

Present the Daily Language Activity. Then have children write one sentence using *I* and another using *me*.

WRITING Assign the daily Writing Prompt on page 150C.

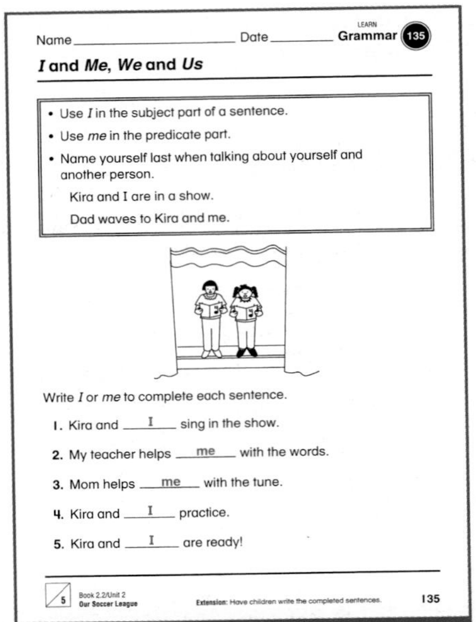
Name ______ Date ______ LEARN Grammar 135

I* and *Me*, *We* and *Us

- Use *I* in the subject part of a sentence.
- Use *me* in the predicate part.
- Name yourself last when talking about yourself and another person.

Kira and I are in a show.
Dad waves to Kira and me.

Write *I* or *me* to complete each sentence.

1. Kira and __I__ sing in the show.
2. My teacher helps __me__ with the words.
3. Mom helps __me__ with the tune.
4. Kira and __I__ practice.
5. Kira and __I__ are ready!

Book 2.2/Unit 2 Our Soccer League — Extension: Have children write the completed sentences. 135

GRAMMAR PRACTICE BOOK, PAGE 135

DAY 2 Teach the Concept

Review *I* and *Me* Remind children that *I* is used in the subject of a sentence and *me* is used in the predicate.

Introducing *We* and *Us* Write these sentences on the chalkboard: *We went to school. Pat talked to us.* Ask children to identify in which part of the sentences the words us and we are used. Present:

We* and *Us

- Use *we* and *us* when you talk about yourself and another person.
- Use *we* in the subject part of the sentence.
- Use *us* in the predicate part.

Present the Daily Language Activity. Then have children write two sentences, one using the pronoun *we* and another using the pronoun *us*.

WRITING Assign the daily Writing Prompt on page 150C.

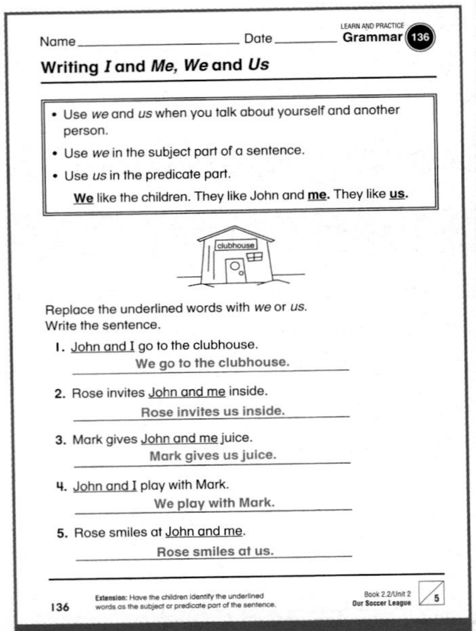
Name ______ Date ______ LEARN AND PRACTICE Grammar 136

Writing *I* and *Me*, *We* and *Us*

- Use *we* and *us* when you talk about yourself and another person.
- Use *we* in the subject part of a sentence.
- Use *us* in the predicate part.

We like the children. They like John and **me**. They like **us**.

clubhouse

Replace the underlined words with *we* or *us*. Write the sentence.

1. John and I go to the clubhouse.
   We go to the clubhouse.
2. Rose invites John and me inside.
   Rose invites us inside.
3. Mark gives John and me juice.
   Mark gives us juice.
4. John and I play with Mark.
   We play with Mark.
5. Rose smiles at John and me.
   Rose smiles at us.

136 Extension: Have the children identify the underlined words as the subject or predicate part of the sentence. Book 2.2/Unit 2 Our Soccer League

GRAMMAR PRACTICE BOOK, PAGE 136

I and *Me*, *We* and *Us*

DAY 3 Review and Practice

Learn from the Literature Review *I, me, we,* and *us*. Read the following sentences on pages 158 and 159 of *Our Soccer League*.

> **Moira throws *it* in for *us*.**
>
> ***We* charge down to the Slugger's goal.**

Have children identify the pronouns. Then ask which part of the sentences *we* and *us* are used in.

Writing *I, Me, We, Us* Present the Daily Language Activity and have children correct the sentences orally. Ask children to write a short, simple letter to a friend, inviting him or her to a sports event. Have children be sure to include information about what children will see. Then have volunteers write one of their sentences that include the pronoun *I, me, we,* or *us* on the chalkboard.

WRITING Assign the daily Writing Prompt on page 150D.

Name ______ Date ______ REVIEW AND PRACTICE Grammar 137

Using *I* and *Me*, *We* and *Us*

- Use *I* in the subject part and *me* in the predicate part of a sentence.
- Name yourself last when talking about yourself and another person.
- Use *we* and *us* when you talk about yourself and another person.
- Use *we* in the subject part and *us* in the predicate part of a sentence.

Write the pronoun that completes each sentence. Write the sentences.

1. Aunt Penny and __I__ have fun.
   Aunt Penny and I have fun.
2. "Please take __us__ to the mall," I said to Mom.
   "Please take us to the mall," I said to Mom.
3. "Please take __us__ to the circus," my brother and I said to Aunt Penny.
   "Please take us to the circus," my brother and I said to Aunt Penny.
4. __We__ are very happy to see Aunt Penny.
   We are very happy to see Aunt Penny.
5. "Aunt Penny will take __us__ to a movie," my brother and I said.
   "Aunt Penny will take us to a movie," my brother and I said.

5 Book 2.2/Unit 2 Our Soccer League

Extension: Have children perform actions such as handing a pencil to one another. Then the receiver describes the action using *I, me, we,* and *us.* 137

GRAMMAR PRACTICE BOOK, PAGE 137

DAY 4 Review and Practice

Review *I, Me, We, Us* Write corrected sentences from the Daily Language Activities for Days 1 to 3 on the chalkboard. Have children identify the parts of the sentences where the pronouns appear. Then have children do the Daily Language Activity for Day 4.

Mechanics and Usage Review how to write the pronoun *I*.

> **Pronoun *I***
>
> - The pronoun *I* is always a capital letter.

WRITING Assign the daily Writing Prompt on page 150D.

Name ______ Date ______ MECHANICS Grammar 138

Pronoun *I*

- The pronoun *I* is always a capital letter.
  I will go home soon.

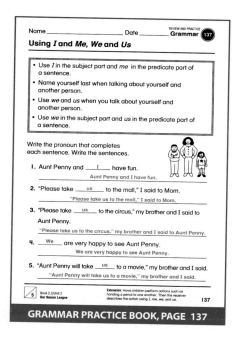

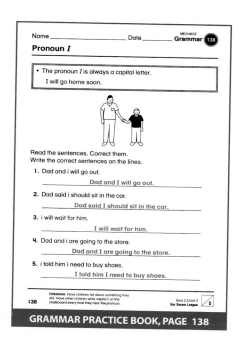

Read the sentences. Correct them. Write the correct sentences on the lines.

1. Dad and i will go out.
   Dad and I will go out.
2. Dad said i should sit in the car.
   Dad said I should sit in the car.
3. i will wait for him.
   I will wait for him.
4. Dad and i are going to the store.
   Dad and I are going to the store.
5. i told him i need to buy shoes.
   I told him I need to buy shoes.

138 **Extensions:** Have children tell about something they did. Have other children write capital I on the chalkboard every time they hear the pronoun.

Book 2.2/Unit 2 Our Soccer League 5

GRAMMAR PRACTICE BOOK, PAGE 138

DAY 5 Assess and Reteach

Assess Use the Daily Language Activity and page 139 of the **Grammar Practice Book** for assessment.

Reteach Review *I, me, we,* and *us* with children. Ask each child to make a statement beginning with the word *I* that describes himself or herself, and then complete another statement ending with the words ... *is important to me.* Then have children work in small groups. Have them come to a general agreement on something they all like to do and complete the statements *We like to ...* and ... *is fun for us.*

Have children write new sentences using the pronouns *I, me, we,* and *us* on individual slips of paper and tape them to the chalkboard.

Use page 140 of the **Grammar Practice Book** for additional reteaching.

WRITING Assign the daily Writing Prompt on page 150D.

Name ______ Date ______ TEST Grammar 139

I* and *Me*, *We* and *Us

Which pronoun fits the sentence? Mark your answer.

1. ______ went to the doctor.
   ⓐ Me
   ⓑ I (marked)
   ⓒ Us
2. The doctor looked ______ over.
   ⓐ me (marked)
   ⓑ we
   ⓒ I
3. ______ went home.
   ⓐ Us
   ⓑ We (marked)
   ⓒ Me
4. The dog was glad to see ______.
   ⓐ we
   ⓑ us (marked)
   ⓒ I
5. The dog and ______ went to the park.
   ⓐ me
   ⓑ I (marked)
   ⓒ we

5 Book 2.2/Unit 2 Our Soccer League 139

GRAMMAR PRACTICE BOOK, PAGE 139

GRAMMAR PRACTICE BOOK, PAGE 140

5 Day Spelling Plan

LANGUAGE SUPPORT

To help students hear both consonants in the blends, make letter cards for the letters *p, b, d,* and *t.* Then write the words *lay, rag, low, raw,* and *rap* on the chalkboard and have students pronounce them. Hold up a letter card to each word to form Spelling Words *play, brag, drag, blow, draw,* and *trap.* Have students repeat each word as you pronounce it.

DICTATION SENTENCES

Spelling Words

1. I try very hard.
2. The sky is blue.
3. Can the baby play with that toy?
4. She likes to brag about her bike.
5. I saw the cat drag the mouse.
6. The clock is made of brass.
7. I have a plan.
8. She can blow it away.
9. You can draw on this page.
10. The mouse went into the trap.

Challenge Words

11. The coaches blew their whistles.
12. The field is green.
13. I know the score.
14. She stretches her arm.
15. He throws the penny.

DAY 1 Pretest

Assess Prior Knowledge Use the Dictation Sentences at left and **Spelling Practice Book** page 135 for the pretest. Allow students to correct their own papers. If students have trouble, have partners give each other a midweek test on Day 3. Students who require a modified list may be tested on the first five words.

Spelling Words		Challenge Words
1. **try**	6. brass	11. **coaches**
2. **blue**	7. plan	12. **field**
3. **play**	8. blow	13. **score**
4. brag	9. draw	14. **stretches**
5. drag	10. trap	15. **throws**

*Note: Words in **dark type** are from the story.*

Word Study On page 136 of the **Spelling Practice Book** are word study steps and an at-home activity.

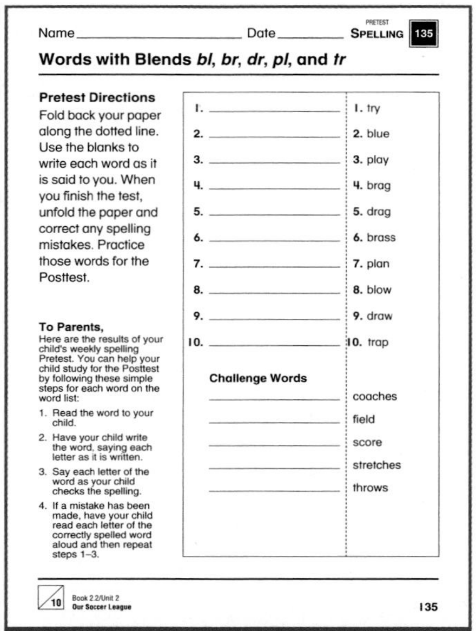

Name______________ Date________ PRETEST SPELLING 135

Words with Blends *bl*, *br*, *dr*, *pl*, and *tr*

Pretest Directions
Fold back your paper along the dotted line. Use the blanks to write each word as it is said to you. When you finish the test, unfold the paper and correct any spelling mistakes. Practice those words for the Posttest.

1. ______	1. try
2. ______	2. blue
3. ______	3. play
4. ______	4. brag
5. ______	5. drag
6. ______	6. brass
7. ______	7. plan
8. ______	8. blow
9. ______	9. draw
10. ______	10. trap

Challenge Words

______	coaches
______	field
______	score
______	stretches
______	throws

To Parents,
Here are the results of your child's weekly spelling Pretest. You can help your child study for the Posttest by following these simple steps for each word on the word list:

1. Read the word to your child.
2. Have your child write the word, saying each letter as it is written.
3. Say each letter of the word as your child checks the spelling.
4. If a mistake has been made, have your child read each letter of the correctly spelled word aloud and then repeat steps 1–3.

10 Book 2.2/Unit 2 Our Soccer League 135

SPELLING PRACTICE BOOK, PAGE 135

WORD STUDY STEPS AND ACTIVITY, PAGE 136

DAY 2 Explore the Pattern

Sort and Spell Words Say the words *blow, brass, draw, plan,* and *trap.* Have students identify the beginning consonant sounds they hear in each word. These words contain initial blends *bl, br, dr, pl,* and *tr.*

Ask students to read aloud the ten spelling words before sorting them according to spelling pattern.

Words beginning with				
bl	***br***	***dr***	***pl***	***tr***
blue	brag	drag	play	try
blow	brass	draw	plan	trap

Word Wall As students read poems and short stories, have them look for new words with initial blends *bl, br, dr, pl,* and *tr* and add them to the classroom word wall, underlining the spelling pattern in each word.

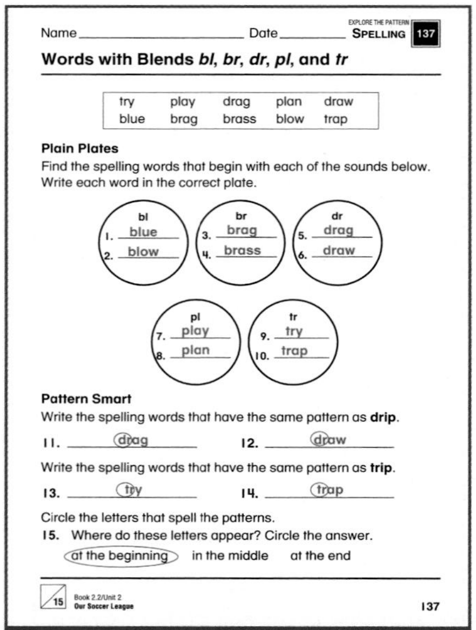

Name______________ Date________ EXPLORE THE PATTERN SPELLING 137

Words with Blends *bl*, *br*, *dr*, *pl*, and *tr*

try	play	drag	plan	draw
blue	brag	brass	blow	trap

Plain Plates
Find the spelling words that begin with each of the sounds below. Write each word in the correct plate.

bl: 1. blue 2. blow
br: 3. brag 4. brass
dr: 5. drag 6. draw
pl: 7. play 8. plan
tr: 9. try 10. trap

Pattern Smart
Write the spelling words that have the same pattern as **drip**.
11. drag 12. draw
Write the spelling words that have the same pattern as **trip**.
13. try 14. trap
Circle the letters that spell the patterns.
15. Where do these letters appear? Circle the answer.
at the beginning   in the middle   at the end

15 Book 2.2/Unit 2 Our Soccer League 137

SPELLING PRACTICE BOOK, PAGE 137

Words with Blends

DAY 3 Practice and Extend

Word Meaning: Endings Tell students that when adding *-ing* to verbs ending in one vowel and one consonant, the final consonant is usually doubled. Write the words *brag, drag, plan,* and *trap* on the chalkboard. Have students write the *-ing* form of each word.

Glossary Have students:

- write each Challenge Word.
- look up a synonym for each word in the Glossary. The synonyms for *coaches, stretches,* and *throws* are listed under their base words *coach, stretch* and *throw*.
- write a synonym beside each Challenge Word.

Name__________ Date______ PRACTICE AND EXTEND SPELLING 138

Words with Blends *bl, br, dr, pl,* and *tr*

try	play	drag	plan	draw
blue	brag	brass	blow	trap

Use a spelling word to complete each sentence.

1. The school bell was made of __brass__.
2. I like to __play__ with my dog.
3. Always __try__ to spell words right.
4. A strong wind began to __blow__ across the street.
5. Carl is wearing a __blue__ shirt today.
6. __Draw__ a circle around the word *tray*.

Word Building

Be a word builder. Double the consonant and add *-ing* to make new words.

Example: flip + p + ing = flipping

7. brag + g + ing = __bragging__
8. drag + g + ing = __dragging__
9. plan + n + ing = __planning__
10. trap + p + ing = __trapping__

138 **Challenge Extension:** Have students write riddles using the words. They may exchange with a partner to answer the riddles. Book 2.2/Unit 2 **Our Soccer League** 10

SPELLING PRACTICE BOOK, PAGE 138

DAY 4 Proofread and Write

Proofread Sentences Write these sentences on the chalkboard, including the misspelled words. Ask students to proofread, circling incorrect spellings and writing the correct spellings. There are two spelling errors in each sentence.

I can tri to plae. (try, play)

The cat can dragg the mouse from the trapp. (drag, trap)

Have students create additional sentences with errors for partners to correct.

WRITING Have students use as many Spelling Words as possible in the daily Writing Prompt on page 150D. Remind students to proofread their writing for errors in spelling, grammar, and punctuation.

Name__________ Date______ PROOFREAD AND WRITE SPELLING 139

Words with Blends *bl, br, dr, pl,* and *tr*

Proofreading Activity

There are six spelling mistakes in the paragraph below. Circle each misspelled word. Write the words correctly on the lines below.

Jody liked to drawe. She would plen every picture and trye to make it beautiful. One day I asked her to playe outside, but Jody wanted to color a new picture. Nothing I said could dragg her away from her picture. She colored some cats bright blu. I said, "Cats aren't that color." She said, "I know, but aren't they beautiful?"

1. __draw__ 2. __plan__ 3. __try__
4. __play__ 5. __drag__ 6. __blue__

Writing Activity

Make up song titles for silly songs. Use four spelling words in your titles. Circle the words you use.

10 Book 2.2/Unit 2 **Our Soccer League** 139

SPELLING PRACTICE BOOK, PAGE 139

DAY 5 Assess and Reteach

Assess Students' Knowledge Use page 140 of the **Spelling Practice Book** or the Dictation Sentences on page 179Q for the posttest.

Personal Word List If students have trouble with any words in the lesson, have them add to their personal list of troublesome words in their journals. Have students write a context sentence for each word.

JOURNAL

Students should refer to their word lists during later writing activities.

Name__________ Date______ POSTTEST SPELLING 140

Words with Blends *bl, br, dr, pl,* and *tr*

Look at the words in each set. One word in each set is spelled correctly. Use a pencil to color in the circle in front of that word. Before you begin, look at the sample sets of words. Sample A has been done for you. Do Sample B by yourself. When you are sure you know what to do, you may go on with the rest of the page.

Sample A
Ⓐ onlee
Ⓑ onley
● only
Ⓓ onely

Sample B
Ⓔ cowver
● cover
Ⓖ cuver
Ⓗ coaver

1. Ⓐ blu ● blue Ⓒ bule Ⓓ bleu
2. Ⓔ blou Ⓕ bloe Ⓖ bolw ● blow
3. Ⓐ brage Ⓑ barg ● brag Ⓓ bragg
4. ● brass Ⓕ bruss Ⓖ brase Ⓗ brasse
5. ● drag Ⓑ drage Ⓒ darg Ⓓ dragg
6. Ⓔ darw ● draw Ⓖ drwe Ⓗ drawe
7. Ⓐ pley Ⓑ paly ● play Ⓓ playe
8. Ⓔ plann Ⓕ paln Ⓖ plen ● plan
9. Ⓐ trie Ⓑ tyr ● try Ⓓ trye
10. ● trap Ⓕ trape Ⓖ trp Ⓗ trappe

140 Book 2.2/Unit 2 **Our Soccer League** 10

SPELLING PRACTICE BOOK, PAGE 140

Reaching All Learners

Concept
- Learning to Read

Comprehension
- Sequence of Events

Phonics
- /ər/*er*, /ən/*en*, and /əl/*el*

Vocabulary
- chance
- favorite
- heavy
- nervous
- office
- wrapped

Anthology

The Wednesday Surprise

Selection Summary Readers will get to figure out what surprise Anna and her grandmother have planned.

To Market! To Market!
To market, to market
With Grandmother today.
We go hand in hand
And we giggle all the way.
The basket we carry
Gets filled to the top.
With things that we buy
From each place that we stop.
And when we go home
Grandmother puts up her feet,
Time to listen to a story
And have something to eat.

Rhyme applies to phonics

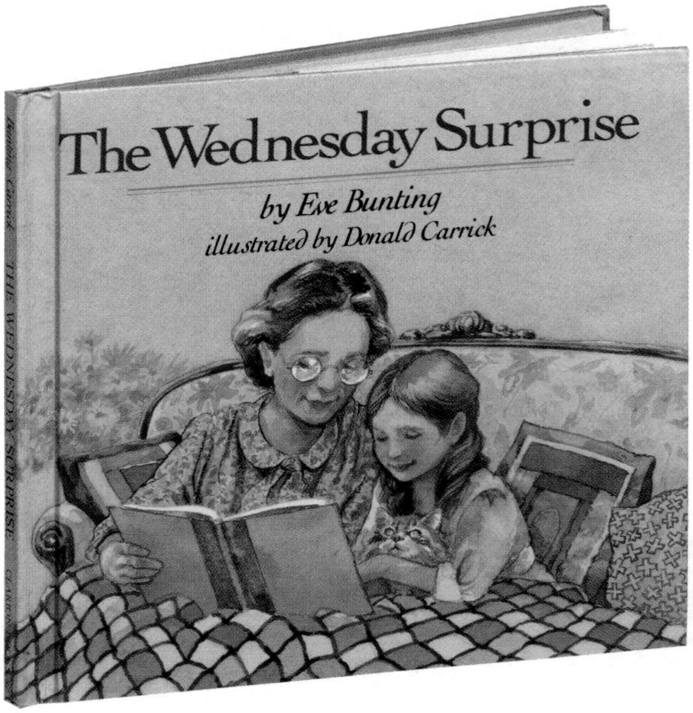
The Wednesday Surprise
by Eve Bunting
illustrated by Donald Carrick

Listening Library

INSTRUCTIONAL pages 182–211

About the Author One of Eve Bunting's friends used picture books to teach her mother, Katina, to read English. "Every day she would bring books home from school or the library, and they would read them together," Ms. Bunting says. "*The Wednesday Surprise* is my book, but it is Katina's story."

About the Illustrator Donald Carrick started drawing as a child. His first job was painting signs and billboards. Later he illustrated newspaper and magazine ads. His wife, Carol, wrote the first children's book he illustrated.

Same Concept, Skills and Vocabulary!

Leveled Books

EASY
Lesson on pages 211A and 211D
DECODABLE

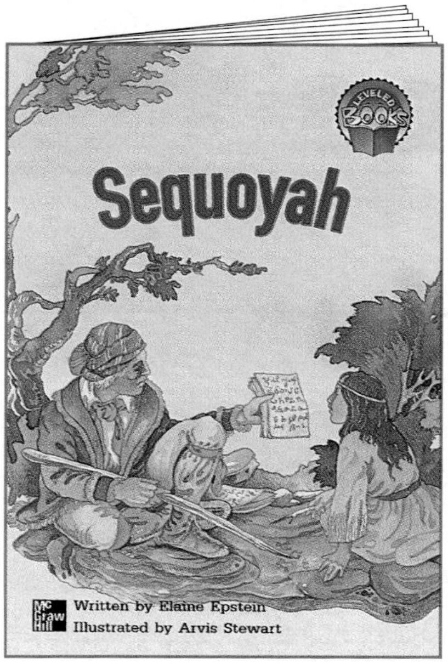

INDEPENDENT
Lesson on pages 211B and 211D
Take-Home version available

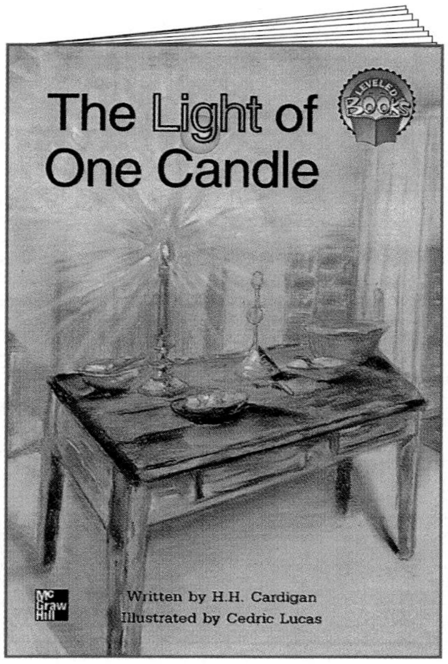

CHALLENGE
Lesson on pages 211C and 211D

Leveled Practice

EASY
Reteach, 185–192 Blackline masters with reteaching opportunities for each assessed skill

INDEPENDENT/ON-LEVEL
Practice, 185–192 Workbook with Take-Home stories and practice opportunities for each assessed skill and story comprehension

CHALLENGE
Extend, 185–192 Blackline masters that offer challenge activities for each assessed skill

Quizzes Prepared by Accelerated Reader

WORKSTATION Activities

Social Studies . . . Learning About Deserts, *194*
Science . . . . What's in a Breath? *184*
Math . . . . Graph Transportation, *200*
Art . . . . What Can You Share? *190*
Language Arts . . Read Aloud, *180E*
Writing . . . . Write About a Book, *208*
Cultural Perspectives . . . . . Birthday Celebrations Around the World, *202*
Research and Inquiry . . . . . . Find Out More, *209*
Internet Activities . . . . www.mhschool.com/reading

Suggested Lesson Planne

READING AND LANGUAGE ARTS	DAY 1 Focus on Reading and Skills	DAY 2 Read the Literatur
Phonics Daily Routines	Daily **Phonics** Routine: **Fluency,** 180H **Phonics CD-ROM**	Daily **Phonics** Routine: **Segmenting,** 182A **Phonics CD-ROM**
Phonological Awareness Phonics /ər/, /ən/, /əl/ Comprehension Vocabulary Study Skills Listening, Speaking, Viewing, Representing	**Read Aloud: Poem,** 180E "Reading to Me" ☑ **Develop Phonological Awareness,** 180F /ər/er, /ən/en, /əl/le ☑ **Review /ər/er, /ən/en, /əl/le,** 180G–180H **Teaching Chart 155** **Reteach, Practice, Extend,** 185 **Phonics/Phonemic Awareness Practice Book,** 121–124 Read **Apply /ər/er, /ən/en, /əl/le,** 180/181 "To Market! To Market!" Intervention Program	**Build Background,** 182A Develop Oral Language **Vocabulary,** 182B–182C *chance* *heavy* *office* *favorite* *nervous* *wrapped* **Word Building Manipulative Cards** **Teaching Chart 156** **Reteach, Practice, Extend,** 186 Read **Read the Selection,** 182–207 Comprehension ☑ /ər/er, /ən/en, /əl/le ☑ Sequence of Events **Genre: Realistic Fiction,** 183 **Writer's Craft: Word Choice,** 204 **Cultural Perspectives,** 202 Intervention Program
Curriculum Connections	Link **Language Arts,** 180E	Link **Language Arts,** 182A
Writing	**Writing Prompt:** Did you or someone you know ever get a surprise present? Tell about it. Or write a paragraph about a present you would like to get.	**Writing Prompt:** Have you ever taugh someone how to do or make something? What did you teach? Who was your student? **Journal Writing** Quick-Write, 207
Grammar	**Introduce the Concept: Possessive Pronouns,** 211O Daily Language Activity: Write possessive nouns correctly. **Grammar Practice Book,** 141	**Teach the Concept: Possessive Pronouns,** 211O Daily Language Activity: Write possessive nouns correctly. **Grammar Practice Book,** 142
Spelling *Blends*	**Pretest: Words with Blends,** 211Q **Spelling Practice Book,** 141–142	**Explore the Pattern: Words with Blends,** 211Q **Spelling Practice Book,** 143

Intervention Program Available

Meeting Individual Needs

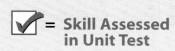

☑ = Skill Assessed in Unit Test

ⓘ Intervention Program Available

Read EVERY DAY

DAY 3 Read the Literature	DAY 4 Build Skills	DAY 5 Build Skills
Daily Phonics Routine: **Writing,** 209 Phonics **CD-ROM**	**Daily Phonics Routine:** **Letter Substitution,** 211F Phonics **CD-ROM**	**Daily Phonics Routine:** **Blending,** 211H Phonics **CD-ROM**
Rereading for Fluency, 206 **Story Questions and Activities,** 208–209 **Reteach, Practice, Extend,** 187 **Study Skills,** 210 ☑ Various Texts **Teaching Chart 157** **Reteach, Practice, Extend,** 188 **Test Power,** 211 Read **Read the Leveled Books,** 211A–211D Guided Reading ☑ /ər/er, /ən/en, /əl/le ☑ Sequence of Events ☑ Instructional Vocabulary ⓘ Intervention Program	Read **Read the Leveled Books and Self-Selected Books** ☑ Review /ər/er; /ən/en; /əl/le, 211E–211F **Teaching Chart 158** **Reteach, Practice, Extend,** 189 **Language Support,** 204 **Phonics/Phonemic Awareness Practice Book,** 121–124 ☑ Review /ər/, /ən/, /əl/; /ü/; /ôr/; /îr/, 211G–211H **Teaching Chart 159** **Reteach, Practice, Extend,** 190 **Language Support,** 205 **Phonics/Phonemic Awareness Practice Book,** 121–124 **Minilessons,** 187, 193, 197, 199, 201 ⓘ Intervention Program	Read **Read Self-Selected Books** ☑ Review Summarize, 211I–211J **Teaching Chart 160** **Reteach, Practice, Extend,** 191 **Language Support,** 206 ☑ Review Suffixes, 211K–211L **Teaching Chart 161** **Reteach, Practice, Extend,** 192 **Language Support,** 207 **Listening, Speaking, Viewing, Representing,** 211N Look at Books Make a Book Cover **Minilessons,** 187, 193, 197, 199, 201 ⓘ Intervention Program
Activity **Science,** 184; **Art,** 190	Activity **Social Studies,** 194	Activity **Math,** 200
Writing Prompt: What new thing would you like to learn? Do you know someone who could teach you? Why do you want to learn to do or make this thing? **Expository Writing,** 211M Prewrite, Draft	**Writing Prompt:** Write an invitation to a surprise party. Be sure to include where and when the party will be, and who it is for. **Expository Writing,** 211M Revise **Meeting Individual Needs for Writing,** 211N	**Writing Prompt:** Think of someone you would like to surprise. What would you do? Tell about it. **Expository Writing,** 211M Edit/Proofread, Publish
Practice and Write: Possessive Pronouns, 211P Daily Language Activity: Write possessive nouns correctly. **Grammar Practice Book,** 143	**Review and Practice: Possessive Pronouns,** 211P Daily Language Activity: Write possessive nouns correctly. **Grammar Practice Book,** 144	**Assess and Reteach: Possessive Pronouns,** 211P Daily Language Activity: Write possessive nouns correctly. **Grammar Practice Book,** 145, 146
Practice and Extend: Words with Blends, 211R **Spelling Practice Book,** 144	**Proofread and Write: Words with Blends,** 211R **Spelling Practice Book,** 145	**Assess and Reteach: Words with Blends,** 211R **Spelling Practice Book,** 146

Link
Language Arts

Read Aloud

Reading to Me

a poem by Jeff Moss

When I was little, Mom would read to me in bed.

I'd lie under the covers with my eyes closed

And the sound of her voice would make me feel safe and sleepy at the same time.

Sometimes, even with the good stories, I'd fall asleep before the end.

Now I'm bigger and I can read by myself but still, every once in a while, when I'm feeling sad or something,

I'll ask Mom and she'll come in and sit on the edge of the bed and touch my head

And read to me again.

Oral Comprehension

LISTENING AND SPEAKING Encourage children to think about the author's purpose by reading aloud this poem. When you have finished, ask, "Why do you think the author wanted to write this poem?" Then ask, "If you were going to write a poem, would you rather write to entertain people or to share a special feeling? Why?"

GENRE STUDY: POETRY Discuss the literary devices and techniques used in "Reading to Me."

- Ask: *Did you enjoy listening to this poem? What types of poems do you enjoy listening to most?*
- Tell children that poems do not always rhyme. Ask children to determine if there is a rhyme scheme in this poem.
- Have children close their eyes and picture the events in the poem. Discuss how the choice of words paints a picture of the events.

Activity Encourage children to express how they feel about a special moment. Suggest that they think of images that might be connected with the moment. Encourage them to paint their feelings about the moment, and to feel free to use colors to express their feelings. ▶ **Visual**

Develop Phonological Awareness

Blend Sounds

Phonemic Awareness

MATERIALS
- Phonics Picture Cards

Teach Hold up the Phonics Picture of the cat. Tell a story, such as the following, asking children to blend each segmented word as you say it. *My cat's name is* /t/-/e/-/d/. (Ted) *He likes to hide under the* /t/-/a/-/b/-/əl/. (table) *His favorite* /f/-/ü/-/d/ *is fish.* (food) *His whiskers make me* /g/-/i/-/g/-/əl/. (giggle)

Practice Use the following list of words and the Phonics Picture for *turtle* to create other blending stories: *turtle, clue, large, hawk, dinner, apple, feather,* and *oven.*

Segment Sounds

Phonemic Awareness

Teach Invite children to play a variation of Duck-Duck-Goose called Sounds and Words. Sit children in a circle. Walk around the circle tapping them on the head as you say, for example: /w/-/i/-/g/-/əl/, /w/-/i/-/g/-/əl/, /w/-/i/-/g/-/əl/, *wiggle!* Whoever is tapped when you say the whole word is the "goose" and must chase you around the circle until you take a seat or you are tagged.

Practice To continue, whisper one of the following words to the child who is the "goose": *letter, float, boys, home, kitten,* and *marble.*

Substitute Sounds

Phonemic Awareness

MATERIALS
- Word Building Boxes from *Word Building Cards*
- red and yellow counters

Teach Distribute Word Building Boxes and red and yellow counters to each child. Say /b/-/a/-/t-/əl/ as you place a red counter in four word boxes. Then say: *Now I'll change a sound in the word to make it* /r/-/a/-/t-/əl/. Replace the red counter in the first box with a yellow counter.

Practice Have children use their boxes and counters as you continue the exercise with these sound substitutions: *table/cable, seven/sever, goggle/giggle, battle/batter, flower/tower,* and, *tickle/tackle.*

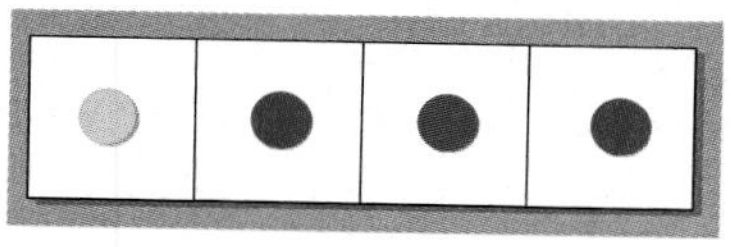

INFORMAL ASSESSMENT

Observe children as they blend, segment, and substitute sounds. If children have difficulty, see Alternate Teaching Strategies on p. T72.

Review /ər/ er; /ən/ en; /əl/ le

TESTED OBJECTIVES

Children will:

- review /ər/ *er*, /ən/ *en*, and /əl/ *le*.
- decode and read /ər/ *er*, /ən/ *en*, and /əl/ *le* words.
- use strategies to decode multisyllabic words.

MATERIALS

- **Teaching Chart 155**
- **Word Building Manipulative Cards**

Skills Finder

/ər/ *er*	
Introduce	B1: 290G-H
Review	B1: 319E-F, 319G-H; B2: 180G-H, 211E-F
Test	B1: Unit 3
Maintain	B2: 55, 257

SPELLING/PHONICS CONNECTIONS

See 5-Day Spelling Plan, pages 211Q–211R.

TEACHING TIP

DECODING MULTISYLLABIC WORDS Write these words on the board: *dinner, happen, candle.* Explain that two or more consonants appear in the middle of each word and that these break into syllables between consonants. Note that there is a vowel in each syllable. Demonstrate segmenting and blending each syllable and then blending the syllables together to pronounce the word.

TEACH

Identify Symbols for /ər/, /ən/, and /əl/ Write the following sentences on the chalkboard:

My brother is seven years older than I am.

We light candles at the table when we eat dinner.

Invite children to read the sentences and underline words containing the sounds /ər/, /ən/, /əl/.

er	en	le
ever	seven	table
brother	happen	candle
water	even	giggle
dinner	oven	handle

Teaching Chart 155

BLENDING Model and Guide Practice with /ər/ er, /ən/ en, and /əl/ le Words

- Display **Teaching Chart 155.**
- Review that /ər/ can be formed with the letters *e* and *r*.
- Model how to add the letters *er* to make the word *ever*. Read aloud the word *ever*. Ask children to identify the letters for the /ər/ sound. Ask children to blend the sounds and repeat the word with you.
- Help children repeat the procedure to form the words *brother, water,* and *dinner.*

Use the Words in Context

- Use the words in sentences to reinforce their meanings. Example: *Did you ever see something so funny?*

Repeat the Procedure

- Repeat the same procedure for the /ən/ *en* and /əl/ *le* words on the chart.

PRACTICE

SEGMENTING Build /ər/ *er*, /ən/ *en*, /əl/ *le* Words with Letter Cards

PARTNERS

Direct children to use letter cards to build, blend, and read aloud *er* words. Then have children work in pairs and repeat the steps with words that contain *en* for /ən/ and *le* for /əl/. Ask them to copy the words onto index cards, using a different color pencil or pen for letters that form /ər/, /ən/, or /əl/. ▶ **Linguistic/Visual**

ASSESS/CLOSE

Build and Read /ər/ *er*, /ən/ *en*, and /əl/ *le* Words

To assess children's ability to build and read /ər/ *er*, /ən/ *en*, and /əl/ *le* words, observe their work during the Practice activity. Ask each child to read and spell aloud one word with /ər/ *er*, /ən/ *en*, or /əl/ *le* , and to use the word orally in a sentence.

ADDITIONAL PHONICS RESOURCES

Phonics/Phonemic Awareness Practice Book, pages 121–124

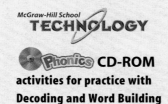

McGraw-Hill School TECHNOLOGY

Phonics CD-ROM activities for practice with Decoding and Word Building

Daily Routines

DAY 1 **Fluency** Ask children to blend the sounds silently in the following words as you point to them on the chalkboard: *another, brother, happen, seven, candle, table.* Then ask volunteers to read each word aloud.

DAY 2 **Segmenting** Write *father, eleven*, and *wiggle* on the chalkboard. Invite children to circle the letters in each word that form the /ər/, /ən/, or /əl/ sound, and to read each word aloud.

DAY 3 **Writing** Have partners write questions and answers using words with the /ər/ *er*, /ən/ *en*, and /əl/ *le* sounds. For example: *Is your mother here? No, she happens to be at the store.*

DAY 4 **Letter Substitution** Invite pairs of children to form new *er, en, le* words from the words *ever, seven*, and *table* using Word Building Manipulative Cards.

DAY 5 **Blending** Write the spelling of each sound in *seven* as you say it. Have children repeat blending the sounds and reading the word. Repeat with *mother, table*, and *water*.

Meeting Individual Needs for Phonics

EASY

Name ________ Date ________ Reteach 185

/ər/ er; /ən/ en; /əl/ le

Listen for the sounds in each word.
/ər/ as in **better**
/ən/ as in **even**
/əl/ as in **apple**

Finish the story by writing words that have the **/ər/**, **/ən/**, or **/əl/** sound in them.

My Brother's Birthday

1. It was my ___brother's___ birthday. (brother's aunt's)
2. We had cake after ___dinner___. (lunch dinner)
3. The cake had some ___candles___ on it. (candles icing)
4. My brother leaned over to blow them out. I saw what was about to ___happen___. (happen fall)
5. He spilled his glass of ___water___. (water milk)
6. I tried not to ___giggle___. (laugh giggle) I helped him clean up. Then I said, "Happy Birthday!"

6 Book 2.2/Unit 2 The Wednesday Surprise — At Home: Have children read the words they wrote aloud. 185

Reteach, 185

ON-LEVEL

Name ________ Date ________ Practice 185

/ər/ er; /ən/ en; /əl/ le

Write the word from the box that completes each sentence.

dinner	candle	wiggle	handle
oven	water	happen	mother

1. We had soup for ___dinner___.
2. We put one red ___candle___ on Billy's cake.
3. Be careful! The ___oven___ is hot.
4. The coat belonged to my ___mother___.
5. Dad washed the dishes in warm ___water___.
6. I can ___wiggle___ like a snake.
7. Anything can ___happen___!
8. The ___handle___ to the teapot broke.

8 Book 2.2/Unit 2 The Wednesday Surprise — At Home: Ask children to suggest a rhyming word for one of the words they wrote. 185

Practice, 185

CHALLENGE

Name ________ Date ________ Extend 185

/ər/ er; /ən/ en; /əl/ le

brother	dinner	seven	candle	giggle

Write a word from the box that rhymes with the last word in each line of the poem.

Juan's Story

Juan played baseball with his mother. ___brother___
The score was nine to eleven. ___seven___
Who was the winner? ___dinner___
He walked home and turned the door handle. ___candle___
His puppy saw him and began to wiggle. ___giggle___

Write two more sentences for the poem using words from the box below.

happen	water

Answers will vary.

Book 2.2/Unit 2 The Wednesday Surprise — At Home: Have children make up a new story about Juan using words from the boxes. 185

Extend, 185

TESTED OBJECTIVES

Children will decode and read /ər/*er*, /ən/*en*, and /əl/*le* words.

Apply /ər/er, /ən/en, and /əl/le

To Market! To Market!
To market, to market
With Grandmother today.
We go hand in hand
And we giggle all the way.
The basket we carry
Gets filled to the top,
With things that we buy
From each place that we stop.
And when we go home
Grandmother puts up her feet,
Time to listen to a story
And have something to eat.

Anthology pages 180–181

Read and Build Fluency

READ THE POEM Have children read the poem "To Market! To Market!" to themselves. Before you read the poem aloud, remind children to listen carefully for the /ər/, /ən/, and /əl/ sounds. As an auditory model, read the poem once more, this time in echo style. Remind children to track the print.

GROUP **REREAD FOR FLUENCY** Organize the class into three groups. Have each group take a turn reading aloud, in choral fashion. For variation, split the poem into three equal sections and have each group read a section. Children who need fluency practice can take turns reading aloud while the rest of their group follows along.

Dictate and Spell

JOURNAL **DICTATE WORDS** Say the word *giggle*. Segment it into its four individual sounds. (/g/-/i/-/g/-/əl/) Repeat the word and say it in a sentence, such as, "The cartoon made Jim giggle." After children repeat the word aloud, have them write it, making sure they have a letter or letter pattern for each sound. Continue with *when*. Then repeat with the words *grandmother* and *listen*. Ask children if they can suggest other words that have the same ending sounds as *giggle*, *happen*, and *grandmother*.

Intervention **Skills Intervention Guide,** for direct instruction and extra practice of /ər/*er*, /ən/*en*, and /əl/*le*

Build Background

Link Language Arts

Concept: Learning to Read

Evaluate Prior Knowledge

CONCEPT: LEARNING TO READ Encourage children to think of examples of things people read. Ask children why they think someone might need or want to read each item they mention.

CREATE A WORD WEB Work with children to create a word web to record different things that people read. ▶ **Linguistic**

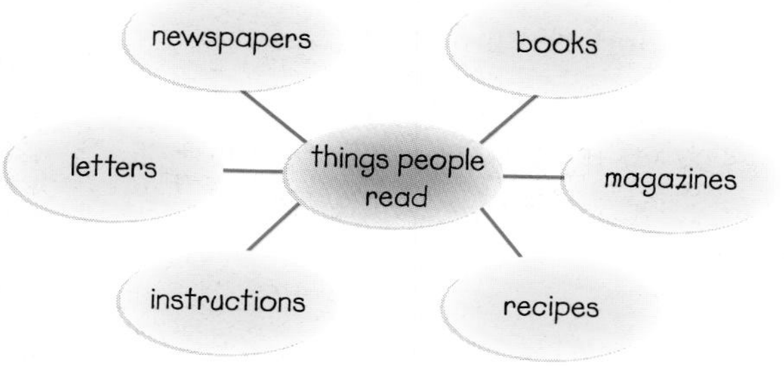

Graphic Organizer 29

DRAW A PICTURE Invite children to draw a picture of a person reading something. Ask them to write a sentence explaining what the person is reading, and why.

ONE WRITING

Develop Oral Language

ROLE-PLAY Ask children to role-play a person who receives an important letter but who has difficulty reading it.

ESL

- How would the person feel?
- Who might he or she ask for help in reading the letter?

Then have children role-play a person who receives a letter and is able to read it easily.

- What does the letter say?

▶ **Kinesthetic/Interpersonal**

Anthology and Leveled Books

DAILY Phonics ROUTINES

DAY 2 **Segmenting** Write *father, eleven,* and *wiggle* on the chalkboard. Invite children to circle the letters in each word that form the /ər/, /ən/, or /əl/ sound, and to read each word aloud.

Phonics CD-ROM

LANGUAGE SUPPORT

See Language Support Book, pages 199–202 to help build background.

TESTED OBJECTIVES

Children will use context and structural clues to determine the meanings of vocabulary words.

Definitions

chance (p. 203) a good opportunity to do something

favorite (p. 194) someone or something that you like best

nervous (p. 194) tense or worried

office (p. 184) a room or building where people work

heavy (p. 194) hard to lift, weighing a lot

wrapped (p. 194) covered with paper or material

Story Words

These words from the selection may be unfamiliar. Before children read, have them check the meanings and pronunciations of the words in a dictionary.

- business, p. 188
- astonished, p. 198
- stuck-up, p. 204

chance
favorite
nervous
office
heavy
wrapped

Vocabulary

Teach Vocabulary in Context

Identify Vocabulary Words Display **Teaching Chart 156** and read the passage with children. Have volunteers circle each vocabulary word and underline other words that are clues to its meaning.

A Birthday Dinner

1. Anna has a chance to cook a birthday dinner for Dad, so she's taking the opportunity. **2.** She decides to make the chocolate cake that he likes best. It is also Anna's favorite cake. **3.** Anna is a little nervous and worried about making the cake by herself. **4.** While Mom is working late at her office, Grandma helps Anna. **5.** Their bag of groceries is so heavy that it is hard for Anna to carry. **6.** After dinner, Dad opens the gifts Mom and Anna wrapped for him.

Teaching Chart 156

Discuss Meanings Ask questions like these to help clarify word meanings:

- When you have a chance to do something, are you allowed to do it?
- Is your favorite game the one you like the least or the best?
- Do you worry when you are nervous?
- Would a candy bar make a bag of groceries heavy? Would a gallon of milk?
- Would you spend a vacation in an office?
- Can you see what is in something that is wrapped?

Activities

Practice

Draw Clues

PARTNERS Children can work in pairs. One partner chooses a vocabulary card and, without speaking, draws a clue about the word's meaning. After the partner guesses, children switch roles.

▶ **Spatial/Linguistic**

Word Building Manipulative Cards

Write Riddles

WRITING PARTNERS Partners can write riddles that give clues about the meaning of each vocabulary word. Have them solve partners' riddles. Have children use the Glossary, as needed.

▶ **Linguistic/Interpersonal**

Assess Vocabulary

Identify Word Meaning in Context

WRITING GROUP Invite small groups to work together to write a paragraph about a surprise they enjoyed recently. Challenge them to use as many of the vocabulary words as possible. Have groups exchange papers with another group and check that the vocabulary words are used correctly.

SPELLING/VOCABULARY CONNECTIONS

See Spelling Challenge Words, pages 211Q–211R.

LANGUAGE SUPPORT

See the Language Support Book, pages 199–202, for teaching suggestions for Vocabulary.

Vocabulary PuzzleMaker

Provides vocabulary activities.

Meeting Individual Needs for Vocabulary

EASY

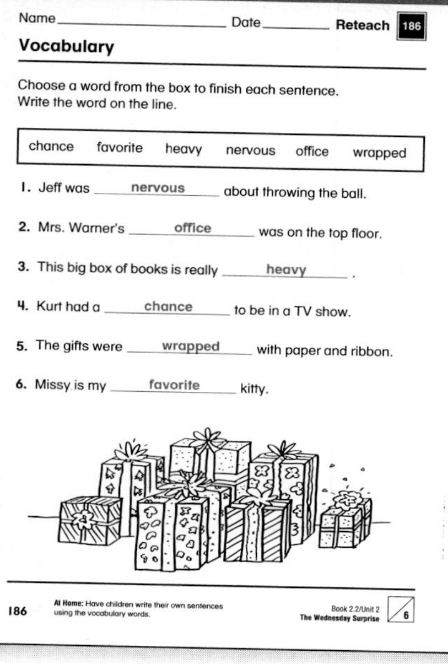

Name________________ Date________ Reteach 186

Vocabulary

Choose a word from the box to finish each sentence. Write the word on the line.

chance favorite heavy nervous office wrapped

1. Jeff was ___nervous___ about throwing the ball.
2. Mrs. Warner's ___office___ was on the top floor.
3. This big box of books is really ___heavy___.
4. Kurt had a ___chance___ to be in a TV show.
5. The gifts were ___wrapped___ with paper and ribbon.
6. Missy is my ___favorite___ kitty.

186 **At Home:** Have children write their own sentences using the vocabulary words. Book 2.2/Unit 2 **The Wednesday Surprise** 6

Reteach, 186

ON-LEVEL

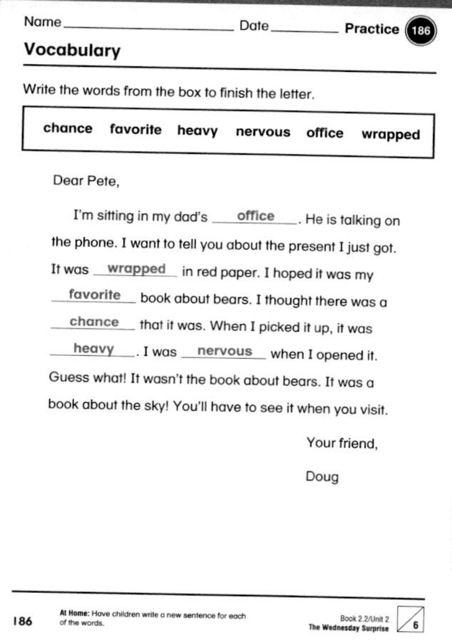

Name________________ Date________ Practice 186

Vocabulary

Write the words from the box to finish the letter.

chance favorite heavy nervous office wrapped

Dear Pete,

I'm sitting in my dad's ___office___. He is talking on the phone. I want to tell you about the present I just got. It was ___wrapped___ in red paper. I hoped it was my ___favorite___ book about bears. I thought there was a ___chance___ that it was. When I picked it up, it was ___heavy___. I was ___nervous___ when I opened it. Guess what! It wasn't the book about bears. It was a book about the sky! You'll have to see it when you visit.

Your friend,

Doug

186 **At Home:** Have children write a new sentence for each of the words. Book 2.2/Unit 2 **The Wednesday Surprise** 6

Practice, 186

ON-LEVEL

MOM'S SECRET

"How did that happen?" I asked.

"When I came to this country I did not know English. I can speak it now. But I never had the chance to learn how to read it."

"I will help you learn now," I said.

And together we sat down to read a book.

McGraw-Hill School Division

At Home: Discuss with children the importance of reading. Why is it important to read? What are some of the children's favorite books?

4

186a

Practice, 186a
Take-Home Story

CHALLENGE

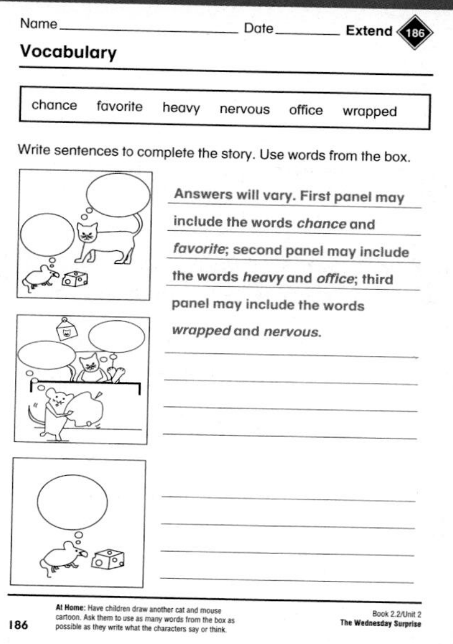

Name________________ Date________ Extend 186

Vocabulary

chance favorite heavy nervous office wrapped

Write sentences to complete the story. Use words from the box.

Answers will vary. First panel may include the words *chance* and *favorite*; second panel may include the words *heavy* and *office*; third panel may include the words *wrapped* and *nervous*.

186 **At Home:** Have children draw another cat and mouse cartoon. Ask them to use as many words from the box as possible as they write what the characters say or think. Book 2.2/Unit 2 **The Wednesday Surprise**

Extend, 186

Comprehension

Prereading Strategies

PREVIEW AND PREDICT Have children read the title and the names of the author and illustrator aloud. Take a **picture walk** through the story's illustrations. Discuss what clues the pictures provide about the story.

- What clues do the pictures show about what the characters will do in the story?
- Is this a realistic story or is it a fable? How can you tell? (Realistic story; it tells about events that could happen in real life.) ***Genre***
- What is this story most likely about?

Have children write their predictions about what will happen in the story in a chart as shown below.

PREDICTIONS	WHAT HAPPENED
The surprise will be for someone's birthday.	
The surprise will be from Anna and Grandma.	

SET PURPOSES Ask children what they would like to learn as they read the story.

THE WEDNESDAY SURPRISE

by Eve Bunting

I like surprises. But the one Grandma and I are planning for Dad's birthday is the best surprise of all.

illustrated by Donald Carrick

182

Meeting Individual Needs • Grouping Suggestions for Strategic Reading

EASY

Read Together Invite children to read aloud as you read, or have them use the **Listening Library.** Model the strategy of paying attention to the sequence of events in the story in order to understand what happens better.

ON-LEVEL

Guided Instruction Read the story with the class, using Comprehension prompts. You may want to have children read the story first on their own. Monitor any difficulties children have while reading on their own to determine what to emphasize. After reading the story with children, have them reread it using the rereading suggestions on page 206.

CHALLENGE

Read Independently Remind children that paying attention to when things happen in a story makes it easier to organize information and to understand events. After reading, have children retell story events in the order in which they occurred. Children can also use the questions on page 208 for a group discussion.

Comprehension

- Phonics Apply /ər/ *er*, /ən/ *en*, /əl/ *le*
- Apply Sequence of Events

STRATEGIC READING When we pay attention to the order in which things happen in a story, it helps us to remember what happens. Before we begin reading, let's prepare Sequence of Events charts so we can write down story notes.

Sequence of Events

↓

Sequence of Events

↓

Sequence of Events

1 **SEQUENCE OF EVENTS** Let's look at the picture on page 183. What are the characters doing as the story begins? (They are reading a book together.)

Genre

Realistic Fiction

Remind children that realistic fiction:

- has believable characters that seem to experience human emotions.
- tells about events that could and often do happen.
- can take place in any setting of the world.

Activity After children read *The Wednesday Surprise,* ask them to find examples in the illustrations of a character showing emotion. Then invite volunteers to compare their experiences with planning or receiving a surprise with the experiences of the characters in the selection. Discuss how the plot might change if the story was set in a different location.

LANGUAGE SUPPORT

A blackline master of the Sequence of Events chart is available in the **Language Support Book**, page 203.

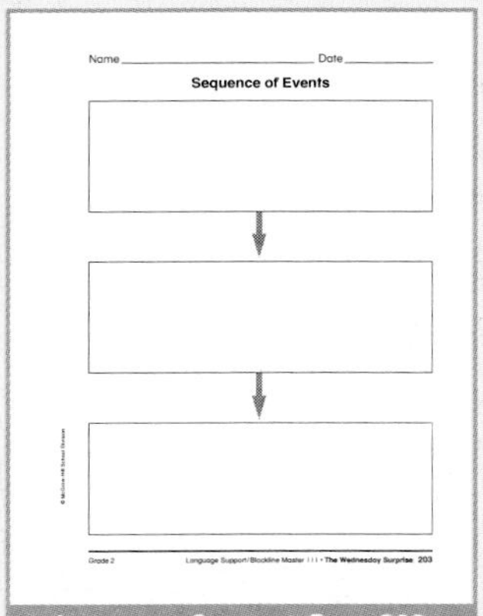
Name Date
Sequence of Events

Language Support, Page 203

Comprehension

2 **SEQUENCE OF EVENTS** Grandma stays with Anna on Wednesday nights. What does Anna do first while she waits for Grandma to arrive? (She makes breath pictures.) When she sees Grandma what does she do next? (She tells Sam.) What does Anna do after Sam answers her? (She goes downstairs to wait.)

MODEL I know that certain words give me clues about the order of events in a story. For example the word *when* is a clue. The story says that *when* she sees Grandma, Anna calls, "Sam! She's here!" Anna does not tell this to Sam before she sees Grandma coming. The word *when* is telling me that something has to happen before something else can happen.

We work on it Wednesday nights. On Wednesdays Mom has to stay late at the office and my brother, Sam, goes to basketball practice at the Y. That's when Grandma rides the bus across town to stay with me.

I watch for her from the window and I blow on the glass
2 to make breath pictures while I wait. When I see her I call:
3 "Sam! She's here!" and he says it's okay to run down, down the
4 long stairs and wait by the door.

"Grandma!" I call.

Activity

Cross Curricular: Science

WHAT'S IN A BREATH? Tell children that they will be doing an experiment that will help them learn what's in a breath.

- Provide drinking glasses, plastic bowls, ice cubes, and paper towels.
- Partners can put a glass in a bowl of ice while counting to 100. One partner wipes off the glass and breathes on it.
- Explain that breath contains tiny droplets of water that appear when they touch the glass.

▶ **Logical/Kinesthetic**

Comprehension

3 **Phonics** **/ər/** Which word in the first paragraph on page 184 has /ər/ at the end? (*brother*) ***Graphophonic Cues***

4 **SEQUENCE OF EVENTS** Remind children that a sequence of events can be identified by the use of "time" words such as *first, then, next,* or *before*. Ask children to look at the text on page 184 and to identify the time words. (*when, while*) Write their answers on the chalkboard. Have children read aloud the sentences that contain these "time" words.

LANGUAGE SUPPORT

ESL Read the second paragraph aloud and ask ꞏhildren how the girl feels about her ꞏrandmother's visit. (She's happy and excited.) Ask how they know this. (She calls out, "Sam! She's here!" and she runs down the stairs to wait by the door.)

Comprehension

5 Look at the illustration on page 186. What are Grandma and Anna doing? (They are preparing dinner.) ***Make Inferences***

6 **SEQUENCE OF EVENTS** After Grandma and Anna meet and hug, what does Anna do? (She helps carry Grandma's bag.)

Fluency

READ DIALOGUE

PARTNERS

Model how to use expression when reading dialogue.

Model the difference in expression between reading a statement, a question, and an exclamation. Guide children to see how your voice rises at the end of a question.

Invite partners to read the parts of Grandma and Anna on page 187. Ask children to make up words for Grandma and Anna to say in place of the narration. Encourage children to make their voices and facial expressions appropriate for the different characters.

"Anna!" She's hurrying, her big, cloth bag bumping against her legs.

We meet and hug. She tells me how much I've grown since last week and I tell her how much she's grown, too, which is our joke. Between us we carry her lumpy bag upstairs. (6)

I show Grandma my breath picture, if it's still there. Mostly she knows what it is. Mostly she's the only one who does.

On Wednesday nights we have hot dogs.

"Have you heard from your dad?" Grandma asks Sam. (7)

187

Comprehension

(7) A new character is introduced in the illustration on page 187. Who is he, and how do you know? (The other person is Sam. He is mentioned in the text.) Based on what Anna has already told you, what do you think Sam will do after dinner? (He will go to basketball practice.) ***Make Inferences***

Let's fill in our sequence chart with what has happened in the story so far.

Sequence of Events

Anna waits for Grandma's visits on Wednesdays.

↓

Grandma, Anna, and Sam eat dinner.

Minilesson

REVIEW

Suffixes

Review the meaning of suffixes. (an ending that changes the meaning of a base word)

- Have children locate words on page 187 that contain a base word and a suffix. Ask children to identify the base word and the suffix for each word.
- Tell students that the *–y* suffix means "full of." As a class, determine the meaning of the word *lumpy*.

Activity Have children write a paragraph describing a big, lumpy bag. Encourage students to use descriptive words and words with suffixes in their writing.

Comprehension

8 **SEQUENCE OF EVENTS** What is the first thing that Grandma and Anna do when Sam leaves? (They do the dishes.) What do they do next? (They start to read together.)

9 How does the illustration on pages 188–189 help you understand the events that are occurring? (Some of the books are out of the bag. Anna and Grandma both have an open book.) ***Make Inferences***

Visual Literacy

VIEWING AND REPRESENTING

Discuss how the artist shows the family resemblance among the characters. Invite children to look carefully at the illustration on pages 188–189. What is the resemblance, if any, between Anna and Grandma? Ask children to look back at the illustration on pages 186–187. In what ways does Sam look like his grandmother and his sister?

"He'll be back Saturday, same as always," Sam says. "In time for his birthday."

"His birthday?" Grandma raises her eyebrows as if she'd forgotten all about that.

Grandma is some actress!

8 When Sam goes she and I do the dishes. Then we get down to business.

I sit beside her on the couch and she takes the first picture book from the bag. We read the story together, out loud, and when we finish one book we start a second.

10 We read for an hour, get some ice cream, then read some more.

11

188

189

Comprehension

10 **Phonics** ***/ən/en*** Ask children to identify the letters that stand for the /ən/ sound. What word(s) can they find that end with /ən/ on page 188? (*forgotten*) ***Graphophonic Cues***

11 What activity do Grandma and Anna do together on Wednesday evenings? (read) In the illustration on page 189, who is reading the story? How do you know? (Grandma; she is holding the book and turning the pages.) ***Make Inferences***

TEACHING TIP

REALISTIC FICTION Remind children of the elements of realistic fiction. Suggest they use the pictures to help identify story elements that are real. Discuss things they eat for lunch and activities they do with their own family members. Compare these to what happens in the story.

Comprehension

12 What do you see in the illustration that tells you Grandma is getting ready to leave? (Anna is holding her coat.)
Make Inferences

Activity

Cross Curricular: Art

WHAT CAN YOU SHARE? Children can share artistic activities with older adults at a local senior center.

- Invite children to share with adults at a local senior center family experiences they have had.
- Help children and adults at the center plan ways to depict these experiences in murals, photo collages, video, drawings, embroidery, crafts, or other artwork.

▶ **Kinesthetic/Interpersonal**

Grandma gives me another hug. “Only seven years old and smart as paint already!”

I’m pleased. “They’re all going to be so surprised on Saturday,” I say. 13

When Sam comes home we play card games, and when Mom comes she plays, too.

“You’ll be here for the birthday dinner?” Mom asks as Grandma is getting ready to leave.

“Oh yes, the birthday,” Grandma says vaguely, as if she’d forgotten again. As if we hadn’t been working on our special surprise for weeks and weeks. Grandma is tricky. 14

“I’ll be here,” she says.

Comprehension

13 Based on what Grandma and Anna are doing and saying, do you think the birthday surprise will be successful? Why or why not? (Yes. Anna says, “They’re all going to be so surprised …” and both Grandma and Anna seem happy.) ***Character/Make Predictions***

14 What do Grandma’s actions tell you about the surprise? (She really wants to keep it a secret.) Do you have enough information now to know what the surprise will be? Why or why not? (Yes, we know that Anna is teaching Grandma to read.) ***Character/Make Inferences***

MODEL When I am planning a surprise for someone in my family, I get very excited, just like Anna. If I am working on the surprise with a friend, we both work really hard to keep it a secret, just like Anna and Grandma are doing in the story. If someone asks me something about the surprise, I might answer vaguely just like Grandma did. Then I won’t give that person any clues about the surprise.

LANGUAGE SUPPORT

ESL Reread aloud the last two paragraphs on page 91, modeling how to say something aguely. Explain that when something said vaguely, it is not clear or definite. Invite children to practice answering the following question vaguely: What are you going to do this weekend?

Comprehension

15 As Sam carries Grandma's bag to the bus stop, he jokingly asks her if she has bricks in it. The author writes, "That makes her smile." Why do you think the author wrote that? (The author wants to show that Grandma knows that Sam doesn't suspect her surprise.) ***Author's Craft***

16 **SEQUENCE OF EVENTS** Let's review what has happened in the story so far by referring to our Sequence of Events chart.

Sequence of Events

Anna waits for Grandma's visits on Wednesdays.

↓

Grandma, Anna, and Sam eat dinner.

↓

Grandma and Anna read together.

↓

Grandma answers Mom's question vaguely about whether she will be there for the birthday dinner.

↓

Dad comes home on Saturday.

Sam walks Grandma to the bus stop. As they're going down the stairs I hear him say: "What have you got in this bag, Grandma? Bricks?" 15

That makes me smile.

Dad comes home Saturday morning, and we rush at him with our *Happy Birthdays*. He has brought Sam a basketball magazine and me a pebble, smooth and speckled as an egg, for my rock collection. 16 17 18

"I found it in the desert, close to the truck stop," he says. "It was half covered with sand."

I hold it, imagining I can still feel the desert sun hot inside it. How long did it lie there? What kind of rock is it?

193

Comprehension

17 Do you think Dad will be surprised? Why or why not? (Yes, he does not know that Anna has been teaching Grandma how to read.) ***Make Predictions***

18 **Phonics** **/əl/** What word on page 193 ends with the /əl/ sound? (*pebble*) What is the spelling for the /əl/ sound? *(le)* ***Graphophonic Cues***

Minilesson

REVIEW/MAINTAIN

Context Clues

Remind children that they can use context clues to find out the meaning of words or phrases they don't understand. They can find clues in the text and picture clues around an unfamiliar word.

Ask children to reread the passage about the pebble on page 193. What words or phrases help the reader to understand the meaning of *pebble*?

Activity Have children use context clues in drawing the pebble Dad bought Anna for her rock collection.

Comprehension

19 Why does Dad go to sleep during the day? (He drove all night.) *Make Inferences*

20 **Phonics** /ər/ Name some words that end with /ər/ on page 194. (*water, dinner*) How is the /ər/ sound spelled? (*er*) ***Graphophonic Cues***

21 **SEQUENCE OF EVENTS** Reread the passage about preparations for the birthday dinner. Which preparations did Anna, Sam, and their mother do first? (They made the pot roast and wrapped the gifts.) How do we know? (The story states: *we've made the pot roast*—it took place in the past. Other preparations are taking place in the present, such as "frost the cake.")

22 Why is Anna nervous? (She is excited about the surprise; she doesn't want the surprise spoiled.) ***Character/Make Inferences***

Dad has stopped to pick wildflowers for Mom. They're wilting and she runs to put them in water. Then Dad has to go to bed because he has been driving
19 his big truck all through the night.

While Dad sleeps, Sam and I hang red and blue streamers in the living room. We help Mom frost the cake. We've made Dad's
20 favorite dinner, pot roast, and
21 our gifts are wrapped and ready.

I watch for Grandma and help carry the bag upstairs. Wow! Sam should feel how heavy it is now! Grandma has brought a ton of books. We hide the bag behind the couch. I am sick from being
22 nervous.
23

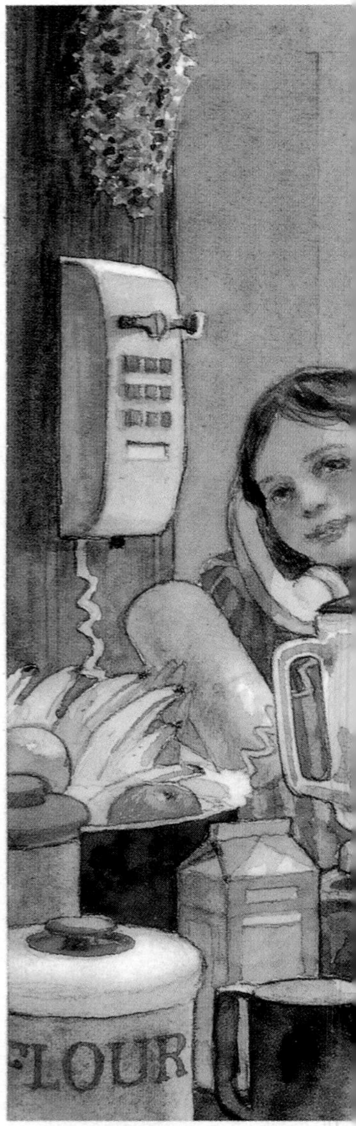

194

Activity

Cross Curricular: Social Studies

LEARNING ABOUT DESERTS In *The Wednesday Surprise,* Dad drives a truck in a desert. Provide children with atlases, reference books about deserts, pencils, and paper. Children will research deserts in the United States.
▶ **Linguistic/Spatial**

RESEARCH AND INQUIRY Divide class into groups. Assign each group to a different desert in the United States.

interNET CONNECTION Children can learn more about deserts by visiting ***www.mhschool.com/reading.***

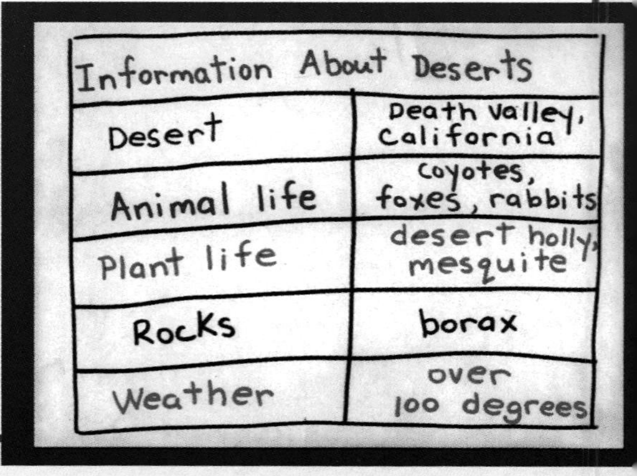

Information About Deserts	
Desert	Death Valley, California
Animal life	coyotes, foxes, rabbits
Plant life	desert holly, mesquite
Rocks	borax
Weather	over 100 degrees

Comprehension

23 The characters' feelings affect their actions and what happens in a story. What actions in the story tell you how the family feels about Dad? (Anna and Grandma are planning a surprise for him. Everyone is working together to make his favorite dinner.) How do you think Grandma feels about Dad? What do you think the title of the story might have to do with how Grandma feels about Dad? (She wants to give him a special surprise to show him how she feels about him.) ***Character***

24 What are the characters doing in the illustration on page 195? Imagine that you are preparing a surprise party for someone. Who would like to role-play? What would you do? ***Role-Play***

LANGUAGE SUPPORT

ESL PARTNERS Reread the last paragraph on ɔage 194. Point out the phrase *a ton of ɔooks*. Ask children if they know the meaning of a *ton*. Explain to children hat the author uses the word *ton* in his sentence to help the reader imagine the heaviness of Grandma's bag. ell children that in the context of this paragraph the word *ton* means "a lot of something." Have the children work with a partner to write sentences using the word *ton* to describe something. (Answers will vary. For example: Dad packed a ton of clothes inside his suitcase. Mom and I bought a ton of food at the grocery store.)

Comprehension

25 Look closely at the illustration on page 196. Do you think Anna's Dad knows what the surprise is yet? Why or why not? (No, Grandma is not reading with Anna in the picture.) ***Make Inferences***

26 **SEQUENCE OF EVENTS** Let's fill in our chart with what we know so far.

Sequence of Events

Anna waits for Grandma's visits on Wednesdays.

↓

Grandma, Anna, and Sam eat dinner.

↓

Grandma and Anna read together.

↓

Grandma answers Mom's question vaguely about whether she will be there for the birthday dinner.

↓

Dad comes home on Saturday.

↓

While Dad sleeps, everyone prepares for the birthday dinner.

↓

Grandma and Anna hide the bag of books.

196

Grandma usually has seconds but tonight she doesn't. I don't either. I can tell Mom is worried about the pot roast but Grandma tells her it's very good. **26**

"Are you feeling well, Mama?" Dad asks Grandma. "How are your knees?"

"Fine. Fine. The knees are fine."

Dad blows out the birthday candles and we give him his gifts. Then Grandma shoots a glance in my direction and I go for the big bag and drag it across to the table. I settle it on the floor between us. **27**

"Another present?" Dad asks.

"It's a special surprise for your birthday, Dad, from Grandma and me." **28**

197

Comprehension

27 What does Dad think is going to happen after Anna puts Grandma's bag on the floor? (He is going to get another present.) What do you think is going to happen next? (Grandma is going to read.) ***Make Predictions***

28 How do you think Anna's Mom and Dad are feeling when Anna tells them that a surprise is in the bag? (curious) ***Character/Make Inferences***

P/I **CONTRACTIONS** Ask children to find three words with apostrophes in the first paragraph. (*doesn't, don't, it's*) Do they know why the apostrophes are there?

P/I PREVENTION/INTERVENTION

ONTRACTIONS Write *doesn't,* *›n't,* and *it's* on the chalkboard. ›mind children that they are called ›ntractions and that the apostrophe kes the place of a letter or letters. ave volunteers write the two words r which each contraction stands.

Have the class brainstorm a list of other contractions and the words for which they stand. *Syntactic Cues*

Minilesson

REVIEW/MAINTAIN

Phonics and Decoding Consonant Blends /pr/*pr*

Have children read aloud the question: *"Another present?" Dad asks* on page 197.

Ask children to identify the two letters that form the /pr/ sound. Then ask children to find other words in the story that contain the /pr/ sound and write them in their own sentences.

Activity Have children brainstorm other /pr/ words and write them on index cards. Put the children's index cards in a box. Have each child pick a card from the box and write a sentence using the word on the card.

Phonics CD-ROM Have children use the interactive phonics activities on the CD-ROM for more reinforcement.

Comprehension

29 What is "The Wednesday Surprise"? (The surprise is that Grandma has learned to read.) Did you think that Anna's parents would be surprised? Why or why not? ***Draw Conclusions/Character***

30 After Grandma finishes reading *Popcorn,* she gives the book back to whom? (Anna) How do you know? (The quote is, "She gives the book back to me." *Me,* or the narrator in the story, is Anna.) ***Make Inferences***

SELF-MONITORING STRATEGY

REREAD Use this opportunity to explore whether children were surprised to discover that Grandma, not Anna, was the person learning to read. Ask the children to read the story again. The author was very clever about hiding the real surprise. What clues falsely suggested that Anna was the student? Did any clues hint at the real surprise?

MODEL I was very surprised to find out that Anna was teaching Grandma to read and not the other way around. What made me think that Anna was the student? Maybe it was the fact that Anna was seven. I'm going to look back through the story to see what else I can find.

My heart's beating awfully fast as I unzip the bag and give the first book to Grandma. It's called *Popcorn.* I squeeze Grandma's hand and she stands
29 and begins to read.

Mom and Dad and Sam are all astonished.

Dad jumps up and says: "What's this?" but Mom shushes him and pulls him back down.

Grandma has the floor. She finishes *Popcorn,* which takes quite a while, gives the book
30 back to me and beams all over her face.

Comprehension

31 What do you think Anna is feeling as Grandma reads *Popcorn*? (She feels happy and proud.) How do you know? (She is smiling in the picture on page 199.) ***Make Inferences***

32 How do you think Grandma is feeling as she reads the book? (She is proud.) Who wishes to volunteer role-playing Grandma reading *Popcorn*? ***Make Inferences***

Minilesson

REVIEW/MAINTAIN

Summarize

Remind children that summarizing a story retells the main events that have happened so far. Work with children to write a summary of the story. Have them:

- refer to their sequence of events charts.
- look at what Anna and Grandma are doing in the pictures.

Activity Ask children to make story maps to add to their Sequence of Events chart. First, ask them to fill in the story's main character(s), setting, and the beginning or first main event. Complete the chart listing other important events in the order in which they occur. Encourage children to use the chart as a guide to retell the story to another classmate.

Comprehension

33 Why do you think Grandma chose to go to Anna to learn to read rather than to classes as Anna's mother had suggested? (Responses will vary: She felt more comfortable with family; she knew it would help Anna's confidence; it was something they could share together.) ***Character***

34 How does Mom feel about Grandma's surprise? (She is excited.) How do you know? (She is beaming.) Role-play Mom's reaction to Grandma's surprise. ***Role-Play***

"My goodness!" Mom is beaming too. "When did this wonderful thing happen? When did you learn to read?"

"Anna taught me," Grandma says.

"On Wednesday nights," I add. "And she took the books home, and practiced."

33 "You were always telling me to go to classes, classes, classes," Grandma says to Dad. She looks at Mom. "You must learn to read, you say. So? I come to Anna."

34

200

Activity

Cross Curricular: Math

GRAPH TRANSPORTATION In *The Wednesday Surprise,* Grandma takes the bus to Anna's house. Make a bar graph on the chalkboard that shows the number of children in the class in increments of five up the left side, and across the bottom, modes of transportation. Suggest they make each bar a different color when recording data.

- Ask children to help you list types of transportation.
- Record the number of children who have used each listed type of transportation. ▶ **Logical/Spatial**

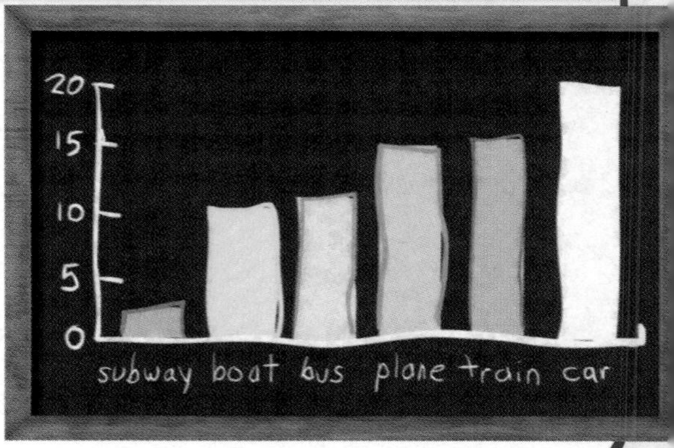

Comprehension

BLENDING with /ü/*oo, ue* Which sound do you hear in the word *too* that you also hear in the word *blue*? (/ü/) ***Graphophonic Cues***

35 Look at the illustration on page 201. How does Anna feel about Grandma's accomplishment? (She is proud.) How do you know? (She is holding the book and smiling.) ***Make Inferences***

PREVENTION/INTERVENTION

LENDING with /ü/*oo, ue* Remind ıildren that there are different ›ellings for the /ü/ sound. Write the ›ords *too* and *blue* on the chalkboard. ›vite a volunteer to underline the let- ›rs that stand for /ü/ in each word.

- Brainstorm with children other words with /ü/ and write them on the chalkboard. Some examples are: *true, broom, afternoon, glue, clue, tooth*. Have volunteers blend the sounds in each word together and read the word. Then tell the children to underline the spelling of /ü/ in each word.
- Invite children to use the words in sentences that reinforce their meanings. *Graphophonic Cues*

Minilesson

REVIEW/MAINTAIN

Making Inferences

Remind children that when we make inferences, we think about what we have read and what we already know. This helps us understand a selection.

- Ask the class to reread the last paragraph on page 200. What inferences can they make about why Grandma chose Anna as her teacher. (Answers will vary.)
- Ask children to make an inference about how Grandma feels about Dad. What clues were used to form their inferences?

Activity Ask children how they might make inferences about what is inside a wrapped package. (Answers will vary.) Invite children to pantomime their special techniques.

▶ **Kinesthetic**

Comprehension

36 How does Grandma feel? (proud) What does it make her want to do? (read more books) ***Character***

37 Writers may leave out or only give hints about certain parts of a story. Readers can then draw conclusions based on facts they already have or their own experience to help them understand what the story leaves out. Look at the illustration on these pages and reread page 203. Try to draw a conclusion about why Grandma never learned to read. What are some possible reasons why Grandma never learned to read? (She had to leave school at an early age.) ***Draw Conclusions***

202

CULTURAL PERSPECTIVES

BIRTHDAY CELEBRATIONS AROUND THE WORLD Share with children that birthdays are celebrated in many different ways around the world. For example, in Denmark a flag is flown outside a window to designate that someone who lives in that house is having a birthday.

RESEARCH AND INQUIRY Have children research how birthdays are celebrated in other countries by using children's reference materials. Then help them make a class video depicting birthdays around the world.
▶ **Kinesthetic/Visual**

In Mexico, children try to break open a pinata filled with small candy, fruit and toys.

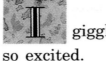

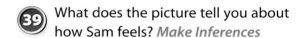

I giggle because I'm so excited. 36

Grandma reads and acts out *The Easter Pig*. And *The Velveteen Rabbit*. 37

"It's much smarter if you learn to read when you're young," she tells Sam sternly. "The chance may pass along with the years." 38

Sam looks hurt. "But I *can* read, Grandma."

Comprehension

SUFFIX *-ly* Reread the third paragraph on this page. What do you think *sternly* means? (Grandma is speaking in a stern, or firm, way.)

38 What reasons might Grandma have for telling Sam about the importance of learning to read when you are young? (Reading is important for most jobs and adds enjoyment to your life.) Do you agree with her? Explain your answer. ***Make Inferences***

39 What does the picture tell you about how Sam feels? ***Make Inferences***

PREVENTION/INTERVENTION

UFFIX: *-ly* Remind students that hen *-ly* is added to a word, it forms n adverb that describes a way of acting. Why is Grandma speaking to Sam a stern way or *sternly*? (She wants to ommunicate to Sam how important it is to learn how to read.) Write the following words on the chalkboard: *quickly, quietly*. Have students use each word in a sentence that describes a way of acting. ***Semantic Cues***

Comprehension

40 Why does Dad think Grandma wants to read everything in the world? (She takes out another book.) Do you think she and Anna might continue to read together on Wednesdays? Is it possible that Anna and Grandma might choose to read together at a different time now? Why or why not? (They don't need to keep their reading a secret.) ***Make Inferences***

Writer's Craft

WORD CHOICE

Explain: An author chooses words carefully to make a story interesting. Vivid language can help enhance the mood of a story and give the story greater meaning.

Direct children to the following example on page 204: *He's grinning, but his eyes are brimming over with tears and he and Mom are holding hands across the table.* Discuss how the words "brimming over" help the reader to better understand that Dad is overwhelmed with pride.

WRITING Write about a time when you were proud about something you accomplished. Use descriptive words to tell how the people around you reacted.

"Nevertheless." She takes out another book.

"Are you going to read everything in that bag, Mama?" Dad asks her. He's grinning, but his eyes are brimming over with tears and he and Mom are holding hands across the table.

40 "Maybe I will read everything
41 in the world now that I've started," Grandma says in a stuck-up way. "I've got time." She winks at me.

"So, Anna? What do you think? Was it a good surprise?"

I run to her and she puts her cheek against mine. "The best
42 ever," I say.

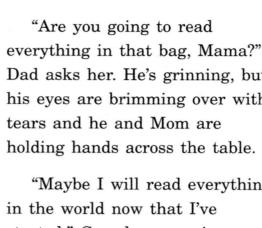

204

Comprehension

41 Let's read the following sentence on page 204: *He's grinning, but his eyes are brimming over with tears …* What pictures form in your minds when you hear that description? Look through the story for details that help form strong pictures in your mind. ***Story Elements***

42 How does Anna feel about the surprise? Why does she think it was the best ever? (Anna is overjoyed that she gave a gift that made her Grandma's life better.) ***Make Inferences***

Comprehension

43 **SEQUENCE OF EVENTS** Let's finish our charts. What events happened after Grandma and Anna hid the books?

Sequence of Events

↓

Grandma reads *Popcorn* to the family.

↓

Grandma explains that Anna taught her to read.

↓

They agree that the surprise was the best ever.

RETELL THE STORY Invite volunteers to retell important events from this story. Write the events on sentence strips and put them in "scrambled" order. Encourage children to help you rearrange the strips so events are in the correct order.

STUDENT SELF-ASSESSMENT

Have children ask themselves the following questions to assess how they are reading:

- How did paying attention to the sequence of events help me understand this story?
- How did I use words like *when* and *next* to help me figure out the order in which things were happening in the story?

TRANSFERRING THE STRATEGIES

- How can I use these strategies to help me read other stories?

43 *Meet*

Eve Bunting

There's a story about *The Wednesday Surprise,* and Eve Bunting tells about it like this: "A friend took me out to dinner and began talking about her mother, Katina, who was quite a character.

"She told a story about how she taught her mother to read English with her picture books. Every day she would bring books home from school or the library, and they would read them together. *The Wednesday Surprise* is my book, but it's Katina's story."

Ms. Bunting loves Donald Carrick's illustrations. She asked him if the kitchen in *The Wednesday Surprise* was like his kitchen. He said to her, "Oh, yes. There's always a bit of my house in my books."

206

REREADING FOR *Fluency*

Children who need fluency practice can read along silently or aloud as they listen to the recording of the story.

READING RATE When you evaluate reading rate, have children read aloud from the story for one minute. Place a stick-on note after the last word read. Count words read. To evaluate children's performance, see Running Record in the **Fluency Assessment** book.

Intervention For leveled fluency passages, lessons, and norms charts, see **Skills Intervention Guide**, Part 5, Fluency.

READ TOGETHER

Meet Donald Carrick

Donald Carrick started drawing pictures as a child, and he kept on drawing his whole life. His first job was painting signs and billboards. Later, he painted pictures for newspaper and magazine ads. His wife, Carol, wrote the first children's book he ever illustrated, *The Old Barn.* After that, Donald Carrick illustrated more than eighty picture books. Some of the most popular ones are about a boy named Christopher and his two dogs. Two other well-known books are about a boy named Patrick who imagines there are dinosaurs everywhere.

207

LITERARY RESPONSE

JICK-WRITE Invite children to record their thoughts about the story in their journals.

URNAL

ey may wish to draw pictures of the rthday celebration.

RAL RESPONSE Have children e their journal entries to discuss ese questions:

What are some other ways that Grandma could have learned to read?

- How would you describe how Anna and her grandmother feel about each other?
- If you were Anna's mother or father, what might you have said to her after the surprise?
- What do you think Grandma and Anna might want to do now that Grandma can read?

Comprehension

Return to Predictions and Purposes

Reread children's predictions about the story. Discuss the predictions, noting which needed to be revised. Then ask children if the story answered the questions they had before they read.

Have children talk about the strategy of using Sequence of Events charts. Did they feel that these were helpful in understanding what happens in the story? Why?

INFORMAL ASSESSMENT

HOW TO ASSESS

Phonics /ər/, /ən/, /əl/ Have children turn to page 204 and find and read any words with /ər/, /ən/, and /əl/. (another, table, ever)

SEQUENCE OF EVENTS Remind children how paying attention to when things happen in a story makes it easier to understand what is happening in the story. Have children role-play how the story would be different if the sequence of events were changed. (For example: Dad comes home Wednesday night while Anna and Grandma are reading.)

FOLLOW UP

Phonics /ər/, /ən/, /əl/ Continue to use words with these sounds. Have children underline the letters that represent the sounds.

SEQUENCE OF EVENTS Children who are having difficulty understanding sequence of events can draw pictures to illustrate their Sequence of Events charts.

Story Questions

Have children discuss or write answers to the questions on page 208.

Answers:

1. The surprise is that Anna has taught Grandma how to read. *Literal/Plot*
2. Anna's Dad is so happy that his mother knows how to read. *Inferential*
3. Anna feels excited and proud. *Inferential/Sequence of Events*
4. The story is about a girl and her grandmother who plan a very special surprise for the girl's father. *Critical/Summarize*
5. Fernando gives Carmina a small tree; Grandma's gift to Dad is that she learns to read. *Critical/Reading Across Texts*

Write About a Book For a full writing process lesson on expository writing, see pages 211M–211N.

Story Questions & Activities

READ TOGETHER

1. What is the surprise that Anna and Grandma have planned for Dad's birthday?
2. Why does Anna's dad cry at the surprise party?
3. How does Anna feel after Grandma starts to read?
4. What is this story mainly about?
5. Compare the gift Fernando gives Carmina in "Fernando's Gift" to Grandma's gift to Dad. What makes these gifts special?

Write About a Book

Write a report about a book you like. Include the names of the author and illustrator. Explain what the book is about and what happens in it. Include a beginning, middle, and end in your book report.

Meeting Individual Needs

EASY

Name________ Date______ Reteach 187

Story Comprehension

Fill in the circular story map with information from "The Wednesday Surprise." Answers may vary.

1. FIRST: Grandma comes over.
2. THEN: We eat dinner.
3. THEN: I help Grandma do the dishes.
4. NEXT: Grandma and I read.
5. NEXT: We play card games.
6. THEN: Dad comes home on Saturday.
7. THEN: We give Dad his birthday gifts.
8. FINALLY: Grandma reads to Dad.

Book 2.2/Unit 2 The Wednesday Surprise

At Home: Have children use a story map like the one on this page to describe a trip they took or a place they visited. 187

Reteach, 187

ON-LEVEL

Name________ Date______ Practice 187

Story Comprehension

Think about "The Wednesday Surprise." Finish each sentence by underlining the answer.

1. Grandma takes care of Anna _____.
   a. every day
   b. only on Wednesdays
2. Anna's dad is a _____.
   a. truck driver
   b. pilot
3. Anna and Grandma want to surprise Dad because _____.
   a. it is his birthday
   b. he got a new job
4. Anna and Grandma have worked together to _____.
   a. teach Anna how to read
   b. teach Grandma how to read
5. Sam and Anna decorate the house because _____.
   a. it is Dad's birthday
   b. it is a holiday
6. Grandma doesn't have seconds because _____.
   a. she is thinking about reading
   b. she is full
7. Anna is nervous at the party because _____.
   a. she wants Grandma to read well
   b. she wants to read well
8. Dad is crying at the end of the story because _____.
   a. he is sad that his surprise is over
   b. Grandma can read

Book 2.2/Unit 2 The Wednesday Surprise

At Home: Have children draw a picture of their favorite part of the story. Then ask them to write a sentence about it. 187

Practice, 187

CHALLENGE

Name________ Date______ Extend 187

Story Comprehension

Look for pictures that show students understand the story.

Draw a picture to answer each question about "The Wednesday Surprise."

1. How does Anna feel about Grandma?
2. How does Grandma feel about learning to read?
3. How does Dad feel about his family when he gets home?
4. How does Anna feel right before she gives Dad his surprise?

What would the story be like if Grandma had not learned to read? Write a sentence or two telling what might have happened. Make up a title to go with this story.

Answers will vary.

Book 2.2/Unit 2 The Wednesday Surprise

At Home: Have children draw a picture of a surprise they would like to give someone for their birthday. Ask them to write a sentence or two telling why that person would like the surprise. 187

Extend, 187

16

Make a Calendar

Anna needed to know how many days she and Grandma had to work on their surprise. A calendar would tell her. Make a calendar for yourself. Mark important days such as holidays, birthdays, and vacation dates.

ake a Book Cover

ıks are very important to Grandma and Anna. ke a book cover to protect your favorite book. brown paper bags or large sheets of paper ırap your book. Draw a scene from the book the front cover. On the back write: This k belongs to [your name goes here].

ind Out More

rthdays can be special days. hat are some other special ys that you and your family ebrate? Choose a holiday and l out more about it. Write a stcard to a friend telling what kes the day special.

209

Story Activities

Make a Calendar

Materials: paper, felt-tipped markers, ruler

GROUP Have children help you list on the chalkboard the kinds of information that appear on a calendar. Using this information, help children brainstorm ways a calendar could be organized. Ask them to draw some of their ideas. Display and discuss work.

Make a Book Cover

Materials: brown paper bags or large sheets of paper, scissors

ONE Display a variety of book covers. Have students compare and contrast what is on them. Ask children to tell what they like and what they don't like about each of them.

Find Out More

Have children pick a holiday and share how their family celebrates it. Invite them to discuss what they find special about their celebration.

*inter***NET** **CONNECTION** Have children find out more about holidays by visiting ***www.mhschool.com/reading.***

FORMAL ASSESSMENT

After page 209, see Selection Assessment.

DAILY Phonics ROUTINES

DAY 3 **Writing** Have partners write questions and answers using words with /ər/*er*, /ən/*en*, and /əl/*le* sounds. (For example: *Is your mother here? No, she happens to be at the store.*)

Phonics CD-ROM

Study Skills

VARIOUS TEXTS

TESTED OBJECTIVES

Children will use a calendar to:

- identify the day and date events occur.
- identify the number of times an event will occur.
- identify how much time is left until a certain event occurs.

PREPARE Display **Teaching Chart 157.** Tell children that Grandma and Anna use a calendar to plan their surprise. As each day passes, Anna marks the day with an *X*.

TEACH Help children use the calendar to answer the questions. Have them note which days of the week fall on which dates. Point out the special dates.

PRACTICE Have children answer questions 1–5. Review the answers with them.
1. Anna and Grandma will get new books on Monday, March 19th. **2.** four times **3.** two more times **4.** fourteen days, two weeks **5.** (Answers will vary.)

STUDY SKILLS

READ TOGETHER

Use a Calendar

Anna and Grandma use this calendar to plan their surprise. Anna marks off with an X each day that passes.

March						
Sunday	Monday	Tuesday	Wednesday	Thursday	Friday	Saturday
				1 X	2 X	3 X
4 X	5 X	6 X	7 ~~Practice reading~~	8 X	9 X	10 X
11 X	12 X	13 X	14 ~~Practice reading~~	15 X	16 X	17 X
18	19 Get new books	20	21 Practice reading	22	23	24
25	26	27	28 Practice reading	29	30 Bake cake	31 Dad's party

1. When will Anna and Grandma get new books?
2. How many days do Grandma and Anna practice reading in all?
3. How many reading days do they have left?
4. How many days are left until Dad's party?
5. On what day should Grandma and Anna mail party invitations? How many days before the party is that?

Meeting Individual Needs

EASY

Name__________ Date______ Reteach 188

Use a Calendar

A **calendar** shows you the days of the year.

Study the calendar below. It shows only two weeks of a month. Notice the days of the week along the top.

JULY						
Sun	Mon	Tues	Wed	Thurs	Fri	Sat
		1	2 vacation begins	3	4 Independence Day	5
6	7 Kate comes for a visit	8 piano lesson	9 doctor's appointment	10	11	12

Complete the questions using the calendar.

1. How many weeks does this calendar show you? 2
2. What month is this calendar showing you? July
3. What holiday is on July 4th? Independence Day
4. What happens on July 7th? Kate comes for a visit
5. Why don't the first Sunday and Monday on this calendar have numbers on them? they are not part of this month

188 **At Home:** Challenge children to look at a calendar of the year and identify the days of the week that popular holidays fall on. Book 2.2/Unit 2 **The Wednesday Surprise** 5

Reteach, 188

ON-LEVEL

Name__________ Date______ Practice 188

Use a Calendar

A **calendar** tells you the month and the day.

NOVEMBER						
Sun	Mon	Tues	Wed	Thurs	Fri	Sat
					1	2
3	4	5 Soccer	6	7	8	9
10	11	12 Soccer	13	14	15	16
17	18	19 Soccer	20	21	22	23
24	25	26 Soccer	27	28 Thanksgiving	29	30

Follow the instructions below.

1. The days of the week go in the boxes along the top. Start with Sunday in the first box. What day did you put in the last box? Saturday
2. Start the calendar with November 1 on a Friday. Then put a number in every box. There are thirty days in November. What day of the week is the 25th day? Monday
3. Put Thanksgiving in the box for the fourth Thursday of the month. What day of the month is that? 28
4. You have soccer practice every Tuesday. Mark that on the calendar. What dates did you mark? 5, 12, 19, 26

188 **At Home:** Have children mark November 17-23 with an **X** and write **vacation** through those days. Book 2.2/Unit 2 **The Wednesday Surprise** 4

Practice, 188

CHALLENGE

Name__________ Date______ Extend 188

Use a Calendar

Anna has a lot to do in March. Fill in the calendar to help Anna remember what to do each day. Write only the words that will remind Anna what she must do.

MARCH						
Sunday	Monday	Tuesday	Wednesday	Thursday	Friday	Saturday
			1 Doctor	2	3	4
5	6	7	8	9 party	10	11 Sal's house
12	13	14	15	16	17	18 swim meet
19	20	21 walk dog	22	23	24	25
26	27 book fair	28	29 band practice	30	31	

1. On Wednesday, March 1, Anna goes to the doctor.
2. On Tuesday, March 21, Anna walks Nick's dog.
3. On Thursday , March 9, Anna goes to a party.
4. On Wednesday, March 29, Anna has band practice.
5. On Saturday, March 11, Anna goes to her friend Sal's house.
6. On Monday, March 27, Anna goes to the Book Fair.
7. On Saturday, March 18, Anna has a swim meet.

Answers may vary. Sample answers are shown.

188 **At Home:** Have children make a twelve-month calendar, using one page per month. Provide old magazines and catalogues and have children cut out appropriate pictures for each month to illustrate their calendars. Book 2.2/Unit 2 **The Wednesday Surprise**

Extend, 188

TEST POWER

Read each answer before you choose the best one.

IRECTIONS:

ead the story. Then read each question about the story.

AMPLE

A Trip for Science Class

Our class took a trip to the ›ach to study the seashore. Each ›rson had a partner. Our teacher, r. Ranja, gave us a list of things look for. Mr. Ranja told us to ›ite down what we learned.

1. Find three different shells. What makes each one different?
2. Look carefully at the sand. What does it look like? Is it soft or hard?
3. Look at the seaweed. What does it look like? What other plants do you see on the beach?

1 What are the students supposed to do first?

- ○ Look at plants
- ● Find three different shells
- ○ Look at the sand
- ○ Find ten different shells

2 What's the best summary for this story?

- ● Mr. Ranja's class looked at many things at the beach.
- ○ The sand at the beach is hard.
- ○ Mr. Ranja's class took a trip to the museum.
- ○ We had partners at the beach.

211

Test Power

THE PRINCETON REVIEW

Read the Page

Explain to children that you will be reading this story as a group. You will read the story, and they will follow along in their books.

Request that children put pens, pencils, and markers away, since they will not be writing.

Discuss the Questions

QUESTION 1: Children should reread the story and look for the first task on the list, which is to find three different shells.

QUESTION 2: The children went to the beach, not to the museum, so the third choice must be wrong. Point out to children that most of the story has to do with the list of things to look for. The most reasonable choice is the first one.

Leveled Books

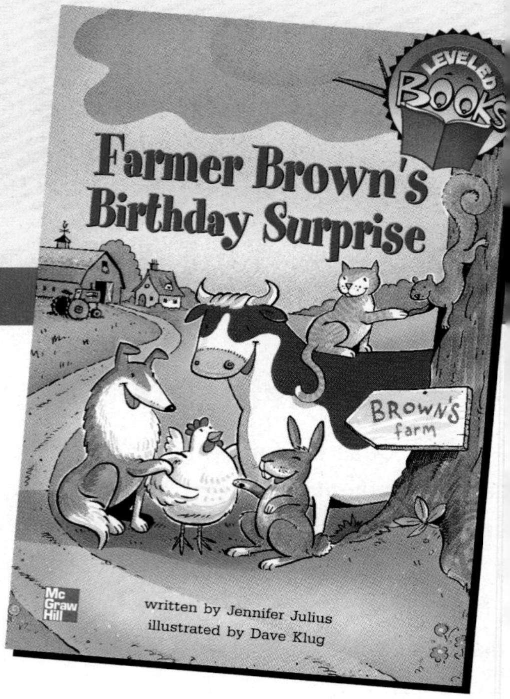

EASY

Farmer Brown's Birthday Surprise

- Phonics /ər/ *er*; /ən/ *en*; /əl/ *le*
- **Sequence of Events**
- **Instructional Vocabulary:** ***chance, favorite, heavy, nervous, office, wrapped***

Guided Reading

PREVIEW AND PREDICT Take a **picture walk** with children through page 5 of the story. Have them predict what the story is about.

SET PURPOSES Have children write and draw why they want to read *Farmer Brown's Birthday Surprise*.

READ THE BOOK Use the following questions to guide children's reading or after they have read the story independently.

Page 2: Point to the word *Farmer*. Say the sound the letters *er* make in the word. (ər) Name some other words that have the /ər/ sound. ***Phonics and Decoding***

Page 3–4: Which animal spoke first? (dog) Which animal spoke next? (chicken) ***Sequence of Events***

Page 7: Find the word *favorite*. What does squirrel think would make him Farmer Brown's favorite animal? (if Farmer Brown knew him better) ***Vocabulary***

Page 16: What did Farmer Brown do before he ate the carrot cake? (He thanked all the animals first.) ***Sequence of Events***

RETURN TO PREDICTIONS AND PURPOSES Discuss children's predictions. Ask which were close to the story and why. Did they find out what they wanted to know?

LITERARY RESPONSE Discuss these questions:

- What does this story tell you about working together?
- Do you think Farmer Brown really had a favorite animal? Why?

Also see the story questions and activity in *Farmer Brown's Birthday Surprise*.

See the Phonics **CD-ROM** for practice using words with /ər/, /ən/, and /əl/.

Intervention **Skills**

Intervention Guide, for direct instruction and extra practice of vocabulary and comprehension

Answers to Story Questions

1. Carrot cake
2. Because the animals on the farm could provide all the missing ingredients.
3. 4, 3, 2, 1, 5, eat the cake
4. The animals on the farm work together to help make a carrot cake for Farmer Brown's birthday.
5. She would have read the recipe and baked the cake.

The Story Questions and Activity below appear in the Easy Book.

Story Questions and Writing Activity

1. What kind of cake did the animals on the farm help to make?
2. Why did Dog choose to make that kind of cake?
3. In baking a cake, which of these things should you do first? Second? Third? Fourth? Fifth? After doing all these things, what would you do?
   1. Put the cake in the oven.
   2. Pour the batter into a pan.
   3. Measure everything and mix the ingredients.
   4. Look at a cookbook.
   5. Take the cake out of the oven.
4. What is the story mostly about?
5. If the grandmother from *The Wednesday Surprise* had lived on the Brown farm, how would she have helped?

Pour It On!

Look at the recipe on page 11. If you added the flour and sugar at the same time, how many total cups would you add? How many cups if you added the nuts and the milk together? The sugar and the nuts?

from *Farmer Brown's Birthday Surprise*

Leveled Books

INDEPENDENT

Sequoyah

- ☑ Phonics /ər/ *er*; /ən/ *en*; /əl/ *le*
- ☑ Sequence of Events
- ☑ Instructional Vocabulary: *chance, favorite, heavy, nervous, office, wrapped*

Guided Reading

PREVIEW AND PREDICT Take a **picture walk** to page 7. Record children's predictions.

SET PURPOSES Have children write or draw pictures that show why they want to read *Sequoyah*. For example: *I want to find out who Sequoyah is and why he is famous.*

READ THE BOOK Use questions like the following to guide children's reading or after they have read the story independently.

Page 2: Find the word *people*. Say the sound the letters *le* make in the word *people*. Look at this word. (Write the word *steeple* on the chalkboard.) Say the sound the letters *le* make in this word. ***Phonics and Decoding***

Page 5: What did Sequoyah do before he wrote the Cherokee language? (He listened for and counted the sounds in Cherokee.) ***Sequence of Events***

Page 10: Find the word *office*. Where did John Ross want to meet with the Cherokee chiefs? (his office) What is an office? What might you find in an office? ***Vocabulary***

Page 16: If someone asked you to describe Sequoyah and his work, what would you tell them? ***Summarize***

RETURN TO PREDICTIONS AND PURPOSES Discuss children's predictions. Ask which were close to the story and why. Have children review their purposes for reading. Did they find out what they wanted to know?

LITERARY RESPONSE Discuss these questions:

- Do you think Sequoyah was a hero? Why?
- Why was inventing an alphabet so important?

Also see the story questions and activity in *Sequoyah*.

See the Phonics **CD-ROM** for practice using words with /ər/, /ən/, and /əl/.

Answers to Story Questions

1. He was a Cherokee Indian.
2. They were scared.
3. Sequoyah finishes his alphabet, Sequoyah meets with John Ross, Cherokee people have their own newspaper.
4. How Sequoyah gave the Cherokee people their alphabet.
5. Answers will vary.

The Story Questions and Activity below appear in the Independent Book.

Story Questions and Writing Activity

1. Who was Sequoyah?
2. Why were the people of Sequoyah's village angry about his work with the alphabet?
3. Which of these things happens first, next, and last in the story? Sequoyah meets with John Ross, Sequoyah finishes his alphabet, Cherokee people have their own newspaper.
4. What is the main idea of the book?
5. If Anna from *The Wednesday Surprise* were to meet Ah-yoka, what might they talk about?

Secret Messages

Think about a new alphabet you could use to send secret messages to friends. Write the letters of our real alphabet. Then write a new picture or shape for some or all of the letters. Use a new alphabet to write a message.

from *Sequoyah*

Leveled Books

CHALLENGE

The Light of One Candle

- ☑ Phonics /ər/ *er*; /ən/ *en*; /əl/ *le*
- ☑ Sequence of Events
- ☑ Instructional Vocabulary: *chance, favorite, heavy, nervous, office, wrapped*

Guided Reading

PREVIEW AND PREDICT Take a **picture walk** with children through page 7 of the story. As children study the illustrations, have them predict what the story is about.

SET PURPOSES List reasons why children want to read *The Light of One Candle* on the chalkboard. Discuss their purposes.

READ THE BOOK Use questions like the following to guide children's reading or after they have read the story independently.

Page 2: Find the word *seven*. Say the sound the letters *en* make. Look at these words. (Write the words *eleven* and *heaven* on the chalkboard.) Say the sound the letters *en* make in these words. ***Phonics and Decoding***

Page 4: Find the word *chance*. What kind of *chance* did Mrs. Wheatley take? (She decided she wanted Phillis.) Have you ever taken a chance? What happened? ***Vocabulary***

Page 14: What happened to Phillis first in 1773? (She was granted her freedom) What happened to her next? (She went to England and published a book.) ***Sequence of Events***

Page 16: What did Phillis achieve in her lifetime? (She wrote poetry, and she wrote about religion and slavery.) ***Summarize***

RETURN TO PREDICTIONS AND PURPOSES Discuss children's predictions. Were children's purposes for reading the story met?

LITERARY RESPONSE Discuss these questions:

- What do you think was the best thing Mrs. Wheatley gave to Phillis? Why?
- Why was Phillis Wheatley's writing important to the whole world?

Also see the story questions and activity in *The Light of One Candle*.

See the Phonics **CD-ROM** for practice using words with /ər/, /ən/, and /əl/.

Answers to Story Questions

1. She is a young girl who is sold as a slave to the Wheatleys of Boston.
2. She had few chores to do; other slaves had a lot of work.
3. She may have felt Phillis was better because she knew how to read and write.
4. Phillis Wheatley was the first African American poet.
5. Both Phillis and Grandma wanted to learn to read.

The Story Questions and Activity below appear in the Challenge Book.

Story Questions and Writing Activity

1. Who is Phillis?
2. What about Phillis's life was different from that of other slaves?
3. Why do you think Mrs. Wheatley kept Phillis from spending time with other slaves?
4. What was the main idea of this story?
5. How is Phillis Wheatley in this story like Grandma in *The Wednesday Surprise?*

Phillis's Diary

Write a section from an imaginary diary that Phillis Wheatley might have written. Draw a picture that shows how she might feel to go with it.

from *The Light of One Candle*

Bringing Groups Together

Anthology and Leveled Books

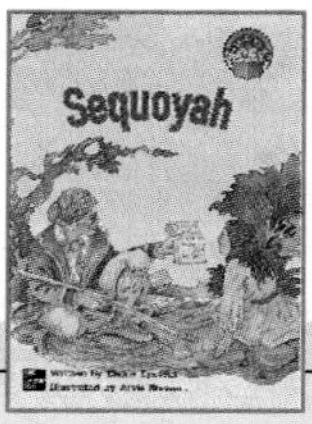

Connecting Texts

CHARACTER CHARTS
Start a Word Web on the chalkboard. In the center of the web, write the word *Achievements.* Write the story titles around the center of the web. Have children list the characters' achievements under each story title.

ACHIEVEMENTS

The Wednesday Surprise

- Grandmother learns to read.
- She is taught to read by her granddaughter.

Farmer Brown's Birthday Surprise

- Dog has the animals work together to provide a birthday cake for Farmer Brown's birthday gift.

Sequoyah

- Sequoyah develops the Cherokee alphabet so that his people can communicate.

The Light of One Candle

- Phillis, a slave, is a very smart girl.
- Phillis grows up to be free and to write and publish poetry.

Viewing/Representing

GROUP PRESENTATIONS Divide the class into four groups to represent each story in the lesson. Have each group work together to create a drawing, a poem, or another form of writing that demonstrates the major achievements in each story.

AUDIENCE RESPONSE
Have children look carefully at the completed project of each group. Allow time for questions.

Research and Inquiry

MORE ABOUT ACHIEVEMENTS Invite children to learn more about people who achieved in some way. They can:

- do research in classroom books and school library books.
- invite a speaker to talk to the class about a person who has made a major contribution to our country.
- visit a history museum to learn about achievements of famous and not-so-famous Americans.

*inter*NET CONNECTION For more information about people and their achievements, have children log on to ***www.mhschool.com/reading.***

Review /ər/er; /ən/en; /əl/le

TESTED OBJECTIVES

Children will:

- review /ər/*er*, /ən/*en*, and /əl/*le*.
- blend and read words with /ər/*er*, /ən/*en*, and /əl/*le*.

MATERIALS

- **Word Building Manipulative Cards**
- **Teaching Chart 158**

Skills Finder

/ər/ er	
Introduce	B1: 290G-H
Review	B1: 319E-F, 319G-H; B2: 180G-H, 211E-F
Test	B1: Unit 3
Maintain	B2: 55, 257

ALTERNATE TEACHING STRATEGY

REVIEW /ər/, /ən/, /əl/

For a different approach to teaching this skill, see page T73.

PREPARE

Listen for Words with /ər/, /ən/, /əl/

Read the following sentence aloud and have children raise a hand whenever they hear a word with the /ər/, /ən/, or /əl/ sound.

She met seven people for dinner at the table at the front of the restaurant.

TEACH

BLENDING Model and Guide Practice with /ər/*er*, /ən/*en*, /əl/*le* Words

- Display **Teaching Chart 158**. Tell children that they can form words by choosing one of the vowel patterns to fill in the blank.
- Write the letters *er* on the blank in the first example. Blend the sounds together to read the word *dinner*. d i n n er dinner.
- Repeat, having children blend and read the word.

er	le	en
dinner	table	listen
together	candle	happen
brother	apple	seven
never	little	often
better	able	open

Teaching Chart 158

Use the Word in Context

Have volunteers use the word in a sentence to reinforce its meaning. Example: *Did you eat soup for dinner?*

Repeat the Procedure

Repeat the same procedure to model and guide practice to complete the chart. Have volunteers fill in the blanks and blend the sounds together to form real words.

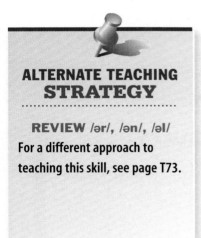

PRACTICE

SEGMENTING Discriminate Between /ər/er, /ən/en, /əl/le Words

Have children work in groups to build words with /ər/*er*, /ən/*en*, and /əl/*le* sounds. Ask children to copy their words onto blank cards, read the words, and circle the letters that stand for /ər/, /ən/, and /əl/ in each. ▶**Linguistic/Auditory**

GROUP

puddle

even

sister

ASSESS/CLOSE

Read, Spell, and Use /ər/er, /ən/en, /əl/le Words in Context

To assess children's ability to build and read /ər/*er*, /ən/*en*, /əl/*le* words, observe them as they work on the Practice activity. Ask each child to read and spell aloud a word with /ər/*er*, /ən/*en*, and /əl/*le*. Then have children use the words in sentences.

ADDITIONAL PHONICS RESOURCES

Phonics/Phonemic Awareness Practice Book, pages 121–124

McGraw-Hill School **TECHNOLOGY**

Phonics CD-ROM activities for practice with Decoding and Discriminating

Meeting Individual Needs for Phonics

EASY

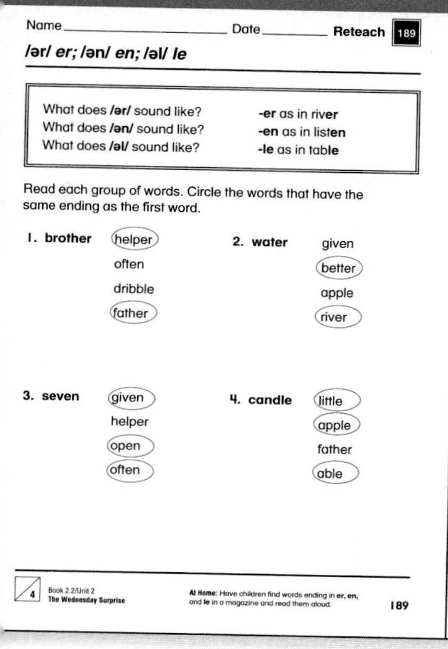

Name ________ Date ________ Reteach 189

/ər/ er; /ən/ en; /əl/ le

What does **/ər/** sound like?	**-er** as in river
What does **/ən/** sound like?	**-en** as in listen
What does **/əl/** sound like?	**-le** as in table

Read each group of words. Circle the words that have the same ending as the first word.

1. **brother** — helper, often, dribble, father
2. **water** — given, better, apple, river
3. **seven** — given, helper, open, often
4. **candle** — little, apple, father, able

4 Book 2.2/Unit 2 The Wednesday Surprise — **At Home:** Have children find words ending in **er, en,** and **le** in a magazine and read them aloud. 189

Reteach, 189

ON-LEVEL

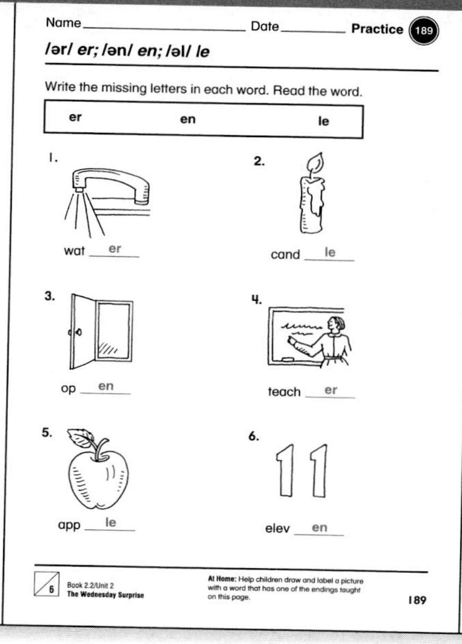

Name ________ Date ________ Practice 189

/ər/ er; /ən/ en; /əl/ le

Write the missing letters in each word. Read the word.

er	en	le

1. wat er
2. cand le
3. op en
4. teach er
5. app le
6. elev en

6 Book 2.2/Unit 2 The Wednesday Surprise — **At Home:** Help children draw and label a picture with a word that has one of the endings taught on this page. 189

Practice, 189

CHALLENGE

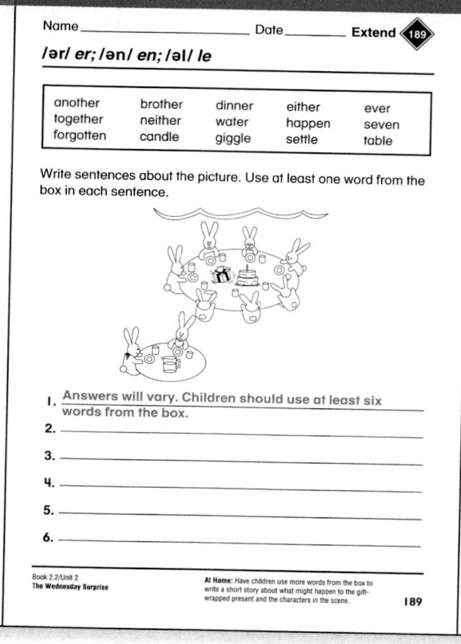

Name ________ Date ________ Extend 189

/ər/ er; /ən/ en; /əl/ le

another	brother	dinner	either	ever
together	neither	water	happen	seven
forgotten	candle	giggle	settle	table

Write sentences about the picture. Use at least one word from the box in each sentence.

1. Answers will vary. Children should use at least six words from the box.
2. ________
3. ________
4. ________
5. ________
6. ________

Book 2.2/Unit 2 The Wednesday Surprise — **At Home:** Have children use more words from the box to write a short story about what might happen to the gift-wrapped present and the characters in the scene. 189

Extend, 189

LANGUAGE SUPPORT

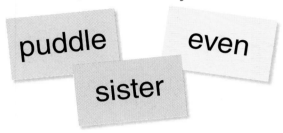

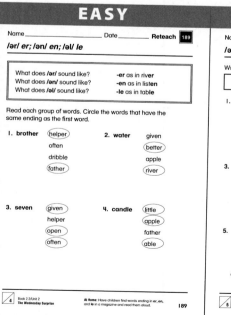

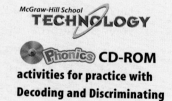

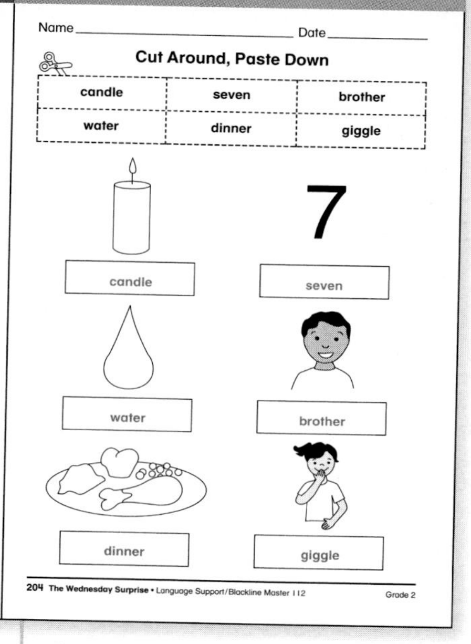

Name ________ Date ________

Cut Around, Paste Down

candle	seven	brother
water	dinner	giggle

204 The Wednesday Surprise • Language Support/Blackline Master 112 — Grade 2

Language Support, 204

DAILY **Phonics** ROUTINES

DAY 4 Letter Substitution Invite pairs of children to form new *er, en, le* words from the words *ever, seven,* and *table* using Word Building Manipulative Cards.

Phonics CD-ROM

SPELLING/PHONICS CONNECTIONS

See the 5-Day Spelling Plan, pages 211Q–211R.

Intervention Skills

Intervention Guide, for direct instruction and extra practice of /ər/ *er;* /ən/ *en;* /əl/ *el*

TESTED **OBJECTIVES**

Children will:

- review /ər/*er*, /ən/*en*, /əl/*le*.
- review /ü/*oo, ue, ew*.
- review /ôr/*or, ore*; /îr/*ear*.
- build and read words with *er, en, le, oo, ue, ew, or, ore, ear*.

MATERIALS

- **Teaching Chart 159**

Skills Finder

/ər/ *er*	
Introduce	B1: 290G-H
Review	B1: 319E-F, 319G-H; B2: 180G-H, 211E-F
Test	B1: Unit 3
Maintain	B2: 55, 257

Review /ər/, /ən/, /əl/; /ü/; /ôr/; /îr/

PREPARE

Identify Words with the /ü/*oo, ue, ew*; /ôr/ *or, ore*; /îr/ *ear*; /ər/ *er*; /ən/ *en*; /əl/*le* Sounds Ask children to read aloud the following words on the chalkboard: *brother, boot, blue, for, score, hear, table, giggle, seven.* For each word, have a volunteer tell whether it contains /ü/, /ôr/, /îr/, /ər/, /ən/, or /əl/, and circle the letters that stand for the sound.

TEACH

BLENDING Model and Guide Practice with /ü/*oo, ue, ew*; /ôr/ *or, ore*; /îr/ *ear*; /ər/ *er*; /ən/ *en*; /əl/*le*

- Display **Teaching Chart 159.** Challenge children to find eight words hidden in the chart.
- Circle the word *table*. Read the word, running your hand underneath it and smoothly blending the letters together.
- Have children repeat after you.
- Have a volunteer underline one of these letter combinations in each word they find: *oo, ue, ew, or en, ear, le,* or *er.* You may suggest that for those words children find written vertically on the chart, they write them horizontally on paper. This will make it easier for them to blend the sounds together.

Use the Words in Context Have volunteers use the words in sentences to reinforce their meanings. Example: *We sit at the cafeteria table for lunch.*

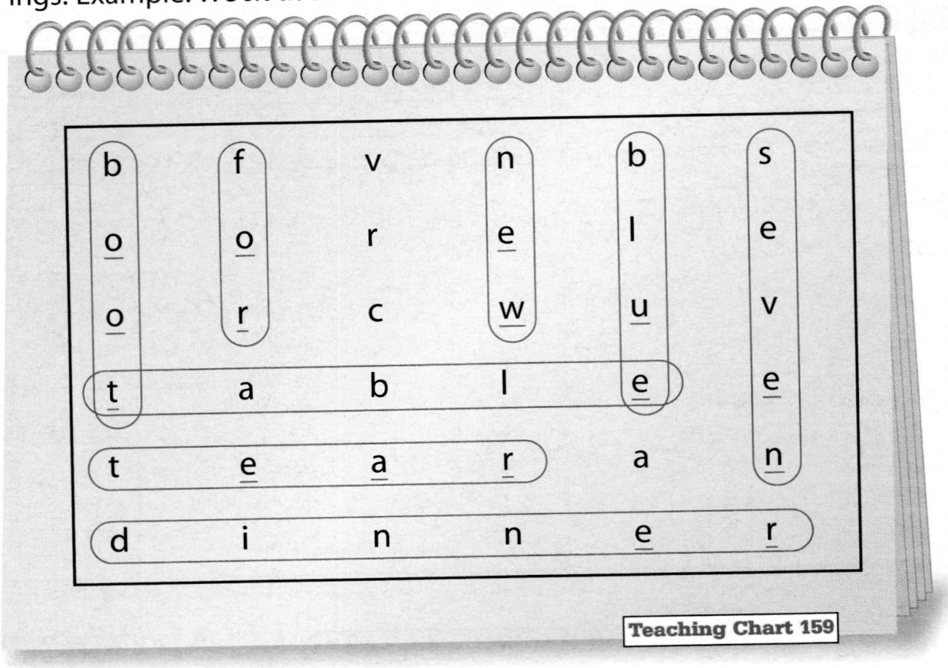

Repeat the Procedure Repeat the same procedure for the remaining hidden words on the chart.

PRACTICE

BLENDING
Read Words with Schwa and Variant Vowels

GROUP

Place the following words on pieces of paper in a hat: *dinner, mother, hammer, little, middle, even, listen, clear, blue, moon, spoon, more, for, store, stew*. Have children sit in a circle and pass around the hat. As each child receives the "hot potato," she or he selects a word from the hat and reads it aloud. ▶**Linguistic/Auditory**

blue | moon

ASSESS/CLOSE

Read and Write Words with /ər/er; /ən/en; /əl/le; /ü/oo, ue, ew; and /ôr/or, ore; /îr/ear

To assess children's ability to build and read schwa and variant-vowel words, observe them as they read words in the Practice activity. Ask each child to write a new word for one of the sounds and read it aloud. Children can use their words in context sentences to demonstrate that they understand their meanings.

ADDITIONAL PHONICS RESOURCES

Phonics/Phonemic Awareness Practice Book, pages 121–124

McGraw-Hill School TECHNOLOGY

Phonics CD-ROM activities for practice with Decoding and Discriminating

DAILY Phonics ROUTINES

DAY 5 **Blending** Write the spelling of each sound in *seven* as you say it. Have children repeat blending the sounds and reading the word. Repeat with *mother, table,* and *water*.

Phonics CD-ROM

ALTERNATE TEACHING STRATEGY

/ü/, /ôr/, /îr/, /ər/, /ən/, /əl/

For a different approach to teaching these skills, see pages T65, T70, T73.

Intervention **Skills**

Intervention Guide, for direct instruction and extra practice of /ər/; /ən/; /əl/; /ü/; /ôr/; /îr/

Meeting Individual Needs for Phonics

EASY

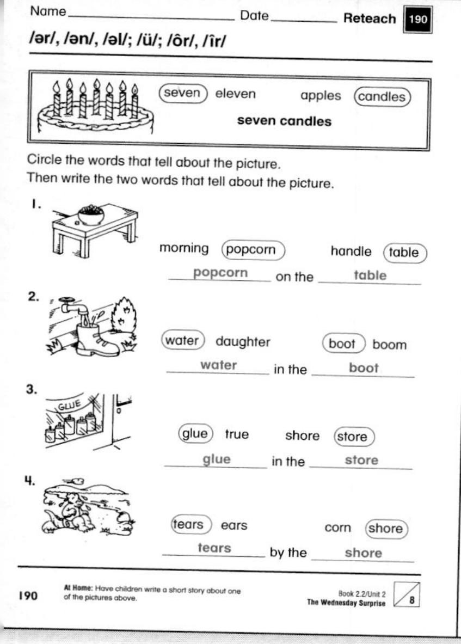

Name____ Date____ **Reteach 190**

/ər/, /ən/, /əl/; /ü/; /ôr/, /îr/

seven eleven apples candles
seven candles

Circle the words that tell about the picture.
Then write the two words that tell about the picture.

1. morning popcorn handle table
popcorn on the table
2. water daughter boot boom
water in the boot
3. glue true shore store
glue in the store
4. tears ears corn shore
tears by the shore

190 **At Home:** Have children write a short story about one of the pictures above. Book 2.2/Unit 2 **The Wednesday Surprise** 8

Reteach, 190

ON-LEVEL

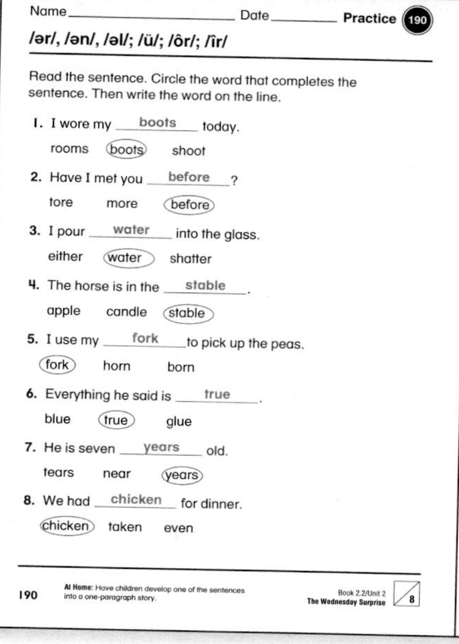

Name____ Date____ **Practice 190**

/ər/, /ən/, /əl/; /ü/; /ôr/; /îr/

Read the sentence. Circle the word that completes the sentence. Then write the word on the line.

1. I wore my boots today.
rooms boots shoot
2. Have I met you before?
tore more before
3. I pour water into the glass.
either water shatter
4. The horse is in the stable.
apple candle stable
5. I use my fork to pick up the peas.
fork horn born
6. Everything he said is true.
blue true glue
7. He is seven years old.
tears near years
8. We had chicken for dinner.
chicken taken even

190 **At Home:** Have children develop one of the sentences into a one-paragraph story. Book 2.2/Unit 2 **The Wednesday Surprise** 8

Practice, 190

CHALLENGE

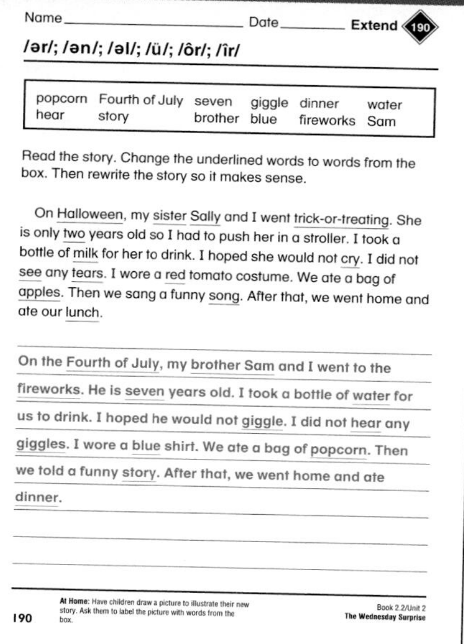

Name____ Date____ **Extend 190**

/ər/; /ən/; /əl/; /ü/; /ôr/; /îr/

popcorn	Fourth of July	seven	giggle	dinner	water
hear	story	brother	blue	fireworks	Sam

Read the story. Change the underlined words to words from the box. Then rewrite the story so it makes sense.

On Halloween, my sister Sally and I went trick-or-treating. She is only two years old so I had to push her in a stroller. I took a bottle of milk for her to drink. I hoped she would not cry. I did not see any tears. I wore a red tomato costume. We ate a bag of apples. Then we sang a funny song. After that, we went home and ate our lunch.

On the Fourth of July, my brother Sam and I went to the fireworks. He is seven years old. I took a bottle of water for us to drink. I hoped he would not giggle. I did not hear any giggles. I wore a blue shirt. We ate a bag of popcorn. Then we told a funny story. After that, we went home and ate dinner.

190 **At Home:** Have children draw a picture to illustrate their new story. Ask them to label the picture with words from the box. Book 2.2/Unit 2 **The Wednesday Surprise**

Extend, 190

LANGUAGE SUPPORT

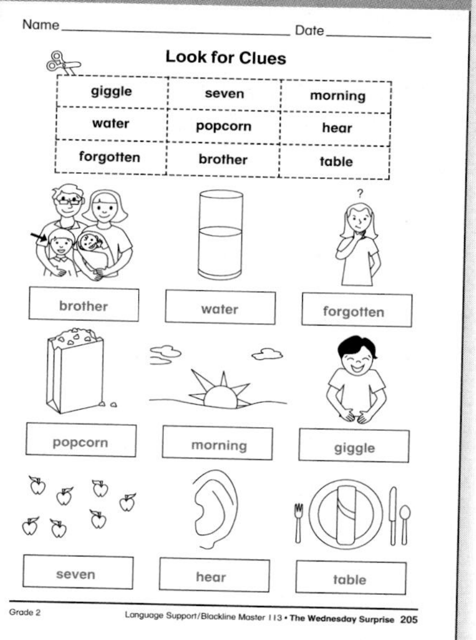

Name____ Date____

Look for Clues

giggle	seven	morning
water	popcorn	hear
forgotten	brother	table

brother | water | forgotten
popcorn | morning | giggle
seven | hear | table

Grade 2 Language Support/Blackline Master 113 • **The Wednesday Surprise** 205

Language Support, 205

TESTED OBJECTIVES

Children will summarize a passage.

MATERIALS

- Teaching Chart 160

Skills Finder

Summarize	
Introduce	B2: 149I-J
Review	B2: 211I-J, 245G-H
Test	B2: Unit 2
Maintain	B2: 271, 303, 323

TEACHING TIP

IMPLIED MAIN IDEA

Cover the title on the teaching chart. Tell children that sometimes the main idea is not stated directly. Ask children to look for clues in the passage that lead them to think about a main idea. Have children summarize the clues to form a main idea. Discuss how each clue adds supporting details to the main idea.

SELF-SELECTED Reading

Children may choose from the following titles.

ANTHOLOGY

- *The Wednesday Surprise*

LEVELED BOOKS

- *Farmer Brown's Birthday Surprise*
- *Sequoyah*
- *The Light of One Candle*

Bibliography, T88–T89

Review Summarize

PREPARE

Discuss Summarizing Remind children that a summary includes only the important information of a passage or story.

TEACH

Summarize *Grandma Visits the Library* Display **Teaching Chart 160**. Read the chart aloud together.

Grandma Visits the Library

Grandma says that she has never been to the library. Anna and Grandma agree to visit the library on Saturday. Grandma tells Anna it will be fun, now that she can read.

On Saturday, Grandma wears her blue dress. When they get to the library, Grandma picks out some books. Then she gets a brand-new library card so that she can check out the books.

On the way home, Anna has a chocolate-chip ice cream cone and Grandma orders vanilla. When they get back to Anna's house, they sit down on the blue couch to read the library books.

Teaching Chart 160

MODEL When I want to summarize a story I need to include only the most important information. In my summary, I will want to tell about Grandma getting a library card, but I do not need to include information about the color of her dress. This information is not important and leaving it out will not change the meaning of the summary.

Have children make a two-column chart listing important information from the passage on the **Teaching Chart** in one column and unimportant details in the other column.

PRACTICE

Use Important Information Have children use the important information from their charts to write a summary of the passage. ▶**Linguistic**

ASSESS/CLOSE

Summarize a Different Story Have children choose a story from an earlier unit to summarize. Ask: If you wanted to tell what the story is about to someone who has never read it, what would you say?

Important Information	Unimportant Details
Grandma and Anna go to the library.	Grandma's dress is blue.

ALTERNATE TEACHING STRATEGY

SUMMARIZE

For a different approach to teaching this skill, see page T67.

Intervention **Skills**

Intervention Guide, for direct instruction and extra practice in summarizing

Comprehension

EASY

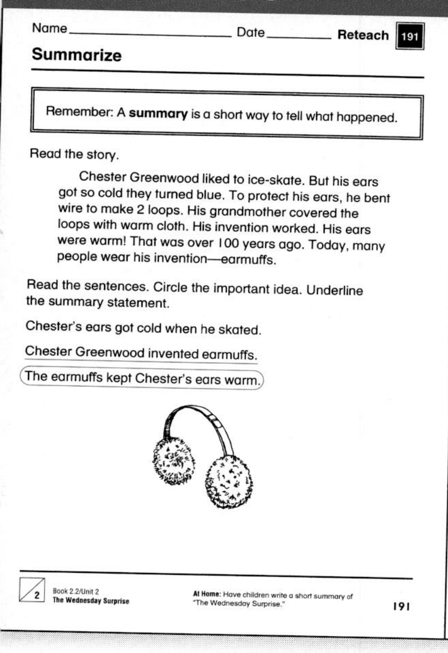
Name________ Date________ Reteach 191

Summarize

Remember: A **summary** is a short way to tell what happened.

Read the story.

Chester Greenwood liked to ice-skate. But his ears got so cold they turned blue. To protect his ears, he bent wire to make 2 loops. His grandmother covered the loops with warm cloth. His invention worked. His ears were warm! That was over 100 years ago. Today, many people wear his invention—earmuffs.

Read the sentences. Circle the important idea. Underline the summary statement.

Chester's ears got cold when he skated.

Chester Greenwood invented earmuffs.

The earmuffs kept Chester's ears warm.

2 Book 2.2/Unit 2 The Wednesday Surprise

At Home: Have children write a short summary of "The Wednesday Surprise."

191

Reteach, 191

ON-LEVEL

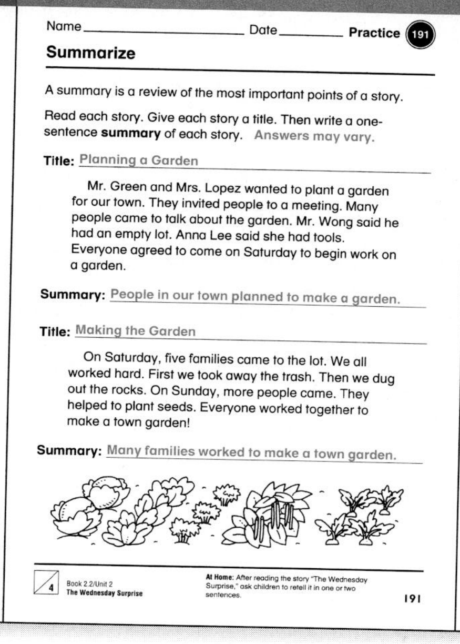
Name________ Date________ Practice 191

Summarize

A summary is a review of the most important points of a story.

Read each story. Give each story a title. Then write a one-sentence **summary** of each story. Answers may vary.

Title: Planning a Garden

Mr. Green and Mrs. Lopez wanted to plant a garden for our town. They invited people to a meeting. Many people came to talk about the garden. Mr. Wong said he had an empty lot. Anna Lee said she had tools. Everyone agreed to come on Saturday to begin work on a garden.

Summary: People in our town planned to make a garden.

Title: Making the Garden

On Saturday, five families came to the lot. We all worked hard. First we took away the trash. Then we dug out the rocks. On Sunday, more people came. They helped to plant seeds. Everyone worked together to make a town garden!

Summary: Many families worked to make a town garden.

4 Book 2.2/Unit 2 The Wednesday Surprise

At Home: After reading the story "The Wednesday Surprise," ask children to retell it in one or two sentences.

191

Practice, 191

CHALLENGE

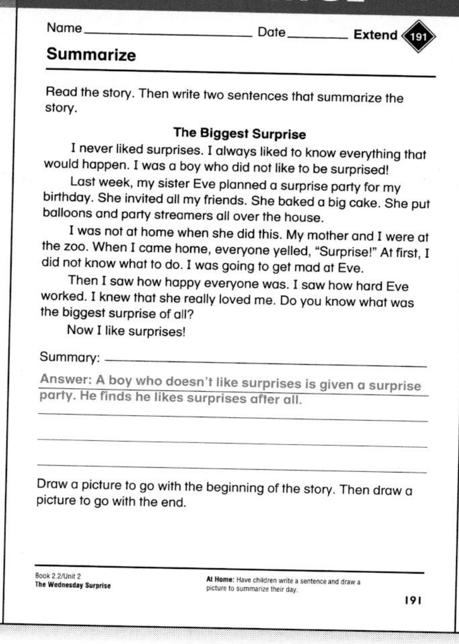
Name________ Date________ Extend 191

Summarize

Read the story. Then write two sentences that summarize the story.

The Biggest Surprise

I never liked surprises. I always liked to know everything that would happen. I was a boy who did not like to be surprised!

Last week, my sister Eve planned a surprise party for my birthday. She invited all my friends. She baked a big cake. She put balloons and party streamers all over the house.

I was not at home when she did this. My mother and I were at the zoo. When I came home, everyone yelled, "Surprise!" At first, I did not know what to do. I was going to get mad at Eve.

Then I saw how happy everyone was. I saw how hard Eve worked. I knew that she really loved me. Do you know what was the biggest surprise of all?

Now I like surprises!

Summary: Answer: A boy who doesn't like surprises is given a surprise party. He finds he likes surprises after all.

Draw a picture to go with the beginning of the story. Then draw a picture to go with the end.

Book 2.2/Unit 2 The Wednesday Surprise

At Home: Have children write a sentence and draw a picture to summarize their day.

191

Extend, 191

LANGUAGE SUPPORT

Name________ Date________

Anna and Grandma's Surprise

206 The Wednesday Surprise • Language Support/Blackline Master 114 Grade 2

Language Support, 206

Review Suffixes

TESTED **OBJECTIVES**

Children will:

- define *suffix.*
- be able to identify the suffixes *-ly* and *-ful* in a passage.
- write words with suffixes *-ly* and *-ful*.

MATERIALS

- **Teaching Chart 161**

Skills Finder

Suffixes	
Introduce	B2: 149K-L
Review	B2: 211K-L, 245K-L
Test	B2: Unit 2
Maintain	B2: 355

TEACHING TIP

SUFFIXES

- In some cases the *y* at the end of a word must be changed to an *i* before adding the suffix *-ly* (*sleepy -y + i + ly = sleepily*).
- Sometimes the final *e* is dropped before adding *ly* (*true - e + ly=truly*).
- The suffix *-ly* can be added to a word that already has the suffix *-ful* (*playfully*).

PREPARE

Define Suffixes Remind children that a suffix is a syllable or syllables added at the end of a word that changes the word's meaning and forms a new word.

TEACH

Read the Passage and Model the Skill Have children read the passage with you on **Teaching Chart 161** and then model the skill.

Dad Returns Home

Dad's birthday surprise is ready. Anna and Sam listen carefully for Dad's truck in the driveway. Finally, the front door opens. "Dad!" they cry joyfully, "Welcome home!"

"It's wonderful to be home," Dad says sleepily. He hugs the children, then goes to his room for a nap.

Mom tells the children to play quietly while she hangs the colorful streamers for the party. When Dad wakes up, he is truly surprised. "Thank you all so much," he says happily.

Teaching Chart 161

MODEL I see lots of words with suffixes in this story. I know that the suffix *-ful* mean "full of" and *-ly* means "in a certain way." When the streamers are described as being *colorful*, the suffix *-ful* at the end of the word tells me that the streamers are "full of" color. When Mom tells the children to play *quietly*, the suffix *-ly* at the end of the word tells me she wants them to play *in a quiet way* so that Dad can get some rest.

PRACTICE

Identify Words with Suffixes

GROUP

Have the children circle the *-ly* words and underline the *-ful* words on **Teaching Chart 161**. Ask a volunteer to point out the words that have both endings. *(carefully, joyfully)*

ASSESS/CLOSE

Use Words with Suffixes

In order to determine children's abilities to identify and write words with suffixes *-ly* and *-ful*, observe them during the Teach and Practice activities. Ask them to make a list of words with suffixes *-ly* and *-ful* that they find in *The Wednesday Surprise* and write each word in a new sentence.

ALTERNATE TEACHING STRATEGY

SUFFIXES

For a different approach to teaching this skill, see page T68.

Intervention Skills

Intervention Guide, for direct instruction and extra practice of suffixes

Meeting Individual Needs for Vocabulary

EASY

Name________ Date________ Reteach 192

Suffixes

The **suffix -ly** means "in the manner of"; the suffix **-ful** means "full of."

joy + **ful** = **joyful**

slow + **ly** = **slowly**

For each of the following words, write the base word and the suffix on the lines.

1. gladly = glad + ly
2. hopeful = hope + ful
3. careful = care + ful
4. sadly = sad + ly
5. suddenly = sudden + ly
6. truthful = truth + ful
7. helpful = help + ful
8. playful = play + ful
9. sternly = stern + ly
10. sweetly = sweet + ly

192 **At Home:** Ask children to tell a short story, using three words that end in -ly or -ful. Book 2.2/Unit 2 The Wednesday Surprise 10

Reteach, 192

ON-LEVEL

Name________ Date________ Practice 192

Suffixes

The suffixes **-ly** and **-ful** change the meaning of the base word to which they are added. The suffix **-ly** means "in the way of." The suffix **-ful** means "full of."

Write a word that means the same as the group of words. Your new word will end in **-ly** or **-ful.**

1. full of power — powerful
2. in a beautiful way — beautifully
3. in a cold way — coldly
4. in a different way — differently
5. full of thanks — thankful
6. in a soft way — softly
7. in a bright way — brightly
8. full of good cheer — cheerful

Write two sentences using some of the new words.
Answers will vary.

9. ________
10. ________

192 **At Home:** Ask children to make a list of other words ending in -ful and -ly. Book 2.2/Unit 2 The Wednesday Surprise 10

Practice, 192

CHALLENGE

Name________ Date________ Extend 192

Suffixes

sternly carefully perfectly beautiful hopeful joyful

This story doesn't make sense! Find the word in each underlined sentence that doesn't make sense. Use a word from the box to change the word.

The Reader and Her Teacher

Once there was a girl and a reading teacher. They were practicing for a reading contest. The girl was hoped that she would win first prize. hopeful She loved to read.

The reading teacher was kind, but sometimes she spoke stern. sternly . She made the reader practice her story until she could read it perfect. perfectly The teacher gave the girl a beauty hat to wear. beautiful She put it on care. carefully At the contest, she won first prize! Her voice was joy as she thanked her teacher. joyful

192 **At Home:** Have children draw pictures to illustrate the story "The Reader and Her Teacher." Book 2.2/Unit 2 The Wednesday Surprise

Extend, 192

LANGUAGE SUPPORT

Name________ Date________

Be Careful and Read Slowly!

1. Grandma vaguely remembered Dad's birthday.

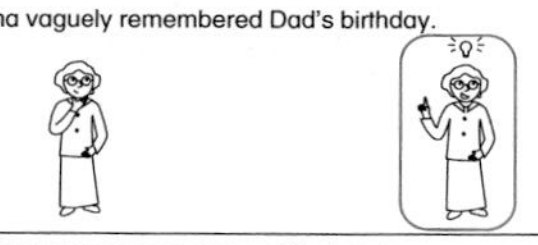

2. Grandma usually comes over on Wednesdays.

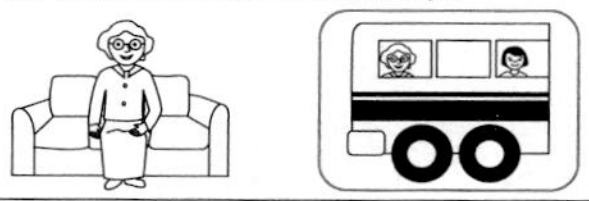

3. Grandma reads each word carefully.

4. Grandma spoke sternly to Sam.

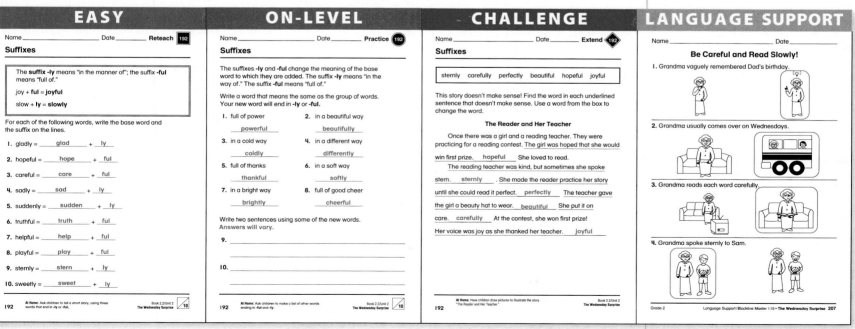

Grade 2 Language Support/Blackline Master 115 • The Wednesday Surprise 207

Language Support, 207

Expository Writing

GRAMMAR/SPELLING CONNECTIONS

See the 5-Day Grammar and Usage Plan on pages 211O–211P.

See the 5-Day Spelling Plan on pages 211Q–211R.

TEACHING TIP

Technology Use your word processing program's thesaurus to find synonyms for words. Instead of using the same word over and over, you can use the thesaurus to find a word that means almost the same thing.

References Ask children to check the spelling of difficult words by using word lists, the dictionary, or a glossary. Remind children that the spell-check feature on a computer does not always list the best choices for spelling a word.

Handwriting CD-ROM

Prewrite

WRITE ABOUT A BOOK Present this writing assignment: Write a report about a book you like. Include the names of the author and illustrator. Explain what the book is about and what happens in it. Include a beginning, middle, and end to your book report.

DEFINE PURPOSE AND AUDIENCE Help children consider the purpose of their writing and who will be reading their reports. Suggest that they ask themselves questions, such as: Who will be reading my report? What do I want to communicate to the readers?

Strategy: Make an Outline Have children make an outline of what they will cover in the beginning, middle, and end of their report. This will help them organize the information.

Draft

USE THE OUTLINE Guide children to draft their ideas without self-editing. They can consult their outline to help keep their reports in order. Encourage them to add details that will show why they like this book.

Revise

SELF-QUESTIONING Ask students to assess their drafts.

- Did I communicate the information in a clear, organized, and interesting way?
- Does my report have a beginning, middle, and end?
- Do I explain why I enjoyed this book?

Edit/Proofread

CHECK FOR ERRORS Students should reread their reports for organization, spelling, grammar, and punctuation.

Publish

ANTHOLOGY Children can compile an anthology of book reports and keep it as part of their classroom library.

"A Letter to Amy"

This is one of my favorite books. It is called "A Letter to Amy" and the author of it is Ezra Jack Keats.

The book is about a boy named Peter who is having a birthday party and writes an invitation to his friend Amy. On the way to the mailbox, Peter bumps into Amy and makes her cry. Peter worries that she will not come to the party, but she shows up at the end and Peter is very happy.

I liked this book because Peter invited Amy even though he was worried about what the boys would think of him for having a girl at the party.

PRESENTATION IDEAS

LOOK AT BOOKS Have children work together in the library to find new books to read. Partners can look at books and discuss what they like and don't like about them.
▶**Viewing/Representing**

MAKE A BOOK COVER Children can design their own covers for the books they used in their reports. Encourage them to use their imaginations, and to draw characters or scenes the way that they pictured them.
▶**Speaking/Listening**

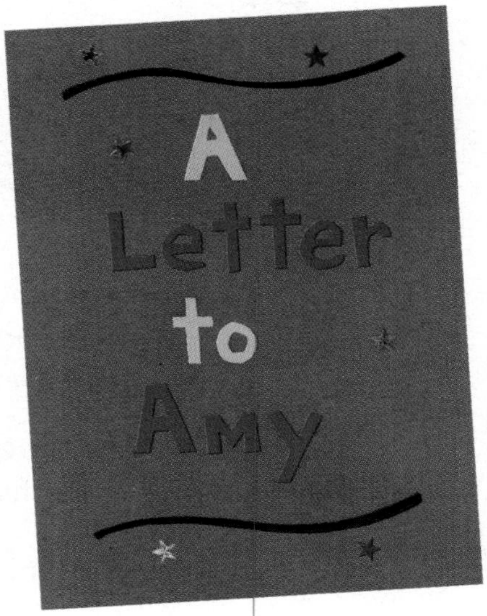

Consider students' creative efforts, possibly adding a plus (+) for originality, wit, and imagination.

Scoring Rubric

Excellent	Good	Fair	Unsatisfactory
4: The writer • explains what the book is about in an interesting and well-organized way. • clearly explains why he or she likes this book in a way that encourages others to read it. • presents no errors in grammar, punctuation, and spelling.	**3:** The writer • explains what the book is about in a well-organized way. • clearly explains why he or she likes this book. • presents few errors in grammar, punctuation, and spelling.	**2:** The writer • tells what the book is about but not very clearly. • states whether he or she likes the book, but does not explain why. • presents some errors in grammar, punctuation, and spelling.	**1:** The writer • explains too briefly, if at all, what the book is about. • does not state whether he or she likes this book. • presents many errors in grammar, punctuation, and spelling.

Incomplete 0: The writer leaves the page blank or fails to respond to the writing task. The student does not address the topic or simply paraphrases the prompt. The response is illegible or incoherent.

Meeting Individual Needs for Writing

EASY

Characterization Have each student choose a character from *The Wednesday Surprise* and write a descriptive sentence without revealing the character's identity. Invite students to read their sentences aloud and have others identify the character.

ON-LEVEL

Book Recommendation Ask children to think about books they have enjoyed reading. Have them select one that they think an older person might enjoy. Ask them to write a paragraph explaining why this older person might enjoy the book. Remind them to include the title of the book.

CHALLENGE

Diary Entry Invite children to imagine that they are an adult who has just learned to read. Have them write a diary entry describing how it feels and what they want to read next.

Listening and Speaking

LISTENING Have children
- listen for details about the book to determine their interest in reading it.
- write down questions they might have about the book.
- maintain eye contact with the speaker.

SPEAKING Encourage children to
- speak with an expressive voice to show interest in the story.
- use notes to assist in remembering the details.
- leave the audience wanting to find out more about the book. Do not tell the ending.

LANGUAGE SUPPORT

ESL Ask ESL students to share the book they have chosen with an English-fluent partner. Have them show and tell their partners what they like and don't like about the book. Suggest that the ESL students, with the help of their partners, write down words or phrases they can use in their reports.

PORTFOLIO Invite children to include their book reports or another writing project in their portfolios.

5 Day Grammar and Usage Plan

LANGUAGE SUPPORT

ESL Ask children to hold up various possessions. Point to these objects one by one and model sentences with possessive pronouns. Say: *That's her key. This is his calculator*. Also model sentences such as *This is our room* and *Those are their chairs*. Ask children to repeat these sample sentences.

DAILY LANGUAGE ACTIVITIES

Write the Daily Language Activities on the chalkboard each day, or use **Transparency 23**. Ask children to correct the formation of possessive pronouns orally.

Day 1

1. The book is on my's desk. my
2. Anna has a pen in she's bag. her
3. Grandma is in you's room. your

Day 2

1. The cake is without it candles. its
2. They's work is good. Their
3. Where are you's books? your

Day 3

1. He's basketball practice is today. His
2. Grandma reads her's book. her
3. Our's grandma is the best! Our

Day 4

1. Dad drives his's large truck. his
2. Mom and Dad ate they dinner. their
3. The book is missing it cover. its

Day 5

1. Dad liked me's gift. my
2. Our's surprise was great. Our
3. Sam and Dad practiced they's game. their

Daily Language Transparency 23

DAY 1 Introduce the Concept

Oral Warm-Up Read this sentence aloud: *Sam brought his basketball*. Ask children to whom *his* refers. (Sam)

Introduce Possessive Pronouns Some pronouns show ownership. Present:

Possessive Pronouns

- A **possessive pronoun** takes the place of a possessive noun.
- A possessive pronoun shows who or what owns something.

These pronouns can replace singular possessive nouns: *my, your, his, her, its*. Ask students which possessive pronoun would replace *Mom's, the boy's, the book's*. (*her, his, its*)

Present the Daily Language Activity and have children correct the possessive pronouns orally. Then ask them to use these pronouns in their own sentences.

WRITING Assign the daily Writing Prompt on page 180C.

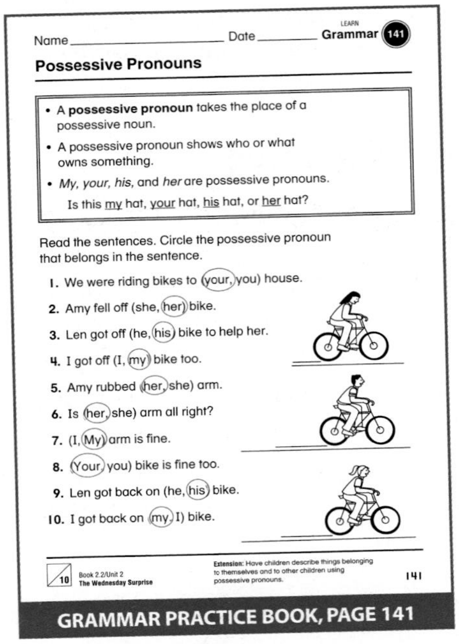

Name ________ Date ________ LEARN Grammar 141

Possessive Pronouns

- A **possessive pronoun** takes the place of a possessive noun.
- A possessive pronoun shows who or what owns something.
- *My, your, his,* and *her* are possessive pronouns.

Is this my hat, your hat, his hat, or her hat?

Read the sentences. Circle the possessive pronoun that belongs in the sentence.

1. We were riding bikes to (your, you) house.
2. Amy fell off (she, her) bike.
3. Len got off (he, his) bike to help her.
4. I got off (I, my) bike too.
5. Amy rubbed (her, she) arm.
6. Is (her, she) arm all right?
7. (I, My) arm is fine.
8. (Your, you) bike is fine too.
9. Len got back on (he, his) bike.
10. I got back on (my, I) bike.

10 Book 2.2/Unit 2 The Wednesday Surprise

Extension: Have children describe things belonging to themselves and to other children using possessive pronouns.

141

GRAMMAR PRACTICE BOOK, PAGE 141

DAY 2 Teach the Concept

Review Possessive Pronouns Ask children how to identify a possessive pronoun, and give examples.

Introduce Plural Possessives Tell children that some possessive pronouns show that more than one person or things own something. They can take the place of plural possessive nouns. List the pronouns *our, your,* and *their*.

Write the following phrases on the chalkboard: *the boys' gifts, the pans' covers, Sally's and my plan*. Ask students to replace the underlined words with possessive pronouns. (*their gifts, their covers, our plan*)

Present the Daily Language Activity. Then ask students to give examples of plural possessive pronouns and write a sentence for each.

WRITING Assign the daily Writing Prompt on page 180C.

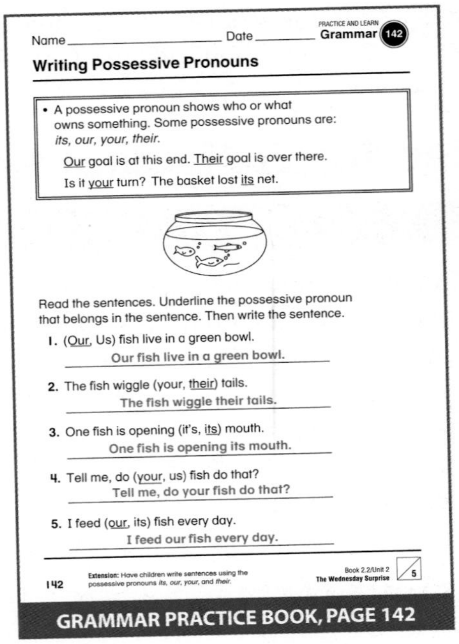

Name ________ Date ________ PRACTICE AND LEARN Grammar 142

Writing Possessive Pronouns

- A possessive pronoun shows who or what owns something. Some possessive pronouns are: *its, our, your, their.*

Our goal is at this end. Their goal is over there.

Is it your turn? The basket lost its net.

Read the sentences. Underline the possessive pronoun that belongs in the sentence. Then write the sentence.

1. (Our, Us) fish live in a green bowl.
   Our fish live in a green bowl.
2. The fish wiggle (your, their) tails.
   The fish wiggle their tails.
3. One fish is opening (it's, its) mouth.
   One fish is opening its mouth.
4. Tell me, do (your, us) fish do that?
   Tell me, do your fish do that?
5. I feed (our, its) fish every day.
   I feed our fish every day.

142

Extension: Have children write sentences using the possessive pronouns *its, our, your,* and *their*.

Book 2.2/Unit 2 The Wednesday Surprise 5

GRAMMAR PRACTICE BOOK, PAGE 142

Possessive Pronouns

DAY 3 Review and Practice

Learn from Literature Review possessive pronouns. Read the following passage on page 188 from *The Wednesday Surprise:*

> **"His birthday?" Grandma raises her eyebrows as if she'd forgotten all about that.**

Have children identify the possessive pronouns. Ask which possessive nouns they take the place of. Children should recall that *his* refers to *Dad's*. Discuss that *her* takes the place of *Grandma's*.

Identify Possessive Pronouns Present the Daily Language Activity. Then ask each child to write three sentences about *The Wednesday Surprise*, including a possessive pronoun in each. Have volunteers present their sentences and ask others to identify the possessive pronoun(s).

WRITING Assign the daily Writing Prompt on page 180D.

DAY 4 Review and Practice

Review Possessive Pronouns Ask children to replace each possessive noun with a possessive pronoun in the following sentences:

- Anna's book is special. Her
- That is Sam's basketball. his
- Mom and Dad's present is a surprise. Their

Present the Daily Language Activity and have students correct the sentences orally.

Mechanics and Usage Before children do the daily Writing Prompt on page 180D, review capitalization. Display and discuss:

> **Capitalization**
>
> - A proper noun begins with a capital letter.
> - The name of a day, month, or holiday begins with a capital letter.

WRITING Assign the daily Writing Prompt on page 180D.

DAY 5 Assess and Reteach

Assess Use the Daily Language Activity and page 145 of the **Grammar Practice Book** for assessment.

Reteach Have children list the possessive pronouns from the lesson.

Assign each child a partner and have them choose a picture book from the classroom library. Direct each pair of children to write a list of possessive pronouns that they find while reading their book together. Attach their word lists to book cover cutouts as part of a word wall activity.

Use page 146 of the **Grammar Practice Book** for additional reteaching.

WRITING Assign the daily Writing Prompt on page 180D.

Name ____________ Date ________ REVIEW AND PRACTICE **Grammar** 143

Choosing Possessive Pronouns

- A **possessive pronoun** takes the place of a possessive noun.
- A possessive pronoun shows who or what owns something. Some possessive pronouns are *my, your* (singular), *his, her, its, our, your* (plural), *their.*

Read the words on the left. Then circle the words on the right that have the same meaning.

1. cat belonging to you	you cat	(your cat)
2. dog belonging to Pete	he dog	(his dog)
3. cat belonging to the children	(their cat)	they cat
4. mouse belonging to Anna	she mouse	(her mouse)
5. fish belonging to me	(my fish)	me fish
6. horses belonging to you and Ed	you're horses	(your horses)
7. ears belonging to the rabbit	it's ears	(its ears)
8. bird belonging to Jack and me	(our bird)	hour bird

8 Book 2.2/Unit 2 **The Wednesday Surprise**

Extension: Have children name objects and their owners. Call on others to supply the correct possessive pronouns.

143

GRAMMAR PRACTICE BOOK, PAGE 143

Name ____________ Date ________ MECHANICS **Grammar** 144

Proper Nouns

- A **proper noun** begins with a capital letter.
- The name of a day, month, or holiday begins with a capital letter.

George's family always celebrates the Fourth of July.

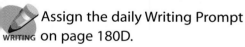

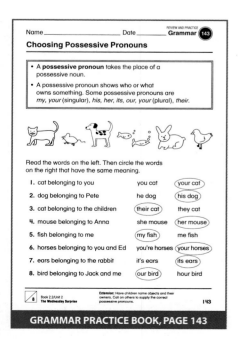

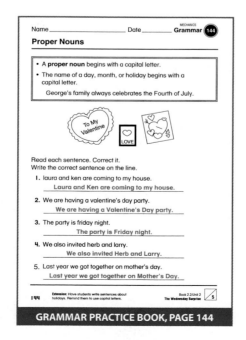

Read each sentence. Correct it.
Write the correct sentence on the line.

1. laura and ken are coming to my house.
   Laura and Ken are coming to my house.
2. We are having a valentine's day party.
   We are having a Valentine's Day party.
3. The party is friday night.
   The party is Friday night.
4. We also invited herb and larry.
   We also invited Herb and Larry.
5. Last year we got together on mother's day.
   Last year we got together on Mother's Day.

144

Extension: Have students write sentences about holidays. Remind them to use capital letters.

Book 2.2/Unit 2 **The Wednesday Surprise** 5

GRAMMAR PRACTICE BOOK, PAGE 144

Name ____________ Date ________ TEST **Grammar** 145

Possessive Pronouns

A. Read the sentences. Underline the possessive pronouns. Write the possessive pronouns on the lines.

1. My cousin tells great jokes. My
2. Your sister is also funny. Your
3. Her stories make me laugh. Her
4. She tells them to our friends. our
5. My brother laughs a lot. My
6. His stories are silly. His
7. Their parties are fun. Their
8. What is your idea? your

B. Read each pair of sentences.
Circle the one with the correct pronoun.

9. a. (When Pam talks, her nose wiggles.)
   b. When Pam talks, she nose wiggles.
10. c. If you pet the dog, it tail wags.
   d. (If you pet the dog, its tail wags.)

10 Book 2.2/Unit 2 **The Wednesday Surprise**

145

GRAMMAR PRACTICE BOOK, PAGE 145

GRAMMAR PRACTICE BOOK, PAGE 146

5 Day Spelling Plan

LANGUAGE SUPPORT

ESL To help students distinguish between initial blends, *sl, sm, sp, st,* and *sw,* write the Spelling Words on the chalkboard and have students repeat each word as you pronounce it. Have children take turns coming to the chalkboard, circling the blend (*sw, sl, st, sm*), and saying the word out loud.

DICTATION SENTENCES

Spelling Words

1. The baby is sweet.
2. She is playing on the slide.
3. They read the story.
4. He is a smart boy.
5. Do not speak to me.
6. Can you start the car?
7. You could slip on the snow.
8. She had a spot on her dress.
9. I could swim all day.
10. That was a smooth ride.

Challenge Words

11. He took a chance.
12. This is my favorite book.
13. The rocks are heavy.
14. She is nervous about the job.
15. The office is clean.

DAY 1 Pretest

Assess Prior Knowledge Use the Dictation Sentences at left and **Spelling Practice Book** page 141 for the pretest. Allow students to correct their own papers. If students have trouble, have partners give each other a midweek test on Day 3. Students who require a modified list may be tested on the first five words.

Spelling Words		Challenge Words
1. sweet	6. **start**	11. **chance**
2. slide	7. slip	12. **favorite**
3. **story**	8. spot	13. **heavy**
4. **smart**	9. swim	14. **nervous**
5. speak	10. smooth	15. **office**

*Note: Words in **dark type** are from the story.*

Word Study On page 142 of the **Spelling Practice Book** are word study steps and an at-home activity.

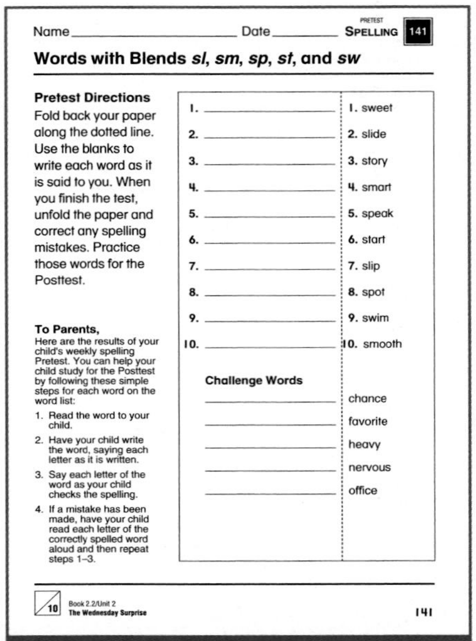

Name ______ Date ______ PRETEST SPELLING 141

Words with Blends *sl*, *sm*, *sp*, *st*, and *sw*

Pretest Directions
Fold back your paper along the dotted line. Use the blanks to write each word as it is said to you. When you finish the test, unfold the paper and correct any spelling mistakes. Practice those words for the Posttest.

To Parents,
Here are the results of your child's weekly spelling Pretest. You can help your child study for the Posttest by following these simple steps for each word on the word list:
1. Read the word to your child.
2. Have your child write the word, saying each letter as it is written.
3. Say each letter of the word as your child checks the spelling.
4. If a mistake has been made, have your child read each letter of the correctly spelled word aloud and then repeat steps 1–3.

1. ______ 1. sweet
2. ______ 2. slide
3. ______ 3. story
4. ______ 4. smart
5. ______ 5. speak
6. ______ 6. start
7. ______ 7. slip
8. ______ 8. spot
9. ______ 9. swim
10. ______ 10. smooth

Challenge Words
______ chance
______ favorite
______ heavy
______ nervous
______ office

10 Book 2.2/Unit 2 The Wednesday Surprise 141

SPELLING PRACTICE BOOK, PAGE 141

WORD STUDY STEPS AND ACTIVITY, PAGE 142

DAY 2 Explore the Pattern

Sort and Spell Words Say the words *slide, smooth, spot, start,* and *swim.* Have students identify the beginning consonant sounds they hear in each word. These words contain initial blends *sl, sm, sp, st,* and *sw.*

Ask students to read aloud the ten spelling words before sorting them according to spelling pattern.

Words beginning with				
sl	***sm***	***sp***	***st***	***sw***
slide	smart	speak	story	sweet
slip	smooth	spot	start	swim

Word Wall As students read other stories, and texts have them look for new words with initial blends *sl, sm, sp, st,* and *sw* and add them to the classroom word wall, underlining the spelling pattern in each word.

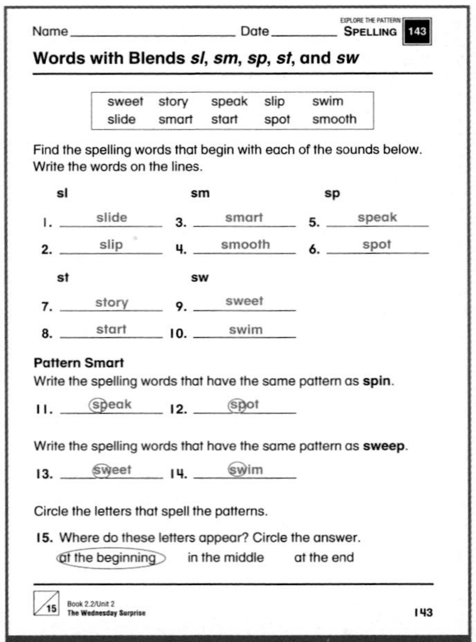

Name ______ Date ______ EXPLORE THE PATTERN SPELLING 143

Words with Blends *sl*, *sm*, *sp*, *st*, and *sw*

sweet story speak slip swim
slide smart start spot smooth

Find the spelling words that begin with each of the sounds below. Write the words on the lines.

sl
1. slide
2. slip

sm
3. smart
4. smooth

sp
5. speak
6. spot

st
7. story
8. start

sw
9. sweet
10. swim

Pattern Smart
Write the spelling words that have the same pattern as **spin**.
11. speak 12. spot

Write the spelling words that have the same pattern as **sweep**.
13. sweet 14. swim

Circle the letters that spell the patterns.

15. Where do these letters appear? Circle the answer.
at the beginning in the middle at the end

15 Book 2.2/Unit 2 The Wednesday Surprise 143

SPELLING PRACTICE BOOK, PAGE 143

Words with Blends

DAY 3 Practice and Extend

Word Meaning: Suffixes Remind students that a suffix is a word part added to the end of a word to give the word a different meaning. Tell them that the suffix *-ly* means "in a certain way." For example, in the sentence "She talked loudly" *loudly* means "in a loud way." Write the words *sweet, smooth, quick, quiet, and soft* on the chalkboard. Have students add *-ly* to each word. Then have them write a sentence using the new form of each word.

Glossary Have students work with partners to:

- look up the synonym or synonyms for each Challenge Word in the Glossary.
- write a sentence using a synonym in place of each Challenge Word.
- exchange papers and rewrite the sentences using the Challenge Words.

Name__________ Date______ PRACTICE AND EXTEND SPELLING 144

Words with Blends *sl*, *sm*, *sp*, *st*, and *sw*

sweet	story	speak	slip	swim
slide	smart	start	spot	smooth

Write a spelling word to complete each sentence.

1. Joey is a smart student and always makes good grades.
2. Be careful not to slip on the ice.
3. The road was full of bumps, it was not smooth.
4. The candy tastes very sweet.
5. It is time to start the test now.
6. My cat has a black spot at the end of his tail.
7. The teacher read a funny story to the class.

Write a spelling word for each picture.

8. slide 9. swim 10. speak

Word Meaning

Be a word builder. Add **ly** to make new words.

Example: nice + ly = nicely

11. sweet + ly = sweetly 12. smooth + ly = smoothly

Write three other words you know that end in **ly**.

13. ______ 14. ______ 15. ______

144 **Challenge Extension:** Scramble the letters in the words and write them on the board. Have students unscramble the words. Book 2.2/Unit 2 The Wednesday Surprise 15

SPELLING PRACTICE BOOK, PAGE 144

DAY 4 Proofread and Write

Proofread Sentences Write these sentences on the chalkboard, including the misspelled words. Ask students to proofread, circling incorrect spellings and writing the correct spellings. There are two spelling errors in each sentence.

> **Pam will starrt the storey.** (start, story)
>
> **We can sllide into the water to swimm.** (slide, swim)

Have students create additional sentences with errors for partners to correct.

WRITING Have students use as many Spelling Words as possible in the daily Writing Prompt on page 180D. Remind students to proofread their writing for errors in spelling, grammar, and punctuation.

Name__________ Date______ PROOFREAD AND WRITE SPELLING 145

Words with Blends *sl*, *sm*, *sp*, *st*, and *sw*

Proofreading Activity

There are six spelling mistakes in the paragraph below. Circle each misspelled word. Write the words correctly on the lines below.

A swete little angel lived on a star. The angel knew his star was special. He kept his star very clean so that it would sparkle. The little angel was smarte. He would shine his star until it was smoothe. Then he would sttart to run. Next, he would slipp and sllidde on the star. Living on his special star was fun!

1. sweet 2. smart 3. smooth
4. start 5. slip 6. slide

Writing Activity

Think about your favorite story. Write sentences about why you like that story. Use four spelling words. Circle the words you use.

10 Book 2.2/Unit 2 The Wednesday Surprise 145

SPELLING PRACTICE BOOK, PAGE 145

DAY 5 Assess and Reteach

Assess Students' Knowledge Use page 146 of the **Spelling Practice Book** or the Dictation Sentences on page 211Q for the posttest.

Personal Word List If students have trouble with any words in the lesson, have them add to their personal list of troublesome words in their journals. Have students write simple poems using words from their list.

JOURNAL

Students should refer to their word lists during later writing activities.

Name__________ Date______ POSTTEST SPELLING 146

Words with Blends *sl*, *sm*, *sp*, *st*, and *sw*

Look at the words in each set. One word in each set is spelled correctly. Use a pencil to color in the circle in front of that word. Before you begin, look at the sample sets of words. Sample A has been done for you. Do Sample B by yourself. When you are sure you know what to do, you may go on with the rest of the page.

Sample A
Ⓐ blu
Ⓑ bloe
Ⓒ bulue
● blue

Sample B
Ⓔ grein
● green
Ⓖ grene
Ⓗ grean

1. Ⓐ spoat Ⓑ spoot ● spot Ⓓ spoth
2. ● smart Ⓕ semart Ⓖ smaart Ⓗ smrt
3. Ⓐ swimm ● swim Ⓒ siwm Ⓓ swime
4. Ⓔ stoorey Ⓕ stry Ⓖ storie ● story
5. Ⓐ slde Ⓑ slied ● slide Ⓓ slidde
6. ● smooth Ⓕ smoothe Ⓖ smoth Ⓗ smothe
7. Ⓐ speke Ⓑ speake Ⓒ spoek ● speak
8. Ⓔ swet ● sweet Ⓖ sweete Ⓗ swte
9. ● slip Ⓑ silip Ⓒ slipe Ⓓ slpe
10. Ⓔ starte Ⓕ strat Ⓖ strt ● start

146 Book 2.2/Unit 2 The Wednesday Surprise 10

SPELLING PRACTICE BOOK, PAGE 146

Lesson Overview

Reaching All Learners

Concept
- Natural History Museums

Comprehension
- Summarize

Phonics
- Diphthongs /ou/, /oi/

Vocabulary
- buried
- creatures
- fossil
- fresh
- layers
- millions

Anthology

Fossils Tell of Long Ago

Selection Summary **Children will visit a natural history museum to figure out how plants and animals become fossils, and what fossils tell us about life forms that existed millions of years ago.**

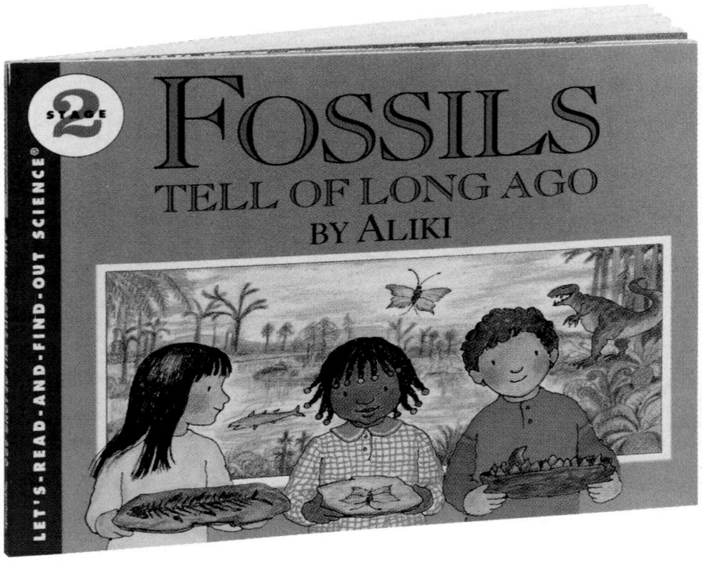

FOSSILS
TELL OF LONG AGO
BY ALIKI
STAGE 2
LET'S-READ-AND-FIND-OUT SCIENCE®

Listening Library

Digging
Digging deep, digging down,
I dug a big hole in the ground.
Soil black, soil brown,
Look at all the things I found.
A little seashell white as snow,
A toy I lost two years ago.
A piece of someone's broken dish,
A fossil shaped just like a fish.
Digging, digging in the ground,
Oh, what special things I found!
213

Rhyme applies to phonics

INSTRUCTIONAL pages 214–235

About the Author/Illustrator Aliki started drawing when she was in preschool and continued throughout her school years. After graduating, she worked as an illustrator for advertising. Finally, she began to illustrate and write both fiction and non-fiction books for children. Aliki, who has won many awards, says, "The words and the pictures should blend so that the pictures add to the words and make them more important." Among her award-winning books are *The Story of William Penn* and *Corn is Maize: the Gift of the Indians.*

Same Concept, Skills and Vocabulary!

Leveled Books

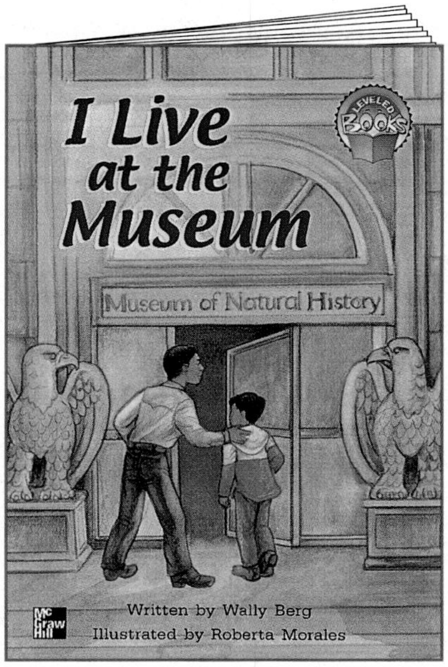

EASY
Lesson on pages 235A and 235D
DECODABLE

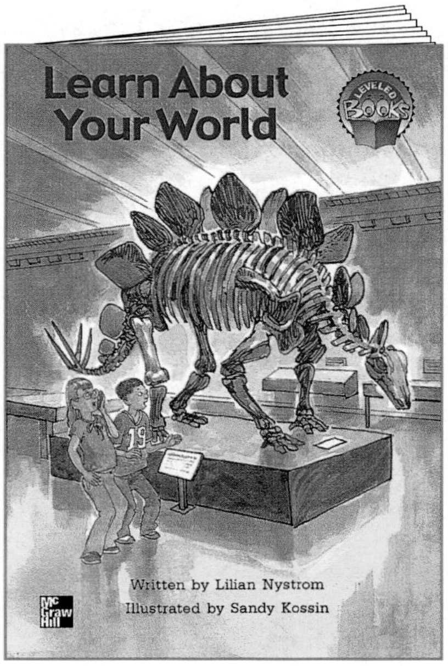

INDEPENDENT
Lesson on pages 235B and 235D
Take-Home version available

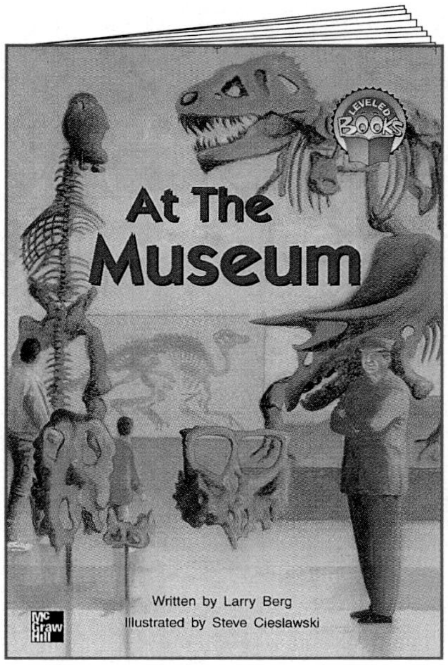

CHALLENGE
Lesson on pages 235C and 235D

Leveled Practice

EASY
Reteach, 193–200 Blackline masters with reteaching opportunities for each assessed skill

INDEPENDENT/ON-LEVEL
Practice, 193–200 Workbook with Take-Home stories and practice opportunities for each assessed skill and story comprehension

CHALLENGE
Extend, 193–200 Blackline masters that offer challenge activities for each assessed skill

Quizzes Prepared by Accelerated Reader

WORKSTATION Activities

Social Studies	Prehistoric Life, *218*
Science	An Imprint Investigation, *220*
Math	Which Is More? Which Is Less? *222*
Art	Make Imprints, *228*
Language Arts	Read Aloud, *212E*
Writing	Write a Speech, *232*
Cultural Perspectives	Dinosaurs, *226*
Research and Inquiry	Find Out More, *233*
Internet Activities	www.mhschool.com/reading

Suggested Lesson Planner

READING AND LANGUAGE ARTS	DAY 1 Focus on Reading and Skills	DAY 2 Read the Literature
Phonics Daily Routines	**Daily Phonics Routine: Segmenting,** 212H Phonics CD-ROM	**Daily Phonics Routines: Blending,** 214A Phonics CD-ROM
Phonological Awareness Phonics /ou/, /oi/ Comprehension Vocabulary Study Skills Listening, Speaking, Viewing, Representing	**Read Aloud: Fantasy,** 212E "The Dinosaur Who Lived in My Backyard" ☑ **Develop Phonological Awareness,** 212F /ou/*ow, ou*; /oi/*oi, oy* ☑ **Review /ou/*ow, ou* and /oi/*oi, oy*,** 212G–212H **Teaching Chart, 162** **Reteach, Practice, Extend,** 193 **Phonics/Phonemic Awareness Practice Book,** 125–128 Read **Apply /ou/*ow, ou*; /oi/*oi, oy*,** 212/213 "Digging" Intervention Program	**Build Background,** 214A Develop Oral Language **Vocabulary,** 214B–214C ***buried*** ***fossils*** ***layers*** ***creatures*** ***fresh*** ***millions*** **Word Building Manipulative Cards** **Teaching Chart 163** **Reteach, Practice, Extend,** 194 Read **Read the Selection,** 214–231 Comprehension ☑ ***/ou/ow, ou; /oi/oi, oy*** ☑ **Summarize** **Genre: Informational Story,** 215 **Cultural Perspectives,** 226 Intervention Program
Curriculum Connections	Link **Language Arts,** 212E	Link **Science,** 214A
Writing	**Writing Prompt:** What do you know about dinosaurs? What do they look like? What do they eat? How big are they? How do you know this information?	**Writing Prompt:** Compare fossils with photographs. How are they the same? How are they different? **Journal Writing** Quick-Write, 231
Grammar	**Introduce the Concept: Pronoun-Verb Agreement,** 235O Daily Language Activity: Write the correct form of the verb to agree with the pronoun. **Grammar Practice Book,** 147	**Teach the Concept: Pronoun-Verb Agreement,** 235O Daily Language Activity: Write the correct form of the verb to agree with the pronoun. **Grammar Practice Book,** 148
Spelling *Blends*	**Pretest: Words with Blends,** 235Q **Spelling Practice Book,** 147, 148	**Explore the Pattern: Words with Blends,** 235Q **Spelling Practice Book,** 149

Intervention Program Available

leeting ndividual leeds

☑ = Skill Assessed in Unit Test

ⓘ Intervention Program Available

Read EVERY DAY

DAY 3 — Read the Literature

Daily Phonics Routine: **Word Building,** 233

Phonics CD-ROM

Rereading for Fluency, 230

Story Questions and Activities, 232–233
- **Reteach, Practice, Extend,** 195

Study Skills, 234
- ☑ Various Texts
- **Teaching Chart 164**
- **Reteach, Practice, Extend,** 196

Test Power, 235

Read the Leveled Books, 235A–235D
- Guided Reading
  - ☑ /ou/*ow, ou*; /oi/*oi, oy*
  - ☑ Summarize
  - ☑ Instructional Vocabulary

ⓘ Intervention Program

Activity **Social Studies,** 218; **Science,** 220

Writing Prompt: Write a story about a boy or girl who finds a fossil. Tell where he or she found it and what it looked like.

Expository Writing, 235M
- Prewrite, Draft

Review and Practice: Pronoun-Verb Agreement, 235P
- Daily Language Activity: Write the correct form of the verb to agree with the pronoun.

Grammar Practice Book, 149

Practice and Extend: Words with Blends, 235R

Spelling Practice Book, 150

DAY 4 — Build Skills

Daily Phonics Routine: **Writing,** 235F

Phonics CD-ROM

Read **Read the Leveled Books and Self-Selected Books**

☑ **Review /ou/*ow, ou* and /oi/*oi, oy*,** 235E–235F
- **Teaching Chart 165**
- **Reteach, Practice, Extend,** 197
- **Language Support,** 213
- **Phonics/Phonemic Awareness Practice Book,** 125–128

☑ **Cumulative Review,** 235G–235H
- **Teaching Chart 166**
- **Reteach, Practice, Extend,** 198
- **Language Support,** 214
- **Phonics/Phonemic Awareness Practice Book,** 125–128

Minilessons, 219, 221, 225, 229

ⓘ Intervention Program

Activity **Math,** 222

Writing Prompt: Write a short review of *Fossils Tell of Long Ago.* Tell what you thought was interesting about it. Be sure to include the title of the book.

Expository Writing, 235M
- Revise

Meeting Individual Needs for Writing, 235N

Review and Practice: Pronoun-Verb Agreement, 235P
- Daily Language Activity: Write the correct form of the verb to agree with the pronoun.

Grammar Practice Book, 150

Proofread and Write: Words with Blends, 235R

Spelling Practice Book, 151

DAY 5 — Build Skills

Daily Phonics Routine: **Fluency,** 235H

Phonics CD-ROM

Read **Read Self-Selected Books**

☑ **Review Sequence of Events,** 235I–235J
- **Teaching Chart 167**
- **Reteach, Practice, Extend,** 199
- **Language Support,** 215

☑ **Review Context Clues,** 235K–235L
- **Teaching Chart 168**
- **Reteach, Practice, Extend,** 200
- **Language Support,** 216

Listening, Speaking, Viewing, Representing, 235N
- Match Speeches to Drawings
- Make an Announcement

Minilessons, 219, 221, 225, 229

ⓘ Intervention Program

Activity **Art,** 228

Writing Prompt: Tell about a museum you have visited or would like to visit. What exhibits do they have there?

Expository Writing, 235M
- Edit/Proofread, Publish

Assess and Reteach: Pronoun-Verb Agreement, 235P
- Daily Language Activity: Write the correct form of the verb to agree with the pronoun.

Grammar Practice Book, 151, 152

Assess and Reteach: Words with Blends, 235R

Spelling Practice Book, 152

Link
Language Arts

Read Aloud

The Dinosaur Who Lived in My Backyard

a fantasy story by B. G. Hennessey

There used to be a dinosaur who lived in my backyard. Sometimes I wish he still lived here.

The dinosaur who lived here hatched from an egg that was as big as a basketball.

By the time he was five, he was as big as our car.

Just one of his dinosaur feet was so big it wouldn't even have fit in my sandbox.

My mother says that if you eat all your vegetables you'll grow very strong. That must be true, because that's all this dinosaur ate. I bet he ate a hundred pounds of vegetables every day. That's a whole lot of lima beans.

This dinosaur was so heavy that he would have made my whole neighborhood shake like pudding if he jumped. He weighed as much as twenty pick-up trucks.

The dinosaur who lived in my backyard was bigger than my school bus. Even bigger than my house.

Continued on page T4

Oral Comprehension

LISTENING AND SPEAKING Ask children, as you read, to use clues in the text to come to conclusions about the dinosaur. When you have finished, ask children: *How long ago did the dinosaur live in the neighborhood? Was it a few years ago or a long, long time ago?* Then ask, *Which words in the story helped you draw that conclusion?*

GENRE STUDY: FANTASY Discuss the literary devices and techniques used in *The Dinosaur Who Lived in My Backyard.*

- Look at the characters in the story. Determine if the characters are realistic. Ask: *In real life, could the characters do what they did in the story? Why?*
- Have children describe the setting of the story. Ask: *Is the setting realistic? Why or why not?*
- Ask children to close their eyes and picture the events in the story. Then have children imagine what would happen if the dinosaur lived in their backyards. Encourage children to describe the dinosaur in their backyard.

Activity Invite children to make drawings of the dinosaur in the story. Encourage them to think about the story's description of the dinosaur. Remind children that the dinosaur in the story only ate plants. Encourage children to research which dinosaurs were only plant-eaters. Have them study pictures of dinosaurs for ideas about how such creatures would look. ▶ **Visual**

Develop Phonological Awareness

Blend Sounds

Phonemic Awareness

MATERIALS
- magazine or storybook pictures or objects

Teach Tell children they are going to say the sounds for some words with you and then blend the sounds to say the word. To demonstrate say, /k/-/l/-/ou/-/n/. *Let's put the sounds together . . . clown.* Show the picture of the clown. Repeat with a piece of chalk.

Practice Using pictures or objects to represent the following words, have children blend the sounds to say the word: *coin, toys, flower, cow, watch, spoon, bird,* and *car.*

Segment Sounds

Phonemic Awareness

MATERIALS
- Word Building Boxes from *Word Building Cards*
- counters

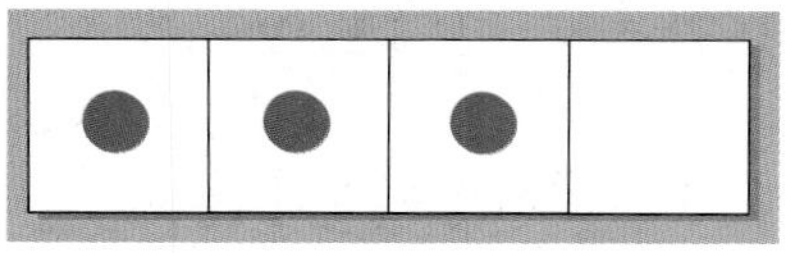

Teach Draw four Word Building Boxes on a transparency to represent sounds in a selected word. Then, using counters, say each sound as you simultaneously put a counter into one box for each sound. Then have children repeat the sound as you point to each counter.

Practice Have children work in pairs to segment the following words using Word Building Boxes and counters: *now, joy, class, flame, down, sound, towel, noise, poke,* and *dream.*

Substitute Sounds

Phonemic Awareness

MATERIALS
- Phonics Pictures from *Word Building Cards*

Teach Hold up the Phonics Picture of the house. Tell children to listen carefully as you tell a story about the house. Tell the following story: *This is my pouse.* (house) *I live here with my pat* (cat) *and my pog.* (dog) *There is a parge* (large) *tree in the front yard. We pit* (sit) *under the tree all day.* After you say each sentence, have children guess the correct word and beginning sound.

Practice Tell other stories, substituting beginning, middle, and ending sounds for the following sets of words: *clown/crown, point/paint, cow/con, boy/toy, pound/found, coil/coin, toil/tail,* and *power/tower.*

INFORMAL ASSESSMENT

Observe children as they blend, segment, and substitute sounds. If children have difficulty, see Alternate Teaching Strategies on p. T75.

Review /ou/ow, ou and /oi/oi, oy

TESTED OBJECTIVES

Children will:

- identify /ou/ words spelled *ow* and *ou.*
- identify /oi/ words spelled with *oy* and *oi.*
- decode and read words with /ou/ or /oi/ sounds.

MATERIALS

- **Word Building Manipulative Cards**
- **Teaching Chart 162**

Skills Finder

/ou/ ow, ou, **and** */oi/ oi, oy*

Introduce	B1: 156G-H
Review	B1: 191E-F, 191G-H; B2: 235E-F, 236G-H
Test	B1: Unit 2

TEACHING TIP

DECODING MULTISYLLABIC WORDS Write the words *about, towel,* and *oyster* on the board with hyphens to indicate syllable breaks. Say the words aloud, stressing the accented syllable. Then have them read the words, stressing the accented syllable.

PREPARE

Identify Spelling Patterns for /ou/ and /oi/

- Review that /ou/ can be formed by the letter combinations *ow* or *ou* and /oi/ can be formed with the letter combinations *oi, oy*.

TEACH

BLENDING Model and Guide Practice with /ou/ and /oi/ Words

- Display **Teaching Chart 162**.
- Ask children to read column one and identify which word in it does not contain the /ou/ sound. Ask a volunteer to circle that word. Ask children to repeat the procedure for column two.

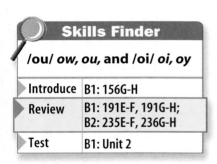

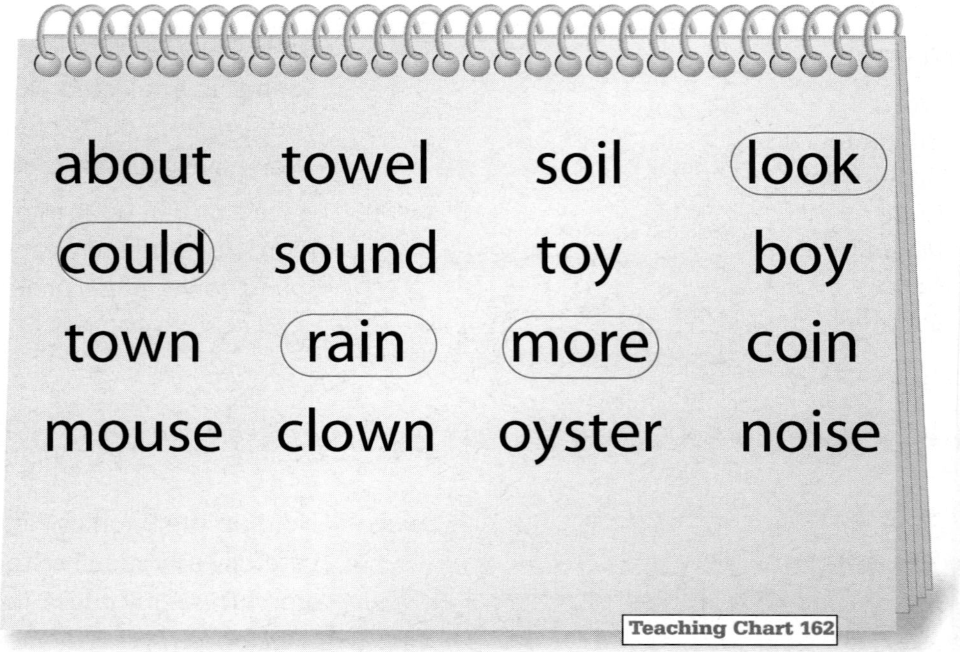

about
towel
soil
look
could
sound
toy
boy
town
rain
more
coin
mouse
clown
oyster
noise
Teaching Chart 162

Use the Words in Context

- Have children use the words in a sentence to reinforce their meanings. For example: *The town was founded about two hundred years ago.*

Repeat the Procedure

- Repeat the procedure to model and guide practice with columns three and four on the chart for words with the sound /oi/.

PRACTICE

WORD BUILDING Build /ou/ and /oi/ Words with Letter Cards

ONE

Use letter and vowel diphthong cards to build words with letter combinations *ow* or *ou* that stand for the /ou/ sound. Have children read each word aloud after they build it and determine if a word rhymes with the previous word. Repeat with letter combinations *oi* or *oy* that stand for the /oi/ sound. ▶ **Linguistic/Visual**

a b o u t

ASSESS/CLOSE

Build and Read /ou/ and /oi/ Words

To assess children's ability to build and decode /ou/ and /oi/ words, observe them as they work on the Practice activity. Ask each child to read aloud and spell a word using the letter combinations for /ou/ and /oi/.

ADDITIONAL PHONICS RESOURCES

Phonics/Phonemic Awareness Practice Book, pages 125–128

McGraw-Hill School TECHNOLOGY

Phonics CD-ROM

activities for practice with Decoding and Word Building

Meeting Individual Needs for Phonics

EASY

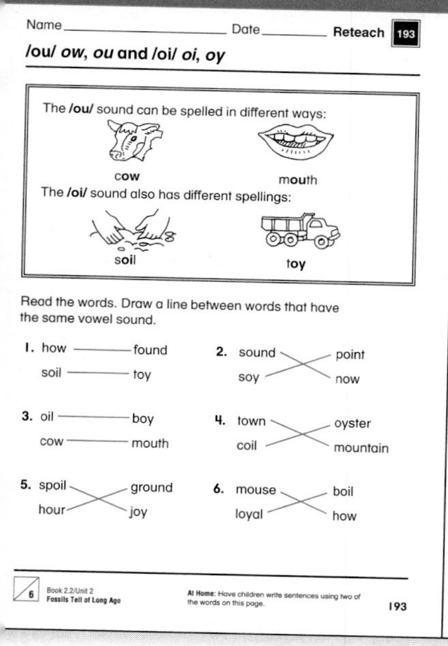

Name ______ Date ______ Reteach 193

/ou/ ow, ou and */oi/ oi, oy*

The **/ou/** sound can be spelled in different ways:

cow — mouth

The **/oi/** sound also has different spellings:

soil — toy

Read the words. Draw a line between words that have the same vowel sound.

1. how — found; soil — toy
2. sound — point; soy — now
3. oil — boy; cow — mouth
4. town — oyster; coil — mountain
5. spoil — ground; hour — joy
6. mouse — boil; loyal — how

6 Book 2.2/Unit 2 Fossils Tell of Long Ago

At Home: Have children write sentences using two of the words on this page.

193

Reteach, 193

ON-LEVEL

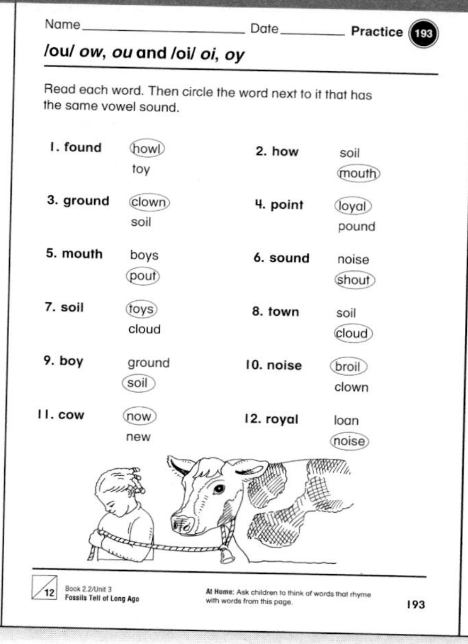

Name ______ Date ______ Practice 193

/ou/ ow, ou and */oi/ oi, oy*

Read each word. Then circle the word next to it that has the same vowel sound.

1. **found** — howl, toy
2. **how** — soil, mouth
3. **ground** — clown, soil
4. **point** — loyal, pound
5. **mouth** — boys, pout
6. **sound** — noise, shout
7. **soil** — toys, cloud
8. **town** — soil, cloud
9. **boy** — ground, soil
10. **noise** — broil, clown
11. **cow** — now, new
12. **royal** — loan, noise

12 Book 2.2/Unit 3 Fossils Tell of Long Ago

At Home: Ask children to think of words that rhyme with words from this page.

193

Practice, 193

CHALLENGE

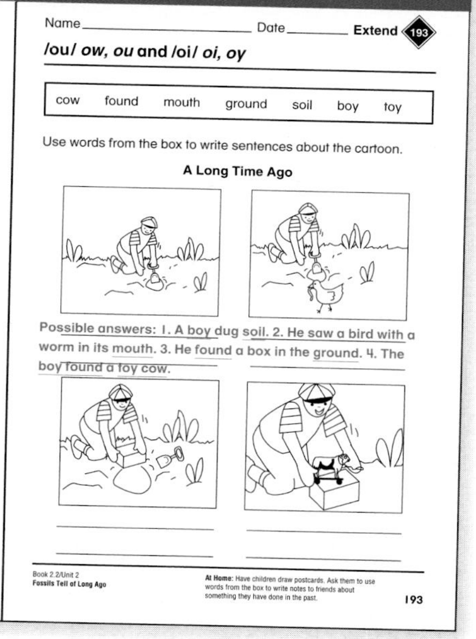

Name ______ Date ______ Extend 193

/ou/ ow, ou and */oi/ oi, oy*

cow	found	mouth	ground	soil	boy	toy

Use words from the box to write sentences about the cartoon.

A Long Time Ago

Possible answers: 1. A boy dug soil. 2. He saw a bird with a worm in its mouth. 3. He found a box in the ground. 4. The boy found a toy cow.

Book 2.2/Unit 2 Fossils Tell of Long Ago

At Home: Have children draw postcards. Ask them to use words from the box to write notes to friends about something they have done in the past.

193

Extend, 193

Daily Routines

DAY 1 **Segmenting** Write *town, loud, join,* and *toy* on the chalkboard. Invite volunteers to circle the letters that stand for the /ou/ sound or /oi/ sound.

DAY 2 **Blending** Write the spelling of each sound in *growl* as you say it. Have children repeat after you. Then ask children to blend the sounds to read the word. Repeat with *mouth, point, toy.*

DAY 3 **Word Building** Divide children into four groups. Assign each group a letter combination: *ou, ow, oy,* or *oi.* Each group can make a list of words with the /ou/ or /oi/ sound.

DAY 4 **Writing** Have groups of children write poems that include the words on their lists from Day 3. Invite one child from each group to read the poem aloud.

DAY 5 **Fluency** Write the following list of words on the chalkboard: *mouth, down, loyal, join.* Point to each word. Ask children to blend the sounds silently and read each word aloud.

Apply /ou/ow, ou and /oi/oi, oy

TESTED OBJECTIVES

Children will decode and read words with /ou/ and /oi/ sounds.

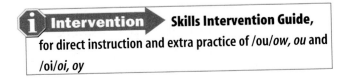

Digging
Digging deep, digging down,
I dug a big hole in the ground.
Soil black, soil brown,
Look at all the things I found.
A little seashell white as snow,
A toy I lost two years ago.
A piece of someone's broken dish,
A fossil shaped just like a fish.
Digging, digging in the ground,
Oh, what special things I found!
212
213

Anthology pages 212–213

Read and Build Fluency

READ THE POEM Invite children to listen closely for the /ou/ and /oi/ sounds as they follow, in their texts, your reading of "Digging." Model fluency by expressively reading the poem line by line. Then, for auditory modeling, ask them to read the poem aloud in unison as you track the print.

PARTNERS **REREAD FOR FLUENCY** Have children take turns rereading the poem with a partner. Ask one child to monitor the text while the other reads aloud. Guide children to pause appropriately when they come to punctuation. Encourage them to pause at end punctuation by cueing them to actually "read" each punctuation mark.

Dictate and Spell

JOURNAL **DICTATE WORDS** Say the /ou/ word *ground.* Segment it into its individual sounds. Repeat the word and use it in a sentence, for example, "The ground was wet from the rain." Encourage children to pronounce the word. Then have them write down the letter or letter patterns for each sound until the word is complete. Repeat the process with other /ou/ and /oi/ words from the poem: *down, found, soil, toy.* Then repeat using words other than those found in the poem: *about, towel, noise, boy.*

Intervention **Skills Intervention Guide, for direct instruction and extra practice of /ou/*ow, ou* and /oi/*oi, oy***

Build Background

ink
Science

Concept: Natural History Museums

Evaluate Prior Knowledge

ONCEPT: NATURAL HISTORY IUSEUMS Ask children if they have ever isited a natural history museum. Invite those ho have to share their experiences. Which as their favorite exhibit? Why? Which xhibit did they like least and why? ncourage those who have not visited a natral history museum to brainstorm what inds of things they might find in it.

SE A TOUR MAP Have children help you fill in the map with drawings and words describing what they might e on a museum tour.
Spatial/Linguistic

WRITING

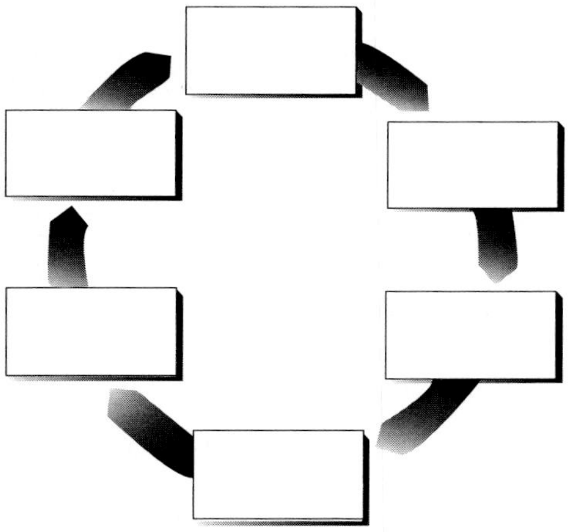

Graphic Organizer 1

ESCRIBE THE EXHIBIT Have children rite brief descriptions of what they saw on eir imaginary tour of a natural istory museum.

Develop Oral Language

CONNECT WORDS AND PICTURES

ESL Show and explain a picture of an exhibit from a natural history museum. Encourage children to show photos or make drawings of exhibits that they might see in a natural history museum. Discuss:

- What are all the exhibits about?
- How old are the items exhibited?
- What's so important about each exhibit? ▶ Spatial/Linguistic

Anthology and Leveled Books

DAILY Phonics ROUTINES

DAY 2 **Blending** Write the spelling of each sound in *growl* as you say it. Have children repeat after you. Then ask children to blend the sounds to read the word. Repeat with *mouth, point, toy.*

LANGUAGE SUPPORT

Use the Language Support Book, pages 208–211, to help build background.

buried
fresh
layers
millions
fossils
creatures

Vocabulary

TESTED **OBJECTIVES**

Children will use context and structural clues to determine the meanings of vocabulary words.

Definitions

buried (p. 220) put underground; covered

fresh (p. 223) having its original qualities; new or recent

layers (p. 220) thicknesses of materials lying one on another

millions (p. 222) 1,000 times 1,000; a great amount

fossils (p. 218) remains or traces of prehistoric plants or animals found in the earth

creatures (p. 226) animals or humans

Story Words

These words from the selection may be unfamiliar. Before children read, have them check the meanings and pronunciations of the words in the Glossary, beginning on page 390, or in a dictionary.

- minerals, p. 221
- extinct, p. 226
- ichthyosaur, p. 227

Teach Vocabulary in Context

Identify Vocabulary Words Display **Teaching Chart 163** and read the passage with children. Have volunteers circle each vocabulary word and underline other words that are clues to its meaning.

Prints from Long Ago

1. Animals and plants died and were buried deep in the muddy ground. **2.** Each left a new imprint in the fresh, soft mud. **3.** Slowly their imprints were covered many times by layers of new mud. **4.** Lots of time passed; in fact, millions of years went by. **5.** Now the remains of the plants or animals are stones called fossils. They are found all over the world. **6.** We use them to learn about creatures that lived long ago.

Teaching Chart 163

Discuss Meanings Ask questions like these to help clarify word meanings:

- If a treasure was buried in the sand, would you be able to see it?
- If your orange juice is fresh, was it squeezed just now or a long time ago?
- What do you call things that are stacked one on top of another?
- What is the name for animal or plant remains that are preserved in stone?
- What is another word for animals or humans?

Activities

Practice

Play "Twenty Questions" GROUP Assign children to small groups. Ask a member of each group to pick a vocabulary card from a pile and not reveal it. Other members of the group play "Twenty Questions" with the card-holder and try to identify the "mystery" word.
▶ **Linguistic/Interpersonal**

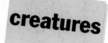

fossils **millions** **creatures**

Word Building Manipulative Cards

Swap Sentences PARTNERS WRITING Ask children to write a context sentence for each vocabulary word. Assign partners. Have partners read each other's sentences and edit them when necessary. Have children refer to the Glossary as needed. ▶ **Linguistic/Oral**

Assess Vocabulary

Identify Word Meaning in Context PARTNERS WRITING Encourage children to write questions for each of the vocabulary words. Have them include context clues in the questions to help show the meanings of the words. Then ask children to exchange their questions with partners. Partners should write answers to the questions, using the vocabulary words whenever possible.

SPELLING/VOCABULARY CONNECTIONS

See Spelling Challenge Words, pages 245Q.

LANGUAGE SUPPORT

See the Language Support Book, pages 208–211, for teaching suggestions for Vocabulary.

Vocabulary PuzzleMaker

Provides vocabulary activities.

Meeting Individual Needs for Vocabulary

EASY

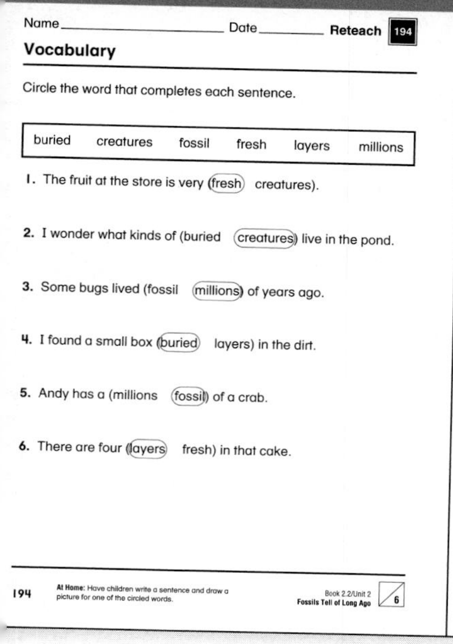

Name______ Date______ Reteach 194

Vocabulary

Circle the word that completes each sentence.

buried creatures fossil fresh layers millions

1. The fruit at the store is very (fresh creatures).
2. I wonder what kinds of (buried creatures) live in the pond.
3. Some bugs lived (fossil millions) of years ago.
4. I found a small box (buried layers) in the dirt.
5. Andy has a (millions fossil) of a crab.
6. There are four (layers fresh) in that cake.

Reteach, 194

ON-LEVEL

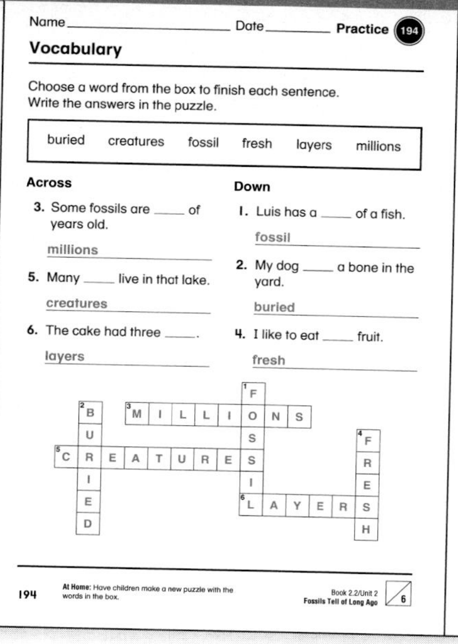

Name______ Date______ Practice 194

Vocabulary

Choose a word from the box to finish each sentence. Write the answers in the puzzle.

buried creatures fossil fresh layers millions

Across
3. Some fossils are ___ of years old. millions
5. Many ___ live in that lake. creatures
6. The cake had three ___. layers

Down
1. Luis has a ___ of a fish. fossil
2. My dog ___ a bone in the yard. buried
4. I like to eat ___ fruit. fresh

Practice, 194

ON-LEVEL

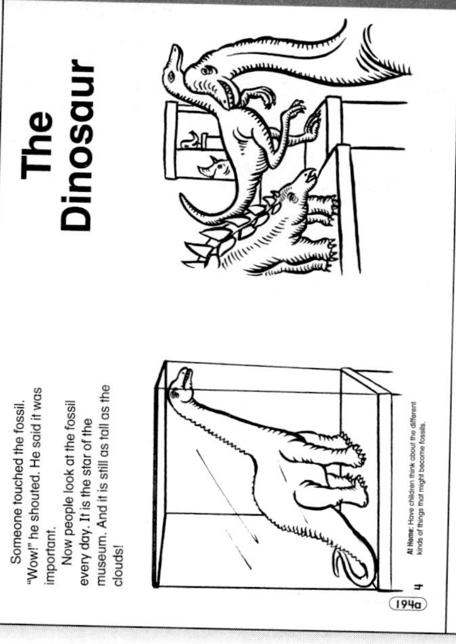

The Dinosaur

Someone touched the fossil. "Wow!" he shouted. He said it was important.

Now people look at the fossil every day. It is the star of the museum. And it is still as tall as the clouds!

4 194a

Practice, 194a
Take-Home Story

CHALLENGE

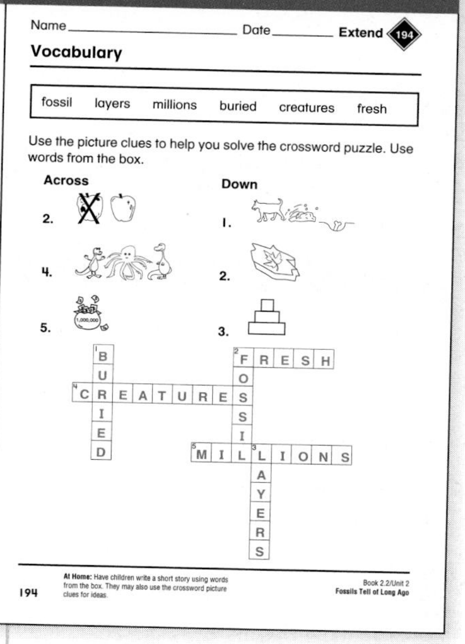

Name______ Date______ Extend 194

Vocabulary

fossil layers millions buried creatures fresh

Use the picture clues to help you solve the crossword puzzle. Use words from the box.

Across 2. 4. 5.
Down 1. 2. 3.

Extend, 194

Comprehension

Prereading Strategies

PREVIEW AND PREDICT Have the children read the title and author's name. Take a **picture walk** through the illustrations.

- What clues do the pictures give about the story?
- What do you think a fossil is?
- Will the story be a realistic one or a fable? How can you tell? (Realistic; pictures show real things that lived in the past and modern people.) ***Genre***

Have children make predictions about the story.

PREDICTIONS	WHAT HAPPENED
The children in the story will learn about fossils.	
They will visit a museum.	

SET PURPOSES What do the children want to find out by reading the story? For example:

- How are fossils made?
- Where are fossils found?

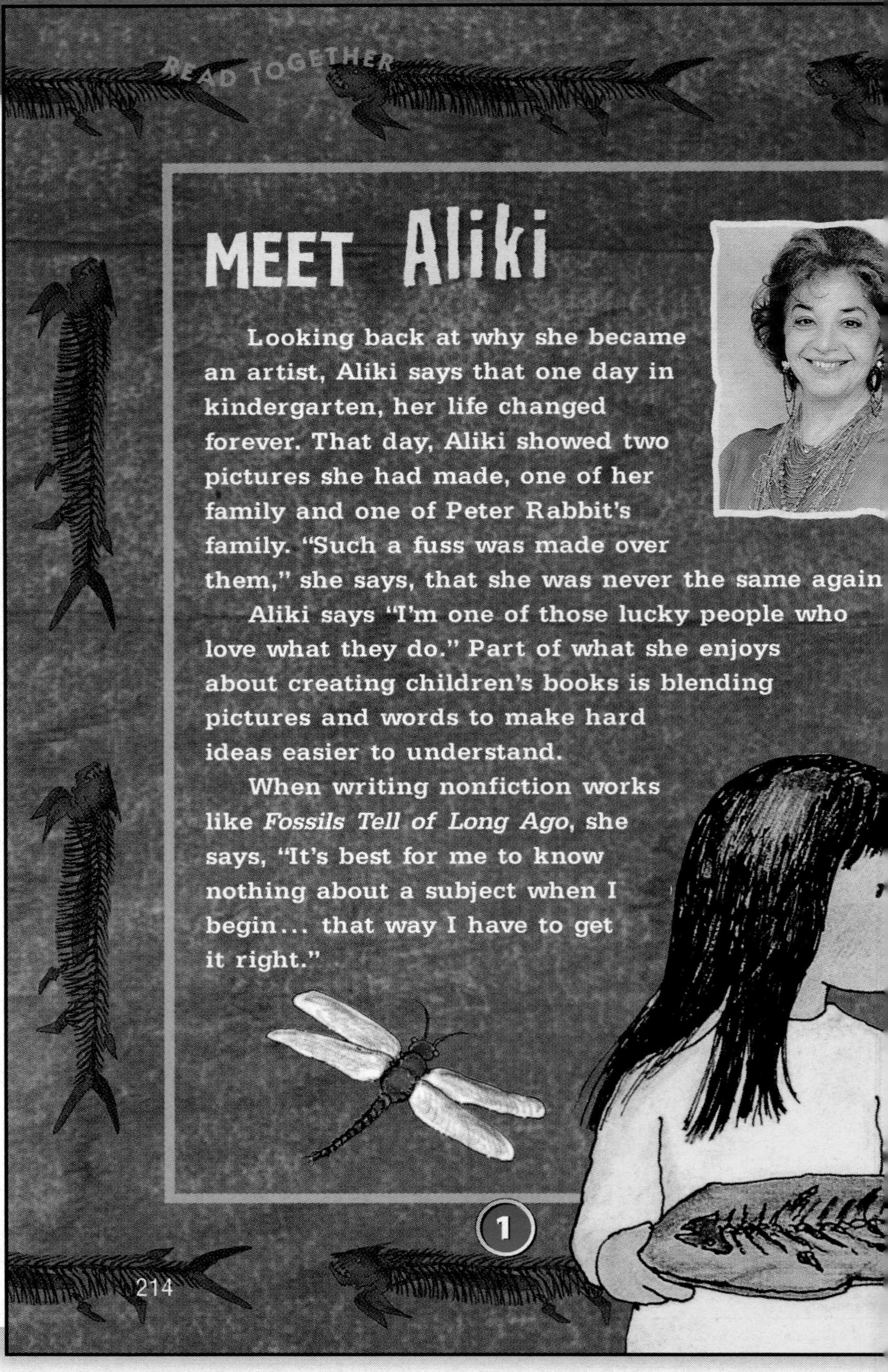
READ TOGETHER

MEET Aliki

Looking back at why she became an artist, Aliki says that one day in kindergarten, her life changed forever. That day, Aliki showed two pictures she had made, one of her family and one of Peter Rabbit's family. "Such a fuss was made over them," she says, that she was never the same again

Aliki says "I'm one of those lucky people who love what they do." Part of what she enjoys about creating children's books is blending pictures and words to make hard ideas easier to understand.

When writing nonfiction works like *Fossils Tell of Long Ago*, she says, "It's best for me to know nothing about a subject when I begin... that way I have to get it right."

1

214

Meeting Individual Needs • Grouping Suggestions for Strategic Reading

EASY

Read Together Have children look at pages 218–219 and then close their books. Read aloud 220–221, telling children to visualize the events as you read. After this introduction, read the story aloud and invite children to read aloud with you. As you read, model the strategy of summarizing chunks of story information.

ON-LEVEL

Guided Instruction Read the story with the class using Comprehension prompts. You may want to have the children read the story first on their own. Monitor any difficulties in reading the children may have in order to determine which parts of Comprehension to emphasize.

CHALLENGE

Read Independently Remind students that learning how to summarize important events can help them understand and better remember what happens in the story. After reading, have children summarize selection information in their own words.

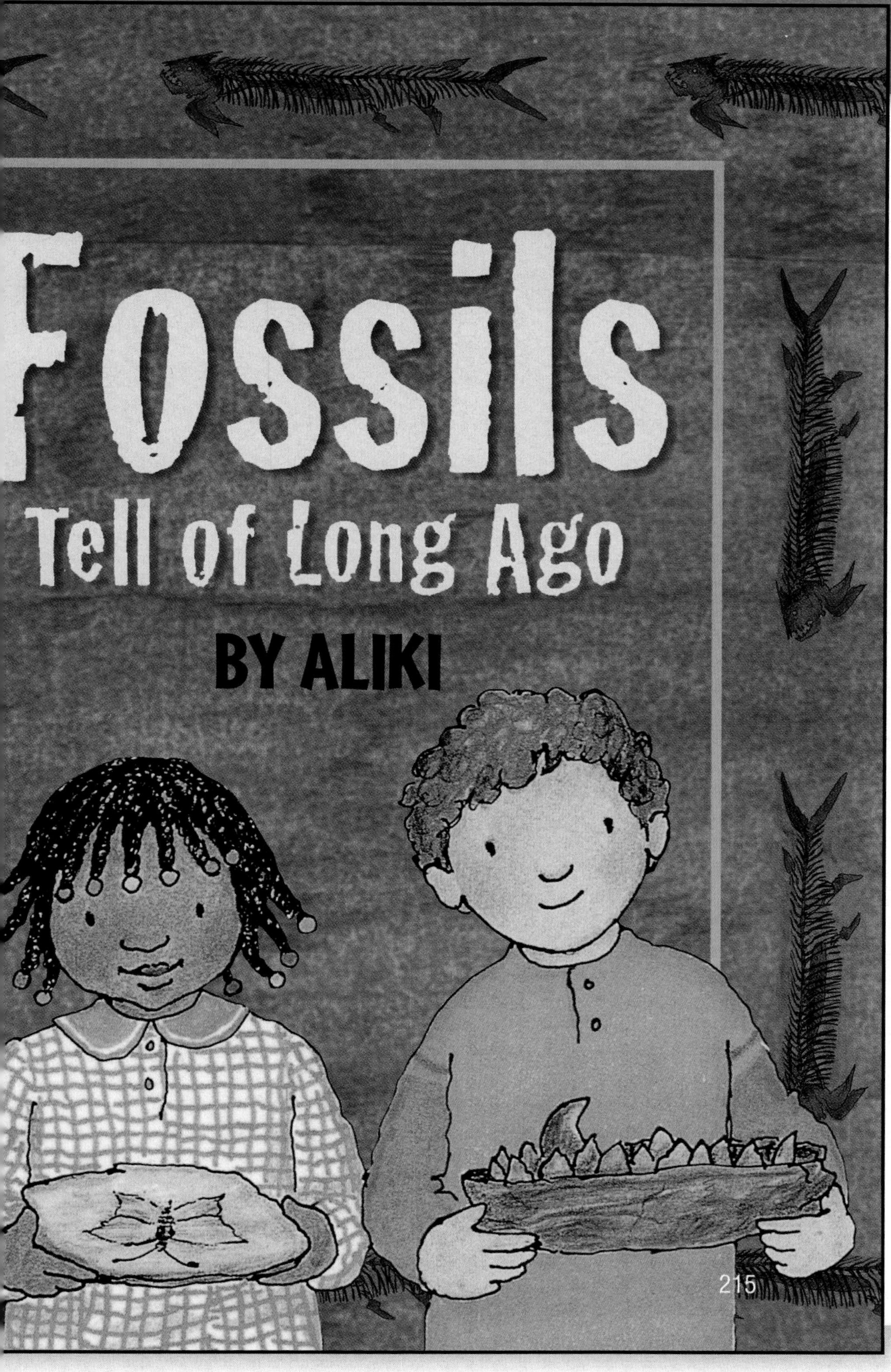

Comprehension

Phonics Apply /ou/ and /oi/

Apply Summarize

STRATEGIC READING Explain to students that if they were to tell someone else about this selection, they would summarize, or tell only the main facts. Tell them they will fill in a story map with important facts that build on one another. This will help them to understand and summarize the story better.

Fossils Tell of Long Ago
↓

1 Look at the illustrations on pages 214–215. What do you think a fossil is, from looking at the pictures? *Make Inferences*

Genre

Informational Story

Tell children that an informational story:

- has believable characters and realistic settings.
- tells a story with a simple plot.
- gives information in an easy-to-understand way.

Activity After children read *Fossils Tell of Long Ago,* have them compare this selection to *Fernando's Gift,* in Book 2-Unit 1. Ask children to examine both informational stories for similarities and differences. Have them focus on character development, setting, and the way information is presented. Invite children to share their preference for drawn illustrations or photographs.

LANGUAGE SUPPORT

A blackline master of the story map is available in the **Language Support Book**.

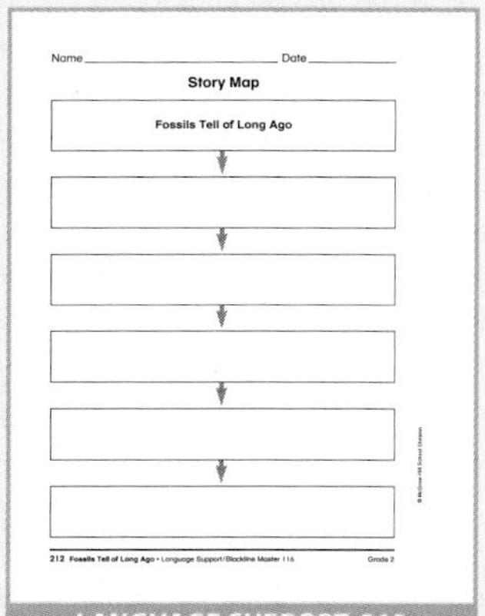
Name ________ Date ________

Story Map

Fossils Tell of Long Ago

LANGUAGE SUPPORT, 212

Comprehension

2 What did the big fish do? (It ate the little fish whole.) Why? (It was hungry.)
Cause and Effect

3 **SUMMARIZE** What do you think is the most important event on pages 216 and 217?

MODEL These pages give me some information, but I only need to include the most important facts when I summarize. I think the most important information here is that a big fish died ninety million years ago. That's what I will add to my story map.

Fossils Tell of Long Ago

↓

A big fish died in mud ninety million years ago.

Fluency

READING ALOUD

PARTNERS Have partners take turns reading to each other.

- While one child reads, have the other child track the print with his/her finger.
- Remind children to focus on punctuation, and to notice how your voice changes when asking a question.

Once upon a time a huge fish was swimming around when along came a smaller fish.

2 The big fish was so hungry it swallowed the other fish whole.

216

The big fish died and sank to the bottom of the sea. This happened ninety million years ago. How do we know?

3

4

5

217

Comprehension

4 Reread page 217 and look at the illustration. How do you think scientists can tell that the fish sank to the bottom of the sea millions of years ago? (The scientist found its fossil.) ***Make Inferences/Make Predictions***

5 Does the author make you want to keep reading the story? How does she do this? (Yes, she ends the page with a question.) ***Author's Craft***

TEACHING TIP

CONTEXT CLUES **Explain that phrases, words, and parts of words (such as prefixes and suffixes) often provide clues about when an event happens. *Once upon a time*, for example, is a phrase used to suggest a long, long time ago. The *-ed* ending in the word *happened*, on page 217, tells the reader that something took place in the past.**

LANGUAGE SUPPORT

ESL Write the word *swallow* on the chalkboard and ›monstrate its meaning. Then write e word *swallowed* on the chalk- ›ard. Draw a line between the base ord and the *-ed* suffix. Explain that ›ing the *-ed* suffix means that the :tion took place in the past. Ask chil- en to find other words that end in *-ed* (died, happened) and discuss the meaning of each. Remind children that many past tense verbs don't end in *-ed*. Then ask them to find past tense verbs on these pages that don't end in *-ed*. (was, sank) Ask children to give the present tense equivalent of each.

Comprehension

6 Reread this page and look closely at the illustration again. Describe the illustration on pages 218–219. (It is a fish fossil.) How can a scientist determine the age of a fossil? (By figuring out the approximate age of the stone.) ***Make Inferences***

7 Why might fossils be important to scientists? (They help scientists study what life was like many years ago.) ***Make Inferences***

TEACHING TIP

BACKGROUND INFORMATION Contact the Archaeological Institute of America or your local Archeological Society for information, educational programs, and guest speakers. Also, provide other picture books or magazines about fossils and archeology for students to examine. Encourage children to verify the accuracy of information in their book.

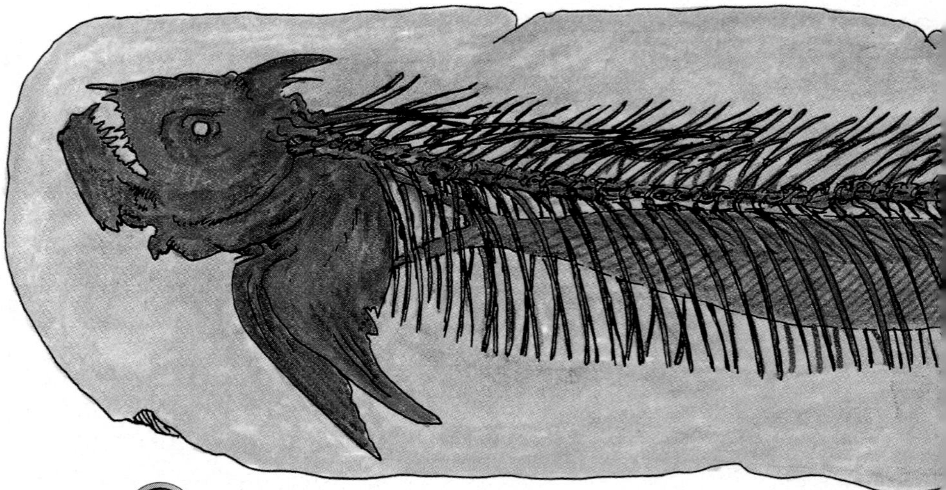

6

We know because the fish turned to stone. The fish became a fossil. A plant or animal that has turned to stone is called a fossil.

7 Scientists can tell how old stones are. They could tell how old the fish fossil was.

How did the fish become a fossil?

218

Activity

Cross Curricular: Social Studies

PREHISTORIC LIFE Discuss the meaning of *prehistoric*. Write a list of places on the chalkboard where prehistoric people lived, for example, Çatal Huyuk, Turkey; Oaxaca, Mexico; and Yangtze Valley, China.

RESEARCH AND INQUIRY Have children choose a place to research. Ask them to write a few sentences that describe the shelters in which people lived, the clothes they wore, and what they did to get food.
▶ **Linguistic**

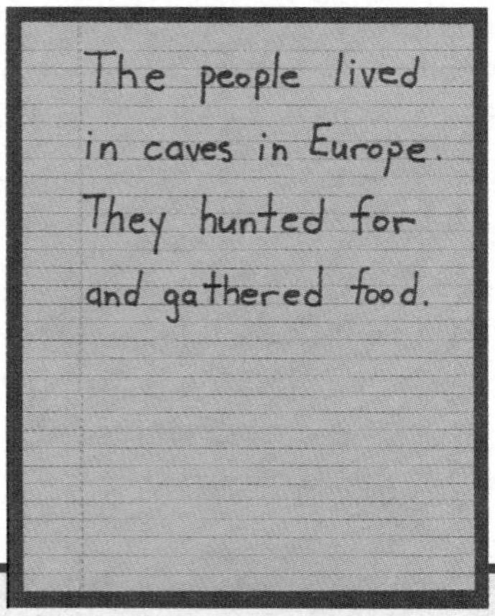

The people lived
in caves in Europe.
They hunted for
and gathered food.

Most animals and plants do not become fossils when they die. Some rot.

Others dry up, crumble, and blow away. No trace of them is left. This could have happened to the big fish. We would never know it had lived. Instead, the fish became a fossil. This is how it happened.

219

PREVENTION/INTERVENTION

HONICS AND DECODING

emind children that the letters *le* can make the sound /əl/. Write the following vords on the chalkboard as you blend the sounds together emphasizing the /əl/ ound in each one: *little, crumble, bubble, twinkle.* Encourage children to blend the ounds together to read the words and underline the letters *le* that make the /əl/ ound. Finally, tell children to use each word in a sentence. *Graphophonic Cues*

Comprehension

PHONICS AND DECODING Find the word spelled c-r-u-m-b-l-e. Point to it, and read it. Use your finger to help you to remember to blend the sounds of the letters together. (c r u m b le crumble)
Graphophonic Cues

8 Where do you think these children are? (at an exhibit in a museum)
Setting/Make Inferences

Minilesson

REVIEW/MAINTAIN

Decoding Multisyllabic Words

Tell children that if they come across a multisyllabic word they cannot pronounce, they can try breaking it into syllables. Review that most often, when two or more consonants appear in the middle of a word, you can divide it into syllables (digraphs are the exception).

- Remind children that these words often have short vowel sounds in both syllables.
- Have children locate *fossil, crumble,* and *instead* on page 219. Tell them to break these words into syllables.

Activity Have children create a list of other words in this selection that can be divided between consonants. Encourage them to divide and then blend the syllables to pronounce the word.

Comprehension

9 What happened after the big fish died? (It sank to the bottom of the sea and rotted.) ***Sequence of Events***

10 What remained? (The skeleton of the big fish and the smaller fish.) What happened next? (Layers of mud covered the skeleton.) ***Sequence of Events***

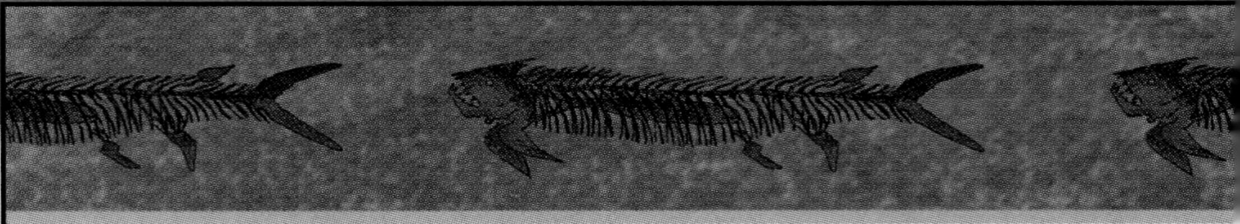

When the big fish died, it sank into the
9 mud at the bottom of the sea. Slowly, the soft parts of the fish rotted away. Only its hard bones were left. The bones of the fish it had eaten were left, too. The skeleton of the fish
10 lay buried and protected deep in the mud.

Thousands of years went by. More layers of mud covered the fish. Tons and tons of mud piled up. After a long time, the surface of the earth changed. The sea where the fish was buried dried out.

Activity

Cross Curricular: Science

AN IMPRINT INVESTIGATION An imprint in a fossil can help a scientist identify it. How does a fingerprint help identify you?

Have students work with partners to make fingerprints with their thumbs, using clay or fingerpaints. Ask students to look closely at the fingerprints. How are the fingerprints different from their partners? How are they alike? Have students write their observations on paper and share their findings with the class.
▶ **Kinesthetic/Logical**

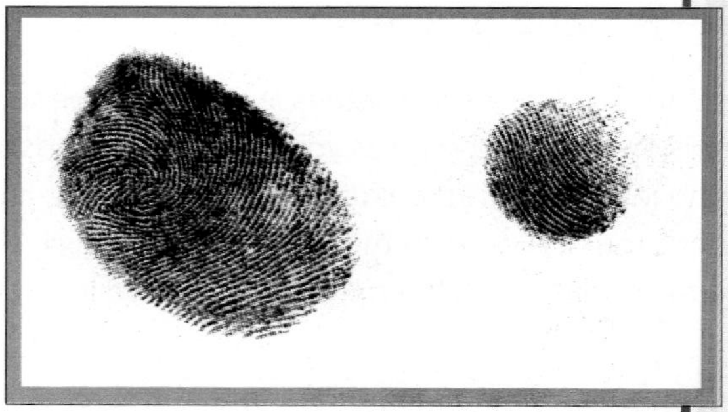

The weight of the layers of mud pressed down. Slowly, the mud turned to rock. As that happened, ground water seeped through the changing layers of mud. (11)

Minerals were dissolved in the water. The water seeped into all the tiny holes in the fish bones. (12)

The minerals in the water were left behind in the fish bones. After a very long time the bones turned to stone. The fish was a fossil.

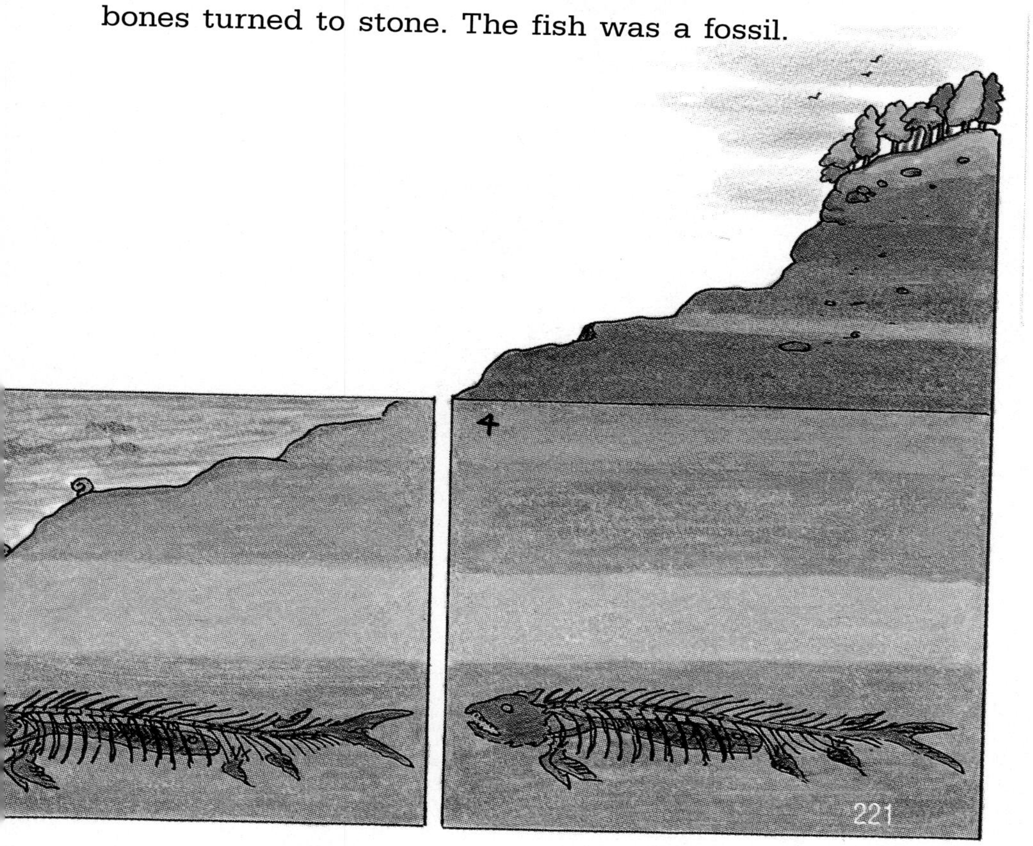

Comprehension

11 **Phonics** ***/ou/*** Find the words with /ou/ on page 221. How is /ou/ spelled in each word? (*ou, ow; down, ground*) Where is the vowel sound in each word? (middle: *down, ground*) ***Graphophonic Cues***

12 **SUMMARIZE** What are the most important events that happened on these pages? Let's add to our story map.

A big fish died in mud ninety million years ago.

↓

Parts of the fish rotted away and only its bones were left protected deep in the mud.

↓

Slowly, the bones turned to stone.

Minilesson

REVIEW/MAINTAIN

/j/ ge and /s/ ce

Write the word *changed* on the chalkboard and have children read it aloud. Ask children to identify the letters in the word that stand for /j/. (*ge*) Next, write the word *surface* on the board. Ask the students to identify the letters that stand for /s/. (*s, ce*)

Activity Assign groups. Ask each group to write lists of words that contain *ge* for /j/ and *ce* for /s/. Have groups share word lists and use a word with *ge* for /j/ and a word with *ce* for /s/ in context sentences.

Phonics CD-ROM Have children use the interactive phonics activities on the CD-ROM for reinforcement.

Comprehension

13 Read page 222. What are some of the differences among fossils? (Some are actual parts of plants or animals; some are imprints of plants or animals.) ***Compare and Contrast***

14 **Phonics** **/oi/** Cover the last two letters in *soil* and pronounce the word you see. (*so*) Cover the first letter and pronounce the word you see. (*oil*) What makes the vowel sound in *oil* and *soil* different from *so*? (the *oi* together) ***Graphophonic Cues***

15 Describe the process in which a leaf turns into a fossil. What happens first? (A leaf falls onto the ground.) What happens next? (The leaf rots and the peat hardens.) ***Sequence of Events***

13 Some fossils, like the fish, are actual parts of plants or animals that have turned to stone. Sometimes a fossil is only an imprint of a plant or animal.

14 Millions of years ago, a leaf fell off a fernlike plant. It dropped onto the swampy forest soil, which is called peat. The leaf rotted away.

15 But it left the mark of its shape in the peat. The peat, with the imprint of the leaf, hardened. It became a rock called coal. Coal is a fossil, too.

222

Activity

Cross Curricular: Math

WHICH IS MORE? WHICH IS LESS?
Review *greater than, less than* concepts. Help rank quantities of time.

Have children fill in the blanks on paper with the symbols > (greater than) or < (less than) to show comparisons of these quantities on the chalkboard:

- 100 years ______1 year
- 2 months _______1 year
- 1 hour ______1 minute

Have children create their own comparisons.
▶ **Logical/Mathematical**

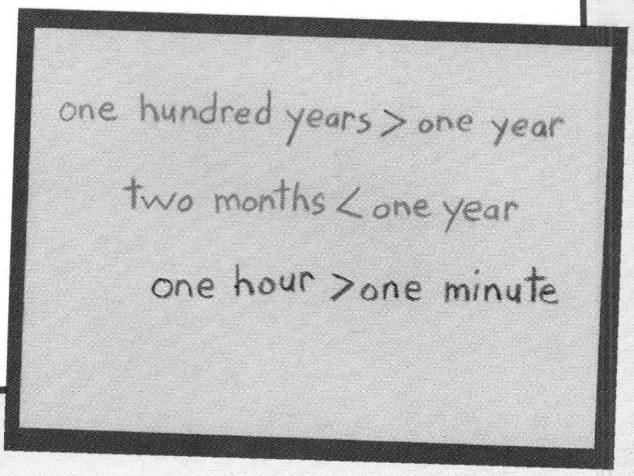

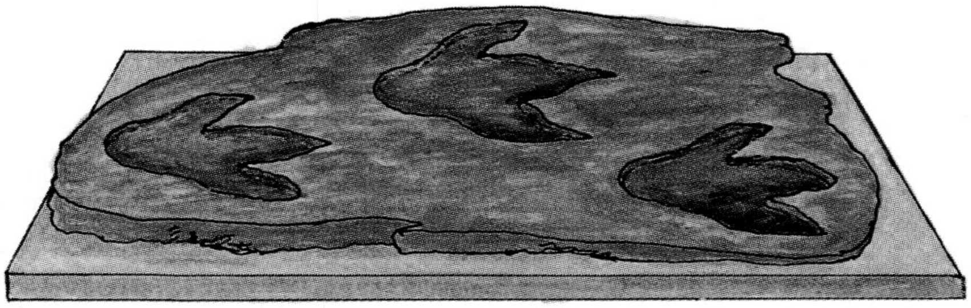

These are dinosaur tracks. They were made in fresh mud 115 million years ago.

Sand filled the dinosaur's footprints in the mud. The sand hardened into a rock called sandstone. Millions of years later fossil hunters dug through the rock. They found the fossil tracks—exact imprints of the dinosaur's foot. 16

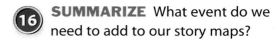

se footprints
us a lot about
Iguanodon.
Scientists can tell
how big it was.
And how fast
it moved.
And that it walked
on two legs.

223

Comprehension

COMPOUND WORDS Read the first two sentences in the second paragraph. What are *footprints* and *sandstone*? How can you figure out their meanings? (by figuring out the meaning of each smaller word in the compound word)

16 **SUMMARIZE** What event do we need to add to our story maps?

Slowly, the bones turn to stone.
↓
Some fossils are actual parts of animals or plants. Others are imprints.

PREVENTION/INTERVENTION

:OMPOUND WORDS Discuss with :hildren that just as we sound out let-ers to read a whole word, we can often ind smaller parts to help show the neaning of the whole word.

ootprint and *sandstone* are compound vords. They are each made up of two maller words. Identifying the meaning of each word helps us figure out the neaning of the whole compound word:

footprints: prints made by a foot

sandstone: stone made of sand

Have children identify smaller words in these compounds, define the compound, and use it in a sentence:

footstep football

Semantic Cues

Comprehension

17 How do fossils tell us that there "once were forests where now there are deserts"? (Fossils of plants and trees are found in the desert.) ***Draw Conclusions***

18 How do fossils tell us that there "once were seas where now there are mountains"? (Fossils of fish are found in the mountains.) ***Draw Conclusions***

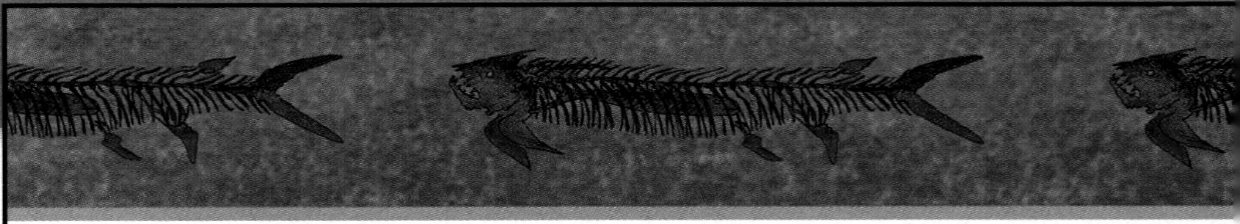

17 Fossils tell us about the past. Fossils tell us there once were forests where now there are deserts.

224

Visual Literacy

VIEWING AND REPRESENTING

Invite children to discuss the style of the drawings found in the story. Are they realistic or not? How can you tell if a drawing is realistic or not realistic? (If a drawing is realistic, the object's color and shape are like the real thing. It resembles the actual object.)

If the drawings had been more realistic and less cartoonlike, how would that have changed the children's perception of the story? (Opinions may vary, but it might have seemed more serious. Drawings made the story fun.)

LANGUAGE SUPPORT

ESL On page 224, an illustration shows a girl referring to "the petrified forest." Remind children that when they see an unknown word, they should look for other words or picture clues nearby that can help them understand its meaning. On page 225, the term is defined and the picture shows what the petrified forest looks like.

Point out that the pictures on pages 224 and 225 are pictures of the same place, but at different times.

Fossils tell us there once were seas where now there are mountains. Many lands that are cold today were once warm. We find fossils of tropical plants in very cold places. (18) (19)

225

Comprehension

(19) What might your town have been like 200 million years ago? (Answers will vary. Possible response: Since our town is in a warm climate, it might have been a cold one 200 million years ago.) ***Make Inferences***

Minilesson

REVIEW/MAINTAIN

Form Generalizations

Explain to students that generalizations can be made by observing, or looking closely, for what is the same among a group of persons, places, or things.

Activity Sort objects or pictures as Fossils and Not Fossils by placing a self-stick note on each to identify it. Have students help you make a list of what fossils have in common. (Examples: prehistoric; were buried; hardened into rock)

Have students form a generalization about fossils. Encourage them to consider things that are not fossilized (soft parts) as well as things that are. (Sample generalization: Fossils are usually formed from hard parts of plants and animals.)

Comprehension

20 Can you name an example of an extinct creature? (dinosaurs) Read the first five lines on this page. Explain what the word *extinct* means. (A creature that is no longer in existence.) ***Make Inferences***

21 How can you recognize a fossil? (A plant or animal is part of the stone; there is an imprint of a plant or animal in the stone or coal.) ***Draw Conclusions***

TEACHING TIP

USING CONTEXT CLUES Encourage children to use context clues to determine the meaning of an unknown word. The surrounding words provide information to help decipher the meaning. Think about the meaning of the word *extinct* in the following example: *They have all died out. We say they are extinct.*

20 Fossils tell us about strange creatures that lived on earth long ago. No such creatures are alive today. They have all died out. We say they are extinct.

21 Some fossils are found by scientists who dig for them. Some fossils are found by accident. You, too, might find a fossil if you look hard. When you see a stone, look at it carefully. It may be a fossil of something that once lived.

CULTURAL PERSPECTIVES

DINOSAURS Explain to children that dinosaur fossils have been found all over the world.

RESEARCH AND INQUIRY Have groups choose one kind of dinosaur and research the places where the fossils were found and who discovered them. Have groups create a museum exhibit based on their findings.

interNET CONNECTION Students can learn more about dinosaurs by visiting ***www.mhschool.com/reading.***

▶**Interpersonal/Linguistic**

That's Pteranodon, the flying reptile.
Here's an ichthyosaur!
It was quite a swimmer.
I love museums!

227

Comprehension

PHONOLOGICAL AWARENESS Point to the word *museums* in the speech bubble. How many syllables are in the word *museum*? How can you figure it out? (three; by clapping and counting the parts)

SELF-MONITORING STRATEGY

PARAPHRASE Paraphrasing, or retelling the information in your own words, can help you to understand facts and important details in nonfiction stories.

MODEL It's hard for me to remember all the information that I have read so far. I will go back through the story, and look at the pictures and captions to remind myself of important facts. Then I will retell the information that I have learned so far in my own words.

PREVENTION/INTERVENTION

HONOLOGICAL AWARENESS Have children listen as you say the word *nuseum* aloud. Ask them to clap for each syllable, or part, that they hear in the vord. Continue by saying the following two- and three-syllable words aloud. ncourage children to clap for each syllable they hear in the words: *fossils, deserts, inosaur, skeleton*. *Graphophonic Cues*

Comprehension

(22) **SUMMARIZE** Let's complete our story map with the rest of the main events or main points of the story.

A big fish died in mud ninety million years ago.
↓
Parts of the fish rotted away and only its bones were left protected deep in the mud.
↓
Slowly, the bones turned to stones.
↓
Some fossils are actual parts of animals or plants. Others are imprints.
↓
Fossils tell us about places, creatures, and plants that are extinct.

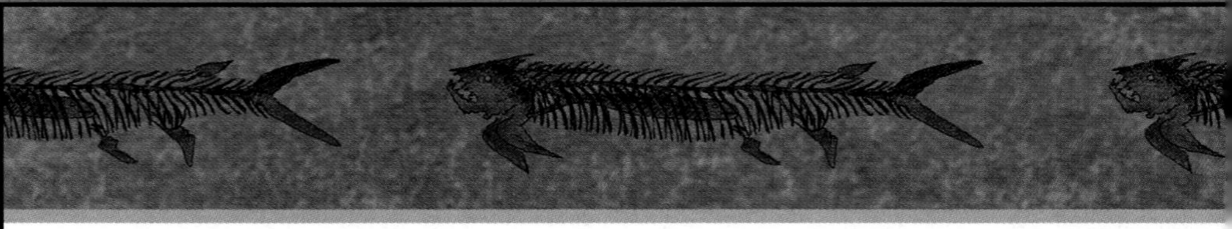

How would you like to make a fossil? Not a one-million-year-old fossil. A one-minute-old fossil. Make a clay imprint of your hand.

(22) The imprint shows what your hand is like, the way a dinosaur's track shows us what its foot was like.

First you take some clay.
Then you flatten it out.
Press your hand in the clay.
Then lift your hand away.

228

Activity

Cross Curricular: Art

MAKE IMPRINTS In *Fossils Tell of Long Ago*, there are instructions for the reader on how to make a clay imprint with his or her hand.

Explain that imprints can be made in many ways with many different materials. Assign children into groups and assign each group to make an imprint in a different way. For example, one group could make stamp imprints on paper, another group could fingerpaint pictures on paper, and a third group could make soap imprints.

▶ **Visual/Kinesthetic**

Suppose, when it dried out, you buried your clay imprint. Suppose, a million years from now, someone found it. Your imprint would be as hard as stone. It would be a fossil of your hand. It would tell the finder something about you. It would tell something about life on earth a million years earlier. 23

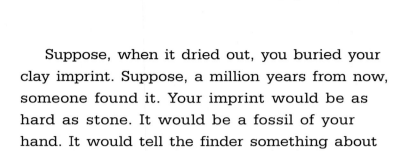

Comprehension

23 Explain the steps needed to make your own fossil. (First, I would make a clay imprint of my hands, then I would bury it. In millions of years, it would turn to stone.)
Steps in a Process

Minilesson
REVIEW/MAINTAIN

Main Idea

Tell children that knowing the main idea, or purpose, of a story helps us to understand what the author is trying to explain. Supporting details elaborate on and reinforce the main idea.

Activity Invite children to look through the story and write down what they think is the main idea of the story. Then have them list supporting details for the main idea. If students used the summarizing strategy during Comprehension, they might use their notes for this activity.

Comprehension

(24) **SUMMARIZE** Ask the children to summarize what they learned in the story by referring to their story map.

A big fish died in mud ninety million years ago.
↓
Parts of the fish rotted away, and only its bones were left protected deep in the mud.
↓
Slowly, the bones turned to stone.
↓
Some fossils are actual parts of animals or plants. Others are imprints.
↓
Fossils tell us about creatures and plants that are extinct.

RETELL THE STORY Have volunteers retell the story in their own words. They may use their story map for reference.

STUDENT SELF-ASSESSMENT

- How did the story map help me summarize what happened?

TRANSFERRING THE STRATEGY

- How can I use this strategy to help me read other stories and books?

(24) Every time someone finds a fossil, we learn more about life on earth long ago.

Someday you may find a fossil—one that is millions and millions of years old.

230

REREADING FOR *Fluency*

ONE Children who need fluency practice can read along silently or aloud as they listen to a recording of the story.

READING RATE When you evaluate reading rate, have children read aloud from the story for one minute. Place a stick-on note after the last word read. Count words read. To evaluate children's performance, see Running Record in the **Fluency Assessment** book.

Intervention For leveled fluency passages, lessons, and norms charts, see **Skills Intervention Guide**, Part 5, Fluency.

You may discover something
no one knows today.

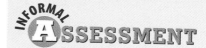

231

Comprehension

Return to Predictions and Purposes

Reread children's predictions, noting which ones needed to be revised and why. Then ask children if the story answered the questions they had before they read it.

PREDICTIONS	WHAT HAPPENED
The children in the story will learn about fossils.	They learned about all kinds of fossils and how they are formed.
They will visit a museum.	They visited museums and saw fossil exhibits.

INFORMAL ASSESSMENT

HOW TO ASSESS

/ou/ AND /oi/ Have children make a list of words from the story with /ou/ or /oi/.

SUMMARIZE Remind children that identifying the main points in what they read helps them to remember information better. Have them tell what they learned from the story.

FOLLOW UP /ou/ AND /oi/ Continue to model the blending of words with /ou/ and /oi/ for children who are having difficulty.

SUMMARIZE If children have difficulty, have them draw their own pictures of important parts of the selection and write about each picture.

LITERARY RESPONSE

QUICK-WRITE Have children draw a picture of a type of fossil in their journals, and write a few sentences about it based on facts that they learned from the story.

JOURNAL

ORAL RESPONSE Have children share their journal entries to discuss these questions:

- What types of things become fossils?
- How are fossils created?
- How long does it take something to become a fossil?

Story Questions

Have students discuss or write answers to the questions on page 232.

Answers:

1. Coal is peat that hardened into rock. *Literal/Detail*
2. The kinds of plants and animals have changed, and places where it is hot or cold have changed. *Literal/Compare and Contrast*
3. Fossils tell scientists what life on Earth might have been like millions of years ago. *Make Inferences*
4. This story tells how fossils were formed and what fossils tell us about the world that existed long ago. *Critical/Summarize*
5. Amanda might have found fossils in the La Brea Tar Pits. *Critical/Reading Across Texts*

Write a Speech For a full writing-process lesson, see expository writing on page 235M.

Story Questions & Activities

READ TOGETHER

1. What is a fossil?
2. Has Earth changed much since the dinosaurs?
3. Why are fossils important to scientists?
4. What is the main idea of this selection?
5. Where do you think Amanda from "The Best Vacation Ever" might have found fossils?

Write a Speech

What if you found a fossil? Write a speech that tells all about your discovery. What is your fossil made of? How did it become a fossil? What else can you learn from your fossil?

Meeting Individual Needs

EASY

Name________ Date______ Reteach 195

Story Comprehension

Think about "Fossils Tell of Long Ago." Read the statements below. If a statement is correct, write **true**. If it is not correct, write **false**.

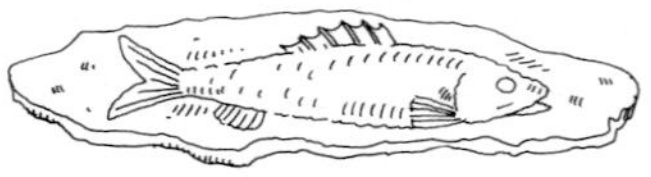

1. Animal bones that have turned to stone are called fossils. true
2. Scientists can't tell how old fossils are. false
3. All fossils of fish are at the bottom of the sea. false
4. Scientists study fossils to learn about life long ago. true
5. A plant cannot become a fossil. false
6. Some fossils are footprints of dinosaurs. true
7. A fossil can show us what an animal ate. true
8. You can see fossils in museums. true

8 Book 2.2/Unit 2 **Fossils Tell of Long Ago**
At Home: Have children use clay to make their own fossils of such things as a handprint, a leaf, or a shell. 195

Reteach, 195

ON-LEVEL

Name________ Date______ Practice 195

Story Comprehension

Think about what you learned from the story "Fossils Tell of Long Ago." Then answer these questions.

1. Does every animal turn into a fossil?
   No; most animals simply rot and disappear.
2. What kinds of things can become fossils?
   Possible answers: animals, plants, insects, footprints, fish
3. Name three things we can learn from fossils. Answers will vary. Possible answers: We can learn what ancient animals looked like and where they lived. We can learn where and when there were forests, mountains, and seas. Footprints can tell us how big an animal was, how fast it moved, and how many legs it walked on.

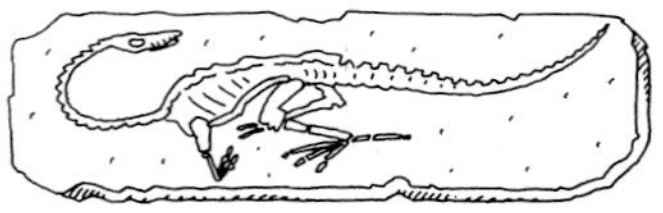

5 Book 2.2/Unit 2 **Fossils Tell of Long Ago**
At Home: Have children make a drawing of a fossil that they would like to find. 195

Practice, 195

CHALLENGE

Name________ Date______ Extend 195

Story Comprehension

How many objects in this scene could become fossils? Circle them.

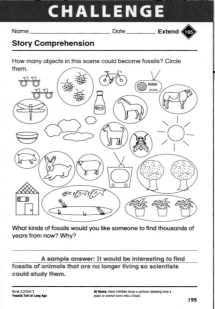

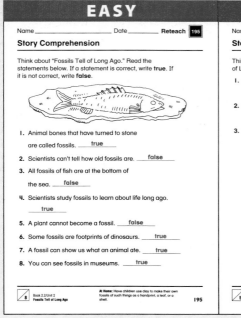

What kinds of fossils would you like someone to find thousands of years from now? Why?

A sample answer: It would be interesting to find fossils of animals that are no longer living so scientists could study them.

Book 2.2/Unit 2 **Fossils Tell of Long Ago**
At Home: Have children draw a cartoon showing how a plant or animal turns into a fossil. 195

Extend, 195

Make a Fossil

Make a clay imprint of your hand. Flatten some clay. Press your hand in the clay. Take your hand away. Carve your name and today's date underneath your handprint. Let the clay dry out and harden for a few days before moving your fossil.

Create a Mural

Fossils can tell us about the plants and animals that lived in a particular place. What plants and animals live in your community? Plan a mural that shows some of these plants and animals. Remember to add a title and to sign the mural in the corner.

Find Out More

Giant dinosaurs roamed Earth long before humans did. Find out more about dinosaurs. Choose a dinosaur to research and write a list of facts about it. When did it live? What did it eat? About how big was it?

233

DAILY Phonics ROUTINES

DAY 3 **Word Building** Divide children into four groups. Assign each group a letter combination: *ou, ow, oy,* or *oi*. Each group can make a list of words with the /ou/ or /oi/ sound.

Phonics CD-ROM

Story Activities

MAKE A FOSSIL

Materials: clay, toothpicks

ONE Show an example of an imprint and discuss the meaning of the word. Brainstorm with students how the imprint may have been made. Assign students into groups, and ask them to create a list of other examples of imprints in the classroom. Have groups share examples.

CREATE A MURAL

Materials: poster, felt-tipped markers, magazines to cut out pictures

GROUP Ask students to describe the plants and animals that live in the community. Organize and write the information in a graphic organizer on the chalkboard or on chart paper.

FIND OUT MORE

RESEARCH AND INQUIRY Have students work with index cards and a chart. They can write facts they know and facts they learn on index cards as they work. Invite children to visit **www.mhschool.com/reading.**

MY DINOSAUR: STEGOSAURUS	
What I Want to Know	Where I Can Find Out

FORMAL ASSESSMENT

After page 233, see Selection Assessment.

Study Skills

VARIOUS TEXTS

TESTED OBJECTIVES

Children will read and interpret signs.

PREPARE Ask children about signs they see every day. Read the paragraph. Display **Teaching Chart 164.**

TEACH Help students to interpret what each sign means. Have volunteers explain what the signs are directing them to do.

PRACTICE Have children answer questions 1–5. Then review the answers with them. **1.** 2nd floor **2.** behind the lobby **3.** information desk **4.** It means be careful because the floor may be wet. **5.** yes; the sign with the dinosaur picture has an arrow pointing to the left, on the same floor.

ASSESS/CLOSE Have children make drawings of their homes, and include signs giving directions to where various rooms are located.

STUDY SKILLS

READ TOGETHER

Interpret Signs

Fossils can tell us about animals and plants from the past. Many science museums have shows about fossils. This picture shows the main lobby of a science museum.

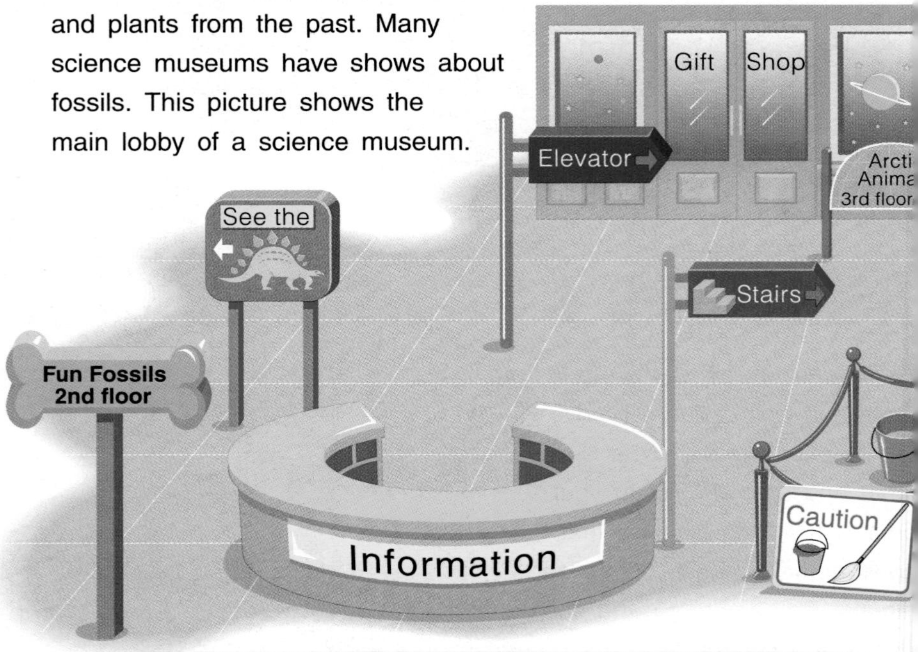

1. On which floor is the fossil exhibit?
2. Where is the gift shop?
3. Where would you ask for directions?
4. What does the sign near the ropes mean?
5. Do you think the dinosaur show is on the same floor as the lobby? Explain your answer.

Meeting Individual Needs

EASY

Name__________ Date________ **Reteach 196**

Interpret Signs

Signs are messages that call our attention to things. Signs can warn us, help us, and point us in the right direction. But signs can mislead us if we don't read them correctly. A good sign gets the message across quickly.

Below are examples of signs you see every day. On the line beside each sign, write what it means. Choose from the list of messages.

Stairway Down This Way | Tickets Sold Here
Deer Crossing | Stop | Don't Walk

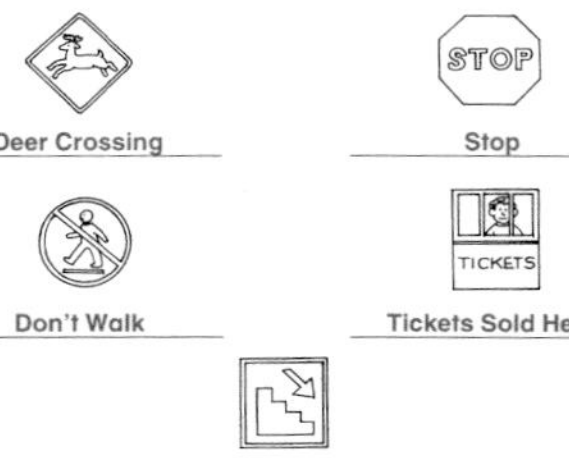

Deer Crossing
Stop
Don't Walk
Tickets Sold Here
Stairway Down This Way

196 **At Home:** Ask children to draw a sign they see on their way home from school. Book 2.2/Unit 2 **Fossils Tell of Long Ago** 5

Reteach, 196

ON-LEVEL

Name__________ Date________ **Practice 196**

Interpret Signs

Find the signs that show the messages listed below. Write the letter of the sign on the line beside each message.

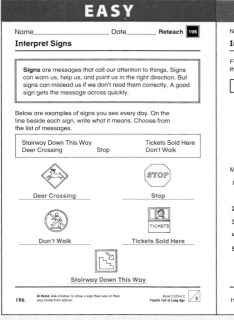

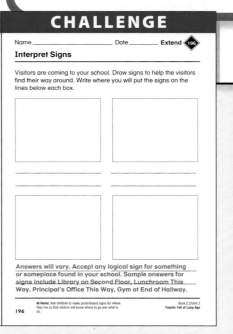

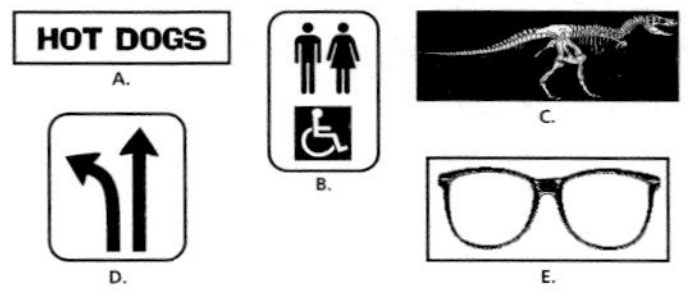

Messages:

1. The road is splitting up ahead to the right and to the left. D
2. Here is the dinosaur museum. C
3. Eyeglasses are sold in this store. E
4. A restroom is here for disabled people. B
5. Hot dogs are for sale. A

196 **At Home:** Have children draw pictures of any signs that they see on the way home from school. Explain the meanings of these signs. Book 2.2/Unit 2 **Fossils Tell of Long Ago** 5

Practice, 196

CHALLENGE

Name__________ Date________ **Extend 196**

Interpret Signs

Visitors are coming to your school. Draw signs to help the visitors find their way around. Write where you will put the signs on the lines below each box.

Answers will vary. Accept any logical sign for something or someplace found in your school. Sample answers for signs include Library on Second Floor, Lunchroom This Way, Principal's Office This Way, Gym at End of Hallway.

196 **At Home:** Ask children to make posterboard signs for where they live so that visitors will know where to go and what to do. Book 2.2/Unit 2 **Fossils Tell of Long Ago**

Extend, 196

TEST POWER

Check your understanding of the story as you read it.

DIRECTIONS:
Read the story. Then read each question about the story.

SAMPLE

A Present for Dad

Marci and her mother went shopping to buy a present. They walked into the store. They asked a salesperson for help. The salesperson showed them a list of everything in the store.

	Floor
Men's Clothing	3
Men's Shoes	3
Boys' Clothing	2
Girls' Clothing	2
Women's Clothing	1
Women's Shoes	1

Marci and her mother went to the third floor. They found a red necktie that Marci liked. Marci took the tie home. She put it in a box. Then, she wrapped the box in blue paper.

She made a card for her dad and put it on top. The next day, Marci gave the present to her father. He liked it so much that he wore it that same day.

1 What is the best summary for this story?
- ● Marci goes shopping for a present.
- ○ Marci and her mother like to shop.
- ○ Marci bought a box.
- ○ Marci likes the color red.

2 What did Marci and her mother do first?
- ● They asked for help.
- ○ They took the tie home.
- ○ They bought shoes.
- ○ Marci made a card.

235

Test Power

THE PRINCETON REVIEW

Read the Page

Explain to children that you will be reading this story as a group. You will read the story, and they will follow along in their books.

Request that children put pens, pencils, and markers away, since they will not be writing in their books.

Discuss the Questions

QUESTION 1: Remind children that the title often has clues to the main idea of the story. Also point out that the story ends with Marci giving her father a present.

QUESTION 2: Children should reread the story from the beginning, looking for what happened first. Of the choices listed, asking for help (third sentence) comes first.

Leveled Books

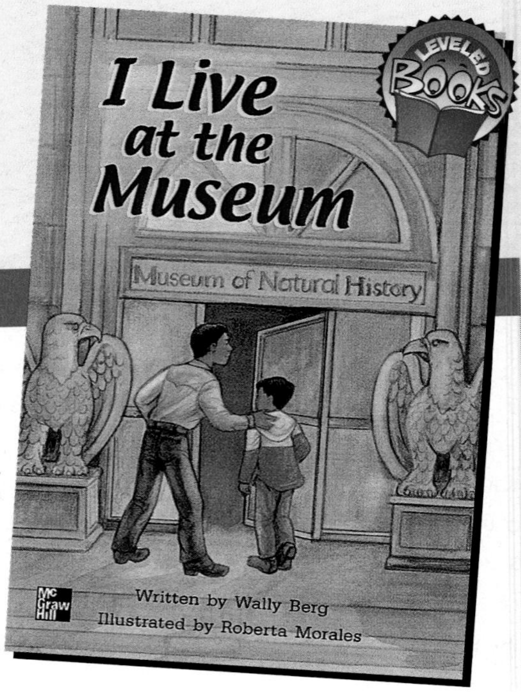

EASY

I Live at the Museum

- ☑ Phonics Diphthongs/ou/, /oi/
- ☑ Summarize
- ☑ Instructional Vocabulary: ***buried, creatures, fossil, fresh, layers, millions***

Guided Reading

PREVIEW AND PREDICT Take a **picture walk** with children through the story. Have children look closely at the illustrations and try to predict what the story will be about. Chart children's ideas.

SET PURPOSES Have children draw pictures of what they expect to learn by reading *I Live at the Museum*. For example, children might draw pictures of exhibits they hope to learn more about.

READ THE BOOK Use the following questions to guide children's reading or to ask after they have read the story independently.

Pages 4–6: What displays have Pete and his father seen so far? (They've seen North American animals and stars and planets.) ***Summarize***

Page 5: Find the word *owl*. Blend the letters *ow*. What sound do the letters make? (ou) Can you think of other words that use *ow* to make the /ou/ sound? *(cow, how, now)* ***Phonics and Decoding***

Page 12: Find the word *fossils*. Are fossils things that are old or new? What words help you figure out the meaning of *fossils*? (millions of years old) ***Instructional Vocabulary***

Pages 14–15: Summarize, or tell what is the most important idea, on these two pages. (Native Americans care about Earth.) ***Summarize***

RETURN TO PREDICTIONS AND PURPOSES Discuss children's predictions. Have children review their purposes for reading. Did they find out what they wanted to know?

LITERARY RESPONSE Discuss the following questions:

- Would you like to visit a museum like the one in the story? What would be your favorite room?
- Why do you think Pete wants a room of the museum named after him? What do you think he means?

Also see the story questions and activity in *I Live at the Museum*.

See the Phonics **CD-ROM** for practice using diphthongs /ou/ and /oi/.

Intervention Skills

Intervention Guide, for direct instruction and extra practice of vocabulary and comprehension

Answers to Story Questions

1. Pete and his father.
2. So he can learn about natural history.
3. What Pete is making believe, what Pete is thinking, etc.
4. Pete likes it at the museum.
5. Answers will vary.

The Story Questions and Activity below appear in the Easy Book.

Story Questions and Writing Activity

1. Who in this story are Native Americans?
2. Why, do you think, did Pete's dad take him to the natural history museum?
3. Some of the drawings in this book have two kinds of pictures. One kind of picture shows what is really happening at the museum. What does the other kind of picture show?
4. What is the main idea of the story?
5. What do you think Pete might tell the children in *Fossils Tell of Long Ago?*

Your Own Museum

If you could have your own natural history museum, what would you put in it? Look at the map on page 3, and then draw a map for your museum. Label each of the rooms.

from *I Live at the Museum*

Leveled Books

INDEPENDENT

Learn About Your World

- ☑ Phonics Diphthongs/ou/, /oi/
- ☑ Summarize
- ☑ Instructional Vocabulary
  buried, creatures, fossil, fresh, layers, millions

Guided Reading

PREVIEW AND PREDICT As you take the **picture walk**, see if children can predict what they will find out in *Learn About Your World*. Chart their ideas.

SET PURPOSES Have children write several sentences that describe why they want to read *Learn About Your World*. For example, children may want more information about specific scientific subjects, such as dinosaurs, natural disasters, or animals.

READ THE BOOK Use the following questions to guide children's reading or to ask after they have read the story independently.

Page 5: Find the word *layers* in the first sentence. Do you think the fossils are buried deep under the ground or are near the top if they are under layers of mud? ***Instructional Vocabulary***

Page 8: Find the word *out*. What sound do the letters *ou* make in the word *out?* Can you find another word on this page spelled with an *ou* that makes the /ou/ sound? (thousands) ***Phonics and Decoding***

Page 12–13: You have read about many different birds on these two pages. Give a one or two sentence summary that tells the most important things you learned about birds. (Birds live all over the world. Some birds fly and others swim.) ***Summarize***

Page 16: What kinds of things can you learn about Earth if you visit a natural history museum? ***Summarize***

RETURN TO PREDICTIONS AND PURPOSES Review children's predictions and reasons for reading.

LITERARY RESPONSE Discuss these questions with children:

- If you were to visit a natural history museum, what would be your favorite room? Why?
- Did you learn something new from reading the story? What did you learn?

Also see the story questions and activity from *Learn About Your World*.

See the Phonics **CD-ROM** for practice using diphthongs /ou/ and /oi/.

Answers to Story Questions

1. You can learn about Earth, Space, and the Ocean.
2. The World of Birds
3. At the museum, you can see things that are real and alive. You can observe things about the creatures for yourself. This gives you an experience that is very different from looking at a picture in a book or reading information on a page.
4. You can learn many new things if you visit a natural history museum.
5. The dinosaur fossil exhibit.

The Story Questions and Activity below appear in the Independent Book.

Story Questions and Writing Activity

1. What three parts of the world can you learn about at this natural history museum?
2. If you wanted to learn something about the Bald Eagle, which exhibit would you go to?
3. How is learning from a museum different from learning from a book?
4. What is the main idea of the book?
5. What exhibit in the museum might the author of *Fossils Tell of Long Ago* have visited to do research?

Create Your Own Exhibit

Think of an exhibit that you would like to create for a natural history museum. Draw the exhibit and be sure to label everything in it. Write a few words about why you chose this exhibit.

from *Learn About Your World*

Leveled Books

CHALLENGE

At the Museum

- ☑ Phonics Diphthongs /ou/, /oi/
- ☑ Summarize
- ☑ Instructional Vocabulary: ***buried, creatures, fossil, fresh, layers, millions***

Guided Reading

PREVIEW AND PREDICT Take a **picture walk** through the story. Ask children to predict what the story will be about. Chart their ideas.

SET PURPOSES Have children write why they want to read *At the Museum*. For example, children may be curious about all the different rooms inside a museum of natural history.

READ THE BOOK Use the following questions to guide children's reading or to ask after they have read the story independently.

Page 2: Find the word *enjoy*. What sound do the letters *oy* make? (oi) What other words can you think of that are spelled with *oy* and make the /oi/ sound? *(toy, boy, joy)* ***Phonics and Decoding***

Pages 3–6: What does Mark do during the day? (makes sure people don't touch exhibits, gives directions, answers questions) ***Summarize***

Page 11: Find the word *millions*. This is one of our new words. Are millions more than thousands? Less than billions? What other new vocabulary words can you find on this page? *(layers, buried)* ***Instructional Vocabulary***

Page 11–14: What does Mark describe on these pages? (dinosaurs, fossils, minerals, the moon) ***Summarize***

RETURN TO PREDICTIONS AND PURPOSES Discuss children's predictions. Ask which were close to the story and why. Have children review their purposes for reading.

LITERARY RESPONSE Discuss the following questions:

- If you met Mark, what would you ask him about the museum?
- What other exhibits might be in the museum? What would you want to see?

Also see the story questions and activity from *At the Museum.*

See the Phonics **CD-ROM** for practice using diphthongs /ou/ and /oi/.

Answers to Story Questions

1. He likes to go into the room with the African animals.
2. He remembers the map.
3. Things about animals, etc. and also about people who visit the museum.
4. Mark guards things in the museum; Mark enjoys going through the museum at night; Mark loves his family.
5. Answers will vary. He might tell them facts about fossils.

The Story Questions and Activity below appear in the Challenge Book.

Story Questions and Writing Activity

1. What is the first thing Mark likes to do when the people leave the museum?
2. Reread page 4. What does Mark mean when he says, "I have the map in my head"?
3. On page 5, Mark says, "But I have learned a lot, working at the museum." What kinds of things do you think he has learned?
4. What is the main idea of the book?
5. If Mark met the children from the story, *Fossils Tell of Long Ago,* what might he tell them?

Visiting the Museum

Look at the map of the museum on page 4. Now imagine that you are at the museum and want to find these things: 1. A picture of the Sun. 2. A model of a bear. 3. Information about a fossil. Write where you would find each of those things, and how you would get to them.

from *At the Museum*

Bringing Groups Together

Anthology and Leveled Books

Connecting Texts

WORD WEB
Write the story titles on the upper and lower right- and left-hand corners of a chart. Draw a circle with the word *Museum* in the middle of the chart. Have children identify animals/objects found in the museums in each story. Write the words under each story title. Then draw a line from the word *Museum* in the center of the chart to each of the words children contribute under the different story titles.

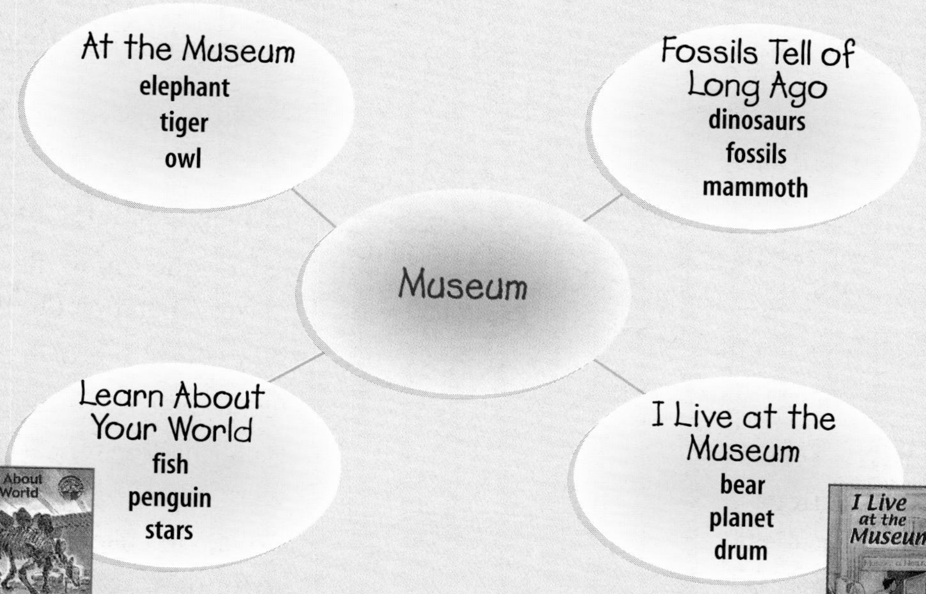

Viewing/Representing

GROUP PRESENTATIONS Divide the class into four groups. Have each group pretend to be tour guides giving a tour of a science museum or a museum of natural history. Have all group members participate in explaining some of the museums' exhibits to the rest of the class.

AUDIENCE RESPONSE Ask children to pay close attention during these imaginary tours. Encourage them to ask questions as they are introduced to the different "exhibits."

Research and Inquiry

MORE ABOUT MUSEUMS Have children ask themselves what other things they would like to know about museums. Then invite them to do the following:

- Visit a local museum.
- Investigate museums in picture books and reference books found in your school library.

*inter***NET CONNECTION** Have children go to ***www.mhschool.com/reading*** for more information or activities about museums.

Review /ou/ow, ou and /oi/oi, oy

TESTED OBJECTIVES

Children will:

- review /ou/ and /oi/.
- blend and read words with /ou/ *ow, ou* and /oi/ *oi, oy.*

MATERIALS

- **Teaching Chart 165**
- **Word Building Manipulative Cards**

Skills Finder

/ou/ *ow, ou,* and /oi/ *oi, oy*

Introduce	B1: 156G-H
Review	B1: 191E-F; B2: 212G-H, 235E-F, 235G-H
Test	B1: Unit 2

TEACHING TIP

MANAGEMENT Create card games such as word lotto using words with /ou/ and /oi/ sounds. Keep them on a classroom shelf where students can use them at an appropriate time for practice.

ALTERNATE TEACHING STRATEGY

/ou/ow, ou* AND */oi/oi, oy

For a different approach to teaching this skill, see page T76.

PREPARE

Listen for /ou/ and /oi/ Read the following sentence aloud and have children raise their hands whenever they hear a word with /ou/ or /oi/.

The town was joyful about the dinosaur find.

TEACH

BLENDING Model and Guide Practice with /ou/ and /oi/ Words

- Display **Teaching Chart 165**.
- Review the sound that each letter combination in the letter bank makes. Then point to the first example.
- Write the letters *oi* in the blank space.
- Blend the sounds together and read the word *point.*
- Have children repeat the blending process with you, reading the word *point.*
- Explain to children that they can continue filling in the blanks to form words by choosing a letter pair from the letter bank. Tell children that not all letter pairs will make up real words.

ou ow oi oy

p oi nt	c ow s	m ou th
j oy	pr ou d	b oy*
r ou nd	t oy	t ow n
s oi l	c oi n	cr ow d

*other possible answer: bow

Teaching Chart 165

Use the Word in Context

- Have children use the word in a sentence to reinforce its meaning. Example: *The point on the pencil broke.*

Repeat the Procedure

- Repeat this procedure until the chart is completed.

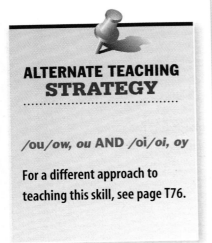

PRACTICE

BLENDING
Build Words with the Sounds /ou/ and /oi/

GROUP

Using the letter and vowel diphthong cards, have children work in groups to form as many words as possible containing /ou/ *ou, ow* and /oi/ *oi, oy*. Have each group list their words on index cards. Then have a volunteer from each group tack the words onto a bulletin board labeled *ou, ow, oi, oy*. Encourage children to classify the words based on their word families. ▶ **Interpersonal/Linguistic**

ASSESS/CLOSE

Read and Use /ou/ and /oi/ Words in Sentences

To assess children's mastery of blending and reading /ou/ and /oi/ words, observe them as they work together in the Practice activity. Ask each child to read two of the words from the chalkboard and use both in one sentence.

ADDITIONAL PHONICS RESOURCES

Phonics/Phonemic Awareness Practice Book, pages 125–128

McGraw-Hill School **TECHNOLOGY**

Phonics CD-ROM
activities for practice with Blending and Segmenting

DAILY Phonics ROUTINES

DAY 4 **Writing** Have groups of children write poems that include the words on their lists from Day 3. Invite one child from each group to read the poem aloud.

Phonics CD-ROM

SPELLING/PHONICS CONNECTIONS

See the 5-Day Spelling Plan, pages 235Q–235R.

Intervention Skills

Intervention Guide, for direct instruction and extra practice of /ou/ *ow, ou* and /oi/ *oi, oy*

Meeting Individual Needs for Phonics

EASY

Name ______ Date ______ **Reteach 197**

/ou/ *ow, ou* and /oi/ *oi, oy*

Read these words aloud. Both of them have the **/ou/** sound.
found how
Read these words aloud. Both of them have the **/oi/** sound.
joy point

Name each picture. Write letters from the box to complete each word.

ow	ou	oi	oy

1.  b __oy__
2.  c __oi__ ns
3.  cl __ou__ d
4.  t __oy__ s
5.  m __ou__ th
6.  c __ow__

6 Book 2.2/Unit 2 **Fossils Tell of Long Ago**
At Home: Have children think of two more words that contain these sounds. Ask them to write the words and draw a picture of each one. 197

Reteach, 197

ON-LEVEL

Name ______ Date ______ **Practice 197**

/ou/ *ow, ou* and /oi/ *oi, oy*

Write the words from the list that have the same sound as **ou** in **mouth** or **oi** in **soil**. Then circle the letters in each word that create the sound.

ground	how	south	point
foil	loud	joy	spoil
boy	sound	now	toy
soil	cow	join	found

mouth	soil
1. found	9. point
2. loud	10. foil
3. ground	11. soil
4. sound	12. boy
5. south	13. toy
6. cow	14. join
7. how	15. joy
8. now	16. spoil

16 Book 2.2/Unit 2 **Fossils Tell of Long Ago**
At Home: Recite the words, "How now, brown cow?" Encourage children to write a one-line verse using words from the page. 197

Practice, 197

CHALLENGE

Name ______ Date ______ **Extend 197**

/ou/ *ow, ou* and /oi/ *oi, oy*

Use words from the box to finish the rhymes in the story.

about	around	mouth	ground	soil	toy

One day I heard someone shout,
And I said, What's the noise __about__?
I heard another sound,
Then I looked to the __ground__.
Suddenly, I saw a snake!
It was not a fossil, not a fake.
The snake made a coil,
Down there on the __soil__.
Then I saw a boy,
Who was holding a __toy__.
I said, "Look what I found,
Please turn __around__."
To see the snake, the boy looked south.
There was the snake with a toy in its __mouth__!

Book 2.2/Unit 2 **Fossils Tell of Long Ago**
At Home: Have children write what might have happened next in the story. Encourage them to use words from the box. 197

Extend, 197

LANGUAGE SUPPORT

Name ______ Date ______

Fossil Moments

soil	mouth	ground	found

1. I __found__ a fossil!

2. This dinosaur had a big __mouth__.

3. Peat is a kind of swampy forest __soil__.

4. The mammoth was found in the frozen __ground__.

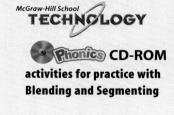

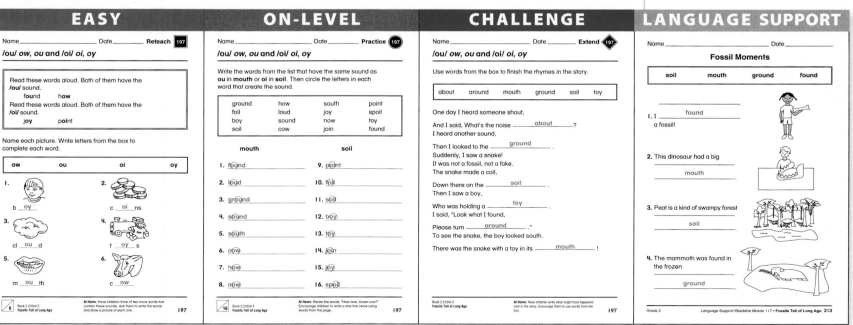

Grade 2 Language Support/Blackline Master 117 • **Fossils Tell of Long Ago** 213

Language Support, 213

Review /ou/; /oi/; /ər/, /ən/, /əl/; /âr/

TESTED OBJECTIVES

Children will:

- review /ou/ *ou, ow*; /oi/ *oi, oy*; /âr/ *are*; /ər/ *er*; /əl/ *le*; /ən/*en*.
- blend and read words with /ou/ *ou, ow*; /oi/ *oi, oy*; /âr/ *are*; /ər/ *er*; /əl/ *le*; /ən/*en*.

MATERIALS

- Word Building Manipulative Cards
- Teaching Chart 166

Skills Finder

/ou/ *ow, ou,* and /oi/ *oi, oy*

Introduce	B1: 156G-H
Review	B1: 191E-F, 191G-H; B2: 212G-H, 235G-H
Test	B1: Unit 2

LANGUAGE SUPPORT

ESL Write words that contain the /ou/, /oi/, and /âr/ sounds on the chalkboard. Read each word aloud, and have children repeat after you as you point to it. Invite children to demonstrate the meaning of each word through drawing, pantomime, or verbal clues.

PREPARE

Review /ou/, /oi/, /âr/, /ər/, /ən/, /əl/

Write this sentence on the chalkboard: *If you share the golden apple you found, everyone can enjoy it.* Ask volunteers to underline the letters that represent the sounds /ou/, /oi/, /âr/, /ər/, /ən/, /əl/. Explain that you will now review those sounds with their different spellings.

TEACH

BLENDING Model and Guide Practice with /ou/, /oi/, /âr/, /ər/, /əl/, /ən/ Words

- Display **Teaching Chart 166.**
- Read the words *ground* and *how* with children, blending the sounds in each word together.
- Ask children what sound the words *ground* and *how* both contain. (/ou/)
- Have children underline the spelling for /ou/ in each word.

ground	how
soil	boy
layers	water
hardened	happened
crumble	carefully

Teaching Chart 166

Use the Words in Context Have volunteers use the words from the **Teaching Chart** in sentences. Example: *They did not know how the ground changed.*

Repeat the Procedure Repeat the procedure with the remaining words on the chart.

PRACTICE

WORD BUILDING
Building Words and Sentences

ONE

Have children build words with letter, variant vowel, and vowel diphthong cards that contain the /ou/, /oi/, /âr/, /ər/, /ən/, and /əl/ sounds. Then have them write each word in a context sentence, underlining the target word. ▶ **Linguistic/Kinesthetic**

ASSESS/CLOSE

Read Sentences with /ou/, /oi/, /ər/, /ən/, /əl/, /âr/ Words

To assess children's ability to form and read words with the /ou/, /oi/, /ər/, /ən/, /əl/, and /âr/ sounds, observe them in the Practice activity. Then have children exchange their sentences and read them aloud.

ADDITIONAL PHONICS RESOURCES

Phonics/Phonemic Awareness Practice Book, pages 125–128

McGraw-Hill School TECHNOLOGY

Phonics CD-ROM

activities for practice with Blending and Word Building

DAILY Phonics ROUTINES

DAY 5 **Fluency** Write the following list of words on the chalkboard: *mouth, down, loyal, join*. Point to each word. Ask children to blend the sounds silently, and read each word aloud.

Phonics CD-ROM

ALTERNATE TEACHING STRATEGY

/ou/, /oi/, /ər/, /ən/, /əl/, /âr/

For a different approach to teaching these skills, see pages T65, T73, and T76.

Intervention Skills

Intervention Guide, for direct instruction and extra practice of /ou/; /oi/; /ən; /əl; /âr/

Meeting Individual Needs for Phonics

EASY

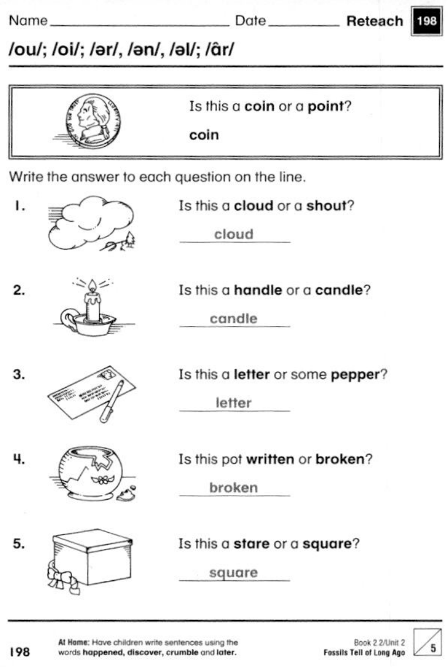

Name ______ Date ______ Reteach 198

/ou/; /oi/; /ər/, /ən/, /əl/; /âr/

Is this a coin or a point? coin

Write the answer to each question on the line.

1. Is this a cloud or a shout? cloud
2. Is this a handle or a candle? candle
3. Is this a letter or some pepper? letter
4. Is this pot written or broken? broken
5. Is this a stare or a square? square

198 At Home: Have children write sentences using the words happened, discover, crumble and later. Book 2.2/Unit 2 Fossils Tell of Long Ago 5

Reteach, 198

ON-LEVEL

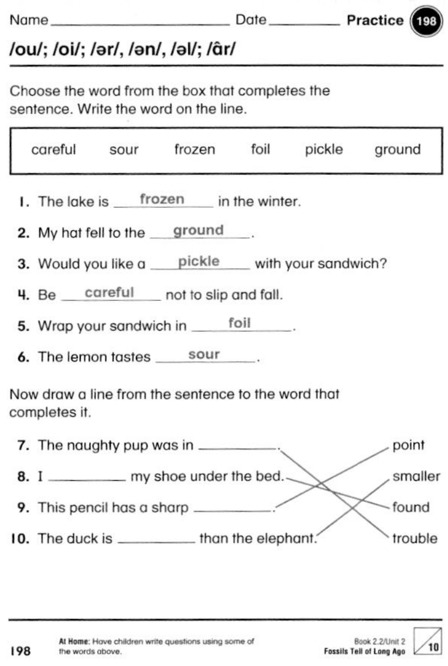

Name ______ Date ______ Practice 198

/ou/; /oi/; /ər/, /ən/, /əl/; /âr/

Choose the word from the box that completes the sentence. Write the word on the line.

careful sour frozen foil pickle ground

1. The lake is frozen in the winter.
2. My hat fell to the ground.
3. Would you like a pickle with your sandwich?
4. Be careful not to slip and fall.
5. Wrap your sandwich in foil.
6. The lemon tastes sour.

Now draw a line from the sentence to the word that completes it.

7. The naughty pup was in ______. point
8. I ______ my shoe under the bed. smaller
9. This pencil has a sharp ______. found
10. The duck is ______ than the elephant. trouble

198 At Home: Have children write questions using some of the words above. Book 2.2/Unit 2 Fossils Tell of Long Ago 10

Practice, 198

CHALLENGE

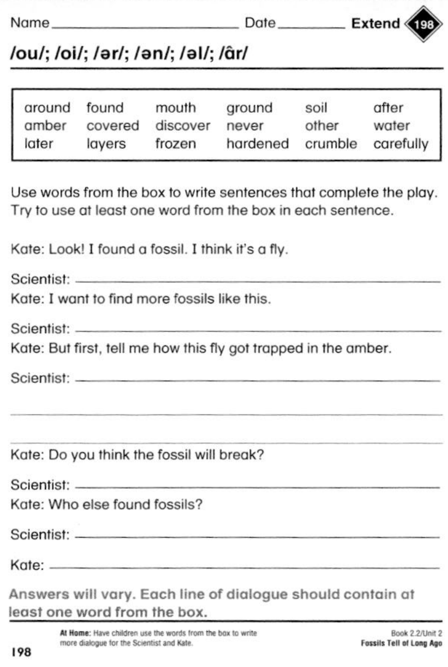

Name ______ Date ______ Extend 198

/ou/; /oi/; /ər/; /ən/; /əl/; /âr/

around found mouth ground soil after
amber covered discover never other water
later layers frozen hardened crumble carefully

Use words from the box to write sentences that complete the play. Try to use at least one word from the box in each sentence.

Kate: Look! I found a fossil. I think it's a fly.
Scientist: ______
Kate: I want to find more fossils like this.
Scientist: ______
Kate: But first, tell me how this fly got trapped in the amber.
Scientist: ______
Kate: Do you think the fossil will break?
Scientist: ______
Kate: Who else found fossils?
Scientist: ______
Kate: ______

Answers will vary. Each line of dialogue should contain at least one word from the box.

198 At Home: Have children use the words from the box to write more dialogue for the Scientist and Kate. Book 2.2/Unit 2 Fossils Tell of Long Ago

Extend, 198

LANGUAGE SUPPORT

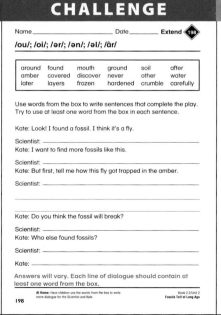

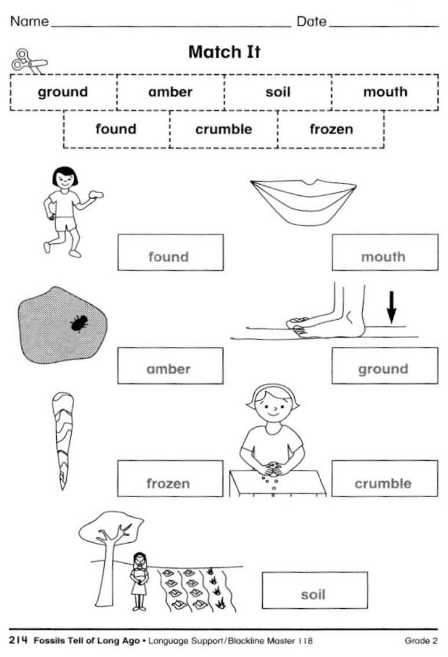

Name ______ Date ______

Match It

ground amber soil mouth found crumble frozen

found mouth amber ground frozen crumble soil

214 Fossils Tell of Long Ago • Language Support/Blackline Master 118 Grade 2

Language Support, 214

Review Sequence of Events

TESTED OBJECTIVES

Children will identify and list a sequence of events.

Skills Finder

Sequence of Events

Introduce	B2: 179I-J
Review	B2: 235I-J, 245E-F
Test	B2: Unit 2
Maintain	B1: 207, 229

TEACHING TIP

IMPLIED SEQUENCE OF EVENTS Explain that even if a scientific process does not contain a numbered list of items, it is still explained step by step. The steps or events are listed in the sequence in which they occur.

SELF-SELECTED Reading

Children may choose from the following titles.

ANTHOLOGY

- *Fossils Tell of Long Ago*

LEVELED BOOKS

- *I Live at the Museum*
- *Learn About Your World*
- *At the Museum*

Bibliography, pages T88–T89

PREPARE

Discuss Sequence of Events

Tell children that a good way to keep track of the sequence of events in a story is to make a list of events in the order they occurred. If you wanted to know how a fossil is formed, you would keep a list of each step in the process.

TEACH

How a Fossil Is Formed/Steps in a Process

Display **Teaching Chart 167**. Read the chart aloud with children.

How a Fossil Is Formed

1. A fish dies and sinks to the bottom of the sea.
2. The soft parts of the fish rot away.
3. The bones of the fish are buried in the mud.
4. Layers and layers of mud cover the fish over thousands of years.
5. The sea dries out and the mud turns to rock.
6. Minerals in the ground water seep into the fish bones.
7. After a very long time, the bones turn to stone.
8. The fish becomes a fossil.

Teaching Chart 167

Have children discuss the eight steps in the process of how a fossil is formed. Guide them to see that listing the steps in the proper order helps them to understand the entire process.

PRACTICE

Steps in a Process

PARTNERS

Have partners scramble the order of the eight events or steps on the **Teaching Chart** and then take turns putting them in the correct order. Have children reread page 223 in the story and make a list of the steps in the process of how dinosaur tracks became fossils.

▶ **Interpersonal/Linguistic**

ASSESS/CLOSE

Compare Process Steps

Have partners exchange their lists and compare how their lists are the same or different. Encourage them to work together to make one list that covers all the steps in the proper sequence. Ask volunteers to read their lists to the class.

ALTERNATE TEACHING STRATEGY

SEQUENCE OF EVENTS

For a different approach to teaching this skill, see page T71.

Intervention **Skills**

Intervention Guide, for direct instruction and extra practice of sequence of events

Meeting Individual Needs for Comprehension

EASY	ON-LEVEL	CHALLENGE	LANGUAGE SUPPORT

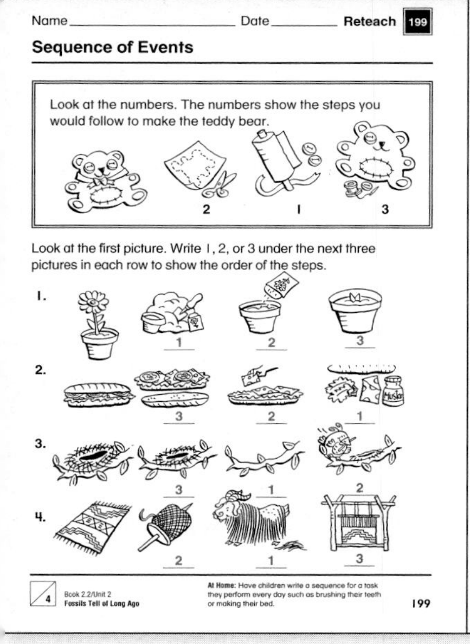
Name ________ Date ________ Reteach 199

Sequence of Events

Look at the numbers. The numbers show the steps you would follow to make the teddy bear.

Look at the first picture. Write 1, 2, or 3 under the next three pictures in each row to show the order of the steps.

1. 1 2 3
2. 3 2 1
3. 3 1 2
4. 2 1 3

4 Book 2.2/Unit 2 Fossils Tell of Long Ago — At Home: Have children write a sequence for a task they perform every day such as brushing their teeth or making their bed. 199

Reteach, 199

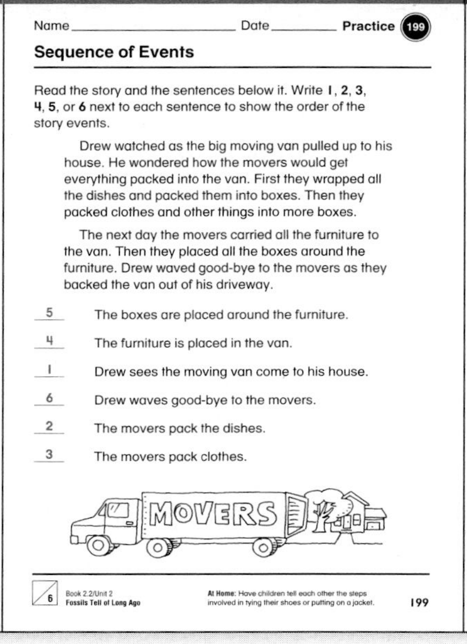
Name ________ Date ________ Practice 199

Sequence of Events

Read the story and the sentences below it. Write 1, 2, 3, 4, 5, or 6 next to each sentence to show the order of the story events.

Drew watched as the big moving van pulled up to his house. He wondered how the movers would get everything packed into the van. First they wrapped all the dishes and packed them into boxes. Then they packed clothes and other things into more boxes.

The next day the movers carried all the furniture to the van. Then they placed all the boxes around the furniture. Drew waved good-bye to the movers as they backed the van out of his driveway.

5 The boxes are placed around the furniture.
4 The furniture is placed in the van.
1 Drew sees the moving van come to his house.
6 Drew waves good-bye to the movers.
2 The movers pack the dishes.
3 The movers pack clothes.

5 Book 2.2/Unit 2 Fossils Tell of Long Ago — At Home: Have children tell each other the steps involved in tying their shoes or putting on a jacket. 199

Practice, 199

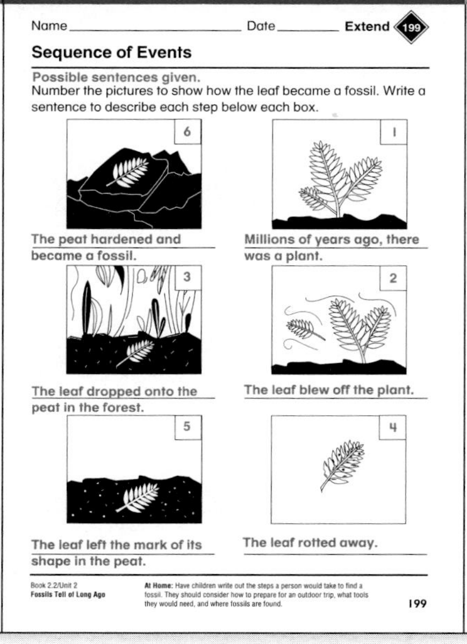
Name ________ Date ________ Extend 199

Sequence of Events

Possible sentences given.
Number the pictures to show how the leaf became a fossil. Write a sentence to describe each step below each box.

6 The peat hardened and became a fossil.
1 Millions of years ago, there was a plant.
3 The leaf dropped onto the peat in the forest.
2 The leaf blew off the plant.
5 The leaf left the mark of its shape in the peat.
4 The leaf rotted away.

Book 2.2/Unit 2 Fossils Tell of Long Ago — At Home: Have children write out the steps a person would take to find a fossil. They should consider how to prepare for an outdoor trip, what tools they would need, and where fossils are found. 199

Extend, 199

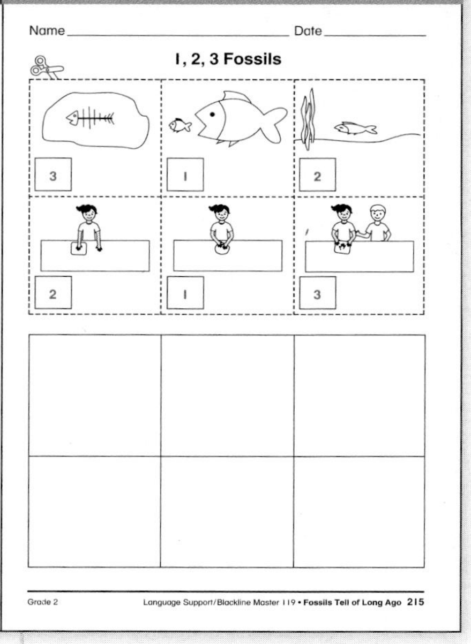
Name ________ Date ________

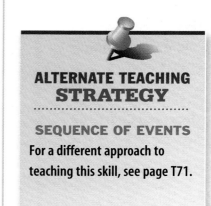

1, 2, 3 Fossils

3 1 2
2 1 3

Grade 2 — Language Support/Blackline Master 119 • Fossils Tell of Long Ago 215

Language Support, 215

TESTED **OBJECTIVES**

Children will identify context clues.

MATERIALS

- **Teaching Chart 168**

Skills Finder

Context Clues

Introduce	B1: 91K-L
Review	B1: 113K-L, 123I-J; B2: 179K-L, 245I-J
Test	B1: Unit 1
Maintain	B2: 139, 193, 269, 295

TEACHING TIP

USING REFERENCE MATERIALS Remind children that they can use a dictionary or glossary to find out the meaning of a word that they can't figure out from context clues.

Review Context Clues

PREPARE

Discuss Context Clues Ask children to raise their hands if they found unfamiliar words in the story *Fossils Tell of Long Ago*. Remind children that they can use nearby words to figure out the meaning of a word they do not know. Discuss how a science writer often defines or explains the meaning of an unfamiliar word in the same sentence or paragraph. The writer may also give examples that clarify the meaning of a scientific word.

TEACH

Identify Context Clues Display **Teaching Chart 168** and read the first sentence with children. Model how to figure out the meaning of the circled words.

1. A fossil is a dead animal or plant that has turned to stone.
2. The leaf fell to the swampy ground of the woods and rotted away in the peat.
3. Only the fish's bones were left. This hard skeleton was buried in the mud.
4. The dinosaur's feet made imprints in the mud. The tracks were easy to see. The hunters knew right away that they were a dinosaur's footprints.

Teaching Chart 168

MODEL I don't know what *fossil* means, but the rest of the words in the sentence explain what it is: a dead animal or plant that has turned to stone.

Then read the second sentence with children and discuss how they can use nearby words to figure out the meaning of the word *peat*.

PRACTICE

Identify Context Clues (PARTNERS)

Have volunteers underline the words in the sentences on **Teaching Chart 168** that can help them figure out the meaning of each circled word. Have partners discuss the meaning of each circled word and use it in a new sentence. ▶ **Linguistic/Interpersonal**

ASSESS/CLOSE

Write Context Clues

Have children write their own sentences using context clues. Ask them to think of a difficult word that they know, or a word from the story, and put it in a sentence that helps the reader understand its meaning. Have them circle the word. Then have the partners trade sentences and identify each other's context clues by underlining them. Encourage them to use the word in a new sentence.

ALTERNATE TEACHING STRATEGY

CONTEXT CLUES

For a different approach, see alternate teaching strategy on page T74.

Intervention ▶ Skills

Intervention Guide, for direct instruction and extra practice of Context Clues

Meeting Individual Needs for Vocabulary

EASY

Name ______ Date ______ **Reteach 200**

Context Clues

You can use **context clues** to find the meaning of words you don't know.

A plant or animal that has turned to stone is called a **fossil.**

Read the story. Then match each new word in dark type below with its meaning in the story.

The rain forest is hot and rainy. It is a **tropical** place. There are **millions** of different animals and plants there. No one can count them all.

Scientists look for helpful plants in the rain forest. They **discover** plants that can save people's lives. People work to protect the rain forest so the plants and animals do not become **extinct.** If a plant dies out forever, we can never know how special it is.

1. a **tropical** place is — hot and wet / cold and wet
2. **millions** means — different / a very large number
3. **discover** means — to hide / to find
4. to be **extinct** means — to have died out / to search for

200 **At Home:** Have children circle the context clues in the story that helped them decide on the meaning of the words in dark type. Book 2.2/Unit 2 **Fossils Tell of Long Ago** 4

Reteach, 200

ON-LEVEL

Name ______ Date ______ **Practice 200**

Context Clues

Sometimes you can figure out the meaning of unfamiliar words by looking at the words around them.

Read the story. Some of the underlined words will be new to you. Look for clues to discover each new word's meaning.

In the Desert

Rob and Jill went for a walk in the desert. The air was hot and dry. The ground was hot and dry too. The soil was mostly sand so few plants grew there. Jill saw tracks made by the feet of small animals. She knew creatures like mice and lizards had walked there. When Rob looked for minerals, he found some interesting red rocks and brown rocks. He rubbed and polished a stone to make it shiny.

Draw a line from the word in the first column to its definition in the second.

1. desert	animals
2. soil	marks made by feet
3. tracks	rubbed to make shiny
4. creatures	a dry and hot place
5. minerals	what rocks are made of
6. polished	the top layer of earth, where plants grow

200 **At Home:** Ask children to tell you what context clues they used to figure out the meanings of the words in the exercise. Book 2.2/Unit 2 **Fossils Tell of Long Ago** 6

Practice, 200

CHALLENGE

Name ______ Date ______ **Extend 200**

Context Clues

Use the sentences to show what the girl said in the cartoon.

Here are fossils of other sea creatures!
I found a fossil of a fish!
What is buried in this ground?
I bet these fossils are millions of years old!

What is buried in this ground?
I found a fossil of a fish!
Here are fossils of other sea creatures!
I bet these fossils are millions of years old!

200 **At Home:** Have children draw another cartoon about fossils. Ask them to use some of these words in the characters' speech balloons: *bones, coal, peat, preserved, amber, minerals, imprint, and tracks.* Book 2.2/Unit 2 **Fossils Tell of Long Ago**

Extend, 200

LANGUAGE SUPPORT

Name ______ Date ______

Matching Up

coal
layers
sap
mammoth
fossil
imprint

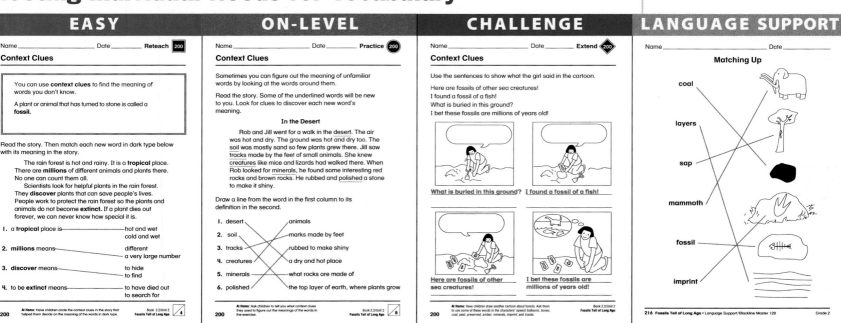

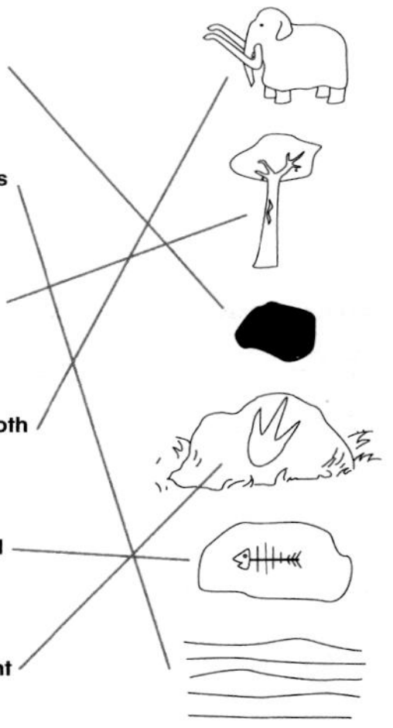

216 **Fossils Tell of Long Ago** • Language Support/Blackline Master 120 Grade 2

Language Support, 216

Expository Writing

GRAMMAR/SPELLING CONNECTIONS

See the 5-Day Grammar and Usage Plan on pages 2350–235P.

See the 5-Day Spelling Plan on pages 235R–235Q.

TEACHING TIP

Technology
Revise your work on the computer by highlighting information you no longer want and pressing the *delete* key. To add new information, click your mouse where you want to insert words and type.

Handwriting
Remind children to take their time to write neatly. All capital letters should be the same size, and all small letters should be the same size.

Handwriting CD-ROM

Prewrite

WRITE A SPEECH Present this writing assignment: What if you found a fossil? Write a speech that tells about your great discovery. What is your fossil made of? What is in your fossil? How did it become a fossil? What else can you learn from your fossil?

VISUALIZING Have children close their eyes and visualize themselves finding a fossil. Where did they find their fossil? What is the fossil they found and what does it look like?

Strategy: Make a Drawing Have the children open their eyes and draw the fossil they visualized in their minds.

Elaborate: Remind children to include details about the place where they found the fossil, as well as details of the fossil itself. The children's drawings will serve as references for their speeches. They can also make notes on their drawings to elaborate on the fossil.

Draft

USE THE DRAWING Guide children to use their drawings to recall the most important details about their fossil discovery. Remind them that speeches should contain an introduction of the topic, a middle section, which includes supporting details, and a conclusion.

Revise

WORK WITH A PARTNER Children work in pairs and share their fossil discovery speeches. Guide them to comment clearly on the most interesting parts of each other's writing. Invite them to share questions about each other's fossils to clarify their ideas and descriptions.

PARTNERS

Edit/Proofread

CHECK FOR ERRORS Students should reread their speeches to check spelling, grammar, and punctuation. Encourage them to pick a quiet spot and read their speeches aloud to each other.

Publish

BULLETIN-BOARD DISPLAY Have children create a wall display of their speeches and drawings. Guide them to discuss each fossil discovery and state the most interesting points.

THE FISH FOSSIL IN MY BACKYARD

I was digging in my garden and found the skeleton of a fish. The skeleton had turned into stone.

The fish died millions of years ago and was buried under layers of soil. After all that time, it turned to stone and became a fossil.

The more fossils that are found, the more we learn about the creatures who lived long ago. Where fossils are found is also important. This fossil tells me that a fish lived in my backyard a million years ago and that there was water there, instead of a garden.

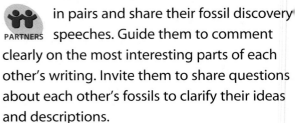

Presentation Ideas

MATCH SPEECHES TO DRAWINGS
Display a few drawings and ask children to study them. Reread a few speeches. Ask children to match drawings with speeches.
▶ **Viewing/Representing**

MAKE AN ANNOUNCEMENT Have children imagine that they are at a press conference announcing their great fossil discovery. Encourage the audience to ask questions.
▶ **Speaking/Listening**

Consider students' creative efforts, possibly adding a plus (+) for originality, wit, and imagination.

Scoring Rubric

Excellent	Good	Fair	Unsatisfactory
4: The writer • vividly presents the facts of his or her fossil discovery. • provides rich supporting information, details, and description. • explains clearly the significance of the discovery.	**3:** The writer • clearly presents the facts of his or her fossil discovery. • provides adequate supporting information, details, and description. • attempts to explain significance of the discovery.	**2:** The writer • states the discovery, but does not include pertinent facts. • provides few supporting details. • does not explain significance of the discovery.	**1:** The writer • does not clearly present a fossil discovery. • provides incomplete or unclear details. • does not present significance of the discovery.

Incomplete 0: The writer leaves the page blank or fails to respond to the writing task. The writer does not address the topic or simply paraphrases the prompt. The response is illegible or incoherent.

Meeting Individual Needs for Writing

EASY

Invitation Have children write an invitation to the members of the media to come to a press conference featuring their fossil discovery. Remind them to include the subject, place, date, and time.

ON-LEVEL

Caption Have children write display captions to go with their fossil discovery, for a public viewing. Remind them to include the name of the fossil, where it was found, by whom, and how old it is.

CHALLENGE

News Bulletin Have children write a news bulletin that tells about the amazing fossil discovery they have just learned about at a press conference. Tell them to include all the information that newspapers would need to write a story.

Listening and Speaking

LISTENING Have children
- listen for new and interesting details about the fossil.
- try to determine if the information is based on facts or opinions.
- visualize the fossil as it is described.

SPEAKING Encourage children to
- speak loudly and clearly so children from all areas of the room can hear.
- choose descriptive words to tell about the fossil.
- maintain eye contact with various areas of the room.

LANGUAGE SUPPORT

ESL Pair each ESL student with an English-fluent child. Suggest that they both rehearse the presentation using the picture cards. As they do this, have them ask each other questions and make helpful suggestions.

PORTFOLIO Invite children to include their speeches or another writing project in their portfolios.

5 Day Grammar and Usage Plan

LANGUAGE SUPPORT

ESL Write this sentence on the board: *I live in (town).* Look at a student and say, *You live in (town).* Next point to a girl and say to the class, *She lives in (town).* Then point to a boy and say, *He lives in (town).* Write all four sentences on the board. Point out the *s* at the end of the verbs used with *he* and *she*.

DAILY LANGUAGE ACTIVITES

Write the Daily Language Activities on the chalkboard each day or use **Transparency 24**. Have children orally correct the verb in each sentence.

Day 1

1. She find a fossil. finds
2. It come from a stone. comes
3. He make a clay imprint. makes

Day 2

1. They finds tracks. find
2. We walks in the forest. walk
3. You looks for fossils. look

Day 3

1. It tell of long ago. tells
2. She fill the footprints with sand. fills
3. We discovers something. discover

Day 4

1. It live in the sea. lives
2. She dig for a fossil. digs
3. He drop it into the swamp. drops

Day 5

1. It turn to stone. turns
2. She lift her hand from the clay. lifts
3. We shows her the imprint. show

Daily Language Transparency 24

DAY 1 Introduce the Concept

Oral Warm-Up Write these sentences on the board: *He wants to play. They want to play.* Explain that when the subject of the sentence changes from *he* to *they*, the form of the verb must change from *wants* to *want.*

Introduce Pronoun-Verb Agreement Explain that present-tense verbs must agree with their subjects and that this is also true when the subject is a pronoun. Present the following:

Pronoun-Verb Agreement

- A present-tense verb must agree with a pronoun in the subject part of a sentence.
- With the pronouns *he, she,* and *it,* add *-s* to most action verbs in the present tense.

Present the Daily Language Activity. Then have children write a sentence using *he, she,* or *it* and underline the form the verb takes in the sentence.

WRITING Assign the daily Writing Prompt on page 212C.

Name ______ Date ______ LEARN Grammar 147

Pronoun-Verb Agreement

- A present-tense verb must agree with its subject when the subject is a noun. It must also agree with its subject when the subject is a pronoun.
- A present-tense verb must agree with a pronoun in the subject part of the sentence.
- With the pronouns *he, she,* and *it,* add *-s* to most action verbs in the present tense.

He visits the Ramos family every year.
She goes with him.

Underline the correct verb in each sentence.
Then write the sentence.

1. It (take, takes) two hours to drive there.
   It takes two hours to drive there.
2. She (show, shows) us the river.
   She shows us the river.
3. He (meets, meet) Ana and Diego.
   He meets Ana and Diego.
4. He (shake, shakes) hands with them.
   He shakes hands with them.
5. He (see, sees) the new car.
   He sees the new car.

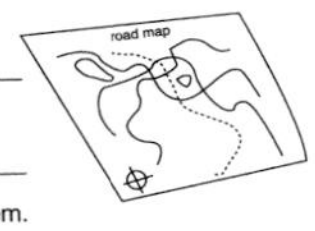

5 Book 2.2/Unit 2 Fossils Tell of Long Ago — **Extension:** Have the children write sentences for the remaining verbs. — 147

GRAMMAR PRACTICE BOOK, PAGE 147

DAY 2 Teach the Concept

Review Pronoun-Verb Agreement Remind children that present-tense verbs must agree with their pronoun subjects. Have them use *it* in a sentence with an action verb.

Introduce More Pronouns Present the following:

Pronoun-Action Verb Agreement

With the pronouns *I, we, you,* and *they,* do not add *s* to most action verbs in the present tense.

Review when a present-tense verb ends in *-s* and when it doesn't. For example, show how the action verb *find* changes when used with different pronouns.

Present the Daily Language Activity. Then have children write a sentence including the pronoun *I, we, you,* or *they* and an action verb.

WRITING Assign the daily Writing Prompt on page 212C.

Name ______ Date ______ LEARN AND PRACTICE Grammar 148

Pronoun and Verb Agreement

- With the pronouns *I, we, you,* and *they,* do not add *-s* to most action verbs in the present tense.

I sing	we sing
you sing	you sing
he, she, it sings	they sing

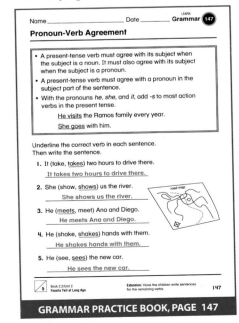

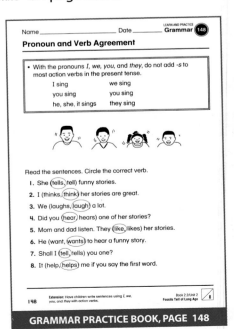

Read the sentences. Circle the correct verb.

1. She (tells, tell) funny stories.
2. I (thinks, think) her stories are great.
3. We (laughs, laugh) a lot.
4. Did you (hear, hears) one of her stories?
5. Mom and dad listen. They (like, likes) her stories.
6. He (want, wants) to hear a funny story.
7. Shall I (tell, tells) you one?
8. It (help, helps) me if you say the first word.

148 — **Extension:** Have children write sentences using *I, we, you,* and *they* with action verbs. — Book 2.2/Unit 2 Fossils Tell of Long Ago 8

GRAMMAR PRACTICE BOOK, PAGE 148

Pronoun-Verb Agreement

DAY 3 Review and Practice

Learn from the Literature Review pronoun-verb agreement. Read the second sentence on page 225 of *Fossils Tell of Long Ago*.

We find fossils of tropical plants in very cold places.

Have children identify the subject pronoun and action verb in the sentence. Ask them to explain why the word *find* was used instead of *finds*.

Write Sentences Present the Daily Language Activity and have children correct the sentences orally. Ask them to write three sentences, one using the pronoun *I*, one using the pronoun *we*, and one using the pronoun *he*. Have volunteers write one of their sentences on the chalkboard. Ask others in the group to identify the pronoun subject and verb in each sentence.

WRITING Assign the daily Writing Prompt on page 212D.

Name________ Date______ REVIEW AND PRACTICE Grammar 149

Matching Pronouns and Verbs

- A present-tense verb must agree with a pronoun in the subject part of the sentence.
- With the pronouns *he, she,* and *it*, add *-s* to most action verbs in the present tense.
- With the pronouns *I, we, you,* and *they*, do not add *-s* to most action verbs in the present tense.

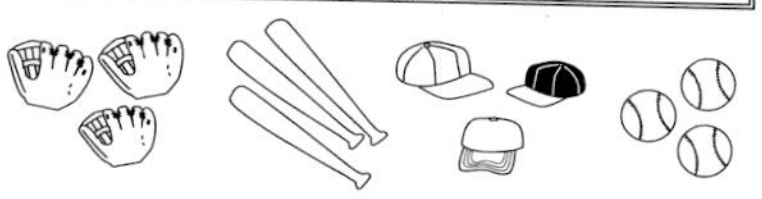

Read the sentence beginnings. Find an ending that could go with each beginning. Draw a line to connect them.

1. Carmen is quick. She — misses the ball sometimes.
2. The other team is new. They — calls the player out.
3. The umpire is fair. He — shakes his head.
4. The sun is bright. It — shines in our eyes.
5. Cliff is a beginner. He — find our team hard to beat.
6. Ron misses the ball. He — runs very fast.

6 Book 2.2/Unit 2 **Fossils Tell of Long Ago**

Extension: Have children use sentence strips to write sentences using pronouns and action verbs. They can cut them in half between pronoun and verb, mix them up, and try to reassemble them.

149

GRAMMAR PRACTICE BOOK, PAGE 149

DAY 4 Review and Practice

Review Pronoun-Verb Agreement Write the pronouns and action verbs from the Daily Language Activities for Days 1–3 on the board. Ask students to explain how to make each verb agree with its pronoun subject. Then present the Daily Language Activity for Day 4.

Mechanics and Usage Before children do the daily Writing Prompt on page 212 review how to write book titles. Display and discuss.

Book Titles

- Begin the first word and each important word in a book title with a capital letter.
- Underline all the words in the title of a book.

WRITING Assign the daily Writing Prompt on page 212D.

Name________ Date______ MECHANICS Grammar 150

Titles and Capital Letters

- Begin the first word and each important word in a book title with a capital letter.
- Underline all the words in the title of a book.

My Trip to Alaska

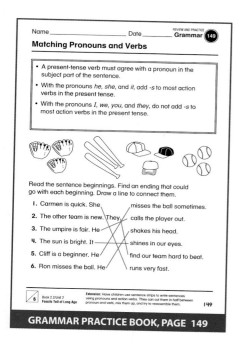

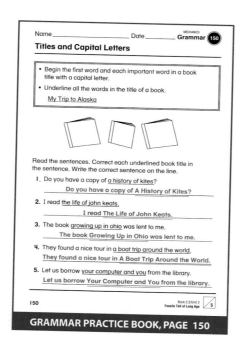

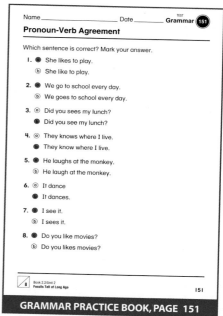

Read the sentences. Correct each underlined book title in the sentence. Write the correct sentence on the line.

1. Do you have a copy of a history of kites?
   Do you have a copy of A History of Kites?
2. I read the life of john keats.
   I read The Life of John Keats.
3. The book growing up in ohio was lent to me.
   The book Growing Up in Ohio was lent to me.
4. They found a nice tour in a boat trip around the world.
   They found a nice tour in A Boat Trip Around the World.
5. Let us borrow your computer and you from the library.
   Let us borrow Your Computer and You from the library.

150 Book 2.2/Unit 2 **Fossils Tell of Long Ago** 5

GRAMMAR PRACTICE BOOK, PAGE 150

DAY 5 Assess and Reteach

Assess Use the Daily Language Activity and page 151 of the **Grammar Practice Book** for assessment.

Reteach Write the following action verbs on the board: *write, clap, jump, eat, sleep.* Ask one child to pantomime each action verb while others describe it, using the subject pronoun *he* or *she*. Emphasize how the form of the verb changes when the subject is the singular *he* or *she*. Then give out index cards to two groups of children. Have one group write the pronouns *he, she, it, I, we, you,* and *they* on individual cards. Have another group write action verbs on index cards, some ending in *-s*. Then have children pin the cards on the bulletin board, placing each pronoun beside the correct form of an action verb.

Use page 152 of the **Grammar Practice Book** for additional reteaching.

WRITING Assign the daily Writing Prompt on page 212D.

Name________ Date______ TEST Grammar 151

Pronoun-Verb Agreement

Which sentence is correct? Mark your answer.

1. ● She likes to play.
   ⓑ She like to play.
2. ● We go to school every day.
   ⓑ We goes to school every day.
3. ⓐ Did you sees my lunch?
   ● Did you see my lunch?
4. ⓐ They knows where I live.
   ● They know where I live.
5. ● He laughs at the monkey.
   ⓑ He laugh at the monkey.
6. ⓐ It dance
   ● It dances.
7. ● I see it.
   ⓑ I sees it.
8. ● Do you like movies?
   ⓑ Do you likes movies?

8 Book 2.2/Unit 2 **Fossils Tell of Long Ago**

151

GRAMMAR PRACTICE BOOK, PAGE 151

GRAMMAR PRACTICE BOOK, PAGE 152

5 Day Spelling Plan

LANGUAGE SUPPORT

ESL Some languages do not have final consonant clusters at the ends of words. Write these clusters on the board: *nd, ft, st, nk*. Then say each spelling word and ask children to repeat it. Repeat the word again and ask a child to come to the board and point to the final cluster in that word.

DICTATION SENTENCES

Spelling Words

1. The ground is dry.
2. She left her hat on the desk.
3. My hand is cold.
4. We went past the turn.
5. The boat sank into the sea.
6. I put the money in the bank.
7. How does the story end?
8. The chest is made of wood.
9. The snow is soft and white.
10. That was a hard test.

Challenge Words

11. The car was buried under the snow.
12. The creatures look scary.
13. The fossil is very old.
14. There are several layers of soil.
15. Millions of people live there.

DAY 1 Pretest

Assess Prior Knowledge Use the Dictation Sentences at left and **Spelling Practice Book** page 147 for the pretest. Allow students to correct their own papers. If students have trouble, have partners give each other a midweek test on Day 3. Students who require a modified list may be tested on the first five words.

Spelling Words		Challenge Words
1. **ground**	6. bank	11. **buried**
2. left	7. end	12. **creatures**
3. **hand**	8. chest	13. **fossil**
4. **past**	9. soft	14. **layers**
5. **sank**	10. test	15. **millions**

*Note: Words in **dark type** are from the story.*

Word Study On page 148 of the **Spelling Practice Book** are word study steps and an at-home activity.

Name ______________ Date ________ PRETEST SPELLING 147

Words with Blends *nk, nd, ft, st*

Pretest Directions
Fold back your paper along the dotted line. Use the blanks to write each word as it is said to you. When you finish the test, unfold the paper and correct any spelling mistakes. Practice those words for the Posttest.

To Parents,
Here are the results of your child's weekly spelling Pretest. You can help your child study for the Posttest by following these simple steps for each word on the word list:
1. Read the word to your child.
2. Have your child write the word, saying each letter as it is written.
3. Say each letter of the word as your child checks the spelling.
4. If a mistake has been made, have your child read each letter of the correctly spelled word aloud and then repeat steps 1–3.

1. ______ 1. ground
2. ______ 2. left
3. ______ 3. hand
4. ______ 4. past
5. ______ 5. sank
6. ______ 6. bank
7. ______ 7. end
8. ______ 8. chest
9. ______ 9. soft
10. ______ 10. test

Challenge Words
______ buried
______ creatures
______ fossil
______ layers
______ millions

10 Book 2.2/Unit 2 Fossils Tell of Long Ago 147

SPELLING PRACTICE BOOK, PAGE 147

WORD STUDY STEPS AND ACTIVITY, PAGE 148

DAY 2 Explore the Pattern

Sort and Spell Words Say the words *left, ground, bank,* and *test*. Have student identify the ending consonant sounds they hear in each word. These words con tain final blends *ft, nd, nk,* and *st*.

Ask students to read aloud the ten spelling words before sorting them according to spelling pattern.

Words ending with			
ft	***nd***	***nk***	***st***
left	ground	sank	past
soft	hand	bank	chest
	end		test

Word Wall Have students look throug song books and sheet music for new words with the final blends *ft, nd, nk,* anc *st* and add them to the classroom word wall, underlining the spelling pattern in each word.

Name ______________ Date ________ EXPLORE THE PATTERN SPELLING 149

Words with Blends *nk, nd, ft, st*

ground	hand	sank	end	soft
left	past	bank	chest	test

Find the spelling words that end with each of the sounds below. Write the words on the lines.

nk
1. sank
2. bank

nd
3. ground
4. hand
5. end

ft
6. left
7. soft

st
8. past
9. chest
10. test

Pattern Smart
Write the spelling words that have the same pattern as **lift**.
11. left 12. soft

Write the spelling words that have the same pattern as **think**.
13. sank 14. bank

Circle the letters that spell the pattern in each word you wrote.

15. Where do these letters appear? Circle the answer.
at the beginning in the middle at the end

15 Book 2.2/Unit 2 Fossils Tell of Long Ago 149

SPELLING PRACTICE BOOK, PAGE 149

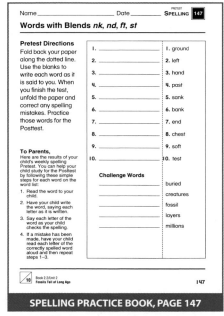

Words with Blends

DAY 3 Practice and Extend

Word Meaning: Antonyms Remind students that an *antonym* is a word that has the opposite meaning of another word. Ask students to think of antonyms for as many of the spelling words as they can (examples: left, right; soft, hard; past, present; end, begin).

Glossary Remind students that words with endings can be found in the glossary in their base-word form. Point out the verb forms and plural forms of the main entry. Have students:

- look up each Challenge Word.
- write each word as it appears in the main listing in the Glossary.
- write the form or forms given at the end of the Glossary entry.

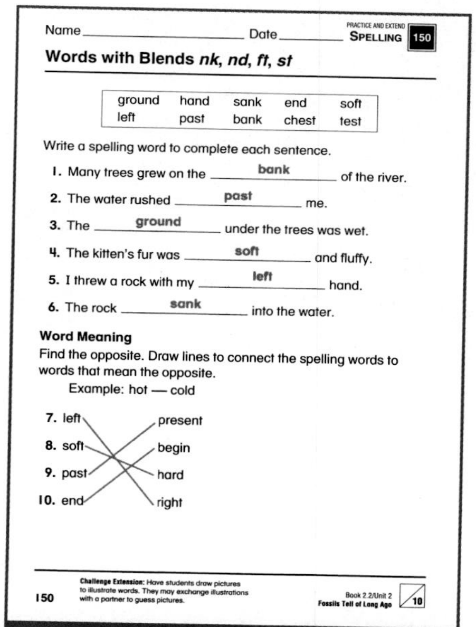

Name________ Date_____ PRACTICE AND EXTEND SPELLING 150

Words with Blends *nk, nd, ft, st*

ground	hand	sank	end	soft
left	past	bank	chest	test

Write a spelling word to complete each sentence.

1. Many trees grew on the __bank__ of the river.
2. The water rushed __past__ me.
3. The __ground__ under the trees was wet.
4. The kitten's fur was __soft__ and fluffy.
5. I threw a rock with my __left__ hand.
6. The rock __sank__ into the water.

Word Meaning

Find the opposite. Draw lines to connect the spelling words to words that mean the opposite.

Example: hot — cold

7. left	present
8. soft	begin
9. past	hard
10. end	right

150 **Challenge Extension:** Have students draw pictures to illustrate words. They may exchange illustrations with a partner to guess pictures. Book 2.2/Unit 2 Fossils Tell of Long Ago /10

SPELLING PRACTICE BOOK, PAGE 150

DAY 4 Proofread and Write

Proofread Sentences Write these sentences on the chalkboard, including the misspelled words. Ask students to proofread, circling incorrect spellings and writing the correct spellings. There are two spelling errors in each sentence.

The bird leaft the groun. (left, ground)

The chesst sanck into the mud (chest, sank)

Have students create additional sentences with errors for partners to correct.

Have students use as many Spelling Words as possible in the daily Writing Prompt on page 212D. Remind students to proofread their writing for errors in spelling, grammar, and punctuation.

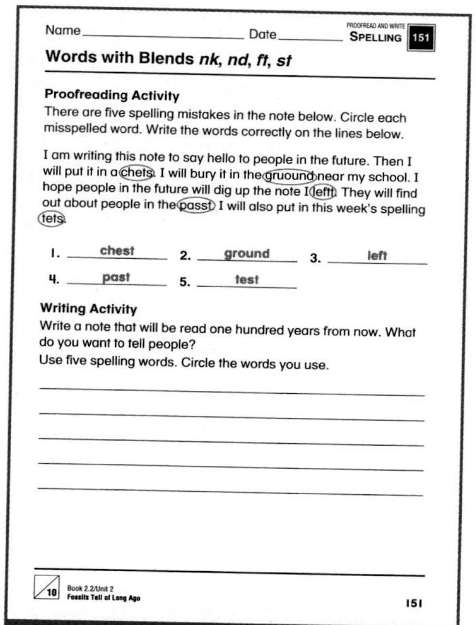

Name________ Date_____ PROOFREAD AND WRITE SPELLING 151

Words with Blends *nk, nd, ft, st*

Proofreading Activity

There are five spelling mistakes in the note below. Circle each misspelled word. Write the words correctly on the lines below.

I am writing this note to say hello to people in the future. Then I will put it in a chets. I will bury it in the gruound near my school. I hope people in the future will dig up the note I leftt. They will find out about people in the passt. I will also put in this week's spelling tets.

1. __chest__ 2. __ground__ 3. __left__
4. __past__ 5. __test__

Writing Activity

Write a note that will be read one hundred years from now. What do you want to tell people?

Use five spelling words. Circle the words you use.

/10 Book 2.2/Unit 2 Fossils Tell of Long Ago 151

SPELLING PRACTICE BOOK, PAGE 151

DAY 5 Assess and Reteach

Assess Students' Knowledge Use page 152 of the **Spelling Practice Book** or the Dictation Sentences on page 235Q for the posttest.

Personal Word List If students have

trouble with any words in the lesson, have them add to their personal list of troublesome words in their journals. Have students write a simple riddle for each word. Example: What is below our feet? (ground)

Students should refer to their word lists during later writing activities.

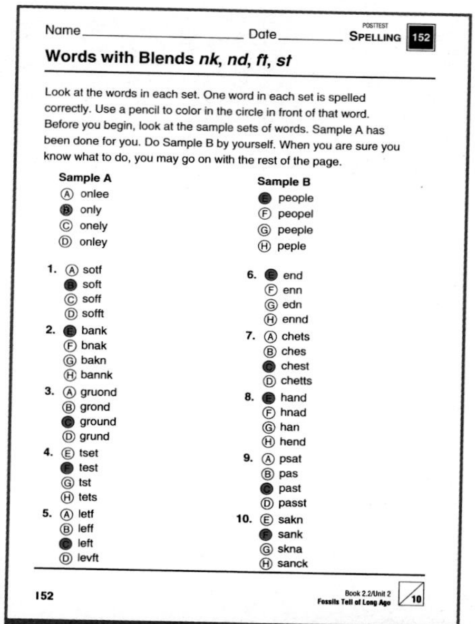

Name________ Date_____ POSTTEST SPELLING 152

Words with Blends *nk, nd, ft, st*

Look at the words in each set. One word in each set is spelled correctly. Use a pencil to color in the circle in front of that word. Before you begin, look at the sample sets of words. Sample A has been done for you. Do Sample B by yourself. When you are sure you know what to do, you may go on with the rest of the page.

Sample A
Ⓐ onlee
● only
Ⓒ onely
Ⓓ onley

Sample B
● people
Ⓕ peopel
Ⓖ peeple
Ⓗ peple

1. Ⓐ sotf ● soft Ⓒ soff Ⓓ sofft
2. ● bank Ⓕ bnak Ⓖ bakn Ⓗ bannk
3. Ⓐ gruond Ⓑ grond ● ground Ⓓ grund
4. Ⓔ tset ● test Ⓖ tst Ⓗ tets
5. Ⓐ letf Ⓑ leff ● left Ⓓ levft
6. ● end Ⓕ enn Ⓖ edn Ⓗ ennd
7. Ⓐ chets Ⓑ ches ● chest Ⓓ chetts
8. ● hand Ⓕ hnad Ⓖ han Ⓗ hend
9. Ⓐ psat Ⓑ pas ● past Ⓓ passt
10. Ⓔ sakn ● sank Ⓖ skna Ⓗ sanck

152 Book 2.2/Unit 2 Fossils Tell of Long Ago /10

SPELLING PRACTICE BOOK, PAGE 152

Cumulative Review with Expository Text

Time to Review

Anthology

Are You a Fossil Fan?

Selection Summary **A teenage fossil hunter named Sam makes discoveries that surprise even adult scientists.**

TIME
FOR KIDS
SPECIAL REPORT
Are You a Fossil Fan?
This dragonfly fossil is millions of years old.

Listening Library

INSTRUCTIONAL pages 238–245

If you're digging up a clue

Then nothing new will do

Old toys could tell you how
Life happened up till now.
You can add them to your list

Rhyme applies to phonics

Time to Reread

Reread Leveled Books

EASY
Lesson on pages 245A and 245D
DECODABLE

INDEPENDENT
Lesson on pages 245B and 245D
Take-Home version available

CHALLENGE
Lesson on pages 245C and 245D

Leveled Practice

EASY
Reteach, 201–210 Blackline masters with reteaching opportunities for each assessed skill

INDEPENDENT/ON-LEVEL
Practice, 201–210 Workbook with Take-Home stories and practice opportunities for each assessed skill and story comprehension

CHALLENGE
Extend, 201–210 Blackline masters that offer challenge activities for each assessed skill

Quizzes Prepared by Accelerated Reader

WORKSTATION Activities

Science .... Be a Fossil Finder, *243*
Create Leaf Fossils, *243*

Language Arts .. Read Aloud, *236E*

Writing .... Write a Report, *242*

Research and Inquiry ...... Find Out More, *243*

Internet Activities .... www.mhschool.com/reading

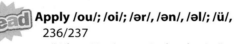

Suggested Lesson Planne

READING AND LANGUAGE ARTS	DAY 1 Focus on Reading and Skills	DAY 2 Read the Literatur
Phonics Daily Routines	**Daily Phonics Routine: Segmenting,** 236H Phonics **CD-ROM**	**Daily Phonics Routine: Discriminating,** 238A Phonics **CD-ROM**
Phonological Awareness Phonics *Review* Comprehension Vocabulary Study Skills Listening, Speaking, Viewing, Representing	**Read Aloud and Motivate,** 236E "Gotta Find a Footprint" ☑ **Develop Phonological Awareness,** 236F Review ☑ **Review /ou/; /oi/; /ər/, /ən/, /əl/; /ü/,** 236G–236H **Teaching Chart 169** **Reteach, Practice, Extend,** 201 **Phonics/Phonemic Awareness Practice Book,** 129–132 Read **Apply /ou/; /oi/; /ər/, /ən/, /əl/; /ü/,** 236/237 "When You're an Archeologist" Intervention Program	**Build Background,** 238A Develop Oral Language **Vocabulary,** 238B–238C ***change hunt piece glue magazine tooth*** **Word Building Manipulative Card** **Teaching Chart 170** **Reteach, Practice, Extend,** 202 Read **Read the Selection,** 238–241 Comprehension ☑ **Phonics Review** ☑ **Sequence of Events** **Genre: Science Magazine Article,** 239 Intervention Program
Curriculum Connections	Link **Language Arts,** 236E	Link **Science,** 238A
Writing	**Writing Prompt:** Would you like to be a fossil finder? Why or why not?	**Writing Prompt:** You are a reporter spending the day with the Fossil Finder. Describe what you do and see on the dig with Sam. **Journal Writing** Quick-Write, 241
Grammar	**Introduce the Concept: Contractions,** 245O Daily Language Activity: Write contractions correctly. **Grammar Practice Book,** 153	**Teach the Concept: Contractions,** 245O Daily Language Activity: Write contractions correctly. **Grammar Practice Book,** 154
Spelling *Words from Social Studies*	**Pretest: Words from Social Studies,** 245Q **Spelling Practice Book,** 153, 154	**Explore the Pattern: Words from Social Studies,** 245Q **Spelling Practice Book,** 155

Intervention Program Available

Meeting Individual Needs

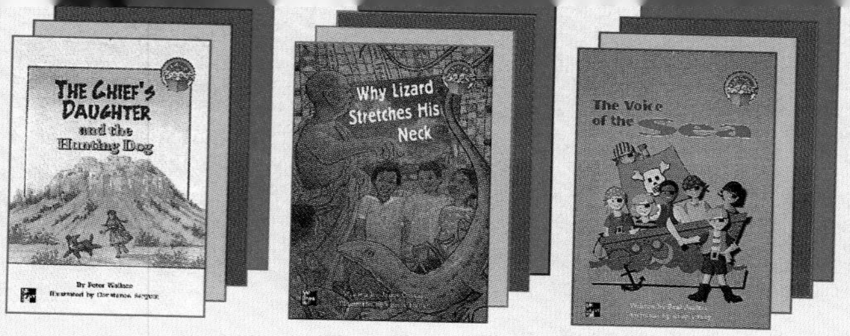

☑ = Skill Assessed in Unit Test

ⓘ Intervention Program Available

Read EVERY DAY

DAY 3 Read the Literature	DAY 4 Build Skills	DAY 5 Build Skills
Daily Phonics Routine: **Blending,** 243 Phonics CD-ROM	**Daily Phonics Routine:** **Fluency,** 245F Phonics CD-ROM	**Daily Phonics Routine:** **Writing,** 245H Phonics CD-ROM
Rereading for Fluency, 240 **Story Questions and Activities,** 242–243 **Reteach, Practice, Extend,** 203 **Study Skills,** 244 ☑ **Various Texts** **Teaching Chart 171** **Reteach, Practice, Extend,** 204 **Test Power,** 245 Read **Read the Leveled Books,** 245A–245D Guided Reading ☑ **Phonics Review** ☑ **Comprehension** ⓘ Intervention Program	Read **Read the Leveled Books and Self-Selected Books** ☑ **Review Sequence of Events,** 245E–245F **Teaching Chart 172** **Reteach, Practice, Extend,** 205 **Language Support,** 222 ☑ **Review Summarize,** 245G–245H **Teaching Chart 173** **Reteach, Practice, Extend,** 206 **Language Support,** 223 ⓘ Intervention Program	Read **Read Self-Selected Books** ☑ **Review Context Clues,** 245I–245J **Teaching Chart 174** **Reteach, Practice, Extend,** 207 **Language Support,** 224 ☑ **Review Suffixes,** 245K–245L **Teaching Chart 175** **Reteach, Practice, Extend,** 208 **Language Support,** 225 **Listening, Speaking, Viewing, Representing,** 245N Illustrate Your Article Make a Speech ⓘ Intervention Program
Activity **Art,** 243		
Writing Prompt: How do fossils help us learn about people and things from long ago? **Expository Writing,** 245M Prewrite, Draft	**Writing Prompt:** What equipment does an archeologist need to bring on a dig? Describe the tools and other useful items he or she might carry. **Expository Writing,** 245M Revise **Meeting Individual Needs for Writing,** 245N	**Writing Prompt:** Why is it important to save and study fossils? **Expository Writing,** 245M Edit/Proofread, Publish
Review and Practice: Contractions, 245P Daily Language Activity: Write contractions correctly. **Grammar Practice Book,** 155	**Review and Practice: Contractions,** 245P Daily Language Activity: Write contractions correctly. **Grammar Practice Book,** 156	**Assess and Reteach: Contractions,** 245P Daily Language Activity: Write contractions correctly. **Grammar Practice Book,** 157, 158
Practice and Extend: Words from Social Studies, 245R **Spelling Practice Book,** 156	**Proofread and Write: Words from Social Studies,** 245R **Spelling Practice Book,** 157	**Assess and Reteach: Words from Social Studies,** 245R **Spelling Practice Book,** 158

Link Language Arts

Read Aloud

Gotta Find a Footprint

a poem by Jeff Moss

Gotta find a footprint, a bone, or
a tooth
To grab yourself a piece of dinosaur
truth.
All the dino knowledge that we've
ever known
Comes from a footprint, a tooth, or
a bone.

A tooth can tell you what a dino
would eat,
A sharp tooth tells you that he
dined on meat.
A blunt tooth tells you that she
dined on plants.
No teeth at all? Well, perhaps they
slurped ants.

Gotta find a footprint, a bone, or
a tooth
To grab yourself a piece of dinosaur
truth.
All the dino knowledge that we've
ever known
Comes from a footprint, a tooth, or
a bone.

Footprints can tell you a dinosaur's
size,
And how fast he ran when he raced
with the guys.
Count all the footprints, you'll easily
see
If he traveled alone or with a family.

Continued on page T4

Oral Comprehension

LISTENING AND SPEAKING Ask children to think about the main idea of the poem as you read it to them. When you have finished, ask: "What was the main idea in this poem?" Then ask: "How did you decide this?" Remind children to look for main ideas and supporting details as they read other stories and poems.

GENRE STUDY: POETRY Discuss the literary devices and techniques used in *Gotta Find a Footprint.*

- List the words that rhyme in the poem. Determine if there is a pattern to the rhyming words.
- Read the poem a second time. Encourage children to listen to the rhythm of the words. As the poem progresses, have children tap their fingers to the rhythm.
- Discuss the repetition in the poem. Ask: *What section of the poem is repeated?* Discuss how the poem would be different without the repetition.

Activity Help children make foot portraits. Have them make an outline of one foot and then decorate it with drawings, photographs, stamps, and stickers that tell something about who they are. Encourage students to write a poem about their footprint using one of the genre elements discussed.

▶ **Visual/Spatial**

Develop **Phonological Awareness**

Blend Sounds

Phonemic Awareness

MATERIALS
- Phonics Pictures from *Word Building Cards*

Teach Place the Phonics Picture for *turtle* behind your back so the children cannot see it. Say /t/-/ûr/-/t/-/əl/ . . . *turtle* and then show the card. Repeat with the pictures for *feather, raccoon,* and *house.*

Practice Have children blend sounds together for the following words: *care, born, grew, clue, dear, room, middle,* and *round.*

Segment Sounds

Phonemic Awareness

MATERIALS
- magazine or storybook pictures

Teach Show children a picture and ask them to say the word for the picture sound-by-sound. Demonstrate by holding up a picture of a candle and saying, /k/-/a/-/n/-/d/-/əl/. Have children repeat the sounds.

Practice Using pictures of the words below, have children segment the words: *fork, buckle, crown, mouse, boot, spear, moon, letter, boy,* and *apple.*

Delete Sounds

Phonemic Awareness

Teach Say: *store . . . Now I'll say some of the sounds in the word . . .* /s/-/ôr/. *What sound did I leave off?* (/t/) Then ask, *If I leave off the* /t/ *sound in store, what new word do I make?* (sore) Have children repeat both words, *store/sore.*

Practice Repeat the procedure with the words below.

spell/without the *p*	*flew*/without the *l*
truck/without the *r*	*skunk*/without the first *k*
drip/without the *r*	*play*/without the *l*
drew/without the *r*	*skip*/without the *k*

INFORMAL ASSESSMENT

Observe children as they blend, segment, and delete sounds. If children have difficulty, see Alternate Teaching Strategies on pp. T64, T69, T72, and T75.

TESTED OBJECTIVES

Children will:

- review /ou/, /oi/; /ər/, /ən/, /əl/; /ü/.
- decode and read words with /ou/, /oi/.

MATERIALS

- Teaching Chart 169
- Word Building Manipulative Cards
- Word building boxes

Skills Finder

/ou/ ow, ou, and /oi/ oi, oy

Introduce	B1: 156G-H
Review	B1: 191E-F; B2: 212G-H, 235E-F, 235G-H
Test	B1: Unit 2

TEACHING TIP

SPELLING PATTERNS
Point out that each of these letter pairs spells other sounds in other words. For example, *oo* can also spell /u̇/ as in book. Make sure children can distinguish the vowel sounds in *boot* and *book*.

Review /ou/; /oi/; /ər/, /ən/, /əl/; /ü/

PREPARE

Read Words with /ou/, /oi/, /ər/, /ən/, /əl/, /ü/

Review the spelling of the vowel sounds heard at the end of the following words: *how, boy, over, even, battle,* and *boo.* Explain that for the sounds /ou/, /oi/, and /ü/ more than one letter combination can make the sound. The letters *ow* and *ou* make the /ou/ sound; the letters *oi* and *oy* make the /oy/ sound; the letters *oo, ue,* and *ew* make the /ü/ sound.

TEACH

BLENDING Model and Guide Practice with /ou/ Words

- Display **Teaching Chart 169** and say the word *loud* in the first row.
- Ask children to blend the sounds as you run a finger under the word.
- Ask volunteers to complete the other words in the first row by adding letters that spell the /ou/ sound.

ou, ow	loud	cow	mouth	plow
oi, oy	toy	noise	boys	moist
er	other	center	never	father
en	even	happen	seven	broken
le	candle	bugle	middle	little
oo, ue, ew	too	glue	dew*	boot

* other possible answer: due

Teaching Chart 169

Use the Words in Context

- Have children use words in sentences to reinforce their meanings. Example: *That cow had a loud mouth.*

Repeat the Procedure

- Repeat the procedure with the next five rows of the chart.

PRACTICE

WORD BUILDING Unscramble Words

GROUP

Use Word Building Manipulative Cards to build words such as: *out, toy, sister, heaven, bundle, room, chew, true.* Have children read aloud each word with you. Then jumble the letters and invite volunteers to rebuild and read each word. Have children work in groups to build other words with /ou/; /oi/; /ər/; /ən/; /əl/; /ü/. Each group should jumble six words on paper for another group to solve.

▶ **Interpersonal/Linguistic**

ASSESS/CLOSE

Read Unscrambled Words with /ü/, /ou/, /oi/, /ər/, /ən/, /əl/

To assess children's ability to build and read words with /ü/, /ou/, /oi/, /ər/,/ən/, and /əl/, observe their work on the Practice activity, and ask each child to read aloud three words from their solved jumbles list. Have children read the phonics rhyme on page 237 in their books.

ADDITIONAL PHONICS RESOURCES

Phonics/Phonemic Awareness Practice Book, pages 129–132

McGraw-Hill School TECHNOLOGY

Phonics CD-ROM **activities for practice with Blending and Word Building**

Meeting Individual Needs for Phonics

EASY

Name__________ Date______ Reteach 201

/ou/; /oi/; /ər/, /ən/, /əl/; /ü/

You have learned different spellings for several sounds.
/ou/ as in m**ou**th or c**ow** **/oi/** as in t**oy** or s**oi**l
/ər/ as in bett**er** **/əl/** as in app**le** **/ən/** as in op**en**
/ü/ as in sp**oo**n, bl**ue**, or fl**ew**

Circle the word or words in each group that have the same sound as the letters in dark type.

1. m**ou**th — (cow) (found) boat
2. s**oi**l — (boy) (coin) brother
3. b**oo**t — also (boom) (flew)
4. broth**er** — (another) settle (neither)
5. ov**er** — open (dinner) hear
6. cand**le** — care mouth (giggle)
7. happ**en** — (seven) river found
8. bl**ue** — boil (few) (true)

8 Book 2.2/Unit 2 **Are You a Fossil Fan?** **At Home:** Have children think of one more word that has the same sound as each of the underlined sounds. 201

Reteach, 201

ON-LEVEL

Name__________ Date______ Practice 201

/ou/; /oi/; /ər/, /ən/, /əl/; /ü/

Read the words on the list. List each one underneath the word that shares the same underlined sound. Then cross the word off the list.

found	apple	river	cow	noise	seven
giggle	blue	toy	open	too	teacher

m**ou**th
1. found
2. cow

b**oo**t
3. too
4. blue

happ**en**
5. seven
6. open

ov**er**
7. river
8. teacher

cand**le**
9. giggle
10. apple

s**oi**l
11. toy
12. noise

12 Book 2.2/Unit 2 **Are You a Fossil Fan?** **At Home:** Have children circle the letters in each word that create the underlined sound. 201

Practice, 201

CHALLENGE

Name__________ Date______ Extend 201

/ou/; /oi/; /ər/, /ən/, /əl/; /ü/

careful	scared	for	morning	hear	blue
too	found	ground	soil	brother	
dinner	happen	seven	candle	giggle	

Use words from the box to write a story for telling out loud. Use at least five words from the box in your story.

Stories will vary. Children should use at least five words from the box.

Book 2.2/Unit 2 **Are You a Fossil Fan?** **At Home:** Have children tell the story they wrote. Encourage them to use words from the box. 201

Extend, 201

Daily Routines

DAY 1 **Segmenting** Distribute word building boxes. Read the following words aloud: *hoot, drew, sound, joint, candle, ever,* and *even*. Ask children to write the spelling of each sound in the appropriate box.

DAY 2 **Discriminating** Write these pairs: *cook/hoot, clue/cut, foot/boot, good/ food*. Invite children to read aloud all the words. For each pair, ask a volunteer to underline the word with /ü/ spelled *oo, ew,* or *ue*.

DAY 3 **Blending** Write the letters *oo, ew,* and *ue* on the chalkboard. Call on volunteers to add letters to build words with the /ü/ sound. Have children say each word, blending the sounds.

DAY 4 **Fluency** Write the following words on the chalkboard: *roof, knew, middle, broken, noise,* and *true*. Point to each word, asking children to blend the sounds silently. Ask a child to read each word aloud.

DAY 5 **Writing** Ask partners to create rhyming couplets, using /ü/. Review that the rhyming words can be spelled with *oo, ew,* or *ue*. Have each pair read aloud their rhyme.

TESTED OBJECTIVES

Children will review /ou/, /oi/; /ər/, /ən/, /əl/; /ü/.

Apply /ou/, /oi/; /ər/, /ən/, /əl/; /ü/

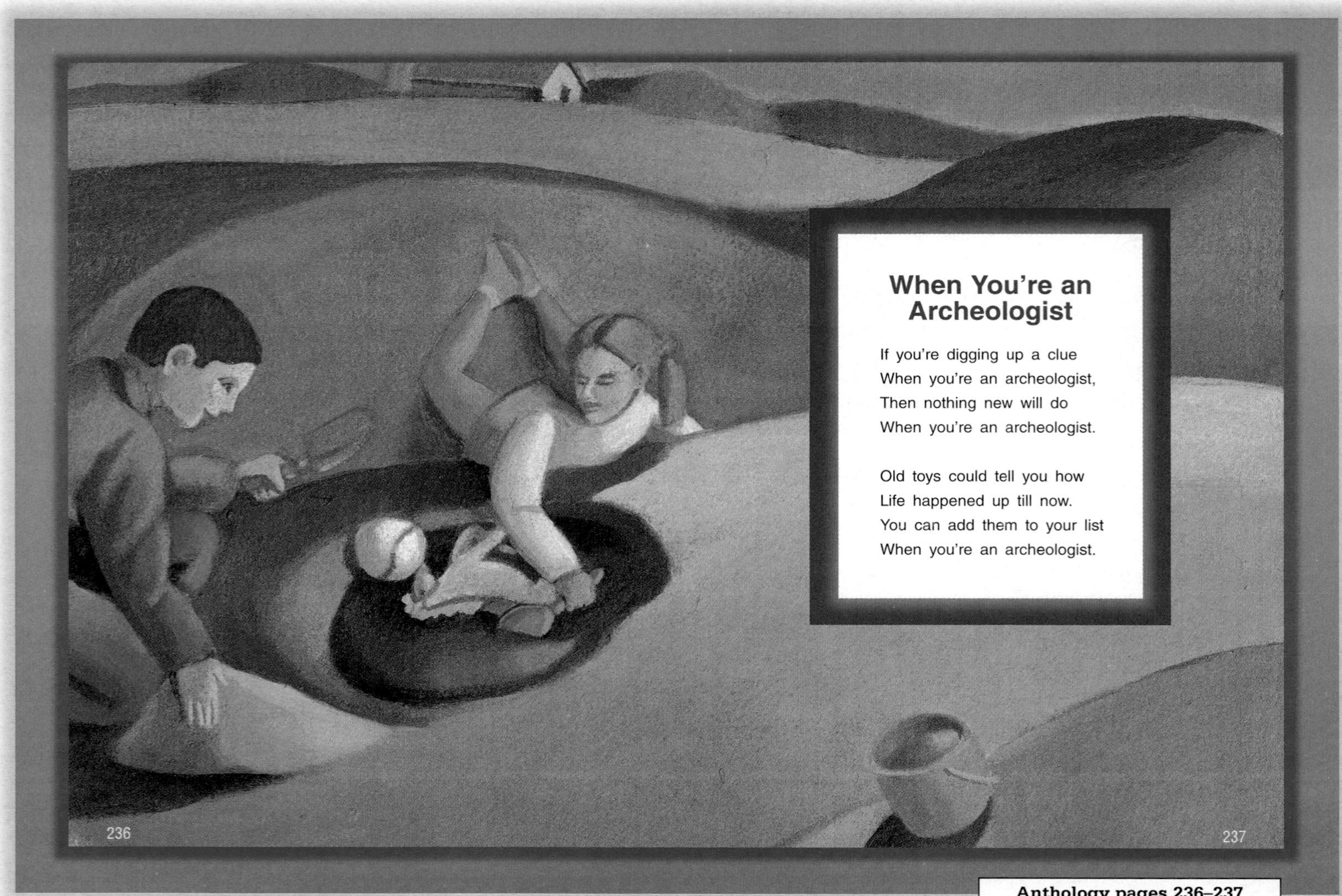
When You're an Archeologist
If you're digging up a clue
When you're an archeologist,
Then nothing new will do
When you're an archeologist.

Old toys could tell you how
Life happened up till now.
You can add them to your list
When you're an archeologist.
236
237

Anthology pages 236–237

Read and Build Fluency

READ THE POEM Tell children they will read a poem called "When You're an Archeologist." Encourage them to listen and follow along in the text while you read the poem as an auditory model. Then track the print and ask children to engage in a shared reading with you.

GROUP **REREAD FOR FLUENCY** Pair children of varying reading levels for thirty-second timed readings. Tell readers to read slowly and expressively, starting over again if time allows. Have the listening partner track the text and place a self-stick note after the last word read. Set and monitor the time for the whole class. Then have pairs count the number of words read. Have partners switch roles and continue the exercise.

Dictate and Spell

JOURNAL **DICTATE WORDS** Write the following list on the chalkboard and underline the reviewed phonemic element in each as you say the word aloud: *now, toys, oven, wiggle, ever, clue.* Ask children to copy the list and circle the important review sound in each word. Say the word *mouth* as you write it on the chalkboard. Ask children what review sound they hear and have them circle it. Continue the exercise with the words *moist, center, seven, middle,* and *boot.*

Intervention **Skills Intervention Guide,** for direct instruction and extra practice of /ou/, /oi/; /ər/, /ən/, /əl/; /ü/

Build Background

Link Science

Concept: Fossils

Evaluate Prior Knowledge

CONCEPT: FOSSILS Ask children to explain how fossils are formed, and to share other memorable facts about fossils. Encourage them to recall what they learned from the previous selection, *Fossils Tell of Long Ago*.

MAKE A FOSSIL FACT CHART Help children create a question-and-answer chart about fossils. Suggest that they include questions such as: What are fossils? Where are fossils found? What are some examples of fossils? ▶ **Linguistic/Logical**

QUESTIONS	ANSWERS
What are fossils?	the remains of plants and animals that have turned to stone
Where are fossils found?	in the ground
What are some examples of fossils?	leaves, dinosaur bones, fish skeleton

DESCRIBE FINDING A FOSSIL Ask ONE WRITING children to pretend they are scientists and to write a short account of finding an important fossil. Encourage them to draw illustrations for their descriptions.

Develop Oral Language

CONNECT WORDS AND ACTIONS Ask ESL children to act out how they came across their imaginary fossils. Guide them by asking:

- Show me how you found your fossil.
- How big is your fossil?
- What kind of fossil is it?
- Where did you find it?

As children pantomime *hunting, digging,* and so on, describe their actions aloud.

▶ **Kinesthetic/Linguistic**

DAILY Phonics ROUTINES

DAY 2 **Discriminating** Write these pairs: *cook/hoot, clue/cut, foot/boot, good/food.* Invite children to read aloud all the words. For each pair, ask a volunteer to underline the word with /ü/ spelled *oo, ew,* or *ue.*

Phonics CD-ROM

LANGUAGE SUPPORT

Use the **Language Support Book**, pages 217–220, to help build background.

TESTED OBJECTIVES

Children will use context and structural clues to determine the meanings of vocabulary words.

Definitions

hunt (p. 239) to look for something

magazine (p. 241) printed collection of stories, articles, and pictures

piece (p. 240) part of something

glue (p. 240) substance that sticks things together

tooth (p. 240) bony part of mouth for biting and chewing

change (p. 239) to make or become different

Story Words

These words from the selection may be unfamiliar. Before children read, have them check the meanings and pronunciations of the words in the Glossary beginning on page 390, or in a dictionary.

- teenager, p. 239
- mastodon, p. 240
- termite, p. 240

hunt
magazine
piece
glue
tooth
change

Vocabulary

Teach Vocabulary in Context

Identify Vocabulary Words Display **Teaching Chart 170** and read the passage with children. Have volunteers circle each vocabulary word and underline other words that are clues to its meaning.

Fossil Hunt

1. Mike and Jen carefully look through the dirt as they hunt for fossils. **2.** Jen got the idea from a page in a magazine filled with articles about fossils. **3.** The article she and Mike liked best was about a boy who found a broken piece of bone, and then dug some more and found other little parts of the bone. **4.** Mike used glue to stick them together. **5.** It was a sharp tooth from the front of a dinosaur's mouth. **6.** Mike and Jen also read about how animals and plants change and turn into fossils.

Teaching Chart 170

Discuss Meanings Ask questions like these to help clarify word meanings:

- When you hunt for something are you trying to find it or throw it away?
- How is a magazine different from a book? How is it like a book?
- If something changes, does it stay the same or become different?
- If you wanted to share a cake with friends, how many pieces would you cut it into?
- What is something you could use for glue?
- Have you ever lost a tooth? Was it hard to chew your food after your tooth fell out?

Activities

Practice

Demonstrate Word Meaning

GROUP Invite children to play 20 Questions with Key Vocabulary Words. Have one child choose a vocabulary card. Other children should ask yes/no questions to try to guess the word.
▶ **Interpersonal/Linguistic**

Word Building Manipulative Cards

Write a Story

WRITING

ONE Have children use vocabulary words in a very short story about a real or imaginary animal. Have them refer to their Glossary if needed. Invite children to illustrate their stories, and to read them aloud. ▶ **Linguistic/Spatial**

Assess Vocabulary

Identify Word Meaning in Context

WRITING

PARTNERS Encourage partners to write context sentences for the vocabulary words. Instead of using the actual vocabulary word, however, ask them to substitute the word *fossils*. After partners exchange papers, have them write the vocabulary word that *fossils* stands for in each sentence. Also ask them to underline the context clues that helped them guess the vocabulary word.

SPELLING/VOCABULARY CONNECTIONS

See Spelling Challenge Words, pages 245P–245Q.

LANGUAGE SUPPORT

See the Language Support Book, pages 217–220, for teaching suggestions for Vocabulary.

Vocabulary PuzzleMaker

Provides vocabulary activities.

Meeting Individual Needs for Vocabulary

EASY

Name__________ Date______ Reteach 202

Vocabulary

Choose a word from the box to complete each sentence. Write the word on the line.

piece magazine tooth change glue hunt

1. Sal likes to look at the pictures in the ___magazine___.
2. I used some ___glue___ to fix my broken truck.
3. Johnny needs to ___change___ his clothes for the party.
4. I lost a ___tooth___ when I bit into an apple.
5. Would you like a ___piece___ of my orange?
6. We will have to ___hunt___ for the lost ball.

202 At Home: Have children write a new sentence for each word in the box. Book 2.2/Unit 2 Are You a Fossil Fan? 6

Reteach, 202

ON-LEVEL

Name__________ Date______ Practice 202

Vocabulary

Read each group of sentences. One word is missing from each group. Find the missing word and fill in the circle next to it.

1. Billy is making a birthday card. He is using ______ to stick a picture on the inside.
   ○ a. soap ● b. glue ○ c. hurry
2. The picture shows a lion near a tree. Billy cut it out of a ______.
   ● a. magazine ○ b. homework ○ c. garden
3. Sally and Becky played out in the rain. They got wet. Now they have to ______ their clothes.
   ○ a. grow ○ b. sell ● c. change
4. Sally and Becky are playing with blocks. They can't find the red one. They will have to ______ for it.
   ● a. hunt ○ b. worry ○ c. sing
5. Emile has trouble chewing. Last night he lost a ______. He thought it would come out last week. It took a long time.
   ○ a. card ● b. tooth ○ c. dog
6. Emile's mother made an apple pie. She cut it and gave him a ______ of it. The pie was soft and tasted good!
   ● a. piece ○ b. door ○ c. week

202 At Home: Have children point out the clues in each example that helped them make the word choices. Book 2.2/Unit 2 Are You a Fossil Fan? 6

Practice, 202

ON-LEVEL

Amber's Hunt

Amber looked in the mirror. Right in the front of her mouth a huge tooth had grown in.
"Aha!" said Amber. "Here is the missing piece to my life! I don't have to change my life. Now I have everything I need!"
And from that day on Amber felt happy!

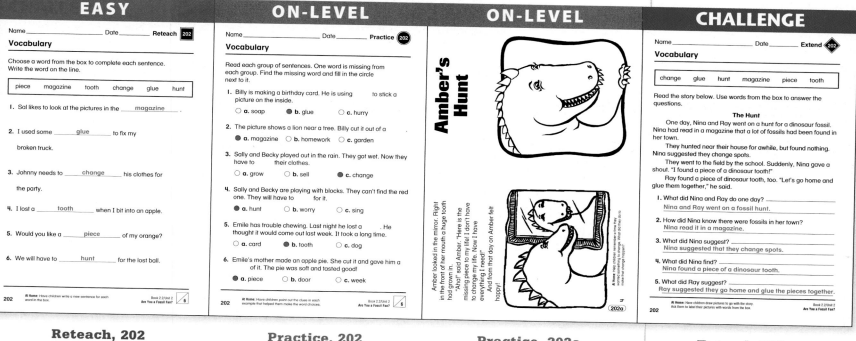

At Home: Help children remember a time they wanted something to change. What did they do to make that change happen?

4 (202a)

Practice, 202a
Take-Home Story

CHALLENGE

Name__________ Date______ Extend 202

Vocabulary

change glue hunt magazine piece tooth

Read the story below. Use words from the box to answer the questions.

The Hunt

One day, Nina and Ray went on a hunt for a dinosaur fossil. Nina had read in a magazine that a lot of fossils had been found in her town.

They hunted near their house for awhile, but found nothing. Nina suggested they change spots.

They went to the field by the school. Suddenly, Nina gave a shout. "I found a piece of a dinosaur tooth!"

Ray found a piece of dinosaur tooth, too. "Let's go home and glue them together," he said.

1. What did Nina and Ray do one day? Nina and Ray went on a fossil hunt.
2. How did Nina know there were fossils in her town? Nina read it in a magazine.
3. What did Nina suggest? Nina suggested that they change spots.
4. What did Nina find? Nina found a piece of a dinosaur tooth.
5. What did Ray suggest? Ray suggested they go home and glue the pieces together.

202 At Home: Have children draw pictures to go with the story. Ask them to label their pictures with words from the box. Book 2.2/Unit 2 Are You a Fossil Fan?

Extend, 202

Comprehension

Prereading Strategies

PREVIEW AND PREDICT Have children read the title of the article. Take a **picture walk** through the illustrations. Discuss with children how the title, pictures, and fact boxes give clues to what they will read in the selection.

- What clues do the pictures and title give about the boy on page 239?
- Is the article nonfiction or fiction? How can you tell? (Nonfiction; it uses photographs that look real.) ***Genre***
- What is this article most likely about?

Have children record their predictions about the article.

SET PURPOSES What do children want to find out by reading the article? For example:

- What are fossils made of?
- What do people learn from fossils?

TIME
FOR KIDS
SPECIAL REPORT
Are
You a
Fossil
Fan?
This dragonfly fossil i
millions of years old.
238

Meeting Individual Needs • Grouping Suggestions for Strategic Reading

EASY	ON-LEVEL	CHALLENGE
Read Together Read the article together with children. As you read, model the strategy of using the Sequence of Events chart to record what happens in the article. Show how this can help children to understand and remember what they read.	**Guided Instruction** Read the article with the children using the Comprehension prompts. You may want to have children read the article on their own first. As they read, have children use the Sequence of Events chart to record events from the article.	**Read Independently** Remind children that keeping track of the chain of events in an article or story will help them to better understand what they are reading. Have children use their Sequence of Events charts as they read. After reading, they can use their charts to summarize the article.

The Fossil Kid

This boy has been digging since he was eight.

When Sam Girouard was eight years old, he visited his grandmother in Alabama. On that visit, Sam and his grandmother made a big discovery. They found all kinds of fossils. "Ferns, plants, things like that. I still have all those fossils," says Sam. Those fossils changed Sam's life forever. (1) (2)

Sam is now a teenager. He is also a scientist. Sam knows a lot about fossils. (Fossils are the remains of plants and animals that died a long time ago. Over time, the remains turned to stone.)

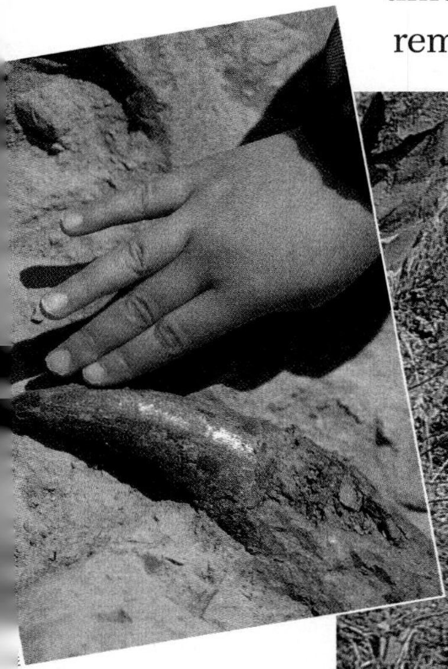

A *T. rex* dinosaur tooth is larger than a kid's hand.

Sam Girouard hunts for fossils near his home in Washington State.

Comprehension

Phonics Apply /ü/ *oo, ue, ew*

Apply Sequence of Events

STRATEGIC READING Before we begin reading, let's set up a Sequence of Events chart. Keeping track of events as they happen may help you to understand and remember the article.

(1) **SEQUENCE OF EVENTS** How old was Sam when he found his first fossil? (eight) Do you know how old Sam is now? (He is a teenager.)

(2) How did finding a fossil change Sam's life? (Sam and his grandmother found some fossils. He got interested in fossils. Now Sam is a scientist who knows a lot about fossils.) *Critical Thinking*

Genre

Science Magazine Article

Explain that magazine articles:

- contain headings, captions, diagrams, and different typefaces.
- give a short description of discoveries, ideas, or events.
- often include sidebars and other text features.

Activity When children have read *Are You a Fossil Fan?*, invite volunteers to find examples of captions, headers, and different typefaces. Point out the sidebar on page 241. Ask them to discuss how these text features provide information to the reader.

LANGUAGE SUPPORT

This chart is available as a blackline master in the **Language Support Book**.

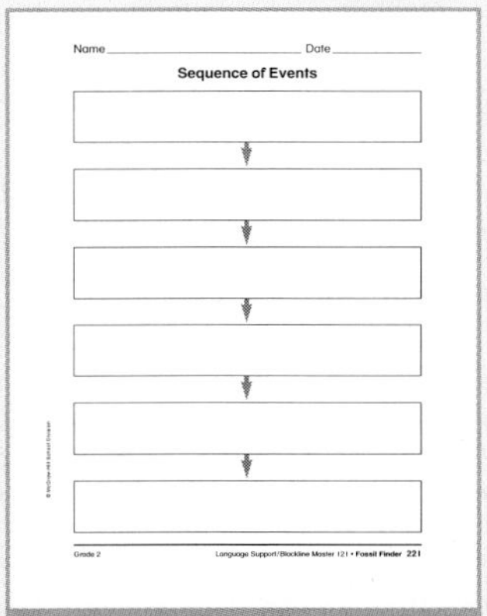
Name_____ Date_____

Sequence of Events

LANGUAGE SUPPORT, 221

Comprehension

3 **SEQUENCE OF EVENTS** Use the words *first*, *then*, *next*, and *finally* to describe how Sam found and repaired a dinosaur tooth.

MODEL First, he spent hours digging for fossils. Then, he found pieces of bone that were fossils. Next, he found more little pieces. Finally, he glued the pieces together to make a whole tooth.

4 **Phonics** ***/ü/ oo, ue*** Find any two words in the first paragraph on this page that have the /ü/ sound. (*glued, tooth*) What letters stand for /ü/ in each word? (*ue, oo*) ***Graphophonic Cues***

5 **SEQUENCE OF EVENTS** Let's fill in our chart with events from Sam's life that tell about his work with fossils.

Event 1: Sam found fossils of ferns and other plants when he was eight.
↓
Event 2: Sam found pieces of a dinosaur tooth.
↓
Event 3: Sam found the oldest American mastodon fossil ever found.

ORGANIZE INFORMATION Call on children to tell the major events of the selection. Tell children they may refer to the Sequence of Events chart, but encourage them to use their own words. ***Summarize***

RIGHT: JOHN CANCALOSI/STOCK BOSTON; MIDDLE: KEVIN SCHAFER/PETER ARNOLD; FAR RIGHT: JOHN CANCALOSI/PETER ARNOLD; BELOW: LAYNE KENNEDY/CORBIS

Fossils of a fern, a bird, and a fish are each millions of years old.

3 Sam spends hours and hours digging for fossils. Once, Sam found a few tiny pieces of bone. Sam knew he had found something important. So he spent the day on his hands and knees looking for more bone. He picked up all the tiny pieces he could find. Then he
4 glued them together. The pieces made up a dinosaur tooth. The dinosaur had lived millions of years ago!

Sam has found other kinds of fossils, too. He's found the wrist bone of an American mastodon. Tests showed that it was more than four million years old. It was the oldest
5 American mastodon fossil ever found.

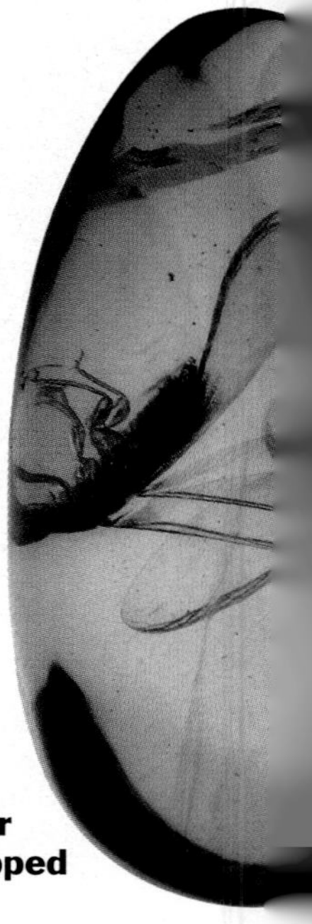

A large termite is trapped in amber. Amber comes from sticky tree sap. Bugs get trapped in it. Over time, it hardens into amber.

240

REREADING FOR *Fluency*

GROUP Have children choose one page of the article to read aloud to a partner. Encourage them to pause when appropriate and to read with expression.

READING RATE When you evaluate reading rate, have children read aloud from the story for one minute. Place a stick-on note after the last word read. Count words read. To evaluate children's performance, see Running Record in the **Fluency Assessment** book.

Intervention For leveled fluency passages, lessons, and norms charts, see **Skills Intervention Guide**, Part 5, Fluency.

TIME FOR KIDS

Sam has found a fossil of a raindrop. It is the only raindrop fossil ever found in Washington. He has also found a wing of a fly. The fly lived millions of years ago.

When Sam finds an unusual fossil, he writes about it for a magazine. The magazine is read by many scientists. Sometimes grown-up scientists are surprised to learn that Sam is a teenager. Sam says that if some scientists knew he was a kid, they would not take his work seriously. "I want people to see that I'm doing science. Then they can hear about my age," says Sam.

DID YOU KNOW?
FOSSIL FACTS

- The oldest reptile fossil nests ever found were discovered in Arizona. The nests are 220 million years old. The reptiles were cousins of today's crocodiles and turtles.
- Scientists study fossils to find out about the history of Earth and of the plants and animals that have lived here.
- You can find fossils in every state, and there are a lot to go around. But fossils tell only a small part of the story of all the plants and animals that have lived on Earth.
- The oldest fossils are about $3\frac{1}{2}$ billion years old.

FIND OUT MORE
Visit our website:
www.mhschool.com/reading

interNET CONNECTION

Based on an article in *TIME FOR KIDS.*

241

LITERARY RESPONSE

QUICK-WRITE Have children record their thoughts about the article. Prompt them with questions such as: How does one hunt for fossils? Do you think you would like to look for fossils?

JOURNAL

ORAL RESPONSE Have children share their journal entries and discuss what they found most interesting about the article.

interNET CONNECTION For more information or activities on fossils, dinosaurs, and famous archeologists go to ***www.mhschool.com/reading***.

Comprehension

Return to Predictions and Purposes

Reread and discuss children's predictions about the article, noting which ones needed to be revised. Ask children if the article answered the questions they had before they read it.

INFORMAL ASSESSMENT

HOW TO ASSESS

Phonics **/ü/ oo, ue, ew** Write *oo* and *ue* on the chalkboard. Ask: What sound do each of these letter pairs stand for? Ask each child to write three words with /ü/, using each of these spellings for /ü/.

SEQUENCE OF EVENTS Ask children to tell about the time Sam found the pieces of dinosaur bone. Ask them to use words such as *first, then, next,* and *finally* to explain how Sam finds fossils and what he does with them.

FOLLOW UP

Phonics **/ü/ oo, ue, ew** Continue to model blending words with /ü/ sounds for children who are having difficulty.

SEQUENCE OF EVENTS If children have difficulty understanding sequence of events, ask them to describe putting on socks and shoes. Ask questions such as: What do you put on first, socks or shoes? Would you tie your shoes before or after you put them on your feet?

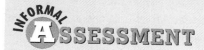

Story Questions

Are You a Fossil Fan?

Help children read the questions on page 242 and discuss answers.

Answers:

1. ferns, a dinosaur tooth, the wrist bone of an American mastodon, the wing of a fly, and a raindrop *Literal/Detail*
2. It was the oldest American mastodon fossil ever found. *Literal/Detail*
3. He thinks people won't take his work seriously if they know how young he is. *Inferential/Draw Conclusions*
4. Sam Girouard is a young scientist and a talented fossil finder. *Inferential/Summarize*
5. Possible answers: adventurous, hard-working, skilled *Character/Reading Across Texts*

Write a Report For a full writing-process lesson related to this writing suggestion, see the lesson on expository writing on pages 245M–245N.

Story Questions & Activities

READ TOGETHER

1. What animals and plant fossils did Sam find
2. Why is the wrist bone of the American mastodon that Sam found so special?
3. Why do you think Sam wants people to read his work before they hear about his age?
4. What is the main idea of this selection?
5. Sam Girouard and the young riders of the Pony Express have done great things. What words might describe both Sam and the Pony Express riders?

Write a Report

Some people know very little about fossils. Write a magazine article that will help them learn about fossils. Explain what fossils are. Tell about some of the fossils Sam has found. Tell where and how he found the fossils.

Meeting Individual Needs

EASY

Name________ Date______ Reteach 203

Story Comprehension

Think about what you learned in "Are You a Fossil Fan?" Then write the word that best completes each statement.

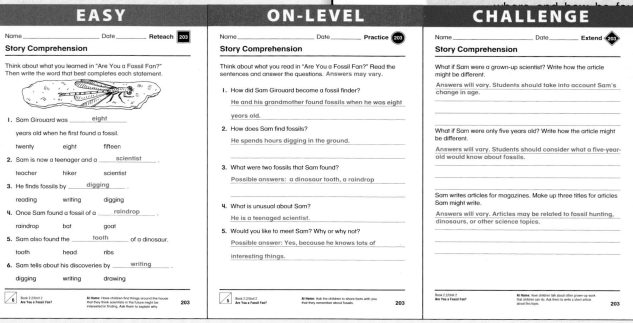

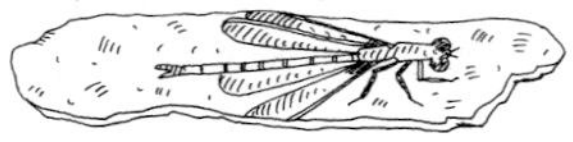

1. Sam Girouard was __eight__ years old when he first found a fossil.
   twenty eight fifteen
2. Sam is now a teenager and a __scientist__.
   teacher hiker scientist
3. He finds fossils by __digging__.
   reading writing digging
4. Once Sam found a fossil of a __raindrop__.
   raindrop bat goat
5. Sam also found the __tooth__ of a dinosaur.
   tooth head ribs
6. Sam tells about his discoveries by __writing__.
   digging writing drawing

6 Book 2.2/Unit 2 **Are You a Fossil Fan?**
At Home: Have children find things around the house that they think scientists in the future might be interested in finding. Ask them to explain why. 203

Reteach, 203

ON-LEVEL

Name________ Date______ Practice 203

Story Comprehension

Think about what you read in "Are You a Fossil Fan?" Read the sentences and answer the questions. Answers may vary.

1. How did Sam Girouard become a fossil finder?
   He and his grandmother found fossils when he was eight years old.
2. How does Sam find fossils?
   He spends hours digging in the ground.
3. What were two fossils that Sam found?
   Possible answers: a dinosaur tooth, a raindrop
4. What is unusual about Sam?
   He is a teenaged scientist.
5. Would you like to meet Sam? Why or why not?
   Possible answer: Yes, because he knows lots of interesting things.

5 Book 2.2/Unit 2 **Are You a Fossil Fan?**
At Home: Ask the children to share facts with you that they remember about fossils. 203

Practice, 203

CHALLENGE

Name________ Date______ Extend 203

Story Comprehension

What if Sam were a grown-up scientist? Write how the article might be different.

Answers will vary. Students should take into account Sam's change in age.

What if Sam were only five years old? Write how the article might be different.

Answers will vary. Students should consider what a five-year-old would know about fossils.

Sam writes articles for magazines. Make up three titles for articles Sam might write.

Answers will vary. Articles may be related to fossil hunting, dinosaurs, or other science topics.

Book 2.2/Unit 2 **Are You a Fossil Fan?**
At Home: Have children talk about other grown-up work that children can do. Ask them to write a short article about this topic. 203

Extend, 203

Be a Fossil Finder

Imagine that you are a scientist who lives a million years from now. You have just made a fantastic fossil discovery that tells about life on Earth around the year 2000. What would you find? Write a short magazine article about your discovery.

Create Leaf Fossils

Collect several different leaves. Then make leaf rubbings to show what the fossils might look like. Follow these steps:

1. Lay the leaf with the underside face up on your desk.
2. Cover the leaf with tracing paper.
3. Rub the paper lightly with a soft pencil, a piece of charcoal, or a crayon.

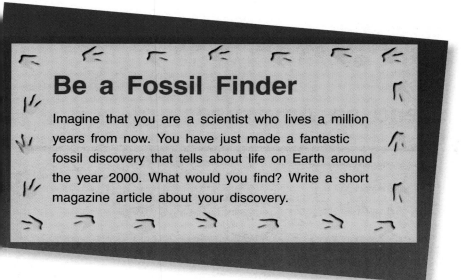

Find Out More

Sam found the wrist bone of an American mastodon. Find out more about mastodons. What were they? When did they live? What did they look like? Draw a picture of a mastodon, and list three facts about it.

243

Story Activities

Be a Fossil Finder

Materials: paper and pencil

GROUP Help children see that human skeletons and the remains of plants and animals can give clues about life on Earth. Distribute books or magazines about archeology or fossils written for children to use as models.

Create Leaf Fossils

Materials: leaves, tracing paper, pencils, charcoal or crayons

ONE Have children collect fallen leaves from trees in the area. Encourage them to find unusual shapes and patterns. You may want to take children on a walk to collect leaves.

Find Out More

PARTNERS **RESEARCH AND INQUIRY** Have children do their research in pairs. Partners can take turns using the Internet and the encyclopedia. Display their findings on a bulletin board.

*inter*NET CONNECTION For more information on mastodons go to ***www.mhschool.com/reading***.

FORMAL ASSESSMENT

After page 243, see Selection and Unit Assessment.

DAILY Phonics ROUTINES

DAY 3 **Blending** Write the letters *oo, ew*, and *ue* on the chalkboard. Call on volunteers to add letters to build words with the /ü/ sound. Have children say each word, blending the sounds.

Phonics CD-ROM

Study Skills

VARIOUS TEXTS

TESTED OBJECTIVES

Children will read and analyze an advertisement.

PREPARE Preview with children the advertisement on **Teaching Chart 171**. Let children know that ads sometimes say things that may "stretch the truth."

TEACH Read the ad with children. Ask whether it makes them want to go on a Super Fossil Dig. Do they trust this ad?

PRACTICE Have children answer questions 1–5. Review the answers with them.
1. to go on a Super Fossil Dig **2.** shell fossils; bugs in amber **3.** to make the reader think he or she will find one of these fossils **4.** to make the reader trust the ad **5.** No; there are no facts in the ad, just opinions.

ASSESS/CLOSE Show children a real advertisement. Ask them to explain what the ad does to convince the reader to do or buy something.

STUDY SKILLS

READ TOGETHER

Read an Advertisement

Use the ad to answer the questions.

1. What is the ad telling you to do?
2. What might you find on a Super Fossil Dig?
3. Why does the ad include pictures?
4. Why do you think the ad tells you that Paul Perkins is a fossil expert?
5. Does the ad prove that Super Fossil Digs are the best? Why or why not?

Meeting Individual Needs

EASY

Name________________ Date________ Reteach 204

Read an Ad

Some **advertisements** are trying to sell you something. Others are trying to convince you of something.

Study the advertisement below.

Own a Piece of the Past!
Fossils—Complete or in Parts—
Can Be Yours for Pennies
T-Rex Teeth!
Stegosaurus Spikes!
Raptor Claws!
Iguanodon Eggs!
Great as Conversation Pieces or Paperweights!
Ancient Art from a Forgotten Time
Archie's Ologies—The Fossil Store
Corner of Broadway and 4th
Send for Our Catalog now!
555-7856

Use this ad to answer the questions below.

1. Who is advertising something here? Archie's Ologies—The Fossil Store
2. Where is this store located? Corner of Broadway and 4th
3. What four things from dinosaurs are offered? T-Rex teeth stegosaurus spikes, iguanodon eggs, raptor claws
4. What is the phone number you can call to order? 555-7856

204 **At Home:** Have children make a collage of advertisements cut out from magazines. Book 2.2/Unit 2 **Are You a Fossil Fan?** 4

Reteach, 204

ON-LEVEL

Name________________ Date________ Practice 204

Read an Ad

Look at the **advertisements** shown below. Decide if each ad is trying to get you to buy something or to do something.
Write **Buy Something** on the blank line if the ad is selling a product. Write **Do Something** if the ad is trying to change your opinion or get you to do something.

Advertising Language:

1. **AT $29.95 THIS IS A GIVEAWAY OFFER! You won't find rain boots like this anywhere else in the city. Act now and we'll throw in a FREE UMBRELLA!** Buy Something
2. ***How would you like it if we dumped our garbage can in the middle of your living room!*** **DON'T LITTER! IT'S DIRTY AND UGLY, AND IT'S NOT POLITE!** Do Something
3. Is your house always cold? **Add Solar Windows** and get warm today. Buy Something
4. You wouldn't wear clothes someone else picked out for you. You wouldn't drive someone else's car. So why let somebody else pick your government? **GET OUT AND VOTE.** Do Something
5. Happiness is a state of mind. Peace is found in living right. Take it easy. Drink Orange Juice. It's just good. Buy Something

204 **At Home:** Help children to make a collage with advertisements clipped from magazines. Ask them whether each ad is trying to get them to buy or to do something. Book 2.2/Unit 2 **Are You a Fossil Fan?** 5

Practice, 204

CHALLENGE

Name________________ Date________ Extend 204

Read an Advertisement

Create an ad for an invention that you could sell.

Write why you think your ad will work.
Answers will vary.

204 **At Home:** Look at different advertisements with children. Have them tell you whether or not they think these ads will work. Book 2.2/Unit 2 **Are You a Fossil Fan?**

Extend, 204

TEST POWER

Directions tell you what to do.

RECTIONS:

ad the story. Then read each question about the story.

MPLE

How to Make a Hand Puppet

Read all of the directions first.
u will need:

an old sock
three buttons
a red marker
yarn, glue, and scissors

Put the sock on your hand.
en and close your hand. This
be the puppet's mouth. Draw
ne around the mouth with the
ker. Draw two dots on the top
he sock. Glue two buttons for
puppet's eyes here. Draw
ther dot where you want the
e to be. Glue the third button
. Cut twenty pieces of yarn.
h piece should be about six
es long. Glue the middle of
each piece of yarn to the top of the sock for hair. Put the puppet aside for an hour so that the glue can dry.

1 What do the directions say to do after you draw the puppet's mouth?

- ● Glue the buttons on.
- ○ Put the sock on your hand.
- ○ Find a sock to use.
- ○ Read the directions.

2 What do you do after you glue the yarn on?

- ● Let the glue dry.
- ○ Draw the eyes.
- ○ Read the directions.
- ○ Open and close your hand.

245

Test Power

THE PRINCETON REVIEW

Read the Page

Explain to children that you will be reading this story as a group. You will read the story, and they will follow along in their books.

Request that children put pens, pencils, and markers away, since they will not be writing in their books.

Discuss the Questions

QUESTION 1: Direct children to find the line where drawing the mouth is discussed. Ask them to read the lines that follow and find the choice that appears on those lines.

QUESTION 2: Direct children to finding the line where gluing the yarn is discussed. Ask them to read the lines that follow and find the choice that appears in those lines.

Self-Selected Reading
Leveled Books

Intervention **Skills**

Intervention Guide, for direct instruction and extra practice in phonics and comprehension

☑ Phonics

- /ü/oo, ue, ew
- /ər/er; /ən/en; /əl/le
- /ou/ow, ou; /oi/oi, oy

☑ Comprehension

- Summarize
- Sequence of Events

Answers will vary. Have children cite examples from the story to support their answers.

EASY

Story Questions for Selected Reading

1. Name the major events of the story.
2. Which story events surprised you? Why?
3. How would you describe the characters in the story?
4. What other title could the story have?
5. Which story character would you like to be? Why?

Draw a Picture

Draw a picture of your favorite character in the story.

EASY

UNIT SKILLS REVIEW

☑ Phonics

☑ Comprehension

Help children self-select an Easy Book to read and apply phonics and comprehension skills.

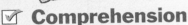

Guided Reading

PREVIEW AND PREDICT Discuss the illustrations in the beginning of the book. As you take the **picture walk**, have children predict what the story will be about. List their ideas.

SET PURPOSES Have children write why they want to read the book. Have them share their purposes.

READ THE BOOK Use items like the following to guide children's reading or to prompt discussion after they have read the story independently. Model blending and other phonics and decoding strategies for students who need help.

- What happened in the story? *Summarize*
- What was the first major event in the story? What happened next? What was the last thing that happened in the story? *Sequence of Events*
- Have children search for words that use the letters *er* to make the /ər/ sound, *ow, ou* to make the /ou/ sound, and *oi, oy* to make the /oi/ sound. *Phonics and Decoding*

RETURN TO PREDICTIONS AND PURPOSES Discuss children's predictions. Ask which were close to the book contents and why. Have children review their purposes for reading. Did they find out what they wanted to know?

LITERARY RESPONSE Have children discuss questions like the following:

- What did you like about the setting of the book? Why?
- What would you like to talk about with the story characters?
- If you could add another character to the story, what would that character be like?

See the Phonics **CD-ROM** for practice with words with /ü/*oo, ue, ew*; /ər/*er*; /ən/*en*; /əl/*le;* and /ou/*ow, ou*; /oi/*oy, oi.*

Self-Selected Reading
Leveled Books

INDEPENDENT

UNIT SKILLS REVIEW

☑ Phonics

☑ Comprehension

Help students self-select an Independent Book to read and apply phonics and comprehension skills.

Guided Reading

PREVIEW AND PREDICT Discuss the illustrations in the beginning of the book. As you take the **picture walk**, have children predict what the story will be about. List their ideas.

SET PURPOSES Have children write why they want to read the book. Have them share their purposes.

READ THE BOOK Use items like the following to guide children's reading or to prompt discussion after they have read the story independently.

- How did the story end? How did you feel about the story ending? ***Summarize***
- Imagine that the last thing that happened in the story happened first. How would that have changed the characters' behavior? ***Sequence of Events***
- What was a problem in the book that the character faced? How was the problem solved? ***Problem and Solution***
- Look back through the story. Can you find three words that have the /ər/ sound spelled *er*? ***Phonics and Decoding***

RETURN TO PREDICTIONS AND PURPOSES Have children review their predictions. Children can talk about whether their purposes were met, and if they have any questions the story left unanswered.

LITERARY RESPONSE The following questions will help focus children's responses:

- How do you think the characters felt at the beginning of the story? How was this different from the way they felt at the end of the story?
- How would you describe this story to someone who was about to read it?
- How did you feel after reading the story?

See the Phonics **CD-ROM** for practice with words with /ü/*oo*, *ue*, *ew*; /ər/*er*; /ən/*en*; /əl/*le;* and /ou/*ow*, *ou*; /oi/*oy*, *oi*.

☑ Phonics

- */ü/oo, ue, ew*
- */ər/er; /ən/en; /əl/le*
- */ou/ow, ou; /oi/oi, oy*

☑ Comprehension

- Summarize
- Sequence of Events

Answers will vary. Have children cite examples from the story to support their answers.

INDEPENDENT

Story Questions for Selected Reading

1. Where does the story take place?
2. What problem do the characters have in the story?
3. How do the characters solve their problem?
4. Could this story really have happened? Why? Why not?
5. What would have made this story more interesting?

Act Out a Scene

Work with a partner and act out a scene from the story.

Self-Selected Reading
Leveled Books

CHALLENGE

UNIT SKILLS REVIEW

☑ Phonics

☑ Comprehension

Help students self-select a Challenge Book to read and apply phonics and comprehension skills.

Guided Reading

PREVIEW AND PREDICT Discuss the illustrations in the beginning of the book. As you take the **picture walk**, have children predict what the story will be about. List their ideas. If the book has chapter headings, ask children to use the headings to predict what will happen in the first chapter.

SET PURPOSES Have children write why they want to read the book. Have them share their purposes.

READ THE BOOK Use items like the following to guide children's reading or after they have read the story independently.

- What happened in the story? *Summarize*
- Describe the events in the beginning of the story in the order in which they happened. *Sequence of Events*
- Who do you think was the most important character in the story? *Character*
- Look back through the book. Can you find any words with the /ü/ sound spelled *oo, ue, ew*? *Phonics and Decoding*

RETURN TO PREDICTIONS AND PURPOSES Discuss children's predictions. Ask which were close to the book contents and why. For books with chapter headings, were the headings useful? How? Have children review their purposes for reading. Did they find out what they wanted to know?

LITERARY RESPONSE Have children discuss questions like the following:

- Did you like the characters in the story? Why?
- Was the setting of the story a place you would like to visit? Why?
- What would you add to the story to make it more interesting or enjoyable?

See the Phonics **CD-ROM** for practice with words with /ü/*oo, ue, ew*; /ər/*er*; /ən/*en*; /əl/*le*; and /ou/*ow, ou*; /oi/*oy, oi*.

☑ Phonics

- /ü/*oo, ue, ew*
- /ər/er; /ən/en; /əl/le
- /ou/*ow, ou*; /oi/*oi, oy*

☑ Comprehension

- Summarize
- Sequence of Events

Answers will vary. Have children cite examples from the story to support their answers.

CHALLENGE

Story Questions for Selected Reading

1. Which part of the story was your favorite?
2. What might be a new title for the story?
3. What did you like about the illustrations?
4. Do you think the story could happen in real life?
5. If the story continued, what do you think might happen next?

Draw a Picture

Draw a picture of something you think might happen to the characters after the story ended.

Activities

Bringing Groups Together

Anthology and Leveled Books

Connecting Texts

CLASS DISCUSSION
Have children discuss connections among the different stories. Then make a chart of their suggestions. For example, write these story titles across the top of four columns: *Are You a Fossil Fan?, Playing Your Best, Farmer Brown's Birthday Surprise*, and *Sequoyah*. Label the chart Figure It Out. Then have children discuss the ways in which the theme Figure It Out relates to the characters in the stories. Write children's suggestions on the chart.

FIGURE IT OUT

Are You a Fossil Fan?	Playing Your Best	Farmer Brown's Birthday Surprise	Sequoyah
• Sam finds tiny pieces of bone and glues them together to form a dinosaur bone.	• Billy figures that playing your best is what is important.	• Dog figures out what to make for Farmer Brown's birthday.	• Sequoyah figures out how to translate the Cherokee language into print.

Viewing/Representing

GROUP PRESENTATIONS Divide the class into groups in which children have all read the same stories. Then have them work together to create a large mural that reflects the contents and mood of the story they have read. Have each group share its mural with the rest of the class.

AUDIENCE RESPONSE Give children time to look at each mural in detail. Encourage them to ask questions of the children in each group about their mural.

Research and Inquiry

CHOOSE A TOPIC Have children decide on a topic to explore. Then invite them to do the following:

- Think about ways they might find more information about their topic: encyclopedias, reference books, audiotapes, and so on.
- Take clear, careful notes as they gather information.
- Make a poster or collage that incorporates the information they have gathered.

*inter*NET CONNECTION For links to Web pages have children log on to ***www.mhschool.com/reading***.

JOURNAL Children can write and draw what they learned in their journals.

TESTED OBJECTIVES

Children will review sequence of events.

MATERIALS

Teaching Chart 172

Skills Finder

Sequence of Events

TEACHING TIP

IMPLIED SEQUENCE OF EVENTS Explain that when the sequence of events is not stated directly, it is called implied sequence of events. Have children describe the sequence of events for a typical day. After each description, have listeners determine if the sequence of events are implied or if words such as *first, next, then* were used to state the sequence.

ALTERNATE TEACHING STRATEGY

SEQUENCE OF EVENTS

For a different approach to teaching this skill, see page T71.

Review Sequence of Events

PREPARE

Discuss Sequence of Events Tell children that looking for words such as *first, second, next*, and *after* will help them figure out the order of events as they read. Remind children that knowing the order of events will help them to understand what they read.

TEACH

Read "Digging for Fossils" and Model the Skill Ask children to pay close attention to sequence as you read **Teaching Chart 172** with them.

Digging for Fossils

Amanda woke early on Saturday to dig for fossils. First, she put on her oldest pants and sweater. Then, she put her tools into her backpack. Next, Amanda packed a big lunch. Digging always made her hungry! Before leaving, she checked to see that she had everything.

Amanda spent all day digging for fossils. She had lots of fun. Even though she had not found any yet, she hoped one day to make a great discovery.

Teaching Chart 172

Discuss the clues in the passage that can help children figure out the sequence of events.

MODEL Amanda does many things to prepare for her fossil dig. When I read the word *first*, I know that the writer is going to list the events in the order in which they occurred.

PRACTICE

Show the Events in Order

ONE

Have children underline clues in the passage that help them find the sequence of events. Then have them list the events in the order in which they happened.

1. got dressed
2. packed tools
3. packed lunch
4. checked that she had everything
5. spent all day looking for fossils
6. did not find any yet

▶ **Interpersonal/Logical**

ASSESS/CLOSE

Show Sequence of Events in Comic Strips

Have partners choose a story that they have already read in their anthologies. Have them make a comic strip, with a different boxed picture for each event in the story. They may want to list the events in time order first. Create a bulletin-board display of their finished work.

DAILY Phonics ROUTINES

DAY 4 **Fluency** Write the following words on the chalkboard: *roof, knew, middle, broken, noise,* and *true*. Point to each word, asking children to blend the sounds silently. Ask a child to read each word aloud.

Phonics CD-ROM

Intervention **Skills**

Intervention Guide, for direct instruction and extra practice of sequence of events

Meeting Individual Needs for Comprehension

EASY

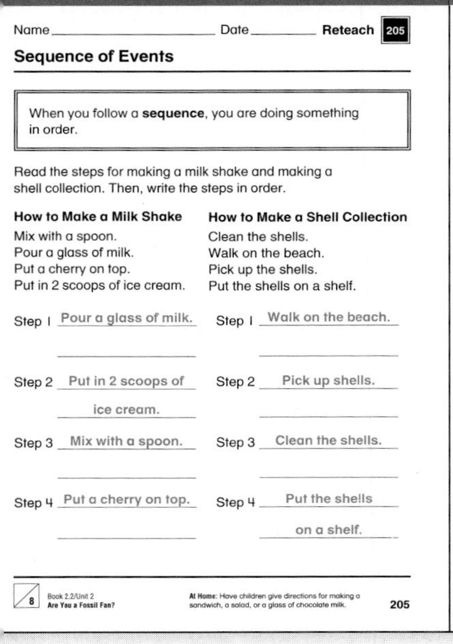

Name ______ Date ______ Reteach 205

Sequence of Events

When you follow a **sequence**, you are doing something in order.

Read the steps for making a milk shake and making a shell collection. Then, write the steps in order.

How to Make a Milk Shake
Mix with a spoon.
Pour a glass of milk.
Put a cherry on top.
Put in 2 scoops of ice cream.

How to Make a Shell Collection
Clean the shells.
Walk on the beach.
Pick up the shells.
Put the shells on a shelf.

Step 1 Pour a glass of milk.
Step 2 Put in 2 scoops of ice cream.
Step 3 Mix with a spoon.
Step 4 Put a cherry on top.

Step 1 Walk on the beach.
Step 2 Pick up shells.
Step 3 Clean the shells.
Step 4 Put the shells on a shelf.

8 Book 2.2/Unit 2 **Are You a Fossil Fan?**

At Home: Have children give directions for making a sandwich, a salad, or a glass of chocolate milk. 205

Reteach, 205

ON-LEVEL

Name ______ Date ______ Practice 205

Sequence of Events

Read the story. Number the pictures to show the order in which they happened in the story.

Grandpa Jake makes the best vegetable soup. First, he boils water in a big pot. Then, he peels carrots and puts them in the pot. Next, he adds corn and green beans. After that, he cuts up potatoes and places them in with everything else to cook. Finally, he adds his own special spices to the soup. My favorite part is eating the soup with fresh bread!

2 1
6 3
5 4

6 Book 2.2/Unit 2 **Are You a Fossil Fan?**

At Home: Ask children to explain the steps they take to make a favorite food. Ask what would happen if they forgot a step or made it in the wrong order. 205

Practice, 205

CHALLENGE

Name ______ Date ______ Extend 205

Sequence of Events

Read the story. Number the pictures to show the order in which they happened in the story.

There were clouds outside. Sheri put on her raincoat and rain boots in case it rained. She got her umbrella out of the closet. Then she locked the door of her house and went outside.

While she was walking, Sheri saw a deer by the side of the road. It was eating berries from a tree. Sheri walked quietly so she wouldn't scare the deer away. Suddenly, a girl on a bicycle raced by, ringing her bell. The deer ran into the woods. Just then, the sun came out.

3 6 7 1
5 2 8 4

Book 2.2/Unit 2 **Are You a Fossil Fan?**

At Home: Have children read a familiar story. Ask them to draw picture clues on individual cards. Then mix up the cards and have them put the cards in the order the pictures appear in the story. 205

Extend, 205

LANGUAGE SUPPORT

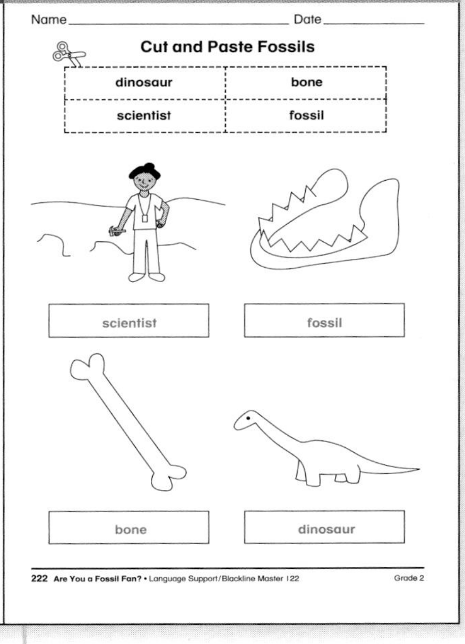

Name ______ Date ______

Cut and Paste Fossils

dinosaur	bone
scientist	fossil

scientist fossil
bone dinosaur

222 **Are You a Fossil Fan?** • Language Support/Blackline Master 122 Grade 2

Language Support, 222

TESTED OBJECTIVES

Children will read and summarize a selection.

MATERIALS
Teaching Chart 173

Skills Finder

Summarize

Introduce	B2: 149I-J
Review	B2: 211I-J, 245G-H
Test	B2: Unit 2
Maintain	B2: 271, 303, 323

TEACHING TIP

SUMMARIZE STEPS
To review, have children write the steps for summarizing a story. Prompt by asking: What do you need to do first? (read the selection) Have volunteers write the steps on the chalkboard to use as a guide with these activities.

SELF-SELECTED Reading

Children may choose from the following titles.

ANTHOLOGY

- *Are You a Fossil Fan?*

LEVELED BOOKS

- All titles for the unit

Bibliography, pages T88–T89

Review Summarize

PREPARE

Discuss Summaries Review that a summary is a short written or oral statement of the main ideas in a selection. Children must have a good understanding of the selection so that they can retell the important points in their own words.

TEACH

Read "All Kinds of Fossils" and Model the Skill Read **Teaching Chart 173** with children and call their attention to the main points. Remind children that when they sum up something they read, they should focus on the big picture, and leave out small details.

All Kinds of Fossils

Fossils have several forms. Petrified fossils are plants and animals that have turned to stone. Molds are the hollowed-out shapes that ancient plants or animals left in the mud that has now hardened.

Prints are a kind of fossil left in mud by such delicate objects as feathers. The rarest kind of fossil is a whole plant or animal that has been preserved in ice or tar. Scientists study all these fossils to understand the past.

Teaching Chart 173

MODEL To summarize this passage, I must find its main points. The title and the first sentence tell me that the passage is about different kinds of fossils. If I write a short description of each one, and tell why they are important, I will have summarized the passage. Let's see. . . the first fossil mentioned is a petrified fossil. I'll write that down.

PRACTICE

Use a Chart to Summarize the Passage

PARTNERS

Work with children to underline the important information in the passage. Then help partners summarize the passage using the chart. Remind children that summaries should be brief.

▶ **Linguistic/Logical**

Title: All Kinds of Fossils

Beginning: Fossils have several forms.

Middle: petrified molds, prints, whole plants and animals

End: Scientists learn about our past from fossils.

Summary: There are many kinds of fossils such as petrified molds, prints and whole plants and animals. Scientists learn about our past from fossils.

ASSESS/CLOSE

Use a Chart to Summarize a Story

Have children summarize the story of a movie or a book they know well, using the chart. Have them each read their summary to a partner. Encourage the listeners to ask questions if the summaries are unclear.

DAILY Phonics ROUTINES

DAY 5 **Writing** Ask partners to create rhyming couplets, using /ü/. Review that the rhyming words can be spelled with *oo*, *ew*, or *ue*. Have each pair read aloud their rhyme.

Phonics CD-ROM

ALTERNATE TEACHING STRATEGY

SUMMARIZE

For a different approach to teaching this skill, see page T67.

Intervention Skills

Intervention Guide, for direct instruction and extra practice in summarizing

Meeting Individual Needs for Comprehension

EASY

Name ____________ Date ________ **Reteach 206**

Summarize

A **summary** is a short way to tell what something is about.

Read the story. Answer the questions. Answers will vary.

Marci buttoned her coat and went outside. The cold wind blew on her face as she looked into the sky. There were dark clouds in the west. There was a ring around the moon. "It's going to snow," Marci whispered. Papa was a weatherman. He had told Marci how to predict the snow. By morning, the snow fell. Marci was right.

1. Who is the story about? Marci
2. What did she see? dark clouds in the west and a ring around the moon
3. What did she think about the weather? Marci thought it was going to snow.
4. What clues helped her make her decision? There was a cold wind, dark clouds, and a ring around the moon.

Write a summary of the story. One day Marci predicted that it was going to snow.

206 **At Home:** Have children look at the headlines of a newspaper. Have children write their own headline summarizing a favorite story. Book 2.2/Unit 2 **Are You a Fossil Fan?** 5

ON-LEVEL

Name ____________ Date ________ **Practice 206**

Summarize

A **summary** is a short way to tell what happens in a story. A summary tells the most important information in a sentence or two.

Read each story, and write a summary. Remember to write each summary in one or two sentences.

Jill opened the black case and looked inside. It was a shiny, new violin. Jill plucked a string. I will never, ever learn to play! she thought.

Jill's brother Owen played the violin very well. He made it look so easy. Jill had always wanted to learn how to play, too. Now she wondered if she could do it.

Summary: Possible answer: Jill has a new violin. She isn't sure she can learn how to play it.

Jill tried to play, but her violin sounded like a sad cat. Then she heard a beautiful sound behind her. Owen was holding his violin and smiling. "I'll play with you," he said.

Together, they played the song over and over. When Owen stopped playing, Jill had a surprise. Music was coming from her own violin! Owen grinned. "All it takes is practice," he said.

Summary: Possible answer: Jill's brother, Owen, helped her to practice playing the violin, and her skills improved.

206 **At Home:** Help children to practice summarizing stories by inviting them to summarize the plot of a cartoon. Book 2.2/ Unit 2 **Are You a Fossil Fan?** 2

CHALLENGE

Name ____________ Date ________ **Extend 206**

Summarize

Read the stories about Sam. Then write a one-sentence summary for each story.

1. When Sam was eight, he loved to dig in the dirt. He found broken toys, marbles, and coins. Once he found a fossil of a dinosaur tooth. He liked finding fossils and learning about the creatures that once lived on the Earth. When Sam grew up, he became a scientist.
   Sample answer: Sam became a scientist because he liked to find fossils and learning about creatures.
2. Sam wrote articles about his work as a scientist. He wrote about the different fossils he had found, and what he learned from them. Once Sam found the wing of a fly that was millions of years old. People enjoyed reading Sam's articles. Sometimes people wrote him letters telling him how much they learned from reading about his work.
   Sample answer: Sam wrote interesting articles about his work as a scientist.

Write a detail from each story that is not important to include in your summaries.

1. Sam found broken toys in the earth.
2. People wrote to Sam.

206 **At Home:** Have children talk about a favorite book. Ask them to summarize the story in one or two sentences. Book 2.2/Unit 2 **Are You a Fossil Fan?**

LANGUAGE SUPPORT

Name ____________ Date ________

Show the Order

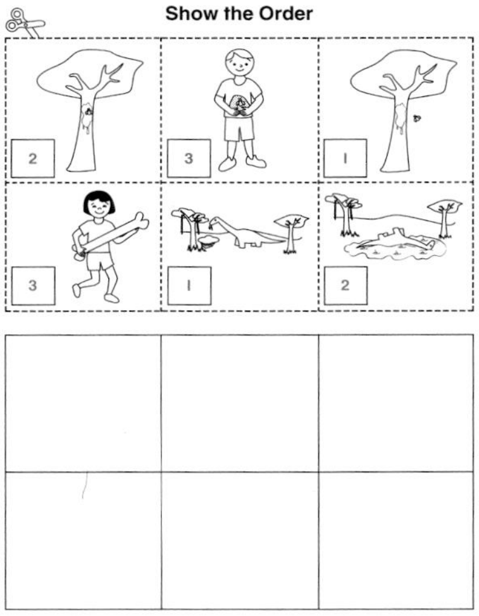

Grade 2 Language Support/Blackline Master 123 • **Are You a Fossil Fan?** 223

Reteach, 206 **Practice, 206** **Extend, 206** **Language Support, 223**

TESTED OBJECTIVES

Children will use context clues to figure out meanings of unfamiliar words and specialized vocabulary.

MATERIALS

Teaching Chart 174

Skills Finder

Context Clues	
Introduce	B1: 91K-L
Review	B1: 113K-L, 123I-J; B2: 179K-L
Test	B1: Unit 1
Maintain	B2: 139, 193, 269, 295

TEACHING TIP

SEMANTIC CUES Have children read through *Are You a Fossil Fan?* and make a list of three unfamiliar words. Model using context clues to help with word meaning. Encourage children to keep a list of troublesome words and to use dictionaries to confirm their meanings.

Review Context Clues

PREPARE

Discuss Context Clues Remind children that they can get clues about the meaning of an unfamiliar word by looking for context clues. Context clues include the surrounding words and sentences and the pictures and illustrations that accompany a story or article.

TEACH

Read the Passage and Model the Skill Have children read the passage on **Teaching Chart 174;** then model the skill beginning with the word *prehistoric.*

Animals of Today and Yesterday

Many animals of today had relatives that lived millions of years ago. Some animals of today look like their relatives from prehistoric times, but certain things have changed over millions of years. The first horse was only one foot tall! It was a miniature version of the horse we know today. The woolly mammoth, with its trunk and tusks, looked a lot like the modern elephant, but it was was covered with fur.

As the earth changed over time, animals also evolved so they would not die out. Those animals' relatives are with us today. Many kinds of animals could not change and became extinct. They are no longer on this planet.

Teaching Chart 174

MODEL I don't know what *prehistoric* means. But I can use the words around it to help me figure out its meaning. The passage says things have changed over millions of years. I think *prehistoric* means "from millions of years ago."

PRACTICE

Identify Context Clues (GROUP)

Work with children to underline the context clues that help determine the meaning of the circled words. ▶ **Linguistic/Logical**

ASSESS/CLOSE

Write Sentences Using Specialized Vocabulary

Have children write sentences to define the circled words on **Teaching Chart 174,** using the context clues they underlined.

ALTERNATE TEACHING STRATEGY

CONTEXT CLUES

For a different approach to teaching this skill, see page T74.

Intervention **Skills**

Intervention Guide, for direct instruction and extra practice of context clues

Meeting Individual Needs for Vocabulary

EASY

Name ____________ Date ______ Reteach 207

Context Clues

Clues in a sentence can tell you the meaning of a new word.

Sap is a liquid that moves inside a tree and brings food to the leaves and branches.

In the sentence above, the words "a liquid that moves inside a tree and brings food to the leaves and branches" tell you what **sap** means.

Read each sentence. Then circle the meaning of the underlined word.

1. We took a walk in the forest. There were trees as far as we could see.
   (a place with many trees) a wet place
2. Dad showed us an ancient redwood tree. He said it was very, very old.
   (very, very old) very, very small
3. The oldest tree was three thousand years old!
   (a big number) a small number
4. In the swamp, the water came up to our knees.
   a rocky place (a wet place)
5. Some of the trees had fuzzy green moss all over them.
   a big animal (a plant that grows on trees)

Book 2.2/Unit 2 Are You a Fossil Fan? — At Home: Ask children to list three new words they learned this week by using clues in the words and pictures. 207

Reteach, 207

ON-LEVEL

Name ____________ Date ______ Practice 207

Context Clues

Read the story. Find clues to the meaning of the underlined words by reading the words around them. Then choose one of the underlined words to answer each question.

Animals in the Snow

Many animals can live in snow. In the coldest winters, the earth is frozen hard. Rabbits and foxes dig holes in the snow to live in. They lie happily buried under a snow bank. They are warm and safe, protected from the cold winds. Some bigger animals, such as the mammoth who lived long ago and the polar bear, can live where it is cold all year. They have warm layers of fat and fur.

1. To be safe and warm is to be ___protected___.
2. To lie underneath something is to be ___buried___.
3. When something grows cold and hard, it is ___frozen___.
4. One big animal that lived long ago was the ___mammoth___.
5. Thicknesses or coats of something are called ___layers___.

Book 2.2/Unit 2 Are You a Fossil Fan? — At Home: Have children draw an illustration for the story and use two of the underlined words to write a caption. 207

Practice, 207

CHALLENGE

Name ____________ Date ______ Extend 207

Context Clues

What are they saying? Use sentences from the box.

1. This is a rare fossil. I have made a big discovery!
2. Here is a fly trapped in amber.
3. Wow! This is the bone of a giant mastodon!
4. Let me do a test on that fossil to find out how old it is.
5. This tooth is from a large dinosaur!

Book 2.2/Unit 2 Are You a Fossil Fan? — At Home: Have children use the picture to make up a story about what the scientists will do next. 207

Extend, 207

LANGUAGE SUPPORT

Name ____________ Date ______

Read These Closely

quickly	seriously	gently

Scientists take their work very ___seriously___.

John ___gently___ glues the tooth together.

John ___quickly___ called the museum when he found the mastodon bone.

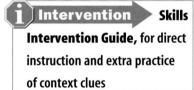

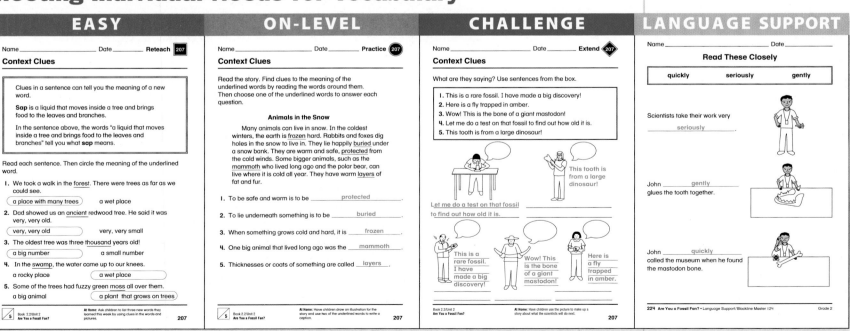

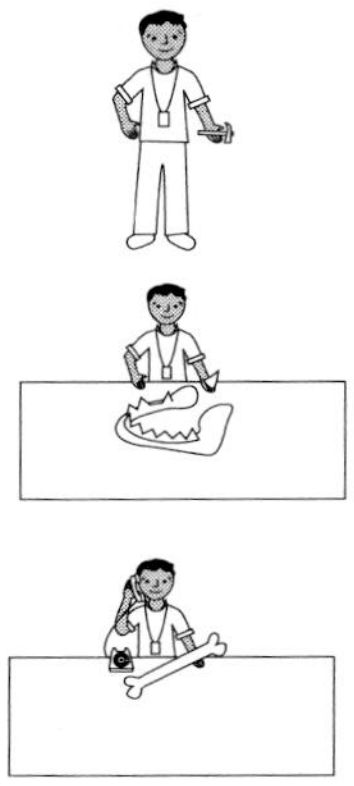

224 Are You a Fossil Fan? • Language Support/Blackline Master 124 Grade 2

Language Support, 224

Review Suffixes

OBJECTIVES

Children will review suffixes *-ly* and *-ful*.

MATERIALS

Teaching Chart 175

Skills Finder

Suffixes	
Introduce	B2: 149K-L
Review	B2: 211K-L, 245K-L
Test	B2: Unit 2
Maintain	B2: 355

TEACHING TIP

SUFFIXES Remind children of the following:

- The suffix *-ly* usually indicates a descriptive word such as *happily, sadly, gently*.
- Change the *y* at the end of a word to *i* before adding *-ly*, as in *merrily*.
- A clue for the meaning of the suffix *-ful* is to think of the word *full*.

PREPARE

Review the Suffixes *-ly* and *-ful* Remind children that suffixes are added to base words to make new words. The suffix *-ly* means "to do something in a certain way." The suffix *-ful* means "full of." By analyzing the base word and its suffix, children should be able to define the new word.

TEACH

Read the Passage and Model the Skill Have children look and listen for words with the suffixes *-ly* and *-ful* as you read the passage on **Teaching Chart 175** with them.

Sam Strikes Amber!

As Sam dug in the ground, he was very careful not to damage anything that might be a fossil. Suddenly, he saw something. He was hopeful that he had found an ancient plant or animal. Sam gently brushed the dirt away from the object to find that it was just a chicken bone. Then he spotted something colorful in the dirt. It turned out to be an orange piece of amber with a perfectly preserved insect in it. Now all his work was worthwhile.

Teaching Chart 175

Ask a volunteer to define the word *careful* by dividing it into *care* and *-ful*. Remind children that *-ful* means the same as *full*.

MODEL I see the word *careful* has the *-ful* suffix. By thinking about the meaning of *care* and *-ful*, I think that I can figure out what *careful* means. The word *care* means "close attention." The suffix *-ful* means "full of." The word *careful* must mean "full of attention or care."

PRACTICE

Define Words with *-ly* and *-ful* Suffixes

PARTNERS

Have children circle all the words with the *-ly* and *-ful* suffixes in the passage. Then have them identify the meaning of each word by defining the base word and suffix. Have children write their definitions down and read them to a partner. ▶ **Linguistic/Logical**

ASSESS/CLOSE

Create Words with *-ly* and *-ful* Suffixes

Tell children to add to the following base words either the *-ly* or the *-ful* suffix. Then have children write short sentences for each of the words.

doubt	**hour**	**cheer**
slow	**quick**	**dread**

ALTERNATE TEACHING STRATEGY

SUFFIXES *-ly* AND *-ful*

For a different approach to teaching this skill see page T68.

Intervention Skills

Intervention Guide, for direct instruction and extra practice of suffixes

Meeting Individual Needs for Vocabulary

EASY

Name ____________ Date ________ **Reteach 208**

Suffixes

Adding **-ly** or **-ful** to a word changes its meaning. The suffix **-ly** means "in the way of"; the suffix **-ful** means "full of."

Write the correct suffix to complete the sentence.

1. A fossil finder must be very care__ful__ .
   ful ly
2. Scientists take their work serious__ly__ .
   ly ful
3. Everyone polite__ly__ said "thank you" after the party.
   ful ly
4. Maria sang loud__ly__ to wake us up.
   ful ly
5. Glue is use__ful__ for mending broken toys.
   ly ful

208 **At Home:** Have children list three more words that end with the suffix **-ly** and three words that end with **-ful**. Book 2.2/Unit 2 **Are You a Fossil Fan?** 5

Reteach, 208

ON-LEVEL

Name ____________ Date ________ **Practice 208**

Suffixes

Choose a word from the box that means the same as the phrase in parentheses. Rewrite the sentence using the new word.

quickly slowly skillful fearful helpful neatly

1. We ate our lunch (in a slow way).
   We ate our lunch slowly.
2. Matt is (full of skill) with a hammer.
   Matt is skillful with a hammer.
3. The rain fell (in a quick way.)
   The rain fell quickly.
4. Do not be (full of fear) when it is dark.
   Do not be fearful when it is dark.
5. Mom was (full of help) with my science project.
   Mom was helpful with my science project.
6. Lola wrote (in a neat way).
   Lola wrote neatly.

208 **At Home:** Help children make a list of all the words they have learned that end in **-ly** and **-ful**. Book 2.2/Unit 2 **Are You a Fossil Fan?** 6

Practice, 208

CHALLENGE

Name ____________ Date ________ **Extend 208**

Suffixes

beautiful careful slowly quickly

Use each word from the box in a sentence. Then draw a picture to illustrate each sentence.

1. Answers will vary. Each sentence should contain a word from the box.
2. ____________
3. ____________
4. ____________

208 **At Home:** Have children brainstorm other words with the suffixes **-ly** and **-ful**. Ask them to write a poem about something that they think is beautiful. Have them include words with the suffixes **-ly** and **-ful**. Book 2.2/Unit 2 **Are You a Fossil Fan?**

Extend, 208

LANGUAGE SUPPORT

Name ____________ Date ________

Circle the Words

fearful grateful beautiful plentiful thoughtful awful joyful

x w i (b e a u t i f u l) a s c t i
s c o c r b d h (p l e n t i f u l)
a a c s e m a o c k n c y u l o d
n r a p i w l u q e f a z c b m r
r e s q z a v (g r a t e f u l) v e
i f c e b v a h f r w s r f l x f
f u q z c p c t s r a (a w f u l) t
p l d g r y q (f e a r f u l) w a s
s i y w e t a u a r t h n y a l n
p l i n o t b l p m (j o y f u l) q
t i (t h o u g h t f u l) n y l a j

Grade 2 Language Support/Blackline Master 125 • **Are You a Fossil Fan?** 225

Language Support, 225

GRAMMAR/SPELLING CONNECTIONS

See the 5-Day Grammar and Usage Plan on pages 245O–245P.

See the 5-Day Spelling Plan on pages 245Q–245R.

TEACHING TIP

Technology You can easily fix an error by using the undo feature. Undo will automatically erase the last change you entered.

Handwriting CD-ROM

Expository Writing

Prewrite

WRITE A REPORT Present this writing assignment: Write a magazine article that will teach people about fossils. Explain what fossils are. Tell where and how fossils are found.

FOCUSING QUESTIONS Have children focus on what they want to teach others about fossils by asking questions. Tell them to use the following words to help them write their questions: *Who? What? Where? When? Why?* and *How?*

Strategy: Make Lists Have children work independently to list the questions they formed. For example:

- Who digs for fossils?
- What are fossils?
- Where are they found?
- When were the fossils found?
- Why do we study fossils?
- How were they made?

Draft

FREE WRITE Encourage children to write freely, using the information from their lists. Remind them to place their facts in a clear, logical order. Tell children that using vivid, descriptive language and examples will help give the reader a better understanding of fossils.

Revise

SELF-QUESTIONING Ask children to assess their drafts.

- Do I clearly explain what fossils are?
- Is my information in a logical order?
- Do I use descriptions and examples to make my explanations clearer?

PARTNERS Have children trade their articles with partners for feedback.

Edit/Proofread

CHECK FOR ERRORS Children should check their articles for spelling, grammar, and punctuation errors.

Publish

SHARE THE ARTICLES Have children share their articles with other classes. Encourage the readers to ask questions.

All About Fossils
by Lyssa Weitz

Fossils are parts of animals and plants that have been preserved in stone or amber. They can be millions of years old. Some are even 3 1/2 billion years old! Scientists can learn a lot about the history of the earth by studying these fossils.

Fossils are found all over the world. Anyone can find them. People find fossils by digging in the ground. They must be very careful as they dig, so they don't damage any fossils. People have found dinosaur eggs, teeth, and footprints. Sometimes even whole animals or plants are found.

Presentation Ideas

ILLUSTRATE YOUR ARTICLE Have children illustrate their articles with pictures of fossils or of people digging for fossils.
▶ **Viewing/Representing**

MAKE A SPEECH Have children imagine they are presenting their articles to an audience who wants to learn about fossils. Invite members of the audience to ask questions.
▶ **Speaking/Listening**

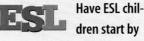

Consider children's creative efforts, possibly adding a plus (+) for originality, wit, and imagination.

Scoring Rubric

Excellent	Good	Fair	Unsatisfactory
4: The writer • clearly and fully explains fossils. • presents the information in a clear and organized way. • uses vivid, descriptive language to bring details to life.	**3:** The writer • clearly defines fossils. • presents organized information. • presents important details and descriptions.	**2:** The writer • gives a sketchy definition of fossils. • has made an attempt to organize information. • presents only a few important or interesting details.	**1:** The writer • does not define fossils. • writes without considering the order of information. • includes few or no details.

Incomplete 0: The writer leaves the page blank or fails to respond to the writing task. The student does not address the topic or simply paraphrases the prompt. The response is illegible or incoherent.

Meeting Individual Needs for Writing

EASY

Make a Poster Have children make simple fossil posters by photocopying a few examples of the following: fossils, dig sites, and supplies used to find fossils. Have them label their pictures to help others understand the topic.

ON-LEVEL

Write an Interview Have children write an imaginary interview with Sam Girouard. Their interviews should cover the same material as the magazine articles but should be presented in a question-and-answer format.

CHALLENGE

Apply for a Job Have children write a letter to an excavating leader explaining how they could be of help to the expedition. Have them tell all they know about fossils and fossil finding. Have them explain why they should be invited to go on the excavation.

Viewing and Speaking

VIEWING Have children
- look for details about the fossils.
- determine the setting of the picture.
- discover how details from the picture match details from the speech.

SPEAKING Encourage children to
- speak clearly and at a pace that is easy to understand.
- look at various members of the audience while speaking.
- refer to your picture to support your thoughts.

LANGUAGE SUPPORT

ESL Have ESL children start by writing the following words in their native language: *Who? What? Where? When? Why?* and *How?* Then help them translate each word. Next have ESL children work with a native English-speaking partner to brainstorm questions for their articles.

PORTFOLIO Encourage children to include their magazine articles in their portfolios.

5 Day Grammar and Usage Plan

LANGUAGE SUPPORT

ESL Write these equivalents on the board:

I am = I'm
He is = He's
She is = She's

Point to each contraction and ask children to say things about themselves and others using the contracted forms. Say: *We use contractions most of the time when we are speaking.*

DAILY LANGUAGE ACTIVITIES

Write the Daily Language Activities on the chalkboard each day or use **Transparency 25**. Have children orally make changes to form properly punctuated contractions. Prompt them to spell aloud each contraction, including apostrophes where needed.

Day 1

1. David says hes going fossil hunting. he's
2. Im going to ask Jen to come along. I'm
3. Shes never seen a fossil. She's

Day 2

1. Its time to start digging. It's
2. W'ere going to find some cool things. We're
3. Youre going to be excited! You're

Day 3

1. Theyre going to come with us. They're
2. Shes been digging for a long time. She's
3. Dan says hes going to help. he's

Day 4

1. Your going to be amazed. You're
2. Its four million years old. It's
3. Tell me when their ready. they're

Day 5

1. Sam says their buried right here. they're
2. Take a break if your tired. you're
3. Im sitting down to rest. I'm

Daily Language Transparency 25

DAY 1 Introduce the Concept

Oral Warm-Up Read aloud the following statements: *I am here. He is here.* Ask children to identify the pronouns.

Introduce Pronoun-Verb Contractions Review the following:

Contractions

- A **contraction** is a short form of two words.
- An **apostrophe (')** takes the place of the letters that are left out.

Explain that some contractions are formed from pronouns and verbs. Present and discuss the following pronoun-verb pairs and their contractions: *I am/I'm, he is/he's, she is/she's.* Ask children what letter was replaced by the apostrophe in each contraction.

Present the Daily Language Activity. Then have each child write three sentences using these contractions.

WRITING Assign the daily Writing Prompt on page 236C.

Name ____________ Date ________ LEARN Grammar 153

Contractions

- A **contraction** is a short form of two words.
- An **apostrophe** (') takes the place of the letters that are left out.

I am I'm
he is he's
she is she's

He's tall. She's short. I'm in the middle.

Write the contraction for the underlined words in each sentence.

1. He is my brother. He's
2. She is my sister. She's
3. I am the youngest. I'm
4. He is the oldest. He's
5. She is funny. She's

Write the words the contractions mean.

6. I'm here. I am
7. She's my friend. She is
8. He's a nice boy. He is

8 Book 2.2/Unit 2 Are You a Fossil Fan? Extension: Have the children write more sentences with *I'm, he's,* and *she's.* 153

GRAMMAR PRACTICE BOOK, PAGE 153

DAY 2 Teach the Concept

Review Contractions Prompt children to explain what contractions are, and what takes the place of the missing letters in the shortened word.

Introduce More Contractions Write on the chalkboard the following pronoun-verb pairs and their contractions: *it is/it's, they are/they're, we are/we're, you are/you're.* Have children spell aloud each contraction and identify the letter that was replaced by the apostrophe.

Present the Daily Language Activity. Then have each child write two sentences using contractions. Invite volunteers to read aloud their sentences, and to say the two words each contraction is formed from.

WRITING Assign the daily Writing Prompt on page 236C.

Name ____________ Date ________ PRACTICE AND LEARN Grammar 154

Using Contractions

- A **contraction** is a short form of two words.
- An **apostrophe** (') takes the place of the letters that are left out.

it is it's we are we're
they are they're you are you're

They're here. *You're* here. *We're* all here.

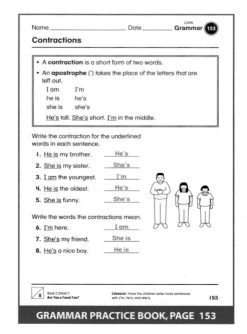

Write the contraction for the underlined words in each sentence.

1. We are waiting for the bus. We're
2. It is late. It's
3. You are late too. You're
4. I see a bus. It is not running. It's
5. They are all not running! They're
6. It is getting late. It's
7. We are going to walk. We're
8. You are sure to miss your class. You're

154 Extension: Have the children write their own sentences with the contractions. Book 2.2/Unit 2 Are You a Fossil Fan? 8

GRAMMAR PRACTICE BOOK, PAGE 154

Contractions

DAY 3 Review and Practice

.earn from the Literature Review :ontractions. Read aloud this sentence rom page 240 of *Are You a Fossil Fan?*

> **He's found the wristbone of an American mastodon.**

\sk children to identify the contraction in he sentence and state what two words ire joined in it. *(He* and *has)* Challenge :hildren to find another contraction on)age 241. *(I'm)*

Vrite Contractions Present the Daily .anguage Activity and have children cor- ect orally. Write on the chalkboard the vord pairs *I am, he is, she is, it is, they are, ve are, you are.* Ask each child to write hree sentences that include as many of hese word pairs as possible. Then have :hildren trade with partners, and rewrite heir partners' sentences, replacing each vord pair with a contraction.

WRITING Assign the daily Writing Prompt on page 236D.

Name ____________ Date ________ REVIEW AND PRACTICE Grammar 155

More Contractions

- A **contraction** is a short form of two words.
- An **apostrophe** (') takes the place of the letters that are left out.

I am	I'm	we are	we're
you are	you're	you are	you're
he is	he's	they are	they're
she is	she's		
it is	it's		

Read the sentences. Write the contraction for the two underlined words.

1. I am taking a bath. I'm
2. She is taking a shower. She's
3. It is not time for his bath. It's
4. They are taking showers. They're
5. We are taking baths soon. We're
6. You are ready for bed. You're
7. He is staying up late. He's
8. They are going out. They're

8 Book 2.2/Unit 2 **Are You a Fossil Fan?** **Extension:** Have children write sentences using all the contractions in the chart at the top of the page. 155

GRAMMAR PRACTICE BOOK, PAGE 155

DAY 4 Review and Practice

Review Contractions with Pronouns Write contractions from Daily Language Activity sentences for Days 1 through 3 on the chalkboard. Ask children what two words each contraction is formed from. Then present the Daily Language Activity for Day 4.

Mechanics and Usage Review possessive pronouns: *my, your, his, her, their, our, its.* Present:

> **Contractions and Possessive Pronouns**
>
> - An apostrophe takes the place of the letters left out of a contraction.
> - Possessive pronouns do not have apostrophes.
> - Do not confuse possessive pronouns with contractions *(they're/their, you're/your, it's/its).*

WRITING Assign the daily Writing Prompt on page 236D.

Name ____________ Date ________ MECHANICS Grammar 156

Contractions

- An **apostrophe** takes the place of the letters left out of a contraction.
- Possessive pronouns do not have apostrophes.
- Do not confuse possessive pronouns with contractions.

they're	their
you're	your
it's	its

Read the sentences. Write the correct pronoun or contraction.

1. Did you lose (you're, your) glasses? your
2. I think (they're, their) on the table. they're
3. The dog put them in (it's, its) mouth. its
4. (You're, Your) lucky I got them. You're
5. (It's, Its) getting late. It's
6. When is (they're, their) party? their
7. (You're, Your) not going to be there. You're
8. Do you know (they're, their) number? their

156 **Extension:** Have the children write the sentences with the correct words. Book 2.2/Unit 2 **Are You a Fossil Fan?** 8

GRAMMAR PRACTICE BOOK, PAGE 156

DAY 5 Assess and Reteach

Assess Use the Daily Language Activity and page 157 of the **Grammar Practice Book** for assessment.

Reteach Have children write the definition of a contraction, and how to form one. Orally state word pairs from the lesson and ask children to write a list of the contractions that can be formed from them. Call on children to say and spell aloud each contraction. Ask children to distinguish between meanings and spellings of *they're/their, you're/your,* and *it's/its.* Have children write sentences using contractions from their lists, using at least one of these three homophone pairs correctly. Have the class build a contraction word wall.

Use page 158 of the **Grammar Practice Book** for additional reteaching.

WRITING Assign the daily Writing Prompt on page 236D.

Name ____________ Date ________ TEST Grammar 157

Contractions

A. Read each sentence. Change each underlined word to a contraction. Write the contraction on the line.

1. I am cold. I'm
2. He is not cold. He's
3. She is bringing me a cover. She's
4. They are not my covers. They're

B. Read the sentences. Circle each contraction.

5. We're waiting for you.
6. You're going to be late.
7. It's ten o'clock.
8. He's on time.

8 Book 2.2/Unit 2 **Are You a Fossil Fan?** 157

GRAMMAR PRACTICE BOOK, PAGE 157

GRAMMAR PRACTICE BOOK, PAGE 158

5 Day Spelling Plan

LANGUAGE SUPPORT

ESL Have five children stand and hold up cards with the following words on them: *bone, hill, land, remains,* and *deep.* Say the words. Ask the five children to look at the first letter in each word and arrange themselves in alphabetical order. Repeat with other words on cards, some of which must be alphabetized by looking at the second letter.

DICTATION SENTENCES

Spelling Words

1. The hill is high.
2. The stone was on the ground.
3. She broke a bone in her arm.
4. The land is dry.
5. I poured oil into the can.
6. The water is deep.
7. The ocean is blue.
8. A drill is a kind of tool.
9. We saw the remains of the nest.
10. She is digging for clues.

Challenge Words

11. I have to change my clothes.
12. I can glue them together.
13. The hawk can hunt for mice.
14. She read a magazine.
15. Mom had her tooth pulled.

DAY 1 Pretest

Assess Prior Knowledge Use the Dictation Sentences at left and **Spelling Practice Book** page 153 for the pretest. Allow students to correct their own papers. If students have trouble, have partners give each other a midweek test on Day 3. Students who require a modified list may be tested on the first five words.

Spelling Words		Challenge Words
1. hill	6. deep	11. **change**
2. **stone**	7. ocean	12. **glue**
3. **bone**	8. drill	13. **hunt**
4. land	9. **remains**	14. **magazine**
5. oil	10. **digging**	15. **tooth**

*Note: Words in **dark type** are from the story.*

Word Study On page 154 of the **Spelling Practice Book** are word study steps and an at-home activity.

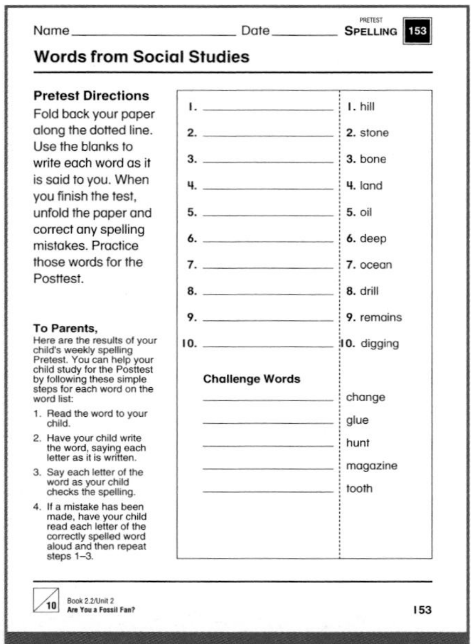

Name __________ Date ______ PRETEST SPELLING 153

Words from Social Studies

Pretest Directions
Fold back your paper along the dotted line. Use the blanks to write each word as it is said to you. When you finish the test, unfold the paper and correct any spelling mistakes. Practice those words for the Posttest.

1. ______ 1. hill
2. ______ 2. stone
3. ______ 3. bone
4. ______ 4. land
5. ______ 5. oil
6. ______ 6. deep
7. ______ 7. ocean
8. ______ 8. drill
9. ______ 9. remains
10. ______ 10. digging

Challenge Words
______ change
______ glue
______ hunt
______ magazine
______ tooth

To Parents,
Here are the results of your child's weekly spelling Pretest. You can help your child study for the Posttest by following these simple steps for each word on the word list:

1. Read the word to your child.
2. Have your child write the word, saying each letter as it is written.
3. Say each letter of the word as your child checks the spelling.
4. If a mistake has been made, have your child read each letter of the correctly spelled word aloud and then repeat steps 1–3.

10 Book 2.2/Unit 2 **Are You a Fossil Fan?** 153

SPELLING PRACTICE BOOK, PAGE 153

WORD STUDY STEPS AND ACTIVITY, PAGE 154

DAY 2 Explore the Pattern

Sort and Spell Words Write the words *deep* and *digging* on the chalkboard. Ask a student which comes first in alphabetical order. Explain that they must look at the second letter in each word.

Ask students to read aloud the ten spelling words before arranging them in alphabetical order.

Alphabetical Order	
bone	land
deep	ocean
digging	oil
drill	remains
hill	stone

Word Wall Ask students to find other words related to social studies and add them in alphabetical order to a classroom word wall.

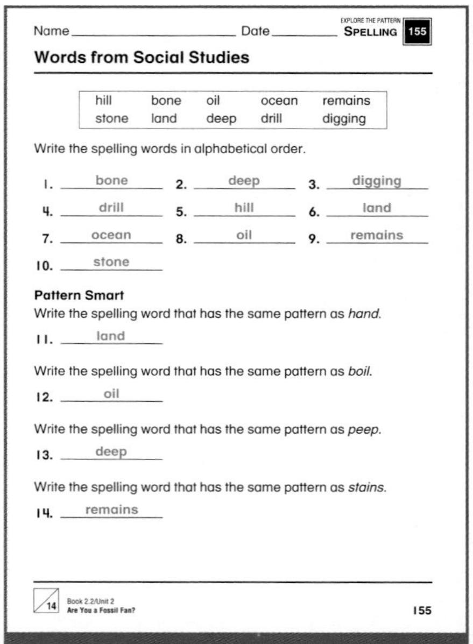

Name __________ Date ______ EXPLORE THE PATTERN SPELLING 155

Words from Social Studies

hill	bone	oil	ocean	remains
stone	land	deep	drill	digging

Write the spelling words in alphabetical order.

1. bone 2. deep 3. digging
4. drill 5. hill 6. land
7. ocean 8. oil 9. remains
10. stone

Pattern Smart
Write the spelling word that has the same pattern as *hand.*
11. land

Write the spelling word that has the same pattern as *boil.*
12. oil

Write the spelling word that has the same pattern as *peep.*
13. deep

Write the spelling word that has the same pattern as *stains.*
14. remains

14 Book 2.2/Unit 2 **Are You a Fossil Fan?** 155

SPELLING PRACTICE BOOK, PAGE 155

Words from Social Studies

DAY 3 Practice and Extend

Word Meaning: Social Studies Tell students that the words from the spelling list are all words from social studies. Write sentences such as the following on the chalkboard and ask students to fill in the blanks with words from the spelling list.

A ______ is a tool you might use to find ______. (drill, oil)

An ______ is a body of water that is very ______. (ocean, deep)

Glossary Have students:

- write each Challenge Word.
- look up the definition of each word in the Glossary.
- write a definition for each Challenge Word.

DAY 4 Proofread and Write

Proofread Sentences Write these sentences on the chalkboard, including the misspelled words. Ask students to proofread, circling incorrect spellings and writing the correct spellings. There are two spelling errors in each sentence.

The bown is on hil. (bone, hill)

The oshin is dep. (ocean, deep)

Have students create additional sentences with errors for partners to correct.

WRITING

Have students use as many spelling words as possible in the daily Writing Prompt on page 236D. Remind students to proofread their writing for errors in spelling, grammar, and punctuation.

DAY 5 Assess and Reteach

Assess Students' Knowledge Use page 158 of the **Spelling Practice Book** or the Dictation Sentences on page 245Q for the posttest.

Personal Word List If students have trouble with any words in the lesson, have them add to their personal list of troublesome words in their journals. Have students write a story using words from their list.

JOURNAL

Students should refer to their word lists during later writing activities.

Name________________ Date________ PRACTICE AND EXTEND SPELLING 156

Words from Social Studies

hill	bone	oil	ocean	remains
stone	land	deep	drill	digging

All in a Set

Use a spelling word to complete each sentence.

1. Where did your dog bury the ___bone___?
2. Jack and Jill climbed a ___hill___.
3. George liked ___digging___ for treasure.
4. Where will the space ship ___land___?
5. I like to watch the waves in the ___ocean___.
6. Always dive into the ___deep___ end of the pool.
7. Another word for **rock** is ___stone___.
8. Tina put gas and ___oil___ in her car.
9. The worker used a ___drill___ to make a hole.
10. Fossils are the ___remains___ of dinosaurs.

156 Book 2.2/Unit 2 Are You a Fossil Fan? 10

SPELLING PRACTICE BOOK, PAGE 156

Name________________ Date________ PROOFREAD AND WRITE SPELLING 157

Words from Social Studies

Proofreading Activity

There are five spelling mistakes in the report below. Circle each misspelled word. Write the words correctly on the lines below.

We learned about Columbus in school. We learned that Columbus was very brave. He sailed across the ocaen to find a new ladn. Our class wanted to show our depe respect for Columbus. We wrote a play about him. Then we placed a special stoan on a hille to honor him.

1. ___ocean___ 2. ___land___ 3. ___deep___
4. ___stone___ 5. ___hill___

Writing Activity

Write a story about a dinosaur who visits your school. Use five spelling words in your story. Circle the words you use.

10 Book 2.2/Unit 2 Are You a Fossil Fan? 157

SPELLING PRACTICE BOOK, PAGE 157

Name________________ Date________ POSTTEST SPELLING 158

Words from Social Studies

Look at the words in each set. One word in each set is spelled correctly. Use a pencil to color in the circle in front of that word. Before you begin, look at the sample sets of words. Sample A has been done for you. Do Sample B by yourself. When you are sure you know what to do, you may go on with the rest of the page.

Sample A
- (A) one
- (B) twoo
- (C) thwee
- (D) foure

Sample B
- (E) blu
- (F) telo
- (G) red
- (H) whiite

1. (A) hille (B) hil (C) hill (D) hile
2. (E) bne (F) boone (G) bon (H) bone
3. (A) stne (B) stone (C) ston (D) stoen
4. (E) deep (F) deepe (G) depe (H) deap
5. (A) osean (B) ocene (C) ocean (D) osion
6. (E) oil (F) oel (G) ole (H) oyl
7. (A) drle (B) drill (C) drille (D) drele
8. (E) land (F) lande (G) leand (H) lnde
9. (A) diging (B) degging (C) digging (D) digeing
10. (E) remaines (F) remanes (G) remains (H) remaens

158 Book 2.2/Unit 2 Are You a Fossil Fan? 10

SPELLING PRACTICE BOOK, PAGE 158

UNIT 2

Unit Closer

Wrap Up the Theme

Figure It Out

We can solve problems by working together.

REVIEW THE THEME Remind children that all of the selections in this unit relate to the theme Figure it Out. Do children agree that this is so? Encourage them to name other stories or nonfiction pieces they have read that also fit the theme Figure it Out.

READ THE POEM Read aloud "To Catch a Fish" by Eloise Greenfield. Then ask how the poem connects to the theme Figure it Out. Who is figuring out what? Do they think the poet's plan will work?

LISTENING LIBRARY Children can listen to an audio recording of the poem.

GROUP **MAKE CONNECTIONS** Have children work in small groups to brainstorm a list of ways that the stories, poems, and the *Time for Kids* magazine article relate to the theme Figure it Out. Groups can then compare their lists as they share them with the class.

Have children name their favorite selections. Encourage them to think about other books they might like by the same author or on the same topic.

READ TOGETHER

To Catch a Fish

It takes more than a wish
to catch a fish
you take the hook
you add the bait
you concentrate
and then you wait
you wait you wait
but not a bite
the fish don't have
an appetite
so tell them what
good bait you've got
and how your bait
can hit the spot
this works a whole
lot better than
a wish
if you really
want to catch
a fish

by Eloise Greenfield

246

LOOKING AT GENRE

Have children review *The Bremen Town Musicians* and *The Wednesday Surprise*. What are the differences between a play and a story?

Help children list the key characteristics of each genre. Can they name other selections they have read that have the same characteristics?

PLAY *The Bremen Town Musicians*	FICTION *The Wednesday Surprise*
• Characters are listed at beginning of play.	• Characters are not listed.
• Dialogue follows character's name and colon.	• Dialogue is in quotation marks.

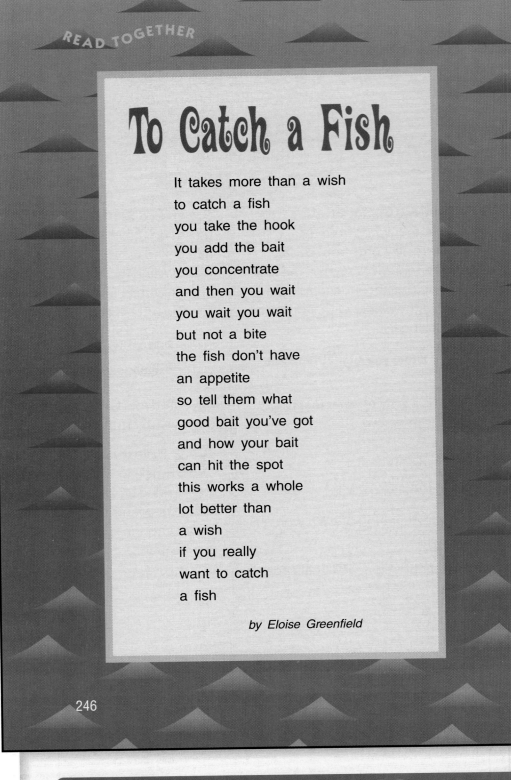

LEARNING ABOUT POETRY

Literary Devices: No Punctuation Point out that there are no capital letters or punctuation of any kind in this poem. Thus, the whole poem can be read without pausing. Encourage children to try this.

Guide children to understand that the lack of punctuation combined with the uneven rhyme scheme make the poem funny and interesting.

WRITING **Poetry Activity** Have children write a poem about a sport or game they play. They can use the same format as "To Catch a Fish," or you may choose to model another poem for them to follow.

Activity

Research and Inquiry

GROUP **Complete the Theme Project** Have children work in teams to complete their group projects and decide how to present them. Encourage children to share the tasks of writing and illustrating so that each member of the team can contribute to the project.

Make a Classroom Presentation Explain to children that if they speak in a lively manner, expressing themselves with their hands and faces as well as their voices, they will more likely capture the attention of their audience. Have the teams present their riddles. Then have the other teams try to solve them. The team that solves the riddle first gets a point. The team with the most points wins.

Draw Conclusions Have children draw conclusions about what they learned from researching and preparing their projects. Was the resource chart they made helpful? What other resources did they use? For example, did they use the Internet? Was working in a group helpful for creating riddles? What conclusions can they draw from this?

Ask More Questions What other questions came up during the course of preparing the project? Did team members have any problems working together? How did they solve the problems? You might encourage teams to create more riddles and prepare new presentations.

Reading Research

Learning to check the information you read is an important skill. Facts in different books or sources may disagree with each other. Information may be out of date. The questions below can help you check your facts.

It says that
blue whales can grow to
100 feet (30 meters) long. I
can check this fact out in the
encyclopedia!

Check Facts

1. **Does the information make sense?** Does it fit with what you already know?
2. **Where can I check?** Look in an encyclopedia or a book on the topic.
3. **Whom can I ask?** Ask an adult at school or at home. This person might help you find out if a fact is correct.
4. **Is there newer information?** It is important to use information that is up-to-date.

1. **Does it make sense?** I know that whales are very big.
2. **Where can I check?** I could look in an encyclopedia.
3. **Whom can I ask?** I could ask the librarian.
4. **Is there newer information?** Is this still true?

Nonfiction Book

BLUE WHALES

The blue whale is probably the largest animal that has ever lived. Its body is bigger than the largest dinosaur. It makes a sound so loud that it can be heard 100 miles (160 km) away.

Blue whales look like large fish, but they are not. Blue whales keep a constant body temperature, the same as you do. Fish do not. Blue whales have lungs and cannot breathe underwater. Fish use their gills to breathe underwater.

Most blue whales live in Earth's southern oceans. Laws protect these whales from being hunted. Even so, only a small number remain.

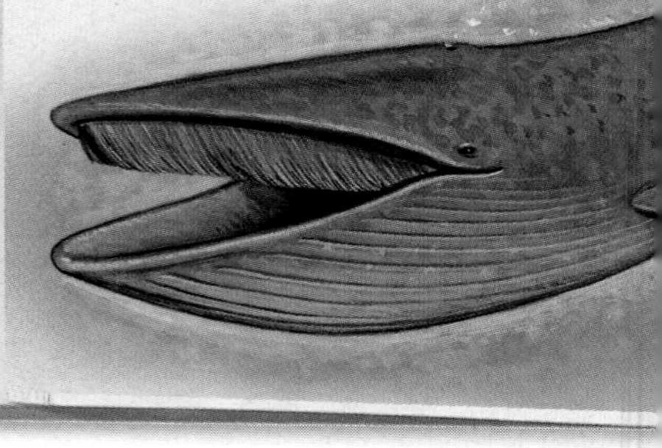

Reading Research

Anthology pages 382–383

Research: Checking Facts

OBJECTIVES Children will:

- check whether information presented is true by asking others and using another source.
- use the media center and available technology as sources of information.
- use text features to aid comprehension.

INTRODUCE Discuss whether every fact in books, newspapers, magazines, or on the Internet is true. Why would information not be true?

MODEL One step says "Does the information make sense?" When I read that blue whales can be 100 feet long, that seems about right. If it said they were 10 feet or 1,000 feet long, I would know that those numbers do not make sense.

PRACTICE/APPLY Have children **preview** page 383, including **text features** such as headings. Then have them read and apply the strategy to pages 384 and 385. Ask:

- **Does it make sense that dinosaurs hatched from eggs? Why or why not?** (yes, because other reptiles hatch from eggs, including snakes and alligators)
- **Where could you check the information about the discovery in China?** (new reference books, science magazines, online encyclopedias the Internet)
- **How do you know if you are reading the newest information?** (I can check the copyright date or the publication date of the source.)

Have children review the encyclopedia entry and magazine article and answer the questions on page 385.

Encyclopedia

dinosaur

Dinosaurs

Dinosaur bones have been found all over the world. Scientists who study the bones have learned that some dinosaurs ate meat and others ate plants. Some dinosaurs walked on two legs, while others walked on four legs.

Some scientists think dinosaurs died when a huge meteor crashed into Earth. It caused dust to fly into the air and block the sunlight. Without sun, plants could not grow. The dinosaurs that ate plants died. Then, dinosaurs that ate meat had nothing to eat. They died, too.

Magazine

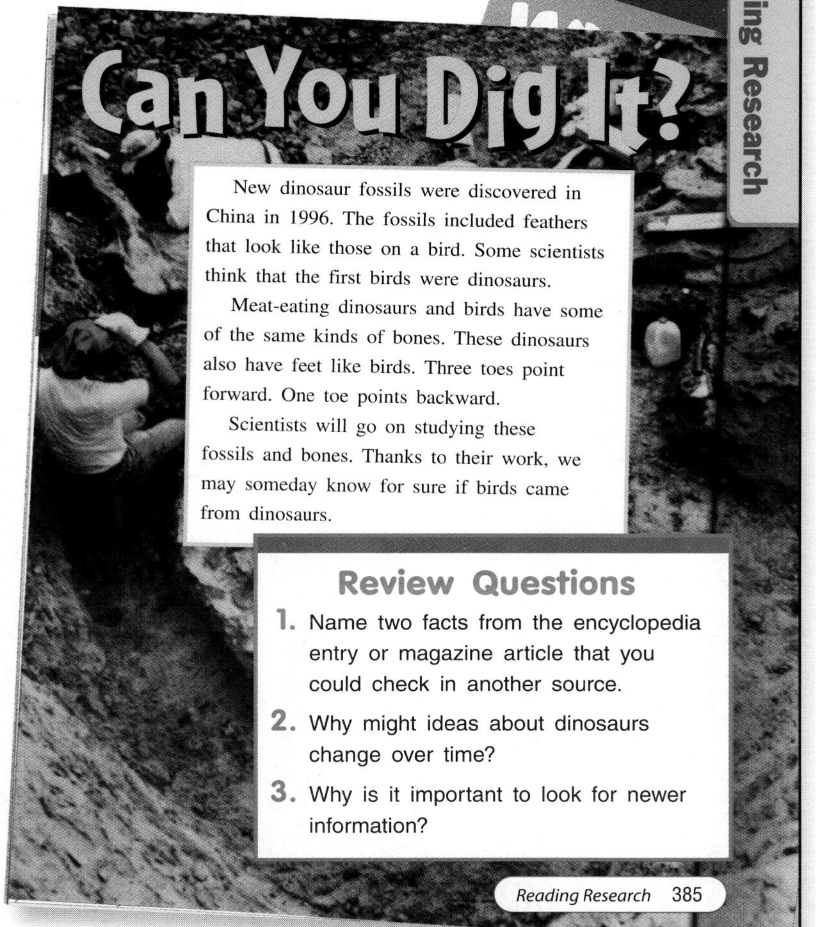

Can You Dig It?

New dinosaur fossils were discovered in China in 1996. The fossils included feathers that look like those on a bird. Some scientists think that the first birds were dinosaurs.

Meat-eating dinosaurs and birds have some of the same kinds of bones. These dinosaurs also have feet like birds. Three toes point forward. One toe points backward.

Scientists will go on studying these fossils and bones. Thanks to their work, we may someday know for sure if birds came from dinosaurs.

Review Questions

1. Name two facts from the encyclopedia entry or magazine article that you could check in another source.
2. Why might ideas about dinosaurs change over time?
3. Why is it important to look for newer information?

Anthology pages 384–385

ANSWERS TO REVIEW QUESTIONS

1. Possible answers: what dinosaurs ate, how they walked, why they died, what was discovered in China and in which year, if first birds were dinosaurs.
2. Scientists constantly discover new dinosaur fossils and learn more about old ones.
3. New discoveries are being made every day, even about old topics.

TRANSFER THE STRATEGY

Ask: How would the strategy on page 382 help you check the facts about another animal?

Discuss: Every day we hear and read information. Why is it important to make sure facts are correct?

Activity

True or False?

What to Do:

Mark each statement *T* for *true* or *F* for *false*. Then use the steps on page 382 to check your answers.

T F **1.** Many dinosaurs lived on Earth 200 million years ago.

T F **2.** Dinosaurs are related to lions.

T F **3.** Scientists who study dinosaurs are called paleontologists.

T F **4.** All dinosaurs are now extinct.

T F **5.** The dinosaur called Tyrannosaurus Rex weighed more than ten tons.

T F **6.** Tyrannosaurus Rex ate mostly plants.

Answers: 1, T; 2, F; 3, T; 4, T; 5, F; 6, F

Expository Writing

CONNECT TO LITERATURE In *The Bremen Town Musicians*, the characters GROUP work together to solve their problem. Have the class discuss how the animals help each other. Have children list their classmates' responses.

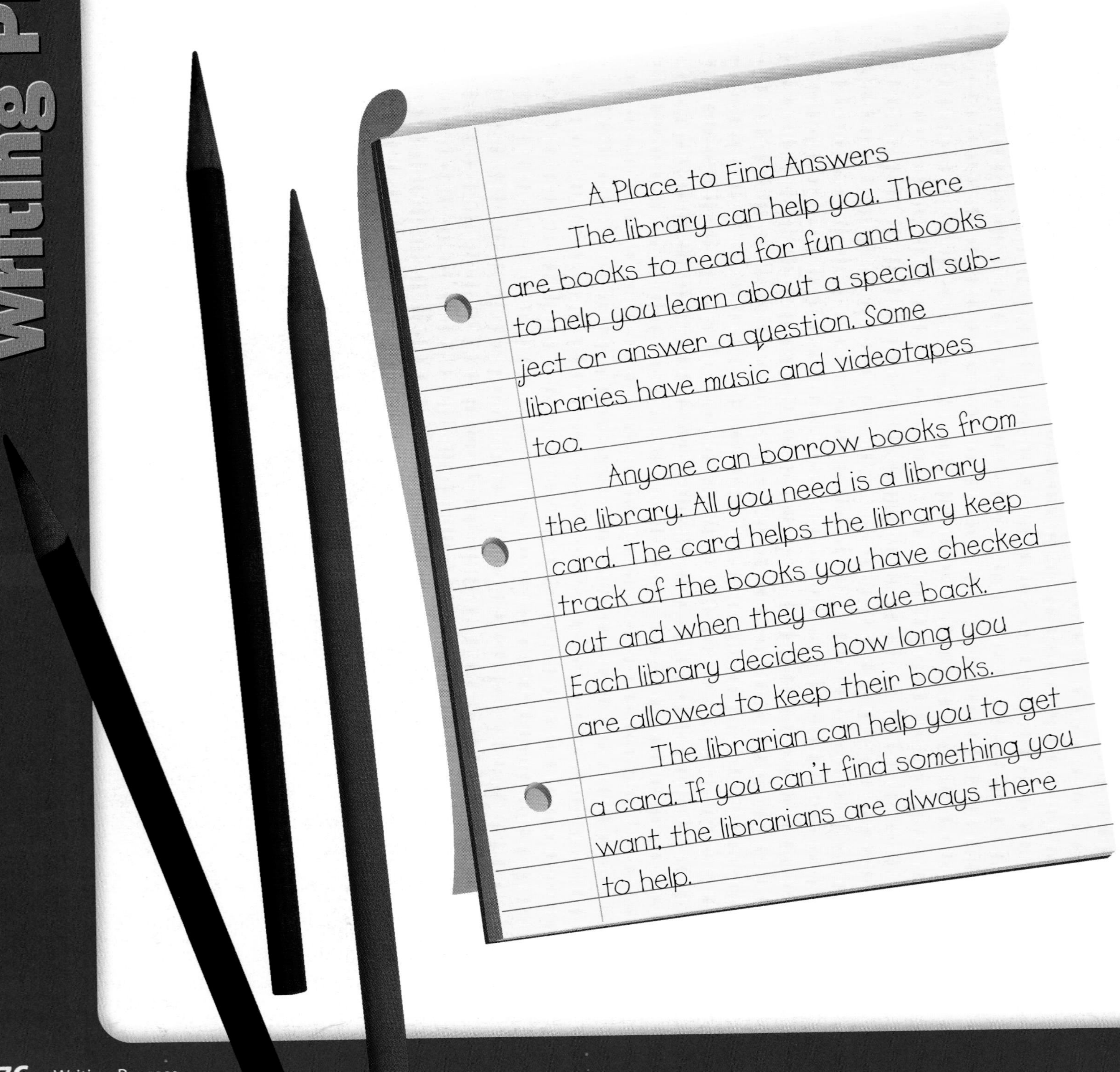
A Place to Find Answers
The library can help you. There
are books to read for fun and books
to help you learn about a special subject or answer a question. Some
libraries have music and videotapes
too.
Anyone can borrow books from
the library. All you need is a library
card. The card helps the library keep
track of the books you have checked
out and when they are due back.
Each library decides how long you
are allowed to keep their books.
The librarian can help you to get
a card. If you can't find something you
want, the librarians are always there
to help.

Prewrite

PURPOSE AND AUDIENCE Tell children that they will write a report about a person or place that helps them to find information. Explain that the purpose of the report is to inform the reader by presenting facts about this person or place.

STRATEGY: MAKE AN OUTLINE Present children with a few topic options. Include their suggestions as well. Ask them to choose a topic and explain why they chose it. Then show them how to make an outline.

Use **Writing Transparency 5A** to model an outline.

FEATURES OF EXPOSITORY WRITING

- States a specific topic.
- Presents facts that inform on the topic.
- Has a logical beginning, middle, and end.
- Ends with a conclusion based on the facts.

TEACHING TIP

ORGANIZATION Show children how to make the best use of their outlines. Have them put their ideas in order under each relevant category in their reports. Encourage them to be very specific in stating their topic heading.

***PREWRITE* TRANSPARENCY**

THE MAIN IDEA:
The library can help you in many ways.

A. What's in a library?
1. Books to read for fun
2. Books to help you learn something new and interesting
3. Sometimes music and videos

B. How do you use the library?
1. Use a library card
2. Return books when they are due
3. Find books by the author's name or the subject
4. Ask the librarian for help

C. Why do you like the library?
1. It can help you answer questions
2. There are books to read and learn from

Book 2.2/Unit 2: Expository Writing / Prewriting 5A

Expository Writing

Draft

STRATEGY: EXPAND THE MAIN IDEA Instruct students to begin with a sentence that introduces their main idea. Encourage them to use concrete examples or personal experiences to illustrate or support the main idea. At this stage, they should write their ideas freely, without self-editing.

Use **Writing Transparency 5B** to model a first draft.

WORD CHOICE Take the children around their school library. Instruct them to list important words that pertain to the library. Ask them to use each word in a new sentence about the library. Have them file the lists and sentences in their writing portfolios.

LANGUAGE SUPPORT

Work directly with children who need help focusing or expanding on their topics. Under each question in their outline, have them write phrases that give examples from their own experiences. Help them list descriptive words to enhance their examples.

***DRAFT* TRANSPARENCY**

The library can help you. There are books to read for fun and books to help you laern about a special subject. Some libraries have music and videotapes too.

Anyone can books borrow from the library. All you need a library card. The card helps the library keep track of the books you have checked out. each library decides how long you are allowed to keep the books.

The libarian can help you to get a card, like Ms. Chapter did for me. She said, "You can use this card forever! i like going to the library because there are so many interesting books. There is so much to learn. You can find the answers to many questions in the library!

McGraw-Hill School Division

Book 2.2/Unit 2: Expository Writing / Drafting 5B

Revise

Have children review their work for clarity and expressiveness. Ask them to check the sequence of their thoughts to see if it makes sense. Have partners exchange papers and make constructive, creative suggestions for ways to improve their work.

Use **Writing Process Transparency 5C** for classroom discussion on the revision process. Ask children to comment on how revisions may have improved this writing example.

STRATEGY: ELABORATION Have a class discussion exploring ways children can expand on their drafts. Ask them to consider how a reader might understand and react to their reports. Encourage them to reflect on these questions in the revision process:

- Have I kept to my topic idea?
- What other important information could I add?
- Does my report have a beginning, middle, and end?

TEACHING TIP

TEACHER CONFERENCE

Help children individually to elaborate upon the main idea in their writing. You may begin the process with a conferencing checklist:

- Do you explain why this person or place is helpful?
- Do you show how this person or place can help solve problems?
- Can you support the main idea with details from your own experience?

***REVISE* TRANSPARENCY**

A Place to Find Answers

The library can help you. There are books to read for fun and books to help you laern about a special subject, or answer a question Some libraries have music and videotapes too.

Anyone can books borrow from the library. All you need a library card. The card helps the library keep track of the books you have checked out, and when they are due back each library decides how long you are allowed to keep the books.

The libarian can help you to get a card, like Ms. Chapter did for me. She said, "You can use this card forever! i like going to the library because there are so many interesting books. There is so much to learn. You can find the answers to many questions in the library!

McGraw-Hill School Division

Book 2.2/Unit 2: Expository Writing / Revising 5C

Expository Writing

Edit/Proofread

After students finish revising their reports, have them proofread for final corrections and additions.

GRAMMAR/SPELLING CONNECTIONS

See the 5-Day Grammar and Usage Plans pp. 149O–149P, pp. 179O–179P, pp. 211O–211P, pp. 235O–235P pp. 245O–245P.

See the 5-Day Spelling Plans, pp. 149Q–149R, pp. 179Q–179R, pp. 211Q–211R, pp. 235Q–235R, pp. 245Q–245R.

GRAMMAR, MECHANICS, USAGE

- A pronoun must agree with the noun it replaces.
- Do not confuse possessive pronouns with contractions.
- An abbreviation begins with a capital letter and ends with a period.

Publish

Children can read their reports to the class. You can bind their reports in a class book and put a copy in the school library.

Use **Writing Process Transparency 5D** as a proofreading model and **Writing Process Transparency 5E** to discuss presentation ideas.

PROOFREAD **TRANSPARENCY**

A Place to Find Answers

¶ The library can help you. There are books to read for fun and books to help you laern (learn) about a special subject (or answer a question). Some libraries have music and videotapes, too.

Anyone can books borrow from the library. All you need a (is) library card. The card helps the library keep track of the books you have checked out (and when they are due back). each library decides how long you are allowed to keep the books.

The libarian can help you to get a card, like Ms. Chapter did for me. She said, "You can use this card forever! ¶ i like going to the library because there are so many interesting books. There is so much to learn. You can find the answers to many questions in the library!

McGraw-Hill School Division

Book 2.2/Unit 2: Expository Writing / Proofreading 5D

PUBLISH **TRANSPARENCY**

A Place to Find Answers

The library can help you. There are books to read for fun and books to help you learn about a special subject or answer a question. Some libraries have music and videotapes, too.

Anyone can borrow books from the library. All you need is a library card. The card helps the library keep track of the books you have checked out and when they are due back. Each library decides how long you are allowed to keep the books.

The librarian can help you to get a card, like Ms. Chapter did for me. She said, "You can use this card forever!"

I like going to the library because there are so many interesting books. There is so much to learn. You can find the answers to many questions in the library!

McGraw-Hill School Division

Book 2.2/Unit 2: Expository Writing / Publishing 5E

Presentation Ideas

MAKE A CLASS ANTHOLOGY Bind children's reports into a class guide called "Ways to Solve Problems." Encourage children to comment on each other's reports. ▶ **Representing/Speaking**

MAKE AN AUDIOTAPE Record the reports, and invite children to listen to them and share their responses. ▶ **Listening/Speaking**

Assessment

SCORING RUBRIC When using the rubric, please consider childrens' creative efforts, possibly adding a plus (+) for originality, wit, and imagination.

SELF-ASSESSMENT Present the Features of Expository Writing from page 247B in question form. Have students use these questions to self-assess their writing.

Listening and Speaking

LISTENING STRATEGIES

- Sit comfortably, facing speaker.
- Listen closely for topic and related facts.
- Write down unfamiliar words or ideas.

SPEAKING STRATEGIES

- Raise hand and wait to be called upon before speaking.
- Ask a written question to better understand the topic.
- Share ideas you have on the topic.

Scoring Rubric: 6-Trait Writing

4 Excellent	3 Good	2 Fair	1 Unsatisfactory
Ideas & Content • devises a focused report, with elaborate details that show how a problem was solved by a familiar person or place.	Ideas & Content • presents a clear, well-thought-out report; details show knowledge of the person or place, and clarify the problem-solution events.	Ideas & Content • has some control of the topic, but may not offer thorough details; ideas are vague or undeveloped.	Ideas & Content • does not successfully report on a person, problem, or a solution.
Organization • crafts an effective plan that moves a reader logically through the text; facts, ideas, and sentences are tied together.	Organization • has a capable, easy-to-follow structure; logic is easy to follow from beginning to end; details and observations fit, and reinforce the facts.	Organization • tries to shape a report, but may have trouble sequencing information; reader may be confused by vague or disconnected facts and details.	Organization • shows extreme lack of organization; logic is hard to follow; details are vague or irrelevant to the topic.
Voice • shows deep involvement with the topic; distinct personal style brings the information to life.	Voice • sounds like a real person behind the words; personal style connects to the topic and audience.	Voice • gives some hint of who is behind the words; may not relate personal observations to the topic of solving a problem.	Voice • is not involved in the topic; does not address an audience, or attempt a personal tone.
Word Choice • makes imaginative use of accurate language; vocabulary is striking, varied, and natural; creates clear images for the reader.	Word Choice • uses a variety of precise words to create an image for the reader; explores some new words, or tries to use everyday words in a fresh way.	Word Choice • gets the message across, but experiments with few new words; may not describe a clear picture of the problem or solution.	Word Choice • chooses words that don't fit the topic, or which confuse reader; no new words are attempted.
Sentence Fluency • crafts fluid, capable sentences that connect ideas evenly; varying lengths and patterns add interest to the article.	Sentence Fluency • sentences are easy to read and understand; lengths and patterns vary, and fit together.	Sentence Fluency • most sentences are understandable, but may be choppy, monotonous, or awkward; text may be hard to follow or read aloud.	Sentence Fluency • sentences are incomplete or confusing; writing doesn't follow natural sentence patterns, and is hard to follow and read aloud.
Conventions • is skilled in most writing conventions; proper use of the rules of English enhances clarity, style, and cohesion of ideas; editing is largely unnecessary.	Conventions • uses a variety of conventions correctly; some editing may be needed; errors are few and don't interfere with following the text.	Conventions • makes repeated noticeable mistakes that interfere with reading the text; extensive need for editing and revision.	Conventions • has severe, repeated errors in spelling, word choice, punctuation and usage; reader has a hard time getting through the text.

Incomplete This piece is either blank, or fails to respond to the writing task. The topic is not addressed, or the child simply paraphrases the prompt. The response may be illegible or incoherent.

VOCABULARY

GROUP Children take turns choosing words from the review words and mime them. The other children try to guess the word that is being mimed.

Unit Review

The Bremen Town Musicians

daughter	scare	voice
music	third	whistle

Our Soccer League

coaches	score	throws
field	stretches	touch

The Wednesday Surprise

chance	heavy	office
favorite	nervous	wrapped

Fossils Tell of Long Ago

buried	fossil	layers
creatures	fresh	millions

Are You a Fossil Fan?

change	hunt	piece
glue	magazine	tooth

Name__________ Date______ **Practice 209**

Unit 2 Vocabulary Review

A. Put a check mark next to each true sentence.

✓ **1.** People can play music on a piano.
✓ **2.** Your favorite food is the food that you like best.
___ **3.** People play baseball in an office.
✓ **4.** People glue things to hold them together.
___ **5.** You can taste a voice.

B. Complete the crossword puzzle using the words in the box.

magazine	scare	field	daughter	wrapped

DOWN

1. He read a ___ while he waited.
2. I ___ his gift in paper.

ACROSS

3. They have one ___ and three sons.
4. The noise will ___ the birds away.
5. The baseball team ran onto the ___ .

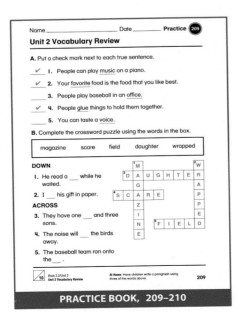

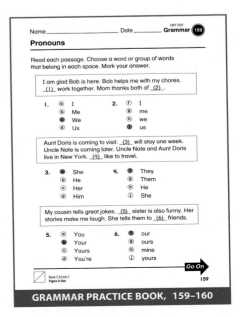

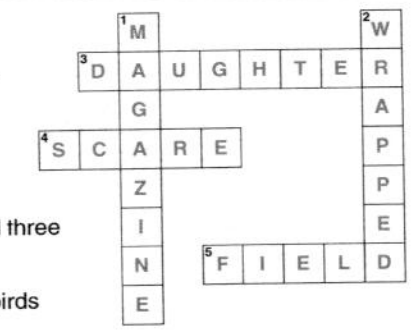

10 Book 2.2/Unit 2 Unit 2 Vocabulary Review — **At Home:** Have children write a paragraph using three of the words above. 209

PRACTICE BOOK, 209–210

GRAMMAR

ONE Children write poems about something they love to eat. The poems should describe the food, tell how it feels in their mouths, and how they feel when they eat it.

Unit Review

The Bremen Town Musicians
Pronouns

Our Soccer League
I and *Me*, *We* and *Us*

The Wednesday Surprise
Possessive Pronouns

Fossils Tell of Long Ago
Pronoun-Verb Agreement

Are You a Fossil Fan?
Contractions

Name__________ Date______ UNIT TEST **Grammar 159**

Pronouns

Read each passage. Choose a word or group of words that belong in each space. Mark your answer.

I am glad Bob is here. Bob helps me with my chores. _(1)_ work together. Mom thanks both of _(2)_.

1. ⓐ I ⓑ Me ● We ⓓ Us
2. ⓕ I ⓖ me ⓗ we ● us

Aunt Doris is coming to visit. _(3)_ will stay one week. Uncle Nate is coming later. Uncle Nate and Aunt Doris live in New York. _(4)_ like to travel.

3. ● She ⓑ He ⓒ Her ⓓ Him
4. ● They ⓖ Them ⓗ He ⓙ She

My cousin tells great jokes. _(5)_ sister is also funny. Her stories make me laugh. She tells them to _(6)_ friends.

5. ⓐ You ● Your ⓒ Yours ⓓ You're
6. ● our ⓖ ours ⓗ mine ⓙ yours

Go On

Book 2.2/Unit 2 Figure It Out 159

GRAMMAR PRACTICE BOOK, 159–160

SPELLING

GROUP Each team chooses two review words and creates a riddle for each one. The teams then take turns presenting their riddles. The team that guesses the riddle first wins.

Unit Review

_c, k_ and _ck_
- come
- work
- bake
- sick

Blends
- hand
- sank
- chest
- soft

Blends
- try
- play
- brag
- draw

Social Studies Words
- stone
- bone
- remains
- digging

Blends
- slide
- speak
- swim
- smooth

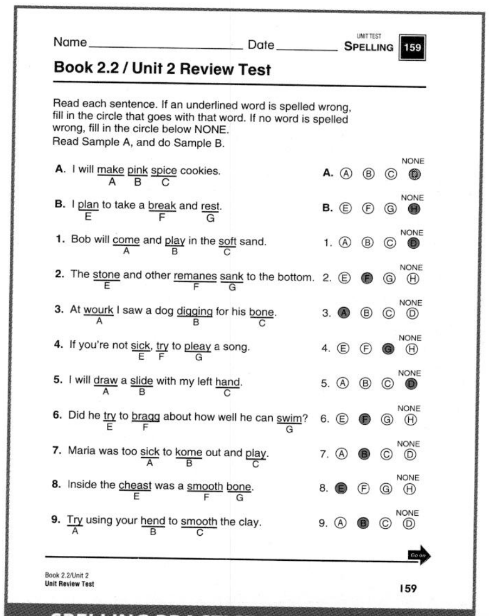
Name__________ Date_______ UNIT TEST SPELLING 159

Book 2.2 / Unit 2 Review Test

Read each sentence. If an underlined word is spelled wrong, fill in the circle that goes with that word. If no word is spelled wrong, fill in the circle below NONE.
Read Sample A, and do Sample B.

A. I will make (A) pink (B) spice (C) cookies. — A. Ⓐ Ⓑ Ⓒ NONE ●

B. I plan (E) to take a break (F) and rest (G). — B. Ⓔ Ⓕ Ⓖ NONE ●

1. Bob will come (A) and play (B) in the soft (C) sand. — 1. Ⓐ Ⓑ Ⓒ NONE ●
2. The stone (E) and other remanes (F) sank (G) to the bottom. — 2. Ⓔ ● Ⓖ NONE Ⓗ
3. At wourk (A) I saw a dog digging (B) for his bone (C). — 3. ● Ⓑ Ⓒ NONE Ⓓ
4. If you're not sick (E), try (F) to pleay (G) a song. — 4. Ⓔ Ⓕ ● NONE Ⓗ
5. I will draw (A) a slide (B) with my left hand (C). — 5. Ⓐ Ⓑ Ⓒ NONE ●
6. Did he try (E) to bragg (F) about how well he can swim (G)? — 6. Ⓔ ● Ⓖ NONE Ⓗ
7. Maria was too sick (A) to kome (B) out and play (C). — 7. Ⓐ ● Ⓒ NONE Ⓓ
8. Inside the cheast (E) was a smooth (F) bone (G). — 8. ● Ⓕ Ⓖ NONE Ⓗ
9. Try (A) using your hend (B) to smooth (C) the clay. — 9. Ⓐ ● Ⓒ NONE Ⓓ

Go on

Book 2.2/Unit 2
Unit Review Test

159

SPELLING PRACTICE BOOK, 159–160

SKILLS & STRATEGIES

Phonics and Decoding
- ☑ /âr/*are*; /ôr/*or, ore*; /îr/*ear*
- ☑ /ü/*oo, ue, ew*
- ☑ /ər/*er*; /ən/*en*; /əl/*le*
- ☑ /ou/*ow, ou* and /oi/*oi, oy*

Comprehension
- ☑ Summarize
- ☑ Sequence of Events

Vocabulary Strategies
- ☑ Suffixes
- ☑ Context Clues

Study Skills
- ☑ Various Texts

Writing
- ☑ Expository Writing

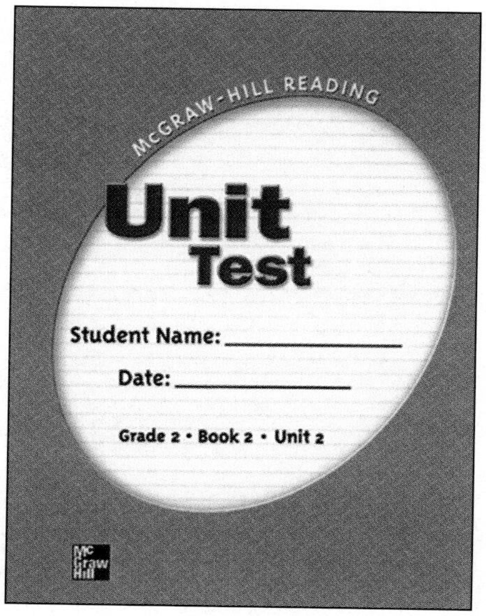

Assessment Follow-Up

Use the results of the informal and formal assessment opportunities in the unit to help you make decisions about future instruction.

SKILLS AND STRATEGIES	Reteaching Blackline Masters	Alternate Teaching Strategies	Skills Intervention Guide
Phonics and Decoding			
/âr/*are*; /ôr/*or, ore*; /îr/*ear*	169, 173, 174, 182, 190, 198	T65	✓
/ü/*oo, ue, ew*	177, 181, 182, 190, 201	T70	✓
/ər/*er*; /ən/*en*; /əl/*le*	185, 189, 190, 198, 201	T73	✓
/ou/*ow, ou* and /oi/*oi, oy*	193, 197, 198, 201	T76	✓
Comprehension			
Summarize	175, 191, 206	T67	✓
Sequence of Events	183, 199, 205	T71	✓
Vocabulary Strategies			
Suffixes	176, 192, 208	T68	✓
Context Clues	184, 200, 207	T74	✓
Study Skills			
Various Texts	172, 180, 188, 196, 204	T66	✓

	Alternate Writing Project–Easy	Unit Writing Process Lesson
Writing		
Expository Writing	149N, 179N, 211N, 235N, 245N	247C-247H

McGraw-Hill School TECHNOLOGY

Phonics **CD-ROM** Provides extra phonics support.

*inter*NET CONNECTION Research & Inquiry ideas. Visit ***www.mhschool.com/reading.***

Glossary

Introduce children to the Glossary by reading through the introduction and looking over the pages with them. Encourage the class to talk about what they see.

Words in a glossary, like words in a dictionary, are listed in **alphabetical order.** Point out the **guide words** at the top of each page that tell the first and last words appearing on that page.

Point out examples of **entries** and **main entries.** Read through a simple entry with the class, identifying each part. Have children note the order in which information is given: entry word(s), definition(s), example sentence(s), syllable division, pronunciation respelling, part of speech, plural/verb/adjective forms.

Note that if more than one definition is given for a word, the definitions are numbered. Note also the format used for a word that is more than one part of speech.

Review the parts of speech by identifying each in a sentence:

inter.	*adj.*	*n.*	*conj.*	*adj.*	*n.*
Wow!	**A**	**dictionary**	**and**	**a**	**glossary**
v.	*adv.*	*pron.*	*prep.*	*n.*	
tell	**almost**	**everything**	**about**	**words!**	

Explain the use of the **pronunciation key** (either the **short key,** at the bottom of every other page, or the **long key,** at the beginning of the Glossary). Demonstrate the difference between **primary** stress and **secondary** stress by pronouncing a word with both.

Point out an example of the small triangle signaling a homophone. **Homophones** are words with different spellings and meanings but with the same pronunciation. Explain that a pair of words with the superscripts **1** and **2** are **homographs**—words that have the same spelling, but different origins and meanings, and in some cases, different pronunciations.

The **Word History** feature tells what language a word comes from and what changes have occurred in its spelling and/or meaning. Many everyday words have interesting and surprising stories behind them. Note that word histories can help us remember the meanings of difficult words.

Allow time for children to further explore the Glossary and make their own discoveries.

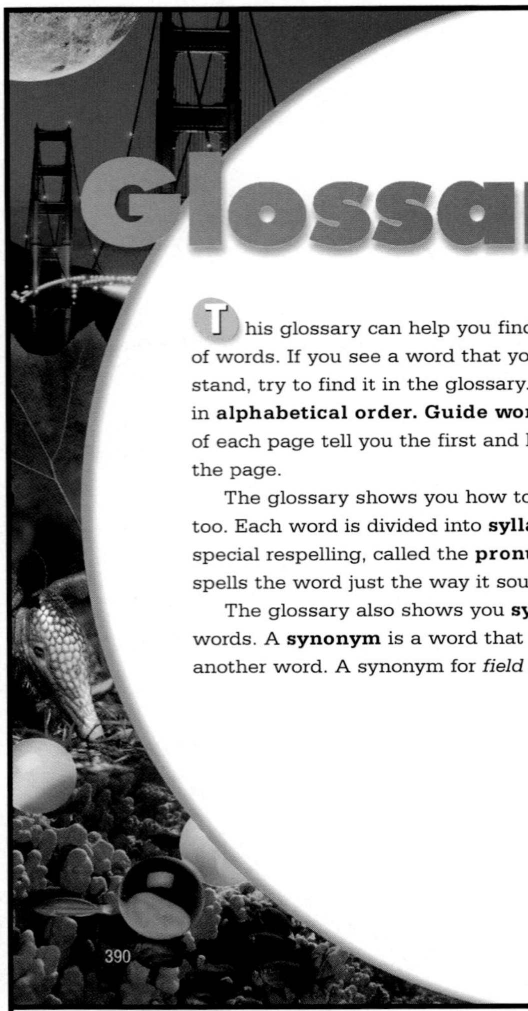

Glossary

This glossary can help you find the **meanings** of words. If you see a word that you don't understand, try to find it in the glossary. The words are in **alphabetical order. Guide words** at the top of each page tell you the first and last words on the page.

The glossary shows you how to say the words, too. Each word is divided into **syllables.** Next, a special respelling, called the **pronunciation,** spells the word just the way it sounds.

The glossary also shows you **synonyms** for words. A **synonym** is a word that can be used for another word. A synonym for *field* is *grass.*

Guide Words

accident / binoculars

First word on the page — Last word on the page

Sample Entry

creature A living person or animal. Bears and wolves are *creatures* of the forest. ▲ **Synonym:** being.
crea•ture (KREE chuhr) *noun, plural* **creatures.**

Main entry · Example sentence · Syllable division · Definition · Synonym · Part of speech · Plural form · Pronunciation

Use the **Pronunciation Key** below to find examples for the sounds you see in the **pronunciation** spellings.

Phonetic Spelling	Examples	Phonetic Spelling	Examples
a	cat	oh	go, home
ah	father	aw	saw, fall
ay	late, day	or	more, four
air	there, hair	oo	too, do
b	bit, rabbit	oy	toy
ch	chin	ow	out, cow
d	dog	p	pig
e	met	r	run, carry
ee	he, see	s	song, mess
f	fine, off	sh	shout, fish
g	go, bag, bigger	t	ten, better
h	hat	th	thin
hw	wheel	thh	them
ih	sit	u	sun
ī	fine, tiger, my	u̇	look, should
ihr	near, deer, here	yoo	music, new
j	jump, page	ur	turn, learn
k	cat, back	v	very, of
l	line, hill	w	we
m	mine, hammer	y	yes
n	nice, funny	z	has, zoo
ng	sing	zh	treasure, division
o	top	uh	about, happen, lemon

Aa

accident Something unlucky that happens without warning. There were many *accidents* the day of the snowstorm. ▲ **Synonym:** mishap.
ac•ci•dent (AK sih duhnt) *noun, plural* **accidents.**

afraid Feeling fear; frightened. There is no reason to be *afraid* of bats. ▲ **Synonym:** scared.
a•fraid (uh FRAYD) *adjective.*

Alamo (AL uh moh)

alyssum A plant of the mustard family that bears small white or yellow flowers.
a•lys•sum (uh LIHS um) *noun, plural* **alyssum.**

audience A group of people gathered to hear and see something. My family was in the *audience* to watch my school play ▲ **Synonyms:** spectators, listeners.
au•di•ence (AW dee uhns) *noun, plural* **audiences.**

auditorium A large room or building where people can gather. The concert will be in the school *auditorium.*
au•di•to•ri•um (aw dih TOR ee uhm) *noun, plural* **auditoriums.**

Bb

binoculars A device that makes distant objects look larger and closer, made up of two small telescopes joined together. We needed *binoculars* to see the ship on the horizon.
bi•noc•u•lars (buh NAHK yoo luhrz) *plural noun.*

borrow To take something to use for a while. Hector let me *borrow* his roller skates.
bor•row (BAHR oh) *verb,* **borrowed, borrowing.**

brachiopod Any of a large group of sea animals having a shell with a top and bottom half. We saw several different *brachiopods* while scuba diving.
bra•chi•o•pod (BRAY kee uh pahd) *noun, plural* **brachiopods.**

brave Having courage. The *brave* lifeguard jumped into the water to save the child.
brave (BRAYV) *adjective,* **braver, bravest.**

bravo Well done! Good! Excellent! The grateful audience clapped and cried *"Bravo!"*
bra•vo (BRAH voh) *interjection, plural* **bravos** or **bravoes.**

breath Air drawn into and forced out of the lungs; respiration. The doctor asked me to take a big *breath.*
breath (BRETH) *noun, plural* **breaths.**

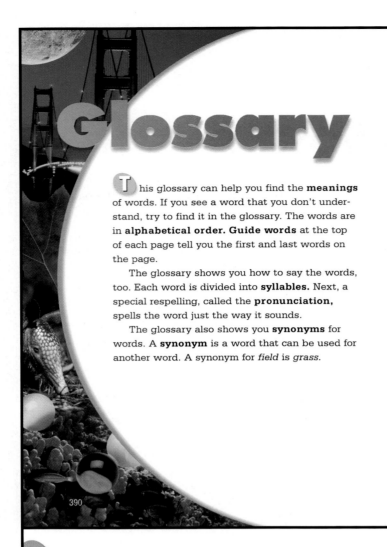

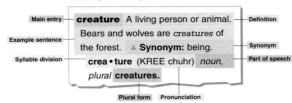

Buenas noches Spanish for "good night." (BWAY nuhs NOH chez)

bulletin board A board for putting up notices, announcements, and pictures. She pinned the advertisement on the *bulletin board.*
bul•le•tin board (BÚL ih tihn bord) *noun, plural* **bulletin boards.**

bumblebee A large bee with a thick, hairy body. Most *bumblebees* have yellow and black stripes.
bum•ble•bee (BUHM buhl bee) *noun, plural* **bumblebees.**

burrito A Mexican food made of a tortilla wrapped around a filling. We had a choice of *burritos* or pizza for dinner.
bur•ri•to (bur EE toh) *noun, plural* **burritos.**

bury To cover up; hide. The letter was *buried* in a pile of papers.
▲**Synonyms:** conceal, hide.
bur•y (BER ee) *verb,* **buried, burying.**

Cc

chance 1. A turn to do something. Each child will have a *chance* to ride the pony. **2.** The possibility that something might happen. There is a *chance* that it may snow tomorrow.
▲**Synonym:** opportunity.
chance (CHANS) *noun, plural* **chances.**

change 1. To make or become different. I will *change* the way I sign my name. *Verb.* **2.** The money that is given back when something costs less than the amount paid for it. I gave the ice cream man a dollar and got back twenty cents in *change. Noun.*
change (CHAYNJ) *verb,* **changed, changing;** *noun, plural* **changes.**

cheer The shout you make to give someone hope or courage.
cheer (CHIHR) *noun, plural* **cheers.**

chocolate A food used in making sweet things to eat. Billy unwrapped the bar of *chocolate.*
choc•o•late (CHAWK liht) *noun, plural* **chocolates.**

clear 1. To remove things from. I *cleared* the dishes after supper. *Verb.* **2.** Free from anything that darkens; bright. The sky is *clear* today. *Adjective.*
clear (KLIHR) *verb,* **cleared, clearing;** *adjective,* **clearer, clearest.**

clothes Things worn to cover the body. Coats, dresses, pants, and jackets are kinds of *clothes.*
▲**Synonym:** clothing.
clothes (KLOHZ *or* KLOHTHHZ) *plural noun.*

coach A person who trains athletes. The *coach* made the team practice every day.
▲**Synonym:** trainer.
coach (KOHCH) *noun, plural* **coaches.**

collide To crash against each other. The two players *collided* as they chased the ball.
col•lide (kuh LĪD) *verb,* **collided, colliding.**

colony 1. A group of animals of the same kind that live together. Ants live in *colonies.* **2.** A territory ruled by another country. The British *colonies* became the United States.
col•ony (KOL uh nee) *noun, plural* **colonies.**

coral 1. A hard, stony substance found in tropical seas. We saw huge pieces of *coral* while scuba-diving. *Noun.* **2.** A pinkish red color. Her nail polish matched her *coral* sweater. *Adjective.*
cor•al (KOR uhl) *noun, plural* **corals.**

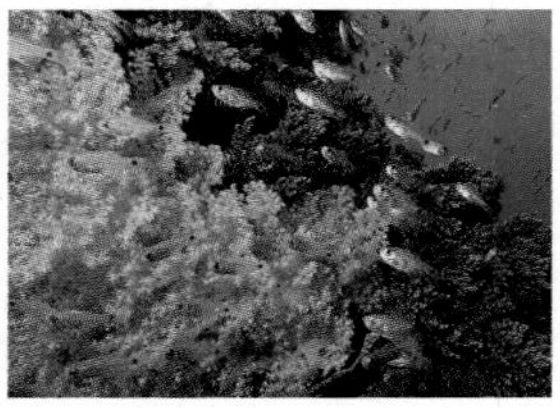

Costa Rica A country in Central America. (KOH stuh REE kuh)

cousin The child of an aunt or uncle. My *cousin* and I have the same grandfather.
cou•sin (KUZ ihn) *noun, plural* **cousins.**

cover 1. To put something on or over. *Cover* your head with a hat in cold weather. *Verb.* **2.** Something that is put on or over something else. The *cover* will keep the juice from spilling. *Noun.*
cov•er (KUV uhr) *verb,* **covered, covering;** *noun, plural* **covers.**

creature A living person or animal. Bears and wolves are *creatures* of the forest.
▲**Synonym:** being.
crea•ture (KREE chuhr) *noun, plural* **creatures.**

crinoid Any of a group of colorful, flower-shaped saltwater animals. Crinoids are usually found in deep tropical waters. The glass-bottom boat let us see the colorful *crinoids* and coral on the ocean floor.
cri•noid (KRĪ noyd) *noun, plural* **crinoids.**

Cristobal (KRIHS tuh bahl)

crocodile A long animal with short legs, thick, scaly skin, and a long, powerful tail. *Crocodiles* have longer heads than alligators.
croc•o•dile (KROK uh dil) *noun, plural* **crocodiles.**

crop Plants grown to be used as food. I grew my own *crop* of tomatoes in our garden.
crop (KROP) *noun, plural* **crops.**

crowd 1. To put or force too many people or things into too small a space. My cousin *crowded* the shelf with books. *Verb.* **2.** A large group of people in one place. The *crowd* waited for the game to start. *Noun.*
▲**Synonyms:** swarm, flock, assembly.
crowd (KROWD) *verb,* **crowded, crowding;** *noun, plural* **crowds.**

Dd

darkness Little or no light. *Darkness* comes earlier in the winter.
dark•ness (DAHRK nihss) *noun.*

daughter The female child of a mother and a father. Claire is the *daughter* of her mother and father. Claire's mother is the *daughter* of Claire's grandmother and grandfather.
daugh•ter (DAW tuhr) *noun, plural* **daughters.**

desert A hot, dry, sandy area of land. It can be hard to find water in the *desert.*
des•ert (DEZ uhrt) *noun, plural* **deserts.**

Glossary

disappear 1. To go out of sight. We watched the moon *disappear* behind the clouds. **2.** To become extinct. The dinosaurs *disappeared* from the earth millions of years ago.
dis•ap•pear (dihs uh PIHR) *verb,* **disappeared, disappearing.**

disturb To break in on; to interrupt. The telephone call *disturbed* everyone's sleep.
▲ **Synonym:** bother.
dis•turb (dihs TURB) *verb,* **disturbed, disturbing.**

dive To go into the water with your head first. When Maria and Carlos took swimming lessons, they learned how to *dive*.
▲ **Synonym:** plunge.
dive (DĪV) *verb,* **dived** or **dove, dived, diving.**

dribble To move a ball along by bouncing or kicking it. Players *dribble* the basketball.
drib•ble (DRIHB uhl) *verb,* **dribbled, dribbling.**

Ee

echolocation A method of determining the location of objects by bouncing sound waves off the objects.
ech•o•lo•ca•tion (EK oh loh KAY shun) *noun.*

eel A long, thin fish that looks like a snake. The *eel* darted swiftly through the water.
eel (EEL) *noun, plural* **eels.**

endanger To threaten with becoming extinct. Pollution *endangers* many species.
en•dan•ger (en DAYN juhr) *verb,* **endangered, endangering.**

envy 1. A feeling of disliking or desiring another person's good luck or belongings. I felt *envy* for your new toy. *Noun.*
▲ **Synonym:** jealousy.
2. To feel envy toward. Everyone in our class *envies* you because of your good grades. *Verb.*
en•vy (EN vee) *noun, plural* **envies;** *verb,* **envied, envying.**

escape To get away from something. People knew a storm was coming and could *escape* before it started.
es•cape (es KAYP) *verb,* **escaped, escaping.**

evening The time of day when it starts to get dark, between afternoon and night. We eat dinner at 6 o'clock in the *evening*.
▲ **Synonyms:** dusk, nightfall, twilight.
eve•ning (EEV ning) *noun, plural* **evenings.**

explain To give a reason for. *Explain* why you were late.
▲ **Synonyms:** make clear, say.
ex•plain (ek SPLAYN) *verb,* **explained, explaining.**

explore To look around a place and discover new things. Nancy and Robert couldn't wait to *explore* their new neighborhood.
▲ **Synonym:** search.
ex•plore (ek SPLOR) *verb,* **explored, exploring.**

extinct No longer existing. The dodo bird became *extinct* because people hunted it.
ex•tinct (ek STINGKT) *adjective;* **extinction** *noun.*

Ff

fact Something that is real or true. It is a *fact* that there are 50 states in the United States.
▲ **Synonym:** truth.
fact (FAKT) *noun, plural* **facts.**

favorite Liked best. I always wear my *favorite* cap.
▲ **Synonym:** preferred.
fa•vor•ite (FAY vuhr iht) *adjective.*

Fernando (fur NAN doh)

field 1. An area of land where some games are played. Football is played on a football *field*. **2.** An area of land that has no trees, used for growing grass or food. We planted corn in this *field*.
▲ **Synonym:** grass. **field** (FEELD) *noun, plural* **fields.**

fierce Wild and dangerous. A hungry lion is *fierce*.
▲ **Synonyms:** ferocious, savage. **fierce** (FIHRS) *adjective,* **fiercer, fiercest.**

forest A large area of land covered by trees and plants. They camped in the *forest*.
▲ **Synonym:** woods.
for•est (FOR ist) *noun, plural* **forests.**

forever 1. For all time; without ever coming to an end. Things cannot stay the same *forever*. **2.** Always; on and on. That grouch is *forever* complaining.
for•ev•er (for EV uhr) *adverb.*

fossil What is left of an animal or plant that lived a long time ago. Fossils are found in rocks, earth, or clay. The bones and footprints of dinosaurs are *fossils*.
▲ **Synonyms:** relic, remains
fos•sil (FOS uhl) *noun, plural* **fossils.**

fresh Newly made, done, or gathered. We ate *fresh* tomatoes from June's garden.
▲ **Synonyms:** sweet, new, unused. **fresh** (FRESH) *adjective,* **fresher, freshest.**

Gg

glue 1. A material used for sticking things together. I used *glue* to stick the magazine pictures on the paper. *Noun.* **2.** To stick things together with glue. Please *glue* the pieces of the vase together. *Verb.*
glue (GLOO) *noun, plural* **glues;** *verb,* **glued, gluing.**

goalie The player who defends the goal in soccer, hockey, and some other games. The *goalie* stopped the puck.
goal•ie (GOHL ee) *noun, plural* **goalies.**

golden 1. Made of or containing gold. My mother has a pair of *golden* earrings. **2.** Having the color or shine of gold; bright or shining. The field of *golden* wheat swayed in the wind.
gol•den (GOHL duhn) *adjective.*

guess 1. To form an opinion without sure knowledge. Did you *guess* how much that would cost? *Verb.* **2.** An opinion formed without enough information. My *guess* is that the trip will take four hours. *Noun*
guess (GES) *verb,* **guessed, guessing;** *noun, plural* **guesses.**

Hh

halftime A rest period in the middle of some games. The players had a chance to cool off at *halftime*.
half•time (HAF tim) *noun, plural* **halftimes.**

hammock A swinging bed made from a long piece of canvas or netting. She fell asleep in the *hammock*.
ham•mock (HAM uhk) *noun, plural* **hammocks.**

harm An injury. She put the baby where he would be safe from *harm. Noun.*
▲ **Synonyms:** hurt, wrong.
harm (HAHRM) *noun, plural* **harms;** *verb,* **harmed, harming.**

heavy Hard to lift or move. The bag of groceries was too *heavy* for Derek to lift.
▲ **Synonyms:** hefty, weighty.
heav•y (HEV ee) *adjective,* **heavier, heaviest.**

hibernate To spend the winter sleeping. Some bears, woodchucks, frogs, and snakes *hibernate* all winter.
hi•ber•nate (HĪ buhr nayt) *verb,* **hibernated, hibernating;** *noun,* **hibernation.**

hidden Past participle of **hide.** To put yourself or something else in a place where it cannot be seen. My cat likes to stay *hidden* under my bed.
▲ **Synonym:** unseen.
hide (HĪD) *verb,* **hid, hidden** (HIHD uhn) or **hid, hiding.**

hunt 1. To look hard to find something or someone. I will *hunt* all over my room until I find my watch. *Verb.* **2.** A search to try to find something or someone. We went on a *hunt* through all the stores to find the toy he wanted. *Noun.*
hunt (HUNT) *verb,* **hunted, hunting;** *noun, plural* **hunts.**

Ii

ichthyosaur Any of an extinct group of porpoise-like marine reptiles. **ich•thy•o•saur** (IHK thee oh sor) *noun.*

iguanodon (ih GWAH nuh don)

insect Any of a large group of small animals without a backbone. Insects have a body divided into three parts, with three pairs of legs and usually two pairs of wings. Flies, ants, grasshoppers, and beetles are *insects.*
in•sect (IN sekt) *noun, plural* **insects.**

intercept To stop or take something on its way from one person or place to another. I tried to pass the ball to a teammate, but a player on the other team *intercepted* it.
in•ter•cept (IHN tuhr sept) *verb,* **intercepted, intercepting.**

Ll

La Brea (lah BRAY uh)

layer One thickness of something. A *layer* of dust covered the table. **lay•er** (LAY uhr) *noun, plural* **layers.**

lily A large flower shaped like a trumpet. **lil•y** (LIHL ee) *noun, plural* **lilies.**

Mm

machine A thing invented to do a particular job. Airplanes are *machines* that fly.
▲ **Synonyms:** device, mechanism. **ma•chine** (muh SHEEN) *noun, plural* **machines.**

magazine A printed collection of stories, articles, and pictures usually bound in a paper cover. I read that article about fossils in a nature *magazine.*
mag•a•zine (MAG uh zeen) *noun, plural* **magazines.**

marigold A garden plant that bears yellow, orange, or red flowers in the summer.
mar•i•gold (MAR ih gohld) *noun, plural* **marigolds.**

marvel 1. A wonderful or amazing thing. Space travel is one of the *marvels* of modern science. *Noun.* **2.** To feel wonder and astonishment. We *marveled* at the acrobat's skill. *Verb.*
mar•vel (MAHR vuhl) *noun, plural* **marvels;** *verb,* **marveled, marveling.**

medusa A jellyfish.
me•du•sa (muh DOO suh) *noun, plural* **medusas** or **medusae.**

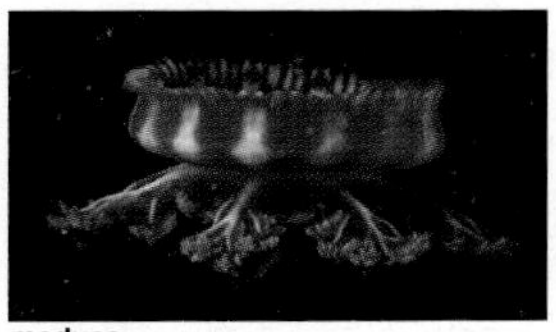

medusa

membrane A thin, flexible layer of skin or tissue that lines parts of the body. The skin that connects a bat's wing bones to its body is called a *membrane.*
mem•brane (MEM brayn) *noun, plural* **membranes.**

middle A place halfway between two points or sides. Noon is in the *middle* of the day.
▲ **Synonym:** center.
mid•dle (MIHD uhl) *noun, plural* **middles.**

midnight Twelve o'clock at night; the middle of the night. Cinderella's coach turned into a pumpkin at *midnight.*
mid•night (MIHD nīt) *noun.*

miller A person who owns or operates a mill, especially one for grinding grain. The *miller* sold the wheat to the baker.
mill•er (MIHL uhr) *noun, plural* **millers.**

million 1. One thousand times one thousand; 1,000,000. *Noun.* **2.** Having a very large number. It looks like a *million* stars in the sky. *Adjective.*
mil•lion (MIHL yuhn) *noun, plural* **millions;** *adjective.*

mine A large area dug out in or under the ground. Coal and gold are dug out of *mines.*
mine (MĪN) *noun, plural* **mines.**

mosquito A small insect with two wings. The female gives a sting or bite that itches. There were hundreds of *mosquitoes* near the swamp.
mos•qui•to (muh SKEE toh) *noun, plural* **mosquitoes** or **mosquitos.**

museum A building where pieces of art, science displays, or objects from history are kept for people to see. I saw one of George Washington's hats at the history *museum.*
mu•se•um (myoo ZEE uhm) *noun, plural* **museums.**

music A beautiful combination of sounds. When you sing or play an instrument, you are making *music.*
mu•sic (MYOO zihk) *noun.*

musician A person who is skilled in playing a musical instrument, writing music, or singing. The *musician* prepared to play for the audience.
mu•si•cian (myoo ZIHSH uhn) *noun, plural* **musicians.**

mussel An animal that looks like a clam. Saltwater *mussels* have bluish-black shells.
▲ Another word that sounds like this is *muscle.* **mus•sel** (MUS uhl) *noun, plural* **mussels.**

Nn

nature All things in the world that are not made by people. Plants, animals, mountains, and oceans are all part of *nature.*
na•ture (NAY chuhr) *noun.*

nervous 1. Not able to relax. Loud noises make me *nervous.* **2.** Fearful or timid. I am very *nervous* about taking the test.
▲ **Synonym:** anxious.
nerv•ous (NUR vuhs) *adjective.*

noisy Making harsh or loud sounds. It is *noisy* at the airport.
▲ **Synonym:** loud.
nois•y (NOY zee) *adjective,* **noisier, noisiest.**

Oo

object Anything that can be seen and touched. Is that large, round *object* an orange?
▲ **Synonym:** thing.
ob•ject (OB jihkt) *noun, plural* **objects.**

offer To present for someone to take or refuse. Mom *offered* to pick us up if it gets dark before the game ends.
▲ **Synonym:** volunteer, give.
of•fer (AHF uhr) *verb,* **offered, offering.**

office A place where people work. The principal's *office* is at the end of the hall.
▲ **Synonym:** workplace.
of•fice (AHF ihs) *noun, plural* **offices.**

out-of-bounds In sports, outside the area of play allowed. I kicked the ball *out-of-bounds,* so the other team was given the ball.
out•of•bounds (OWT uv BOWNDZ) *adverb, adjective.*

Pp

package A thing or group of things that are packed in a box, wrapped up, or tied in a bundle. We sent a *package* of treats to my sister at camp.
▲ **Synonyms:** bundle, parcel.
pack•age (PAK ihj) *noun, plural* **packages.**

Parthenon (PAHR thuh nahn)

piece A part that has been broken, cut, or torn from something. There are *pieces* of broken glass on the floor.
piece (PEES) *noun, plural* **pieces.**

practice To do something over and over to gain skill. I *practice* playing guitar every day.
prac•tice (PRAK tihs) *verb,* **practiced, practicing.**

preserve To keep from being damaged, decayed, or lost; protect. You can *preserve* the wood of the table by waxing it.
pre•serve (prih ZURV) *verb,* **preserved, preserving.**

princess The daughter of a king or queen; a female member of a royal family other than a queen; the wife of a prince. The people of the kingdom bowed to the *princess.*
prin•cess (PRIHN sihs *or* PRIHN ses) *noun, plural* **princesses.**

principal The person who is the head of a school. The *principal* gave a speech.
▲ Another word that sounds like this is *principle.* **prin•ci•pal** (PRIHN suh puhl) *noun, plural* **principals.**

problem Anything that causes trouble and must be dealt with. A barking dog can be a *problem.*
prob•lem (PRAHB luhm) *noun, plural* **problems.**

prowl To move or roam quietly or secretly. The tiger *prowled* through the forest.
prowl (PROWL) *verb,* **prowled, prowling.**

Rr

reptile One of a class of cold-blooded animals with a backbone and dry, scaly skin. Lizards are *reptiles.*
rep•tile (REP til) *noun, plural* **reptiles.**

restaurant A place where food is prepared and served. We ate at the *restaurant.*
res•tau•rant (RES tuh ruhnt *or* RES tuh rahnt) *noun, plural* **restaurants.**

roof The top part of a building. There was a leak in the *roof.*
roof (ROOF *or* RŬF) *noun, plural* **roofs.**

Ss

save 1. To keep from harm; to make safe. The cat *saved* her kittens from the fire. **2.** To set aside for future use. I will *save* some cookies to eat later.
save (SAYV) *verb,* **saved, saving.**

scare To make afraid. Loud noises always *scare* the puppy.
▲ **Synonyms:** alarm, frighten.
scare (SKAIR) *verb,* **scared, scaring.**

scary Causing alarm or fear; frightening. Your monster costume is very *scary.*
scar•y (SKAIR ee) *adjective,* **scarier, scariest.**

score 1. To get a point or points in a game or on a test. The baseball team *scored* five runs in one inning. *Verb.* **2.** The points gotten in a game or on a test. The final *score* was 5 to 4. *Noun.*
▲ **Synonym:** tally. **score** (SKOR) *verb,* **scored, scoring;** *noun, plural* **scores.**

sea anemone A sea animal shaped like a tube that attaches itself to rocks and to other objects.
sea a•nem•o•ne (SEE uh NEM uh nee) *noun, plural* **sea anemones.**

seaweed Any plant or plants that grows in the sea, especially certain kinds of algae.
sea•weed (SEE weed) *noun.*

señor Sir; mister. Spanish form of respectful or polite address for a man. **se•ñor** (sen YOR)

señora Mistress; madam. Spanish form of respectful or polite address for a woman.
se•ño•ra (sen YOR uh)

servant A person hired to work for the comfort or protection of others. The *servant* brought in their dinner.
serv•ant (SUR vuhnt) *noun, plural* **servants.**

several More than two, but not many. We saw *several* of our friends at the parade.
▲ **Synonym:** various.
sev•er•al (SEV uhr ul *or* SEV ruhl) *adjective; noun.*

shoulder The part on either side of the body from the neck to where the arm joins. I carry the sack over my *shoulder.*
shoul•der (SHOHL duhr) *noun, plural* **shoulders.**

skeleton A framework that supports and protects the body. Birds, fish, and humans have *skeletons* made of bones.
skel•e•ton (SKEL uh tuhn) *noun, plural* **skeletons.**

slip To slide and fall down. Be careful not to *slip* on the wet floor.
▲ **Synonyms:** slide, skid.
slip (SLIHP) *verb,* **slipped, slipping.**

soil The top part of the ground in which plants grow. There is sandy *soil* near the coast.
▲ **Synonyms:** dirt, earth.
soil (SOYL) *noun, plural* **soils.**

station A place of business where something specific is done. We get gas for a car at a gas *station.* Police officers work in a police *station.*
▲ **Synonym:** precinct.
sta•tion (STAY shuhn) *noun, plural* **stations.**

stepmother A woman who has married a person's father after the death or divorce of the natural mother. Dan's *stepmother* came to his school play.
step•moth•er (STEP muthh uhr) *noun, plural* **stepmothers.**

storyteller A person who tells or writes stories.
sto•ry•tell•er (STOR ee tel uhr) *noun, plural* **storytellers.**

stretch To spread out to full length. The lazy cat *stretched* and then went back to sleep.
▲ **Synonym:** extend. **stretch** (STRECH) *verb,* **stretched, stretching.**

study To try to learn by reading, thinking about, or looking; examine closely. A detective *studies* clues carefully.
stud•y (STUD ee) *verb,* **studied, studying.**

sway To move back and forth. The tree branches *swayed.*
▲ **Synonyms:** swing, wave, lean.
sway (SWAY) *verb,* **swayed, swaying.**

swift Moving or able to move very quickly. The rider had a *swift* horse.
▲ **Synonyms:** speedy, fast.
swift (SWIHFT) *adjective,* **swifter, swiftest.**

swivel chair A chair with a seat that spins. She spun around on the *swivel chair.*
swi•vel chair (SWIHV uhl chair) *noun, plural* **swivel chairs.**

Tt

teenager A person who is between the ages of thirteen and nineteen.
teen•a•ger (TEEN ay juhr) *noun, plural* **teenagers.**

termite An insect that eats wood, paper, and other materials. The *termites* ate through the floor of the old house.
ter•mite (TUR mit) *noun, plural* **termites.**

therapy Treatment for a disability, injury, psychological problem, or illness. He needed physical *therapy* to help heal his broken leg.
ther•a•py (THER uh pee) *noun, plural* **therapies.**

third Next after the second one. We had seats in the *third* row of the theater.
third (THURD) *adjective.*

throne 1. The chair that a king or queen sits on during ceremonies and other special occasions. **2.** The power or authority of a king or queen.
throne (THROHN) *noun, plural* **thrones.**

throw To send something through the air. *Throw* the ball to the dog, and she will bring it back to you.
▲ **Synonyms:** toss, fling, pitch.
throw (THROH) *verb,* **threw, thrown, throwing.**

thumbtack A tack with a flat, round head that can be pressed into a wall or board with the thumb. Notices are often pinned to bulletin boards with *thumbtacks.*
thumb•tack (THUM tak) *noun, plural* **thumbtacks.**

ton A measure of weight equal to 2,000 pounds in the United States and Canada, and 2,240 pounds in Great Britain.
ton (tun) *noun, plural* **tons.**

tooth One of the hard, white, bony parts in the mouth used for biting and chewing. I got a filling in my front *tooth.*
tooth (TOOTH) *noun, plural* **teeth.**

touch To put your hand on or against something. If you *touch* the stove, you will get burned.
▲ **Synonym:** feel.
touch (TUCH) *verb,* **touched, touching.**

trilobite An extinct sea animal that lived hundreds of millions of years ago.
tri•lo•bite (TRĪ loh bīt) *noun, plural* **trilobites.**

Uu

upstairs 1. On or to a higher floor. My bedroom is *upstairs. Adverb.* **2.** On an upper floor. The *upstairs* bathroom was just cleaned. *Adjective.*
up•stairs (UP stairz) *adverb; adjective.*

Vv

vacation A period of rest or freedom. Summer *vacation* begins next week.
va•ca•tion (vay KAY shuhn) *noun, plural* **vacations.**

village A small town. The streets of the *village* were paved with stones.
▲ **Synonym:** community.
vil•lage (VIHL ihj) *noun, plural* **villages.**

voice The sound you make through your mouth. You use your *voice* when you sing.
voice (VOYS) *noun, plural* **voices.**

Ww

warn alert; To tell about something before it happens.
warn (WORN) *verb,* **warned, warning.**

waterfall A natural stream of water falling from a high place. We had a picnic by the *waterfall.* **wa•ter•fall** (WAH tuhr fawl) *noun, plural* **waterfalls.**

wheelchair A chair on wheels that is used by someone who cannot walk to get from one place to another. He needed a *wheelchair* until his leg healed. **wheel•chair** (HWEEL chair *or* WEEL chair) *noun, plural* **wheelchairs.**

whistle 1. To make a sound by pushing air out through your lips or teeth. My dog comes when I *whistle. Verb.* **2.** Something you blow into that makes a whistling sound. The police officer blew his *whistle. Noun.* **whis•tle** (HWIS uhl *or* WIS uhl) *verb,* **whistled, whistling;** *noun, plural* **whistles.**

wipe To clean or dry by rubbing. ▲ **Synonym:** clean. **wipe** (WĪP) *verb,* **wiped, wiping.**

wonder 1. To want to know or learn; be curious about. I *wonder* why the sky is blue. *Verb.* **2.** A surprising or impressive thing. *Noun.* **won•der** (WUN duhr) *verb,* **wondered, wondering;** *noun, plural* **wonders.**

world Place where all things live. **world** (WURLD) *noun, plural* **worlds.**

wrap To cover something by putting something else around it. We will *wrap* the package. **wrap** (RAP) *verb,* **wrapped, wrapping.**

Xx

xiphactinus (zee FAK ti nus)

Zz

zinnia A garden flower. **zin•ni•a** (ZIHN nee uh) *noun, plural* **zinnias.**

ACKNOWLEDGMENTS

The publisher gratefully acknowledges permission to reprint the following copyrighted material:

"Charlie Anderson" by Barbara Abercrombie, illustrated by Mark Graham. Text copyright © 1990 by Barbara Abercrombie. Illustrations copyright © 1990 by Mark Graham. Reprinted with permission of Margaret K. McElderry Books, Simon & Schuster Children's Publishing Division.

"Fernando's Gift" by Douglas Keister. Copyright © 1995 by Douglas Keister. Reprinted by permission of Sierra Club Books For Children.

"Fossils Tell of Long Ago" by Aliki. Copyright © 1972, 1990 by Aliki Brandenberg. Used by permission of HarperCollins Publishers.

"Neighbors" by Marchette Chute from RHYMES ABOUT US. by Marchette Chute. Published 1974 by E.P. Dutton. Reprinted with permission of Elizabeth Hauser.

"Officer Buckle and Gloria" by Peggy Rathmann. Copyright ©, Peggy Rathmann, 1995. Published by arrangement with Penguin Putnam Books for Young Readers, a division of Penguin Putnam Inc.

"Our Soccer League" from OUR SOCCER LEAGUE by Chuck Solomon. Text copyright © 1988 by Chuck Solomon. Reprinted by arrangement with Random House Children's Books, a division of Random House, Inc.

"Princess Pooh" is the entire text from PRINCESS POOH by Kathleen M. Muldoon with illustrations by Linda Shute. Text copyright © 1989 by Kathleen M. Muldoon. Illustrations copyright © 1989 by Linda Shute. Originally published in hardcover by Albert Whitman & Company. All rights reserved. Used with permission.

"River Winding" from RIVER WINDING by Charlotte Zolotow. Copyright © 1970 by Charlotte Zolotow. Reprinted by permission of S©ott Treimel New York.

"Swimmy" from SWIMMY by Leo Lionni. Copyright © 1963 by Leo Lionni. Copyright renewed 1991 by Leo Lionni. Reprinted by arrangement with Random House Children's Books, a division of Random House, Inc.

"To Catch a Fish" by Eloise Greenfield from UNDER THE SUNDAY TREE. Text copyright © 1988 by Eloise Greenfield. Paintings copyright © 1988 by Amos Ferguson. Reprinted by permission of HarperTrophy, a division of HarperCollins Publishers.

"Tomás and the Library Lady" by Pat Mora. Text copyright © 1977 by Pat Mora. Illustrations copyright © 1997 by Raul Colón. Reprinted by permission of Alfred A. Knopf.

"The Wednesday Surprise" from THE WEDNESDAY SURPRISE by Eve Bunting with illustrations by Donald Carrick. Text copyright © 1989 by Eve Bunting. Illustrations copyright © 1989 by Donald Carrick. Reprinted by permission of Clarion Books, a Houghton Mifflin Co. imprint.

"What Is It?" by Eve Merriam from HIGGLE WIGGLE (MORROW JR BOOKS). Text copyright © 1994 by the Estate of Eve Merriam by Marian Reiner, Literary Executor. Used by permission of Marian Reiner.

"Which?" from CRICKETY CRICKET! THE BEST LOVED POEMS OF JAMES S. TIPPETT. Text copyright © 1933, copyright renewed © 1973 by Martha K. Tippett. Illustrations copyright © 1973 by Mary Chalmers. Reprinted by permission of HarperCollins Publishers.

"Zipping, Zapping, Zooming Bats" by Ann Earle. Text copyright © 1995 by Ann Earle. Illustrations copyright © 1995 by Henry Cole. Reprinted by permission of HarperCollins Children's Books, a division of HarperCollins Publishers.

Illustration

Matt Straub, 12–13; Leonor Glynn, 42; Claude Martinot, 43; Kuenhee Lee, 44–45; Myron Grossman, 67; Annette Cable, 68–69; Cecily Lang, 70–87; Claude Martinot, 91; Tim Raglin, 92–93; Claude Martinot, 115; Melinda Levine, 130–131; Mary GrandPre, 132–145; Julia Gorton, 149; Tom Barrett, 150–151; Myron Grossman, 179; Joe Cepeda, 180–181; Leonor Glynn, 210; Julia Gorton, 211; Suling Wang, 212–213; Vilma Ortiz–Dillon, 234; Myron Grossman, 235; Anne Lunsford, 282–283; Myron Grossman, 309; Jerry Smath, 250–251; Julia Gorton, 281; Abby Carter, 310–311; Claude Martinot, 339; Carol Inouye, 340–341; Claude Martinot, 361; Robert Crawford, 10–11; Taylor Bruce, 126–127; Russ Willms, 128–129; Marina Thompson, 248–249; Sonja Lamut, 372–373; Tom Leonard, 116–117; Myron Grossman, 125, 371; Michael Welch, 236–237; Claude Martinot, 245; Alexandra Wallner, 362–363; John Carozza, 410; Holly Jones, 394, 403; Miles Parnell, 398, 407, 412.

Photography

4: b. Douglas Keister; 5: b. Merline Tuttle/Photo Researchers; 7: b, John Cancalosis/Peter Arnold; 9: b. David Muench/Corbis; 41: r. Renee Lynn/Photo Researchers/l. Renee Lynn/Photo Researchers/Dough Plummer/Photonica; 42: b.r. Renee Lynn/Photo Researchers; 65: b. Andrea Pistolesi/The Image Bank; 70: b.r. Courtesy of Cecily Lang Studio/t.l. Courtesy of Diane Hoyt–Goldsmith; 75: t. Roy Morsch/The Stock Market/b. Brown Brothers; 77: r. Wernher Kruten/Liaison International/l. Chad Ehlers/Tony Stone Images; 79: Zigy Kalunzy/Tony Stone Images; 81: Merlin D. Tuttle/Bat Conservation International; 83: t. Wesley Hitt/Liaison International/b. Superstock; 84: Howard Grey/Tony Stone Images; 85: Robert Landau/Westlight; 87: t.r. Hiroyuki Matsumoto/Tony Stone Images/b.r. Marc Biggins/Liaison International/b.l. Tom Bean/Tony Stone/t.l. Superstock; 89: b. Merlin D. Tuttle/Bat Conservation International/t. Wesley Hitt/Liaison International; 94: t.l. Courtesy of HarperCollins Publishers; 113: b. T. Sawada/Photonica; 114: m.l. Merlin D. Tuttle/Bat Conservation International/t.r. Merlin D. Tuttle/Bat Conservation International/t.l. Merlin D. Tuttle/Bat Conservation International/b.r. Stephen Dalton/Photo Researchers; 122: t. Merlin D. Tuttle/Photo Researchers/m. Joe Mcdonald/Animals Animals/b. Merlin Tuttle/Bat Conservation International; 123 b. PhotoDisc; 132: Courtesy of the artist; 176-177: David Madison/Tony Stone Images; 214: T. Carolina Ambida. 233: b. Jeffrey Sylvester/FPG International; 242: t.l. PhotoDisc/b.r. Howard Grey/Tony Stone Images/m.l. PhotoDisc; 244: l. PhotoDisc/r. Howard Grey/Tony Stone Images; 252: t. Courtesy of Penguin Putnam Inc.; 279: m.r. Jonathan Nourok/Photo Edit/b. Tom Nebbia/Corbis-Bettman/m.c. David Young-Wolff/Photo Edit/m.l. Spencer Grant/Photo Edit; 284: t.l. Courtesy Random House/b.r. Courtesy of Raul Colon/t.l. Courtesy Alfred A. Knopf Inc.; 306-307: Tony Freeman/Photo Edit; 337: b. Jim Cummins/FPG International/m.r. PhotoDisc; 360: t. PhotoDisc/b. PhotoDisc; 368; m. Kit Latham/FPG.

Reading for Information

All photographs are by Macmillan/McGraw-Hill (MMH); Michael Groen for MMH; Ken Karp for MMH; and Chuck Solomon for MMH, except as noted below.

Table of Contents, pp. 374–375

Chess pieces, tl, Wides + Hall/FPG; Earth, mcl, M. Burns/Picture Perfect; CD's, mcl, Michael Simpson/FPG; Newspapers, bl, Craig Orsini/Index Stock/PictureQuest; Clock, tc, Steve McAlister/The Image Bank; Kids circle, bc, Daniel Pangbourne Media/FPG; Pencils, tr, W. Cody/Corbis; Starfish, tc, Darryl Torckler/Stone; Keys, cr, Randy Faris/Corbis; Cells, br, Spike Walker/Stone; Stamps, tr, Michael W. Thomas/Focus Group/PictureQuest; Books, cr, Siede Preis/PhotoDisc; Sunflower, cr, Jeff LePore/Natural Selection; Mouse, br, Andrew Hall/Stone; Apples, tr, Siede Preis/PhotoDisc; Watermelons, br, Neil Beer/PhotoDisc; Butterfly, br, Stockbyte

377: t.r. George Godfrey/Earth Scenes/b.r. Leonard Lee Rue/Stock Boston; 378-379: bkgd. Tom Walker/Stock Boston; 380: m.l. George Bernard/Animals Animals/m.r. M. MC. Chamberlain/DRK Photo/b.l. David Baron/Animals Animals: 380-381 bkgd. William Johnson/Stock Boston; 381: t.l. Fritz Polking/Dembinsky Photo Assoc./b.l. E. R. Dergginger/Dembinsky Photo Assoc.; 390: l. PhotoDisc; 392: Ron Chapple/FPG International; 393: Jose Azel/Aurora/PNI; 395: David Stockein/The Stock Market; 396: Mark A. Johnson/The Stock Market; 397: Tom Dean/The Stock Market; 398: Wayne Levin/FPG International; 400: Eric Meola/The Image Bank; 401: David Brooks/The Stock Market; 402: Michel Renaudeau/Liaison; 405: Don Perdue/Liaison; 406: Richard H. Johnston/FPG International; 408: Rick Rusing/Tony Stone Images; 409: Darryl Torchker/Tony Stone Images; 411: Hank de Lespinasse/Image Bank; 412: Adam Woolfitt/Woodfin Camp, Inc.

Art/Illustration

Linda Weller, 44F; Richard Kolding, 180F

Photography

125A: M. Burns, Picture Perfect; Daniel Pagbourne, Media/FPG; 127A: Jeff LaPore/Natural Selection; Stockbyte

Cover Illustration: Kenneth Spengler

The publisher gratefully acknowledges permission to reprint the following copyrighted material:

"All Living Things" by W. Jay Cawley. Words and music copyright © 1992 by W. Jay Cawley.

"The Bat" from BEAST FEAST by Douglas Florian. Copyright © 1984 by Douglas Florian. Used by permission of Voyager Books, Harcourt Brace & Company.

"Behind the Museum Door" from GOOD RHYMES, GOOD TIMES by Lee Bennett Hopkins. Copyright © 1973, 1995 by Lee Bennett Hopkins. Used by permission of Curtis Brown Ltd.

"Brothers" from SNIPPETS by Charlotte Zolotow. Copyright © 1993 by Charlotte Zolotow. Illustrations copyright © 1993 by Melissa Sweet. Used by permission of HarperCollins Publishers.

"The Bundle of Sticks" from THE CHILDREN'S AESOP: SELECTED FABLES retold by Stephanie Calmenson. Used by permission of Caroline House, Boyds Mills Press, Inc.

"The Cat Came Back" arranged by Mary Goetze. Copyright © 1984 MMB Music, Inc.

"Covers" from VACATION TIME: POEMS FOR CHILDREN by Nikki Giovanni. Copyright © 1980 by Nikki Giovanni. Used by permission of William Morrow & Company, Inc.

"The Day the Sun Hid" from MICHAEL FOREMAN'S WORLD OF FAIRY TALES. Copyright © 1991 by Pavilion Books Limited. Used by permission of Arcade Publishing, Inc.

"The Dinosaur Who Lived in My Backyard" by B. G. Hennessey. Copyright © 1988 by B. G. Hennessey. Used by permission of Viking Books, a division of Penguin Books USA Inc.

"The Discontented Fish" from Tales from Africa by Kathleen Arnott. Copyright © 1962 by Kathleen Arnott. Used by permission of Oxford University Press.

"The Golden Touch" retold by Margaret H. Lippert from TEACHER'S READ ALOUD ANTHOLOGY. Copyright © 1993 by Macmillan/McGraw-Hill School Publishing Company.

"Gotta Find a Footprint" from BONE POEMS by Jeff Moss. Text copyright © 1997 by Jeff Moss. Illustrations copyright © 1997 by Tom Leigh. Used by permission of Workman Publishing Company, Inc.

"The Great Ball Game: A Muskogee Story" by Joseph Bruchac. Copyright © 1994 by Joseph Bruchac. Used by permission of Dial Books.

"Lemonade Stand" reprinted with the permission of Margaret K. McElderry Books, an imprint of Simon & Schuster Children's Publishing Division from WORLDS I KNOW and Other Poems by Myra Cohn Livingston. Text copyright © 1985 by Myra Cohn Livingston.

"The Letter" from FROG AND TOAD ARE FRIENDS by Arnold Lobel. Copyright © 1970 by Arnold Lobel. Used by permission of HarperCollins Publishers.

"The Library" by Barbara A. Huff from THE RANDOM HOUSE BOOK OF POETRY FOR CHILDREN. Copyright © 1983 by Barbara A. Huff.

"The Lion and the Mouse" from ONCE IN A WOOD: TEN TALES FROM AESOP adapted and illustrated by Eve Rice. Copyright © 1979 by Eve Rice. Used by permission of Greenwillow Books, a division of William Morrow & Company, Inc.

"Me I Am!" copyright © 1983 by Jack Prelutsky from THE RANDOM HOUSE BOOK OF POETRY FOR CHILDREN by Jack Prelutsky. Used by permission of Random House Children's Books, a division of Random House, Inc.

"Penguins" from A HIPPOPOTAMUSN'T AND OTHER ANIMAL VERSES by J. Patrick Lewis. Text copyright © 1990 by J. Patrick Lewis. Pictures copyright © 1990 by Victoria Chess. Used by permission of Dial Books for Young Readers, a division of Penguin Books USA Inc.

"Reading to Me" from THE OTHER SIDE OF THE DOOR by Jeff Moss. Text copyright © 1991 by Jeff Moss. Illustrations copyright © 1991 by Chris Demarest. Used by permission of Bantam Books, a division of Bantam Doubleday Dell Publishing Group, Inc.

"The Sharks" from IN THE SWIM by Douglas Florian. Copyright © 1997 by Douglas Florian. Used by permission of Harcourt Brace & Company.

"Summer Goes" from EGG THOUGHTS AND OTHER FRANCES SONGS by Russell Hoban. Copyright © 1964, 1974 by Russell Hoban. Used by permission of HarperCollins Publishers.

"A Superduper Pet" from SUPERDUPER TEDDY by Johanna Hurwitz. Text copyright © 1980 by Johanna Hurwitz. Illustrations copyright © 1990 by Lillian Hoban. Used by permission of William Morrow and Company, Inc.

"The Tall Tales," "The Tiger Story," and "Two Foolish Friends" by Tanya Lee, from FLOATING CLOUDS, FLOATING DREAMS: FAVORITE ASIAN FOLKTALES by I.K. Junne. Copyright © 1974 by I.K. Junne. Used by permission of Doubleday & Company, Inc.

"Thinking Green" from 50 SIMPLE THINGS KIDS CAN DO TO SAVE THE EARTH by The EarthWorks Group. Copyright © 1989 by John Javna, The EarthWorks Group. Used by permission of Andrew McMeel Publishers.

Untitled from A CHINESE ZOO: FABLES AND PROVERBS by Demi. Copyright © 1987. Used by permission of Harcourt Brace Jovanovich Publishers.

"Vacation" from FATHERS, MOTHERS, SISTERS, BROTHERS by Mary Ann Hoberman. Text copyright © 1991 by Mary Ann Hoberman. Illustrations copyright © 1991 by Marylin Hafner. Used by permission of Little, Brown and Company.

ZB Font Method Copyright © 1996 Zaner-Bloser. Handwriting Models, Manuscript and Cursive. Used by permission.

Backmatter Contents

The Bundle of Sticks

a fable by Aesop
retold by Stephanie Calmenson

One evening, a Father who was about to set off on a long journey gathered his children together and said, "There is something important I want you to know. But rather than tell you in words, I will show you what I mean."

The Father handed a bundle of sticks to his Eldest Son.

"I want you to break this bundle of sticks in two," he said.

"Yes, Father," said the Eldest Son. He took the bundle in his hands and, with a mighty effort, tried to break the sticks. Again and again he tried. But he could not do it.

"It is no use, Father," he said. "I cannot break the bundle in two."

"Pass the bundle to your Sister and let her try," the Father said.

The Sister took her turn trying to break the bundle of sticks, but could not do it either.

"Now let your youngest brother try," said their Father.

▶ The Youngest Son tried as hard as the others, but it was no use. He could not break the bundle in two, so he handed it back to his Father.

The Father untied the bundle and gave one stick to each of his children. "See if you can break the sticks now," he said.

Of course, the sticks broke easily.

"Have I made myself clear?" asked the Father.

"Yes," said the Youngest Son. "If we stand together like the bundle of sticks, we will be strong."

"But if we become divided and stand alone," continued the Sister,"we can easily be broken."

The Eldest Son said it this way:

Moral: *In union there is strength.*

The Great Ball Game

a Muskogee story
retold by Joseph Bruchac

Long ago the Birds and Animals had a great argument.

"We who have wings are better than you," said the Birds.

"That is not so," the Animals replied. "We who have teeth are better."

The two sides argued back and forth. Their quarrel went on and on, until it seemed they would go to war because of it.

Then Crane, the leader of the Birds, and Bear, the leader of the Animals, had an idea.

"Let us have a ball game," Crane said. "The first side to score a goal will win the argument."

"This idea is good," said Bear. "The side that loses will have to accept the penalty given by the other side."

So they walked and flew to a field, and there they divided up into two teams.

On one side went all those who had wings. They were the Birds.

On the other side went those with teeth. They were the Animals.

▶ But when the teams were formed, one creature was left out: Bat. He had wings *and* teeth. He flew back and forth between the two sides.

First he went to the Animals. "I have teeth," he said. "I must be on your side."

But Bear shook his head. "It would not be fair," he said. "You have wings. You must be a Bird."

So Bat flew to the other side. "Take me," he said to the Birds, "for you see I have wings."

But the Birds laughed at him. "You are too little to help us. We don't want you," they jeered.

Then Bat went back to the Animals. "Please let me join your team," he begged them. "The Birds laughed at me and would not accept me."

So Bear took pity on the little bat. "You are not very big," said Bear, "but sometimes even the small ones can help. We will accept you as an Animal, but you must hold back and let the bigger Animals play first."

Two poles were set up as the goalposts at each end of the field. Then the game began.

Each team played hard. On the Animals' side Fox and Deer were swift runners, and Bear cleared the way for them as they played. Crane and Hawk, though, were even swifter, and they stole the ball each time before the Animals could reach their goal.

Soon it became clear that the Birds had the advantage. Whenever they got the ball, they would fly up into the air and the Animals could not reach them.

The Animals guarded their goal well, but they soon grew tired as the sun began to set.

Just as the sun sank below the horizon, Crane took the ball and flew toward the poles. Bear tried to stop him, but stumbled in the dim light and fell. It seemed as if the Birds would surely win.

Suddenly a small dark shape flew onto the field and stole the ball from Crane just as he was about to reach the poles. It was Bat. He darted from side to side across the field, for he did not need light to find his way. None of the Birds could catch him or block him.

Holding the ball, Bat flew right between the poles at the other end! The Animals had won!

This is how Bat came to be accepted as an Animal. He was allowed to set the penalty for the Birds.

"You Birds," Bat said, "must leave this land for half of each year."

So it is that the Birds fly south each winter.

And every day at dusk Bat still comes flying to see if the Animals need him to play ball.

Reading to Me

Jeff Moss

When I was little, Mom would read to me in bed.
I'd lie under the covers with my eyes closed
And the sound of her voice would make me feel safe and sleepy at the same time.
Sometimes, even with the good stories, I'd fall asleep before the end.
Now I'm bigger and I can read by myself but still, every once in a while, when I'm feeling sad or something,
I'll ask Mom and she'll come in and sit on the edge of the bed and touch my head
And read to me again.

The Dinosaur Who Lived in My Backyard

by B.G. Hennessey

There used to be a dinosaur who lived in my backyard. Sometimes I wish he still lived here.

The dinosaur who lived here hatched from an egg that was as big as a basketball.

By the time he was five, he was as big as our car.

Just one of his dinosaur feet was so big it wouldn't even have fit in my sandbox.

My mother says that if you eat all your vegetables you'll grow very strong. That must be true, because that's all this dinosaur ate. I bet he ate a hundred pounds of vegetables every day. That's a whole lot of lima beans.

This dinosaur was so heavy that he would have made my whole neighborhood shake like pudding if he jumped. He weighed as much as twenty pick-up trucks.

The dinosaur who lived in my backyard was bigger than my school-bus. Even bigger than my house.

▶ He had many other dinosaur friends.

Sometimes they played hide-and-seek.

Sometimes they had terrible fights.

The dinosaur who used to live here was allowed to sleep outside every night. It's a good thing he didn't need a tent. He was so big he would have needed a circus tent to keep him covered.

Back when the dinosaur lived here, my town was a big swamp.

This dinosaur needed a lot of water. If he still lived here we'd have to keep the sprinkler on all the time.

My dinosaur had a very long neck so he could eat the leaves at the top of trees. If he still lived here, I bet he could rescue my kite.

That's all I know about the dinosaur who used to live in my backyard.

He hasn't been around for a very long time. Sometimes I wish he still lived here.

It would be pretty hard to keep a dinosaur happy. But my sister and I are saving all our lima beans—just in case.

Gotta Find a Footprint

Jeff Moss

Gotta find a footprint, a bone, or a tooth
To grab yourself a piece of dinosaur truth.
All the dino knowledge that we've ever known
Comes from a footprint, a tooth, or a bone.

A tooth can tell you what a dino would eat,
A sharp tooth tells you that he dined on meat.
A blunt tooth tells you that she dined on plants.
No teeth at all? Well, perhaps they slurped ants.

Gotta find a footprint, a bone, or a tooth
To grab yourself a piece of dinosaur truth.
All the dino knowledge that we've ever known
Comes from a footprint, a tooth, or a bone.

▶ Footprints can tell you a dinosaur's size,
And how fast he ran when he raced with the guys.
Count all the footprints, you'll easily see
If he traveled alone or with a family.

Gotta find a footprint, a bone, or a tooth
To grab yourself a piece of dinosaur truth.
All the dino knowledge that we've ever known
Comes from a footprint, a tooth, or a bone.

Her bones will tell you if she stood up tall,
If she had a big tail or no tail at all.
Put the bones together and see how they look,
Pretty enough to get their picture took!

Yeah, gotta find a footprint, a bone, or a tooth
To grab yourself a piece of dinosaur truth.
All the dino knowledge that we've ever known
Comes from a footprint, a tooth, or a bone.

The Bremen Town Musicians • PRACTICE

Name ______________ Date ________ **Practice 169**

/âr/ are; /ôr/ or, ore; /îr/ ear

Write a word from the box to complete each sentence.

careful	scared	story	for	stored	morning	more	hear

1. Kitty waited ___for___ Sally.
2. The loud noise ___scared___ us.
3. Mom reads me a ___story___ every night.
4. I am ___careful___ when I ride my bike.
5. We eat breakfast every ___morning___.
6. I'm cold, so put on ___more___ heat.
7. Luis wanted to ___hear___ the song.
8. The clothes are ___stored___ in the closet.

At Home: Invite children to write a story using words from the box.

Name ______________ Date ________ **Practice 170**

Vocabulary

scare	third	daughter	music	voice	whistle

Read each sentence. Choose a word from the box that means almost the same thing as the words in dark type. Write it on the line.

1. They took their (**girl child**) to the movies. ___daughter___
2. Alex can (**make a sound with his lips**). ___whistle___
3. John lost his key for the (**three in a row**) time. ___third___
4. The children (**make people afraid**) with their masks. ___scare___
5. I love to play (**nice sounds**) on the guitar. ___music___
6. Luke has a strong speaking (**sound from his mouth**). ___voice___

At Home: Have children make up questions using three of the vocabulary words.

Lina Saves the Play

At the play Lina was scared. Still, she said her lines. But Sandy did not turn on the music, and José did not wake Maria. Luckily, Lina whistled the song and woke the daughter.

Everyone yelled, "More! More!"

"You saved the day, Lina," said Mrs. Rose.

At Home: Have children write about a time they were scared, and what they did to get through their fear.

Mrs. Rose's class was putting on the third play of the school year.

"The play is about a queen's daughter," said Mrs. Rose. "She is put under a spell and falls asleep."

"I want to be the daughter," said Lina.

"No," said Mrs. Rose. "You have a nice voice. You will be the storyteller. She talks clearly through the whole play so people can hear."

"Do I have to?" asked Lina.

"Yes," said Mrs. Rose. "You tell the story. Sandy will take care of the music. José will wake the daughter. And Maria will play the daughter."

I am glad I got the part of the daughter, Maria thought. If I had to talk, it would scare me.

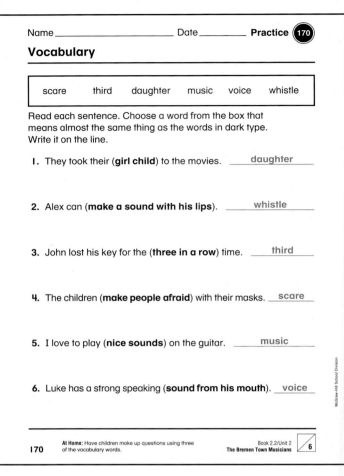

Name______________________ Date__________ **Practice 171**

Story Comprehension

Think about what happened in "The Bremen Town Musicians." Then answer the questions.

1. Why did the donkey run away?
   The farmer wanted to sell him.
2. Why did the dog run away?
   His master was angry with him.
3. Why did the cat run away?
   The cat's owner wanted to throw the cat in the lake.
4. Why did the rooster run away?
   His master wanted to make him into soup.
5. Where did the animals go?
   to a robbers' house
6. Why did the robbers run away?
   The animals made noises that scared them away.

At Home: Invite children to tell what happened next in the story.

Name______________________ Date__________ **Practice 172**

Follow Directions

Learning a task is easier when it's divided into parts. Below is a list of **directions** you follow when you are brushing your teeth. Rewrite the directions in the proper order so that they make sense.

Rinse your mouth.
Find your toothbrush and your tube of toothpaste.
Dry your face.
Put your toothbrush and tube of toothpaste away.
Put toothpaste on the toothbrush.
Brush your teeth.

1. Find your toothbrush and your tube of toothpaste.
2. Put toothpaste on the toothbrush.
3. Brush your teeth.
4. Rinse your mouth.
5. Dry your face.
6. Put your toothbrush and tube of toothpaste away.

At Home: Help children to write the directions for a simple receipe.

Name______________________ Date__________ **Practice 173**

/âr/ *are*; /ôr/ *or*, *ore*; /îr/ *ear*

Complete the words by writing in the correct letters. Then write the full word after the sentence.

are	or	ore	ear

1. The letter began, "D<u>ear</u> Linda." dear
2. Baseball and football are great sp<u>or</u>ts. sports
3. Don't be sc<u>are</u>d. It is safe here. scared
4. We buy milk at the st<u>or</u>e. store
5. The rooster crows in the m<u>or</u>ning. morning
6. After the rain, the sky was cl<u>ear</u>. clear
7. It is good to sh<u>are</u> with others. share
8. Please open the door f<u>or</u> me. for

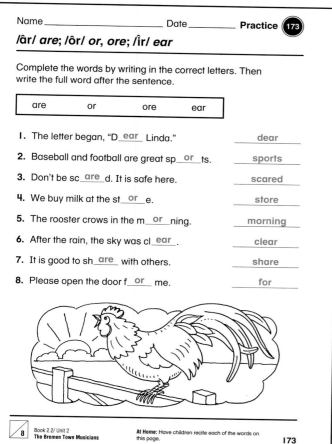

At Home: Have children recite each of the words on this page.

Name______________________ Date__________ **Practice 174**

/âr/ *are*; /ôr/ *or*, *ore*; /îr/ *ear*

Write the word from the box that completes each sentence.

tears	care	thorns	share	more
storm	sore	scare	store	clear

1. That was tasty! Can I have some <u>more</u>?
2. Wipe those <u>tears</u> from your eyes.
3. Some bushes have sharp <u>thorns</u>.
4. Tina and Toni like to <u>share</u> their toys.
5. A tree fell during the <u>storm</u>.
6. I <u>care</u> about all animals.
7. My legs are <u>sore</u> from running.
8. Go to the <u>store</u> and buy a pencil.
9. I don't see any clouds; the sky is blue and <u>clear</u>.
10. Don't yell. You will <u>scare</u> the baby.

At Home: Have children write a story using the words in the box above.

Name____________________ Date________ **Practice 175**

Summarize

Read each story. Then put a line under the best summary.

1. Jay has a blue bird. Min has a black bird. Mary has two white birds.
   - a. The birds like the children.
   - b. All the children have birds.
   - c. Birds make good pets.
2. We saw a black animal with white stripes. As we got closer, we saw that it was starting to get angry. We left it alone!
   - a. We saw a skunk.
   - b. We got angry.
   - c. We left the black animal.
3. Jake puts the towels and beach balls in the car. Then his dad packs the lunches. Jake can't wait to jump in the waves!
   - a. Jake and his dad eat lunch.
   - b. Jake's family goes to the beach.
   - c. Jake throws beach balls.
4. I draw animals all the time. I also like to draw people. Sometimes I like to draw people while they work.
   - a. I only draw people.
   - b. I draw animals well.
   - c. I like to draw.
5. We unpacked the boxes. We hung our pictures, and we moved our furniture. Now we are home!
   - a. We moved the pictures.
   - b. We bought new furniture.
   - c. We moved into a new home.

At Home: Have children write a summary of their day.

Name____________________ Date________ **Practice 176**

Suffixes

You can add **-ful** and **-ly** to some words to make new words.

thank + **-ful** = thankful   quick + **-ly** = quickly

Thankful means "full of thanks." Quickly means "in a quick way."

Read each sentence. Write a word with **-ful** or **-ly** that means the same as the underlined words in each sentence.

1. My mom drives in a slow way past the school. slowly
2. Please be full of care when you cross the street. careful
3. The circus tent was full of color. colorful
4. The storm came in a sudden way from the west. suddenly
5. We are full of hope that the rain will stop soon. hopeful
6. Lulu tiptoed in a quiet way past the baby. quietly
7. My little brother smiled in a shy way. shyly
8. Everyone at the party was full of joy. joyful

At Home: Ask children to add **-ly** or **-ful** to these words to make new words: **eager, glad, firm, fear.**

Name__________________ Date________ **Reteach 169**

/âr/ are; /ôr/ or, ore; /îr/ ear

Look at the spellings for these sounds.
/âr/ as in st**are** **/îr/** as in n**ear** **/ôr/** as in b**or**n or st**ore**

Choose letters from the list below and write them on the line to complete a word. Answers may vary.

are	ear	or	ore

1. c __are__ ful
2. st __or__ m
3. sc __are__ d or scored
4. n __ear__ or nor
5. f __or__ or fear, fore, or fare
6. h __ear__ or hare
7. sh __or__ t
8. t __ore__ or tear
9. st __or__ yteller
10. m __or__ ning
11. m __ore__ or mare
12. sh __are__ or shore or shear

At Home: Have children write a short poem using the words on this page.

Name__________________ Date________ **Reteach 170**

Vocabulary

Find the word in the box below that completes each sentence. Write the letter of the answer on the line in front of the sentence.

daughter	music	scare	third	voice	whistle

__e__ 1. Your ___ sounds very nice when you sing. **a.** whistle

__c__ 2. I like to ___ my friends in the dark. **b.** daughter

__f__ 3. This is the ___ time Rick saw the movie. **c.** scare

__a__ 4. I heard the wind ___ around the corner. **d.** music

__d__ 5. Lou plays beautiful ___ on his piano. **e.** voice

__b__ 6. That girl is the ___ of my teacher. **f.** third

At Home: Encourage children to write a story using the vocabulary words in the box.

Name__________________ Date________ **Reteach 171**

Story Comprehension

Think about what happens to the characters in the "The Bremen Town Musicians." Then draw a line from each sentence to the character who might say it.

1. "I'm too old. No one wants a donkey like me."

2. "We must go and never come back."

3. "I sleep too late to wake them up."

4. "Last night I let a fox run away with a big chicken."

5. "I can't catch mice because my teeth are not sharp anymore."

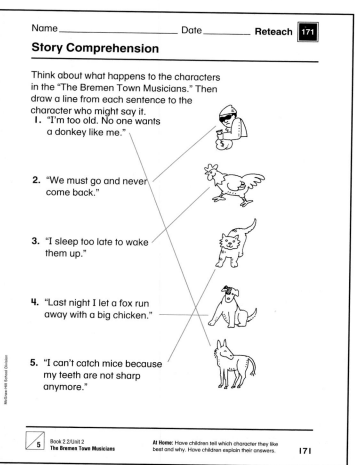

At Home: Have children tell which character they like best and why. Have children explain their answers.

Name__________________ Date________ **Reteach 172**

Follow Directions

Directions are a step-by-step way to do something.

The directions below will tell you how to make a kazoo.

Step 1: Take an empty toilet paper roll, a rubber band, and a piece of waxpaper. You will also need a pencil and scissors.
Step 2: Cut out a square of wax paper large enough to fit completely over one end of the paper roll.
Step 3: Place the wax paper over the end of the roll.
Step 4: Secure the wax paper by wrapping the rubber band around the wax paper on the roll. Make sure the wax paper is pulled tightly.
Step 5: Use the pencil to poke a small hole in the toilet paper roll near the wax paper end.
Step 6: Hum into the other end and blow slightly. Kazoo Music will come out!

Answer these questions using the directions above.

1. How big should the piece of wax paper be? __large enough to fit completely over one end of the paper roll__
2. Where do you poke a small hole? __in the toilet paper roll near the wax paper end__
3. What is the rubber band for? __to hold the wax paper in place__
4. How do you make music with this kazoo? __hum into the uncovered end and blow slightly__

At Home: Have children write step-by-step instructions for completing a simple art project.

Name __________ Date ______ **Reteach 173**

/âr/*are*; /ôr/*or, ore*; /îr/*ear*

Read the words. What sound do you hear in each word?

st**are** 

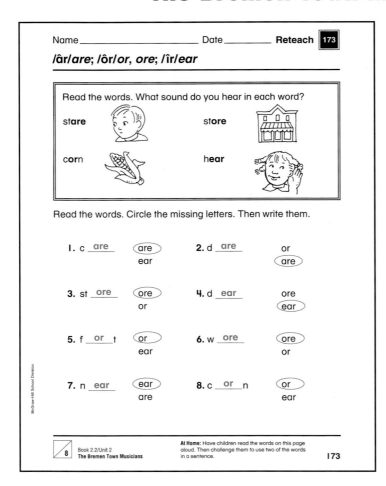

st**ore** 

c**or**n 

h**ear** 

Read the words. Circle the missing letters. Then write them.

1. c _are_ — (are) / ear
2. d _are_ — or / (are)
3. st _ore_ — (ore) / or
4. d _ear_ — ore / (ear)
5. f _or_ t — (or) / ear
6. w _ore_ — (ore) / or
7. n _ear_ — (ear) / are
8. c _or_ n — (or) / ear

At Home: Have children read the words on this page aloud. Then challenge them to use two of the words in a sentence.

Name __________ Date ______ **Reteach 174**

/âr/ *are;* /ôr/ *or, ore;* /îr/ *ear*

porch

Choose the word from the box that names each picture. Write the word on the line.

store	fork	ear	corn	stare

1.  _ear_
2.  _store_
3.  _corn_
4.  _stare_
5.  _fork_

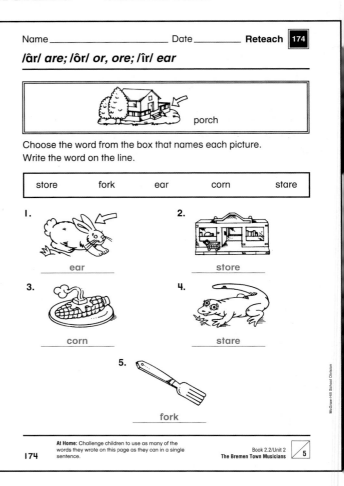

At Home: Challenge children to use as many of the words they wrote on this page as they can in a single sentence.

Name __________ Date ______ **Reteach 175**

Summarize

The sisters like their swimming lessons. They play games. They play with toys. They dive in the water.

Summary: The sisters have fun at swimming lessons.

Read each story. Then draw a line under the best summary.

1. Bob waits for winter. He loves to go sledding and to ice skate. He even likes to go ice fishing!

a. Bob goes sledding.
b. Ice fishing is a winter sport.
c. Bob loves winter sports.

2. Ann likes to care for her dog, Ruff. She feeds her friend's cat when she goes on a trip. Ann likes to brush her horse, too.

a. Ann likes to care for animals.
b. Ann can ride a horse.
c. Ann feeds her friend's cat.

3. Phil's birthday is coming, and he is having a party. He will think about who is coming. Then, he will decide what food he needs to buy.

a. Phil is invited to a party.
b. Phil is planning a party.
c. Phil buys food for dinner.

4. Mary can whistle. Her brother taught her how. Mary's mom and dad can whistle many songs. Even Mary's bird knows how to whistle them!

a. Mary has a bird.
b. Mary's brother is a teacher.
c. Mary's family can whistle!

At Home: Have children summarize "The Bremen Town Musicians."

Name __________ Date ______ **Reteach 176**

Suffixes

The **suffixes -ly** and **-ful** change the meaning of the word to which they are added. The suffix **-ly** means "in a (base word) manner"; **-ful** means "full of (base word)."

Write the word from the box that has the opposite meaning of the underlined word.

quietly	slowly	beautiful	careful	useful

1. I am not careless. I am _careful_.
2. I am not ugly. I am _beautiful_.
3. I am not talking loudly. I am talking _quietly_.
4. I am not going quickly. I am going _slowly_.
5. We are not useless. We are _useful_.

At Home: Ask children to add **-ful** or **-ly** to each of the following words and to use them in sentences: **hope, sad, friend,** and **thought.**

Name________________ Date________ **Extend 169**

/âr/ are; /ôr/ or, ore; /îr/ ear

Help Sam find the gold. Circle all the words with the *ear* sound. Then draw a path.

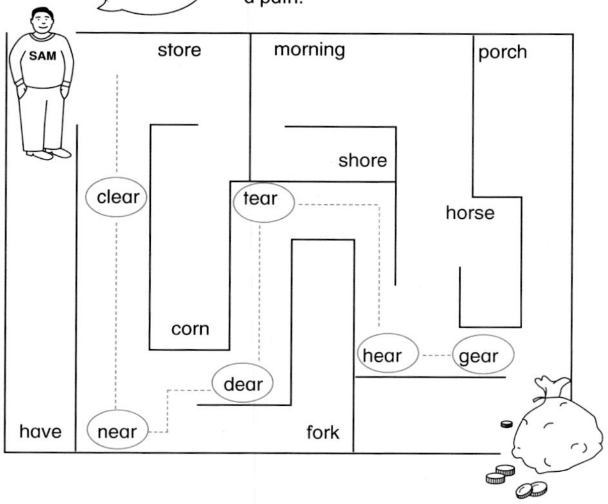

Write two sentences telling what Sam will do with his gold. Use words from the maze.

Sam will buy corn.

Sam will buy a hare.

At Home: Invite children to make a maze using the words *careful, scared, scary, dare, hare, mare,* and *dared* along the path. Have them put other words in the maze to make the maze tricky. They can give their maze to a friend to solve.

Name________________ Date________ **Extend 170**

Vocabulary

daughter	music	scare	third	voice	whistle

Write a word from the box that answers each riddle.

1. She is not a son. daughter
2. You blow through me to make a high sound. whistle
3. I am between the second and the fourth. third
4. You need me to sing, talk, or whisper. voice
5. Musicians read me to play their instruments. music
6. This is what you get when someone sneaks up on you. scare

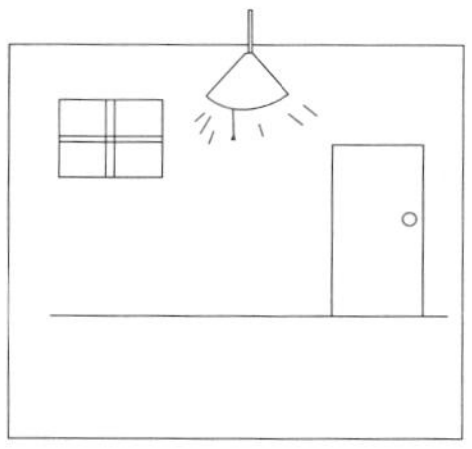

Write a title for this scene.

Title: The Music Room

At Home: Invite children to write the vocabulary words on individual cards. Put them in a stack facing down. Have children choose a card and use the word in a sentence.

Name________________ Date________ **Extend 171**

Story Comprehension

Here are three new endings to "The Bremen Town Musicians." Write a sentence that tells what might have happened.

Answers will vary. Sentences should relate to the picture.

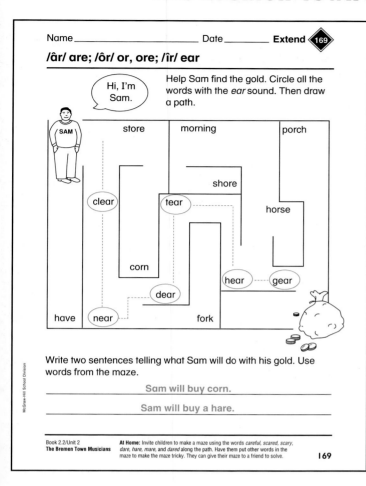

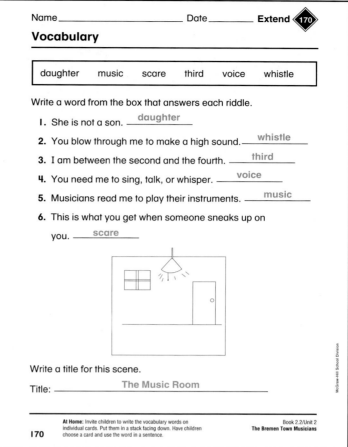

At Home: Have children draw a picture and write a sentence showing what might have happened to each animal if they had never met each other.

Name________________ Date________ **Extend 172**

Follow Directions

Think about something you know how to do. Write the steps that tell how to do it.

You can write directions for:

- Making a puppet
- Solving a math problem
- Writing a story
- Drawing an animal
- Or anything you choose!

Follow These Steps

Look for directions that are complete and in proper sequence.

Give your directions to a partner to follow. See if your partner can follow the steps. Change your directions if you have to.

At Home: Have children draw pictures with missing parts. Ask them to write directions for drawing in the parts in the picture.

Name ______________ Date ________ **Extend 173**

/âr/ are; /ôr/ or, ore; /îr/ ear

Color words with **are** red. Color words with **ore** or **or** blue. Color words with **ear** green. Find the object hidden in the puzzle.

ear	care	scare	dear
story	rare	more	gear
fear	hare	mare	corn
morning	dare	hear	wore
clear	careful	scared	near

Write a riddle telling the name of the object hidden in the puzzle.

Children will write a riddle for the letter E.

At Home: Have children use the *ear* words they colored green to write rhymes.

Name ______________ Date ________ **Extend 174**

âr/ are; /ôr/ or, ore; /îr/ ear

rare	acorn	score	care	dear	dare	scare

Use the words in the box to complete the crossword puzzle.

Across

2. a risk or a challenge

3. something valuable or worth a lot

5. a loud noise might cause this

Down

1. when you like or worry about someone

2. a word you call someone you like

4. an oak tree grows from this

5. the number of points a team has during a game

Now create your own crossword puzzle.

At Home: Have children write sentences for each word in the puzzle on cards. Invite them to draw a picture illustrating each word on separate cards. Children can play a game of concentration in which they match picture cards to sentence cards.

Name ______________ Date ________ **Extend 175**

Summarize

Read the sentences. Put a ✔ next to the four sentences that tell the story of "The Bremen Town Musicians." Write each sentence on a line below a box. Draw a picture in each box.

1. A dog lay in the road.

2. A donkey, a dog, a cat, and a rooster went to Bremen to be musicians. ✔

3. A cat's teeth were not sharp.

4. The animals saw robbers in a house. ✔

5. A rooster crowed late in the morning.

6. The animals made a plan to scare the robbers. ✔

7. The robbers ran away, and the animals found what they wanted. ✔

1	2
Sentence 2	Sentence 4

3	4
Sentence 6	Sentence 7

At Home: Have children draw four pictures that summarize a favorite story. Ask them to write a sentence for each picture.

Name ______________ Date ________ **Extend 176**

Suffixes

suddenly	fearful	careful	luckily	beautiful
slowly	brightly	loudly	quickly	thankful

Add the suffix **-ly** or **-ful** to each word in dark type so the story makes sense. Use words from the box.

It was a **beauti** _ful_ summer day. The sun shone **bright** _ly_. I was **care** _ful_ to wear my sunglasses when I went outside. It got hot **quick** _ly_. I took my time and walked **slow** _ly_ toward the beach. **Sudden** _ly_, lightning flashed across the sky. Thunder rumbled **loud** _ly_. I was **fear** _ful_ that my day at the beach would be spoiled. **Lucki** _ly_, the storm only lasted for five minutes. Boy, was I **thank** _ful_!

Write two more sentences telling what happened next. Use two words from the box. Sample answers given.

I spent a beautiful day on the beach.

I had so much fun that the day went quickly.

At Home: Have children write a short story using three or four words with **-ful** and **-ly** suffixes.

The Bremen Town Musicians • GRAMMAR

Name ______________________ Date __________ LEARN Grammar 129

Pronouns

- A **pronoun** is a word that takes the place of a noun or nouns.
- A pronoun must agree with the noun it replaces.
- The pronouns *I, he, she, it,* and *you* can take the place of a singular noun.

She put her hat on. She put it on her head.
He took his hat off. I saw him.
Did you see him?

Look at the underlined noun. Choose the pronoun that could be used in its place. Mark the answer.

1. Billy only eats spinach.
   ⓐ He ⓑ She
2. Billy loves spinach.
   ⓐ he ⓑ it
3. Billy's mother gave him rice.
   ⓐ He ⓑ She
4. Billy's dad gave him pie.
   ⓐ He ⓑ She
5. Billy gave the pie to the dog.
   ⓐ he ⓑ it

Extension: Have children continue the story about Billy, using the pronouns *I, he, she, it,* and *you.*

Name ______________________ Date __________ PRACTICE AND LEARN Grammar 130

Pronouns

- The pronouns *we, you,* and *they* can take the place of a plural noun.

Beans are good for you. Ned and I are friends.
They are good for you. We are friends.

Underline the pronoun that completes the sentence.

1. Mike is here. We're glad to see (we, you), Mike.
2. Now (we, you) can go to the party.
3. Bob and Jill are late. (You, They) told us to go.
4. (We, You) can come with us.
5. Did you see my friends? (They, You) will be here soon.
6. (We, You) are going together.
7. Call Alice and Peter. (You, They) need a ride.
8. Hurry or we will go without (they, you).

Extension: Have the children write the noun that each pronoun replaces.

Name ______________________ Date __________ REVIEW AND PRACTICE Grammar 131

Writing Pronouns

- A **pronoun** is a word that takes the place of a noun or nouns.
- A pronoun must agree with the noun it replaces.
- The pronouns *I, he, she, it,* and *you* can take the place of a singular noun.
- The pronouns *we, you,* and *they* can take the place of a plural noun.

Replace each underlined word or words with a pronoun. Then write the sentence.

1. Joe and Pam wrote a song together.
   They wrote a song together.
2. Pam wrote the music.
   She wrote the music.
3. Joe wrote the words.
   He wrote the words.
4. The song is funny.
   It is funny.
5. You and I can sing it.
   We can sing it.

Extension: Have children say sentences with proper nouns. Have other children substitute *he, she,* and *they* for them.

Name ______________________ Date __________ MECHANICS Grammar 132

Using Quotation Marks

- Use quotation marks at the beginning and end of what a person says.

"Go home," Jon told the dog.

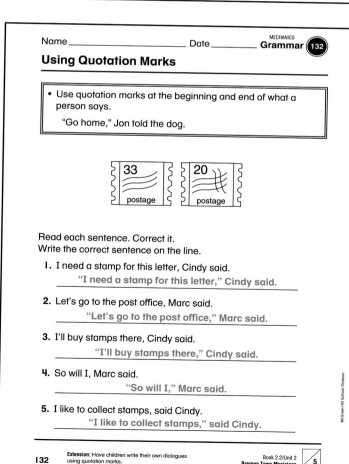

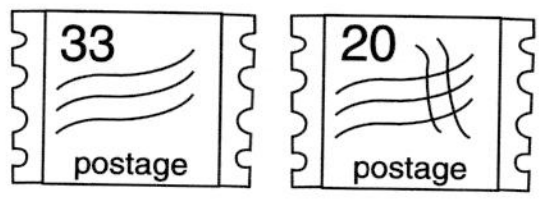

Read each sentence. Correct it.
Write the correct sentence on the line.

1. I need a stamp for this letter, Cindy said.
   "I need a stamp for this letter," Cindy said.
2. Let's go to the post office, Marc said.
   "Let's go to the post office," Marc said.
3. I'll buy stamps there, Cindy said.
   "I'll buy stamps there," Cindy said.
4. So will I, Marc said.
   "So will I," Marc said.
5. I like to collect stamps, said Cindy.
   "I like to collect stamps," said Cindy.

Extension: Have children write their own dialogues using quotation marks.

Name ____________________ Date __________ TEST Grammar 133

Test

A. Read each sentence. Write the pronoun that can take the place of the underlined words.

1. Aunt Doris is coming to visit. She
2. Aunt Doris will stay one week. She
3. Uncle Nate is staying home. He
4. Uncle Nate and Aunt Doris live in New York. They
5. "Uncle Nate will come later," said Aunt Doris. He
6. Uncle Nate and Aunt Doris like to travel. They

B. Read each pair of lines. Write the pronoun that can take the place of the underlined words.

7. Aunt Doris brought a big bag.
   The big bag was heavy. It
8. Uncle Nate gave me something special.
   Uncle Nate wants me to give it to you. He
9. Uncle Nate and Aunt Doris went to the museum.
   The museum was very interesting. It
10. Uncle Nate and Aunt Doris went home.
    Uncle Nate and Aunt Doris had a good time. They

Name ____________________ Date __________ MORE PRACTICE Grammar 134

Pronouns

- A **pronoun** takes the place of a noun or nouns.
- A pronoun must agree with the noun it replaces.
- The pronouns *I, he, she, it,* and *you* can take the place of a singular noun.
- The pronouns *we, you,* and *they* can take the place of a plural noun.

Look at the pictures. Read the sentences. Find the pronouns. Draw a line under each pronoun. Draw another line to the picture each one names.

1. Jan is playing.
   She likes the park.
2. Jan has gloves.
   They keep her hands warm.
3. Jan has boots.
   They keep her feet warm.
4. Jan likes her hat because it is pretty.
5. Jan builds a snowman.
   It will be big.

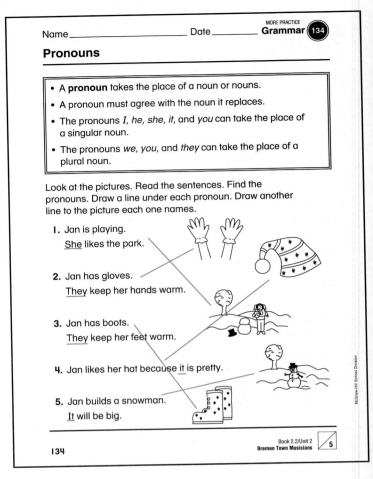

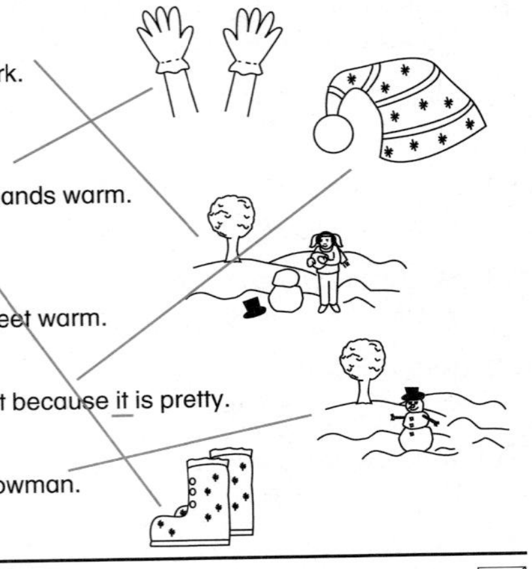

The Bremen Town Musicians • SPELLING

Name ______________ Date ________ PRETEST SPELLING **129**

Words with *c*, *k*, and *ck*

Pretest Directions

Fold back your paper along the dotted line. Use the blanks to write each word as it is said to you. When you finish the test, unfold the paper and correct any spelling mistakes. Practice those words for the Posttest.

1. ________	1. come
2. ________	2. act
3. ________	3. work
4. ________	4. luck
5. ________	5. like
6. ________	6. kind
7. ________	7. wake
8. ________	8. bake
9. ________	9. sick
10. ________	10. cover

Challenge Words

________	daughter
________	music
________	third
________	voice
________	whistle

To Parents,

Here are the results of your child's weekly spelling Pretest. You can help your child study for the Posttest by following these simple steps for each word on the word list:

1. Read the word to your child.
2. Have your child write the word, saying each letter as it is written.
3. Say each letter of the word as your child checks the spelling.
4. If a mistake has been made, have your child read each letter of the correctly spelled word aloud and then repeat steps 1–3.

Name ______________ Date ________ AT-HOME WORD STUDY SPELLING **130**

Words with *c*, *k*, and *ck*

Using the Word Study Steps

1. LOOK at the word.
2. SAY the word aloud.
3. STUDY the letters in the word.
4. WRITE the word.
5. CHECK the word. Did you spell the word right? If not, go back to step 1.

Spelling Tip

The **ck** spelling of the sound /k/ appears only at the end of a word or syllable and never appears at the beginning of a word. Examples:

lu**ck**, du**ck**

Find the Hidden Words

Circle the spelling words hidden in the words of the paragraph.

As a small child she was often ill. But when she grew older, she was to overcome her sickness. She was lucky. She became an actress. In her first starring role, she played a kind old woman who worked in a bakery. She liked covering the doughnuts in powdered sugar while she was acting.

To Parents or Helpers:

Using the Word Study Steps above as your child comes across any new words will help him or her spell well. Review the steps as you both go over this week's spelling words.

Go over the Spelling Tip with your child. Have him or her list other words ending with **ck**.

Help your child find and circle the spelling words in the paragraph.

Name ______________ Date ________ EXPLORE THE PATTERN SPELLING **131**

Words with *c*, *k*, and *ck*

come	work	like	wake	sick
act	luck	kind	bake	cover

Pattern Smart

Write the words with **c**.

1. come
2. act
3. cover

Write the words with **ck**.

4. luck
5. sick

Write the words with **k**.

6. work
7. like
8. kind
9. wake
10. bake

Which spelling of the sound /k/ only appears at the end of a word and never appears at the beginning of a word?

11. ck

Write two spelling words that end with that spelling.

12. clock
13. sick

14. Write the spelling word that completes this rhyme.

Tick Tock
Is the sound of the clock.

Name ______________ Date ________ PRACTICE AND EXTEND SPELLING **132**

Words with *c*, *k*, and *ck*

come	work	like	wake	sick
act	luck	kind	bake	cover

Write the words that complete each sentence.

1. My father rides the bus to work.
2. What kind of sandwich do you want?
3. You should cover your mouth when you sneeze.
4. Tony likes to bake cookies.
5. It's time to wake up from your nap.
6. Is Maria sick with a cold?

Word Meaning

Say it another way. Draw a line from each spelling word to the word that means almost the same.

7. kind	cook
8. cover	ill
9. bake	lid
10. sick	nice

Challenge Extension: Have students write fill-in sentences using the words. They may exchange with a partner to complete the sentences.

Name ______________________ Date __________ PROOFREAD AND WRITE SPELLING 133

Words with *c*, *k*, and *ck*

Proofreading Activity

There are six spelling mistakes in the paragraph below. Circle each misspelled word. Write the words correctly on the lines below.

It takes a lot of werk to make cookies. Pat asked her friend May to cume help. "What keind shall we make?" May asked. "I like chocolate chip!" Pat said. Pat's father put the cookies in the oven to backe. "Waak me when they are done," he said. Pat told May to cuver some cookies and take them home to her mother.

1. work 2. come 3. kind

4. bake 5. Wake 6. cover

Writing Activity

Write a recipe using four spelling words. Circle the spelling words in your recipe.

____

____

____

____

____

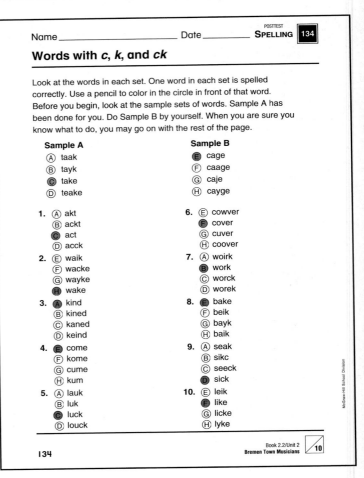

Name ______________________ Date __________ POSTTEST SPELLING 134

Words with *c*, *k*, and *ck*

Look at the words in each set. One word in each set is spelled correctly. Use a pencil to color in the circle in front of that word. Before you begin, look at the sample sets of words. Sample A has been done for you. Do Sample B by yourself. When you are sure you know what to do, you may go on with the rest of the page.

Sample A
- Ⓐ taak
- Ⓑ tayk
- ● take
- Ⓓ teake

Sample B
- ● cage
- Ⓕ caage
- Ⓖ caje
- Ⓗ cayge

1. Ⓐ akt / Ⓑ ackt / ● act / Ⓓ acck
2. Ⓔ waik / Ⓕ wacke / Ⓖ wayke / ● wake
3. ● kind / Ⓑ kined / Ⓒ kaned / Ⓓ keind
4. ● come / Ⓕ kome / Ⓖ cume / Ⓗ kum
5. Ⓐ lauk / Ⓑ luk / ● luck / Ⓓ louck
6. Ⓔ cowver / ● cover / Ⓖ cuver / Ⓗ coover
7. Ⓐ woirk / ● work / Ⓒ worck / Ⓓ worek
8. ● bake / Ⓕ beik / Ⓖ bayk / Ⓗ baik
9. Ⓐ seak / Ⓑ sikc / Ⓒ seeck / ● sick
10. Ⓔ leik / ● like / Ⓖ licke / Ⓗ lyke

Name________________ Date________ **Practice 177**

/ü/ oo, ue, ew

Circle the word that fits in the sentence. Then write the word.

1. I wear a __boot__ on one foot.
   (boot) beet boat
2. A __boom__ is a loud sound.
   broom (boom) bone
3. The sky is __blue__
   blew (blue) blow
4. The bird __flew__ away.
   few flaw (flew)
5. Joe wants to come, __too__.
   toe tow (too)
6. Last night, the wind __blew__ hard.
   blue (blew) blow
7. __Glue__ the broken vase back together.
   Clue (Glue) Blew
8. We eat at __noon__ every day.
   (noon) tune soon

At Home: Ask children to think of a riddle or a rhyme using **oo, ue,** or **ew** words.

Name________________ Date________ **Practice 178**

Vocabulary

Circle the word that answers the riddle. Then write the word on the line.

coaches	**field**	**score**	**stretches**	**throws**	**touch**

1. These are good to do before you play sports. __stretches__
   field (stretches) objects
2. This is what David does with a ball. __throws__
   (throws) whistles scares
3. You can do this to a table, a book, or a chair. __touch__
   sleep score (touch)
4. We are the people who run the team. __coaches__
   (coaches) police nurses
5. This is what happens when a ball goes in the goal. __score__
   safe (score) wild
6. I am the place where ball games are played. __field__
   house barn (field)

At Home: Have children make up riddles using some of the words that they didn't circle.

The Blue Birds

"Now we are going to lose big time!" I say.

"That's not true! Wait and see," says Martha.

Boom! Ted hits the ball! Then Joe hits the ball! Then I hit a home run, too! We win!

"You see," says Martha. "I knew you were a good team all along. You just had to believe in yourselves!"

At Home: Have children draw a picture and write a few sentences about their favorite sport. Who is their favorite player. Why?

The Blue Birds! What an awful baseball team! Every time we get on the field we lose. We never touch base or score.

The coaches try to be nice. "You will do better next time," say Mr. Rivera and Mrs. Nelson.

We know better, though. We do not do our stretches. We do not want to practice. We are losers.

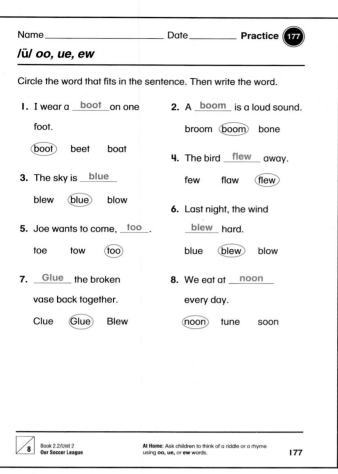

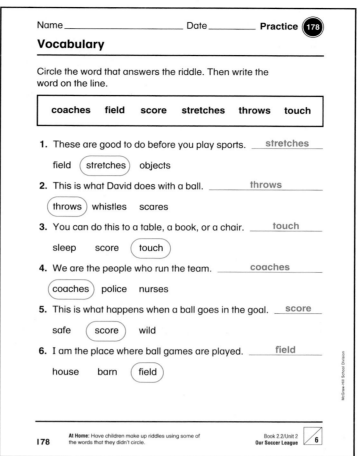

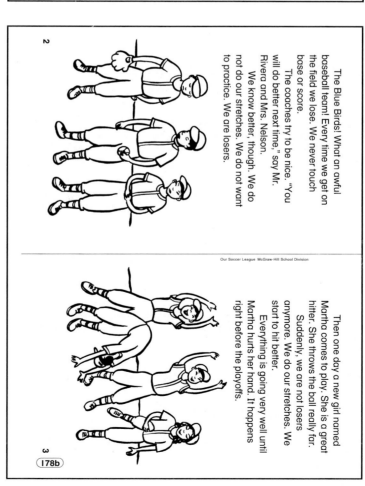

Then one day a new girl named Martha comes to play. She is a great hitter. She throws the ball really far.

Suddenly, we are not losers anymore. We do our stretches. We start to hit better.

Everything is going very well until Martha hurts her hand. It happens right before the playoffs.

Name ______________________ Date __________ **Practice 179**

Story Comprehension

Think about the story "Our Soccer League." Draw pictures to show six things you learned about soccer. Write a label for each picture. **Answers will vary.**

1. Possibly: the goalie	**2.** Possibly: foot dribble
3. Possibly: the goal	**4.** Possibly: header
5. Possibly: pass	**6.** Possibly: hand ball

At Home: Have children pretend to be sports announcers, announcing the players and moves in a soccer game.

Name ______________________ Date __________ **Practice 180**

Read a Newsletter

Different **newsletters** are aimed at different readers.

Newsletter #1

CHESS CLUB NEWS
by Peter Kingsley

The final match of the chess tournament was played Tuesday after school. Tanya Quigly went head to head with Victor Sing. The winner was the first to gain three points. A win was worth one point. A draw was worth a half point. Victor won the first match. Tanya pulled out a tie in the second. And then Tanya got a checkmate in sixteen moves in the third. But Victor won two straight games. They were both close but Victor is our new champion!

Newsletter #2

GABRIEL STREET BLOCK ASSOCIATION NEWSLETTER

Block clean-up Saturday! All day!
Be there or be square! Bring a friend!
Take pride in our block. The city is sending a special garbage truck just for us. The vacant lot will be cleared. Trees will be planted. Bus benches will be painted. Gabby's Deli is bringing sandwiches. If you have anything to bring to the block yard sale, call Tom 555-2345. A clean block is a happy block!!

Use the information in the two newsletters above to answer the questions that follow.

1. Which newsletter was written for the people who lived in a certain area? #2
2. Which newsletter told who wrote it? #1
3. Who won the final match of the chess club? Victor Sing
4. When is the big block clean up? Saturday all day
5. What is the main idea of each newsletter?
   Newsletter #1: to tell who won the big chess match
   Newsletter #2: to tell about the block clean-up

At Home: Have children write newsletters about their lives to send to family and friends.

Name ______________________ Date __________ **Practice 181**

/ü/ *oo, ue, ew*

The answer to each riddle has the same ending sound as cl**ue**, st**ew**, or t**oo**. Circle the word. Write each answer on the line.

1. What does a ghost say? boo — (boo) boom bow
2. What do you do with food? chew — clue (chew) bow
3. What did the flower do? grew — gray (grew) good
4. What is the name of a color? blue — blew buy (blue)
5. What does a cow say? moo — boom (moo) too
6. What is sticky? glue — (glue) grow glow
7. Which word means **also**? too — (too) room to
8. Which word means **not old**? new — no now (new)

At Home: Help children use the words they wrote in a sentence.

Name ______________________ Date __________ **Practice 182**

/ü/ *oo, ue;* /ôr/ *or, ore*

Underline the word that completes the sentence. Then write the answer.

1. Fish is my favorite food.
   food boot hoot
2. The score of the soccer game is tied.
   score tore store
3. The sky is blue today.
   clue blue true
4. I wake up in the morning.
   born morning worn
5. We needed glue for our art project.
   blue true glue
6. My sister plays the horn.
   core short horn

At Home: Have children illustrate one of the sentences above.

Name____________________ Date________ Practice 183

Sequence of Events

Read the story. Then write first, next, then, and last below the sentence to show when Lisa did each thing.

Teams	1st half	2nd half	Final
Tigers	3	2	5
Cubs	2	0	2

Lisa keeps score for the Tigers. Today they are playing the Cubs. In the first half, the Tigers scored 3 goals. The Cubs scored 2 goals. The Tigers played hard during the second half. Jeff scored a goal. Meg kicked a goal, too. Lisa put a 2 on the scoreboard. The whistle blew. The game was over. Lisa counted up the goals. She put the number in the last box. The Tigers won!

Lisa wrote a 5 in the box.

Last

Lisa gave the Tigers a 3

First

Lisa gave the Cubs a 2.

Next

The Cubs scored 0 and the Tigers scored 2.

Then

At Home: Have children tell about common events or activities that involve a sequence, for example, getting dressed or planting a seed.

Name____________________ Date________ Practice 184

Context Clues

Read each sentence. You can find clues about the meaning of the underlined word by reading the rest of the sentence. Color in the circle next to the word's definition.

1. In this game you throw a ball through a basket.
   - ● an open net on a metal ring
   - ⓑ a swimming pool
2. At halftime, we take a break.
   - ⓐ a young player
   - ● when the game is half over
3. The score is ten to twelve.
   - ● the number of points made in a game
   - ⓑ a very big number
4. The coach helps us learn to throw.
   - ⓐ a special throw
   - ● a teacher in sports
5. The players charge down the court.
   - ⓐ pay for with a credit card
   - ● run fast

At Home: Read a picture caption from the sports section of your newspaper and help your child learn new words by using clues given in words and pictures.

Name__________________ Date________ **Reteach 177**

/ü/oo, ue, ew

Say these words. What sound do you hear that is the same in each word?

b**oo**t	br**oo**m	fl**ew**	bl**ue**

Look at each picture below. Choose a word in the box that names a picture. Write the word below the picture it names.

1.

boot

2.

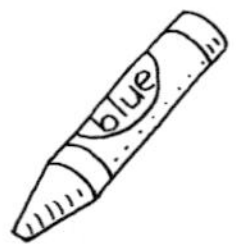

blue

3.

flew

4.

broom

At Home: Have children look at book covers and newspaper headlines to find words with the same vowel sound as the words they wrote.

Name__________________ Date________ **Reteach 178**

Vocabulary

Choose a word from the box to complete each sentence. Write the word on the line.

coaches	field	score	stretches	throws	touch

1. Sue ___throws___ a softball very far.

2. Please don't ___touch___ the wet paint.

3. We did sit-ups and ___stretches___ on the floor.

4. Ben added up the ___score___ to see who won.

5. Our parents are the ___coaches___ of our team.

6. Tall grass grew in the ___field___ .

At Home: Ask children to draw a picture for one of the vocabulary words.

Name__________________ Date________ **Reteach 179**

Story Comprehension

In "Our Soccer League," you learned many things about the game of soccer. Read each statement. Then circle **T** if the sentence is true, or **F** if it is false.

1.	"Our Soccer League" tells about a game.	(T)	F
2.	In soccer, you dribble with your feet.	(T)	F
3.	Goalies can touch the ball.	(T)	F
4.	Everyone can touch the ball.	T	(F)
5.	Soccer is a team sport.	(T)	F
6.	Only boys play soccer.	T	(F)
7.	When you run out of bounds, it is called a "header."	T	(F)
8.	The game is over when time runs out.	(T)	F
9.	The Sluggers are a baseball team.	T	(F)
10.	The Falcons lose the game.	(T)	F

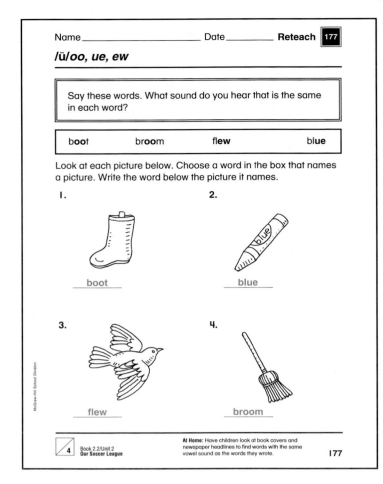

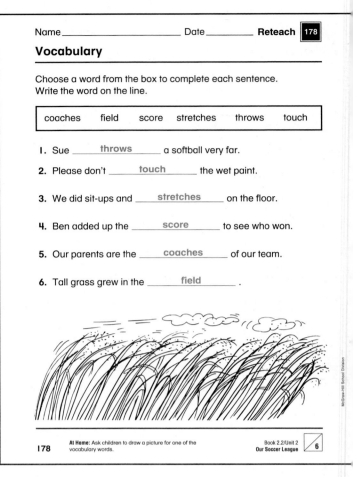

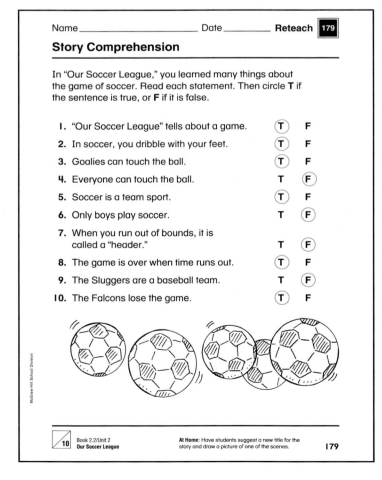

At Home: Have students suggest a new title for the story and draw a picture of one of the scenes.

Name__________________ Date________ **Reteach 180**

Read a Newsletter

A **newsletter** is like a small newspaper. It is usually written about one topic, such as a club, a sport, or a neighborhood.

Girls Basketball Digest

The B-Ball Newsletter of Kennedy Grade School — January 2000

Division Winners Rule
by Kenesha Winterly

The Kennedy hoopsters marched right through the Winter Tournament. Six straight victories! That makes us the winners of our division!

Joleen Larsen led the way with sixteen points in the last three games. Yours truly scored the most points ever. Two! Luckily, the rest of the team scored a lot more points.

Dates To Keep In Mind:

Feb. 4:	Practice for Playoffs	4 P.M.
Feb. 6:	First playoff game	1 P.M.
March 16:	Awards party	7 P.M.

Don't Forget

Coach Remington says all uniforms must be returned to her office after the last game. They must be cleaned and folded. Go Kennedy Girls!

Use the information in the newsletter to answer these questions.

1. When is the first play-off game? Feb. 6, 1 p.m.

2. How many points did Joleen Larsen score in the last three games? 16

3. What is the date of this newsletter? January 2000

4. What did Coach Remington say? all uniforms must be returned to her office after the last game

At Home: Invite children to produce a newsletter about the neighborhood.

Our Soccer League • RETEACH

Name________________ Date________ **Reteach 181**

/ü/oo, ue, ew

> Read the sentence.
> My dog **chewed** on my **blue boot.**

Finish each sentence below. Circle the word that completes the sentence. Then write the answer.

1. We both tripped over the tree root.
   boot (root) boom
2. There were only a few people at the show.
   dew (few) crew
3. Jane thought the answer was true.
   (true) clue glue
4. I am going to the zoo tomorrow.
   tool cool (zoo)
5. Our class has a new chalkboard.
   drew (new) blew
6. Harry found his other boot under the bed.
   pool new (boot)

At Home: Have children create a rhyming sentence or short verse using some of the words above.

Name________________ Date________ **Reteach 182**

/ü/ oo, ue; /ôr/ or, ore

(thorn) corn

Circle the word that names each picture. Then write the word.

1. 
   fork (boot)
   boot
2. 
   (glue) story
   glue
3. 
   zoo (corn)
   corn
4. 
   (core) moon
   core

At Home: Have children write a sentence using one of the words they circled.

Name________________ Date________ **Reteach 183**

Sequence of Events

> The **sequence of events** is the order in which things happen.

Read the story. Then number the pictures to show the order in which things happen.

Mark always warms up before he plays soccer. First, he starts with leg stretches. Next, he warms up his feet by running in place. Then, Mark's coach has the team do something funny to end the warm-ups. He tells the players to squat down and waddle like a duck. "Quack! Quack!" laughs Mark. At last, it's time to play soccer!

Warm-Ups

2

4

3

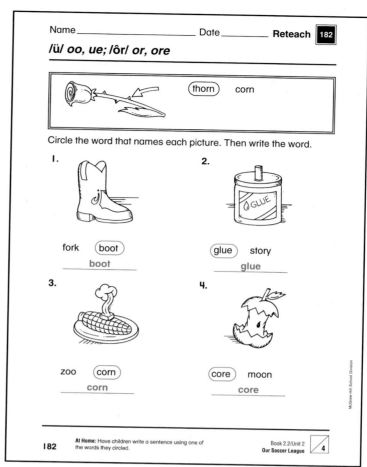

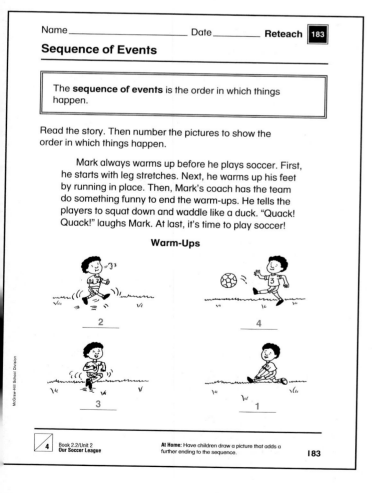

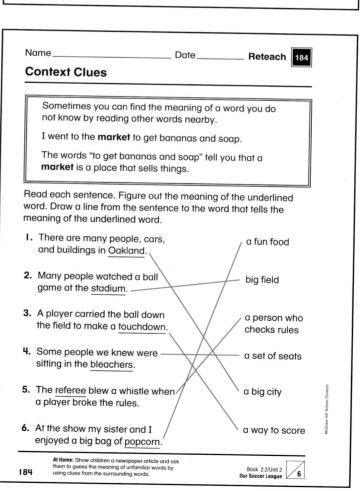

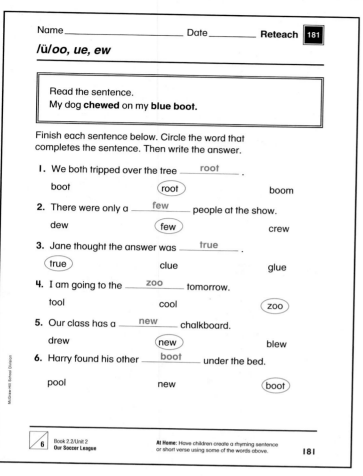

1

At Home: Have children draw a picture that adds a further ending to the sequence.

Name________________ Date________ **Reteach 184**

Context Clues

> Sometimes you can find the meaning of a word you do not know by reading other words nearby.
>
> I went to the **market** to get bananas and soap.
>
> The words "to get bananas and soap" tell you that a **market** is a place that sells things.

Read each sentence. Figure out the meaning of the underlined word. Draw a line from the sentence to the word that tells the meaning of the underlined word.

1. There are many people, cars, and buildings in Oakland. — a big city
2. Many people watched a ball game at the stadium. — big field
3. A player carried the ball down the field to make a touchdown. — a way to score
4. Some people we knew were sitting in the bleachers. — a set of seats
5. The referee blew a whistle when a player broke the rules. — a person who checks rules
6. At the show my sister and I enjoyed a big bag of popcorn. — a fun food

Choices: a fun food; big field; a person who checks rules; a set of seats; a big city; a way to score

At Home: Show children a newspaper article and ask them to guess the meaning of unfamiliar words by using clues from the surrounding words.

Name ____________________ Date ________ **Extend 177**

/ü/ oo, ue, ew

Read the play.

Dog: I'd like to chew a boot.
Cat: Don't chew that blue boot.
Dog: Why not? You should chew it, too.
Cat: No. There are too few boots. The people in the house will get mad at us.
Dog: You're right. Then there will be no more good food!
Cat: Stay away from that boot!

Write a sentence in each speech balloon. Use words from the box.

boot	blue	too	few	food

At Home: Have children draw two more cartoon panels with the same characters. Ask them to use words from the box to write dialogue.

Name ____________________ Date ________ **Extend 178**

Vocabulary

touch	stretches	score	coaches	throws	field

Use the clues in the soccer balls to name a word from the box.

score

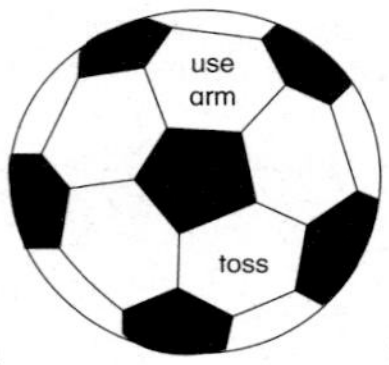

throws

touch

coaches

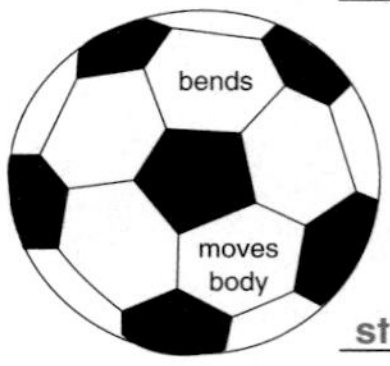

stretches

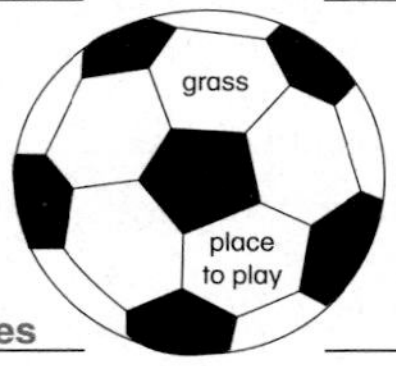

field

At Home: Have children use the vocabulary words to write stories about games they have seen or played. Invite them to draw pictures illustrating their story.

Name ____________________ Date ________ **Extend 179**

Story Comprehension

Sample answers are shown.

Write a sentence to answer the questions.

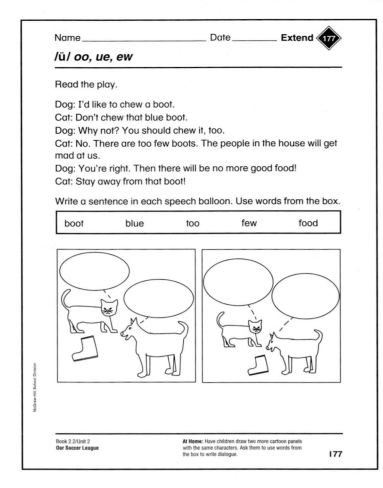

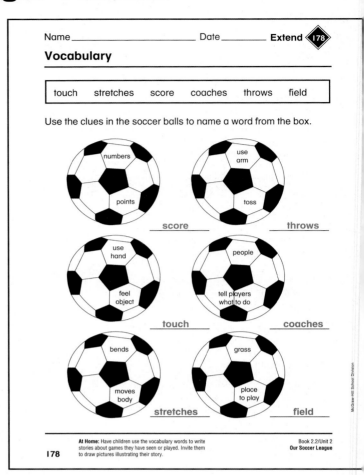

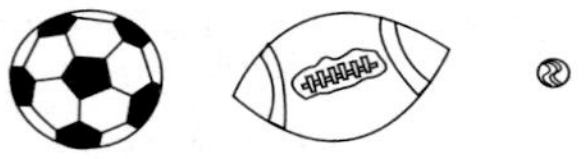

1. What if a soccer ball were the size of a marble? Would it be easy or hard to play soccer with such a small ball?
   It would be hard to play soccer with such a small ball.
2. What if a soccer ball were shaped like a football? Would it be easy or hard to play soccer with a differently shaped ball?
   It would be hard to play soccer with a football.
3. What if there were only two people on each team? Could soccer still be played? How?
   You could play soccer with two people if the two people took turns trying to make a goal and being the goalie.
4. What would happen if it started to rain or snow during the game? Write what you think would happen.
   If it rained or snowed during the game, the field would be slippery.
5. Would you like to be a goalie? Why or why not?
   I would like to be goalie because I like to stop the ball from going in the net.
6. What if there were no coaches? Write what you think would happen during a game.
   If there were no coaches, the players might lose the game.

At Home: Have children make a poster advertising a soccer game. Ask them to make up names for teams, and to include the place, time, date, and fun facts about the players.

Name ____________________ Date ________ **Extend 180**

Read a Newsletter

Read the newsletter. Write a word or words to complete the article. Illustrate the newsletter. **Sample answers given.**

Banner: **Barnhart Elementary** School Newsletter

Date: **November, 2000**

Headine: **Barnhart Tigers** Win Again!

By-line: by **June Moon**

Article: Last Saturday, the **Barnhart Tigers** soccer team beat the **Hollyville Heroes**. The score was **3 to 2**. It was a very exciting game! In the beginning, the goalie of the **Tigers** blocked two kicks. People **were cheering** for the **Tigers**. Then the **Heroes** scored two goals in a row. It looked bad for the **Tigers**, until they **scored** three goals and **won the game**.

At Home: Invite children to create a newsletter about themselves. Ask them to illustrate their pages, and to interview friends and family members for quotes about themselves to include in the newsletter.

Name____________________ Date________ **Extend 181**

/ü/ *oo, ue, ew*

boot	boom	too	blue	few

Look at the code. Read each riddle. Use the code and the riddle to write a word from the box on each line.

CODE

f: ● l: (triangle with lines)
m: ⊜ u: (triangle with dot)
o: ◈ w: ▦
t: ◆ b: ■
e: ▲

1. We lost the game because our team only scored a ● ▲ ▦ points. few

2. When you want to go with us, you say, "Me, ◆ ◈ ◈ !" too

3. A hard kick causes a soccer ball to go ■ ◈ ◈ ⊜. boom

Spell **blue** in code. Write a riddle to go with your code for someone else to solve.

____

____

MY RIDDLE

____

At Home: Brainstorm more words spelled with *oo, ue,* or *ew* with children. Have them make up a code and use the words in secret messages.

Name____________________ Date________ **Extend 182**

/ü/ oo, ue; /ôr/ or, ore

boot	for	score	blue	boom	too

Write a sentence about each picture. Use one word from the box in each sentence. Answers: Sample sentences are given.

1.  **2.**  **3.** 

4.  **5.** 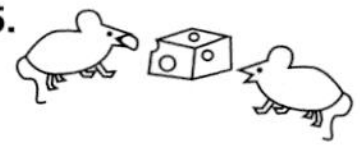 **6.** 

1. This present is for you.
2. The score is 44 to 23.
3. The blocks went boom.
4. The boot fell out of the box.
5. May I have some cheese too?
6. The sky is blue today.

At Home: Have children make a crossword puzzle for the words in the box. Ask them to write clues for each word. Suggest that they use the sentences they wrote to help them.

Name____________________ Date________ **Extend 183**

Sequence of Events

Draw the missing scenes. Write a sentence that tells what is happening in your picture. Answers will vary. Accept any scenes that could occur in the sequence.

First, we stretch. ____________

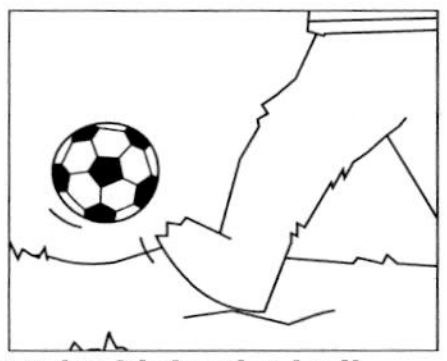

Next, he kicks the ball. ____________

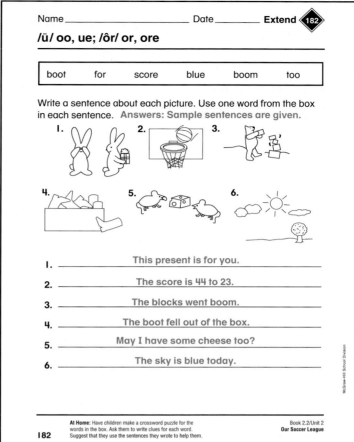

The Bears are going to score! ____________

At Home: Have children make little cartoon books showing the sequence of events of their favorite game or hobby. Each page can be labeled and numbered to show the order of what happens.

Name____________________ Date________ **Extend 184**

Context Clues

Write new sentences using each of the underlined words or phrases in the story.

Teams	1st half	2nd half	Final
Bears	1	0	1
Tigers	0	1	1

What an exciting game! In the first half, the Bears charge to the goal. They run so fast! Then there is a kick to the goal. Barney Bear boots the ball through the goal. The goalie, Tina Tiger, makes a save. There is no point scored this time. Then the Tigers kick the ball out-of-bounds. The Bears get to throw it back in to the field. Then Barney scores. In the end, the Tigers tie the game.

Answers will vary. Look for sentences that use the underlined words or phrases correctly.

____

____

____

At Home: Brainstorm a list of words used in a sport, such as *base hit, shortstop,* and *foul* used in baseball. Have children use the words to write a short story about the game.

Name ______________________ Date __________ LEARN Grammar 135

I and *Me*, *We* and *Us*

- Use *I* in the subject part of a sentence.
- Use *me* in the predicate part.
- Name yourself last when talking about yourself and another person.

  Kira and I are in a show.

  Dad waves to Kira and me.

Write *I* or *me* to complete each sentence.

1. Kira and __I__ sing in the show.
2. My teacher helps __me__ with the words.
3. Mom helps __me__ with the tune.
4. Kira and __I__ practice.
5. Kira and __I__ are ready!

Extension: Have children write the completed sentences.

Name ______________________ Date __________ LEARN AND PRACTICE Grammar 136

Writing *I* and *Me*, *We* and *Us*

- Use *we* and *us* when you talk about yourself and another person.
- Use *we* in the subject part of a sentence.
- Use *us* in the predicate part.

  We like the children. They like John and **me**. They like **us**.

Replace the underlined words with *we* or *us*.
Write the sentence.

1. John and I go to the clubhouse.
   We go to the clubhouse.
2. Rose invites John and me inside.
   Rose invites us inside.
3. Mark gives John and me juice.
   Mark gives us juice.
4. John and I play with Mark.
   We play with Mark.
5. Rose smiles at John and me.
   Rose smiles at us.

Extension: Have the children identify the underlined words as the subject or predicate part of the sentence.

Name ______________________ Date __________ REVIEW AND PRACTICE Grammar 137

Using *I* and *Me*, *We* and *Us*

- Use *I* in the subject part and *me* in the predicate part of a sentence.
- Name yourself last when talking about yourself and another person.
- Use *we* and *us* when you talk about yourself and another person.
- Use *we* in the subject part and *us* in the predicate part of a sentence.

Write the pronoun that completes each sentence. Write the sentences.

1. Aunt Penny and __I__ have fun.
   Aunt Penny and I have fun.
2. "Please take __us__ to the mall," I said to Mom.
   "Please take us to the mall," I said to Mom.
3. "Please take __us__ to the circus," my brother and I said to Aunt Penny.
   "Please take us to the circus," my brother and I said to Aunt Penny.
4. __We__ are very happy to see Aunt Penny.
   We are very happy to see Aunt Penny.
5. "Aunt Penny will take __us__ to a movie," my brother and I said.
   "Aunt Penny will take us to a movie," my brother and I said.

Extension: Have children perform actions such as handing a pencil to one another. Then the receiver describes the action using *I, me, we,* and *us.*

Name ______________________ Date __________ MECHANICS Grammar 138

Pronoun *I*

- The pronoun *I* is always a capital letter.

  I will go home soon.

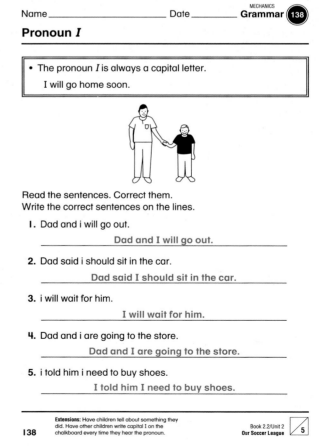

Read the sentences. Correct them.
Write the correct sentences on the lines.

1. Dad and i will go out.
   Dad and I will go out.
2. Dad said i should sit in the car.
   Dad said I should sit in the car.
3. i will wait for him.
   I will wait for him.
4. Dad and i are going to the store.
   Dad and I are going to the store.
5. i told him i need to buy shoes.
   I told him I need to buy shoes.

Extensions: Have children tell about something they did. Have other children write capital I on the chalkboard every time they hear the pronoun.

Name____________________ Date_________ TEST Grammar 139

I and *Me, We* and *Us*

Which pronoun fits the sentence? Mark your answer.

1. _____ went to the doctor.
   - ⓐ Me
   - ⓑ I (marked)
   - ⓒ Us
2. The doctor looked _____ over.
   - ⓐ me (marked)
   - ⓑ we
   - ⓒ I
3. _____ went home.
   - ⓐ Us
   - ⓑ We (marked)
   - ⓒ Me
4. The dog was glad to see _____.
   - ⓐ we
   - ⓑ us (marked)
   - ⓒ I
5. The dog and _____ went to the park.
   - ⓐ me
   - ⓑ I (marked)
   - ⓒ we

Name____________________ Date_________ MORE PRACTICE Grammar 140

Pronouns *I, Me, We, Us*

- Use *I* and *we* in the subject part of a sentence.
- Use *me* and *us* in the predicate part.
- Use *we* and *us* when you talk about yourself and another person.

Read each sentence. Correct it. Write the correct sentence.

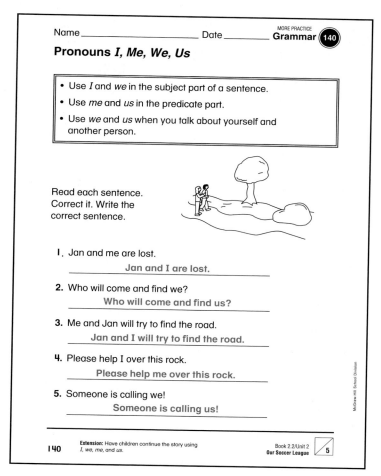

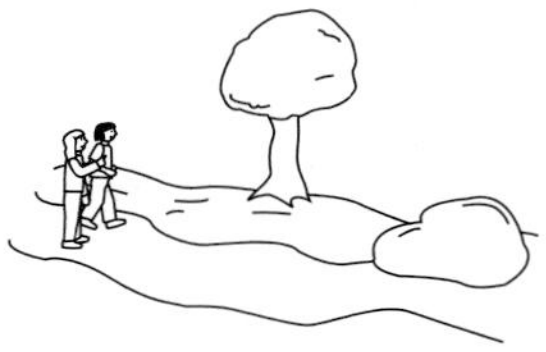

1. Jan and me are lost.
   Jan and I are lost.
2. Who will come and find we?
   Who will come and find us?
3. Me and Jan will try to find the road.
   Jan and I will try to find the road.
4. Please help I over this rock.
   Please help me over this rock.
5. Someone is calling we!
   Someone is calling us!

Extension: Have children continue the story using *I, we, me,* and *us.*

Name __________ Date ______ PRETEST SPELLING 135

Words with Blends *bl*, *br*, *dr*, *pl*, and *tr*

Pretest Directions
Fold back your paper along the dotted line. Use the blanks to write each word as it is said to you. When you finish the test, unfold the paper and correct any spelling mistakes. Practice those words for the Posttest.

To Parents,
Here are the results of your child's weekly spelling Pretest. You can help your child study for the Posttest by following these simple steps for each word on the word list:

1. Read the word to your child.
2. Have your child write the word, saying each letter as it is written.
3. Say each letter of the word as your child checks the spelling.
4. If a mistake has been made, have your child read each letter of the correctly spelled word aloud and then repeat steps 1–3.

1. ______ 1. try
2. ______ 2. blue
3. ______ 3. play
4. ______ 4. brag
5. ______ 5. drag
6. ______ 6. brass
7. ______ 7. plan
8. ______ 8. blow
9. ______ 9. draw
10. ______ 10. trap

Challenge Words

______ coaches
______ field
______ score
______ stretches
______ throws

Name __________ Date ______ AT-HOME WORD STUDY SPELLING 136

Words with Blends

Using the Word Study Steps

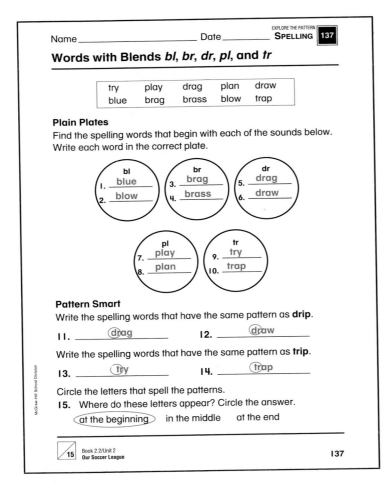

1. LOOK at the word.
2. SAY the word aloud.
3. STUDY the letters in the word.
4. WRITE the word.
5. CHECK the word.
   Did you spell the word right?
   If not, go back to step 1.

Spelling Tip
When a one- syllable word ends in one vowel followed by one consonant, double the consonant before adding an ending that begins with a vowel.
brag + ing = bragging
drag + ed = dragged

Word Scramble
Unscramble each set of letters to make a spelling word.

1. uelb blue
2. wrad draw
3. layp play
4. prat trap
5. grab brag
6. rty try
7. srabs brass
8. grad drag
9. wolb blow
10. nlap plan

To Parents or Helpers:
Using the Word Study Steps above as your child comes across any new words will help him or her spell well. Review the steps as you both go over this week's spelling words.
Go over the Spelling Tip with your child. Ask your child to find other new one syllable words that double the final consonant before adding an ending that begins with a vowel.
Help your child unscramble the letters to spell words.

Name __________ Date ______ EXPLORE THE PATTERN SPELLING 137

Words with Blends *bl*, *br*, *dr*, *pl*, and *tr*

try	play	drag	plan	draw
blue	brag	brass	blow	trap

Plain Plates
Find the spelling words that begin with each of the sounds below. Write each word in the correct plate.

bl: 1. blue 2. blow
br: 3. brag 4. brass
dr: 5. drag 6. draw
pl: 7. play 8. plan
tr: 9. try 10. trap

Pattern Smart
Write the spelling words that have the same pattern as **drip**.

11. drag 12. draw

Write the spelling words that have the same pattern as **trip**.

13. try 14. trap

Circle the letters that spell the patterns.

15. Where do these letters appear? Circle the answer.
at the beginning (circled) in the middle at the end

Name __________ Date ______ PRACTICE AND EXTEND SPELLING 138

Words with Blends *bl*, *br*, *dr*, *pl*, and *tr*

try	play	drag	plan	draw
blue	brag	brass	blow	trap

Use a spelling word to complete each sentence.

1. The school bell was made of brass.
2. I like to play with my dog.
3. Always try to spell words right.
4. A strong wind began to blow across the street.
5. Carl is wearing a blue shirt today.
6. Draw a circle around the word *tray*.

Word Building
Be a word builder. Double the consonant and add *-ing* to make new words.
Example: flip + p + ing = flipping

7. brag + g + ing = bragging
8. drag + g + ing = dragging
9. plan + n + ing = planning
10. trap + p + ing = trapping

Challenge Extension: Have students write riddles using the words. They may exchange with a partner to answer the riddles.

Name________________________ Date__________ PROOFREAD AND WRITE SPELLING 139

Words with Blends *bl*, *br*, *dr*, *pl*, and *tr*

Proofreading Activity

There are six spelling mistakes in the paragraph below. Circle each misspelled word. Write the words correctly on the lines below.

Jody liked to drawe. She would plen every picture and trye to make it beautiful. One day I asked her to playe outside, but Jody wanted to color a new picture. Nothing I said could dragg her away from her picture. She colored some cats bright blu. I said, "Cats aren't that color." She said, "I know, but aren't they beautiful?"

1. draw 2. plan 3. try
4. play 5. drag 6. blue

Writing Activity

Make up song titles for silly songs. Use four spelling words in your titles. Circle the words you use.

____
____
____
____
____

Name________________________ Date__________ POSTTEST SPELLING 140

Words with Blends *bl*, *br*, *dr*, *pl*, and *tr*

Look at the words in each set. One word in each set is spelled correctly. Use a pencil to color in the circle in front of that word. Before you begin, look at the sample sets of words. Sample A has been done for you. Do Sample B by yourself. When you are sure you know what to do, you may go on with the rest of the page.

Sample A
- Ⓐ onlee
- Ⓑ onley
- ● only (C)
- Ⓓ onely

Sample B
- Ⓔ cowver
- ● cover (F)
- Ⓖ cuver
- Ⓗ coaver

1. Ⓐ blu ● (B) blue Ⓒ bule Ⓓ bleu
2. Ⓔ blou Ⓕ bloe Ⓖ bolw ● (H) blow
3. Ⓐ brage Ⓑ barg ● (C) brag Ⓓ bragg
4. ● (E) brass Ⓕ bruss Ⓖ brase Ⓗ brasse
5. ● (A) drag Ⓑ drage Ⓒ darg Ⓓ dragg
6. Ⓔ darw ● (F) draw Ⓖ drwe Ⓗ drawe
7. Ⓐ pley Ⓑ paly ● (C) play Ⓓ playe
8. Ⓔ plann Ⓕ paln Ⓖ plen ● (H) plan
9. Ⓐ trie Ⓑ tyr ● (C) try Ⓓ trye
10. ● (E) trap Ⓕ trape Ⓖ trp Ⓗ trappe

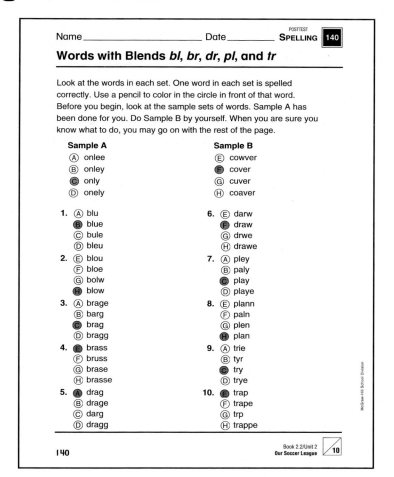

The Wednesday Surprise • PRACTICE

Name ________________ Date ________ **Practice 185**

/ər/ er; /ən/ en; /əl/ le

Write the word from the box that completes each sentence.

dinner	candle	wiggle	handle
oven	water	happen	mother

1. We had soup for ___dinner___.
2. We put one red ___candle___ on Billy's cake.
3. Be careful! The ___oven___ is hot.
4. The coat belonged to my ___mother___.
5. Dad washed the dishes in warm ___water___.
6. I can ___wiggle___ like a snake.
7. Anything can ___happen___!
8. The ___handle___ to the teapot broke.

At Home: Ask children to suggest a rhyming word for one of the words they wrote.

Name ________________ Date ________ **Practice 186**

Vocabulary

Write the words from the box to finish the letter.

chance	**favorite**	**heavy**	**nervous**	**office**	**wrapped**

Dear Pete,

I'm sitting in my dad's ___office___. He is talking on the phone. I want to tell you about the present I just got. It was ___wrapped___ in red paper. I hoped it was my ___favorite___ book about bears. I thought there was a ___chance___ that it was. When I picked it up, it was ___heavy___. I was ___nervous___ when I opened it. Guess what! It wasn't the book about bears. It was a book about the sky! You'll have to see it when you visit.

Your friend,

Doug

At Home: Have children write a new sentence for each of the words.

MOM'S SECRET

"How did that happen?" I asked.
"When I came to this country I did not know English. I can speak it now. But I never had the chance to learn how to read it."
"I will help you learn now," I said.
And together we sat down to read a book.

At Home: Discuss with children the importance of reading. Why is it important to read? What are some of the children's favorite books?

It all began when I was seven. I was at the dinner table reading a heavy book.
"Put the book away," Mom said.
"But it is my favorite book," I said. "Would you like to see it?"
"It is time for dinner now," she said.

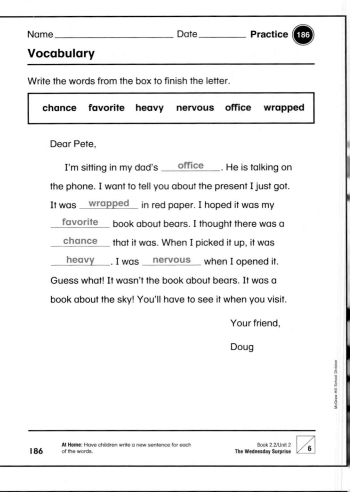

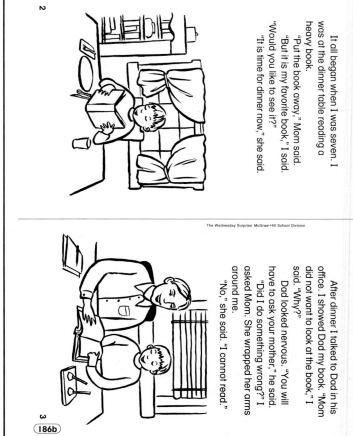

After dinner I talked to Dad in his office. I showed Dad my book. "Mom did not want to look at the book," I said. "Why?"
Dad looked nervous. "You will have to ask your mother," he said.
"Did I do something wrong?" I asked Mom. She wrapped her arms around me.
"No," she said. "I cannot read."

The Wednesday Surprise • PRACTICE

Name____________________ Date________ **Practice 187**

Story Comprehension

Think about "The Wednesday Surprise." Finish each sentence by underlining the answer.

1. Grandma takes care of Anna _______.
   a. every day
   b. only on Wednesdays
2. Anna's dad is a _______.
   a. truck driver
   b. pilot
3. Anna and Grandma want to surprise Dad because _______.
   a. it is his birthday
   b. he got a new job
4. Anna and Grandma have worked together to _______.
   a. teach Anna how to read
   b. teach Grandma how to read
5. Sam and Anna decorate the house because _______.
   a. it is Dad's birthday
   b. it is a holiday
6. Grandma doesn't have seconds because _______.
   a. she is thinking about reading
   b. she is full
7. Anna is nervous at the party because _______.
   a. she wants Grandma to read well
   b. she wants to read well
8. Dad is crying at the end of the story because _______.
   a. he is sad that his surprise is over
   b. Grandma can read

At Home: Have children draw a picture of their favorite part of the story. Then ask them to write a sentence about it.

Name____________________ Date________ **Practice 188**

Use a Calendar

A **calendar** tells you the month and the day.

NOVEMBER

Sun	Mon	Tues	Wed	Thurs	Fri	Sat
					1	2
3	4	5 Soccer	6	7	8	9
10	11	12 Soccer	13	14	15	16
17	18	19 Soccer	20	21	22	23
24	25	26 Soccer	27	28 Thanksgiving	29	30

Follow the instructions below.

1. The days of the week go in the boxes along the top. Start with Sunday in the first box. What day did you put in the last box? Saturday
2. Start the calendar with November 1 on a Friday. Then put a number in every box. There are thirty days in November. What day of the week is the 25th day? Monday
3. Put Thanksgiving in the box for the fourth Thursday of the month. What day of the month is that? 28
4. You have soccer practice every Tuesday. Mark that on the calendar. What dates did you mark? 5, 12, 19, 26

At Home: Have children mark November 17-23 with an **X** and write **vacation** through those days.

Name____________________ Date________ **Practice 189**

/ər/ er; /ən/ en; /əl/ le

Write the missing letters in each word. Read the word.

er	en	le

1. 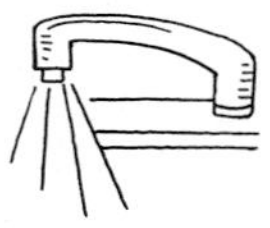
   wat er
2. 
   cand le
3. 
   op en
4. 
   teach er
5. 
   app le
6. 
   elev en

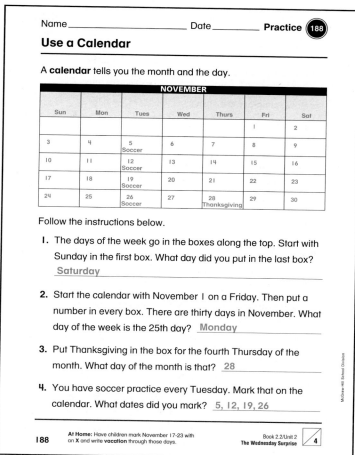

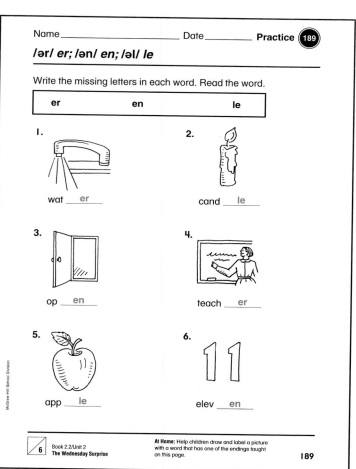

At Home: Help children draw and label a picture with a word that has one of the endings taught on this page.

Name____________________ Date________ **Practice 190**

/ər/, /ən/, /əl/; /ü/; /ôr/; /îr/

Read the sentence. Circle the word that completes the sentence. Then write the word on the line.

1. I wore my boots today.
   rooms (boots) shoot
2. Have I met you before ?
   tore more (before)
3. I pour water into the glass.
   either (water) shatter
4. The horse is in the stable .
   apple candle (stable)
5. I use my fork to pick up the peas.
   (fork) horn born
6. Everything he said is true .
   blue (true) glue
7. He is seven years old.
   tears near (years)
8. We had chicken for dinner.
   (chicken) taken even

At Home: Have children develop one of the sentences into a one-paragraph story.

Name________________ Date________ **Practice 191**

Summarize

A summary is a review of the most important points of a story.

Read each story. Give each story a title. Then write a one-sentence **summary** of each story. **Answers may vary.**

Title: Planning a Garden

Mr. Green and Mrs. Lopez wanted to plant a garden for our town. They invited people to a meeting. Many people came to talk about the garden. Mr. Wong said he had an empty lot. Anna Lee said she had tools. Everyone agreed to come on Saturday to begin work on a garden.

Summary: People in our town planned to make a garden.

Title: Making the Garden

On Saturday, five families came to the lot. We all worked hard. First we took away the trash. Then we dug out the rocks. On Sunday, more people came. They helped to plant seeds. Everyone worked together to make a town garden!

Summary: Many families worked to make a town garden.

At Home: After reading the story "The Wednesday Surprise," ask children to retell it in one or two sentences.

Name________________ Date________ **Practice 192**

Suffixes

The suffixes **-ly** and **-ful** change the meaning of the base word to which they are added. The suffix **-ly** means "in the way of." The suffix **-ful** means "full of."

Write a word that means the same as the group of words. Your new word will end in **-ly** or **-ful.**

1. full of power — powerful

2. in a beautiful way — beautifully

3. in a cold way — coldly

4. in a different way — differently

5. full of thanks — thankful

6. in a soft way — softly

7. in a bright way — brightly

8. full of good cheer — cheerful

Write two sentences using some of the new words. **Answers will vary.**

9. ________________

10. ________________

At Home: Ask children to make a list of other words ending in **-ful** and **-ly**.

Name________________________ Date__________ **Reteach 185**

/ər/ er; /ən/ en; /əl/ le

Listen for the sounds in each word.
/ər/ as in bett**er**
/ən/ as in ev**en**
/əl/ as in app**le**

Finish the story by writing words that have the **/ər/**, **/ən/**, or **/əl/** sound in them.

My Brother's Birthday

1. It was my ___brother's___ birthday. (brother's aunt's)
2. We had cake after ___dinner___. (lunch dinner)
3. The cake had some ___candles___ on it. (candles icing)
4. My brother leaned over to blow them out. I saw what was about to ___happen___. (happen fall)
5. He spilled his glass of ___water___. (water milk)
6. I tried not to ___giggle___. (laugh giggle)

I helped him clean up.

Then I said, "Happy Birthday!"

At Home: Have children read the words they wrote aloud.

Name________________________ Date__________ **Reteach 186**

Vocabulary

Choose a word from the box to finish each sentence.
Write the word on the line.

chance	favorite	heavy	nervous	office	wrapped

1. Jeff was ___nervous___ about throwing the ball.
2. Mrs. Warner's ___office___ was on the top floor.
3. This big box of books is really ___heavy___.
4. Kurt had a ___chance___ to be in a TV show.
5. The gifts were ___wrapped___ with paper and ribbon.
6. Missy is my ___favorite___ kitty.

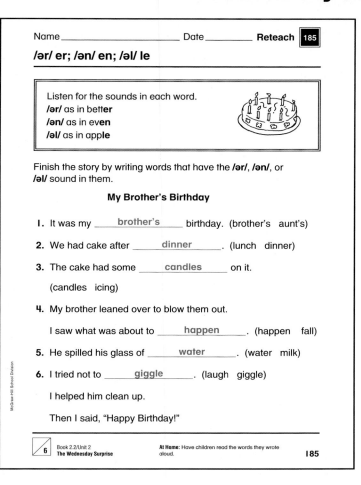

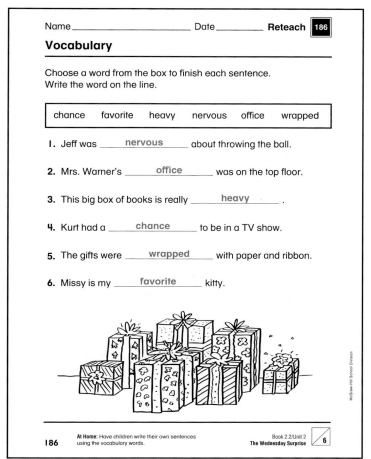

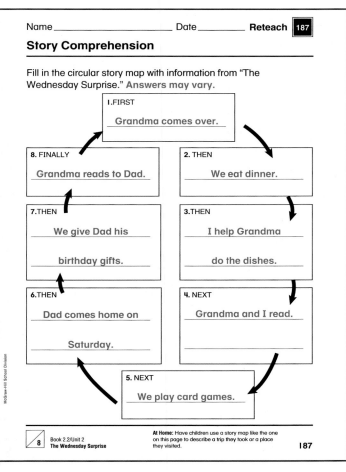

At Home: Have children write their own sentences using the vocabulary words.

Name________________________ Date__________ **Reteach 187**

Story Comprehension

Fill in the circular story map with information from "The Wednesday Surprise." **Answers may vary.**

1. FIRST: Grandma comes over.
2. THEN: We eat dinner.
3. THEN: I help Grandma do the dishes.
4. NEXT: Grandma and I read.
5. NEXT: We play card games.
6. THEN: Dad comes home on Saturday.
7. THEN: We give Dad his birthday gifts.
8. FINALLY: Grandma reads to Dad.

At Home: Have children use a story map like the one on this page to describe a trip they took or a place they visited.

Name________________________ Date__________ **Reteach 188**

Use a Calendar

A **calendar** shows you the days of the year.

Study the calendar below. It shows only two weeks of a month. Notice the days of the week along the top.

JULY

Sun	Mon	Tues	Wed	Thurs	Fri	Sat
		1	2 vacation begins	3	4 Independence Day	5
6	7 Kate comes for a visit	8 piano lesson	9 doctor's appointment	10	11	12

Complete the questions using the calendar.

1. How many weeks does this calendar show you? ___2___
2. What month is this calendar showing you? ___July___
3. What holiday is on July 4th? ___Independence Day___
4. What happens on July 7th? ___Kate comes for a visit___
5. Why don't the first Sunday and Monday on this calendar have numbers on them? ___they are not part of this month___

At Home: Challenge children to look at a calendar of the year and identify the days of the week that popular holidays fall on.

Name ____________ Date ________ **Reteach 189**

/ər/ er; /ən/ en; /əl/ le

What does **/ər/** sound like?	**-er** as in riv**er**
What does **/ən/** sound like?	**-en** as in list**en**
What does **/əl/** sound like?	**-le** as in tab**le**

Read each group of words. Circle the words that have the same ending as the first word.

1. brother helper, often, dribble, father

2. water given, better, apple, river

3. seven given, helper, open, often

4. candle little, apple, father, able

At Home: Have children find words ending in **er, en,** and **le** in a magazine and read them aloud.

Name ____________ Date ________ **Reteach 190**

/ər/, /ən/, /əl/; /ü/; /ôr/, /îr/

seven eleven apples candles

seven candles

Circle the words that tell about the picture.
Then write the two words that tell about the picture.

1. 

morning popcorn handle table

popcorn on the table

2. 

water daughter boot boom

water in the boot

3. 

glue true shore store

glue in the store

4. 

tears ears corn shore

tears by the shore

At Home: Have children write a short story about one of the pictures above.

Name ____________ Date ________ **Reteach 191**

Summarize

Remember: A **summary** is a short way to tell what happened.

Read the story.

Chester Greenwood liked to ice-skate. But his ears got so cold they turned blue. To protect his ears, he bent wire to make 2 loops. His grandmother covered the loops with warm cloth. His invention worked. His ears were warm! That was over 100 years ago. Today, many people wear his invention—earmuffs.

Read the sentences. Circle the important idea. Underline the summary statement.

Chester's ears got cold when he skated.

Chester Greenwood invented earmuffs.

The earmuffs kept Chester's ears warm.

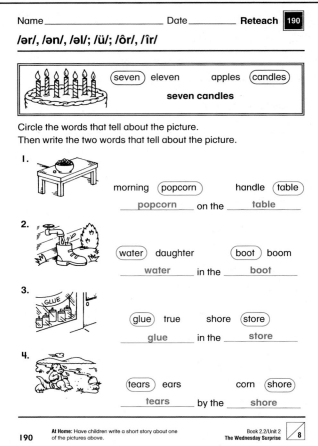

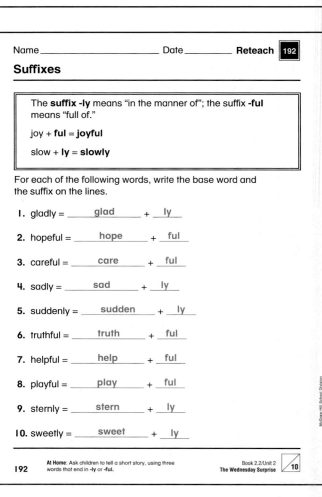

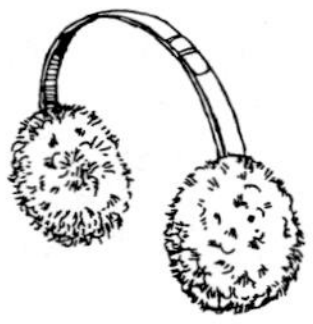

At Home: Have children write a short summary of "The Wednesday Surprise."

Name ____________ Date ________ **Reteach 192**

Suffixes

The **suffix -ly** means "in the manner of"; the suffix **-ful** means "full of."

joy + **ful** = **joyful**

slow + **ly** = **slowly**

For each of the following words, write the base word and the suffix on the lines.

1. gladly = glad + ly
2. hopeful = hope + ful
3. careful = care + ful
4. sadly = sad + ly
5. suddenly = sudden + ly
6. truthful = truth + ful
7. helpful = help + ful
8. playful = play + ful
9. sternly = stern + ly
10. sweetly = sweet + ly

At Home: Ask children to tell a short story, using three words that end in **-ly** or **-ful.**

Name____________________ Date________ **Extend 185**

/ər/ er; /ən/ en; /əl/ le

brother	dinner	seven	candle	giggle

Write a word from the box that rhymes with the last word in each line of the poem.

Juan's Story

Juan played baseball with his mother. brother

The score was nine to eleven. seven

Who was the winner? dinner

He walked home and turned the door handle. candle

His puppy saw him and began to wiggle. giggle

Write two more sentences for the poem using words from the box below.

happen	water

Answers will vary.

At Home: Have children make up a new story about Juan using words from the boxes.

Name____________________ Date________ **Extend 186**

Vocabulary

chance	favorite	heavy	nervous	office	wrapped

Write sentences to complete the story. Use words from the box.

Answers will vary. First panel may include the words *chance* and *favorite*; second panel may include the words *heavy* and *office*; third panel may include the words *wrapped* and *nervous.*

At Home: Have children draw another cat and mouse cartoon. Ask them to use as many words from the box as possible as they write what the characters say or think.

Name____________________ Date________ **Extend 187**

Story Comprehension

Look for pictures that show students understand the story.

Draw a picture to answer each question about "The Wednesday Surprise."

1. How does Anna feel about Grandma?
2. How does Grandma feel about learning to read?
3. How does Dad feel about his family when he gets home?
4. How does Anna feel right before she gives Dad his surprise?

What would the story be like if Grandma had not learned to read? Write a sentence or two telling what might have happened. Make up a title to go with this story.

Answers will vary.

At Home: Have children draw a picture of a surprise they would like to give someone for their birthday. Ask them to write a sentence or two telling why that person would like the surprise.

Name____________________ Date________ **Extend 188**

Use a Calendar

Anna has a lot to do in March. Fill in the calendar to help Anna remember what to do each day. Write only the words that will remind Anna what she must do.

MARCH

Sunday	Monday	Tuesday	Wednesday	Thursday	Friday	Saturday
			1 Doctor	2	3	4
5	6	7	8	9 party	10	11 Sal's house
12	13	14	15	16	17	18 swim meet
19	20	21 walk dog	22	23	24	25
26	27 book fair	28	29 band practice	30	31	

1. On Wednesday, March 1, Anna goes to the doctor.
2. On Tuesday, March 21, Anna walks Nick's dog.
3. On Thursday , March 9, Anna goes to a party.
4. On Wednesday, March 29, Anna has band practice.
5. On Saturday, March 11, Anna goes to her friend Sal's house.
6. On Monday, March 27, Anna goes to the Book Fair.
7. On Saturday, March 18, Anna has a swim meet.

Answers may vary. Sample answers are shown.

At Home: Have children make a twelve-month calendar, using one page per month. Provide old magazines and catalogues and have children cut out appropriate pictures for each month to illustrate their calendars.

Name ________________________ Date __________ **Extend 189**

/ər/ er; /ən/ en; /əl/ le

another	brother	dinner	either	ever
together	neither	water	happen	seven
forgotten	candle	giggle	settle	table

Write sentences about the picture. Use at least one word from the box in each sentence.

1. Answers will vary. Children should use at least six words from the box.
2. ______________________________
3. ______________________________
4. ______________________________
5. ______________________________
6. ______________________________

At Home: Have children use more words from the box to write a short story about what might happen to the gift-wrapped present and the characters in the scene.

Name ________________________ Date __________ **Extend 190**

/ər/; /ən/; /əl/; /ü/; /ôr/; /îr/

popcorn	Fourth of July	seven	giggle	dinner	water
hear	story	brother	blue	fireworks	Sam

Read the story. Change the underlined words to words from the box. Then rewrite the story so it makes sense.

On <u>Halloween</u>, my <u>sister</u> <u>Sally</u> and I went <u>trick-or-treating</u>. She is only <u>two</u> years old so I had to push her in a stroller. I took a bottle of <u>milk</u> for her to drink. I hoped she would not <u>cry</u>. I did not <u>see</u> any <u>tears</u>. I wore a <u>red</u> tomato costume. We ate a bag of <u>apples</u>. Then we sang a funny <u>song</u>. After that, we went home and ate our <u>lunch</u>.

On the <u>Fourth of July</u>, my <u>brother</u> <u>Sam</u> and I went to the <u>fireworks</u>. He is <u>seven</u> years old. I took a bottle of <u>water</u> for us to drink. I hoped he would not <u>giggle</u>. I did not <u>hear</u> any <u>giggles</u>. I wore a <u>blue</u> shirt. We ate a bag of <u>popcorn</u>. Then we told a funny <u>story</u>. After that, we went home and ate <u>dinner</u>.

At Home: Have children draw a picture to illustrate their new story. Ask them to label the picture with words from the box.

Name ________________________ Date __________ **Extend 191**

Summarize

Read the story. Then write two sentences that summarize the story.

The Biggest Surprise

I never liked surprises. I always liked to know everything that would happen. I was a boy who did not like to be surprised!

Last week, my sister Eve planned a surprise party for my birthday. She invited all my friends. She baked a big cake. She put balloons and party streamers all over the house.

I was not at home when she did this. My mother and I were at the zoo. When I came home, everyone yelled, "Surprise!" At first, I did not know what to do. I was going to get mad at Eve.

Then I saw how happy everyone was. I saw how hard Eve worked. I knew that she really loved me. Do you know what was the biggest surprise of all?

Now I like surprises!

Summary: ______________________________

Answer: A boy who doesn't like surprises is given a surprise party. He finds he likes surprises after all.

Draw a picture to go with the beginning of the story. Then draw a picture to go with the end.

At Home: Have children write a sentence and draw a picture to summarize their day.

Name ________________________ Date __________ **Extend 192**

Suffixes

sternly	carefully	perfectly	beautiful	hopeful	joyful

This story doesn't make sense! Find the word in each underlined sentence that doesn't make sense. Use a word from the box to change the word.

The Reader and Her Teacher

Once there was a girl and a reading teacher. They were practicing for a reading contest. <u>The girl was hoped that she would win first prize.</u> **hopeful** She loved to read.

<u>The reading teacher was kind, but sometimes she spoke stern.</u> **sternly** . <u>She made the reader practice her story until she could read it perfect.</u> **perfectly** <u>The teacher gave the girl a beauty hat to wear.</u> **beautiful** <u>She put it on care.</u> **carefully** At the contest, she won first prize! <u>Her voice was joy as she thanked her teacher.</u> **joyful**

At Home: Have children draw pictures to illustrate the story "The Reader and Her Teacher."

Name ____________________ Date __________ LEARN Grammar 141

Possessive Pronouns

- A **possessive pronoun** takes the place of a possessive noun.
- A possessive pronoun shows who or what owns something.
- *My, your, his,* and *her* are possessive pronouns.

  Is this my hat, your hat, his hat, or her hat?

Read the sentences. Circle the possessive pronoun that belongs in the sentence.

1. We were riding bikes to (**your**, you) house.
2. Amy fell off (she, **her**) bike.
3. Len got off (he, **his**) bike to help her.
4. I got off (I, **my**) bike too.
5. Amy rubbed (**her**, she) arm.
6. Is (**her**, she) arm all right?
7. (I, **My**) arm is fine.
8. (**Your**, you) bike is fine too.
9. Len got back on (he, **his**) bike.
10. I got back on (**my**, I) bike.

Extension: Have children describe things belonging to themselves and to other children using possessive pronouns.

Name ____________________ Date __________ PRACTICE AND LEARN Grammar 142

Writing Possessive Pronouns

- A possessive pronoun shows who or what owns something. Some possessive pronouns are: *its, our, your, their.*

  Our goal is at this end. Their goal is over there.

  Is it your turn? The basket lost its net.

Read the sentences. Underline the possessive pronoun that belongs in the sentence. Then write the sentence.

1. (Our, Us) fish live in a green bowl.
   Our fish live in a green bowl.
2. The fish wiggle (your, their) tails.
   The fish wiggle their tails.
3. One fish is opening (it's, its) mouth.
   One fish is opening its mouth.
4. Tell me, do (your, us) fish do that?
   Tell me, do your fish do that?
5. I feed (our, its) fish every day.
   I feed our fish every day.

Extension: Have children write sentences using the possessive pronouns *its, our, your,* and *their.*

Name ____________________ Date __________ REVIEW AND PRACTICE Grammar 143

Choosing Possessive Pronouns

- A **possessive pronoun** takes the place of a possessive noun.
- A possessive pronoun shows who or what owns something. Some possessive pronouns are *my, your* (singular), *his, her, its, our, your* (plural), *their.*

Read the words on the left. Then circle the words on the right that have the same meaning.

1. cat belonging to you	you cat	**your cat**
2. dog belonging to Pete	he dog	**his dog**
3. cat belonging to the children	**their cat**	they cat
4. mouse belonging to Anna	she mouse	**her mouse**
5. fish belonging to me	**my fish**	me fish
6. horses belonging to you and Ed	you're horses	**your horses**
7. ears belonging to the rabbit	it's ears	**its ears**
8. bird belonging to Jack and me	**our bird**	hour bird

Extension: Have children name objects and their owners. Call on others to supply the correct possessive pronouns.

Name ____________________ Date __________ MECHANICS Grammar 144

Proper Nouns

- A **proper noun** begins with a capital letter.
- The name of a day, month, or holiday begins with a capital letter.

  George's family always celebrates the Fourth of July.

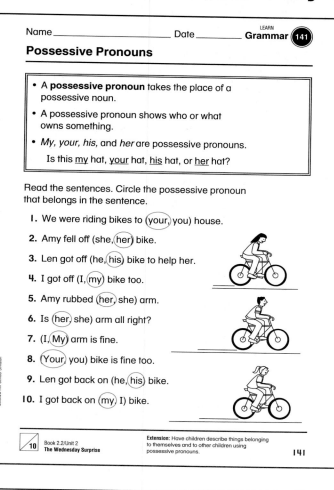

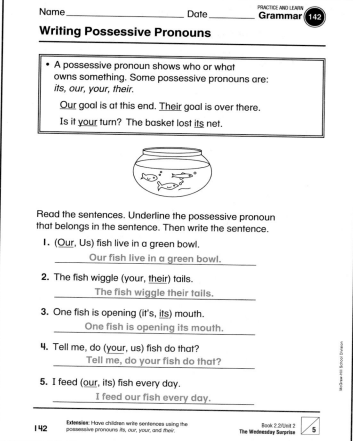

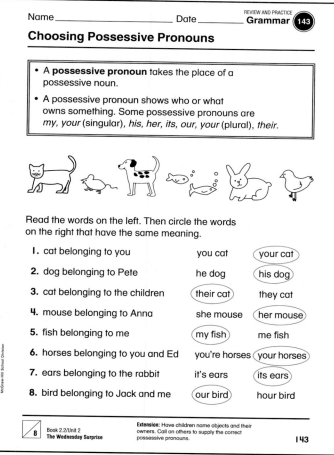

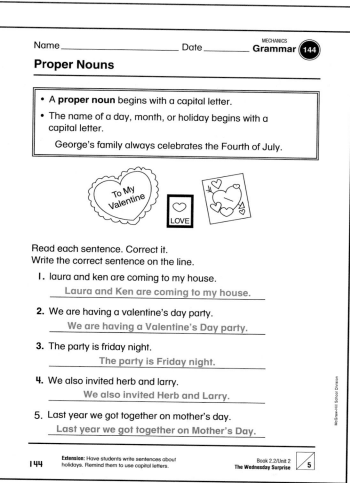

Read each sentence. Correct it.
Write the correct sentence on the line.

1. laura and ken are coming to my house.
   Laura and Ken are coming to my house.
2. We are having a valentine's day party.
   We are having a Valentine's Day party.
3. The party is friday night.
   The party is Friday night.
4. We also invited herb and larry.
   We also invited Herb and Larry.
5. Last year we got together on mother's day.
   Last year we got together on Mother's Day.

Extension: Have students write sentences about holidays. Remind them to use capital letters.

Name ____________ Date ________ TEST Grammar 145

Possessive Pronouns

A. Read the sentences. Underline the possessive pronouns. Write the possessive pronouns on the lines.

1. My cousin tells great jokes. My
2. Your sister is also funny. Your
3. Her stories make me laugh. Her
4. She tells them to our friends. our
5. My brother laughs a lot. My
6. His stories are silly. His
7. Their parties are fun. Their
8. What is your idea? your

B. Read each pair of sentences. Circle the one with the correct pronoun.

9. **a.** When Pam talks, her nose wiggles. (circled)
   b. When Pam talks, she nose wiggles.
10. **c.** If you pet the dog, it tail wags.
    d. If you pet the dog, its tail wags. (circled)

Name ____________ Date ________ MORE PRACTICE Grammar 146

Possessive Pronouns

- A **possessive pronoun** takes the place of a possessive noun.
- A possessive pronoun shows who or what owns something.
- Possessive pronouns include: *my, your, his, its, our, your, their.*

Mechanics
- Begin a sentence with a capital letter.
- End every sentence with a special mark.

Read the sentences aloud. Underline the possessive pronouns. Write the sentences correctly.

1. this is my favorite book
   This is my favorite book.

2. put your pen on the table
   Put your pen on the table.
3. quick, hide their pens
   Quick, hide their pens.

4. take their books home
   Take their books home.
5. place your story on top
   Place your story on top.

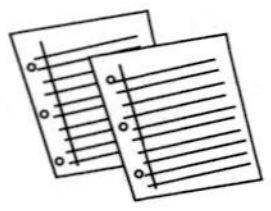

6. who left his bike outside
   Who left his bike outside?

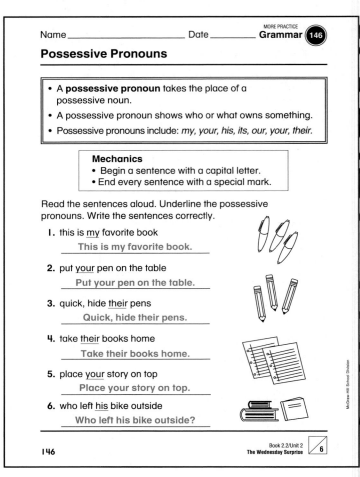

Name ______________________ Date __________ PRETEST SPELLING **141**

Words with Blends *sl*, *sm*, *sp*, *st*, and *sw*

Pretest Directions
Fold back your paper along the dotted line. Use the blanks to write each word as it is said to you. When you finish the test, unfold the paper and correct any spelling mistakes. Practice those words for the Posttest.

1. ________ 1. sweet
2. ________ 2. slide
3. ________ 3. story
4. ________ 4. smart
5. ________ 5. speak
6. ________ 6. start
7. ________ 7. slip
8. ________ 8. spot
9. ________ 9. swim
10. ________ 10. smooth

Challenge Words

________ chance
________ favorite
________ heavy
________ nervous
________ office

To Parents,
Here are the results of your child's weekly spelling Pretest. You can help your child study for the Posttest by following these simple steps for each word on the word list:

1. Read the word to your child.
2. Have your child write the word, saying each letter as it is written.
3. Say each letter of the word as your child checks the spelling.
4. If a mistake has been made, have your child read each letter of the correctly spelled word aloud and then repeat steps 1–3.

Name ______________________ Date __________ AT-HOME WORD STUDY SPELLING **142**

Words with Blends *sl*, *sm*, *sp*, *st*, and *sw*

Using the Word Study Steps

1. LOOK at the word.
2. SAY the word aloud.
3. STUDY the letters in the word.
4. WRITE the word.
5. CHECK the word.
   Did you spell the word right?
   If not, go back to step 1.

Spelling Tip
Use words you know how to spell to help you spell new words. Word beginnings and endings can help.
Example:
star + part = start

Find and Circle
Where are the spelling words?

s	w	e	e	t	a	s	b	s	l	i	d	e	h
l	s	t	o	r	y	p	v	w	s	t	a	r	t
i	s	p	e	a	k	o	g	i	t	s	r	m	o
p	w	s	m	a	r	t	s	m	o	o	t	h	v

To Parents or Helpers:
Using the Word Study Steps above as your child comes across any new words will help him or her spell well. Review the steps as you both go over this week's spelling words.
Go over the Spelling Tip with your child. Help your child spell new words by using words he or she already knows.
Help your child find and circle the spelling words in the puzzle.

Name ______________________ Date __________ EXPLORE THE PATTERN SPELLING **143**

Words with Blends *sl*, *sm*, *sp*, *st*, and *sw*

sweet	story	speak	slip	swim
slide	smart	start	spot	smooth

Find the spelling words that begin with each of the sounds below. Write the words on the lines.

sl
1. slide
2. slip

sm
3. smart
4. smooth

sp
5. speak
6. spot

st
7. story
8. start

sw
9. sweet
10. swim

Pattern Smart
Write the spelling words that have the same pattern as **spin**.

11. speak 12. spot

Write the spelling words that have the same pattern as **sweep**.

13. sweet 14. swim

Circle the letters that spell the patterns.

15. Where do these letters appear? Circle the answer.
at the beginning   in the middle   at the end

Name ______________________ Date __________ PRACTICE AND EXTEND SPELLING **144**

Words with Blends *sl*, *sm*, *sp*, *st*, and *sw*

sweet	story	speak	slip	swim
slide	smart	start	spot	smooth

Write a spelling word to complete each sentence.

1. Joey is a smart student and always makes good grades.
2. Be careful not to slip on the ice.
3. The road was full of bumps, it was not smooth.
4. The candy tastes very sweet.
5. It is time to start the test now.
6. My cat has a black spot at the end of his tail.
7. The teacher read a funny story to the class.

Write a spelling word for each picture.

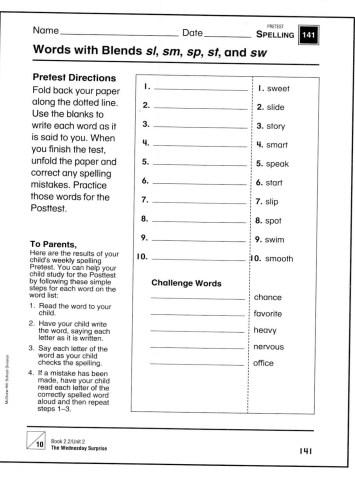

8. slide 9. swim 10. speak

Word Meaning
Be a word builder. Add **ly** to make new words.
Example: nice + ly = nicely

11. sweet + ly = sweetly 12. smooth + ly = smoothly

Write three other words you know that end in **ly**.

13. ________ 14. ________ 15. ________

Challenge Extension: Scramble the letters in the words and write them on the board. Have students unscramble the words.

Name ______________________ Date __________ PROOFREAD AND WRITE SPELLING 145

Words with Blends *sl*, *sm*, *sp*, *st*, and *sw*

Proofreading Activity

There are six spelling mistakes in the paragraph below. Circle each misspelled word. Write the words correctly on the lines below.

A swete little angel lived on a star. The angel knew his star was special. He kept his star very clean so that it would sparkle. The little angel was smarte. He would shine his star until it was smoothe. Then he would sttart to run. Next, he would slipp and sllidde on the star. Living on his special star was fun!

1. sweet 2. smart 3. smooth
4. start 5. slip 6. slide

Writing Activity

Think about your favorite story. Write sentences about why you like that story. Use four spelling words. Circle the words you use.

____
____
____
____
____

Name ______________________ Date __________ POSTTEST SPELLING 146

Words with Blends *sl*, *sm*, *sp*, *st*, and *sw*

Look at the words in each set. One word in each set is spelled correctly. Use a pencil to color in the circle in front of that word. Before you begin, look at the sample sets of words. Sample A has been done for you. Do Sample B by yourself. When you are sure you know what to do, you may go on with the rest of the page.

Sample A
- (A) blu
- (B) bloe
- (C) bulue
- (D) blue ●

Sample B
- (E) grein
- (F) green ●
- (G) grene
- (H) grean

1. (A) spoat (B) spoot (C) spot ● (D) spoth
2. (E) smart ● (F) semart (G) smaart (H) smrt
3. (A) swimm (B) swim ● (C) siwm (D) swime
4. (E) stoorey (F) stry (G) storie (H) story ●
5. (A) slde (B) slied (C) slide ● (D) slidde
6. (E) smooth ● (F) smoothe (G) smoth (H) smothe
7. (A) speke (B) speake (C) spoek (D) speak ●
8. (E) swet (F) sweet ● (G) sweete (H) swte
9. (A) slip ● (B) silip (C) slipe (D) slpe
10. (E) starte (F) strat (G) strt (H) start ●

Fossils Tell of Long Ago • PRACTICE

Name ______________________ Date __________ **Practice 193**

/ou/ *ow, ou* and /oi/ *oi, oy*

Read each word. Then circle the word next to it that has the same vowel sound.

1. found	(howl) toy	**2. how**	soil (mouth)
3. ground	(clown) soil	**4. point**	(loyal) pound
5. mouth	boys (pout)	**6. sound**	noise (shout)
7. soil	(toys) cloud	**8. town**	soil (cloud)
9. boy	ground (soil)	**10. noise**	(broil) clown
11. cow	(now) new	**12. royal**	loan (noise)

At Home: Ask children to think of words that rhyme with words from this page.

Name ______________________ Date __________ **Practice 194**

Vocabulary

Choose a word from the box to finish each sentence. Write the answers in the puzzle.

buried	creatures	fossil	fresh	layers	millions

Across

3. Some fossils are _____ of years old.
millions

5. Many _____ live in that lake.
creatures

6. The cake had three _____.
layers

Down

1. Luis has a _____ of a fish.
fossil

2. My dog _____ a bone in the yard.
buried

4. I like to eat _____ fruit.
fresh

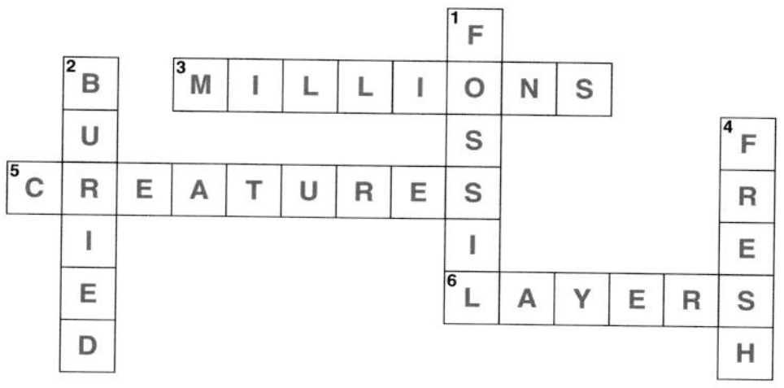

At Home: Have children make a new puzzle with the words in the box.

The Dinosaur

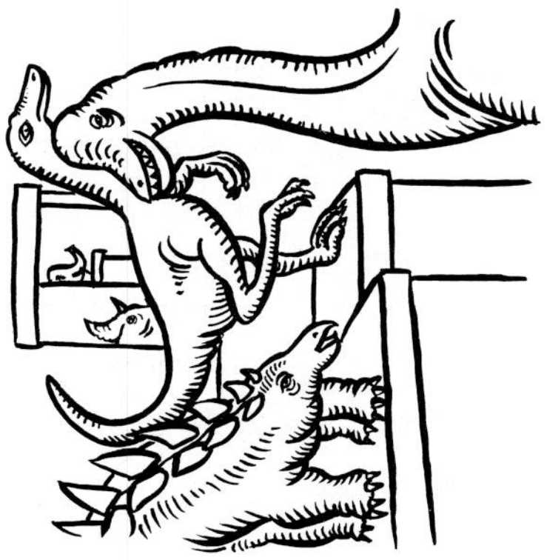

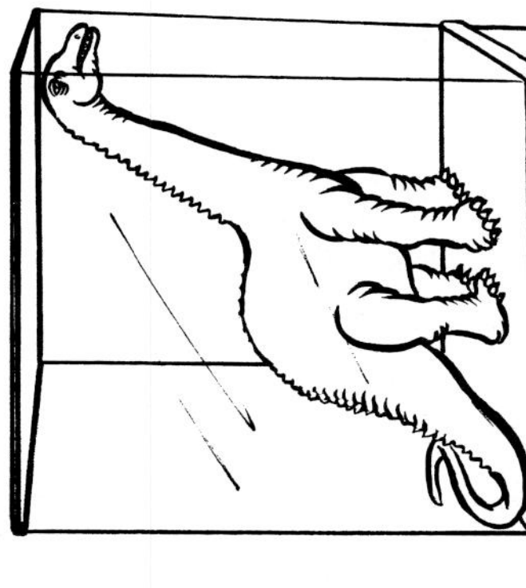

Someone touched the fossil. "Wow!" he shouted. He said it was important.

Now people look at the fossil every day. It is the star of the museum. And it is still as tall as the clouds!

At Home: Have children think about the different kinds of things that might become fossils.

It was one of the creatures from long ago. It ate grass and drank fresh water. It was as tall as the clouds!

But one day it went to sleep on the ground and did not wake up. Instead, it went to sleep forever. Slowly it was covered by soil.

Millions of years went by. It turned to stone. That is what happens when something is buried under many layers of soil. It was a fossil.

Then one day a crowd of people came. They dug down through all that soil and those layers of mud.

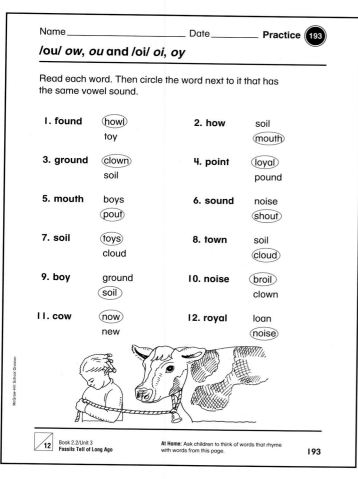

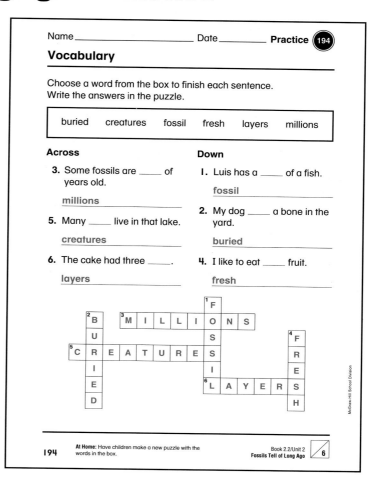

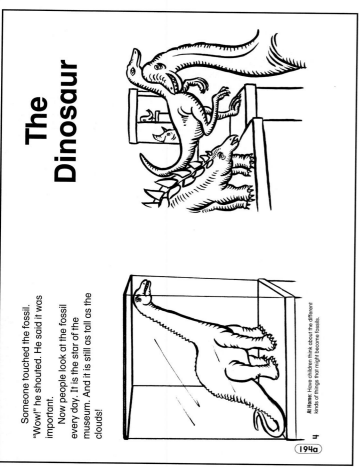

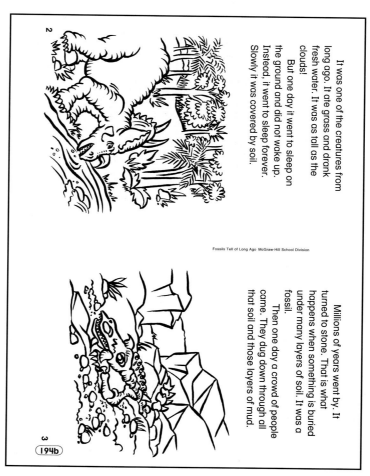

Fossils Tell of Long Ago • PRACTICE

Name ____________ Date ________ **Practice 195**

Story Comprehension

Think about what you learned from the story "Fossils Tell of Long Ago." Then answer these questions.

1. Does every animal turn into a fossil?
   No; most animals simply rot and disappear.
2. What kinds of things can become fossils?
   Possible answers: animals, plants, insects, footprints, fish
3. Name three things we can learn from fossils. Answers will vary. Possible answers: We can learn what ancient animals looked like and where they lived. We can learn where and when there were forests, mountains, and seas. Footprints can tell us how big an animal was, how fast it moved, and how many legs it walked on.

At Home: Have children make a drawing of a fossil that they would like to find.

Name ____________ Date ________ **Practice 196**

Interpret Signs

Find the signs that show the messages listed below. Write the letter of the sign on the line beside each message.

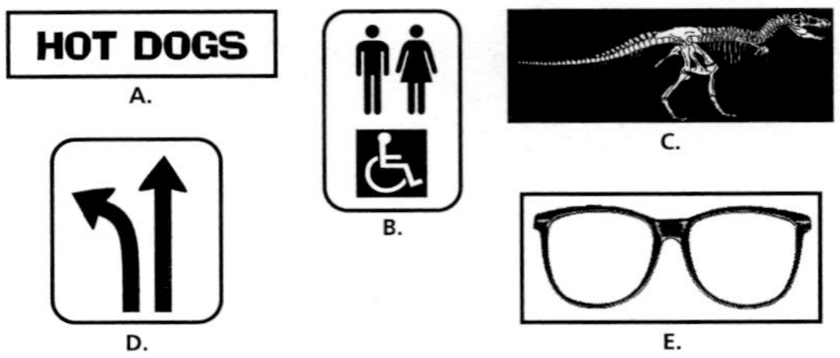

Messages:

1. The road is splitting up ahead to the right and to the left. D
2. Here is the dinosaur museum. C
3. Eyeglasses are sold in this store. E
4. A restroom is here for disabled people. B
5. Hot dogs are for sale. A

At Home: Have children draw pictures of any signs that they see on the way home from school. Explain the meanings of these signs.

Name ____________ Date ________ **Practice 197**

/ou/ *ow, ou* and /oi/ *oi, oy*

Write the words from the list that have the same sound as **ou** in **mouth** or **oi** in **soil**. Then circle the letters in each word that create the sound.

ground	how	south	point
foil	loud	joy	spoil
boy	sound	now	toy
soil	cow	join	found

mouth	soil
1. found	9. point
2. loud	10. foil
3. ground	11. soil
4. sound	12. boy
5. south	13. toy
6. cow	14. join
7. how	15. joy
8. now	16. spoil

At Home: Recite the words, "How now, brown cow?" Encourage children to write a one-line verse using words from the page.

Name ____________ Date ________ **Practice 198**

/ou/; /oi/; /ər/, /ən/, /əl/; /âr/

Choose the word from the box that completes the sentence. Write the word on the line.

careful	sour	frozen	foil	pickle	ground

1. The lake is frozen in the winter.
2. My hat fell to the ground.
3. Would you like a pickle with your sandwich?
4. Be careful not to slip and fall.
5. Wrap your sandwich in foil.
6. The lemon tastes sour.

Now draw a line from the sentence to the word that completes it.

7. The naughty pup was in ________. — point
8. I ________ my shoe under the bed. — smaller
9. This pencil has a sharp ________. — found
10. The duck is ________ than the elephant. — trouble

At Home: Have children write questions using some of the words above.

Name____________________ Date__________ **Practice 199**

Sequence of Events

Read the story and the sentences below it. Write **1**, **2**, **3**, **4**, **5**, or **6** next to each sentence to show the order of the story events.

Drew watched as the big moving van pulled up to his house. He wondered how the movers would get everything packed into the van. First they wrapped all the dishes and packed them into boxes. Then they packed clothes and other things into more boxes.

The next day the movers carried all the furniture to the van. Then they placed all the boxes around the furniture. Drew waved good-bye to the movers as they backed the van out of his driveway.

5 The boxes are placed around the furniture.

4 The furniture is placed in the van.

1 Drew sees the moving van come to his house.

6 Drew waves good-bye to the movers.

2 The movers pack the dishes.

3 The movers pack clothes.

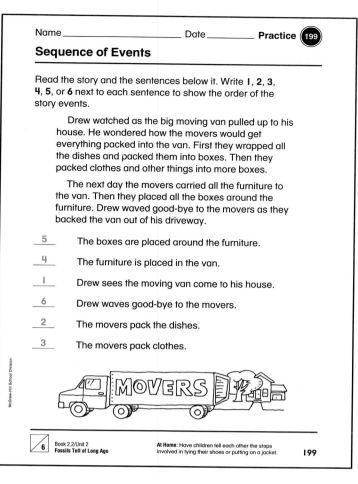

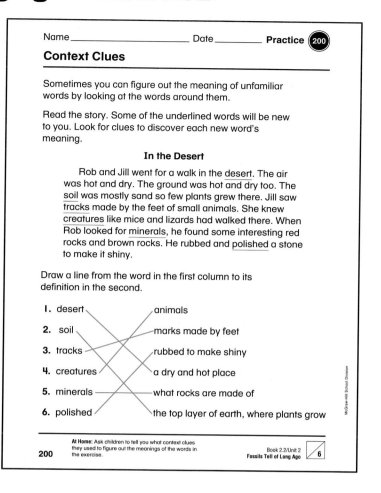

At Home: Have children tell each other the steps involved in tying their shoes or putting on a jacket.

Name____________________ Date__________ **Practice 200**

Context Clues

Sometimes you can figure out the meaning of unfamiliar words by looking at the words around them.

Read the story. Some of the underlined words will be new to you. Look for clues to discover each new word's meaning.

In the Desert

Rob and Jill went for a walk in the desert. The air was hot and dry. The ground was hot and dry too. The soil was mostly sand so few plants grew there. Jill saw tracks made by the feet of small animals. She knew creatures like mice and lizards had walked there. When Rob looked for minerals, he found some interesting red rocks and brown rocks. He rubbed and polished a stone to make it shiny.

Draw a line from the word in the first column to its definition in the second.

1. desert	animals
2. soil	marks made by feet
3. tracks	rubbed to make shiny
4. creatures	a dry and hot place
5. minerals	what rocks are made of
6. polished	the top layer of earth, where plants grow

At Home: Ask children to tell you what context clues they used to figure out the meanings of the words in the exercise.

Name ________________________ Date __________ **Reteach 193**

/ou/ *ow, ou* and /oi/ *oi, oy*

The **/ou/** sound can be spelled in different ways:

c**ow**

m**ou**th

The **/oi/** sound also has different spellings:

s**oi**l

t**oy**

Read the words. Draw a line between words that have the same vowel sound.

1. how — found; soil — toy
2. sound — now; soy — point
3. oil — boy; cow — mouth
4. town — mountain; coil — oyster
5. spoil — joy; hour — ground
6. mouse — how; loyal — boil

At Home: Have children write sentences using two of the words on this page.

Name ________________________ Date __________ **Reteach 194**

Vocabulary

Circle the word that completes each sentence.

buried	creatures	fossil	fresh	layers	millions

1. The fruit at the store is very (fresh creatures).
2. I wonder what kinds of (buried creatures) live in the pond.
3. Some bugs lived (fossil millions) of years ago.
4. I found a small box (buried layers) in the dirt.
5. Andy has a (millions fossil) of a crab.
6. There are four (layers fresh) in that cake.

At Home: Have children write a sentence and draw a picture for one of the circled words.

Name ________________________ Date __________ **Reteach 195**

Story Comprehension

Think about "Fossils Tell of Long Ago." Read the statements below. If a statement is correct, write **true**. If it is not correct, write **false**.

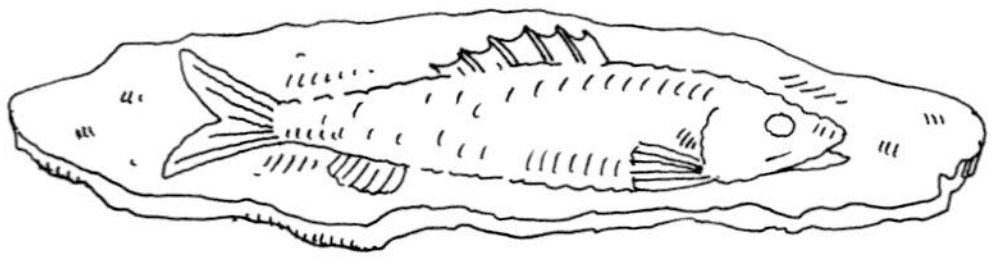

1. Animal bones that have turned to stone are called fossils. true
2. Scientists can't tell how old fossils are. false
3. All fossils of fish are at the bottom of the sea. false
4. Scientists study fossils to learn about life long ago. true
5. A plant cannot become a fossil. false
6. Some fossils are footprints of dinosaurs. true
7. A fossil can show us what an animal ate. true
8. You can see fossils in museums. true

At Home: Have children use clay to make their own fossils of such things as a handprint, a leaf, or a shell.

Name ________________________ Date __________ **Reteach 196**

Interpret Signs

Signs are messages that call our attention to things. Signs can warn us, help us, and point us in the right direction. But signs can mislead us if we don't read them correctly. A good sign gets the message across quickly.

Below are examples of signs you see every day. On the line beside each sign, write what it means. Choose from the list of messages.

Stairway Down This Way		Tickets Sold Here
Deer Crossing	Stop	Don't Walk

Deer Crossing

Stop

Don't Walk

Tickets Sold Here

Stairway Down This Way

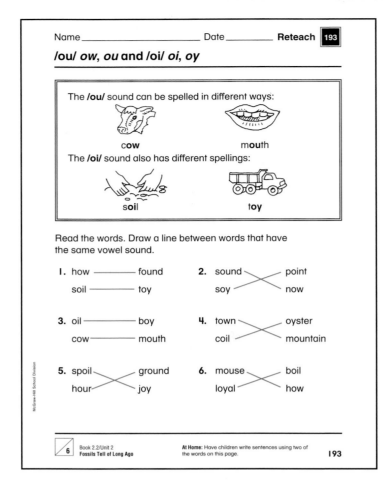

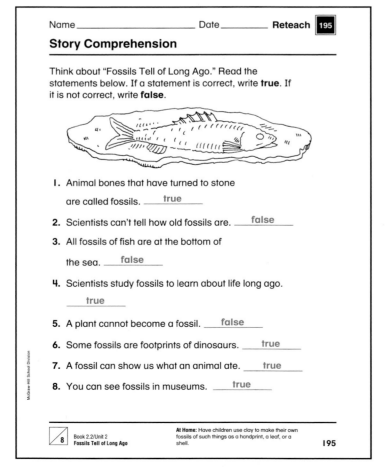

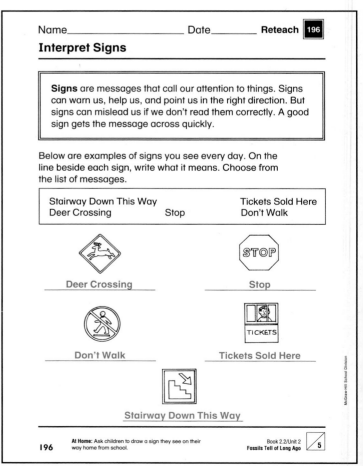

At Home: Ask children to draw a sign they see on their way home from school.

Name____________________ Date_________ **Reteach 197**

/ou/ *ow, ou* and /oi/ *oi, oy*

Read these words aloud. Both of them have the **/ou/** sound.

found **how**

Read these words aloud. Both of them have the **/oi/** sound.

joy **poi**nt

Name each picture. Write letters from the box to complete each word.

ow	ou	oi	oy

1. 
b oy

2. 
c oi ns

3. 
cl ou d

4. 
t oy s

5. 
m ou th

6. 
c ow

At Home: Have children think of two more words that contain these sounds. Ask them to write the words and draw a picture of each one.

Name____________________ Date_________ **Reteach 198**

/ou/; /oi/; /ər/, /ən/, /əl/; /âr/

Is this a **coin** or a **point**?

coin

Write the answer to each question on the line.

1. 
Is this a **cloud** or a **shout**?
cloud

2. 
Is this a **handle** or a **candle**?
candle

3. 
Is this a **letter** or some **pepper**?
letter

4. 
Is this pot **written** or **broken**?
broken

5. 
Is this a **stare** or a **square**?
square

At Home: Have children write sentences using the words **happened, discover, crumble** and **later.**

Name____________________ Date_________ **Reteach 199**

Sequence of Events

Look at the numbers. The numbers show the steps you would follow to make the teddy bear.

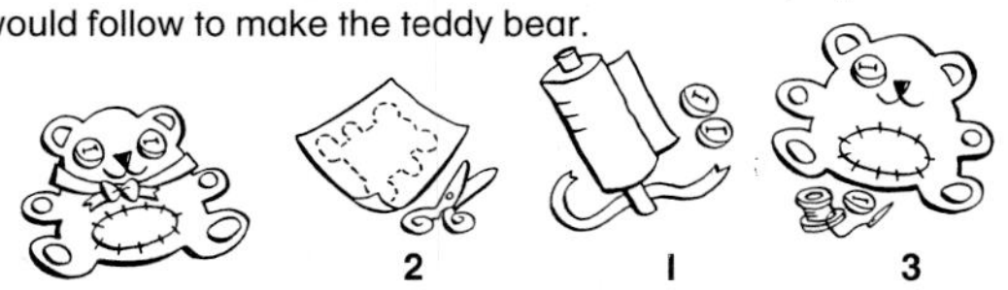

2 1 3

Look at the first picture. Write 1, 2, or 3 under the next three pictures in each row to show the order of the steps.

1. 
1 2 3

2. 

3 2 1

3. 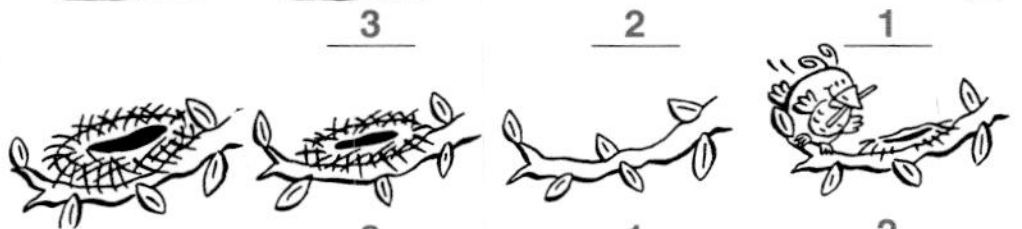
3 1 2

4. 
2 1 3

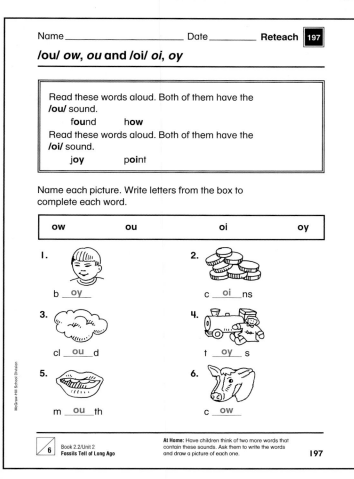

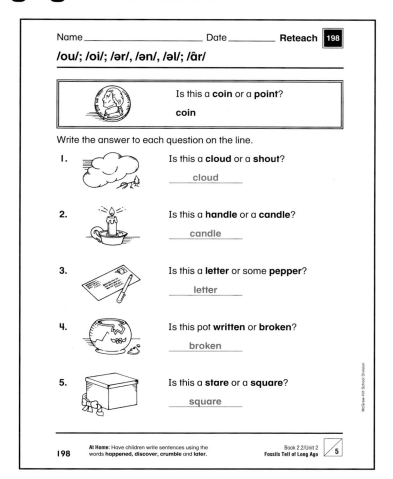

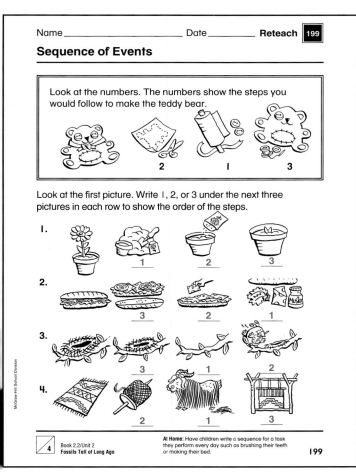

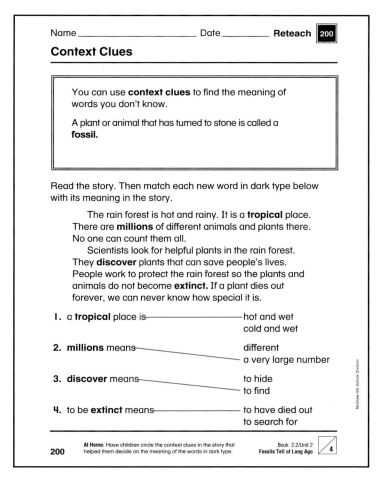

At Home: Have children write a sequence for a task they perform every day such as brushing their teeth or making their bed.

Name____________________ Date_________ **Reteach 200**

Context Clues

You can use **context clues** to find the meaning of words you don't know.

A plant or animal that has turned to stone is called a **fossil.**

Read the story. Then match each new word in dark type below with its meaning in the story.

The rain forest is hot and rainy. It is a **tropical** place. There are **millions** of different animals and plants there. No one can count them all.

Scientists look for helpful plants in the rain forest. They **discover** plants that can save people's lives. People work to protect the rain forest so the plants and animals do not become **extinct.** If a plant dies out forever, we can never know how special it is.

1. a **tropical** place is	hot and wet / cold and wet
2. **millions** means	different / a very large number
3. **discover** means	to hide / to find
4. to be **extinct** means	to have died out / to search for

(Answers: 1 — hot and wet; 2 — a very large number; 3 — to find; 4 — to have died out)

At Home: Have children circle the context clues in the story that helped them decide on the meaning of the words in dark type.

Name ____________________ Date __________ **Extend 193**

/ou/ *ow, ou* and /oi/ *oi, oy*

cow	found	mouth	ground	soil	boy	toy

Use words from the box to write sentences about the cartoon.

A Long Time Ago

Possible answers: 1. A boy dug soil. 2. He saw a bird with a worm in its mouth. 3. He found a box in the ground. 4. The boy found a toy cow.

At Home: Have children draw postcards. Ask them to use words from the box to write notes to friends about something they have done in the past.

Name ____________________ Date __________ **Extend 194**

Vocabulary

fossil	layers	millions	buried	creatures	fresh

Use the picture clues to help you solve the crossword puzzle. Use words from the box.

Across 2. 4. 5.

Down 1. 2. 3.

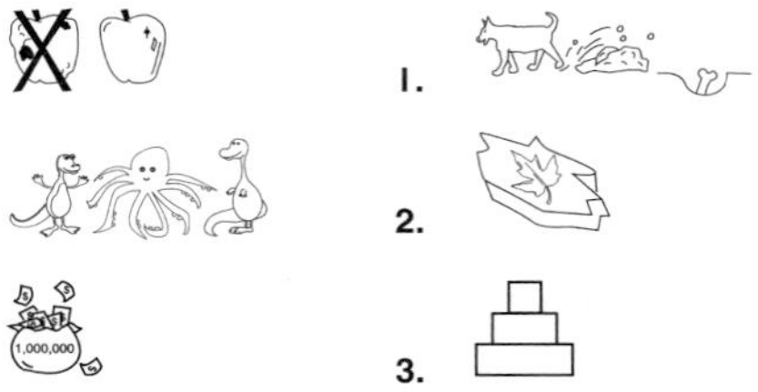

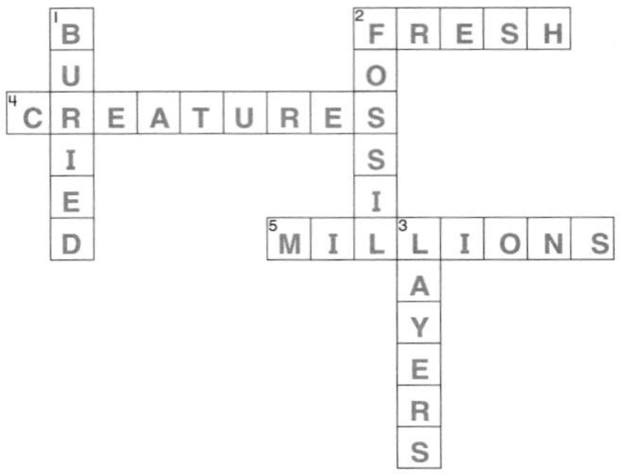

At Home: Have children write a short story using words from the box. They may also use the crossword picture clues for ideas.

Name ____________________ Date __________ **Extend 195**

Story Comprehension

How many objects in this scene could become fossils? Circle them.

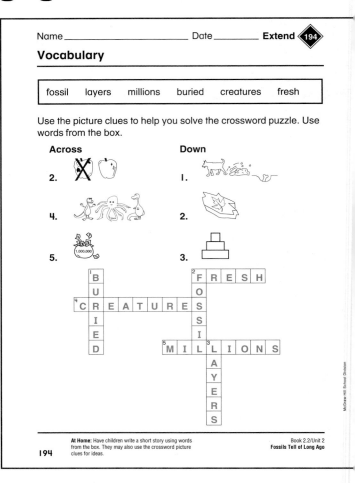

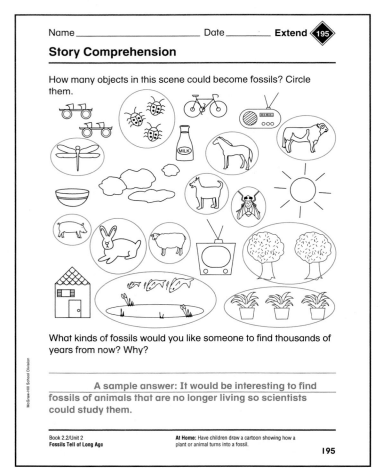

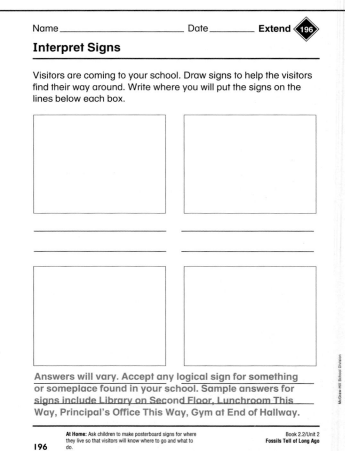

What kinds of fossils would you like someone to find thousands of years from now? Why?

A sample answer: It would be interesting to find fossils of animals that are no longer living so scientists could study them.

At Home: Have children draw a cartoon showing how a plant or animal turns into a fossil.

Name ____________________ Date __________ **Extend 196**

Interpret Signs

Visitors are coming to your school. Draw signs to help the visitors find their way around. Write where you will put the signs on the lines below each box.

Answers will vary. Accept any logical sign for something or someplace found in your school. Sample answers for signs include Library on Second Floor, Lunchroom This Way, Principal's Office This Way, Gym at End of Hallway.

At Home: Ask children to make posterboard signs for where they live so that visitors will know where to go and what to do.

Name__________________ Date________ Extend 197

/ou/ *ow, ou* and /oi/ *oi, oy*

Use words from the box to finish the rhymes in the story.

about	around	mouth	ground	soil	toy

One day I heard someone shout,
And I said, What's the noise **about**?
I heard another sound,
Then I looked to the **ground**.
Suddenly, I saw a snake!
It was not a fossil, not a fake.
The snake made a coil,
Down there on the **soil**.
Then I saw a boy,
Who was holding a **toy**.
I said, "Look what I found,
Please turn **around**."
To see the snake, the boy looked south.
There was the snake with a toy in its **mouth**!

At Home: Have children write what might have happened next in the story. Encourage them to use words from the box.

Name__________________ Date________ Extend 198

/ou/; /oi/; /ər/; /ən/; /əl/; /âr/

around	found	mouth	ground	soil	after
amber	covered	discover	never	other	water
later	layers	frozen	hardened	crumble	carefully

Use words from the box to write sentences that complete the play. Try to use at least one word from the box in each sentence.

Kate: Look! I found a fossil. I think it's a fly.

Scientist: ______________________________

Kate: I want to find more fossils like this.

Scientist: ______________________________

Kate: But first, tell me how this fly got trapped in the amber.

Scientist: ______________________________

____

____

Kate: Do you think the fossil will break?

Scientist: ______________________________

Kate: Who else found fossils?

Scientist: ______________________________

Kate: ______________________________

Answers will vary. Each line of dialogue should contain at least one word from the box.

At Home: Have children use the words from the box to write more dialogue for the Scientist and Kate.

Name__________________ Date________ Extend 199

Sequence of Events

Possible sentences given.
Number the pictures to show how the leaf became a fossil. Write a sentence to describe each step below each box.

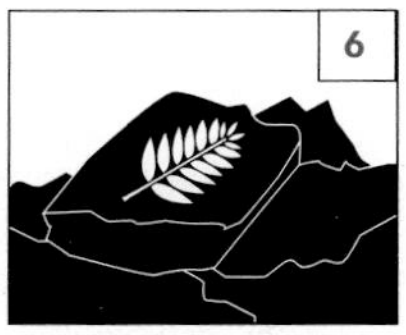

The peat hardened and became a fossil.

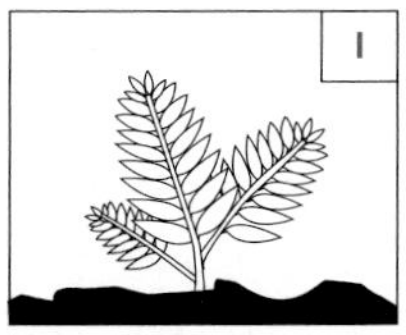

Millions of years ago, there was a plant.

The leaf dropped onto the peat in the forest.

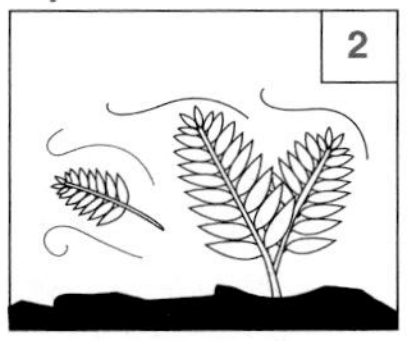

The leaf blew off the plant.

The leaf left the mark of its shape in the peat.

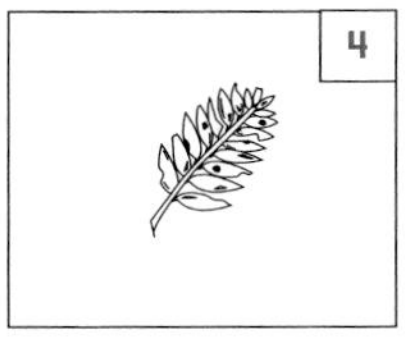

The leaf rotted away.

At Home: Have children write out the steps a person would take to find a fossil. They should consider how to prepare for an outdoor trip, what tools they would need, and where fossils are found.

Name__________________ Date________ Extend 200

Context Clues

Use the sentences to show what the girl said in the cartoon.

Here are fossils of other sea creatures!
I found a fossil of a fish!
What is buried in this ground?
I bet these fossils are millions of years old!

What is buried in this ground?

I found a fossil of a fish!

Here are fossils of other sea creatures!

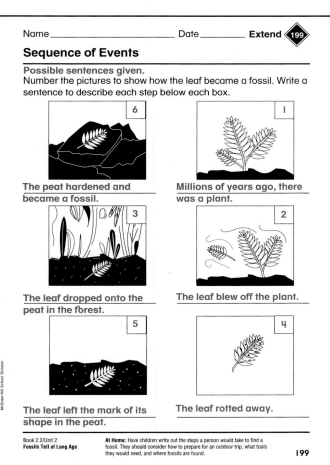

I bet these fossils are millions of years old!

At Home: Have children draw another cartoon about fossils. Ask them to use some of these words in the characters' speech balloons: *bones, coal, peat, preserved, amber, minerals, imprint,* and *tracks.*

Name ______________________ Date _________ LEARN Grammar 147

Pronoun-Verb Agreement

- A present-tense verb must agree with its subject when the subject is a noun. It must also agree with its subject when the subject is a pronoun.
- A present-tense verb must agree with a pronoun in the subject part of the sentence.
- With the pronouns *he, she,* and *it*, add *-s* to most action verbs in the present tense.

  He visits the Ramos family every year.

  She goes with him.

Underline the correct verb in each sentence. Then write the sentence.

1. It (take, takes) two hours to drive there.
   It takes two hours to drive there.
2. She (show, shows) us the river.
   She shows us the river.

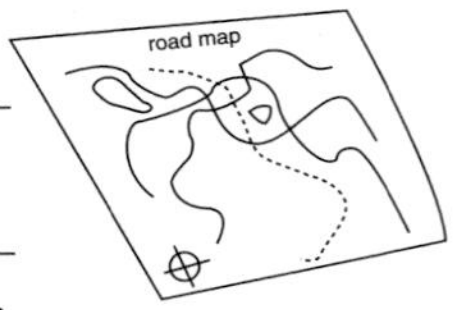

3. He (meets, meet) Ana and Diego.
   He meets Ana and Diego.
4. He (shake, shakes) hands with them.
   He shakes hands with them.
5. He (see, sees) the new car.
   He sees the new car.

Extension: Have the children write sentences for the remaining verbs.

Name ______________________ Date _________ LEARN AND PRACTICE Grammar 148

Pronoun and Verb Agreement

- With the pronouns *I, we, you,* and *they*, do not add *-s* to most action verbs in the present tense.

I sing	we sing
you sing	you sing
he, she, it sings	they sing

Read the sentences. Circle the correct verb.

1. She (tells, tell) funny stories.
2. I (thinks, think) her stories are great.
3. We (laughs, laugh) a lot.
4. Did you (hear, hears) one of her stories?
5. Mom and dad listen. They (like, likes) her stories.
6. He (want, wants) to hear a funny story.
7. Shall I (tell, tells) you one?
8. It (help, helps) me if you say the first word.

Extension: Have children write sentences using *I, we, you,* and *they* with action verbs.

Name ______________________ Date _________ REVIEW AND PRACTICE Grammar 149

Matching Pronouns and Verbs

- A present-tense verb must agree with a pronoun in the subject part of the sentence.
- With the pronouns *he, she,* and *it*, add *-s* to most action verbs in the present tense.
- With the pronouns *I, we, you,* and *they*, do not add *-s* to most action verbs in the present tense.

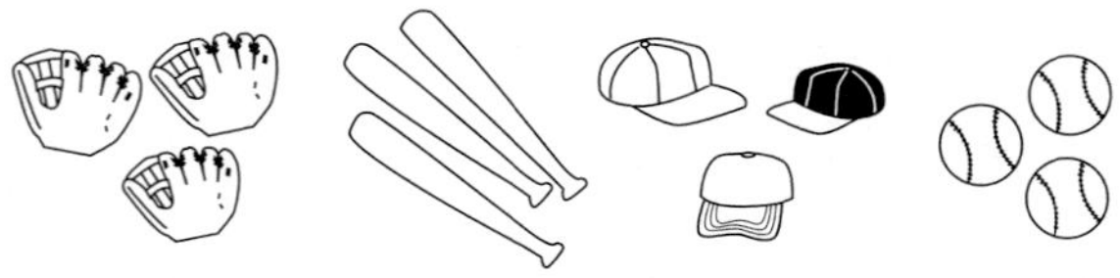

Read the sentence beginnings. Find an ending that could go with each beginning. Draw a line to connect them.

1. Carmen is quick. She	misses the ball sometimes.
2. The other team is new. They	calls the player out.
3. The umpire is fair. He	shakes his head.
4. The sun is bright. It	shines in our eyes.
5. Cliff is a beginner. He	find our team hard to beat.
6. Ron misses the ball. He	runs very fast.

Extension: Have children use sentence strips to write sentences using pronouns and action verbs. They can cut them in half between pronoun and verb, mix them up, and try to reassemble them.

Name ______________________ Date _________ MECHANICS Grammar 150

Titles and Capital Letters

- Begin the first word and each important word in a book title with a capital letter.
- Underline all the words in the title of a book.

  My Trip to Alaska

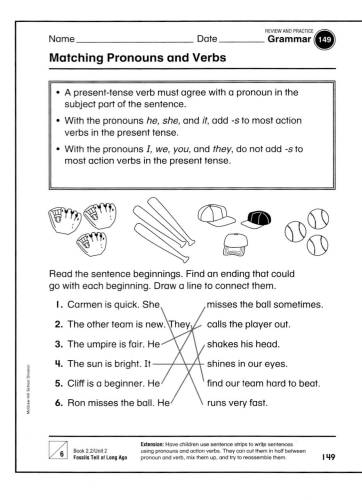

Read the sentences. Correct each underlined book title in the sentence. Write the correct sentence on the line.

1. Do you have a copy of a history of kites?
   Do you have a copy of A History of Kites?
2. I read the life of john keats.
   I read The Life of John Keats.
3. The book growing up in ohio was lent to me.
   The book Growing Up in Ohio was lent to me.
4. They found a nice tour in a boat trip around the world.
   They found a nice tour in A Boat Trip Around the World.
5. Let us borrow your computer and you from the library.
   Let us borrow Your Computer and You from the library.

Name ______________________ Date __________ TEST Grammar 151

Pronoun-Verb Agreement

Which sentence is correct? Mark your answer.

1. ● She likes to play.
   ⓑ She like to play.
2. ● We go to school every day.
   ⓑ We goes to school every day.
3. ⓐ Did you sees my lunch?
   ● Did you see my lunch?
4. ⓐ They knows where I live.
   ● They know where I live.
5. ● He laughs at the monkey.
   ⓑ He laugh at the monkey.
6. ⓐ It dance
   ● It dances.
7. ● I see it.
   ⓑ I sees it.
8. ● Do you like movies?
   ⓑ Do you likes movies?

Name ______________________ Date __________ MORE PRACTICE Grammar 152

Pronoun-Verb Agreement

- A present-tense verb must agree with a pronoun in the subject part of the sentence.
- With the pronouns *he, she,* and *it,* add *-s* in the present tense.
- With the pronouns *I, we, you,* and *they,* do not add *-s* to most action verbs in the present tense.

Read each sentence aloud.
Underline the correct verb in each sentence.

1. I (helps, help) mom with the baby.
2. Then she (help, helps) me with my music.
3. We (plays, play) the piano together.
4. She (call, calls) my two brothers.
5. They (like, likes) to hear us play.
6. He (dance, dances) to the music.
7. It (make, makes) us laugh.
8. I (think, thinks) they are funny.

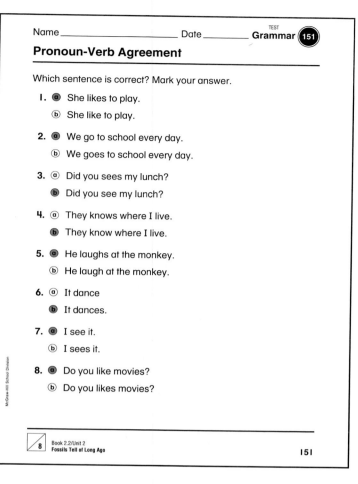

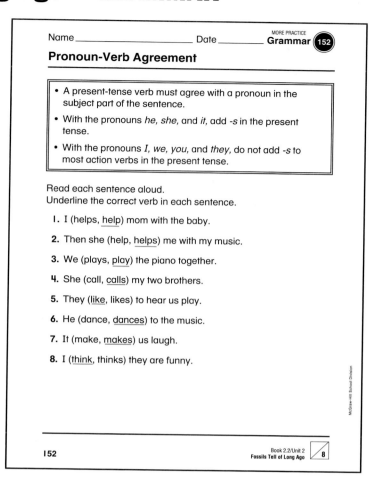

Name ____________ Date ________ PRETEST SPELLING **147**

Words with Blends *nk, nd, ft, st*

Pretest Directions
Fold back your paper along the dotted line. Use the blanks to write each word as it is said to you. When you finish the test, unfold the paper and correct any spelling mistakes. Practice those words for the Posttest.

1. ________	1. ground
2. ________	2. left
3. ________	3. hand
4. ________	4. past
5. ________	5. sank
6. ________	6. bank
7. ________	7. end
8. ________	8. chest
9. ________	9. soft
10. ________	10. test

Challenge Words

________	buried
________	creatures
________	fossil
________	layers
________	millions

To Parents,
Here are the results of your child's weekly spelling Pretest. You can help your child study for the Posttest by following these simple steps for each word on the word list:

1. Read the word to your child.
2. Have your child write the word, saying each letter as it is written.
3. Say each letter of the word as your child checks the spelling.
4. If a mistake has been made, have your child read each letter of the correctly spelled word aloud and then repeat steps 1–3.

Name ____________ Date ________ AT-HOME WORD STUDY SPELLING **148**

Words with Blends *nk, nd, ft, st*

Using the Word Study Steps

1. LOOK at the word.
2. SAY the word aloud.
3. STUDY the letters in the word.
4. WRITE the word.
5. CHECK the word.
   Did you spell the word right?
   If not, go back to step 1.

Spelling Tip
Think of a word that rhymes with the new word. Rhyming words often have the same spelling pattern.
s + **ank** = sank
b + **ank** = bank

X the word
Look at the endings in each row of spelling words. In each row, put an X on the word that does not belong.

ground	hand	~~left~~
past	~~sank~~	chest
sank	bank	~~soft~~
test	~~end~~	chest
hand	~~past~~	end

To Parents or Helpers:
Using the Word Study Steps above as your child comes across any new words will help him or her spell well. Review the steps as you both go over this week's spelling words.
Go over the Spelling Tip with your child. Ask if he or she knows other words that rhyme with the spelling words.
Help your child find and cross out the word that does not belong.

Name ____________ Date ________ EXPLORE THE PATTERN SPELLING **149**

Words with Blends *nk, nd, ft, st*

ground	hand	sank	end	soft
left	past	bank	chest	test

Find the spelling words that end with each of the sounds below. Write the words on the lines.

nk
1. sank
2. bank

nd
3. ground
4. hand
5. end

ft
6. left
7. soft

st
8. past
9. chest
10. test

Pattern Smart
Write the spelling words that have the same pattern as **lift**.
11. left 12. soft

Write the spelling words that have the same pattern as **think**.
13. sank 14. bank

Circle the letters that spell the pattern in each word you wrote.

15. Where do these letters appear? Circle the answer.
at the beginning in the middle (at the end)

Name ____________ Date ________ PRACTICE AND EXTEND SPELLING **150**

Words with Blends *nk, nd, ft, st*

ground	hand	sank	end	soft
left	past	bank	chest	test

Write a spelling word to complete each sentence.

1. Many trees grew on the bank of the river.
2. The water rushed past me.
3. The ground under the trees was wet.
4. The kitten's fur was soft and fluffy.
5. I threw a rock with my left hand.
6. The rock sank into the water.

Word Meaning
Find the opposite. Draw lines to connect the spelling words to words that mean the opposite.
Example: hot — cold

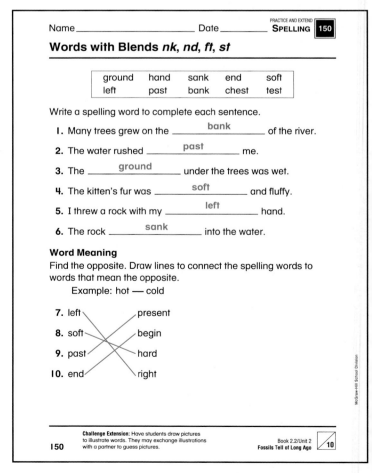

7. left — right
8. soft — hard
9. past — present
10. end — begin

Challenge Extension: Have students draw pictures to illustrate words. They may exchange illustrations with a partner to guess pictures.

Fossils Tell of Long Ago • SPELLING

Words with Blends *nk, nd, ft, st*

Proofreading Activity
There are five spelling mistakes in the note below. Circle each misspelled word. Write the words correctly on the lines below.

I am writing this note to say hello to people in the future. Then I will put it in a (chets). I will bury it in the (gruound) near my school. I hope people in the future will dig up the note I (leftt). They will find out about people in the (passt). I will also put in this week's spelling (tets).

1. ___chest___ 2. ___ground___ 3. ___left___

4. ___past___ 5. ___test___

Writing Activity
Write a note that will be read one hundred years from now. What do you want to tell people?
Use five spelling words. Circle the words you use.

Words with Blends *nk, nd, ft, st*

Look at the words in each set. One word in each set is spelled correctly. Use a pencil to color in the circle in front of that word. Before you begin, look at the sample sets of words. Sample A has been done for you. Do Sample B by yourself. When you are sure you know what to do, you may go on with the rest of the page.

Sample A
- Ⓐ onlee
- Ⓑ only ●
- Ⓒ onely
- Ⓓ onley

Sample B
- Ⓔ people ●
- Ⓕ peopel
- Ⓖ peeple
- Ⓗ peple

1.
- Ⓐ sotf
- Ⓑ soft ●
- Ⓒ soff
- Ⓓ sofft

2.
- Ⓔ bank ●
- Ⓕ bnak
- Ⓖ bakn
- Ⓗ bannk

3.
- Ⓐ gruond
- Ⓑ grond
- Ⓒ ground ●
- Ⓓ grund

4.
- Ⓔ tset
- Ⓕ test ●
- Ⓖ tst
- Ⓗ tets

5.
- Ⓐ letf
- Ⓑ leff
- Ⓒ left ●
- Ⓓ levft

6.
- Ⓔ end ●
- Ⓕ enn
- Ⓖ edn
- Ⓗ ennd

7.
- Ⓐ chets
- Ⓑ ches
- Ⓒ chest ●
- Ⓓ chetts

8.
- Ⓔ hand ●
- Ⓕ hnad
- Ⓖ han
- Ⓗ hend

9.
- Ⓐ psat
- Ⓑ pas
- Ⓒ past ●
- Ⓓ passt

10.
- Ⓔ sakn
- Ⓕ sank ●
- Ⓖ skna
- Ⓗ sanck

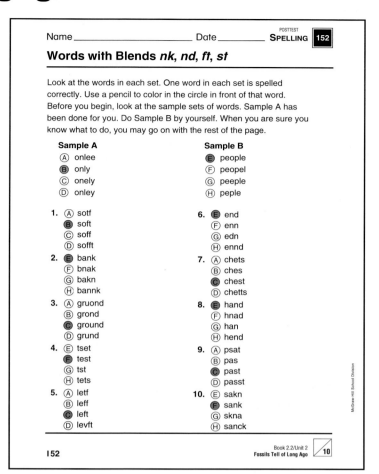

Are You a Fossil Fan? • PRACTICE

Name____________________ Date_________ **Practice 201**

/ou/; /oi/; /ər/, /ən/, /əl/; /ü/

Read the words on the list. List each one underneath the word that shares the same underlined sound. Then cross the word off the list.

found	apple	river	cow	noise	seven
giggle	blue	toy	open	too	teacher

m**ou**th
1. found
2. cow

b**oo**t
3. too
4. blue

happ**en**
5. seven
6. open

ov**er**
7. river
8. teacher

cand**le**
9. giggle
10. apple

s**oi**l
11. toy
12. noise

At Home: Have children circle the letters in each word that create the underlined sound.

Name____________________ Date_________ **Practice 202**

Vocabulary

Read each group of sentences. One word is missing from each group. Find the missing word and fill in the circle next to it.

1. Billy is making a birthday card. He is using _____ to stick a picture on the inside.
   - ○ **a.** soap ● **b.** glue ○ **c.** hurry
2. The picture shows a lion near a tree. Billy cut it out of a _____
   - ● **a.** magazine ○ **b.** homework ○ **c.** garden
3. Sally and Becky played out in the rain. They got wet. Now they have to _____ their clothes.
   - ○ **a.** grow ○ **b.** sell ● **c.** change
4. Sally and Becky are playing with blocks. They can't find the red one. They will have to _____ for it.
   - ● **a.** hunt ○ **b.** worry ○ **c.** sing
5. Emile has trouble chewing. Last night he lost a _____. He thought it would come out last week. It took a long time.
   - ○ **a.** card ● **b.** tooth ○ **c.** dog
6. Emile's mother made an apple pie. She cut it and gave him a _____ of it. The pie was soft and tasted good!
   - ● **a.** piece ○ **b.** door ○ **c.** week

At Home: Have children point out the clues in each example that helped them make the word choices.

Amber's Hunt

Amber looked in the mirror. Right in the front of her mouth a huge tooth had grown in.

"Aha!" said Amber. "Here is the missing piece to my life! I don't have to change my life. Now I have everything I need!"

And from that day on Amber felt happy!

At Home: Help children remember a time they wanted something to change. What did they do to make that change happen?

Amber the dinosaur wanted to change her life. "I want something new to happen," she said. She picked up a magazine. "I will hunt through the pages to see what I can find."

But the magazine did not have what she was looking for.

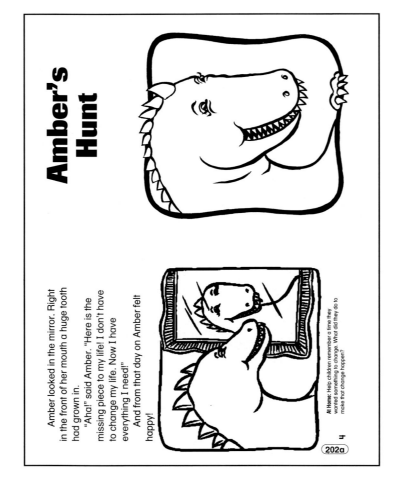

Amber tossed a coin. "Heads, I get a new job. Tails, I travel."

But the coin fell into a jar of glue on Amber's table. Amber could not get it out.

"Now I will never know what to do!" she cried.

Just then Amber felt a pain in her mouth.

"Ouch!"

Name__________________ Date________ **Practice 203**

Story Comprehension

Think about what you read in "Are You a Fossil Fan?" Read the sentences and answer the questions. Answers may vary.

1. How did Sam Girouard become a fossil finder?

   He and his grandmother found fossils when he was eight years old.

2. How does Sam find fossils?

   He spends hours digging in the ground.

3. What were two fossils that Sam found?

   Possible answers: a dinosaur tooth, a raindrop

4. What is unusual about Sam?

   He is a teenaged scientist.

5. Would you like to meet Sam? Why or why not?

   Possible answer: Yes, because he knows lots of interesting things.

At Home: Ask the children to share facts with you that they remember about fossils.

Name__________________ Date________ **Practice 204**

Read an Ad

Look at the **advertisements** shown below. Decide if each ad is trying to get you to buy something or to do something.
Write **Buy Something** on the blank line if the ad is selling a product. Write **Do Something** if the ad is trying to change your opinion or get you to do something.

Advertising Language:

1. **AT $29.95 THIS IS A GIVEAWAY OFFER! You won't find rain boots like this anywhere else in the city. Act now and we'll throw in a FREE UMBRELLA!** — Buy Something

2. *How would you like it if we dumped our garbage can in the middle of your living room!* DON'T LITTER! IT'S DIRTY AND UGLY, AND IT'S NOT POLITE! — Do Something

3. **Is your house always cold? Add Solar Windows and get warm today.** — Buy Something

4. You wouldn't wear clothes someone else picked out for you. You wouldn't drive someone else's car. So why let somebody else pick your government? **GET OUT AND VOTE.** — Do Something

5. Happiness is a state of mind. Peace is found in living right. Take it easy. Drink Orange Juice. It's just good. — Buy Something

At Home: Help children to make a collage with advertisements clipped from magazines. Ask them whether each ad is trying to get them to buy or to do something.

Name__________________ Date________ **Practice 205**

Sequence of Events

Read the story. Number the pictures to show the order in which they happened in the story.

Grandpa Jake makes the best vegetable soup. First, he boils water in a big pot. Then, he peels carrots and puts them in the pot. Next, he adds corn and green beans. After that, he cuts up potatoes and places them in with everything else to cook. Finally, he adds his own special spices to the soup. My favorite part is eating the soup with fresh bread!

2

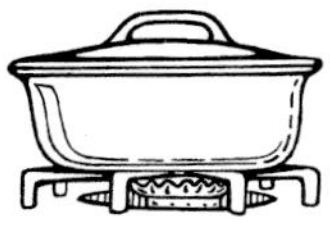

1

6

3

5

4

At Home: Ask children to explain the steps they take to make a favorite food. Ask what would happen if they forgot a step or made it in the wrong order.

Name__________________ Date________ **Practice 206**

Summarize

A **summary** is a short way to tell what happens in a story. A summary tells the most important information in a sentence or two.

Read each story, and write a summary. Remember to write each summary in one or two sentences.

Jill opened the black case and looked inside. It was a shiny, new violin. Jill plucked a string. I will never, ever learn to play! she thought.

Jill's brother Owen played the violin very well. He made it look so easy. Jill had always wanted to learn how to play, too. Now she wondered if she could do it.

Summary: Possible answer: Jill has a new violin. She isn't sure she can learn how to play it.

Jill tried to play, but her violin sounded like a sad cat. Then she heard a beautiful sound behind her. Owen was holding his violin and smiling. "I'll play with you," he said.

Together, they played the song over and over. When Owen stopped playing, Jill had a surprise. Music was coming from her own violin! Owen grinned. "All it takes is practice," he said.

Summary: Possible answer: Jill's brother, Owen, helped her to practice playing the violin, and her skills improved.

At Home: Help children to practice summarizing stories by inviting them to summarize the plot of a cartoon.

Name____________________ Date_________ **Practice 207**

Context Clues

Read the story. Find clues to the meaning of the underlined words by reading the words around them. Then choose one of the underlined words to answer each question.

Animals in the Snow

Many animals can live in snow. In the coldest winters, the earth is frozen hard. Rabbits and foxes dig holes in the snow to live in. They lie happily buried under a snow bank. They are warm and safe, protected from the cold winds. Some bigger animals, such as the mammoth who lived long ago and the polar bear, can live where it is cold all year. They have warm layers of fat and fur.

1. To be safe and warm is to be protected.
2. To lie underneath something is to be buried.
3. When something grows cold and hard, it is frozen.
4. One big animal that lived long ago was the mammoth.
5. Thicknesses or coats of something are called layers.

At Home: Have children draw an illustration for the story and use two of the underlined words to write a caption.

Name____________________ Date_________ **Practice 208**

Suffixes

Choose a word from the box that means the same as the phrase in parentheses. Rewrite the sentence using the new word.

quickly	slowly	skillful	fearful	helpful	neatly

1. We ate our lunch (in a slow way).
   We ate our lunch slowly.
2. Matt is (full of skill) with a hammer.
   Matt is skillful with a hammer.
3. The rain fell (in a quick way.)
   The rain fell quickly.
4. Do not be (full of fear) when it is dark.
   Do not be fearful when it is dark.
5. Mom was (full of help) with my science project.
   Mom was helpful with my science project.
6. Lola wrote (in a neat way).
   Lola wrote neatly.

At Home: Help children make a list of all the words they have learned that end in **-ly** and **-ful**.

Name__________________ Date________ **Reteach 201**

/ou/; /oi/; /ər/, /ən/, /əl/; /ü/

You have learned different spellings for several sounds.
/ou/ as in m**ou**th or c**ow** **/oi/** as in t**oy** or s**oi**l
/ər/ as in bett**er** **/əl/** as in app**le** **/ən/** as in op**en**
/ü/ as in sp**oo**n, bl**ue**, or fl**ew**

Circle the word or words in each group that have the same sound as the letters in dark type.

1. m**ou**th — (cow) (found) boat
2. s**oi**l — (boy) (coin) brother
3. b**oo**t — also (boom) (flew)
4. broth**er** — (another) settle (neither)
5. ov**er** — open (dinner) hear
6. cand**le** — care mouth (giggle)
7. happ**en** — (seven) river found
8. bl**ue** — boil (few) (true)

At Home: Have children think of one more word that has the same sound as each of the underlined sounds.

Name__________________ Date________ **Reteach 202**

Vocabulary

Choose a word from the box to complete each sentence. Write the word on the line.

piece	magazine	tooth	change	glue	hunt

1. Sal likes to look at the pictures in the ___magazine___ .
2. I used some ___glue___ to fix my broken truck.
3. Johnny needs to ___change___ his clothes for the party.
4. I lost a ___tooth___ when I bit into an apple.
5. Would you like a ___piece___ of my orange?
6. We will have to ___hunt___ for the lost ball.

At Home: Have children write a new sentence for each word in the box.

Name__________________ Date________ **Reteach 203**

Story Comprehension

Think about what you learned in "Are You a Fossil Fan?" Then write the word that best completes each statement.

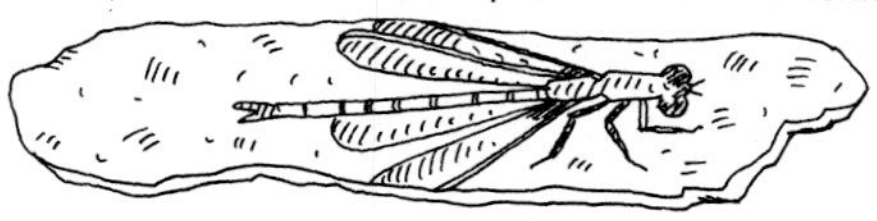

1. Sam Girouard was ___eight___ years old when he first found a fossil.
   twenty eight fifteen
2. Sam is now a teenager and a ___scientist___ .
   teacher hiker scientist
3. He finds fossils by ___digging___ .
   reading writing digging
4. Once Sam found a fossil of a ___raindrop___ .
   raindrop bat goat
5. Sam also found the ___tooth___ of a dinosaur.
   tooth head ribs
6. Sam tells about his discoveries by ___writing___ .
   digging writing drawing

At Home: Have children find things around the house that they think scientists in the future might be interested in finding. Ask them to explain why.

Name__________________ Date________ **Reteach 204**

Read an Ad

Some **advertisements** are trying to sell you something. Others are trying to convince you of something.

Study the advertisement below.

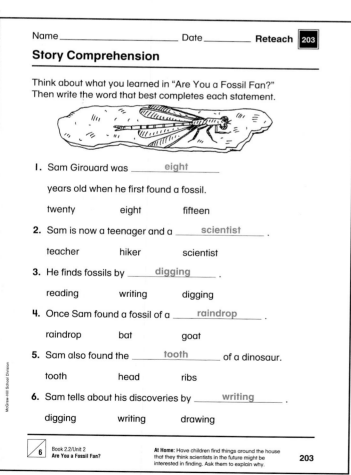

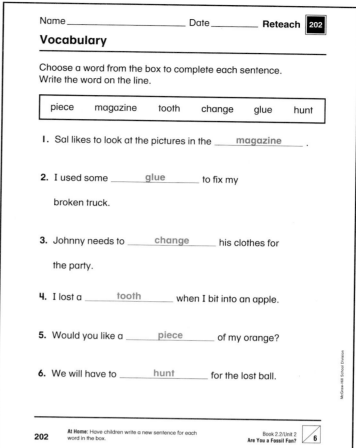

Own a Piece of the Past!
Fossils—Complete or in Parts—
Can Be Yours for Pennies
T-Rex Teeth!
Stegosaurus Spikes!
Raptor Claws!
Iguanodon Eggs!
Great as Conversation Pieces or Paperweights!
Ancient Art from a Forgotten Time
Archie's Ologies—The Fossil Store
Corner of Broadway and 4th
Send for Our Catalog now!
555-7856

Use this ad to answer the questions below.

1. Who is advertising something here? ___Archie's Ologies— The Fossil Store___
2. Where is this store located? ___Corner of Broadway and 4th___
3. What four things from dinosaurs are offered? ___T-Rex teeth stegosaurus spikes, iguanodon eggs, raptor claws___
4. What is the phone number you can call to order? ___555-7856___

At Home: Have children make a collage of advertisements cut out from magazines.

Name________________ Date________ **Reteach 205**

Sequence of Events

When you follow a **sequence**, you are doing something in order.

Read the steps for making a milk shake and making a shell collection. Then, write the steps in order.

How to Make a Milk Shake	**How to Make a Shell Collection**
Mix with a spoon.	Clean the shells.
Pour a glass of milk.	Walk on the beach.
Put a cherry on top.	Pick up the shells.
Put in 2 scoops of ice cream.	Put the shells on a shelf.

Step 1 Pour a glass of milk.	Step 1 Walk on the beach.
Step 2 Put in 2 scoops of ice cream.	Step 2 Pick up shells.
Step 3 Mix with a spoon.	Step 3 Clean the shells.
Step 4 Put a cherry on top.	Step 4 Put the shells on a shelf.

At Home: Have children give directions for making a sandwich, a salad, or a glass of chocolate milk.

Name________________ Date________ **Reteach 206**

Summarize

A **summary** is a short way to tell what something is about.

Read the story. Answer the questions. Answers will vary.

Marci buttoned her coat and went outside. The cold wind blew on her face as she looked into the sky. There were dark clouds in the west. There was a ring around the moon. "It's going to snow," Marci whispered. Papa was a weatherman. He had told Marci how to predict the snow. By morning, the snow fell. Marci was right.

1. Who is the story about? Marci
2. What did she see? dark clouds in the west and a ring around the moon
3. What did she think about the weather? Marci thought it was going to snow.
4. What clues helped her make her decision? There was a cold wind, dark clouds, and a ring around the moon.

Write a summary of the story. One day Marci predicted that it was going to snow.

At Home: Have children look at the headlines of a newspaper. Have children write their own headline summarizing a favorite story.

Name________________ Date________ **Reteach 207**

Context Clues

Clues in a sentence can tell you the meaning of a new word.

Sap is a liquid that moves inside a tree and brings food to the leaves and branches.

In the sentence above, the words "a liquid that moves inside a tree and brings food to the leaves and branches" tell you what **sap** means.

Read each sentence. Then circle the meaning of the underlined word.

1. We took a walk in the forest. There were trees as far as we could see.
   (a place with many trees) a wet place
2. Dad showed us an ancient redwood tree. He said it was very, very old.
   (very, very old) very, very small
3. The oldest tree was three thousand years old!
   (a big number) a small number
4. In the swamp, the water came up to our knees.
   a rocky place (a wet place)
5. Some of the trees had fuzzy green moss all over them.
   a big animal (a plant that grows on trees)

At Home: Ask children to list three new words they learned this week by using clues in the words and pictures.

Name________________ Date________ **Reteach 208**

Suffixes

Adding **-ly** or **-ful** to a word changes its meaning. The suffix **-ly** means "in the way of"; the suffix **-ful** means "full of."

Write the correct suffix to complete the sentence.

1. A fossil finder must be very care<u>ful</u>.
   ful ly
2. Scientists take their work serious<u>ly</u>.
   ly ful
3. Everyone polite<u>ly</u> said "thank you" after the party.
   ful ly
4. Maria sang loud<u>ly</u> to wake us up.
   ful ly
5. Glue is use<u>ful</u> for mending broken toys.
   ly ful

At Home: Have children list three more words that end with the suffix **-ly** and three words that end with **-ful**.

Name ____________ Date ________ Extend 201

/ou/; /oi/; /ər/, /ən/, /əl/; /ü/

careful	scared	for	morning	hear	blue
too	found	ground	soil	brother	
dinner	happen	seven	candle	giggle	

Use words from the box to write a story for telling out loud. Use at least five words from the box in your story.

Stories will vary. Children should use at least five words from the box.

At Home: Have children tell the story they wrote. Encourage them to use words from the box.

Name ____________ Date ________ Extend 202

Vocabulary

change	glue	hunt	magazine	piece	tooth

Read the story below. Use words from the box to answer the questions.

The Hunt

One day, Nina and Ray went on a hunt for a dinosaur fossil. Nina had read in a magazine that a lot of fossils had been found in her town.

They hunted near their house for awhile, but found nothing. Nina suggested they change spots.

They went to the field by the school. Suddenly, Nina gave a shout. "I found a piece of a dinosaur tooth!"

Ray found a piece of dinosaur tooth, too. "Let's go home and glue them together," he said.

1. What did Nina and Ray do one day?
   Nina and Ray went on a fossil hunt.
2. How did Nina know there were fossils in her town?
   Nina read it in a magazine.
3. What did Nina suggest?
   Nina suggested that they change spots.
4. What did Nina find?
   Nina found a piece of a dinosaur tooth.
5. What did Ray suggest?
   Ray suggested they go home and glue the pieces together.

At Home: Have children draw pictures to go with the story. Ask them to label their pictures with words from the box.

Name ____________ Date ________ Extend 203

Story Comprehension

What if Sam were a grown-up scientist? Write how the article might be different.

Answers will vary. Students should take into account Sam's change in age.

What if Sam were only five years old? Write how the article might be different.

Answers will vary. Students should consider what a five-year-old would know about fossils.

Sam writes articles for magazines. Make up three titles for articles Sam might write.

Answers will vary. Articles may be related to fossil hunting, dinosaurs, or other science topics.

At Home: Have children talk about other grown-up work that children can do. Ask them to write a short article about this topic.

Name ____________ Date ________ Extend 204

Read an Advertisement

Create an ad for an invention that you could sell.

Write why you think your ad will work.

Answers will vary.

At Home: Look at different advertisements with children. Have them tell you whether or not they think these ads will work.

Name ______________ Date ________ **Extend 205**

Sequence of Events

Read the story. Number the pictures to show the order in which they happened in the story.

There were clouds outside. Sheri put on her raincoat and rain boots in case it rained. She got her umbrella out of the closet. Then she locked the door of her house and went outside.

While she was walking, Sheri saw a deer by the side of the road. It was eating berries from a tree. Sheri walked quietly so she wouldn't scare the deer away. Suddenly, a girl on a bicycle raced by, ringing her bell. The deer ran into the woods. Just then, the sun came out.

umbrella	tree	bicycle	clouds
3	6	7	1
deer	**boots**	**sun**	**lock**
5	2	8	4

At Home: Have children read a familiar story. Ask them to draw picture clues on individual cards. Then mix up the cards and have them put the cards in the order the pictures appear in the story.

Name ______________ Date ________ **Extend 206**

Summarize

Read the stories about Sam. Then write a one-sentence summary for each story.

1. When Sam was eight, he loved to dig in the dirt. He found broken toys, marbles, and coins. Once he found a fossil of a dinosaur tooth. He liked finding fossils and learning about the creatures that once lived on the Earth. When Sam grew up, he became a scientist.

   Sample answer: Sam became a scientist because he liked to find fossils and learning about creatures.

2. Sam wrote articles about his work as a scientist. He wrote about the different fossils he had found, and what he learned from them. Once Sam found the wing of a fly that was millions of years old. People enjoyed reading Sam's articles. Sometimes people wrote him letters telling him how much they learned from reading about his work.

   Sample answer: Sam wrote interesting articles about his work as a scientist.

Write a detail from each story that is not important to include in your summaries.

1. Sam found broken toys in the earth.
2. People wrote to Sam.

At Home: Have children talk about a favorite book. Ask them to summarize the story in one or two sentences.

Name ______________ Date ________ **Extend 207**

Context Clues

What are they saying? Use sentences from the box.

1. This is a rare fossil. I have made a big discovery!
2. Here is a fly trapped in amber.
3. Wow! This is the bone of a giant mastodon!
4. Let me do a test on that fossil to find out how old it is.
5. This tooth is from a large dinosaur!

This tooth is from a large dinosaur!

Let me do a test on that fossil to find out how old it is.

This is a rare fossil. I have made a big discovery!

Wow! This is the bone of a giant mastodon!

Here is a fly trapped in amber.

At Home: Have children use the picture to make up a story about what the scientists will do next.

Name ______________ Date ________ **Extend 208**

Suffixes

beautiful	careful	slowly	quickly

Use each word from the box in a sentence. Then draw a picture to illustrate each sentence.

1. Answers will vary. Each sentence should contain a word from the box.
2. ______________
3. ______________
4. ______________

At Home: Have children brainstorm other words with the suffixes **-ly** and **-ful**. Ask them to write a poem about something that they think is beautiful. Have them include words with the suffixes **-ly** and **-ful**.

Name ____________________ Date __________ LEARN Grammar 153

Contractions

- A **contraction** is a short form of two words.
- An **apostrophe** (') takes the place of the letters that are left out.

I am	I'm
he is	he's
she is	she's

He's tall. She's short. I'm in the middle.

Write the contraction for the underlined words in each sentence.

1. He is my brother. He's
2. She is my sister. She's
3. I am the youngest. I'm
4. He is the oldest. He's
5. She is funny. She's

Write the words the contractions mean.

6. I'm here. I am
7. She's my friend. She is
8. He's a nice boy. He is

Extension: Have the children write more sentences with *I'm, he's,* and *she's.*

Name ____________________ Date __________ PRACTICE AND LEARN Grammar 154

Using Contractions

- A **contraction** is a short form of two words.
- An **apostrophe** (') takes the place of the letters that are left out.

it is	it's	we are	we're
they are	they're	you are	you're

They're here. *You're* here. *We're* all here.

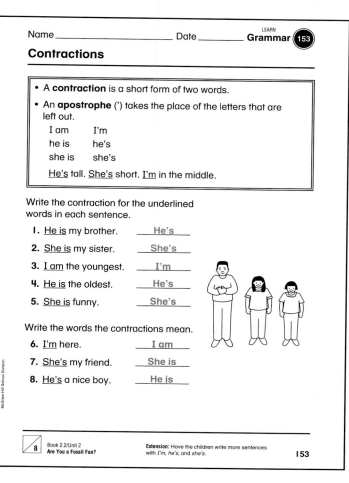

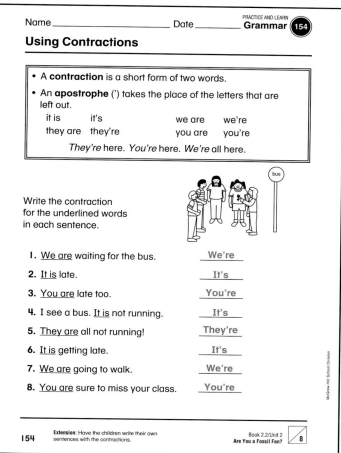

Write the contraction for the underlined words in each sentence.

1. We are waiting for the bus. We're
2. It is late. It's
3. You are late too. You're
4. I see a bus. It is not running. It's
5. They are all not running! They're
6. It is getting late. It's
7. We are going to walk. We're
8. You are sure to miss your class. You're

Extension: Have the children write their own sentences with the contractions.

Name ____________________ Date __________ REVIEW AND PRACTICE Grammar 155

More Contractions

- A **contraction** is a short form of two words.
- An **apostrophe** (') takes the place of the letters that are left out.

I am	I'm	we are	we're
you are	you're	you are	you're
he is	he's	they are	they're
she is	she's		
it is	it's		

Read the sentences. Write the contraction for the two underlined words.

1. I am taking a bath. I'm
2. She is taking a shower. She's
3. It is not time for his bath. It's
4. They are taking showers. They're
5. We are taking baths soon. We're
6. You are ready for bed. You're
7. He is staying up late. He's
8. They are going out. They're

Extension: Have children write sentences using all the contractions in the chart at the top of the page.

Name ____________________ Date __________ MECHANICS Grammar 156

Contractions

- An **apostrophe** takes the place of the letters left out of a contraction.
- Possessive pronouns do not have apostrophes.
- Do not confuse possessive pronouns with contractions.

they're	their
you're	your
it's	its

Read the sentences. Write the correct pronoun or contraction.

1. Did you lose (you're, your) glasses? your
2. I think (they're, their) on the table. they're
3. The dog put them in (it's, its) mouth. its
4. (You're, Your) lucky I got them. You're
5. (It's, Its) getting late. It's
6. When is (they're, their) party? their
7. (You're, Your) not going to be there. You're
8. Do you know (they're, their) number? their

Extension: Have the children write the sentences with the correct words.

Name __________ Date ______ TEST Grammar 157

Contractions

A. Read each sentence. Change each underlined word to a contraction. Write the contraction on the line.

1. I am cold. **I'm**
2. He is not cold. **He's**
3. She is bringing me a cover. **She's**
4. They are not my covers. **They're**

B. Read the sentences. Circle each contraction.

5. (We're) waiting for you.
6. (You're) going to be late.
7. (It's) ten o'clock.
8. (He's) on time.

Name __________ Date ______ MORE PRACTICE Grammar 158

Contractions

- A contraction is a short form of two words.
- Some contractions are: *it's, they're, we're, you're.*

Look at the picture. Read the sentences. Write the sentences correctly.

1. Its' beautiful tonight.
   It's beautiful tonight.
2. Wer'e looking at the stars.
   We're looking at the stars.
3. The'yre as bright as the moon.
   They're as bright as the moon.
4. Im' using Jim's telescope.
   I'm using Jim's telescope.
5. Hes' showing me how to use it.
   He's showing me how to use it.

Name______________ Date________ PRETEST SPELLING 153

Words from Social Studies

Pretest Directions

Fold back your paper along the dotted line. Use the blanks to write each word as it is said to you. When you finish the test, unfold the paper and correct any spelling mistakes. Practice those words for the Posttest.

To Parents,
Here are the results of your child's weekly spelling Pretest. You can help your child study for the Posttest by following these simple steps for each word on the word list:

1. Read the word to your child.
2. Have your child write the word, saying each letter as it is written.
3. Say each letter of the word as your child checks the spelling.
4. If a mistake has been made, have your child read each letter of the correctly spelled word aloud and then repeat steps 1–3.

1. ________ 1. hill
2. ________ 2. stone
3. ________ 3. bone
4. ________ 4. land
5. ________ 5. oil
6. ________ 6. deep
7. ________ 7. ocean
8. ________ 8. drill
9. ________ 9. remains
10. ________ 10. digging

Challenge Words

________ change
________ glue
________ hunt
________ magazine
________ tooth

Name______________ Date________ AT-HOME WORD STUDY SPELLING 154

Words from Social Studies

Using the Word Study Steps

1. LOOK at the word.
2. SAY the word aloud.
3. STUDY the letters in the word.
4. WRITE the word.
5. CHECK the word.
   Did you spell the word right?
   If not, go back to step 1.

Spelling Tip

Think of when you have seen the word before. Think of how it looked. Write the word in different ways to see which one looks correct.
Example:
~~stown~~ ~~stoan~~ stone

Find and Circle

Where are the spelling words?

a	c	b	d	f	h	l	d	r	i	l	l	h	g	j
s	t	o	n	e	i	a	e	k	o	c	e	a	n	n
l	m	n	o	i	l	n	e	r	e	m	a	i	n	s
o	q	e	r	s	l	d	p	d	i	g	g	i	n	g

To Parents or Helpers:
Using the Word Study Steps above as your child comes across any new words will help him or her spell well. Review the steps as you both go over this week's spelling words.
Go over each Spelling Tip with your child. Ask him or her to write a new word in different ways to see which one looks correct. Help your child check the correct spelling in a dictionary.
Help your child find and circle the spelling words in the puzzle.

Name______________ Date________ EXPLORE THE PATTERN SPELLING 155

Words from Social Studies

hill	bone	oil	ocean	remains
stone	land	deep	drill	digging

Write the spelling words in alphabetical order.

1. bone 2. deep 3. digging
4. drill 5. hill 6. land
7. ocean 8. oil 9. remains
10. stone

Pattern Smart

Write the spelling word that has the same pattern as *hand*.

11. land

Write the spelling word that has the same pattern as *boil*.

12. oil

Write the spelling word that has the same pattern as *peep*.

13. deep

Write the spelling word that has the same pattern as *stains*.

14. remains

Name______________ Date________ PRACTICE AND EXTEND SPELLING 156

Words from Social Studies

hill	bone	oil	ocean	remains
stone	land	deep	drill	digging

All in a Set

Use a spelling word to complete each sentence.

1. Where did your dog bury the ____bone____?
2. Jack and Jill climbed a ____hill____.
3. George liked ____digging____ for treasure.
4. Where will the space ship ____land____?
5. I like to watch the waves in the ____ocean____.
6. Always dive into the ____deep____ end of the pool.
7. Another word for **rock** is ____stone____.
8. Tina put gas and ____oil____ in her car.
9. The worker used a ____drill____ to make a hole.
10. Fossils are the ____remains____ of dinosaurs.

Name______________ Date________ PROOFREAD AND WRITE SPELLING 157

Words from Social Studies

Proofreading Activity

There are five spelling mistakes in the report below. Circle each misspelled word. Write the words correctly on the lines below.

We learned about Columbus in school. We learned that Columbus was very brave. He sailed across the ocaen to find a new ladn. Our class wanted to show our depe respect for Columbus. We wrote a play about him. Then we placed a special stoan on a hille to honor him.

1. ocean 2. land 3. deep

4. stone 5. hill

Writing Activity

Write a story about a dinosaur who visits your school. Use five spelling words in your story. Circle the words you use.

____

____

____

____

____

Name______________ Date________ POSTTEST SPELLING 158

Words from Social Studies

Look at the words in each set. One word in each set is spelled correctly. Use a pencil to color in the circle in front of that word. Before you begin, look at the sample sets of words. Sample A has been done for you. Do Sample B by yourself. When you are sure you know what to do, you may go on with the rest of the page.

Sample A
- Ⓐ one (filled)
- Ⓑ twoo
- Ⓒ thwee
- Ⓓ foure

Sample B
- Ⓔ blu
- Ⓕ telo
- Ⓖ red (filled)
- Ⓗ whiite

1. Ⓐ hille Ⓑ hll Ⓒ hill (filled) Ⓓ hile
2. Ⓔ bne Ⓕ boone Ⓖ bon Ⓗ bone (filled)
3. Ⓐ stne Ⓑ stone (filled) Ⓒ ston Ⓓ stoen
4. Ⓔ deep (filled) Ⓕ deepe Ⓖ depe Ⓗ deap
5. Ⓐ osean Ⓑ ocene Ⓒ ocean (filled) Ⓓ osion
6. Ⓔ oil (filled) Ⓕ oel Ⓖ ole Ⓗ oyl
7. Ⓐ drle Ⓑ drill (filled) Ⓒ drille Ⓓ drele
8. Ⓔ land (filled) Ⓕ lande Ⓖ leand Ⓗ lnde
9. Ⓐ diging Ⓑ degging Ⓒ digging (filled) Ⓓ digeing
10. Ⓔ remaines Ⓕ remanes Ⓖ remains (filled) Ⓗ remaens

Name ____________ Date ________ Practice 209

Unit 2 Vocabulary Review

A. Put a check mark next to each true sentence.

✓ **1.** People can play music on a piano.

✓ **2.** Your favorite food is the food that you like best.

___ **3.** People play baseball in an office.

✓ **4.** People glue things to hold them together.

___ **5.** You can taste a voice.

B. Complete the crossword puzzle using the words in the box.

magazine	scare	field	daughter	wrapped

DOWN

1. He read a ___ while he waited.

2. I ___ his gift in paper.

ACROSS

3. They have one ___ and three sons.

4. The noise will ___ the birds away.

5. The baseball team ran onto the ___ .

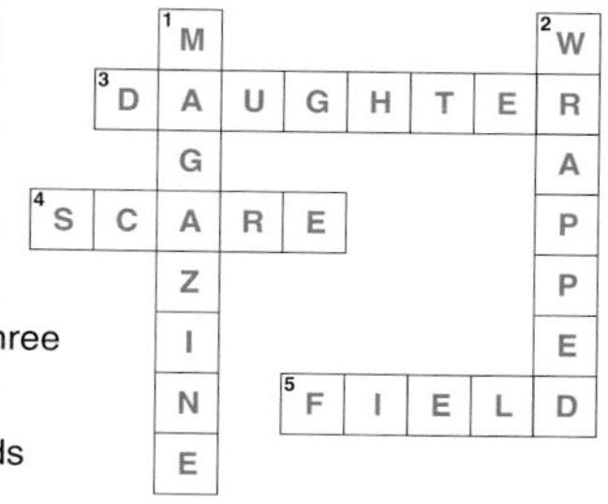

At Home: Have children write a paragraph using three of the words above.

Name ____________ Date ________ Practice 210

Unit 2 Vocabulary Review

A. Circle the word that means the opposite of each word.

1. heavy

a. big **b.** (light) **c.** little

2. nervous

a. (calm) **b.** scared **c.** smart

3. millions

a. many **b.** two **c.** (none)

4. score

a. win a point **b.** (lose a point) **c.** cook

B. Write the word to complete the questions.
Then, answer **Yes** or **No** to the questions. **Answers may vary.**

chance	whistle	touch	piece

1. Do you know how to __whistle__? __Yes.__

2. Would you __touch__ a wild lion? __No.__

3. If you had a __chance__ to ride on a roller coaster, would you? __Yes.__

4. Have you ever eaten a __piece__ of pizza? __Yes.__

At Home: Have children write one true sentence and one false sentence for some of the words above.

Name ____________ Date ________ Reteach 209

Unit 2 Vocabulary Review

A. Find the following words in the word search

coaches	score	creatures	hunt

s e i f j v e i d l e o k (c o a c h e s) e o d c k e i d k e
p o c i e k d o r j f f o v l e o c k d i e i d k c i e h s
e k d i c j d o e l a m s i d i f j r m f p r l g o r j w c
(c r e a t u r e s) d k e i d j v m d o a l s o e a w i e o o
d k e i d j c m d o e p r t u y p a n a m e o m e n i q e r
n b e i d j d c o q q o e i d z m d i l h k e i d o d c k e
p l o i e u d k c i d y a x c o z i k s u d k m e e o h r t
k e n d o z m d o q q i e m y n z o i d n p o r i t c b z e
e o d l c i e l a p l d j f h k c v o e t t e l d o c e i d

B. Fill in the paragraph with the words in the box.

buried	piece	fossil	layers

Yesterday, my friend Max and I went out to look for a __fossil__. Fossils are __buried__ in the ground, so we dug through __layers__ of earth. We didn't find any fossils, but we did find a __piece__ of a broken plate.

At Home: Have children write a paragraph with the words from the word search.

Name ____________ Date ________ Reteach 210

Unit 2 Vocabulary Review

A. Each word below has a definition next to it. Some definitions are wrong. Underline the definitions that are correct.

1. heavy—not light

2. whistle—a type of shirt

3. nervous—happy

4. change—to make or become different

B. Put a check mark in front of the sentences in which the vocabulary words are used correctly.

1. magazine
✓ **a.** I read about it in the *magazine*.
___ **b.** My father is a *magazine* and my mother is a doctor.

2. tooth
___ **a.** We flew to Mexico on a *tooth*.
✓ **b.** My baby brother has a loose *tooth*.

3. stretches
✓ **a.** Everyone *stretches* after gym class.
___ **b.** She *stretches* her homework after school.

4. throws
✓ **a.** She *throws* the ball to me.
___ **b.** The television *throws* down a lot.

At Home: Have children choose one of the sentences that they did not check in Exercise B and illustrate it.

Name ______________ Date ________ Extend 209

Vocabulary Review

heavy	whistle	coaches	field	
favorite	wrapped	stretches	voice	buried

Use the words in the box to complete the sentences.

1. The players ran onto the f i e l d when the game began.
2. We needed two people to lift the h e a v y box.
3. We all enjoy Pam's beautiful singing v o i c e.
4. The team needs the c o a c h e s to teach skills.
5. The dog b u r i e d bones in the ground.
6. The policeman blew his w h i s t l e to get our attention.
7. The players always do s t r e t c h e s before they run.
8. I w r a p p e d the presents for the party.

The word made from the letters in the boxes is:

f a v o r i t e

At Home: Help children make up their own puzzles to form new words.

Name ______________ Date ________ Extend 210

Vocabulary Review

Read the story.

I am so happy. I am at my ***third*** football game. My team has a ***chance*** to win. The players do their ***stretches*** to warm up. The ***coaches*** tell their teams to do the best they can.

The ***whistle*** blows and the game starts. The players run onto the ***field.*** My ***favorite*** player ***throws*** the ball and ***scores!*** I shout with a loud ***voice,*** "YOU ARE THE BEST TEAM!"

I am getting ***nervous.*** The other team throws the ball to their goal. Their player tries to catch the ball to score. He ***touches*** the ball but drops it.

The game isn't over yet! Write what happens next.

At Home: Have children write five sentences and draw five matching pictures on separate cards. Children can play Concentration by picking two cards to try to find a match. If the two cards don't match, they must put them back and try again.

Name ______________ Date ________ UNIT TEST Grammar 159

Pronouns

Read each passage. Choose a word or group of words that belong in each space. Mark your answer.

I am glad Bob is here. Bob helps me with my chores. (1) work together. Mom thanks both of (2).

1. (a) I (b) Me **(c) We** (d) Us
2. (f) I (g) me (h) we **(j) us**

Aunt Doris is coming to visit. (3) will stay one week. Uncle Nate is coming later. Uncle Nate and Aunt Doris live in New York. (4) like to travel.

3. **(a) She** (b) He (c) Her (d) Him
4. **(f) They** (g) Them (h) He (j) She

My cousin tells great jokes. (5) sister is also funny. Her stories make me laugh. She tells them to (6) friends.

5. (a) You **(b) Your** (c) Yours (d) You're
6. **(f) our** (g) ours (h) mine (j) yours

Go On

Name ______________ Date ________ REVIEW Grammar 160

Did you lose your glasses? I think (7) on the table. Don't worry. (8) look for them.

7. (a) they **(b) they're** (c) their (d) theirs
8. (f) I'm (g) I've **(h) I'll** (j) It's

My sister writes books about fossils. She (9) about them in the library. When she borrows books, she asks me, "Can you (10) my books home?"

9. (a) read **(b) reads** (c) reading (d) have read
10. **(f) carry** (g) carrys (h) carries (j) has carried

Hurry up! It's ten o'clock, and (11) going to be late. (12) wait for you at the bus stop.

11. **(a) you're** (b) your (c) yours (d) yo're
12. (f) We're **(g) We'll** (h) We've (j) Weren't

Unit 5 Review • SPELLING

Book 2.2 / Unit 2 Review Test

Name_____ Date_____ UNIT TEST SPELLING 159

Read each sentence. If an underlined word is spelled wrong, fill in the circle that goes with that word. If no word is spelled wrong, fill in the circle below NONE.
Read Sample A, and do Sample B.

A. I will <u>make</u> <u>pink</u> <u>spice</u> cookies.
 A B C
A. Ⓐ Ⓑ Ⓒ ●D (NONE)

B. I <u>plan</u> to take a <u>break</u> and <u>rest</u>.
 E F G
B. Ⓔ Ⓕ Ⓖ ●H (NONE)

1. Bob will <u>come</u> and <u>play</u> in the <u>soft</u> sand.
 A B C
1. Ⓐ Ⓑ Ⓒ ●D (NONE)

2. The <u>stone</u> and other <u>remanes</u> <u>sank</u> to the bottom.
 E F G
2. Ⓔ ●F Ⓖ Ⓗ (NONE)

3. At <u>wourk</u> I saw a dog <u>digging</u> for his <u>bone</u>.
 A B C
3. ●A Ⓑ Ⓒ Ⓓ (NONE)

4. If you're not <u>sick</u>, <u>try</u> to <u>pleay</u> a song.
 E F G
4. Ⓔ Ⓕ ●G Ⓗ (NONE)

5. I will <u>draw</u> a <u>slide</u> with my left <u>hand</u>.
 A B C
5. Ⓐ Ⓑ Ⓒ ●D (NONE)

6. Did he <u>try</u> to <u>bragg</u> about how well he can <u>swim</u>?
 E F G
6. Ⓔ ●F Ⓖ Ⓗ (NONE)

7. Maria was too <u>sick</u> to <u>kome</u> out and <u>play</u>.
 A B C
7. Ⓐ ●B Ⓒ Ⓓ (NONE)

8. Inside the <u>cheast</u> was a <u>smooth</u> <u>bone</u>.
 E F G
8. ●E Ⓕ Ⓖ Ⓗ (NONE)

9. <u>Try</u> using your <u>hend</u> to <u>smooth</u> the clay.
 A B C
9. Ⓐ ●B Ⓒ Ⓓ (NONE)

[Go on →]

Book 2.2 / Unit 2 Review Test

Name_____ Date_____ UNIT TEST SPELLING 160

10. Please <u>come</u> to <u>play</u> on my <u>sliede</u>.
 E F G
10. Ⓔ Ⓕ ●G Ⓗ (NONE)

11. I <u>brag</u> that I can <u>drow</u> a dinosaur <u>bone</u>.
 A B C
11. Ⓐ ●B Ⓒ Ⓓ (NONE)

12. She will <u>speak</u> about <u>digging</u> for the <u>cheste</u>.
 E F G
12. Ⓔ Ⓕ ●G Ⓗ (NONE)

13. I will <u>bake</u> <u>soft</u> cookies at <u>work</u> today.
 A B C
13. Ⓐ Ⓑ Ⓒ ●D (NONE)

14. <u>Come</u> to the lake and <u>swim</u> to the <u>stone</u> wall.
 E F G
14. Ⓔ Ⓕ Ⓖ ●H (NONE)

15. Don't <u>play</u> ball with a broken <u>boan</u> in your <u>hand</u>.
 A B C
15. Ⓐ ●B Ⓒ Ⓓ (NONE)

16. He may <u>play</u> with the <u>smooth</u> ball in the toy <u>chest</u>.
 E F G
16. Ⓔ Ⓕ Ⓖ ●H (NONE)

17. I will <u>try</u> to <u>draw</u> a picture of the boat that <u>sanck</u>.
 A B C
17. Ⓐ Ⓑ ●C Ⓓ (NONE)

18. Raise your <u>hand</u> if you were <u>diggeng</u> near the <u>slide</u>.
 E F G
18. Ⓔ ●F Ⓖ Ⓗ (NONE)

19. I will <u>swimm</u> in the <u>smooth</u> pool if it is <u>chest</u> high.
 A B C
19. ●A Ⓑ Ⓒ Ⓓ (NONE)

20. Tim hurt his <u>hand</u> but he will <u>triy</u> to <u>play</u> ball.
 E F G
20. Ⓔ ●F Ⓖ Ⓗ (NONE)

Phonological Awareness

OBJECTIVES **Children will practice blending and segmenting sounds and deleting the second sound in blends.**

Alternate Activities

Blend Sounds

WHAT'S IN THE JAR?

ONE **Materials:** jar-shaped construction paper

Tell children that they will blend sounds together to determine what item should be drawn in their jars.

- Provide construction paper cut in the shape of a large jar for each child. Tell children that special things belong in these jars. Explain that you are going to tell them what should be in the jar; however, the word will be segmented into individual sounds.
- Ask each child to blend the sounds together to determine the word. Then have children draw the correct item in the jar.
- Say the sounds for the following words for children to blend and then draw inside their jars: *jellybean, popcorn, coin, marble, bee, acorn.*

Segment Sounds

MARCH THE SOUNDS

GROUP **Materials:** music, tape player, marker

Use this game to help children practice segmenting words into individual sounds.

- Organize chairs in a circle around the room. Have each child stand beside a chair. Place a marker on one chair.
- Turn on music and have children walk around the circle. Stop the music periodically and tell them to sit in the closest chair. Invite the child who sits in the chair with the marker to segment a word into individual sounds.
- Use the following words for children to segment while playing the game: *pouch, house, chair, ear, fright, throw, bounce, spoil, morning,* and *short.*

Delete Sounds

WHAT AM I NOW?

GROUP **Materials:** paper and crayons or markers

Tell children that they will delete the second sound in a blend and draw pictures of the new words formed from the remaining sounds.

- Explain the steps children will follow: First, they must repeat the words they hear. Then they will say the sounds in each word. They will take away the second sound, say the rest of the sounds, and the new word formed by these sounds. Finally, they will draw a quick sketch of the new word they made.
- Guide children through an example. Say: *stun, /s/-/t/-/u/-/n/. Take away /t/ makes /s/-/u/-/n/, sun. I'll draw a picture of the sun.*
- Say these words to children, following the pattern shown above (the words children will illustrate are shown in parentheses): *bred (bed), snail (sail), spoil (soil).*

R-controlled Variant Vowels: /âr/*are*; /ôr/*or, ore*; /îr/*ear*

OBJECTIVES Students will recognize and decode words with *r*-controlled vowels.

Alternate Activities

Auditory

MIRROR, MIRROR

GROUP **Materials:** three large cards

Write one of each of the following words on a card: *star, for, clear*. Display the cards to students as you review the sounds of *r*-controlled vowels.

- As you hold up each card, invite a volunteer to repeat the word.
- Invite another volunteer to say a rhyming word with an *r*-controlled vowel. Write the words on the chalkboard to create a word bank.
- Drawing on words from the word bank, have students write and illustrate the word combination, for example: *star car, far tar*.

Visual

SEE IT, SAY IT

GROUP **Materials:** letter cards from the Auditory activity above; noisemakers, such as bells and whistles

Students can play this game to review words with *r*-controlled vowels.

- Give each of three students a different noisemaker in preparation.
- Display one *r*-controlled vowel card at a time. Tell students to sound their noisemakers when they think of a word with the sound represented on the card.
- Call on the first student to sound a noisemaker. If the student's response is correct, he or she scores one point. If it is not correct, ask the next student who sounds a noisemaker.
- Play until one player has three correct responses. Then switch to a new group of players. ▶**Linguistic**

Kinesthetic

MOBILES

ONE **Materials:** wire hangers, fishing line or heavy thread, magazine pictures, markers, scissors, paper

Provide additional practice recognizing words with *r*-controlled vowels as students make mobiles.

- Have students write words or cut out magazine pictures with objects whose names include *r*-controlled vowels spelled: *are; or, ore; ear*.
- Tell students to write a label for each sound, then tie lines or thread to connect the pictures to the labels.
- Have students suspend the pictures and labels from a wire hanger.
- Suspend the completed mobiles in the classroom. ▶**Spatial**

Phonics CD-ROM

See Reteach 169, 173, 174, 182, 190, 198

Various Texts

OBJECTIVES **Students will identify various texts and their characteristics.**

Alternate Activities

Auditory

TEACH EACH OTHER

GROUP **Materials:** variety of types of text, such as: textbook, newspaper, magazine, storybook, poetry book

Provide an opportunity for students to teach classmates about various types of text.

- Organize students into groups of three or four. Give each group a different type of text to examine. Ask groups to answer these questions about the text: *What kinds of information are in this text? Is the information real or make-believe? When would you probably use this type of text?*

WRITING Tell group members to make notes in response to the questions and prepare a very brief report for the class.

- Have each group member share one piece of information in the presentation. **▶Interpersonal**

Kinesthetic

FIND ME

GROUP **Materials:** variety of types of text, such as: textbook, newspaper, magazine, storybook, poetry book

Display a variety of types of texts.

- Provide time for students to look over the materials. Then spread the materials on a table where three students can stand at one time.
- Play *Find Me*, asking questions whose answers identify a type of text. Examples: *You may find rhyming words in me. You'll find today's weather report in me.* Students can answer by holding up samples of material that answer the question. **▶Logical/Mathematical**

Visual

GIANT PAGES

GROUP **Materials:** photocopies of pages from a newspaper, an encyclopedia, a picture book, a textbook; poster board

Students can construct simple displays using photocopies of pages from different types of texts.

- Have students work in four groups. Each group will create one poster that includes only encyclopedia pages, only newspaper pages, only picture book pages, or only textbook pages.

WRITING Tell students to write a list of purposes at the bottom of the poster to explain why they would use the source illustrated. **▶Spatial**

See Reteach 172, 180, 188, 196

Summarize

TESTED OBJECTIVES Students will summarize the events of a story they have read or seen.

Alternate Activities

Auditory

SOUND SUMMARIES

ONE **Materials:** tape recorder

Remind students that a summary contains only the most important information. It does not include minor details.

- Have individual students retell the main events of a story they have read or heard.
- Record students so they can listen to themselves, evaluate whether their summaries are complete and organized, and retape it if necessary. ▶**Intrapersonal**

Kinesthetic

PIECES OF A PUZZLE

PARTNERS **Materials:** heavy paper, pencils, scissors, envelopes

WRITING Have partners write a summary of a story the entire group has read or an experience they have shared.

- Tell students to cut the sentences apart and place the sentence "pieces" in an envelope.
- Have students switch summaries with another pair to reassemble the sentences in a logical order. ▶**Bodily/Kinesthetic**

Visual

CARTOON SUMMARY

ONE **Materials:** drawing paper with three or four blank cartoon frames

Use this activity to help students summarize a television program or play they have watched or a story they have read.

- Have students use the blank cartoon frames to create a cartoon strip that summarizes the plot. Remind them to include only the most important events.

WRITING Tell students to write a caption for each frame. ▶**Spatial**

See Reteach 175, 191, 206

Suffixes

OBJECTIVES **Students will recognize and use words with suffixes *-ly* and *-ful.***

Alternate Activities

Kinesthetic

HANG ONTO YOUR SUFFIX

GROUP **Materials:** heavy paper, hole punch, string, marker

Make name tags for two students to hang around their necks. On one, write *-ly;* on the other, write *-ful.* Prepare name tags for other students with these words and others that can be combined correctly with only one of the suffixes: *sad, sweet, mouth, joy, play, nice, care, tear, mind, glad.*

- Have students wearing the base words stand in a circle. Ask the student wearing the suffix *-ly* to choose others whose words can combine correctly with that suffix to gather in the middle of the circle.
- Ask other students to decide whether each choice is correct.
- Have students return to the edge of the circle and repeat with the *-ful* suffix.
  ▶Bodily/Kinesthetic

Visual

WORD WHEEL

PARTNERS **Materials:** two poster board circles, one smaller than the other, paper fastener

Students will use a word wheel to practice forming words with suffixes.

- Make a word wheel by cutting one large wheel and one small wheel from poster board. Attach the circles with a paper fastener through the center of both. Write words to which the suffix *-ly* or *-ful* can be added around the center of the smaller circle clockwise, as spokes of a wheel. Then choose either of these suffixes and write it on the right side of the larger wheel, where it peeks out from behind the smaller circle.
- Have partners take turns matching the next word with the suffix. Tell them to decide together if the combination makes a real word.

WRITING Ask them to write a list of the words they form. **▶Interpersonal**

Auditory

A MOUTHFUL OF SUFFIXES

GROUP Have students listen for clues and respond orally.

- Give oral clues to words that end with the suffix *-ly* or *-ful.*
- For example: *how you feel when you are full of joy; how you move in a way that is slow.*
- Invite students to say each word with the suffix that fits the clue. **▶Linguistic**

See Reteach 176, 192, 208

Phonological Awareness

OBJECTIVES **Children will practice blending and segmenting sounds and deleting the second sound in blends.**

Alternate Activities

Blend Sounds

STRING A BEAD

GROUP **Materials:** beads and string

Tell children that they will string beads as they blend sounds to form words.

- Give each child a length of string and ten beads.
- Demonstrate by saying the sounds for the word *stool*, /s/-/t/-/ü/-/l/. As you say each sound, put a bead on the string. After you pronounce the final sound, /l/, say *stool*.
- Guide children in joining the activity, stringing their beads as you pronounce the sounds for the following words: *spoon, scoot, strut, clue, broom, stump, stuff, careful*. Then have them say the word. Tell children to remove the beads from the string after they say each word, then continue with the next word.

Segment Sounds

COUNT THE BLUE DOTS

ONE **Materials:** Word Building Boxes from *Word Building Kit*, construction paper, scissors

Have children segment words into individual sounds.

- Ask children to cut six dots from blue construction paper and place their Word Building Boxes in front of them.
- Have children begin the activity with the name *Drew*. Stretch the word out as you pronounce it and ask children to place a blue dot into the Word Building Box to mark each sound.
- Ask children to continue the activity independently by segmenting at least five names of people in their class or family members. If there are more sounds than they have squares on their Word Building Boxes, they can draw additional boxes on the sheet.

Delete Sounds

GOOD-BYE TWO

GROUP **Materials:** construction paper, scissors

Explain to children that they will remove paper squares as they delete sounds.

- Have children cut out construction paper squares.
- Pronounce the following words, segmenting each into individual sounds: *troop, swoop, stool, blew, smash, gray, glass, crash, slight*.
- Children place paper squares in front of them as they repeat the sounds in each word and say the word. Then tell them to say the second sound in the word and remove the square that stands for that sound.
- Now they pronounce the remaining sounds. For example, if children place four squares for *troop*, they say /r/, *toop*. Explain that the remaining sounds may or may not form words.

Variant Vowel /ü/ *oo, ue, ew*

TESTED OBJECTIVES **Students will recognize and decode words with variant vowel /ü/, spelled *oo, ue, ew*.**

Alternate Activities

Auditory

SORT AND SAY

PARTNERS **Materials:** cards, pencils

Provide an opportunity for students to sort /ü/ words by the vowel spelling and read the words aloud.

WRITING Have students brainstorm as many words as they can with the /ü/ sound. Tell them to write each word on a separate card.

- Tell partners to sort the words by the spelling of the vowel sound. Have them form three piles: *oo, ue, ew*.
- Encourage students to display the cards in each pile as flashcards for partners to practice reading the words aloud. ▶**Linguistic**

Kinesthetic

USE GLUE, TOO

ONE **Materials:** squeeze bottles of glue, pencils, drawing paper

Students will prepare a vivid display of /ü/ words.

WRITING Have students write sentences on scrap paper using as many /ü/ words as they can. Correct the spelling, and have students neatly copy their corrected sentences in large letters on drawing paper.

- Tell students to trace over any /ü/ words spelled *oo, ew*, or *ue* with glue and sprinkle glitter over the wet glue.
- When the glue is completely dry, encourage students to share their work with others in a small group. ▶**Spatial**

Visual

MAKE /Ü/ STEW

ONE **Materials:** magazine pictures, scissors, a pot

Help students locate and use pictures representing the /ü/ sound to create a recipe for /ü/ stew.

- Have students search through magazines for pictures of objects whose names have the /ü/ sound.
- As students add each picture to the pot to make /ü/ stew, list the name of each object on chart paper to make a recipe for /ü/ stew.
- To "serve" the stew, "stir" the pictures in the pot. Have each student select one picture and name and spell the word with the /ü/ sound it represents.

Phonics **CD-ROM**

See Reteach 177, 181, 182, 190, 201

Sequence of Events

TESTED OBJECTIVES **Students will correctly identify the sequence of events in a song, a daily schedule, and a story.**

Alternate Activities

Visual

ONE THING AT A TIME

ONE **Materials:** cards, pencils

Students will practice sequencing through the use of a daily schedule.

- Have students reference four events from one day's schedule, writing a sentence or drawing a quick picture of each event on a separate card.
- Have students mix up the cards and then lay them out in order. Ask them to identify what they do first, second, third, and fourth. ▶**Logical/Mathematical**

Auditory

SING A SONG OF SEQUENCE

GROUP Tell students you will sing a song together. Ask them to try to remember the order of the verses.

- Sing a song with several verses, such as *Old McDonald* or *Mary Had a Little Lamb.*
- Ask volunteers to retell what each verse was about—in order. List students' responses on chart paper. ▶**Musical**

Kinesthetic

ACT IT OUT—IN ORDER

GROUP **Materials:** a short story

Tell students to listen for the sequence of events in a story.

- Retell a familiar story, or read a short story to students.
- Call on students to act out the events, as they occurred, in order. Have volunteers briefly describe each event as a student acts it out. Write a phrase on the chalkboard to describe each one.
- Ask the class to confirm the sequence you have listed. Then add numbers or clue words, such as: *first, then, later,* and *finally* next to the corresponding events. ▶**Logical/Mathematical**

See Reteach 183, 199, 205

Phonological Awareness

OBJECTIVES Children will practice blending and segmenting and substituting beginning, middle, and ending sounds.

Alternate Activities

Blend Sounds

LISTEN TO THE LETTER

GROUP Have children listen as you read the letter below. Explain that the writer segmented some of the words as a game. Ask children to listen carefully and blend the sounds to identify each word:

Dear Mom and /D/-/a/-/d/,

I am having fun at /k/-/a/-/m/-/p/. It is /b/-/e/-/t/-/ər/ than last /s/-/u/-/m/-/ər/. We /s/-/w/-/i/-/m/ everyday. We made ice /k/-/r/-/ē/-/m/ yesterday.

Love,

Helen

- Reread the letter. Pause after each segmented word and ask a volunteer to blend the word. Continue reading the letter.

Segment Sounds

NEIGHBOR NAMES

ONE **Materials:** Word Building Boxes from *Word Building Kit,* game markers or pennies

Have children segment the sounds in the names of children who are sitting near them.

- Draw as many squares on the board as there are sounds in your name, say your name, and pronounce it sound by sound, making a mark in a square for each sound as you say it.
- Have children choose the name of a person who is sitting near them, say it softly to themselves, and move a game marker or penny onto a Word Building Box for each sound they hear.
- Explain that children may need to draw one or more additional boxes on their Word Building Box sheet to account for all the sounds in some names.
- Ask children to continue this activity as they say the names of at least four other classroom neighbors.

Substitute Sounds

CLAP, RATTLE, AND STOMP

GROUP **Materials:** musical instruments

Tell children that they will listen to word pairs to determine whether the beginning, middle, or end sound is changed.

- Organize children into three groups.
- Have children listen to the following word pairs: *mare/hare, book/boom, letter/better, pitch/patch, cap/cape, ever/even.*
- Ask children to determine which sound is substituted to make the second word. If there is an initial substitution, have the first group clap their hands. If there is a medial substitution, ask the second group to rattle an instrument, such as a maraca. If there is a final substitution, ask group three to stomp their feet.

/ər/ er; /ən/ en; /əl/ le

TESTED OBJECTIVES Students will recognize and decode words with the sounds /ər/ *er;* /ən/ *en;* /əl/ *le.*

Alternate Activities

Visual

MESSAGE IN A BOTTLE

PARTNERS **Materials:** construction paper, white paper, bottle-shaped pattern, glue, scissors, pencil

Explain that people have used writing to communicate with others for thousands of years.

- Display a bottle, and ask if students have ever heard of sending a message in a bottle.
- Distribute construction paper and patterns, and have students cut in the shape of a bottle.

WRITING Tell students to write a message using words with *er, en,* and *le*. Correct the spelling, and have students make a clean copy.

- Have students glue their messages to the bottles and give them to a partner to read. ▶**Spatial**

Kinesthetic

HOPSCOTCH

GROUP **Materials:** tape or chalk

Use tape or chalk to construct a hopscotch board on the floor or playground.

- In addition to numbering the boxes, write one of these letter combinations in each box: *er, en, le*.
- Have a small group of students play hopscotch. As they land in each box, they must name a word that contains the letters in the box. Encourage students to choose words in which the letters represent one of the following sounds: /ər/, /ən/, /əl/. ▶**Bodily/Kinesthetic**

Auditory

BETTER LISTEN

GROUP This activity requires that students listen carefully for a specific sound.

- For each group of words, tell students to listen for a particular sound. Have them show thumbs up or thumbs down for each word to indicate whether it contains that sound.

/ər/:	<u>brother</u>, friend, ferry
/ər/:	<u>sister</u>, <u>daughter</u>, <u>mother</u>
/ən/:	checker, pattern, <u>broken</u>
/əl/:	<u>trouble</u>, umbrella, better
/əl/:	baby, <u>bottle</u>, bottom
/ər/:	<u>gather</u>, garden, <u>grocer</u>
/ən/:	ticket, <u>taken</u>, talker

▶**Musical**

Phonics CD-ROM

See Reteach 185, 189, 190, 198, 201

Context Clues

TESTED OBJECTIVES **Students will use context clues to answer riddles, follow a treasure map, and determine the meanings of unfamiliar words.**

Alternate Activities

Visual

PICTURE CLUES

ONE **Materials:** list of words, pencils and drawing paper, crayons or markers

- Give each student a secret word that is unfamiliar, and explain privately what the word means.

WRITING Have each student write the word on a piece of drawing paper and draw a number of picture clues to help others interpret the meaning. For example, the word *cattle* might show a herd of cows grazing in a field.

- Encourage students to share their words and drawings, as others use the picture clues to guess the meaning of each word. ▶**Spatial**

Auditory

RIDDLE PLAY

ONE **Materials:** paper, pencils

Model for students how to write riddles that give context clues for guessing the answer.

- Example: *I smell nice. I look pretty. I grow with sun and water. Who am I? (a flower)*

WRITING Have each student write a set of clues for a riddle. Students can read the clues for classmates to guess answers to the riddles.
▶**Logical/Mathematical**

Kinesthetic

TREASURE HUNT

GROUP **Materials:** small pieces of paper, pencils, treats such as crackers or raisins (optional)

Explain that students will prepare clues for a treasure hunt.

WRITING Have groups of students collaborate to write a series of three or four clues that direct others to a place in the school building. Each clue should lead students to the next.

- Clues should include hints about a place or object without identifying it by name. Example: You get two points if you go through me. (basketball hoop) ▶**Logical/Mathematical**

See Reteach 184, 200, 207

Phonological Awareness

OBJECTIVES **Children will practice blending and segmenting sounds and substituting beginning, middle, and ending sounds.**

Alternate Activities

Blend Sounds

TOUCH THE PICTURE

PARTNERS **Materials:** picture books

Tell children that they will use picture books to help them blend words.

- Organize the class into pairs and give each pair a picture book. Tell children they will use the books to choose words to blend.
- Model the activity with a volunteer. Look through a picture book and choose something you see. You might say, for example, /t/-/oi/. The volunteer blends the sounds to make the word *toy* and touches the picture to indicate that he or she blended the word correctly.
- Have partners take turns finding pictures and blending words.

Segment Sounds

DRAW AND COUNT

ONE **Materials:** paper and crayons or markers

Tell children to draw items from various categories and then count the number of sounds in the name of each item.

- Name categories, such as flowers, animals, and toys. Invite children to brainstorm items that fit in each category.
- Model the following procedure: Tell them that if the category were transportation, you might choose bus. Draw a quick sketch of a bus on the chalkboard and say, *bus,* /b/-/u/-/s/. Then make three checkmarks beneath the picture to show the number of sounds in the word.
- Continue the activity, having children draw a picture for an item in each category. Remind them to make a checkmark beneath their drawings for each sound they hear in the word.

Substitute Sounds

PICTURE THIS!

GROUP **Materials:** Phonics Picture Cards and Phonics Pictures from *Word Building Kit*

Have children use picture cards to help them substitute beginning, middle, and ending sounds.

- Show children a picture card and ask them to say the word that names the picture. Then invite them to change a beginning, middle, or ending sound in the word.
- For example, display the picture card for mouse and say, *mouse,* /m/-/ou/-/s/. Then say, *If I substitute the* /m/ *sound in mouse with the* /h/ *sound, that makes house.* Draw a picture of a house on the board.
- Continue the activity with other picture cards, having children change beginning, middle, and ending sounds. Ask them to draw a picture to illustrate the new word.

/ou/ow, ou; /oi/oy, oi

TESTED OBJECTIVES **Students will recognize and decode words with diphthongs /ou/*ow, ou;* /oi/*oy, oi.***

Alternate Activities

Auditory

SILLY SENTENCES

GROUP Focus students' attention on words with diphthongs by brainstorming words that contain the sounds /ou/ and /oi/.

- Say the following sentences slowly, then ask students to repeat them: *How now, brown cow? Noisy toys bring boys joy.*
- Have students work with partners to create other oral sentences that contain /oi/ or /ou/ sounds. Encourage them to share their new sentences with the group. ▶**Linguistic**

Visual

PICTURE THAT

ONE **Materials:** drawing paper, markers or crayons

Tell students to imagine a town filled with flowers and noisy toys. Invite them to create their own pictures of objects whose names contain /oi/ and /ou/ sounds.

- Have students write a caption on the back of the picture. For example: *A brown cow is eating a tower of flowers.*
- Display students' pictures, and invite classmates to guess some of the words in the caption. ▶**Spatial**

Kinesthetic

DIPHTHONG RELAY

ONE **Materials:** two copies of a list of sounds, word cards as described below

Have students play a relay game to discriminate between /ou/ and /oi/.

- Make up a list of words that contain the sound /oi/ or /ou/ in random order. Prepare two sets of cards, each containing words with a same sound for each word on the list. Stack the cards in random order in two piles at one end of the room.
- Have two teams of players line up.
- Give the list to the first player on each team. These players each run to a pile of cards to find a word with that sound. They return the cards to teammates to begin a stack.
- The list goes to the next person, who repeats the steps.
- When each team member has run and returned with a card, check the cards to make sure that they represent the sounds in the same order as those on the list. ▶**Bodily/Kinesthetic**

Phonics **CD-ROM**

See Reteach 193, 197, 198, 201

A Communication Tool

Although typewriters and computers are readily available, many situations continue to require handwriting. Tasks such as keeping journals, completing forms, taking notes, making shopping or organizational lists, and the ability to read handwritten manuscript or cursive writing are a few examples of practical application of this skill.

BEFORE YOU BEGIN

Before children begin to write, certain fine motor skills need to be developed. Examples of activities that can be used as warm-up activities are:

- **Simon Says** Play a game of Simon Says using just finger positions.
- **Finger Plays and Songs** Sing songs that use Signed English, American Sign Language or finger spelling.
- **Mazes** Mazes are available in a wide range of difficulty. You can also create mazes that allow children to move their writing instruments from left to right.

Determining Handedness

Keys to determining handedness in a child:

- Which hand does the child eat with? This is the hand that is likely to become the dominant hand.
- Does the child start coloring with one hand and then switch to the other? This may be due to fatigue rather than lack of hand preference.
- Does the child cross midline to pick things up or use the closest hand? Place items directly in front of the child to see if one hand is preferred.
- Does the child do better with one hand or the other?

The Mechanics of Writing

DESK AND CHAIR

- Chair height should allow for the feet to rest flat on the floor.
- Desk height should be two inches above the level of the elbows when the child is sitting.
- The chair should be pulled in allowing for an inch of space between the child's abdomen and the desk.
- Children sit erect with the elbows resting on the desk.
- Children should have models of letters on the desk or at eye level, not above their heads.

PAPER POSITION

- **Right-handed children** should turn the paper so that the lower left-hand corner of the paper points to the abdomen.

- **Left-handed children** should turn the paper so that the lower right-hand corner of the paper points to the abdomen.

- The nondominant hand should anchor the paper near the top so that the paper doesn't slide.
- The paper should be moved up as the child nears the bottom of the paper. Many children won't think of this and may let their arms hang off the desk when they reach the bottom of a page.

The Writing Instrument Grasp

For handwriting to be functional, the writing instrument must be held in a way that allows for fluid dynamic movement.

FUNCTIONAL GRASP PATTERNS

- **Tripod Grasp** With open web space, the writing instrument is held with the tip of the thumb and the index finger and rests against the side of the third finger. The thumb and index finger form a circle.

- **Quadrupod Grasp** With open web space, the writing instrument is held with the tip of the thumb and index finger and rests against the fourth finger. The thumb and index finger form a circle.

INCORRECT GRASP PATTERNS

- **Fisted Grasp** The writing instrument is held in a fisted hand.

- **Pronated Grasp** The writing instrument is held diagonally within the hand with the tips of the thumb and index finger on the writing instrument but with no support from other fingers.

- **Five-Finger Grasp** The writing instrument is held with the tips of all five fingers.

TO CORRECT WRITING INSTRUMENT GRASPS

- Have children play counting games with an eye dropper and water.
- Have children pick up small objects with a tweezer.
- Do counting games with children picking up small coins using just the thumb and index finger.

FLEXED OR HOOKED WRIST

- The writing instrument can be held in a variety of grasps with the wrist flexed or bent. This is typically seen with left-handed writers but is also present in some right-handed writers. To correct wrist position, have children check their writing posture and paper placement.

Evaluation Checklist

Functional writing is made up of two elements, legibility and functional speed.

LEGIBILITY

MANUSCRIPT

Formation and Strokes

- ☑ Does the child begin letters at the top?
- ☑ Do circles close?
- ☑ Are the horizontal lines straight?
- ☑ Do circular shapes and extender and descender lines touch?
- ☑ Are the heights of all upper-case letters equal?
- ☑ Are the heights of all lower-case letters equal?
- ☑ Are the lengths of the extenders and descenders the same for all letters?

Directionality

- ☑ Are letters and words formed from left to right?
- ☑ Are letters and words formed from top to bottom?

Spacing

- ☑ Are the spaces between letters equidistant?
- ☑ Are the spaces between words equidistant?
- ☑ Do the letters rest on the line?
- ☑ Are the top, bottom and side margins even?

CURSIVE

Formation and Strokes

- ☑ Do circular shapes close?
- ☑ Are the downstrokes parallel?
- ☑ Do circular shapes and downstroke lines touch?
- ☑ Are the heights of all upper-case letters equal?
- ☑ Are the heights of all lower-case letters equal?
- ☑ Are the lengths of the extenders and descenders the same for all letters?
- ☑ Do the letters which finish at the top join the next letter? (*b, o, v, w*)
- ☑ Do the letters which finish at the bottom join the next letter? (*a, c, d, h, i, k, l, m, n, r, s, t, u, x*)
- ☑ Do letters with descenders join the next letter? (*f, g, j, p, q, y, z*)
- ☑ Do all letters touch the line?
- ☑ Is the vertical slant of all letters consistent?

Directionality

- ☑ Are letters and words formed from left to right?
- ☑ Are letters and words formed from top to bottom?

Spacing

- ☑ Are the spaces between letters equidistant?
- ☑ Are the spaces between words equidistant?
- ☑ Do the letters rest on the line?
- ☑ Are the top, bottom and side margins even?

SPEED

The prettiest handwriting is not functional for classroom work if it takes the child three times longer than the rest of the class to complete work assignments. After the children have been introduced to writing individual letters, begin to add time limitations to the completion of copying or writing assignments. Then check the child's work for legibility.

Handwriting Models—Manuscript

A B C D E F G H

I J K L M N O P

Q R S T U V W

X Y Z

a b c d e f g h

i j k l m n o p

q r s t u v w

x y z

Handwriting Models—Cursive

A B C D E F G H I

J K L M N O P Q R

S T U V W X Y Z

a b c d e f g h i j

k l m n o p q r s

t u v w x y z

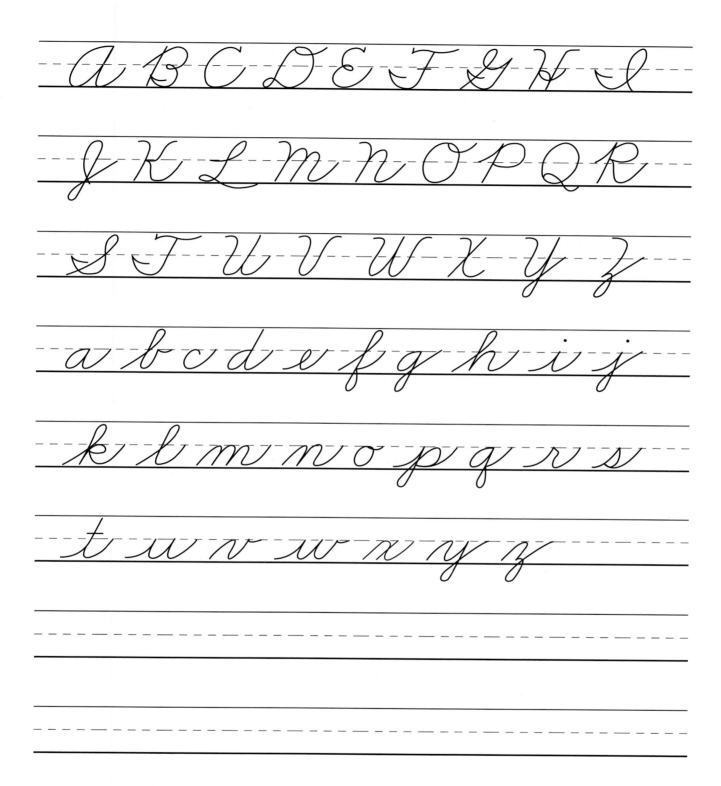

Handwriting Models—Slant

A B C D E F G H

I J K L M N O P

Q R S T U V W

X Y Z

a b c d e f g h

i j k l m n o p

q r s t u v w

x y z

Handwriting Practice

Selection Titles	Honors, Prizes, and Awards
HENRY AND MUDGE Book 1, p.38 by ***Cynthia Rylant*** Illustrated by ***Suçie Stevenson***	**American Book Award Pick of the List (1987)** **Author: *Cynthia Rylant,*** winner of Caldecott Honor (1983) for *When I Was Young in the Mountains;* ALA Notable (1985) for *Waiting to Waltz: A Childhood: Poems;* ALA Notable, Caldecott Honor (1986), New York Times Best Illustrated (1985) for *The Relatives Came;* ALA Notable (1986) for *Blue-Eyed Daisy;* ALA Notable, Newbery Honor (1987) for *Fine White Dust;* ALA Notable (1988) for *Henry and Mudge Under the Yellow Moon;* ALA Notable (1991) for *Henry and Mudge and the Happy Cat;* ALA Notable (1992), Boston Globe-Horn Book Award (1991) for *Appalachia: The Voices of the Sleeping Birds;* ALA Notable (1993) for *Angel for Solomon Singer;* ALA Notable, Newbery Medal (1993), Boston Globe-Horn Book Award (1992) for *Missing May;* ALA Notable (1996) for *Mr. Putter and Tabby Pick the Pears;* ALA Notable (1996) for *Van Gogh Café* **Illustrator: *Suçie Stevenson,*** winner ALA Notable (1988) for *Henry and Mudge Under the Yellow Moon;* ALA Notable (1991) for *Henry and Mudge and the Happy Cat*
ROUNDUP AT RIO RANCH Book 1, p.94 by ***Angela Shelf Medearis***	**Author: *Angela Shelf Medearis,*** winner of IRA-Teachers' Choice Award (1995) for *Our People*
THE MERRY-GO-ROUND Book 1, p.124 by ***Myra Cohn Livingston***	**Poet: *Myra Cohn Livingston,*** winner of National Council of Teachers of English Award for Excellence in Poetry for Children (1980); ALA Notable (1984) for *Christmas Poems;* ALA Notable (1987) for *Cat Poems;* ALA Notable (1992) for *Poem-Making: Ways to Learn Writing Poetry*
A LETTER TO AMY Book 1, p.158 by ***Ezra Jack Keats***	**Author/Illustrator: *Ezra Jack Keats,*** winner of Caldecott Medal (1963) for *The Snowy Day;* Caldecott Honor (1970) for *Goggles;* Boston Globe-Horn Book Award (1970) for *Hi, Cat!*
THE BEST FRIENDS CLUB Book 1, p.194 by ***Elizabeth Winthrop*** Illustrated by ***Martha Weston***	**IRA-CBC Children's Choice (1990)** **Illustrator: *Martha Weston,*** winner of ALA Notable (1989) for *Big Beast Book: Dinosaurs and How They Got That Way*

Selection Titles	Honors, Prizes, and Awards
JAMAICA TAG-ALONG Book 1, p.218 by ***Juanita Havill***	**Author: *Juanita Havill,*** winner of Ezra Jack Keats Award (1987)
FOUR GENERATIONS Book 1, p.254 by ***Mary Ann Hoberman***	**Poet: *Mary Ann Hoberman,*** winner of American Book Award Paperback Picture Book (1983) for *A House Is a House for Me*
CLOUD DRAGONS Book 1, p.256 by ***Pat Mora***	**Author: *Pat Mora,*** winner of National Association for Chicano Studies Creative Writing Award (1983); New America: Woman Artists and Writers of the Southwest Award (1984); Smithsonian Magazine Notable Books for Children (1998) for *Tomás and the Library Lady*
ARTHUR WRITES A STORY Book 1, p.260 by ***Marc Brown***	**IRA-CBC Children's Choice (1997)** **Author/Illustrator: *Marc Brown,*** winner of Boston Globe-Horn Book Honor (1980) for *Why the Tides Ebb and Flow;* ALA Notable (1984) for *The Bionic Bunny Show*
BEST WISHES, ED Book 1, p.292 by ***James Stevenson***	**Author /Illustrator: *James Stevenson,*** winner of Boston Globe-Horn Book Honor (1998) for *Popcorn: Poems;* Christopher Award (1983) for *We Can't Sleep;* ALA Notable (1984) for *What's Under My Bed;* ALA Notable (1987) for *When I Was Nine;* ALA Notable, Boston Globe-Horn Book Honor (1987) for *Georgia Music;* ALA Notable (1988) for *Grandaddy's Place;* ALA Notable (1991) for *July;* ALA Notable (1993) for *Don't You Know There's a War On?;* ALA Notable (1994) for *Grandaddy and Janetta;* Texas Blue Bonnet Master List (1995), ALA Notable (1996) for *Sweet Corn: Poems;* ALA Notable (1996) for *Grandaddy's Stars*
TIME TO PLAY Book 1, p.380 by ***Nikki Grimes***	**Poet: *Nikki Grimes,*** winner of ALA Notable, Coretta Scott King Award (1979) for *Something on My Mind;* ALA Notable (1995) for *Meet Danitra Brown;* ALA Notable (1996) for *Come Sunday*

Selection Titles	Honors, Prizes, and Awards
RIVER WINDING Book 2, p.10 by ***Charlotte Zolotow***	**Poet: *Charlotte Zolotow,*** winner of Caldecott Honor (1953) for *Storm Book;* Caldecott Honor (1962) for *Mr. Rabbit and the Lovely Present;* Christopher Award (1975) for *My Grandson Leo;* ALA Notable (1996) for *When the Wind Stops*
CHARLIE ANDERSON Book 2, p.14 by ***Barbara Abercrombie*** Illustrated by ***Mark Graham***	**Redbook Children's Picture Book Award (1990)**
ZIPPING, ZAPPING, ZOOMING BATS Book 2, p.94 by ***Anne Earle*** Illustrated by ***Henry Cole***	**American Book Award Pick of the List (1995)**
WHAT IS IT? Book 2, p.128 by ***Eve Merriam***	**Poet: *Eve Merriam,*** winner of National Council of Teachers of English Award for Excellence in Poetry for Children (1981)
THE WEDNESDAY SURPRISE Book 2, p.182 by ***Eve Bunting*** Illustrated by ***Donald Carrick***	**ALA Notable Book (1990), IRA-CBC Children's Choice, IRA-Teachers' Choice, School Library Journal Best Book (1989)** **Author: *Eve Bunting,*** winner of ALA Notable (1990) for *Wall;* ALA Notable (1992) for *Fly Away Home;* Edgar Allen Poe Juvenile Award (1993) for *Coffin on a Case;* ALA Notable, Caldecott Medal (1995) for *Smoky Night;* ALA Notable (1997) for *Train to Somewhere;* National Council for Social Studies Notable Children's Book Award (1998) for *Moonstick,* and *I Am the Mummy Heb-Nefert,* and *On Call Back Mountain* **Illustrator: *Donald Carrick,*** winner of ALA Notable (1987) for *What Happened to Patrick's Dinosaurs?*
FOSSILS TELL OF LONG AGO Book 2, p.214 by ***Aliki***	**National Science Teachers' Association Outstanding Science Tradebook for Children (1990), Library of Congress Children's Book of 1972**

Selection Titles	Honors, Prizes, and Awards
TO CATCH A FISH Book 2, p.246 by ***Eloise Greenfield***	**Poet: *Eloise Greenfield,*** winner of Boston Globe-Horn Book Honor (1975) for *She Come Bringing Me That Little Baby Girl;* Jane Addams Book Award (1976) for *Paul Robeson;* Coretta Scott King Award (1978) for *Africa Dream;* Boston Globe-Horn Book Honor (1980) for *Childtimes: A Three Generation Memoir;* ALA Notable (1989) for *Grandpa's Face;* ALA Notable (1989) for *Under the Sunday Tree;* ALA Notable, Coretta Scott King Award (1990) for *Nathaniel Talking;* ALA Notable (1992) for *Night on Neighborhood Street;* National Council of Teachers of English Award for Excellence in Poetry for Children (1997)
OFFICER BUCKLE AND GLORIA Book 2, p.252 by ***Peggy Rathmann***	**Caldecott Medal, ALA Notable (1996)** **Author/Illustrator: *Peggy Rathmann,*** winner of ALA Notable (1995) for *Good Night, Gorilla*
TOMÁS AND THE LIBRARY LADY Book 2, p.284 by ***Pat Mora*** Illustrated by ***Raul Colón***	**Smithsonian Magazine Notable Books for Children (1998)** **Author: *Pat Mora,*** winner of National Association for Chicano Studies Creative Writing Award (1983); New America: Woman Artists and Writers of the Southwest Award (1984) **Illustrator: *Raul Colón,*** winner of ALA Notable (1996) for *My Mama Had a Dancing Heart*
SWIMMY Book 2, p.342 by ***Leo Lionni***	**Caldecott Honor (1961), *New York Times* Best Illustrated (1960)** **Author/Illustrator: *Leo Lionni,*** winner of Caldecott Honor (1961), *New York Times* Best Illustrated (1960) for *Inch by Inch;* Caldecott Honor (1968), *New York Times* Best Illustrated (1967) for *Frederick;* Caldecott Honor (1970) for *Alexander and the Wind-up Mouse*

	Bremen Town Musicians	Our Soccer League
Trade Books **Additional fiction and nonfiction trade books related to each selection can be shared with children throughout the unit.**	**Multicultural Plays for Children—Volume I: Grades K–3** *Pamela Gerke (Smith and Kraus, Inc., 1996)* Stories from around the world in play form, with information on sets, costumes, and techniques. *Play* **East of the Sun & West of the Moon: A Play** *Nancy Willard, illustrated by Barry Moser (Harcourt Brace Jovanovich, 1989)* A play based upon the well-known Norwegian fairy tale about a girl who travels to free her beloved prince. *Play* **Fifty Fabulous Fables: Beginning Readers Theatre** *Suzanne I. Barchers (Teacher Ideas Press, 1997)* Fifty well-known fables are gathered for readers theatre. *Fable*	**Starting Soccer** *Helen Edam and Mike Osborne, illustrated by Norman Young, Harriet Castor (Osborne House, 1993)* A clear explanation of soccer and its techniques is presented in text and illustrations. *Nonfiction* **Olympics!** *B. G. Hennessy, illustrated by Michael D. Chesworth (Viking, 1996)* An overview of the history, preparation, and training of the Olympic Games. *Nonfiction* **Arthur Makes the Team** *Marc Brown (Little, Brown, 1998)* Arthur is worried that he won't be able to play as well as his teammates. *Fiction*
Technology **Multimedia resources can be used to enhance children's understanding of the selections.**	***Bremen Town Musicians*** (BFA Educational Media) Video, 11 min. A dramatic retelling of the literature. ***How to Solve a Problem*** (BFA Educational Media) Video, 13 min. Children work together to come up with a solution to a problem. ***Ultimate Writing and Creativity Center*** (SVE/Churchill Media) CD-ROM Guides students through stages of the writing process. Animated talking figures suggest 100 project ideas and story starters.	***Sports Pages*** (Reading Rainbow/GPN) Video, 30 min. Sports, including bicycling, basketball, weight lifting, and soccer are described. ***Breaking the Sound Barrier: Learning to Value People with Disabilities*** (Coronet/MTI Film and Video) Video, 34 min. Helps children understand and accept people with disabilities. ***Nice Things Kids Can Do, Let's Get Along Series*** (United Learning) Video, 15 min. A program about skills that solve conflicts and differences.

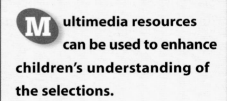

TIME FOR KIDS

The Wednesday Surprise

Jeremiah Learns to Read
Jo Ellen Bogart, illustrated by Laura Fernandez & Rick Jacobson (Orchard Books,1999)

First published in Canada, this story tells of an elderly farmer, who is determined to learn how to read.
Realistic Fiction

Amber on the Mountain
Tony Johnston, illustrated by Robert Duncan (Dial Books for Young Readers, 1994)

Amber, a lonely young girl living on a mountain, meets a friend who teaches her how to read.
Fiction

More Than Anything Else
Marie Bradby, illustrated by Chris K. Soentpiet (Orchard Books, 1996)

Young Booker T. Washington wants to learn how to read more than anything else in the world.
Historical Fiction

The Wednesday Surprise (Coronet/MTI) Videodisc, 14 min. An award-winning version of the literature.

Why We Need Reading: The Piemaker of Ignoramia (Coronet/MTI) Video, 12 min. An animated program that shows children why they need to read.

Today Was a Terrible Day (Pied Piper/AIMS Multimedia) Video or filmstrip, 8 min. Ronald has a terrible day until he discovers that he has learned to read.

Fossils Tell of Long Ago

Dinosaur Bones
Aliki (HarperCollins Children's Books, 1990)

How scientists provide information on dinosaurs from studying fossils.
Nonfiction

Dinosaurs
Gail Gibbons (Holiday House, 1988)

Characteristics and habits of a variety of dinosaurs are described and illustrated.
Nonfiction

The Most Amazing Dinosaur
James Stevenson (Greenwillow, 2000)

Wilfred the Rat finds shelter in a museum and has many adventures there among the exhibits.
Fantasy

Dinosaurs: Lessons from Bones (SRA McGraw-Hill) Video, 25 min. From dig-site to museum, this is an exploration of fossil bones and the secrets they hold.

Fossil Life: An Introduction (United Learning) Video, 19 min. An introduction to fossils.

The Past (SVE/Churchill Media) Video, 12 min. Analyzes clues from the past such as fossils, tree rings, and soil/rock layers that show what happened throughout our natural history.

Are You a Fossil Fan?

Digging Up Dinosaurs
Aliki (HarperCollins Children's Books, 1988)

An introduction to the various types of dinosaurs and an explanation of how scientists uncover, preserve, and study dinosaur bones.
Nonfiction

If You Are a Hunter of Fossils
Byrd Baylor, illustrated by Peter Parnall (Aladdin Books, 1984)

A fossil hunter looking for signs of an ancient sea in the Texas mountain area describes how it must have looked millions of years ago.
Poetry

Archaeologists Dig for Clues
Kate Duke (HarperCollins, 1997)

Learn how scientists study chipped rocks for clues about life thousands of years ago.
Nonfiction

Dinosaurs: The Age of Reptiles (BFA Educational Media) Video, 17 min. A discussion of the painstaking work done by paleontologists and how they strive to provide answers about the past.

A Magical Trip to the Dinosaur Museum (Pied Piper/AIMS) Video, 15 min. In this introduction to fossils and dinosaurs, viewers explore a museum library and an archaeological dig-site.

3-D Dinosaur Adventure (Knowledge Adventure) CD-ROM, Macintosh and Windows. Games and 3-D Technology help children explore the prehistoric world.

Publishers Directory

Abdo & Daughters
4940 Viking Drive, Suite 622
Edina, MN 55435
(800) 458-8399 • www.abdopub.com

Aladdin Paperbacks
(Imprint of Simon & Schuster Children's Publishing)

Atheneum
(Imprint of Simon & Schuster Children's Publishing)

Bantam Doubleday Dell Books for Young Readers
(Imprint of Random House)

Blackbirch Press
260 Amity Rd.
Woodbridge, CT 06525
(203) 387-7525 • (800) 831-9183
www.blackbirch.com

Blue Sky Press
(Imprint of Scholastic)

Boyds Mills Press
815 Church Street
Honesdale, PA 18431
(570) 253-1164 • Fax (570) 253-0179 •
(877) 512-8366
www.boydsmillspress.com

Bradbury Press
(Imprint of Simon & Schuster Children's Publishing)

BridgeWater Books
(Distributed by Penguin Putnam)

Candlewick Press
2067 Masssachusetts Avenue
Cambridge, MA 02140
(617) 661-3330 • Fax (617) 661-0565
www.candlewick.com

Carolrhoda Books
(Division of Lerner Publications Co.)

Children's Press (Division of Grolier, Inc.)
P.O. Box 1795
Danbury, CT 06816-1333
(800) 621-1115 • www.grolier.com

Child's World
P.O. Box 326
Chanhassen, MN 55317-0326
(612) 906-3939 • (800) 599-READ •
www.childsworld.com

Chronicle Books
85 Second Street, Sixth Floor
San Francisco, CA 94105
(415) 537-3730 • Fax (415) 537-4460 •
(800) 722-6657 •
www.chroniclebooks.com

Clarion Books
(Imprint of Houghton Mifflin, Inc.)
215 Park Avenue South
New York, NY 10003
(212) 420-5800 • (800) 726-0600 •
www.houghtonmifflinbooks.com/clarion

Crowell (Imprint of HarperCollins)

Crown Publishing Group
(Imprint of Random House)

Dial Books
(Imprint of Penguin Putnam Inc.)

Dorling Kindersley (DK Publishing)
95 Madison Avenue
New York, NY 10016
(212) 213-4800 • Fax (212) 213-5240 •
(888) 342-5357 • www.dk.com

Doubleday (Imprint of Random House)

E. P. Dutton Children's Books
(Imprint of Penguin Putnam Inc.)

Farrar Straus & Giroux
19 Union Square West
New York, NY 10003
(212) 741-6900 • Fax (212) 741-6973 •
(888) 330-8477

Four Winds Press
(Imprint of Macmillan, see Simon & Schuster Children's Publishing)

Greenwillow Books
(Imprint of William Morrow & Co, Inc.)

Grosset & Dunlap
(Imprint of Penguin Putnam, Inc.)

Harcourt Brace & Co.
6277 Sea Harbor Drive
Orlando, Fl 32887
(407) 345-2000 •
(800) 225-5425 •
www.harcourtbooks.com

Harper & Row (Imprint of HarperCollins)

HarperCollins Children's Books
1350 Avenue of the Americas
New York, NY 10019
(212) 261-6500 • Fax (212) 261-6689 •
(800) 242-7737 •
www.harperchildrens.com

Holiday House
425 Madison Avenue
New York, NY 10017
(212) 688-0085 • Fax (212) 421-6134

Henry Holt and Company
115 West 18th Street
New York, NY 10011
(212) 886-9200 • (212) 633-0748 • (888)
330-8477 • www.henryholt.com/byr/

Houghton Mifflin
222 Berkeley Street
Boston, MA 02116
(617) 351-5000 • Fax (617) 351-1125 •
(800) 225-3362 •
www.houghtonmifflinbooks.com

Hyperion Books
(Division of ABC, Inc.)
77 W. 66th St. 11th floor
New York, NY 10023
(212) 456-0100 • (800) 343-9204 •
www.disney.com

Ideals Children's Books
(Imprint of Hambleton-Hill Publishing, Inc.)
1501 County Hospital Road
Nashville, TN 37218
(615) 254-2451 • (800) 327-5113

Joy Street Books
(Imprint of Little, Brown & Co.)

Just Us Books
356 Glenwood Avenue
E. Orange, NJ 07017
(973) 672-7701 • Fax (973) 677-7570
www.justusbooks.com

Alfred A. Knopf
(Imprint of Random House)

Lee & Low Books
95 Madison Avenue, Room 606
New York, NY 10016
(212) 779-4400 • Fax (212) 683-1894

Lerner Publications Co.
241 First Avenue North
Minneapolis, MN 55401
(612) 332-3344 • Fax (612) 332-7615 •
(800) 328-4929 • www.lernerbooks.com

Little, Brown & Co.
3 Center Plaza
Boston, MA 02108
(617) 227-0730 • Fax (617) 263-2864 •
(800) 759-0190 • www.littlebrown.com

Lothrop Lee & Shepard
(Imprint of William Morrow & Co.)

Macmillan
(Imprint of Simon & Schuster Children's Publishing)

Marshall Cavendish
99 White Plains Road
Tarrytown, NY 10591
(914) 332-8888 • Fax (914) 332-1888 •
(800) 821-9881 •
www.marshallcavendish.com

William Morrow & Co.
(Imprint of HarperCollins)

Morrow Junior Books
(Imprint of HarperCollins)

Mulberry Books
(Imprint of HarperCollins)

National Geographic Society
1145 17th Street, NW
Washington, DC 20036
(202) 857-7345 • (800) 638-4077 •
www.nationalgeographic.com

Northland Publishing
(Division of Justin Industries)
Box 1389
Flagstaff, AZ 86002
(520) 774-5251 • Fax (800) 744-0592 •
(800) 346-3257 • www.northlandpub.com

North-South Books
1123 Broadway, Suite 800
New York, NY 10010
(212) 463-9736 • Fax (212) 633-1004 •
(800) 722-6657 • www.northsouth.com

Orchard Books (A Grolier Company)
95 Madison Avenue
New York, NY 10016
(212) 951-2600 • Fax (212) 213-6435 •
(800) 433-3411 • www.grolier.com

Owlet (Imprint of Henry Holt & Co.)

Penguin Putnam, Inc.
375 Hudson Street
New York, NY 10014
(212) 366-2000 • Fax (212) 366-2636 •
(800) 631-8571 •
www.penguinputnam.com

Willa Perlman Books
(Imprint of Simon & Schuster Children's Publishing)

Philomel Books
(Imprint of Putnam Penguin, Inc.)

Puffin Books
(Imprint of Penguin Putnam, Inc.)

G.P. Putnam's Sons Publishing
(Imprint of Penguin Putnam, Inc.)

Random House
1540 Broadway
New York, NY 10036
(212) 782-9000 • (800) 200-3552 •
Fax (212) 782-9452
www.randomhouse.com/kids

Rourke Corporation
P.O. Box 3328
Vero Beach, FL 32964
(561) 234-6001 • (800) 394-7055 •
www.rourkepublishing.com

Scholastic
555 Broadway
New York, NY 10012
(212) 343-7500 • Fax (212) 965-7442 •
(800) SCHOLASTIC • www.scholastic.com

Charles Scribners's Sons
(Imprint of Simon & Schuster Children's Publishing)

Sierra Club Books for Children
85 Second Street, Second Floor
San Francisco, CA 94105-3441
(415) 977-5500 • Fax (415) 977-5793 •
(800) 935-1056 • www.sierraclub.org

Simon & Schuster Children's Books
1230 Avenue of the Americas
New York, NY 10020
(212) 698-7200 • (800) 223-2336 •
www.simonsays.com/kidzone

Smith & Kraus
177 Lyme Road
Hanover, NH 03755
(603) 643-6431 • Fax (603) 643-1831 •
(800) 895-4331 • www.smithkraus.com

Teacher Ideas Press
(Division of Libraries Unlimited)
P.O. Box 6633
Englewood, CO 80155-6633
(303) 770-1220 • Fax (303) 220-8843 •
(800) 237-6124 • www.lu.com

Ticknor & Fields
(Imprint of Houghton Mifflin, Inc.)

Usborne (Imprint of EDC Publishing)
10302 E. 55th Place, Suite B
Tulsa, OK 74146-6515
(918) 622-4522 • (800) 475-4522 •
www.edcpub.com

Viking Children's Books
(Imprint of Penguin Putnam Inc.)

Watts Publishing
(Imprint of Grolier Publishing; see Children's Press)

Walker & Co.
435 Hudson Street
New York, NY 10014
(212) 727-8300 • (212) 727-0984 •
(800) AT-WALKER

Whispering Coyote Press
300 Crescent Court, Suite 860
Dallas, TX 75201
(800) 929-6104 • Fax (214) 319-7298

Albert Whitman
6340 Oakton Street
Morton Grove, IL 60053-2723
(847) 581-0033 • Fax (847) 581-0039 •
(800) 255-7675 • www.awhitmanco.com

Workman Publishing Co., Inc.
708 Broadway
New York, NY 10003
(212) 254-5900 • Fax (800) 521-1832 •
(800) 722-7202 • www.workman.com

Multimedia Resources

AGC/United Learning
1560 Sherman Avenue, Suite 100
Evanston, IL 60201
(800) 323-9084 •
Fax (847) 328-6706 •
www.unitedlearning.com

AIMS Multimedia
9710 DeSoto Avenue
Chatsworth, CA 91311-4409
(800) 367-2467 •
www.AIMS-multimedia.com

BFA Educational Media
(see Phoenix Learning Group)

Broderbund
(Parsons Technology;
also see The Learning Company)
500 Redwood Blvd
Novato, CA 94997
(800) 395-0277
www.broderbund.com

Carousel Film and Video
260 Fifth Avenue, Suite 705
New York, NY 10001
(212) 683-1660 • e-mail:
carousel@pipeline.com

Cloud 9 Interactive
(888) 662-5683 • www.cloud9int.com

Computer Plus (see ESI)

Coronet/MTI
(see Phoenix Learning Group)

Davidson (see Knowledge Adventure)

Direct Cinema, Ltd.
P.O. Box 10003
Santa Monica, CA 90410-1003
(310) 636-8200 • Fax (310) 396-3233

Disney Interactive
(800) 900-9234 •
www.disneyinteractive.com

DK Multimedia (Dorling Kindersley)
95 Madison Avenue
New York, NY 10016
(212) 213-4800 • Fax: (800) 774-6733 •
(888) 342-5357 • www.dk.com

Edmark Corp.
P.O. Box 97021
Redmond, WA 98073-9721
(800) 362-2890 • www.edmark.com

Encyclopaedia Britannica Educational Corp.
310 South Michigan Avenue
Chicago, IL 60604
(800) 554-9862 • www.eb.com

ESI/Educational Software Institute
4213 S. 94th Street
Omaha, NE 68127
(800) 955-5570 • Fax (402) 592-2017 •
www.edsoft.com

GPN/Reading Rainbow
University of Nebraska-Lincoln
P.O. Box 80669
Lincoln, NE 68501-0669
(800) 228-4630 • Fax (800) 306-2330 •
www.gpn.unl.edu

Hasbro Interactive
(800) 683-5847 • www.hasbro.com

Humongous
13110 NE 177th Pl., Suite B101, Box 180
Woodenville, WA 98072
(800) 499-8386 • www.humongous.com

IBM Corp.
1133 Westchester Ave.
White Plains, NY 10604
(770) 863-1234 • Fax (770) 863-3030 •
(888) 411-1932 •
www.pc.ibm.com/multimedia/crayola

ICE, Inc.
(Distributed by Arch Publishing)
12B W. Main St.
Elmsford, NY 10523
(914) 347-2464 • (800) 843-9497 •
www.educorp.com

Knowledge Adventure
19840 Pioneer Avenue
Torrence, CA 90503
(800) 542-4240 • (800) 545-7677 •
www.knowledgeadventure.com

The Learning Company
6160 Summit Drive North
Minneapolis, MN 55430
(800) 395-0277 • www.learningco.com

Listening Library
A Subsidiary of Random House
One Park Avenue
Greenwich, CT 06870-1727
(800) 243-4504 • www.listeninglib.com

Macmillan/McGraw-Hill
(see SRA/McGraw-Hill)

Maxis
2121 N. California Blvd
Walnut Creek, CA 94596-3572
(925) 933-5630 • Fax (925) 927-3736 •
(800) 245-4525 • www.maxis.com

MECC
(see the Learning Company)

Microsoft
One Microsoft Way
Redmond, WA 98052-6399
(800) 426-9400 • www.microsoft.com/kids

National Geographic Society Educational Services
P.O. Box 10597
Des Moines, IA 50340-0597
(800) 368-2728 • Fax (515) 362-3366
www.nationalgeographic.com/education

National School Products
101 East Broadway
Maryville, TN 37804
(800) 251-9124 • www.ierc.com

PBS Video
1320 Braddock Place
Alexandria, VA 22314
(800) 344-3337 • www.pbs.org

Phoenix Films
(see Phoenix Learning Group)

The Phoenix Learning Group
2348 Chaffee Drive
St. Louis, MO 63146
(800) 221-1274 • e-mail:
phoenixfilms@worldnet.att.net

Pied Piper (see AIMS Multimedia)

Scholastic New Media
555 Broadway
New York, NY 10003
(800) 724-6527 • www.scholastic.com

Simon & Schuster Interactive
(see Knowledge Adventure)

SRA/McGraw-Hill
220 Danieldale Road
De Soto, TX 75115
(800) 843-8855 • Fax (972) 228-1982 •
www.sra4kids.com

SVE/Churchill Media
6677 North Northwest Highway
Chicago, IL 60631
(800) 829-1900 • Fax (800) 624-1678 •
www.svemedia.com

Tom Snyder Productions (also see ESI)
80 Coolidge Hill Rd.
Watertown, MA 02472
(800) 342-0236 • Fax (800) 304-1254 •
www.teachtsp.com

Troll Associates
100 Corporate Drive
Mahwah, NJ 07430
(800) 929-8765 • Fax (800) 979-8765 •
www.troll.com

Voyager (see ESI)

Weston Woods
12 Oakwood Avenue
Norwalk, CT 06850
(800) 243-5020 • Fax (203) 845-0498

Zenger Media
10200 Jefferson Blvd., Room 94,
P.O. Box 802
Culver City, CA 90232-0802
(800) 421-4246 • (800) 944-5432 •
www.Zengermedia.com

BOOK 1, UNIT 1

	Vocabulary	Spelling			
ANN'S FIRST DAY	**carrots** **crawls** **homework** **hurry** **lucky** **shy**	**Words with short vowels**			
		bat **best** clock	**desk** fit hut	**just** **mom**	plant **still**
HENRY AND MUDGE	**different** **hundred** **parents** **searched** **weighed** **worry**	**Long vowels *a, i, o, u* with silent *e***			
		alone bike broke	fine joke late	mine same	take **used**
LUKA'S QUILT	**answered** **garden** **grandmother** **idea** **remember** **serious**	**Long *a* spelled *ai, ay*** **Long *e* spelled *ea, ee, ie***			
		chief clay **dream**	**green** **keep** mail	mean **plain**	seat stay
ROUNDUP AT RIO RANCH	**broken** **carefully** **cattle** **fence** **gently** **safety**	**Long *o* spelled *oa, oe, ow,* and *o*** **Long *i* spelled *i, y,* and *igh***			
		by dry **follow**	load mind old	row sigh	**slow** toe
TIME FOR KIDS: WELCOME TO A NEW MUSEUM	**artist** **body** **famous** **hour** **life** **visit**	**Words from Social Studies**			
		flags law peace	**place** **slave** speech	tax time	trade vote

Boldfaced words appear in the selection.

BOOK 1, UNIT 2

	Vocabulary	Spelling			
LEMONADE FOR SALE		/ü/ spelled *oo, ue, ew*			
	announced **empty** **melted** **poured** **squeezed** **wrong**	blew boot clue	few **new** **room**	school **too**	tool true
A LETTER TO AMY		/ou/ spelled *ou, ow;* /oi/ spelled *oi, oy*			
	candles **corner** **glanced** **repeated** **special** **wild**	brown coin cowboy	**down** **house** joy	loud **now**	**out** point
BEST FRIENDS CLUB		/âr/ spelled *are;* /ôr/ spelled *or, ore;* /îr/ spelled *ear*			
	allowed **leaned** **president** **promise** **rule** **whispered**	bare **care** corn	dear **more** **porch**	shore short	**tore** year
JAMAICA TAG-ALONG		/är/ spelled *ar;* /ûr/spelled *ir, er, ur*			
	building **busy** **edge** **form** **giant** **repair**	arm birthday curl	dirt farm fur	hard **her**	herd **turned**
TIME FOR KIDS: UNDER ATTACK		Words from Science			
	afraid **chew** **danger** **lesson** **trouble** **understand**	**animals** fin **head**	**nets** river **seals**	senses **shark**	tide wave

Boldfaced words appear in the selection.

BOOK 1, UNIT 3

	Vocabulary	Spelling			
		Silent letters *l, b, k, w, gh*			
ARTHUR WRITES A STORY	**decided** **float** **important** **library** **planet** **proud**	half **high** knee	knot **know** lamb	right thumb	write **wrote**
		/ər/ spelled *er*			
BEST WISHES, ED	**climbed** **couple** **drifted** **half** **message** **notice**	corner driver farmer	father **letter** never	**other** **over**	**water** winter
		Short *e* spelled *ea*			
THE PONY EXPRESS	**arrive** **early** **finish** **record** **rush** **success**	bread breakfast feather	instead **leather** meadow	meant ready	spread **weather**
		Long *e* spelled *y, ey*			
NINE-IN-ONE, GRR! GRR!	**earth** **forget** **lonely** **memory** **mountain** **wonderful**	baby **every** **happy**	key lady **many**	money party	penny **tiny**
		Words from Math			
TIME FOR KIDS: CHANGE FOR THE QUARTER	**collect** **honors** **join** **order** **pocket** **worth**	buy **cent** cost	dime dollar exact	nickel price	**quarter** sum

Boldfaced words appear in the selection.

BOOK 2, UNIT 1

	Vocabulary	Spelling			
CHARLIE ANDERSON	**chocolate** **clothes** **middle** **offered** **roof** **upstairs**	/ù/ spelled *oo* book brook cook	 **foot** hood hook	 shook stood	 wood wool
FERNANDO'S GIFT	**diving** **explains** **harm** **noisy** **soil** **village**	Soft *c* and soft *g* **age** cage charge	 dance large mice	 page race	 **rice** space
THE BEST VACATION EVER	**brave** **guess** **museum** **practice** **vacation** **wonder**	/ô/ spelled *a, aw, au, augh* **because** caught fault	 **hawk** lawn paw	 salt straw	 talk taught
ZIPPING, ZAPPING, ZOOMING BATS	**disturb** **explore** **fact** **nature** **object** **several**	Words with *ph, tch, ch* beach **catch** **each**	 graph match patch	 phone **pitch**	 **sandwich** **touch**
TIME FOR KIDS: GOING BATTY FOR BATS	**breath** **cover** **crops** **darkness** **scary** **study**	Words from Science blood **caves** den	 **fly** **insects** **leaves**	 nest sight	 **sleep** wing

Boldfaced words appear in the selection.

BOOK 2, UNIT 2

	Vocabulary	Spelling
Bremen Town Musicians	**daughter** **music** **scare** **third** **voice** **whistle**	**Words with *c, k, ck*** **act**, bake, **come**, cover, kind, **like**, **luck**, sick, **wake**, **work**
Our Soccer League	**coaches** **field** **score** **stretches** **throws** **touch**	**Initial *bl, br, dr, pl,* and *tr*** blow, **blue**, brag, brass, drag, draw, plan, **play**, trap, **try**
The Wednesday Surprise	**chance** **favorite** **heavy** **nervous** **office** **wrapped**	**Initial *sl, sm, sp, st, sw*** slide, slip, **smart**, smooth, speak, spot, **start**, **story**, sweet, swim
Fossils Tell of Long Ago	**buried** **creatures** **fossil** **fresh** **layers** **millions**	**Final *nk, nd, ft, st*** bank, chest, end, **ground**, **hand**, left, **past**, **sank**, soft, test
Time for Kids: Are You a Fossil Fan?	**change** **glue** **hunt** **magazine** **piece** **tooth**	**Words from Social Studies** **bone**, deep, **digging**, drill, hill, land, ocean, oil, **remains**, **stone**

Boldfaced words appear in the selection.

BOOK 2, UNIT 3

	Vocabulary	Spelling			
Officer Buckle and Gloria	**accidents** **audience** **cheered** **slips** **station** **wipe**	Words with *ll, dd, ss, gg* add call egg	fill **kiss** odd	press sell	tell **well**
Tomás and the Library Lady	**borrow** **desert** **evenings** **midnight** **package** **shoulder**	Words with initial *sh, ch* **chair** chase **check**	cheek **children** shape	**shared** shift	**shining** shoe
Princess Pooh	**cousins** **crowded** **golden** **princess** **restaurant** **world**	Words with final *th* and *sh* bath **both** brush	dash fish mouth	**push** **rush**	teeth **with**
Swimmy	**escaped** **fierce** **hidden** **machine** **swaying** **swift**	Words with initial *th* and *wh* **than** **them** **there** **thought**	**through** whale wheel	whimper whirl whisper	
Time for Kids: The World's Plants Are in Danger	**clear** **disappear** **forever** **problem** **save** **warn**	Words from Science bloom bud **bushes**	**cactus** **flower** petal	root **roses**	seed stem

Boldfaced words appear in the selection.

Listening, Speaking, Viewing, Representing

☑ Tested Skill

Tinted panels show skills, strategies, and other teaching opportunities

	K	1	2	3	4	5	6
LISTENING							
Learn the vocabulary of school (numbers, shapes, colors, directions, and categories)							
Identify the musical elements of literary language, such as rhymes, repetition, onomatopoeia, alliteration, assonance							
Determine purposes for listening (get information, solve problems, enjoy and appreciate)							
Understand and follow directions							
Listen critically and responsively; recognize barriers to effective listening							
Ask and answer relevant questions (for clarification; to follow up on ideas)							
Listen critically to interpret and evaluate							
Listen responsively to stories and other texts read aloud, including selections from classic and contemporary works							
Connect and compare own experiences, feelings, ideas, and traditions with those of others							
Apply comprehension strategies in listening activities							
Understand the major ideas and supporting evidence in spoken messages							
Participate in listening activities related to reading and writing (such as discussions, group activities, conferences)							
Listen to learn by taking notes, organizing, and summarizing spoken ideas							
Know personal listening preferences							
SPEAKING							
Use repetition, rhyme, and rhythm in oral texts (such as in reciting songs, poems, and stories with repeating patterns)							
Learn the vocabulary of school (numbers, shapes, colors, directions, and categories)							
Use appropriate language, grammar, and vocabulary learned to describe ideas, feelings, and experiences							
Ask and answer relevant questions (for clarification; to follow up on ideas)							
Communicate effectively in everyday situations (such as discussions, group activities, conferences, conversations)							
Demonstrate speaking skills (audience, purpose, occasion, clarity, volume, pitch, intonation, phrasing, rate, fluency)							
Clarify and support spoken messages and ideas with objects, charts, evidence, elaboration, examples							
Use verbal communication in effective ways, when, for example, making announcements, giving directions, or making introductions							
Use nonverbal communication in effective ways, such as eye contact, facial expressions, gestures							
Retell a story or a spoken message by summarizing or clarifying							
Connect and compare own experiences, ideas, and traditions with those of others							
Determine purposes for speaking (inform, entertain, compare, describe, give directions, persuade, express personal feelings and opinions)							
Recognize differences between formal and informal language							
Demonstrate skills of reporting and providing information							
Demonstrate skills of interviewing, requesting, and providing information							
Apply composition strategies in speaking activities							
Monitor own understanding of spoken message and seek clarification as needed							
VIEWING							
Demonstrate viewing skills (focus attention, organize information)							
Understand and use nonverbal cues							
Respond to audiovisual media in a variety of ways							
Participate in viewing activities related to reading and writing							
Apply comprehension strategies in viewing activities, including main idea and details							
Recognize artists' craft and techniques for conveying meaning							
Interpret information from various formats, such as maps, charts, graphics, video segments, technology							
Know various types of mass media (such as film, video, television, billboards, and newspapers)							
Evaluate purposes of various media, including mass media (information, appreciation, entertainment, directions, persuasion)							
Use media, including mass media, to compare ideas, information, and points of view							
REPRESENTING							
Select, organize, or produce visuals to complement or extend meanings							
Produce communication using appropriate media to develop a class paper, multimedia or video reports							
Show how language, medium, and presentation contribute to the message							

Reading: Alphabetic Principle, Sounds/Symbols

✓ Tested Skill

Tinted panels show skills, strategies, and other teaching opportunities

PRINT AWARENESS	K	1	2	3	4	5	6
Know the order of the alphabet							
Recognize that print represents spoken language and conveys meaning							
Understand directionality (tracking print from left to right; return sweep)							
Understand that written words and sentences are separated by spaces							
Know the difference between individual letters and printed words							
Understand that spoken words are represented in written language by specific sequences of letters							
Recognize that there are correct spellings for words							
Know the difference between capital and lowercase letters							
Recognize how readers use capitalization and punctuation to comprehend							
Recognize the distinguishing features of a letter, word, sentence, paragraph							
Understand appropriate book handling							
Recognize that parts of a book (such as cover/title page and table of contents) offer information							
PHONOLOGICAL AWARENESS							
Listen for environmental sounds							
Identify spoken words and sentences							
Divide spoken sentence into individual words							
Produce rhyming words and distinguish rhyming words from nonrhyming words							
Identify, segment, and combine syllables within spoken words							
Blend and segment onsets and rimes							
Identify and isolate the initial, medial, and final sound of a spoken word							
Add, delete, or substitute sounds to change words (such as *cow* to *how*, *pan* to *fan*)							
Blend sounds to make spoken words							
Segment one-syllable spoken words into individual sounds							
PHONICS AND DECODING							
Alphabetic principle: Letter/sound correspondence	✓	✓	✓				
Blending CVC words	✓	✓					
Segmenting CVC words	✓						
Blending CVC, CVCe, CCVC, CVCC, CVVC words	✓	✓	✓				
Segmenting CVC, CVCe, CCVC, CVCC, CVVC words and sounds	✓	✓	✓				
Initial and final consonants: /n/n, /d/d, /s/s, /m/m, /t/t, /k/c, /f/f, /r/r, /p/p, /l/l, /k/k, /g/g, /b/b, /h/h, /w/w, /v/v, /ks/x, /kw/qu, /j/j, /y/y, /z/z	✓	✓					
Initial and medial short vowels: *a, i, u, o, e*	✓	✓	✓				
Long vowels: *a-e, i-e, o-e, u-e* (vowel-consonant-e)		✓	✓				
Long vowels, including *ay, ai; e, ee, ie, ea; o, oa, oe, ow; i, y, igh*		✓	✓				
Consonant Digraphs: *sh, th, ch, wh*		✓					
Consonant Blends: continuant/continuant, including *sl, sm, sn, fl, fr, ll, ss, ff*		✓					
Consonant Blends: continuant/stop, including *st, sk, sp, ng, nt, nd, mp, ft*		✓					
Consonant Blends: stop/continuant, including *tr, pr, pl, cr, tw*		✓					
Variant vowels: including /ù/*oo*; /ô/*a, aw, au*; /ü/*ue, ew*		✓	✓				
Diphthongs, including /ou/*ou, ow*; /oi/*oi, oy*		✓	✓				
r-controlled vowels, including /âr/*are*; /ôr/*or, ore*; /îr/*ear*			✓				
Soft *c* and soft *g*			✓				
nk		✓	✓				
Consonant Digraphs: *ck*	✓	✓					
Consonant Digraphs: *ph, tch, ch*			✓				
Short *e: ea*			✓				
Long *e: y, ey*			✓				
/ü/*oo*		✓	✓				
/är/*ar*; /ûr/*ir, ur, er*		✓	✓				
Silent letters: including *l, b, k, w, g, h, gh*			✓				
Schwa: /ər/*er*; /ən/*en*; /əl/*le*;			✓				
Reading/identifying multisyllabic words		✓	✓				
Using graphophonic cues							

✓ Tested Skill

Tinted panels show skills, strategies, and other teaching opportunities

Reading: Vocabulary/Word Identification

WORD STRUCTURE	K	1	2	3	4	5	6
Common spelling patterns							
Syllable patterns							
Plurals		✓					
Possessives		✓					
Contractions		✓					
Root, or base, words and inflectional endings (*-s, -es, -ed, -ing*)		✓	✓	✓		✓	
Compound Words		✓	✓	✓	✓	✓	✓
Prefixes and suffixes (such as *un-, re-, dis-, non-; -ly, -y, -ful, -able, -tion*)			✓	✓	✓	✓	✓
Root words and derivational endings				✓	✓	✓	✓
WORD MEANING							
Develop vocabulary through concrete experiences, word walls, other people							
Develop vocabulary through selections read aloud							
Develop vocabulary through reading							
Cueing systems: syntactic, semantic, graphophonic							
Context clues, including semantic clues (word meaning), syntactical clues (word order), and graphophonic clues	✓	✓	✓	✓	✓	✓	✓
High-frequency words (such as *the, a, and, said, was, where, is*)	✓	✓					
Identify words that name persons, places, things, and actions							
Automatic reading of regular and irregular words							
Use resources and references (dictionary, glossary, thesaurus, synonym finder, technology and software, and context)							
Classify and categorize words							
Synonyms and antonyms			✓	✓	✓	✓	✓
Multiple-meaning words			✓		✓	✓	✓
Figurative language			✓	✓	✓	✓	✓
Decode derivatives (root words, such as *like, pay, happy* with affixes, such as *dis-, pre-, un-*)							
Systematic study of words across content areas and in current events							
Locate meanings, pronunciations, and derivations (including dictionaries, glossaries, and other sources)							
Denotation and connotation							✓
Word origins as aid to understanding historical influences on English word meanings							
Homophones, homographs							
Analogies							✓
Idioms							

Reading: Comprehension

PREREADING STRATEGIES	K	1	2	3	4	5	6
Preview and predict							
Use prior knowledge							
Set and adjust purposes for reading							
Build background							
MONITORING STRATEGIES							
Adjust reading rate							
Reread, search for clues, ask questions, ask for help							
Visualize							
Read a portion aloud, use reference aids							
Use decoding and vocabulary strategies							
Paraphrase							
Create story maps, diagrams, charts, story props to help comprehend, analyze, synthesize and evaluate texts							

(continued on next page)

☑ Tested Skill

Tinted panels show skills, strategies, and other teaching opportunities

(Reading: Comprehension continued)

SKILLS AND STRATEGIES	K	1	2	3	4	5	6
Recall story details, including character and setting	☑	☑					
Use illustrations	☑	☑					
Distinguish reality and fantasy	☑	☑	☑				
Classify and categorize	☑						
Make predictions	☑	☑	☑	☑	☑	☑	☑
Recognize sequence of events (tell or act out)	☑	☑	☑	☑	☑	☑	☑
Recognize cause and effect	☑	☑	☑	☑	☑	☑	☑
Compare and contrast	☑	☑	☑	☑	☑	☑	☑
Summarize	☑	☑	☑	☑	☑	☑	☑
Make and explain inferences		☑	☑	☑	☑	☑	☑
Draw conclusions		☑	☑	☑	☑	☑	☑
Distinguish important and unimportant information				☑	☑	☑	☑
Recognize main idea and supporting details	☑	☑	☑	☑	☑	☑	☑
Form conclusions or generalizations and support with evidence from text			☑	☑	☑	☑	☑
Distinguish fact and opinion (including news stories and advertisements)				☑	☑	☑	☑
Recognize problem and solution			☑	☑	☑	☑	☑
Recognize steps in a process		☑	☑	☑	☑	☑	☑
Make judgments and decisions				☑	☑	☑	☑
Distinguish fact and nonfact				☑	☑	☑	☑
Recognize techniques of persuasion and propaganda							☑
Evaluate evidence and sources of information, including checking other sources and asking experts							☑
Identify similarities and differences across texts (including topics, characters, problems, themes, cultural influences, treatment, scope, or organization)							
Practice various questions and tasks (test-like comprehension questions)							
Paraphrase and summarize to recall, inform, and organize							
Answer various types of questions (open-ended, literal, interpretative, test-like such as true-false, multiple choice, short-answer)							
Use study strategies to learn and recall (preview, question, reread, and record)							
LITERARY RESPONSE							
Listen to stories being read aloud							
React, speculate, join in, read along when predictable and patterned selections are read aloud							
Respond to a variety of stories and poems through talk, movement, music, art, drama, and writing							
Show understanding through writing, illustrating, developing demonstrations, and using technology							
Connect ideas and themes across texts							
Support responses by referring to relevant aspects of text and own experiences							
Offer observations, make connections, speculate, interpret, and raise questions in response to texts							
Interpret text ideas through journal writing, discussion, enactment, and media							
TEXT STRUCTURE/LITERARY CONCEPTS							
Distinguish forms and functions of texts (lists, newsletters, signs)							
Use text features to aid comprehension							
Understand story structure							
Identify narrative (for entertainment) and expository (for information) text							
Distinguish fiction from nonfiction, including fact and fantasy							
Understand literary forms (stories, poems, plays, and informational books)							
Understand literary terms by distinguishing between roles of author and illustrator							
Understand title, author, and illustrator across a variety of texts							
Analyze character, character's motive, character's point of view, plot, setting, style, tone, mood		☑	☑	☑	☑	☑	☑
Compare communication in different forms							
Understand terms such as *title, author, illustrator, playwright, theater, stage, act, dialogue,* and *scene*							
Recognize stories, poems, songs, myths, legends, folktales, fables, tall tales, limericks, plays, biographies, autobiographies							
Judge internal logic of story text							
Recognize that authors organize information in specific ways							
Recognize author's purpose: to inform, influence, express, or entertain							
Describe how author's point of view affects text				☑	☑	☑	☑
Recognize biography, historical fiction, realistic fiction, modern fantasy, informational texts, and poetry							
Analyze ways authors present ideas (cause/effect, compare/contrast, inductively, deductively, chronologically)							
Recognize literary techniques such as imagery, repetition, flashback, foreshadowing, symbolism							

(continued on next page)

☑ Tested Skill

Tinted panels show skills, strategies, and other teaching opportunities

(Reading: Comprehension continued)

VARIETY OF TEXT	K	1	2	3	4	5	6
Read a variety of genres and understand their distinguishing features							
Use expository and other informational texts to acquire information							
Read for a variety of purposes							
Select varied sources when reading for information or pleasure							
Know preferences for reading literary and nonfiction texts							
FLUENCY							
Read regularly in independent-level and instructional-level materials							
Read orally with fluency from familiar texts							
Self-select independent-level reading							
Read silently for increasingly longer periods of time							
Demonstrate characteristics of fluent and effective reading							
Adjust reading rate to purpose							
Read aloud in selected texts, showing understanding of text and engaging the listener							
CULTURES							
Connect own experience with culture of others							
Compare experiences of characters across cultures							
Articulate and discuss themes and connections that cross cultures							
CRITICAL THINKING							
Experiences (comprehend, apply, analyze, synthesize, evaluate)							
Making connections (comprehend, apply, analyze, synthesize, evaluate)							
Expression (comprehend, apply, analyze, synthesize, evaluate)							
Inquiry (comprehend, apply, analyze, synthesize, evaluate)							
Problem solving (comprehend, apply, analyze, synthesize, evaluate)							
Making decisions (comprehend, apply, analyze, synthesize, evaluate)							

Study Skills

INQUIRY/RESEARCH AND STUDY STRATEGIES	K	1	2	3	4	5	6
Follow and give directions							
Use alphabetical order							
Use text features and formats to help understand text (such as boldface, italic, or highlighted text; captions; headings and subheadings; numbers or symbols)							
Use study strategies to help read text and to learn and recall information from text (such as preview text, set purposes, and ask questions; use SQRRR; adjust reading rate; skim and scan; use KWL)							
Identify/frame and revise questions for research							
Obtain, organize, and summarize information: classify, take notes, outline, web, diagram							
Evaluate research and raise new questions							
Use technology for research and/or to present information in various formats							
Follow accepted formats for writing research, including documenting sources							
Use test-taking strategies							
Use text organizers (book cover; title page—title, author, illustrator; contents; headings; glossary; index)		☑	☑	☑	☑	☑	☑
Use graphic aids, such as maps, diagrams, charts, graphs, schedules, calendars		☑	☑	☑	☑	☑	☑
Read and interpret varied texts, such as environmental print, signs, lists, encyclopedia, dictionary, glossary, newspaper, advertisement, magazine, calendar, directions, floor plans, online resources		☑	☑	☑	☑	☑	☑
Use print and online reference sources, such as glossary, dictionary, encyclopedia, telephone directory, technology resources, nonfiction books		☑	☑	☑	☑	☑	☑
Recognize Library/Media Center resources, such as computerized references; catalog search—subject, author, title; encyclopedia index		☑	☑	☑	☑	☑	☑

Writing

☑ Tested Skill

Tinted panels show skills, strategies, and other teaching opportunities

MODES AND FORMS	K	1	2	3	4	5	6
Interactive writing							
Descriptive writing			✓				
Personal narrative			✓	✓	✓	✓	✓
Writing that compares		✓	✓	✓	✓	✓	✓
Explanatory writing			✓	✓	✓	✓	✓
Persuasive writing				✓	✓	✓	✓
Writing a story		✓	✓	✓	✓	✓	✓
Expository writing; research report		✓	✓	✓	✓	✓	✓
Write using a variety of formats, such as advertisement, autobiography, biography, book report/report, comparison-contrast, critique/review/editorial, description, essay, how-to, interview, invitation, journal/log/notes, message/list, paragraph/multi-paragraph composition, picture book, play (scene), poem/rhyme, story, summary, note, letter							

PURPOSES/AUDIENCES	K	1	2	3	4	5	6
Dictate sentences and messages, such as news and stories, for others to write							
Write labels, notes, and captions for illustrations, possessions, charts, and centers							
Write to record, to discover and develop ideas, to inform, to influence, to entertain							
Exhibit an identifiable voice							
Use literary devices (suspense, dialogue, and figurative language)							
Produce written texts by organizing ideas, using effective transitions, and choosing precise wording							

PROCESSES	K	1	2	3	4	5	6
Generate ideas for self-selected and assigned topics using prewriting strategies							
Develop drafts							
Revise drafts for varied purposes, elaborate ideas							
Edit for appropriate grammar, spelling, punctuation, and features of published writings							
Proofread own writing and that of others							
Bring pieces to final form and "publish" them for audiences							
Use technology to compose, revise, and present text							
Select and use reference materials and resources for writing, revising, and editing final drafts							

SPELLING	K	1	2	3	4	5	6
Spell own name and write high-frequency words							
Words with short vowels (including CVC and one-syllable words with blends CCVC, CVCC, CCVCC)							
Words with long vowels (including CVCe)							
Words with digraphs, blends, consonant clusters, double consonants							
Words with diphthongs							
Words with variant vowels							
Words with r-controlled vowels							
Words with /ər/, /əl/, and /ən/							
Words with silent letters							
Words with soft *c* and soft *g*							
Inflectional endings (including plurals and past tense and words that drop the final *e* and double a consonant when adding *-ing, -ed*)							
Compound words							
Contractions							
Homonyms							
Suffixes such as *-able, -ly, -ful,* or *-less,* and prefixes such as *dis-, re-, pre-,* or *un-*							
Spell words ending in *-tion* and *-sion,* such as *station* and *procession*							
Accurate spelling of root or base words							
Orthographic patterns and rules such as *keep/can; sack/book; out/now; oil/toy; match/speech; ledge/cage;* consonant doubling, dropping *e,* changing *y* to *i*							
Multisyllabic words using regularly spelled phonogram patterns							
Syllable patterns (including closed, open, syllable boundary patterns)							
Synonyms and antonyms							
Words from Social Studies, Science, Math, and Physical Education							
Words derived from other languages and cultures							
Use resources to find correct spellings, synonyms, and replacement words							
Use conventional spelling of familiar words in writing assignments							
Spell accurately in final drafts							

(continued on next page)

Tested Skill

Tinted panels show skills, strategies, and other teaching opportunities

(Writing continued)

GRAMMAR AND USAGE	K	1	2	3	4	5	6
Understand sentence concepts (word order, statements, questions, exclamations, commands)							
Recognize complete and incomplete sentences							
Nouns (common, proper, singular, plural, irregular plural, possessive)							
Verbs (action, helping, linking, irregular)							
Verb tense (present, past, future, perfect, and progressive)							
Pronouns (possessive, subject and object, pronoun-verb agreement)							
Use objective case pronouns accurately							
Adjectives							
Adverbs that tell how, when, where							
Subjects, predicates							
Subject-verb agreement							
Sentence combining							
Recognize sentence structure (simple, compound, complex)							
Synonyms and antonyms							
Contractions							
Conjunctions							
Prepositions and prepositional phrases							
PENMANSHIP							
Write each letter of alphabet (capital and lowercase) using correct formation, appropriate size and spacing							
Write own name and other important words							
Use phonological knowledge to map sounds to letters in order to write messages							
Write messages that move left to right, top to bottom							
Gain increasing control of penmanship, pencil grip, paper position, beginning stroke							
Use word and letter spacing and margins to make messages readable							
Write legibly by selecting cursive or manuscript, as appropriate							
MECHANICS							
Use capitalization in sentences, proper nouns, titles, abbreviations and the pronoun *I*							
Use end marks correctly (period, question mark, exclamation point)							
Use commas (in dates, in addresses, in a series, in letters, in direct address)							
Use apostrophes in contractions and possessives							
Use quotation marks							
Use hyphens, semicolons, colons							
EVALUATION							
Identify the most effective features of a piece of writing using class/teacher-generated criteria							
Respond constructively to others' writing							
Determine how his/her own writing achieves its purpose							
Use published pieces as models for writing							
Review own written work to monitor growth as a writer							

Scoring Chart

The Scoring Chart is provided for your convenience in grading your students' work.

- Find the column that shows the total number of items.
- Find the row that matches the number of items answered correctly.
- The intersection of the two rows provides the percentage score.

	TOTAL NUMBER OF ITEMS																													
NUMBER CORRECT	1	2	3	4	5	6	7	8	9	10	11	12	13	14	15	16	17	18	19	20	21	22	23	24	25	26	27	28	29	30
1	100	50	33	25	20	17	14	13	11	10	9	8	8	7	7	6	6	6	5	5	5	5	4	4	4	4	4	4	3	3
2		100	66	50	40	33	29	25	22	20	18	17	15	14	13	13	12	11	11	10	10	9	9	8	8	8	7	7	7	7
3			100	75	60	50	43	38	33	30	27	25	23	21	20	19	18	17	16	15	14	14	13	13	12	12	11	11	10	10
4				100	80	67	57	50	44	40	36	33	31	29	27	25	24	22	21	20	19	18	17	17	16	15	15	14	14	13
5					100	83	71	63	56	50	45	42	38	36	33	31	29	28	26	25	24	23	22	21	20	19	19	18	17	17
6						100	86	75	67	60	55	50	46	43	40	38	35	33	32	30	29	27	26	25	24	23	22	21	21	20
7							100	88	78	70	64	58	54	50	47	44	41	39	37	35	33	32	30	29	28	27	26	25	24	23
8								100	89	80	73	67	62	57	53	50	47	44	42	40	38	36	35	33	32	31	30	29	28	27
9									100	90	82	75	69	64	60	56	53	50	47	45	43	41	39	38	36	35	33	32	31	30
10										100	91	83	77	71	67	63	59	56	53	50	48	45	43	42	40	38	37	36	34	33
11											100	92	85	79	73	69	65	61	58	55	52	50	48	46	44	42	41	39	38	37
12												100	92	86	80	75	71	67	63	60	57	55	52	50	48	46	44	43	41	40
13													100	93	87	81	76	72	68	65	62	59	57	54	52	50	48	46	45	43
14														100	93	88	82	78	74	70	67	64	61	58	56	54	52	50	48	47
15															100	94	88	83	79	75	71	68	65	63	60	58	56	54	52	50
16																100	94	89	84	80	76	73	70	67	64	62	59	57	55	53
17																	100	94	89	85	81	77	74	71	68	65	63	61	59	57
18																		100	95	90	86	82	78	75	72	69	67	64	62	60
19																			100	95	90	86	83	79	76	73	70	68	66	63
20																				100	95	91	87	83	80	77	74	71	69	67
21																					100	95	91	88	84	81	78	75	72	70
22																						100	96	92	88	85	81	79	76	73
23																							100	96	92	88	85	82	79	77
24																								100	96	92	89	86	83	80
25																									100	96	93	89	86	83
26																										100	96	93	90	87
27																											100	96	93	90
28																												100	97	93
29																													100	97
30																														100

Expository Writing: Writing About a Person or Place

Scoring Rubric: 6-Trait Writing

6. Exceptional	5. Excellent	4. Good	3. Fair	2. Poor	1. Unsatisfactory
• **Ideas & Content** crafts a clear, fully-detailed report on solving a problem with the help of a person or place. • **Organization** uses careful strategy to help a reader understand impact of the person or place on the writer; ideas are connected; strong beginning and conclusion. • **Voice** shows originality, and deep involvement with the topic; brings a special personal message to the topic and audience. • **Word Choice** uses striking words that animate the information; advanced vocabulary make the report clear and satisfying. • **Sentence Fluency** creates sentences which flow in a smooth, natural rhythm; writing is easy to follow and read aloud; varying lengths, beginnings, and patterns add interest to the content. • **Conventions** is skilled in most writing conventions; proper use of the rules of English enhances clarity, meaning, and style; editing is largely unnecessary.	• **Ideas & Content** crafts a focused, detailed report; has control and knowledge of the topic. • **Organization** has a logical, careful sequence of facts and ideas; strong beginning and satisfying ending; reader moves easily through the ideas. • **Voice** reaches the reader with originality and involvement with the topic; personal style enlivens the facts and observations. • **Word Choice** makes creative use of accurate language; explores new words, or uses everyday words to create a picture for the reader. • **Sentence Fluency** crafts well-paced, fluid sentences; has a variety of lengths, beginnings, and patterns that fit together naturally. • **Conventions** has skills in most conventions; proper use of the rules of English enhances clarity, meaning, and style; editing is largely unnecessary.	• **Ideas & Content** presents a solid, clear report, with details that help the reader understand how a problem was solved. • **Organization** presents information and ideas logically; details fit where they are placed, and help reader understand the message; clear beginning and conclusion. • **Voice** attempts to bring a personal touch to her/his observations; writer connects with the reader; is involved with the topic. • **Word Choice** uses a variety of words that fit the task, but may not create a striking picture of a problem and its solution. • **Sentence Fluency** crafts natural, easy-to-read sentences that vary in length, beginnings, and patterns; text is easy to read aloud. • **Conventions** may make some errors in spelling, capitalization, punctuation or usage which do not interfere with understanding the text; some editing is needed.	• **Ideas & Content** has some control of a report; may include ideas or details which are vague, general, or do not fit the topic. • **Organization** attempts to structure a report, but the logic is sometimes hard to follow; may not draw a pertinent conclusion. • **Voice** may not be very involved with the topic; connection between the writer's message and the audience is unclear. • **Word Choice** describes problem or solution in a limited way; may attempt to use a variety of words, but some do not relate; may overuse some words/expressions. • **Sentence Fluency** writes readable sentences, with limited variety in length and pattern; some rereading may be required to follow the text; some sentences are awkward or incomplete. • **Conventions** has basic control of conventions, but makes enough noticeable errors to interfere with an even reading of the text; significant editing is needed.	• **Ideas & Content** has little control of writing a report, or seems unsure of the topic; ideas are vague; details are few, repeated, or inaccurate. • **Organization** has no clear structure; the order of ideas is hard to follow; details don't fit where they are placed; conclusion is irrelevant, or missing. • **Voice** is not involved in sharing facts or observations with a reader; writing may be lifeless, with no sense of who is behind the words. • **Word Choice** does not choose words that express the topic's full impact; some words are overused, or may detract from the meaning. • **Sentence Fluency** crafts sentences which may be choppy or awkward; patterns are similar or monotonous; text may be hard to follow or read aloud. • **Conventions** makes frequent errors in spelling, word choice, punctuation, and usage; report is difficult to read, and requires extensive revision and editing.	• **Ideas & Content** does not report on a person, place, or problem; writer seems unsure of what he/she wants to say. • **Organization** shows extreme lack of organization; ideas are disconnected; details, if presented, are incomplete or vague. • **Voice** does not try to deal with the topic or audience; does not grasp how to share a personal message or style. • **Word Choice** uses words that do not describe, or are vague and confusing; no new words are attempted; may overuse familiar words. • **Sentence Fluency** uses incomplete, rambling, or confusing sentences which make the text hard to follow and read aloud. • **Conventions** makes severe errors in most conventions; spelling errors may make it hard to guess what words are meant; some parts of the text are impossible to understand.

Incomplete 0: This piece is either blank, or fails to respond to the writing task. The topic is not addressed, or the student simply paraphrases the prompt. The response may be illegible or incoherent.

8-Point Writing Rubric

Expository Writing: Writing About a Person or Place

8-Point Writing Rubric

8	7	6	5	4	3	2	1
The writer • has crafted an exceptionally well-organized report on a person or place, rich in vivid detail and thoughtful commentary. • has elaborated each piece of information with a well-thought-out selection of facts and reasons. • has pertinently related personal experience to the main idea so as to illuminate it. • has used sophisticated vocabulary and a pleasing variety of sentence forms to enhance understanding and fluency. • presents a logical structure with an intriguing introduction, substantive middle, and pointed conclusion. • has reached a carefully considered conclusion based on facts and reasons presented in the report.	The writer • has crafted a well-organized, detailed report on a familiar person or place. • has elaborated each piece of information with at least one fact or reason. • may have pertinently related her/his own experience to the main idea. • may have used sophisticated vocabulary or sentence structure. • presents a logical structure with a beginning, middle, and end. • has drawn an apt conclusion based on facts and reasons in the report.	The writer • presents a solidly thought-out report on a familiar person or place. • has made a consistent effort to elaborate each piece of information. • has made some attempt to use personal comment or experience to enhance the main idea. • exhibits an organizational strategy of some sort. • may have made a strong attempt to draw a conclusion based on the facts and reasons in the report.	The writer • presents a satisfactory report on a familiar person or place. • has made some effort to elaborate each piece of information. • may have attempted to enhance the main idea with personal comment or experience. • may have attempted an organizational strategy but may have a few lapses in presenting a beginning, middle, and end. • may have made some attempt to draw a conclusion based on information in the report.	The writer • has made a minimally successful attempt at reporting on a familiar person or place. • may show an uneven or limited vocabulary for the writing task. • may exhibit organizational problems, such as not introducing the main idea at the beginning of the report. • may show a lack of follow-through on the main idea. • may exhibit a limited control of grammar, mechanics, and usage. • may not have drawn a pertinent conclusion.	The writer • may have made a largely unsuccessful attempt to report on a person or place. • exhibits a limited vocabulary for the writing task. • exhibits organizational problems, such as a lack of a beginning or conclusion. • shows a lack of follow-through on the main idea. • exhibits a limited control of basic grammar, mechanics, and usage. • may not have drawn any conclusion or drawn one unrelated to the writing task.	The writer • has made an unsuccessful attempt to report on a person or place. • has not elaborated on the topic with reasons or facts. • may exhibit serious organizational problems. • may show repeated serious errors in basic grammar, mechanics, and usage. • has not drawn a conclusion or has concluded with a comment unrelated to the topic.	The writer • has made no attempt to report on a familiar person or place. • exhibits extreme organizational problems that interfere with comprehension of the text. • has used only generalities, with no attempt to include specific facts, descriptions, or observations. • displays the most limited grasp of the basic conventions of grammar, mechanics, and usage. • has left the writing unfinished with no attempt at a conclusion.

0: This piece is either blank, or fails to respond to the writing task. The topic is not addressed, or the student simply paraphrases the prompt. The response may be illegible or incoherent.

Notes

Notes

Notes

Notes

Notes

Notes